Window on Humanity

A Concise Introduction to Anthropology

Fifth Edition

Conrad Phillip Kottak

University of Michigan

Connect
Learn
Succeed™

Published by McGraw-Hill, an imprint of The McGraw-Hill Companies, Inc., 1221 Avenue of the Americas, New York, NY 10020. Copyright © 2012, 2010, 2008, 2007, 2005. All rights reserved. No part of this publication may be reproduced or distributed in any form or by any means, or stored in a database or retrieval system, without the prior written consent of The McGraw-Hill Companies, Inc., including, but not limited to, in any network or other electronic storage or transmission, or broadcast for distance learning.

This book is printed on acid-free paper.

1 2 3 4 5 6 7 8 9 0 DOC/DOC 1 0 9 8 7 6 5 4 3 2 1

ISBN: 978-0-07-803489-3
MHID: 0-07-803489-2

Sponsoring Editor: *Gina Boedeker*
Marketing Manager: *Patrick Brown*
Developmental Editor: *Kate Scheinman*
Production Editor: *Jasmin Tokatlian*
Manuscript Editor: *Judith Brown*
Text and Cover Designer: *Allister Fein*
Photo Research: *Nora Agbayani and Barbara Salz*
Buyer: *Louis Swaim*
Media Project Manager: *Jennifer Barrick*
Composition: *10/12 Times by Aptara®, Inc.*
Printing: *PMS 661, 45# New Era Matte Plus, R. R. Donnelley & Sons/Crawfordsville, IN*

Vice President Editorial: *Michael Ryan*
Editorial Director: *William Glass*
Director of Development: *Dawn Groundwater*

Cover: Felix Hug/Lonely Planet Images

Credits: The credits section for this book begins on page 475 and is considered an extension of the copyright page.

Library of Congress Cataloging-in-Publication Data

Kottak, Conrad Phillip.
    Window on humanity: a concise introduction to general anthropology / Conrad Kottak. —5th ed.
        p. cm.
    Includes bibliographical references and index.
    ISBN-13: 978-0-07-803489-3 (alk. paper)
    ISBN-10: 0-07-803489-2 (alk. paper)
    1. Anthropology. I. Title.
    GN25.K68 2011
    301—dc23

                                                                2011033687

The Internet addresses listed in the text were accurate at the time of publication. The inclusion of a website does not indicate an endorsement by the authors or McGraw-Hill, and McGraw-Hill does not guarantee the accuracy of the information presented at these sites.

www.mhhe.com

To my wife,
Isabel Wagley Kottak

Also available from McGraw-Hill by Conrad Phillip Kottak:

Mirror for Humanity: A Concise Introduction to Cultural Anthropology, 8th ed. (2012)

CULTURE, 1st ed. (2012) (Lisa Gezon and Conrad Phillip Kottak)

On Being Different: Diversity and Multiculturalism in the North American Mainstream, 4th ed. (2012) (with Kathryn A. Kozaitis)

Anthropology: Appreciating Human Diversity, 14th ed. (2011)

Cultural Anthropology: Appreciating Cultural Diversity, 14th ed. (2011)

Assault on Paradise: The Globalization of a Little Community in Brazil, 4th ed. (2006)

Brief Contents

Popular Culture Boxes   xiii

Anthropology Today Boxes   xiv

Preface   xv

About the Author   xxvi

1   What Is Anthropology?   1

2   Culture   17

3   Doing Anthropology   40

4   Evolution, Genetics, and Human Variation   67

5   The Primates   96

6   Early Hominins   120

7   The Genus *Homo*   143

8   The First Farmers   174

9   The First Cities and States   195

10   Language and Communication   221

11   Making a Living   246

12   Political Systems   271

13   Families, Kinship, and Marriage   297

14   Gender   324

15   Religion   348

16   The World System and Colonialism   370

17   Ethnicity and Race   393

18   Applying Anthropology   416

19   Anthropology's Role in a Globalizing World   438

GLOSSARY   461

CREDITS   475

BIBLIOGRAPHY   477

INDEX   509

Contents

Popular Culture Boxes   xiii

Anthropology Today Boxes   xiv

Preface   xv

About the Author   xxvi

Chapter 1
What Is Anthropology?   1

Human Adaptability   2
Adaptation, Variation, and Change   3
General Anthropology   4
Cultural Forces Shape Human Biology   5
The Subdisciplines of Anthropology   7
Cultural Anthropology   7
Archaeological Anthropology   7
Applying Anthology to Popular Culture:
Indiana Jones   10
Biological, or Physical, Anthropology   10
Linguistic Anthropology   11
Anthropology and Other Academic
Fields   11
Applied Anthropology   12
*Anthropology Today: Anthropologist's
Son Elected President   13*
Summary   15

Chapter 2
Culture   17

What Is Culture?   18
Culture Is Learned   18
Culture Is Symbolic   18
Culture Is Shared   19
Culture and Nature   20
Culture Is All-Encompassing   20
Culture Is Integrated   20
*Applying Anthropology to Popular
Culture: Popular Songs   21*
*Culture Is Instrumental, Adaptive,
and Maladaptive   21*

Culture's Evolutionary Basis   23
What We Share with Other Primates   24
*How We Differ from Other
Primates   25*
Universality, Generality, and
Particularity   27
Universals and Generalities   27
*Particularity: Patterns of
Culture   27*
Culture and the Individual: Agency
and Practice   28
Popular, Civic, and Public Culture   30
Levels of Culture   30
Ethnocentrism, Cultural Relativism,
and Human Rights   31
Mechanisms of Cultural Change   34
Globalization   34
*Anthropology Today: Experiencing Culture:
Personal Space and Displays
of Affection   36*
Summary   38

Chapter 3
Doing Anthropology   40

Research Methods in Archaeology and
Physical Anthropology   41
Multidisciplinary Approaches   42
Studying the Past   43
Survey and Excavation   43
Kinds of Archaeology   45
Dating the Past   45
Relative Dating   46
Absolute Dating   46
Molecular Anthropology   47
Kinds of Physical Anthropology   48
Bone Biology   48
Anthropometry   49
Primatology   49
*Applying Anthropology to Popular
Culture: Bones   50*

Research Methods in Cultural
Anthropology   50
Ethnography: Anthropology's
Distinctive Strategy   51
Ethnographic Techniques   51
  Observation and Participant
  Observation   52
  Conversation, Interviewing, and
  Interview Schedules   53
  The Genealogical Method   54
  Key Cultural Consultants   55
  Life Histories   55
  Local Beliefs and Perceptions, and
  the Ethnographer's   55
  Problem-Oriented Ethnography   56
  Longitudinal Studies, Team Research,
  and Multisited Ethnography   56
Survey Research   58
Doing Anthropology Right and Wrong:
Ethical Issues   59
  The Code of Ethics   60
  Anthropologists and Terrorism   61
Anthropology Today: Archeologist in
New Orleans Finds a Way to Help
the Living   62
Summary   65

Chapter 4
**Evolution, Genetics, and Human
Variation   67**

The Origin of Species   68
  Theory and Fact   69
Genetics   71
  Mendel's Experiments   72
  Independent Assortment   74
Population Genetics   74
Mechanisms of Genetic
Evolution   75
  Natural Selection   75
  Mutation   78
  Random Genetic Drift   78
  Gene Flow   78
Race: A Discredited Concept in
Biology   80

  Races Are Not Biologically Distinct   82
  Genetic Markers Don't Correlate with
  Phenotype   83
Applying Anthropology to Popular Culture:
Oprah's DNA   84
  Explaining Skin Color   84
Human Biological Adaptation   88
  Genes and Disease   88
Anthropology Today: Genetic Study
Bolsters Columbus Link to
Syphilis   91
  Lactose Tolerance   93
Summary   93

Chapter 5
The Primates   96

Our Place among Primates   96
Applying Anthropology to Popular Culture:
Planet of the Apes   98
Homologies and Analogies   99
Primate Tendencies   100
Prosimians   102
Monkeys   102
  New World Monkeys   103
  Old World Monkeys   104
Apes   105
  Gibbons   106
  Orangutans   106
  Gorillas   107
  Chimpanzees   108
  Bonobos   109
Endangered Primates   110
Primate Evolution   110
Chronology   111
Early Primates   112
  Early Cenozoic Primates   113
  Oligocene Anthropoids   113
Miocene Hominoids   114
  Proconsul   114
  Later Miocene Apes   114
  Pierolapithecus catalaunicus   115
Anthropology Today: Global Economy
Threatens Orangutans   116
Summary   118

Chapter 6
Early Hominins   120

What Makes Us Human?   120
  Bipedalism   120
  *Applying Anthropology to Popular
  Culture: Monkey Bars   122*
    *Brains, Skulls, and Childhood
    Dependency   122*
    Tools   122
    Teeth   122
Chronology of Hominin Evolution   123
Who Were the Earliest Hominins?   123
    Sahelanthropus tchadensis   124
    Orrorin tugenensis   126
    Ardipithecus   126
The Varied Australopithecines   128
    Australopithecus anamensis   129
    Australopithecus afarensis   129
    Gracile and Robust Australopithecines   134
The Australopithecines and Early
Homo   136
Oldowan Tools   137
*Anthropology Today: Anthropologist's Son
Finds New Species of* Australopithecus   *139*
    A. garhi and Early Stone Tools   140
Summary   141

Chapter 7
The Genus *Homo*   143

Early *Homo*   143
    H. rudolfensis *and* H. habilis   *143*
    H. habilis *and* H. erectus   *144*
Out of Africa I: *H. erectus*   147
    Paleolithic Tools   147
    Adaptive Strategies of H. erectus   *149*
    The Evolution and Expansion of
    H. erectus   *150*
Archaic *H. sapiens*   152
    Ice Ages of the Pleistocene   153
    H. antecessor *and*
    H. heidelbergensis   *155*
The Neandertals   156
    Cold-Adapted Neandertals   156
    The Neandertals and Modern People   157

Modern Humans   159
    Out of Africa II   159
    Genetic Evidence for Out of Africa II   161
    The Denisovans   162
The Advent of Behavioral Modernity   162
Advances in Technology   164
*Applying Anthropology to Popular Culture:
So Easy a Caveman Can Do It   166*
Glacial Retreat   166
Settling the Americas   167
Homo floresiensis   168
*Anthropology Today: Neandertal
Cannibalism   170*
Summary   172

Chapter 8
The First Farmers   174

The Mesolithic   174
The Neolithic   175
The First Farmers and Herders in the
Middle East   178
    Genetic Changes and Domestication   180
    Food Production and the State   181
Other Old World Farmers   182
The First American Farmers   185
*Applying Anthropology to Popular Culture:
McDonald's   186*
    *The Tropical Origins of New World
    Domestication   187*
    The Mexican Highlands   189
Explaining the Neolithic   190
    *Geography and the Spread of Food
    Production   191*
*Anthropology Today: The Early Origin of
New World Domestication   192*
Summary   193

Chapter 9
The First Cities and States   195

The Origin of the State   195
    Hydraulic Systems   196
    Long-Distance Trade Routes   196
    Population, War, and Circumscription   196
The Urban Revolution   198

Attributes of States   198
*Applying Anthropology to Popular
Culture: Royalty Today   200*
State Formation in the Middle East   200
  Urban Life   200
  The Elite Level   203
  Social Ranking and Chiefdoms   203
  Advanced Chiefdoms   205
  The Rise of the State   205
Other Early States   208
State Formation in Mesoamerica   210
  Early Chiefdoms and Elites   210
  *Warfare and State Formation:
  The Zapotec Case   212*
  States in the Valley of Mexico   214
Why States Collapse   215
  The Mayan Decline   215
*Anthropology Today: The Fantastic
Claims of Pseudo-Archaeology   217*
Summary   219

Chapter 10
Language and Communication   221

Language   222
Nonhuman Primate Communication   222
  Call Systems   222
  Sign Language   223
  The Origin of Language   226
Nonverbal Communication   226
*Applying Anthropology to Popular Culture:
Facebook and Twitter   227*
The Structure of Language   228
  Speech Sounds   228
Language, Thought, and Culture   231
  The Sapir-Whorf Hypothesis   231
  Focal Vocabulary   232
Sociolinguistics   234
  Social and Linguistic Variation   234
  *Linguistic Diversity within
  Nations   235*
  Gender Speech Contrasts   236
  *Stratification and Symbolic
  Domination   237*
  Black English Vernacular (BEV)   239

Historical Linguistics   240
  Language Loss   242
*Anthropology Today: Linguistic Diversity
and the Internet   243*
Summary   244

Chapter 11
Making a Living   246

Adaptive Strategies   246
  Foraging   247
Adaptive Strategies Based on Food
Production   251
  Horticulture   251
  Agriculture   253
  *Agricultural Intensification: People and
  the Environment   254*
  Pastoralism   255
Economic Systems   256
  Production in Nonindustrial Societies   257
  Means of Production   258
  Alienation in Industrial Economies   258
Economizing and Maximization   261
  Alternative Ends   262
Distribution, Exchange   262
  The Market Principle   262
*Applying Anthropology to Popular
Culture: Hip-Hop Lyrics   263*
  Redistribution   263
  Reciprocity   263
  Coexistence of Exchange Principles   265
  Potlatching   265
*Anthropology Today: Scarcity and the
Betsileo   267*
Summary   269

Chapter 12
Political Systems   271

What Is "The Political"?   271
Types and Trends   272
Bands and Tribes   273
  Foraging Bands   274
  Tribal Cultivators   276
  The Village Head   277
  The "Big Man"   278

Applying Anthropology to Popular Culture: Superheroes 280
    Pantribal Sodalities 280
    Nomadic Politics 282
Chiefdoms 283
    Political and Economic Systems 283
    Status Systems 285
    The Emergence of Stratification 285
State Systems 286
    Population Control 287
    Judiciary 287
    Enforcement 288
    Fiscal Support 288
Social Control 288
    Hegemony and Resistance 289
    Weapons of the Weak 290
    Shame and Gossip 290
    The Igbo Women's War 291
Anthropology Today: Yanomami Update: Venezuela Takes Charge, Problems Arise 292
Summary 295

Chapter 13
Families, Kinship, and Marriage 297

Families 298
    Nuclear and Extended Families 299
    Industrialism and Family Organization 301
    Changes in North American Kinship 302
Applying Anthropology to Popular Culture: TV Families 304
    The Family among Foragers 305
Descent 305
    Descent Groups 306
    Lineages, Clans, and Residence Rules 307
Marriage 308
    Exogamy and Incest 309
    Incest Happens 310
    Endogamy 312
Marital Rights and Same-Sex Marriage 312

Marriage across Cultures 315
    Bridewealth and Dowry 315
    Durable Alliances 316
Divorce 317
Plural Marriages 318
    Polygyny 318
Anthropology Today: Five Wives and 55 Children 320
    Polyandry 321
Summary 322

Chapter 14
Gender 324

Sex and Gender 324
Recurrent Gender Patterns 326
Gender Roles and Gender Stratification 330
    Reduced Gender Stratification— Matrilineal–Matrilocal Societies 331
    Matriarchy 331
    Increased Gender Stratification— Patrilineal–Patrilocal Societies 333
    Patriarchy and Violence 334
Gender in Industrial Societies 334
Applying Anthropology to Popular Culture: Lisa vs. Malibu Stacy 337
    The Feminization of Poverty 337
    Work and Happiness 338
Beyond Male and Female 339
Sexual Orientation 342
Anthropology Today: Changing Images of Masculinity 344
Summary 346

Chapter 15
Religion 348

Expressions of Religion 350
    Spiritual Beings 350
    Powers and Forces 351
    Magic and Religion 352
    Uncertainty, Anxiety, Solace 352
    Rituals 353
    Rites of Passage 354
    Totemism 357

Social Control   357
Kinds of Religion   359
World Religions   360
*Applying Anthropology to Popular
Culture: Muslims and Media   362*
Religion and Change   362
   Revitalization Movements   362
   Cargo Cults   363
   *New and Alternative Religious
   Movements   365*
Secular Rituals   365
*Anthropology Today: Hinduism Takes
Back Yoga   366*
Summary   368

Chapter 16
The World System and
Colonialism   370

The World System   370
   The Emergence of the World System   372
Industrialization   373
   Causes of the Industrial Revolution   373
Socioeconomic Effects of
Industrialization   375
   Industrial Stratification   375
Colonialism   377
   British Colonialism   378
   French Colonialism   380
   Colonialism and Identity   380
   Postcolonial Studies   381
Development   382
   Neoliberalism   383
The Second World   383
   Communism   384
   Postsocialist Transitions   384
The World System Today   385
   *Energy Consumption and Industrial
   Degradation   386*
*Applying Anthropology to Popular Culture:
Avatar   387*
*Anthropology Today: Mining Giant
Compatible with Sustainability
Institute?   388*
Summary   390

Chapter 17
Ethnicity and Race   393

Ethnic Groups and Ethnicity   393
   Shifting Status   394
Race and Ethnicity   396
The Social Construction of Race   397
   *Hypodescent: Race in the United
   States   397*
   Race in the Census   398
   Not Us: Race in Japan   400
   *Phenotype and Fluidity: Race in
   Brazil   402*
Ethnic Groups, Nations, and
Nationalities   404
   *Nationalities and Imagined
   Communities   405*
Ethnic Tolerance and
Accommodation   406
   Assimilation   406
   The Plural Society   406
   *Multiculturalism and Ethnic
   Identity   407*
*Applying Anthropology to Popular
Culture: Diversity on TV   409*
Roots of Ethnic Conflict   409
   Prejudice and Discrimination   410
   Chips in the Mosaic   410
   Aftermaths of Oppression   411
Anthropology Today: From Saturday Night
Fever *to* Jersey Shore   *413*
Summary   414

Chapter 18
Applying Anthropology   416

The Role of the Applied
Anthropologist   417
   Early Applications   417
   Academic and Applied Anthropology   417
   Applied Anthropology Today   418
Development Anthropology   418
   Equity   419
Strategies for Innovation   419
   Overinnovation   420

Applying Anthropology to Popular Culture: Coca-Cola 421

   Underdifferentiation 421

   Indigenous Models 422

Anthropology and Education 423

Urban Anthropology 424

   Urban versus Rural 426

Medical Anthropology 427

Anthropology and Business 431

Careers and Anthropology 432

Anthropology Today: Culturally Appropriate Marketing 434

Summary 436

Chapter 19
Anthropology's Role in a Globalizing World 438

Globalization: Its Meaning and Its Nature 439

Global Climate Change 442

Environmental Anthropology 444

   Global Assaults on Local Autonomy 445

   Deforestation 446

Interethnic Contact 448

   Cultural Imperialism 448

Making and Remaking Culture 450

   Indigenizing Popular Culture 450

   A Global System of Images 451

   A Global Culture of Consumption 451

People in Motion 452

Applying Anthropology to Popular Culture: ET Phone Home 454

Indigenous Peoples 454

   Identity in Indigenous Politics 456

The Continuance of Diversity 456

Anthropology Today: Engulfed by Climate Change, Town Seeks Lifeline 457

Summary 459

Glossary 461

Credits 475

Bibliography 477

Index 509

Popular Culture Boxes

Indiana Jones   10

Popular Songs   21

Bones   50

Oprah's DNA   84

Planet of the Apes   98

Monkey Bars   122

Even a Caveman Can Do It   166

McDonald's   186

Royalty Today   200

Facebook and Twitter   227

Hip-Hop Lyrics   263

Superheroes   280

TV Families   304

Lisa vs. Malibu Stacy   337

Muslims and Media   362

Avatar   387

Diversity on TV   409

Coca-Cola   421

ET Phone Home   454

Anthropology Today Boxes

Anthropologist's Son Elected President   13

Experiencing Culture: Personal Space and Displays of Affection   36

Archaeologist in New Orleans Finds a Way to Help the Living   62

Genetic Study Bolsters Columbus Link to Syphilis   91

Global Economy Threatens Orangutans   116

Anthropologist's Son Finds New Species of *Australopithecus*   139

Neandertal Cannibalism   170

The Early Origin of New World Domestication   192

The Fantastic Claims of Pseudo-Archaeology   217

Linguistic Diversity and the Internet   243

Scarcity and the Betsileo   267

Yanomami Update: Venezuela Takes Charge, Problems Arise   292

Five Wives and 55 Children   320

Changing Images of Masculinity   344

Hinduism Takes Back Yoga   366

Mining Giant Compatible with Sustainability Institute?   388

From *Saturday Night Fever* to *Jersey Shore*   413

Culturally Appropriate Marketing   434

Engulfed by Climate Change, Town seeks Lifeline   457

Preface

Window on Humanity is intended to provide a concise, readable, lower-cost introduction to general (four-field) anthropology. The combination of shorter length and lower cost increases the instructor's options for assigning additional reading—case studies, readers, and other supplements—in a semester course. *Window* also can work well in a quarter system, since traditional anthropology texts may be too long for a one-quarter course.

As a college student, I was drawn to anthropology by its breadth and because of what it could tell me about the human condition, present and past. Since then, I've been fortunate in spending my teaching career at a university (the University of Michigan) that values and unites anthropology's four subdisciplines. I enjoy my contact with members of all the subfields, and by teaching and writing for the four-field introductory anthropology course, I'm happy to keep up with those subfields. I believe that anthropology has compiled an impressive body of knowledge about human diversity in time and space, and I'm eager to introduce that knowledge in the pages that follow. I believe strongly in anthropology's capacity to enlighten and inform. Anthropology's subject matter is intrinsically fascinating, and its focus on diversity helps students understand and interact with their fellow human beings in an increasingly interconnected world and an increasingly diverse North America.

I wrote my first textbook at a time when there were far fewer introductory anthropology texts than there are today. The texts back then tended to be overly encyclopedic. I found them too long and too unfocused for my course and my image of contemporary anthropology. The field of anthropology was changing rapidly. Anthropologists were writing about a "new archaeology" and a "new ethnography." Fresh fossil finds and biochemical studies were challenging our understanding of human and primate evolution. Studies of monkeys and apes in their natural settings were complementing conclusions based on work in zoos. Studies of language as it actually is used in society were revolutionizing formal and static linguistic models. In cultural anthropology, symbolic and interpretive approaches were joining ecological and materialist ones.

Today there are new issues and approaches, such as molecular anthropology and new forms of spatial and historical analysis. The fossil and archaeological records expand every day. Profound changes have affected the people and societies anthropologists traditionally have studied. In cultural anthropology it's increasingly difficult to know when to write in the present tense and when to write in the past tense. Anthropology hasn't lost its excitement. Yet many texts ignore change—except maybe with a chapter tacked on at the end—and are written as though anthropology and the people it studies were the same as they were a generation ago. While any competent anthropology text must present anthropology's core, it also should demonstrate anthropology's relevance to today's globalized world. *Window on Humanity* has been written to present that relevance in clear and simple terms to the beginning student.

Goals

In writing this book, I've been guided by three main goals. First, I wanted to provide a concise, up-to-date, lower-cost, four-field introduction to anthropology. Anthropology is a science—a "systematic field of study or body of knowledge that aims, through experiment, observation, and deduction, to produce reliable explanations of phenomena, with reference to the material and physical world" (*Webster's New World Encyclopedia* 1993, p. 937). Anthropology is a humanistic science devoted to discovering, describing, and explaining similarities and differences in time and space. In *Mirror for Man,* one of the first books I ever read in anthropology, I was impressed by Clyde Kluckhohn's (1944) description of anthropology as "the science of human similarities and differences" (p. 9). Kluckhohn's statement of the need for such a field still stands: "Anthropology provides a scientific basis for dealing with the crucial dilemma of the world today: how can peoples of different appearance, mutually unintelligible languages, and dissimilar ways of life get along peaceably together?" (p. 9).

Anthropology is a science with clear links to the humanities, as it brings a comparative and cross-cultural perspective to forms of creative expression. One might say that anthropology is among the most humanistic academic fields because of its fundamental respect for human diversity. Anthropologists routinely listen to, record, and attempt to represent voices and perspectives from a multitude of times, places, nations, and cultures. Through its four subfields, anthropology brings together biological, social, cultural, linguistic, and historical approaches. Multiple and diverse perspectives offer a fuller understanding of what it means to be human than is provided by academic fields that lack anthropology's broad vision and cross-cultural approach.

My second goal was to write a book that would be good for students. This book would be user-friendly in layout, writing style, approach, and pedagogy. By discussing current events and popular culture in relation to anthropology's core, it would show students how anthropology relates to their own lives and experiences. Throughout this book I've attempted to be fair and objective in covering various and sometimes diverging approaches, but I make my own views known and write in the first person when it seems appropriate. I've heard colleagues who have used other textbooks complain that some authors seem so intent on presenting every conceivable theory about an issue that students are bewildered by the array of possibilities. Anthropology should not be made so complicated that it is impossible for beginning students to appreciate and understand it. The textbook author, like the instructor, must be able to guide the student.

My third goal was to write a book that professors, as well as students, would appreciate. The organization of this text is intended to cover core concepts and basics while also, as mentioned, discussing prominent current interests.

Content and Organization

Window on Humanity covers the core and basics of all four subfields, while also examining current issues and approaches. No single or monolithic theoretical perspective orients this book. My e-mail, along with reviewers' comments, confirms that instructors with a wide range of views and approaches have been pleased with *Window* as a teaching tool.

In Chapter 1, anthropology is introduced as an integrated four-field discipline, with academic and applied dimensions, that examines human biological and cultural diversity in time and space. Anthropology is discussed as a comparative and holistic science, featuring biological, social, cultural, linguistic, humanistic, and historical approaches. Chapter 2 examines the central anthropological concept of culture, including its symbolic and adaptive features. Chapter 3 is about doing anthropology—the methods and ethics of research in anthropology's subfields.

The chapters focusing on physical anthropology and archaeology (4–9) offer up-to-date answers to several key questions: When did we originate, and how did we become what we are? What role do genes, the environment, society, and culture play in human variation and diversity? What can we tell about our origins and nature from the study of our nearest relatives—nonhuman primates? When and how did the primates originate? What key features of their early adaptations are still basic to our abilities, behavior, and perceptions? How did hominids develop from our primate ancestors? When, where, and how did the first hominins emerge and expand? What about the earliest real humans? How do we explain biological diversity in our own species, *Homo sapiens?* What major transitions have taken place since the emergence of *Homo sapiens?*

In Chapters 8 and 9 we learn that the origin of food production (the domestication of plants and animals) was a major change in human adaptation, with profound implications for society and culture. The spread and intensification of food production are tied to the appearance of the first towns, cities, and states, and the emergence of social stratification and major inequalities.

The chapters on linguistic and sociocultural anthropology (10–19) are organized to place related content close together—although they are sufficiently independent to be assigned in any order the instructor might select. Thus "Political Systems" (Chapter 12) logically follows "Making a Living" (Chapter 11). Chapters 13 and 14 ("Families, Kinship, and Marriage" and "Gender," respectively) also form a coherent unit. The chapter on religion (15) covers not just traditional religious practices but also contemporary world religions and religious movements. It is followed by four chapters (16–19) that form a natural unit exploring sociocultural transformations and expressions in today's world.

This concluding unit represents one of the key differences between this text and others. These four chapters address several important questions: How and why did the modern world system emerge and expand? How has world capitalism affected patterns of stratification and inequality within and among nations? What were colonialism, imperialism, and Communism, and what are their legacies? How are race and ethnicity socially constructed and handled in different societies, and how do they generate prejudice, discrimination, and conflict? How do economic development, globalization, and climate change affect the peoples, societies, and communities among which anthropologists traditionally have worked? What is globalization—as fact, as policy, and as ideology? How do people today actively interpret and confront the world system and the products of globalization? What factors threaten continued human diversity? How can anthropologists work to ensure the preservation of that diversity?

Let me focus here as well on two chapters present in *Window on Humanity* but not found consistently in other anthropology texts: "Ethnicity and Race" (Chapter 17) and "Gender" (Chapter 14). I believe that systematic consideration of race, ethnicity, and gender is vital in an introductory anthropology text. Anthropology's distinctive four-field approach can shed special light on these topics. We see this not only in Chapter 17 ("Ethnicity and Race"), but also in Chapter 4 ("Evolution, Genetics, and Human Variation"), in which race is discussed as a problematic concept in biology. Race and gender studies are fields in which anthropology always has taken the lead. I'm convinced that anthropology's special contributions to understanding the biological, social, cultural, and linguistic dimensions of race, ethnicity, and gender should be highlighted in any introductory text.

New in the Fifth Edition

All chapters of *Window on Humanity* have been updated, with charts, tables, and statistics based on the most recent information available. Of the 19 end-of-chapter boxes, 7 are new to this edition, and 2 have been updated substantially. These "Anthropology Today" boxes are intended to bring home anthropology's relevance to current issues and events, as also is the new feature "Applying Anthropology to Popular Culture." With the revised Chapter 19, "Anthropology's Role in a Globalizing World" and other changes, the focus on global themes, trends, and issues has been strengthened even further in this edition.

Chapter-by-Chapter Changes

Chapter 1: What Is Anthropology?

Several users and reviewers felt that the long section on biological race formerly in Chapter 1 interrupted the flow of the introductory chapter. I agree with them and have moved this material to Chapter 4 ("Evolution, Genetics, and Human Variation"), where it fits more appropriately.

Chapter 2: Culture

This chapter contains a new section on pop, civic, and public culture and a new "Anthropology Today" box on public displays of affection.

Chapter 3: Doing Anthropology

I've done a word-by-word revision of Chapter 3, which now is titled "Doing Anthropology." Responding to reviewers' suggestions, the reorganization moves the discussion of archaeology up to precede biological and cultural anthropology. There is a new section on longitudinal, team, and multisited research. The chapter ends with a discussion of ethics and new material on anthropologists, terrorism, and warfare.

Chapter 4: Evolution, Genetics, and Human Variation

This chapter contains a new and revised major section on the problematic concept of race, moved here from Chapter 1 in the previous edition.

Chapter 5: The Primates

Chapter 5 has a new section on endangered primates, a new "Anthropology Today" box on threats to orangutans, and a new discussion of distinguishing traits of apes. I followed reviewers' suggestions to shorten and simplify the primate evolution section. I also moved the material on two possible late Miocene hominins (*Sahelanthropus tchadensis* and *Orrorin tugenensis*) to Chapter 6.

Chapter 6: The Early Hominins

In addition to moving *Sahelanthropus* and *Orrorin* here from Chapter 5, I've added new material on recently described "Ardi" (*Ardipithecus*) and "Lucy's baby." There's also a new "Anthropology Today" on recently discovered *Australopithecus sediba* and a revised discussion of Oldowan tools.

Chapter 7: The Genus *Homo*

Chapter 7 contains a new section, describing "The Denisovans," the recently identified (2010) Asian cousins of Neandertals that interbred with ancestral Melanesians. An abridged section, on "The Advent of Behavioral Modernity," has been moved here from Chapter 2. There's a new section on *H. floresiensis,* aka "hobbits" of Flores island, Indonesia, and a new "Anthropology Today" box on Neandertal cannibalism and social life.

Chapter 8: The First Farmers

This chapter has new material on the Mesolithic and a clarified discussion of New World staples.

Chapter 9: The First Cities and States

Chapter 9 contains a new section, on "The Urban Revolution," and a thoroughly revised "Anthropology Today" on pseudo-archaeology, debunking recent fantastic claims.

Chapter 10: Language and Communication

Chapter 10 includes a new introduction, a new section titled "Social and Linguistic Variation," and a discussion of new media, including texting, Facebook, and Twitter.

Chapter 11: Making a Living

Chapter 11 contains a revised section on alienation and a new table, "Foragers Then and Now."

Chapter 12: Political Systems

Chapter 12 has been revised substantially and word by word. I condensed the early sections and added a new major section, "Social Control" (vs. governmental) that includes these subheads: "Hegemony and Resistance," "Weapons of the Weak," "Shame and Gossip," and "The Igbo Women's War."

Chapter 13: Families, Kinship, and Marriage

I completely revised the section on exogamy and incest, added new material on dowry, updated the discussion of same-sex marriage (and all other statistics), and added a new introduction on family diversity

Chapter 14: Gender

While retaining content that most users and reviewers like, this chapter has been substantially revised. Specific changes include:

- a new major section, "Beyond Male and Female," discussing transgender and chromosomal anomalies creating sex-gender differences;
- an interesting new subsection, "Work and Happiness," discussing the correlation between a national happiness index and female extradomestic employment;
- deletion of sections "Gender among Foragers," "Gender among Horticulturalists," and "Gender among Agriculturalists";
- a new "Anthropology Today" on men's fashion—"Changing Images of Masculinity"— to show that malleable and socially constructed gender attributes apply to males as well as to females.

Chapter 15: Religion

I've done a very thorough word-by-word revision of Chapter 15, reflecting reviewers' suggestions. Specific changes include:

- beginning the chapter with a discussion of how difficult it is to define religion;
- ending the chapter with an expanded discussion of secular rituals;
- adding a new section, "New and Alternative Religious Movements," including new age religion and santeria, voodoo;
- including a new "Anthropology Today" on "Hinduism Takes Back Yoga";
- deleting dated Taliban material;
- adding new material on witchcraft;
- clarifying terms *ecclesiastical* and *Olympian* and eliminating discussion of the Wallace typology.

Chapter 16: The World System and Colonialism

Chapter 16 has been updated, with new and redrawn figures and a substantially revised section, "The World System Today."

Chapter 17: Ethnicity and Race

Thoroughly updated with the latest (2010) census figures, this chapter contains new information on ethnic diversity within countries by region and a new "Anthropology Today" box on *Jersey Shore* and Italian American identity.

Chapter 18: Applying Anthropology

Chapter 18 has undergone a word-by-word revision for clarity and updating.

Chapter 19: Anthropology's Role in a Globalizing World

I've given Chapter 19 a new title and word-by-word revision for clarity and updating. The chapter now begins with an important new major section, "Globalization: Its Meaning and Its Nature," distinguishing between globalization as fact and process, and globalization as ideology and policy.

Pedagogy

This fifth edition incorporates suggestions made by users of my other texts as well as reviewers of previous editions of *Window on Humanity*. The result, I hope, is a sound, well-organized, interesting, and user-friendly introduction to anthropology.

Window contains "Anthropology Today" boxes (seven new and two substantially revised). Placed consistently at the end of each chapter, "Anthropology Today" is intended to give students a chance to consider anthropology's relevance to today's world and to their own lives. Some boxes examine current events or debates. Others are more personal accounts, which add human feeling to the presentation of anthropology's subject matter. Many boxes illustrate a point with examples familiar to students from their enculturation or everyday experience.

The new feature "Applying Anthropology to Popular Culture" (one per chapter) illustrates how easily anthropology can be applied to aspects of popular culture, including music, films, sports, and television. Here again the goal is to foster an appreciation of anthropology within the framework of students' enculturation and everyday experience.

End-of-chapter summaries are numbered, to make major points stand out.

Boldface key terms in each chapter are defined in the glossary at the end of the book. A bibliography contains references cited and relevant reading.

Supplements

Visit our Online Learning Center website at www.mhhe.com/kottak for robust student and instructor resources.

For Students

Student resources include self-quizzes (multiple-choice, true or false, essay), Internet exercises, and additional chapter study aides.

For Instructors

The password-protected instructor portion of the website includes the instructor's manual, a comprehensive computerized test bank, PowerPoint lecture slides, and a variety of additional instructor resources.

CourseSmart eBook

CourseSmart is a new way to find and buy eTextbooks. At CourseSmart you can save up to 50 percent off the cost of a print textbook, reduce your impact on the environment, and gain access to powerful Web tools for learning. CourseSmart has the largest selection of eTextbooks available anywhere, offering thousands of the most commonly adopted textbooks from a wide variety of higher-education publishers. CourseSmart eTextbooks are available in one standard online reader with full text search, notes and highlighting, and e-mail tools for sharing notes between classmates. For further details contact your sales representative or go to www.coursesmart.com.

Tegrity Campus

Tegrity Campus is a service that makes class time available all the time by automatically capturing every lecture in a searchable format for students to review when they study and complete assignments. With a simple one-click start and stop process, you capture all computer screens and corresponding audio. Students replay any part of any class with easy-to-use, browser-based viewing on a PC or Mac.

Educators know that the more students can see, hear, and experience class resources, the better they learn. With Tegrity Campus, students quickly recall key moments by using its unique search feature. This search helps students find what they need, when they need it, across an entire semester of class recordings. Turn all your students' study time into learning moments immediately supported by your lecture.

Acknowledgments

I'm grateful to many colleagues at McGraw-Hill. Gina Boedeker has been supportive and enthusiastic as McGraw-Hill's executive editor for anthropology (along with sociology, women's studies, and criminal justice). As developmental editor, Kate Scheinman once again did an outstanding job synthesizing the reviews and helping me plan and implement the revision, working with me to complete, assemble, and turn over the manuscript, keeping things moving, and catching things even in pages. Thanks as well to Managing Editor Meghan Campbell, William Glass, McGraw-Hill's publisher of anthropology and other social sciences, Marketing Manager Patrick Brown, and Editorial Coordinator Brittany Pogue-Mohammed.

I would like to thank Jasmin Tokatlian for her work as production editor, guiding the manuscript through production and keeping everything moving on schedule. Thanks as well to the entire K4 team. Louis Swaim, Buyer, worked with the printer to make sure everything came out right. It's always a pleasure to work with Barbara Salz, freelance photo researcher, with whom I've worked for two decades. I want to thank Victoria Springer for her work on the Instructor's Manual and Test Bank, Gerry Williams for his work on the PowerPoints, and Maria Perez for her work on the student supplements located on the Online Learning Center website. I also thank Judith Brown for copyediting, Jan Fehler for proofreading, and Allister Fein for executing the design.

Nora Agbayani also deserves thanks as photo research coordinator. Thanks, too, to Jennifer Barrick, media project manager, for creating the OLC. I also thank Karyn Morrison, who has handled the literary permissions.

I'm very grateful to the following prepublication reviewers of this and previous editions of *Window on Humanity* and *Mirror for Humanity:*

Terri Aihoshi
Grant MacEwan College

Sue L. Aki
University of Texas at San Antonio

Linda Allen
Kirkwood Community College

Ari N. Ariyaratne
College of DuPage

Diane Everett Barbolla
San Diego Mesa College

Joshua Barker
University of Toronto

Jeffrey P. Blick
Georgia College & State University

Beau Bowers
Central Piedmont Community College

Jim Brady
California State University, Los Angeles

Larisa Lee Broyles,
California State University, San Bernardino

Stephen Childs
Valdosta State University

William L. Coleman
University of North Carolina, Greensboro

Garrett Cook
Baylor University

Leslie Dawson
Grant MacEwan College

Connie Deroche
Cape Breton University

Barbra E. Erickson
California State University–Fullerton

Charles R. Ewen
East Carolina University

Jason M. Fancher
Washington State University

Les W. Field
University of New Mexico

Elizabeth Fortenbery
Pierce Community College

Elizabeth Fuller-Tarbox
*State University of New
York–Potsdam*

Dan Gardiner
Mohawk College

Maidie R. Golan
Kennesaw State University

David B. Halmo
University of Wisconsin–Parkside

Christopher Hays
*University of Wisconsin–Washington
County*

Marc Healy
Elgin Community College

Katherine Hirschfeld
University of Oklahoma

Patricia Jolly
University of Northern Colorado

Hilary Kahn
Indiana University–Indianapolis

Patricia Kelly-Spurles
Mount Allison University

Yin Lam
University of Victoria

Jami Leibowitz
East Carolina University

William Leons
University of Toledo

Daniel Maher
Westark College

Susan Meswick
CUNY Queens College

Garry Morgan
Northwestern College

Martin Oppenheimer
Kansas State University

Mary Patterson
The University of Melbourne, Australia

Megan A. Perry
East Carolina University

Gerald F. Reid
Sacred Heart University

Carolyn Rock
Valdosta State University

Rita C. Rodabaugh
Central Piedmont Community College

Eugene E. Ruyle
California State University, Long Beach

Carleen Sanchez
University of Nebraska Lincoln

Jon A. Schlenker
University of Maine at Augusta

Pete Sinelli
University of Central Florida

Andris Skreija
University of Nebraska–Omaha

Betty A. Smith
Kennesaw State University

Shannon Speed
University of Texas at Austin

Emily Stovel
Ripon College

Ted Swedenburg
University of Arkansas

Susan Tanner
University of Georgia

Mark Tromans
Broward Community College

Helen Vallianatos
University of Alberta

Salena Wakim
Orange Coast College

Thomas Williamson
St. Olaf College

Students, too, regularly share their insights about *Window* via e-mail. Anyone—student or instructor—with access to e-mail can reach me at the following address: ckottak@ bellsouth.net.

As usual, my family has offered me understanding, support, and inspiration during the preparation of *Window*. Dr. Nicholas Kottak and Dr. Juliet Kottak Mavromatis regularly share their insights with me, as does Isabel Wagley Kottak, my companion in the field and in life for more than four decades, to whom this book is dedicated.

During my long teaching career, I've benefited from the knowledge, help, and advice of so many friends, colleagues, teaching assistants (graduate student instructors—GSIs), and students that I can no longer fit their names into a short preface. I hope they know who they are and accept my thanks. Feedback from students, faculty, and GSIs keeps me up-to-date on the interests, needs, and views of the people for whom *Window* is written, as does my ongoing participation in workshops on the teaching of anthropology. I continue to believe that effective textbooks are based in the enthusiastic practice of teaching. I hope this product of my experience will continue to be helpful to others.

Conrad Phillip Kottak

Seabrook Island, South Carolina

ckottak@bellsouth.net

About the Author

Conrad Phillip Kottak, who received his AB and PhD degrees from Columbia University, is the Julian H. Steward Collegiate Professor Emeritus of Anthropology at the University of Michigan, where he served as anthropology department chair from 1996 to 2006. In 1991 he was honored for his teaching by the university and the state of Michigan. In 1999 the American Anthropological Association (AAA) awarded Professor Kottak its Award for Excellence in the Undergraduate Teaching of Anthropology. In 2005 he was elected to the American Academy of Arts and Sciences, and in 2008 to the National Academy of Sciences. Professor Kottak has done ethnographic fieldwork in Brazil, Madagascar, and the United States. His general interests are in the processes by which local cultures are incorporated—and resist incorporation—into larger systems. This interest links his earlier work on ecology and state formation in Africa and Madagascar to his more recent research on globalization, national and international culture, and the mass media.

The fourth edition of Kottak's popular case study *Assault on Paradise: The Globalization of a Little Community in Brazil,* based on his continuing fieldwork in Arembepe, Bahia, Brazil, was published in 2006 by McGraw-Hill. In a research project during the 1980s, Kottak blended ethnography and survey research in studying "Television's Behavioral Effects in Brazil." That research is the basis of Kottak's book *Prime-Time Society: An Anthropological Analysis of Television and Culture* (updated edition published by Left Coast Press in 2009)—a comparative study of the nature and impact of television in Brazil and the United States.

Kottak's other books include *The Past in the Present: History, Ecology and Cultural Variation in Highland Madagascar* (1980), *Researching American Culture: A Guide for Student Anthropologists* (edited 1982) (both University of Michigan Press), and *Madagascar: Society and History* (1986) (Carolina Academic Press). The most recent editions (14th) of his texts *Anthropology: Appreciating Human Diversity* and *Cultural Anthropology: Appreciating Cultural Diversity* were published by McGraw-Hill in 2010. He also is the author of *Mirror for Humanity: A Concise Introduction to Cultural Anthropology* (8th ed., McGraw-Hill, 2012) and of this book—*Window on Humanity: A Concise Introduction to Anthropology* (5th ed., McGraw-Hill, 2012).

Conrad Kottak's articles have appeared in academic journals, including *American Anthropologist, Journal of Anthropological Research, American Ethnologist, Ethnology, Human Organization,* and *Luso-Brazilian Review.* He also has written for more popular journals, including *Transaction/SOCIETY, Natural History, Psychology Today,* and *General Anthropology.*

In more recent research projects, Kottak and his colleagues have investigated the emergence of ecological awareness in Brazil, the social context of deforestation and biodiversity conservation in Madagascar, and popular participation in economic development planning in northeastern Brazil. Professor Kottak has been active in the University of Michigan's Center for the Ethnography of Everyday Life, supported by the

Alfred P. Sloan Foundation. In that capacity, for a research project titled "Media, Family, and Work in a Middle-Class Midwestern Town," Kottak and his colleague Lara Descartes have investigated how middle-class families draw on various media in planning, managing, and evaluating their choices and solutions with respect to the competing demands of work and family. That research is the basis of their book *Media and Middle Class Moms: Images and Realities of Work and Family* (Descartes and Kottak 2009, Routledge/ Taylor and Francis).

Conrad Kottak appreciates comments about his books from professors and students. He can be reached by e-mail at the following Internet address: **ckottak@bellsouth.net.**

1

What Is Anthropology?

Human Adaptability

Adaptation, Variation, and Change

General Anthropology

Cultural Forces Shape Human Biology

The Subdisciplines of Anthropology

Cultural Anthropology

Archaeological Anthropology

Applying Anthropology to Popular
Culture: Indiana Jones

Biological, or Physical, Anthropology

Linguistic Anthropology

Anthropology and Other Academic Fields

Applied Anthropology

*Anthropology Today: Anthropologist's
Son Elected President*

"That's just human nature." "People are pretty much the same all over the world." Such opinions, which we hear in conversations, in the mass media, and in a dozen scenes in daily life, promote the erroneous idea that people in other countries have the same desires, feelings, values, and aspirations that we do. Such statements proclaim that because people are essentially the same, they are eager to receive the ideas, beliefs, values, institutions, practices, and products of an expansive North American culture. Often this assumption turns out to be wrong.

Anthropology offers a broader view—a distinctive comparative, cross-cultural perspective. Most people think that anthropologists study nonindustrial societies, and they do. My research has taken me to remote villages in Brazil and Madagascar, a large island off the southeast coast of Africa. In Brazil I sailed with fishers in simple sailboats on Atlantic waters. Among Madagascar's Betsileo people I worked in rice fields and took part in ceremonies in which I entered tombs to rewrap the corpses of decaying ancestors.

However, anthropology is much more than the study of nonindustrial peoples. It is a comparative science that examines all societies, ancient and modern, simple and complex. Most of the other social sciences tend to focus on a single society, usually an industrial nation such as the United States or Canada. Anthropology offers a unique cross-cultural perspective, constantly comparing the customs of one society with those of others.

To become a cultural anthropologist, one normally does *ethnography* (the first-hand, personal study of local settings). Ethnographic fieldwork usually entails spending a year or more in another society, living with the local people and learning about their way of life. No matter how much the ethnographer discovers about the society, he or she remains an alien there. That experience of alienation has a profound impact. Having learned to respect other customs and beliefs, anthropologists can never forget that there is a wider world. There are normal ways of thinking and acting other than our own.

Human Adaptability

Anthropologists study human beings wherever and whenever they find them—in a Turkish café, a Mesopotamian tomb, or a North American shopping mall. Anthropology is the exploration of human diversity in time and space. Anthropology studies the whole of the human condition: past, present, and future; biology, society, language, and culture. Of particular interest is the diversity that comes through human adaptability.

Humans are among the world's most adaptable animals. In the Andes of South America, people wake up in villages 16,000 feet above sea level and then trek 1,500 feet higher to work in tin mines. Tribes in the Australian desert worship animals and discuss philosophy. People survive malaria in the tropics. Men have walked on the moon. The model of the starship *Enterprise* in Washington's Smithsonian Institution symbolizes the desire to "seek out new life and civilizations, to boldly go where no one has gone before." Wishes to know the unknown, control the uncontrollable, and create order out of chaos find expression among all peoples. Creativity, adaptability, and flexibility are basic human attributes, and human diversity is the subject matter of anthropology.

Students often are surprised by the breadth of **anthropology,** which is the study of the human species and its immediate ancestors. Anthropology is a uniquely comparative and **holistic** science. Holism refers to the study of the whole of the human condition: past, present, and future; biology, society, language, and culture.

People share **society**—organized life in groups—with other animals, including baboons, wolves, mole rats, and even ants. Culture, however, is more distinctly human. **Cultures** are traditions and customs, transmitted through learning, that form and guide the beliefs and behavior of the people exposed to them. Children learn such a tradition by growing up in a particular society, through a process called enculturation. Cultural traditions include customs and opinions, developed over the generations, about proper and improper behavior. These traditions answer such questions as: How should we do things? How do we make sense of the world? How do we tell right from wrong? What is right, and what is wrong? A culture produces a degree of consistency in behavior and thought among the people who live in a particular society.

The most critical element of cultural traditions is their transmission through learning rather than through biological inheritance. Culture is not itself biological, but it rests on certain features of human biology. For more than a million years, humans have had at least some of the biological capacities on which culture depends. These abilities are to learn, to think symbolically, to use language, and to employ tools and other products in organizing their lives and adapting to their environments.

Anthropology confronts and ponders major questions of human existence as it explores human biological and cultural diversity in time and space. By examining ancient bones and tools, we unravel the mysteries of human origins. When did our ancestors separate from those remote great-aunts and great-uncles whose descendants are the apes? Where and when did *Homo sapiens* originate? How has our species changed? What are we now, and where are we going? How have changes in culture and society influenced biological change? Our genus, *Homo*, has been changing for more than 2 million years. Humans continue to adapt and change both biologically and culturally.

Adaptation, Variation, and Change

Adaptation refers to the processes by which organisms cope with environmental forces and stresses, such as those posed by climate and *topography* or terrains, also called landforms. How do organisms change to fit their environments, such as dry climates or high mountain altitudes? Like other animals, humans use biological means of adaptation. But humans are unique in also having cultural means of adaptation. Table 1.1 summarizes the cultural and biological means that humans use to adapt to high altitudes.

Mountainous terrains pose particular challenges, those associated with high altitude and oxygen deprivation. Consider four ways (one cultural and three biological) in which humans may cope with low oxygen pressure at high altitudes. Illustrating cultural (technological) adaptation would be a pressurized airplane cabin equipped with oxygen masks. There are three ways of adapting biologically to high altitudes: genetic adaptation, long-term physiological adaptation, and short-term physiological adaptation. First, native populations of high-altitude areas, such as the Andes of Peru and the Himalayas of Tibet and Nepal, seem to have acquired certain genetic advantages for life at very high altitudes. The Andean tendency to develop a voluminous chest and lungs probably has a genetic basis. Second, regardless of their genes, people who grow up at a high altitude become physiologically more efficient there than genetically similar people who have grown up at sea level would be. This illustrates long-term physiological adaptation during the body's growth and development. Third, humans also have the capacity for short-term or immediate physiological adaptation. Thus, when lowlanders arrive in the highlands, they immediately increase their breathing and heart

TABLE 1.1　Forms of Cultural and Biological Adaptation (to High Altitude)

Form of Adaptation	Type of Adaptation	Example
Technology	Cultural	Pressurized airplane cabin with oxygen masks
Genetic adaptation (occurs over generations)	Biological	Larger "barrel chests" of native highlanders
Long-term physiological adaptation (occurs during growth and development of the individual organism)	Biological	More efficient respiratory system, to extract oxygen from "thin air"
Short-term physiological adaptation (occurs spontaneously when the individual organism enters a new environment)	Biological	Increased heart rate, hyperventilation

rates. Hyperventilation increases the oxygen in their lungs and arteries. As the pulse also increases, blood reaches their tissues more rapidly. All these varied adaptive responses—cultural and biological—achieve a single goal: maintaining an adequate supply of oxygen to the body.

As human history has unfolded, the social and cultural means of adaptation have become increasingly important. In this process, humans have devised diverse ways of coping with the range of environments they have occupied in time and space. The rate of cultural adaptation and change has accelerated, particularly during the past 10,000 years. For millions of years, hunting and gathering of nature's bounty—*foraging*—was the sole basis of human subsistence. However, it took only a few thousand years for **food production** (the cultivation of plants and domestication of animals), which originated some 12,000–10,000 years ago, to replace foraging in most areas. Between 6000 and 5000 B.P. (before the present), the first civilizations arose. These were large, powerful, and complex societies, such as ancient Egypt, that conquered and governed large geographic areas.

Much more recently, the spread of industrial production has profoundly affected human life. Throughout human history, major innovations have spread at the expense of earlier ones. Each economic revolution has had social and cultural repercussions. Today's global economy and communications link all contemporary people, directly or indirectly, in the modern world system. People must cope with forces generated by progressively larger systems—region, nation, and world. The study of such contemporary adaptations generates new challenges for anthropology: "The cultures of world peoples need to be constantly rediscovered as these people reinvent them in changing historical circumstances" (Marcus and Fischer 1986, p. 24).

General Anthropology

The academic discipline of anthropology, also known as **general anthropology** or "four-field" anthropology, includes four main subdisciplines or subfields. They are sociocultural, archaeological, biological, and linguistic anthropology. (From here on, the shorter term *cultural anthropology* will be used as a synonym for "sociocultural anthropology.") Of the subfields, cultural anthropology has the largest membership. Most departments of anthropology teach courses in all four subfields.

There are historical reasons for the inclusion of four subfields in a single discipline. The origin of anthropology as a scientific field, and of American anthropology in particular, can be traced to the 19th century. Early American anthropologists were concerned especially with the history and cultures of the native peoples of North America. Interest in the origins and diversity of Native Americans brought together studies of customs, social life, language, and physical traits. Anthropologists still are pondering such questions as, Where did Native Americans come from? How many waves of migration brought them to the New World? What are the linguistic, cultural, and biological links among Native Americans and between them and Asia? (Note that a unified four-field anthropology did not develop in Europe, where the subfields tend to exist separately.)

There also are logical reasons for the unity of American anthropology. Each subfield considers variation in time and space (that is, in different geographic areas). Cultural and archaeological anthropologists study (among many other topics) changes in social life and customs. Archaeologists use studies of living societies to imagine what life might have been like in the past. Biological anthropologists examine evolutionary changes in physical form, for example, anatomical changes that might have been associated with the origin of tool use or language. Linguistic anthropologists may reconstruct the basics of ancient languages by studying modern ones.

The subfields influence each other as anthropologists talk to each other, read books and journals, and meet in professional organizations. General anthropology explores the basics of human biology, society, and culture and considers their interrelations. Anthropologists share certain key assumptions. Perhaps the most fundamental is the idea that sound conclusions about "human nature" cannot be derived from studying a single population, nation, society, or cultural tradition. A comparative, cross-cultural approach is essential.

Early American anthropology was especially concerned with the history and cultures of Native North Americans. Ely S. Parker, or Ha-sa-no-an-da, was a Seneca Indian who made important contributions to early anthropology. Parker also served as Commissioner of Indian Affairs for the United States.

Cultural Forces Shape Human Biology

Anthropology's comparative, biocultural perspective recognizes that cultural forces constantly mold human biology. (**Biocultural** refers to the inclusion and combination of both biological and cultural perspectives and approaches to comment on or solve a particular issue or problem.) Culture is a key environmental force in determining how human bodies grow and develop. Cultural traditions promote certain activities and abilities, discourage others, and set standards of physical well-being and attractiveness. Physical activities, including sports, which are influenced by culture, help build the body. For example, North American girls are encouraged to pursue, and therefore do well in, competition involving figure skating, gymnastics, track and field, swimming, diving, and many other sports. Brazilian girls, although excelling in the team sports of basketball and volleyball, haven't fared nearly as well in individual sports as have their American and Canadian counterparts. Why are people encouraged to excel as athletes in some nations but not others? Why do people in some countries invest so much time and effort in competitive sports that their bodies change significantly as a result?

Cultural standards of attractiveness and propriety influence participation and achievement in sports. Americans run or swim not just to compete but to keep trim and fit. Brazil's beauty standards have traditionally accepted more fat, especially in female buttocks and hips. Brazilian men have had some international success in swimming and running, but Brazil rarely sends female swimmers or runners to the Olympics. One reason Brazilian

Brazil rarely sends female swimmers to the Olympics. One exception is Fabiola Molina, who competed in the 2000 and 2008 Olympics. Here, in May 2009, Molina launches herself on a winning swim in the women's 100 meter backstroke final at the Maria Lenk Trophy competition in Rio de Janeiro. How might years of competitive swimming affect phenotype?

women avoid competitive swimming in particular may be that sport's effects on the body. Years of swimming sculpt a distinctive physique: an enlarged upper torso, a massive neck, and powerful shoulders and back. Successful female swimmers tend to be big, strong, and bulky. The countries that produce them most consistently are the United States, Canada, Australia, Germany, the Scandinavian nations, the Netherlands, and the former Soviet Union, where this body type isn't as stigmatized as it is in Latin countries. Swimmers develop hard bodies, but Brazilian culture says that women should be soft, with big hips and buttocks, not big shoulders. Many young female swimmers in Brazil choose to abandon the sport rather than the "feminine" body ideal.

When you grew up, which sport did you appreciate the most—soccer, swimming, football, baseball, tennis, golf, or some other sport (or perhaps none at all)? Is this because of "who you are" or because of the opportunities you had as a child to practice and participate in this particular activity? When you were young, your parents might have told you that drinking milk and eating vegetables would help you grow up "big and strong." They probably didn't as readily recognize the role that *culture* plays in shaping bodies, personalities, and personal health. If nutrition matters in growth, so, too, do cultural guidelines. What is proper behavior for boys and girls? What kinds of work should men and women do? Where should people live? What are proper uses of their leisure time? What role should religion play? How should people relate to their family, friends, and neighbors? Although our genetic attributes provide a foundation for our growth and development, human biology is fairly plastic—that is, it is malleable. Culture is an environmental force that affects our development as much as do nutrition, heat, cold, and altitude. Culture also guides our emotional and cognitive growth and helps determine the kinds of personalities we have as adults.

The Subdisciplines of Anthropology

Cultural Anthropology

Cultural anthropology is the study of human society and culture, the subfield that describes, analyzes, interprets, and explains social and cultural similarities and differences. To study and interpret cultural diversity, cultural anthropologists engage in two kinds of activity: ethnography (based on fieldwork) and ethnology (based on cross-cultural comparison). **Ethnography** provides an account of a particular community, society, or culture. During ethnographic fieldwork, the ethnographer gathers data that he or she organizes, describes, analyzes, and interprets to build and present that account, which may be in the form of a book, article, or film. Traditionally, ethnographers have lived in small communities and studied local behavior, beliefs, customs, social life, economic activities, politics, and religion (see Wolcott 2008).

The anthropological perspective derived from ethnographic fieldwork often differs radically from that of economics or political science. Those fields focus on national and official organizations and policies and often on elites. However, the groups that anthropologists traditionally have studied usually have been relatively poor and powerless. Ethnographers often observe discriminatory practices directed toward such people, who experience food shortages, dietary deficiencies, and other aspects of poverty. Political scientists tend to study programs that national planners develop, while anthropologists discover how these programs work on the local level.

Cultures are not isolated. As noted by Franz Boas (1940/1966) many years ago, contact between neighboring tribes always has existed and has extended over enormous areas. "Human populations construct their cultures in interaction with one another, and not in isolation" (Wolf 1982, p. ix). Villagers increasingly participate in regional, national, and world events. Exposure to external forces comes through the mass media, migration, and modern transportation. City and nation increasingly invade local communities with the arrival of tourists, development agents, government and religious officials, and political candidates. Such linkages are prominent components of regional, national, and international systems of politics, economics, and information. These larger systems increasingly affect the people and places anthropology traditionally has studied. The study of such linkages and systems is part of the subject matter of modern anthropology.

Ethnology examines, interprets, analyzes, and compares the results of ethnography—the data gathered in different societies. It uses such data to compare and contrast and to make generalizations about society and culture. Looking beyond the particular to the more general, ethnologists attempt to identify and explain cultural differences and similarities, to test hypotheses, and to build theory to enhance our understanding of how social and cultural systems work. Ethnology gets its data for comparison not just from ethnography but also from the other subfields, particularly from archaeological anthropology, which reconstructs social systems of the past. (Table 1.2 summarizes the main contrasts between ethnography and ethnology.)

Archaeological Anthropology

Archaeological anthropology (more simply, "archaeology") reconstructs, describes, and interprets human behavior and cultural patterns through material remains. At sites where

TABLE 1.2 **Ethnography and Ethnology—Two Dimensions of Cultural Anthropology**

Ethnography	Ethnology
Requires fieldwork to collect data	Uses data collected by a series of researchers
Often descriptive	Usually synthetic
Group/community specific	Comparative/cross-cultural

people live or have lived, archaeologists find artifacts—material items that humans have made, used, or modified—such as tools, weapons, campsites, buildings, and garbage. Plant and animal remains and ancient garbage tell stories about consumption and activities. Wild and domesticated grains have different characteristics, which allow archaeologists to distinguish between gathering and cultivation. Examination of animal bones reveals the ages of slaughtered animals and provides other information useful in determining whether species were wild or domesticated.

Analyzing such data, archaeologists answer several questions about ancient economies. Did the group get its meat from hunting, or did it domesticate and breed animals, killing only those of a certain age and sex? Did plant food come from wild plants or from sowing, tending, and harvesting crops? Did the residents make, trade for, or buy particular items? Were raw materials available locally? If not, where did they come from? From such information, archaeologists reconstruct patterns of production, trade, and consumption.

An archaeological team works at Harappa, one site from an ancient Indus River civilization dating back some 4,800 years.

Archaeologists have spent much time studying potsherds, fragments of earthenware. Potsherds are more durable than many other artifacts, such as textiles and wood. The quantity of pottery fragments allows estimates of population size and density. The discovery that potters used materials that were not available locally suggests systems of trade. Similarities in manufacture and decoration at different sites may be proof of cultural connections. Groups with similar pots may be historically related. Perhaps they shared common cultural ancestors, traded with each other, or belonged to the same political system.

Many archaeologists examine paleoecology. *Ecology* is the study of interrelations among living things in an environment. The organisms and environment together constitute an *ecosystem,* a patterned arrangement of energy flows and exchanges. Human ecology studies ecosystems that include people, focusing on the ways in which human use "of nature influences and is influenced by social organization and cultural values" (Bennett 1969, pp. 10–11). *Paleoecology* looks at the ecosystems of the past.

In addition to reconstructing ecological patterns, archaeologists may infer cultural transformations, for example, by observing changes in the size and type of sites and the distance between them. A city develops in a region where only towns, villages, and hamlets existed a few centuries earlier. The number of settlement levels (city, town, village, hamlet) in a society is a measure of social complexity. Buildings offer clues about political and religious features. Temples and pyramids suggest that an ancient society had an authority structure capable of marshaling the labor needed to build such monuments. The presence or absence of certain structures, like the pyramids of ancient Egypt and Mexico, reveals differences in function between settlements. For example, some towns were places where people came to attend ceremonies. Others were burial sites; still others were farming communities.

Archaeologists also reconstruct behavior patterns and lifestyles of the past by excavating. This involves digging through a succession of levels at a particular site. In a given area, through time, settlements may change in form and purpose, as may the connections between settlements. Excavation can document changes in economic, social, and political activities.

Although archaeologists are best known for studying prehistory, that is, the period before the invention of writing, they also study the cultures of historical and even living peoples (see Sabloff 2008). Studying sunken ships off the Florida coast, underwater archaeologists have been able to verify the living conditions on the vessels that brought ancestral African Americans to the New World as enslaved people. In a research project begun in 1973 in Tucson, Arizona, archaeologist William Rathje has learned about contemporary life by studying modern garbage. The value of "garbology," as Rathje calls it, is that it provides "evidence of what people did, not what they think they did, what they think they should have done, or what the interviewer thinks they should have done" (Harrison, Rathje, and Hughes 1994, p. 108). What people report may contrast strongly with their real behavior as revealed by garbology. For example, the garbologists discovered that the three Tucson neighborhoods that reported the lowest beer consumption actually had the highest number of discarded beer cans per household (Podolefsky and Brown 1992, p. 100)! Rathje's garbology also has exposed misconceptions about how much of different kinds of trash are in landfills: While most people thought that fast-food containers and disposable diapers were major waste problems, in fact they were

Consider any one of the four *Indiana Jones* movies directed by Steven Spielberg. Archaeologists often complain that these movies distort public perceptions of their field by portraying archaeologists as greedy, adventurous, amoral, unscientific looters. How, if at all, has Indiana Jones influenced your views about archaeology? More generally, do media portrayals of archaeologists make you think more or less of the field of archaeology?

relatively insignificant compared with paper, including environmentally friendly, recyclable paper (Rathje and Murphy 2001).

Biological, or Physical, Anthropology

The subject matter of **biological,** or **physical, anthropology** is human biological diversity in time and space. The focus on biological variation unites five special interests within biological anthropology:

1. Human evolution as revealed by the fossil record (paleoanthropology).
2. Human genetics.
3. Human growth and development.
4. Human biological plasticity (the body's ability to change as it copes with stresses, such as heat, cold, and altitude).
5. The biology, evolution, behavior, and social life of monkeys, apes, and other non-human primates.

These interests link physical anthropology to other fields: biology, zoology, geology, anatomy, physiology, medicine, and public health. Osteology—the study of bones—helps paleoanthropologists, who examine skulls, teeth, and bones, to identify human ancestors and to chart changes in anatomy over time. A paleontologist is a scientist who studies fossils. A paleoanthropologist is one sort of paleontologist, one who studies the fossil record of human evolution. Paleoanthropologists often collaborate with archaeologists, who study artifacts, in reconstructing biological and cultural aspects of human evolution. Fossils and tools often are found together. Different types of tools provide information about the habits, customs, and lifestyles of the ancestral humans who used them.

More than a century ago, Charles Darwin noticed that the variety that exists within any population permits some individuals (those with the favored characteristics) to do better than others at surviving and reproducing. Genetics, which developed later, enlightens us about the causes and transmission of this variety. However, it isn't just genes that cause variety. During any individual's lifetime, the environment works along with heredity to determine biological features. For example, people with a genetic tendency to be tall will be shorter if they are poorly nourished during childhood. Thus, biological anthropology also investigates the influence of environment on the body as it grows and matures. Among the environmental factors that influence the body as it develops are nutrition, altitude, temperature, and disease, as well as cultural factors, such as standards of attractiveness.

Biological anthropology (along with zoology) also includes primatology. The primates include our closest relatives—apes and monkeys. Primatologists study their biology, evolution, behavior, and social life, often in their natural environments. Primatology assists paleoanthropology, because primate behavior may shed light on early human behavior and human nature.

Linguistic Anthropology

We don't know (and probably never will) when our ancestors acquired the ability to speak, although biological anthropologists have looked to the anatomy of the face and the skull to speculate about the origin of language. And primatologists have described the communication systems of monkeys and apes. We do know that well-developed, grammatically complex languages have existed for thousands of years. Linguistic anthropology offers further illustration of anthropology's interest in comparison, variation, and change. **Linguistic anthropology** studies language in its social and cultural context, across space and over time. Some linguistic anthropologists make inferences about universal features of language, linked perhaps to uniformities in the human brain. Others reconstruct ancient languages by comparing their contemporary descendants and in so doing make discoveries about history. Still others study linguistic differences to discover varied perceptions and patterns of thought in different cultures.

Historical linguistics considers variation in time, such as the changes in sounds, grammar, and vocabulary between Middle English (spoken from approximately A.D. 1050 to 1550) and modern English. **Sociolinguistics** investigates relationships between social and linguistic variation. No language is a homogeneous system in which everyone speaks just like everyone else. How do different speakers use a given language? How do linguistic features correlate with social factors, including class and gender differences (Tannen 1990)? One reason for variation is geography, as in regional dialects and accents. Linguistic variation also is expressed in the bilingualism of ethnic groups. Linguistic and cultural anthropologists collaborate in studying links between language and many other aspects of culture, such as how people reckon kinship and how they perceive and classify colors.

Anthropology and Other Academic Fields

As mentioned previously, one of the main differences between anthropology and the other fields that study people is holism, anthropology's unique blend of biological, social, cultural, linguistic, historical, and contemporary perspectives. Paradoxically, while distinguishing anthropology, this breadth is what also links it to many other disciplines. Techniques used to date fossils and artifacts have come to anthropology from physics, chemistry, and geology. Because plant and animal remains often are found with human bones and artifacts, anthropologists collaborate with botanists, zoologists, and paleontologists.

As a discipline that is both scientific and humanistic, anthropology has links with many other academic fields. Anthropology is a **science**—a "systematic field of study or body of knowledge that aims, through experiment, observation, and deduction, to produce reliable explanations of phenomena, with references to the material and physical world" (*Webster's New World Encyclopedia* 1993, p. 937). The following chapters present anthropology as a humanistic science devoted to discovering, describing, understanding, and explaining similarities and differences in time and space among humans and our ancestors. Clyde Kluckhohn (1944) described anthropology as "the science of human similarities and differences" (p. 9). His statement of the need for such a field still stands: "Anthropology provides a scientific basis for dealing with the crucial dilemma of the world today: how can peoples of different appearance, mutually unintelligible languages, and dissimilar ways of life get along peaceably together?" (p. 9). Anthropology has compiled an impressive body of knowledge that this textbook attempts to encapsulate.

Besides its links to the natural sciences (e.g., geology, zoology), and social sciences (e.g., sociology, psychology), anthropology also has strong links to the humanities. The humanities include English, comparative literature, classics, folklore, philosophy, and the arts. These fields study languages, texts, philosophies, arts, music, performances, and other forms of creative expression. Ethnomusicology, which studies forms of musical expression on a worldwide basis, is especially closely related to anthropology. Also linked is folklore, the systematic study of tales, myths, and legends from a variety of cultures. One might well argue that anthropology is among the most humanistic of all academic fields because of its fundamental respect for human diversity. Anthropologists listen to, record, and represent voices from a multitude of nations and cultures. Anthropology values local knowledge, diverse worldviews, and alternative philosophies. Cultural anthropology and linguistic anthropology in particular bring a comparative and nonelitist perspective to forms of creative expression, including language, art, narratives, music, and dance, viewed in their social and cultural context.

Applied Anthropology

Anthropology is not a science of the exotic carried on by quaint scholars in ivory towers. Rather, anthropology has a lot to tell the public. Anthropology's foremost professional organization, the American Anthropological Association (AAA), has formally acknowledged a public service role by recognizing that anthropology has two dimensions: (1) academic or general anthropology and (2) practicing or **applied anthropology.** The latter refers to the application of anthropological data, perspectives, theory, and methods to identify, assess, and solve contemporary social problems. As Erve Chambers (1987, p. 309) states it, applied anthropology is the "field of inquiry concerned with the relationships between anthropological knowledge and the uses of that knowledge in the world beyond anthropology." More and more anthropologists from the four subfields now work in such "applied" areas as public health, family planning, business, economic development, and cultural resource management.

Applied anthropology encompasses any use of the knowledge and/or techniques of the four subfields to identify, assess, and solve practical problems. Because of anthropology's breadth, it has many applications. For example, applied medical anthropologists consider both the sociocultural and the biological contexts and implications of disease and illness. Perceptions of good and bad health, along with actual health threats

Anthropology Today *Anthropologist's Son Elected President*

It is widely known that Barack Obama is the son of a Kenyan father and a White American mother from Kansas. Less recognized is the fact that the 44th president of the United States is the son of an anthropologist— Dr. Stanley Ann Dunham Soetoro (usually called simply Ann Dunham). This account focuses on her life and her attraction to diversity, which led her to a career in anthropology. A sociocultural anthropologist by training, Dunham's work on microfinance and socioeconomic issues affecting Indonesian women illustrates the application of anthropology to identify and solve contemporary problems. In other words, she was both a cultural and an applied anthropologist.

Anthropologists study humanity in varied times and places and in a rapidly changing world. By virtue of his parentage, his enculturation, and his experience abroad, Barack Obama provides an excellent symbol of the diversity and interconnections that characterize such a world. As well, his election is a tribute to an ever more diverse United States of America.

Young Barack Obama with his mother, anthropologist Ann Dunham.

In the capsule version of the Barack Obama story, his mother is simply the white woman from Kansas. . . . On the campaign trail, he has called her his "single mom." But neither description begins to capture the unconventional life of Stanley Ann Dunham Soetoro, the parent who most shaped Mr. Obama. . . .

In Hawaii, she married an African student at age 18. Then she married an Indonesian, moved to Jakarta, became an anthropologist, wrote an 800-page dissertation on peasant blacksmithing in Java, worked for the Ford Foundation, championed women's work and helped bring microcredit to the world's poor.

She had high expectations for her children. In Indonesia, she would wake her son at 4 a.m. for correspondence courses in English before school; she brought home recordings of Mahalia Jackson, speeches by the Rev. Dr. Martin Luther King Jr. And when Mr. Obama asked to stay in Hawaii for high school rather than return to Asia, she accepted living apart— a decision her daughter says was one of the hardest in Ms. Soetoro's life.

"She felt that somehow, wandering through uncharted territory, we might stumble upon something that will, in an instant, seem to represent who we are at the core," said Maya Soetoro-Ng, Mr. Obama's half-sister. "That was very much her philosophy of life—to not be limited by fear or narrow definitions, to not build walls around ourselves and to do our best to find kinship and beauty in unexpected places." . . .

continued

Anthropology Today *continued*

Mr. Obama . . . barely saw his father after the age of 2. Though it is impossible to pinpoint the imprint of a parent on the life of a grown child, people who knew Ms. Soetoro well say they see her influence unmistakably in Mr. Obama. . . .

"She was a very, very big thinker," said Nancy Barry, a former president of Women's World Banking, an international network of microfinance providers, where Ms. Soetoro worked in New York City in the early 1990s. . . .

In a Russian class at the University of Hawaii, she met the college's first African student, Barack Obama. They married and had a son in August 1961, in an era when interracial marriage was rare in the United States. . . .

The marriage was brief. In 1963, Mr. Obama left for Harvard, leaving his wife and child. She then married Lolo Soetoro, an Indonesian student. When he was summoned home in 1966 after the turmoil surrounding the rise of Suharto, Ms. Soetoro and Barack followed . . .

Her second marriage faded, too, in the 1970s. Ms. Soetoro wanted to work, one friend said, and Mr. Soetoro wanted more children. He became more American, she once said, as she became more Javanese. "There's a Javanese belief that if you're married to someone and it doesn't work, it will make you sick," said Alice G. Dewey, an anthropologist and friend. "It's just stupid to stay married.". . .

By 1974, Ms. Soetoro was back in Honolulu, a graduate student and raising Barack and Maya, nine years younger. . . . When Ms. Soetoro decided to return to Indonesia three years later for her field work, Barack chose not to go. . . .

Fluent in Indonesian, Ms. Soetoro moved with Maya first to Yogyakarta, the center of Javanese handicrafts. A weaver in college, she was fascinated with what

Ms. Soetoro-Ng calls "life's gorgeous minutiae." That interest inspired her study of village industries, which became the basis of her 1992 doctoral dissertation.

"She loved living in Java," said Dr. Dewey, who recalled accompanying Ms. Soetoro to a metalworking village. "People said: 'Hi! How are you?' She said: 'How's your wife? Did your daughter have the baby?' They were friends. Then she'd whip out her notebook and she'd say: 'How many of you have electricity? Are you having trouble getting iron?'"

She became a consultant for the United States Agency for International Development on setting up a village credit program, then a Ford Foundation program officer in Jakarta specializing in women's work. Later, she was a consultant in Pakistan, then joined Indonesia's oldest bank to work on what is described as the world's largest sustainable microfinance program, creating services like credit and savings for the poor.

Visitors flowed constantly through her Ford Foundation office in downtown Jakarta and through her house in a neighborhood to the south, where papaya and banana trees grew in the front yard and Javanese dishes . . . were served for dinner. Her guests were leaders in the Indonesian human rights movement, people from women's organizations, representatives of community groups doing grassroots development. . . .

Ms. Soetoro-Ng . . . remembers conversations with her mother about philosophy or politics, books, esoteric Indonesian woodworking motifs. . . .

"She gave us a very broad understanding of the world," her daughter said. "She hated bigotry. She was very determined to be remembered for a life of service and thought that service was really the true measure of a life." Many of her friends see her legacy in Mr. Obama—in his self-assurance and drive, his boundary bridging, even his apparent comfort with strong women. She died in November 1995, as Mr. Obama was starting his first campaign for public office. After a memorial service at the University of Hawaii, one friend said, a small group of friends drove to the South Shore in Oahu. With the wind whipping the waves onto the rocks, Mr. Obama and Ms. Soetoro-Ng placed their mother's ashes in the Pacific, sending them off in the direction of Indonesia.

Source: Janny Scott, "A Free-Spirited Wanderer Who Set Obama's Path," *New York Times,* March 13, 2008. Copyright © 2008 The New York Times. Co. Reprinted by permission.

TABLE 1.3 The Four Subfields and Two Dimensions of Anthropology

Anthropology's Subfields (General Anthropology)	Examples of Application (Applied Anthropology)
Cultural anthropology	Development anthropology
Archaeological anthropology	Cultural resource management (CRM)
Biological or physical anthropology	Forensic anthropology
Linguistic anthropology	Study of linguistic diversity in classrooms

and problems, differ among societies. Various ethnic groups recognize different illnesses, symptoms, and causes and have developed different health-care systems and treatment strategies.

Applied archaeology, usually called *public archaeology,* includes such activities as cultural resource management, contract archaeology, public educational programs, and historic preservation. An important role for public archaeology has been created by legislation requiring evaluation of sites threatened by dams, highways, and other construction activities. To decide what needs saving, and to preserve significant information about the past when sites cannot be saved, is the work of **cultural resource management (CRM).** CRM involves not only preserving sites but also allowing their destruction if they are not significant. The "management" part of the term refers to the evaluation and decision-making process. Cultural resource managers work for federal, state, and county agencies and other clients. Applied cultural anthropologists sometimes work with the public archaeologists, assessing the human problems generated by the proposed change and determining how they can be reduced. Table 1.3 relates anthropology's four subfields to its two dimensions.

Summary

1. Anthropology is the holistic, biocultural, and comparative study of humanity. It is the systematic exploration of human biological and cultural diversity across time and space. Examining the origins of, and changes in, human biology and culture,

anthropology provides explanations for similarities and differences among humans and their societies.

2. The four subfields of general anthropology are (socio)cultural, archaeological, biological, and linguistic. All consider variation in time and space. Each also examines adaptation—the process by which organisms cope with environmental stresses. Anthropology's biocultural perspective is a particularly effective way of approaching interrelations between biology and culture. Cultural forces mold human biology, including our body types and images.

3. Cultural anthropology explores the cultural diversity of the present and the recent past. Archaeology reconstructs cultural patterns, often of prehistoric populations. Biological anthropology documents diversity involving fossils, genetics, growth and development, bodily responses, and nonhuman primates. Linguistic anthropology considers diversity among languages. It also studies how speech changes in social situations and over time.

4. Concerns with biology, society, culture, and language link anthropology to many other fields—natural sciences, social sciences, and humanities.

5. Anthropology has two dimensions: general and applied. The latter uses anthropological perspectives, theory, methods, and data to identify, assess, and solve social problems. The fields in which applied anthropologists work include business, government, economic development, education, and social services, action, and outreach. Applied anthropologists come from all four subfields.

Key Terms

adaptation, *3*
anthropology, *2*
applied
 anthropology, *12*
archaeological
 anthropology, *7*
biocultural, *5*
biological
 (or physical)
 anthropology, *10*

cultural
 anthropology, *7*
cultural resource
 management
 (CRM), *15*
cultures, *2*
ethnography, *7*
ethnology, *7*
food
 production, *4*

general
 anthropology, *4*
holistic, *2*
linguistic
 anthropology, *11*
science, *11*
society, *2*
sociolinguistics, *11*

Go to our Online Learning Center website at **www.mhhe.com/kottak** for Internet resources directly related to the contents of this chapter.

Chapter

Culture

What Is Culture?

Culture Is Learned
Culture Is Symbolic
Culture Is Shared
Culture and Nature
Culture Is All-Encompassing
Culture Is Integrated
Applying Anthropology to Popular
    Culture: Popular Songs
Culture Is Instrumental, Adaptive, and
    Maladaptive

Culture's Evolutionary Basis

What We Share with Other Primates
How We Differ from Other Primates

Universality, Generality, and Particularity

Universals and Generalities
Particularity: Patterns of Culture

Culture and the Individual: Agency and
Practice

Popular, Civic, and Public Culture

Levels of Culture

Ethnocentrism, Cultural Relativism, and
Human Rights

Mechanisms of Cultural Change

Globalization

Anthropology Today: Experiencing
    Culture: Personal Space and Displays
    of Affection

In Chapter 1 we saw that humans share *society,* organized life in groups, with other animals—social animals, such as monkeys, wolves, and ants. Other animals, especially the great apes, have rudimentary cultural abilities, but only humans have fully elaborated cultures—distinctive traditions and customs transmitted over the generations through learning and through language.

The concept of culture has long been basic to anthropology. Well over a century ago, in his book *Primitive Culture,* the British anthropologist Edward Tylor proposed that cultures, systems of human behavior and thought, obey natural laws and therefore can be studied scientifically. Tylor's definition of culture still offers an overview of the subject matter of anthropology and is widely quoted.

"Culture . . . is that complex whole which includes knowledge, belief, arts, morals, law, custom, and any other capabilities and habits acquired by man as a member of society" (Tylor 1871/1958, p. 1). The crucial phrase here is "acquired . . . as a member of society." Tylor's definition focuses on attributes that people acquire not through biological inheritance but by growing up in a particular society in which they are exposed to a specific cultural tradition. **Enculturation** is the process by which a child *learns* his or her culture.

What Is Culture?

Culture Is Learned

The ease with which children absorb any cultural tradition rests on the uniquely elaborated human capacity to learn. Other animals may learn from experience, so that, for example, they avoid fire after discovering that it hurts. Social animals also learn from other members of their group. Wolves, for instance, learn hunting strategies from other pack members. Such social learning is particularly important among monkeys and apes, our closest biological relatives. But our own *cultural learning* depends on the uniquely developed human capacity to use **symbols,** signs that have no necessary or natural connection to the things they stand for or signify.

On the basis of cultural learning, people create, remember, and deal with ideas. They grasp and apply specific systems of symbolic meaning. Anthropologist Clifford Geertz defined culture as ideas based on cultural learning and symbols. Cultures have been characterized as sets of "control mechanisms—plans, recipes, rules, instructions, what computer engineers call programs for the governing of behavior" (Geertz 1973, p. 44). These programs are absorbed by people through enculturation in particular traditions. People gradually internalize a previously established system of meanings and symbols, which helps guide their behavior and perceptions throughout their lives.

Every person begins immediately, through a process of conscious and unconscious learning and interaction with others, to internalize, or incorporate, a cultural tradition through the process of enculturation. Sometimes culture is taught directly, as when parents tell their children to say "thank you" when someone gives them something or does them a favor.

Culture also is transmitted through observation. Children pay attention to the things that go on around them. They modify their behavior not just because other people tell them to do so but as a result of their own observations and growing awareness of what their culture considers right and wrong. Culture also is absorbed unconsciously. North Americans acquire their culture's notions about how far apart people should stand when they talk, not by being told directly to maintain a certain distance but through a gradual process of observation, experience, and conscious and unconscious behavior modification. No one tells Latins to stand closer together than North Americans do; they learn to do so as part of their cultural tradition. (See this chapter's "Anthropology Today.")

Culture Is Symbolic

Symbolic thought is unique and crucial to humans and to cultural learning. A symbol is something verbal or nonverbal, within a particular language or culture, that comes to stand for something else. Anthropologist Leslie White defined culture as

> dependent upon symbolling. . . . Culture consists of tools, implements, utensils, clothing, ornaments, customs, institutions, beliefs, rituals, games, works of art, language, etc.
> (White 1959, p. 3)

For White, culture originated when our ancestors acquired the ability to use symbols, that is, to originate and bestow meaning on a thing or event, and, correspondingly, to grasp and appreciate such meanings (White 1959, p. 3).

There need be no obvious, natural, or necessary connection between the symbol and what it symbolizes. The familiar pet that barks is no more naturally a *dog* than it is a *chien, Hund,* or *mbwa,* the words for "dog" in French, German, and Swahili, respectively. Language is one of the distinctive possessions of *Homo sapiens.* No other animal has developed anything approaching the complexity of language, with its multitude of symbols.

Symbols often are linguistic. There also are myriad nonverbal symbols, such as flags, which stand for various countries, and the arches that symbolize a particular hamburger chain. Holy water is a potent symbol in Roman Catholicism. As is true of all symbols, the association between a symbol (water) and what is symbolized (holiness) is arbitrary and conventional. Water probably is not intrinsically holier than milk, blood, or other natural liquids. Nor is holy water chemically different from ordinary water. Holy water is a symbol within Roman Catholicism, which is part of an international cultural system. A natural thing has been associated arbitrarily with a particular meaning for Catholics, who share common beliefs and experiences that are based on learning and that are transmitted across the generations.

All humans possess the abilities on which culture rests—the abilities to learn, to think symbolically, to manipulate language, and to use tools and other cultural products in organizing their lives and coping with their environments. Every contemporary human population has the ability to use symbols and thus to create and maintain culture. Our nearest relatives—chimpanzees and gorillas—have rudimentary cultural abilities. However, no other animal has elaborated cultural abilities to the extent that *Homo* has.

Culture Is Shared

Culture is an attribute not of individuals per se but of individuals as members of *groups.* Culture is transmitted in society. Don't we learn our culture by observing, listening, talking, and interacting with many other people? Shared beliefs, values, memories, and expectations link people who grow up in the same culture. Enculturation unifies people by providing us with common experiences.

People in the United States sometimes have trouble understanding the power of culture because of the value that American culture places on the idea of the individual. Americans are fond of saying that everyone is unique and special in some way. However, in American culture individualism itself is a distinctive shared value. Individualism is transmitted through hundreds of statements and settings in our daily lives. From the late Mr. Rogers on TV to parents, grandparents, and teachers, our enculturative agents insist that we are all "someone special."

Today's parents were yesterday's children. If they grew up in North America, they absorbed certain values and beliefs transmitted over the generations. People become agents in the enculturation of their children, just as their parents were for them. Although a culture constantly changes, certain fundamental beliefs, values, worldviews, and child-rearing practices endure. Consider a simple American example of enduring shared enculturation. As children, when we didn't finish a meal, our parents may have reminded us of starving children in some foreign country, just as our grandparents might have done a generation earlier. The specific country changes (China, India, Bangladesh, Ethiopia, Somalia, Rwanda—what was it in your home?). Still, American culture goes on transmitting the idea that by eating all our brussels sprouts or broccoli, we can justify our own good fortune, compared to a hungry child in an impoverished or war-ravaged country.

Culture and Nature

Culture takes the natural biological urges we share with other animals and teaches us how to express them in particular ways. People have to eat, but culture teaches us what, when, and how. In many cultures people have their main meal at noon, but most North Americans prefer a large dinner. English people eat fish for breakfast, but North Americans prefer hot cakes and cold cereals. Brazilians put hot milk into strong coffee, whereas many North Americans pour cold milk into a weaker brew. Midwesterners dine at five or six, Spaniards at ten.

Cultural habits, perceptions, and inventions mold "human nature" into many forms. People have to eliminate wastes from their bodies. But some cultures teach people to defecate standing, while others tell them to do it sitting down. Peasant women in the Andean highlands squat in the streets and urinate, getting all the privacy they need from their massive skirts. All these habits are parts of cultural traditions that have converted natural acts into cultural customs.

Our culture—and cultural changes—affect how we perceive nature, human nature, and "the natural." Through science, invention, and discovery, cultural advances have overcome many "natural" limitations. We prevent and cure diseases such as polio and smallpox, which felled our ancestors. We use Viagra to enhance or restore sexual potency. Through cloning, scientists have challenged the way we think about biological identity and the meaning of life itself. Culture, of course, does not always protect us from natural threats. Hurricanes, floods, earthquakes, and other natural forces regularly overthrow our wishes to modify the environment through building, development, and expansion. Can you think of other ways in which nature strikes back at culture?

Culture Is All-Encompassing

For anthropologists, culture includes much more than refinement, good taste, sophistication, education, and appreciation of the fine arts. Not only college graduates but all people are "cultured." The most interesting and significant cultural forces are those that affect people every day of their lives, particularly those that influence children during enculturation.

Culture, as defined anthropologically, encompasses features that are sometimes regarded as trivial or unworthy of serious study, such as those of "popular" culture. To understand contemporary North American culture, we must consider television, fast-food restaurants, sports, and games. As a cultural manifestation, a rock star may be as interesting as a symphony conductor (or vice versa); a comic book may be as significant as a book-award winner.

Culture Is Integrated

Cultures are not haphazard collections of customs and beliefs. Cultures are integrated, patterned systems. If one part of the system (the overall economy, for instance) changes,

We can learn a lot about a culture by analyzing the ideas, images, and themes reflected in its popular songs. See what you can learn about contemporary American culture by studying the lyrics of a few of the current top-10 songs. (Lists are available at "The Billboard Hot 100" or www.top10songs.com.)

other parts change as well. For example, during the 1950s most American women planned domestic careers as homemakers and mothers. Most of today's college women, by contrast, hope to get paying jobs when they graduate.

What are some of the social repercussions of this particular economic change? Attitudes and behavior regarding marriage, family, and children have changed. Late marriage, "living together," and divorce have become more common. Work competes with marriage and family responsibilities and reduces the time available to invest in child care.

Cultures are integrated not simply by their dominant economic activities and related social patterns but also by sets of values, ideas, symbols, and judgments. Cultures train their individual members to share certain personality traits. A set of characteristic **core values** (key, basic, central values) integrates each culture and helps distinguish it from others. For instance, the work ethic and individualism are core values that have integrated American culture for generations. Different sets of dominant values influence the patterns of other cultures.

Culture Is Instrumental, Adaptive, and Maladaptive

Culture is the main reason for human adaptability and success. Other animals rely on biological means of adaptation (such as fur or blubber, which are adaptations to cold). Humans also adapt biologically—for example, by shivering when we get cold or sweating when we get hot. But in addition to biological responses, people also have cultural ways of adapting. To cope with environmental stresses we habitually use technology, or tools. We hunt cold-adapted animals and use their fur coats as our own. We turn the thermostat up in the winter and down in the summer. Or we plan action to increase our comfort. We have a cold drink, jump in a pool, or travel to someplace cooler in the summer or warmer in the winter. People use culture *instrumentally,* that is, to fulfill their basic biological needs for food, drink, shelter, comfort, and reproduction.

People also use culture to fulfill psychological and emotional needs, such as friendship, companionship, approval, and being desired sexually. People seek *informal support*—help from people who care about them—as well as *formal support* from associations and institutions. To these ends, individuals cultivate ties with others on the basis of common experiences, political interests, aesthetic sensibilities, or personal attraction.

On one level, cultural traits (e.g., air conditioning) may be called *adaptive* if they help individuals cope with environmental stresses. But, on a different level, such traits can also

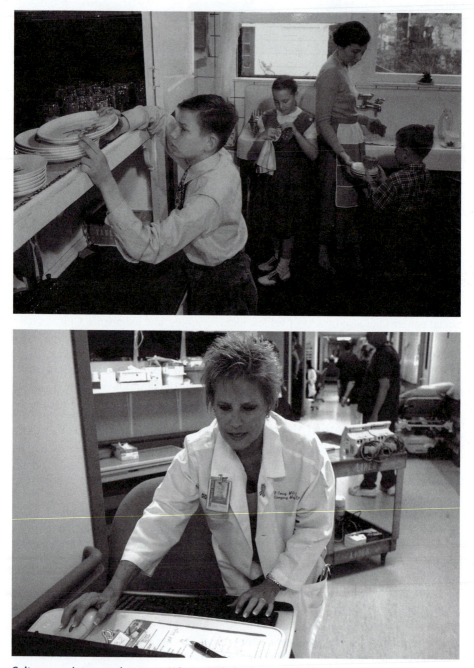

Cultures are integrated systems. When one behavior pattern changes, others also change. During the 1950s, most American women expected to have careers as wives, mothers, and domestic managers. As more and more women have entered the workforce, attitudes toward work and family have changed. On the top, mom and kids do the dishes in 1952. On the bottom, in this 2010 photo, an emergency room physician in Tampa, Florida types patient information into a computer. What do you imagine she does when she gets home?

be *maladaptive.* That is, they may threaten a group's continued existence. Thus chloro-fluorocarbons from air conditioners deplete the ozone layer and, by doing so, can harm humans and other life. Many modern cultural patterns may be maladaptive in the long run. Some examples of maladaptive aspects of culture are policies that encourage over-population, poor food-distribution systems, overconsumption, and industrial pollution of the environment.

Culture's Evolutionary Basis

The human capacity for culture has an evolutionary basis that extends back at least 2.6 million years to early toolmakers. Evidence for these toolmakers exists in the archaeological record. However, based on observation of tool use and manufacture by apes, scientists believe the evolutionary basis for culture may extend even further back.

Similarities between humans and apes, our closest relatives, are evident in anatomy, brain structure, genetics, and biochemistry. Most closely related to us are the African great apes: chimpanzees and gorillas. *Hominidae* is the zoological family that includes fossil and living humans, as well as chimps and gorillas. We refer to members of this family as **hominids.** The term **hominins** is used for the group that leads to humans but not to chimps and gorillas and that encompasses all the human species that ever have existed.

Many human traits reflect the fact that our primate ancestors lived in the trees. These traits include grasping ability and manual dexterity (especially opposable thumbs), depth and color vision, learning ability based on a large brain, substantial parental investment in a limited number of offspring, and tendencies toward sociality and cooperation. Like other primates, humans have flexible, five-fingered hands and *opposable thumbs:* each thumb can touch all the other fingers on the same hand. Like monkeys and apes, humans also have excellent depth and color vision. Our eyes are placed forward in the skull and look directly ahead, so that their fields of vision overlap. Depth perception, impossible without overlapping visual fields, proved adaptive—e.g., for judging distance—in the trees. Having color and depth vision also facilitates the identification of various food sources, as well as mutual grooming—picking out burrs, insects, and other small objects from hair. Such grooming is one way of forming and maintaining social bonds.

The combination of manual dexterity and depth perception allows monkeys, apes, and humans to pick up small objects, hold them in front of their eyes, and appraise them. Our ability to thread a needle reflects an intricate interplay of hands and eyes that took millions of years of primate evolution to achieve. Such dexterity, including the opposable thumb, confers a tremendous advantage in manipulating objects and is essential to a major human adaptive capacity: tool making. In primates, and especially in humans, the ratio of brain size to body size exceeds that of most mammals. Even more important, the brain's outer layer—concerned with memory, association, and integration—is relatively larger. Monkeys, apes, and humans store an array of images in their memories, which permits them to learn more. Such a capacity for learning is another tremendous adaptive advantage. Like most other primates, humans usually give birth to a single offspring rather than a litter. Receiving more parental attention, that one infant has enhanced learning opportunities. The need for longer and more attentive care of offspring places a selective value on support by a social group. Humans have developed considerably the primate tendency to be social animals, living and interacting regularly with other members of their species.

What We Share with Other Primates

There is a substantial gap between primate *society* (organized life in groups) and fully developed human *culture,* which is based on symbolic thought. Nevertheless, studies of nonhuman primates reveal many similarities with humans, such as the ability to learn from experience and change behavior as a result. Apes and monkeys, like humans, learn throughout their lives. In one group of Japanese macaques (land-dwelling monkeys), for example, a three-year-old female started washing sweet potatoes before she ate them. First her mother, then her age peers, and finally the entire troop began washing sweet potatoes as well. The ability to benefit from experience confers a tremendous adaptive advantage, permitting the avoidance of fatal mistakes. Faced with environmental change, humans and other primates don't have to wait for a genetic or physiological response. They can modify learned behavior and social patterns instead.

Although humans employ tools much more than any other animal does, tool use also turns up among several nonhuman species, including birds, beavers, sea otters, and especially apes (see Mayell 2003). Humans are not the only animals that make tools with a specific purpose in mind. Chimpanzees living in the Tai forest of Ivory Coast make and use stone tools to break open hard, golfball-sized nuts (Mercader, Panger, and Boesch 2002; Wilford 2007*b*). At specific sites, the chimps gather nuts, place them on stumps or flat rocks, which are used as anvils, and pound the nuts with heavy stones. The chimps must select hammer stones suited to smashing the nuts and carry them to where the nut trees grow. Nut cracking is a learned skill, with mothers showing their young how to do it.

In 1960, Jane Goodall (1996) began observing wild chimps—including their tool use and hunting behavior—at Gombe Stream National Park in Tanzania, East Africa. The most studied form of ape tool making involves "termiting," in which chimps make tools to probe termite hills. They choose twigs, which they modify by removing leaves and peeling off bark to expose the sticky surface beneath. They carry the twigs to termite hills, dig holes with their fingers, and insert the twigs. Finally, they pull out the twigs and dine on termites that were attracted to the sticky surface. Given what is known about ape tool use and manufacture, it is almost certain that early hominins shared this ability, although the first evidence for hominin stone tool making dates back only 2.6 million years. In addition, bipedalism (moving around upright on two legs) would have permitted the carrying and use of tools and weapons against predators and competitors in an open grassland habitat.

The apes have other abilities essential to culture. Wild chimps and orangs aim and throw objects. Gorillas build nests, and they throw branches, grass, vines, and other objects. Hominins have elaborated the capacity to aim and throw, without which we never would have developed projectile technology and weaponry—or baseball.

Like tool making, hunting once was cited as a distinctive human activity not shared with the apes. Again, however, primate research shows that other primates, especially

Tool use by chimps. These chimps in Liberia are using stone tools to crack palm nuts, as described in the text.

chimpanzees, are habitual hunters. For example, in Uganda's Kibale National Park chimps form large hunting parties, including an average of 26 individuals (almost always adult and adolescent males). Most hunts (78 percent) result in at least one prey item being caught—a much higher success rate than that among lions (26 percent), hyenas (34 percent), or cheetahs (30 percent). Chimps' favored prey there is the red colobus monkey (Mitani and Watts 1999).

Archaeological evidence suggests that humans hunted by at least 2.6 million years ago, based on stone tools found in Ethiopia and, later, at Olduvai Gorge in Tanzania. Given our current understanding of chimp hunting and tool making, we can infer that hominids may have been hunting much earlier than the first archaeological evidence attests. However, because chimps typically devour the monkeys they kill, leaving few remains, we may never find archaeological evidence for the first hominin hunt, especially if it was done without stone tools.

How We Differ from Other Primates

Although chimps often share meat from a hunt, apes and monkeys (except for nursing infants) tend to feed themselves individually. Cooperation and sharing are much more developed among humans. Until fairly recently (12,000 to 10,000 years ago), all humans were hunter-gatherers who lived in small social groups called bands. In some world areas, the hunter-gatherer way of life persisted into recent times, permitting study by ethnographers. In such societies, men and women bring resources back to the camp and share them. Everyone shares the meat from a large animal. Nourished and protected by younger band members, elders live past reproductive age and are respected for their knowledge and experience. Humans are among the most cooperative of the primates—in the food quest and other social activities. As well, the amount of information stored in a human band is far greater than that in any other primate group.

Another difference between humans and other primates involves mating. Among baboons and chimps, most mating occurs when females enter **estrus,** during which they ovulate. In estrus, the vaginal area swells and reddens, and receptive females form temporary bonds with, and mate with, males. Human females, by contrast, lack a visible estrus cycle, and their ovulation is concealed. Not knowing when ovulation is occurring, humans maximize their reproductive success by mating throughout the year. Human pair bonds for mating are more exclusive and more durable than are those of chimps. Related to our more constant sexuality, all human societies have some form of marriage. Marriage gives mating a reliable basis and grants to each spouse special, though not always exclusive, sexual rights in the other.

Marriage creates another major contrast between humans and nonhuman primates: exogamy and kinship systems. Most cultures have rules of exogamy requiring marriage outside one's kin or local group. Coupled with the recognition of kinship, exogamy confers adaptive advantages because it creates ties between the spouses' different kin groups. Their children have relatives, and therefore allies, in two kin groups rather than just one. The key point here is that ties of affection and mutual support between members of different local groups tend to be absent among primates other than *Homo.* Other primates tend to disperse at adolescence. Among chimps and gorillas, females tend to migrate, seeking mates in other groups. Humans also choose mates from outside the natal group, and usually at least one spouse moves. However, *humans maintain lifelong ties with sons and daughters.* The systems of kinship and marriage that preserve these links provide a major contrast between humans and other primates. Table 2.1 lists differences in the cultural abilities of humans and chimpanzees, our nearest relatives.

TABLE 2.1 **Cultural Features of Chimpanzees (Rudimentary) and Humans (Fully Developed)**

	Chimpanzees	Humans
Cultural Learning	Rudimentary	Fully developed
Tool Use	Occasional	Habitual
Tool Manufacture	Occasional: hammer stones, termiting	Habitual and sophisticated
Aimed Throwing	Occasional objects, not tools	Projectile technology
Hunting	Significant, but no tools	Basic hominin subsistence strategy, with tools
Food Sharing	Meat sharing after hunt	Basic to human life
Cooperation	Occasional in hunting	Basic to human life
Mating and Marriage	Female estrus cycle, limited pair bonds	Year-round mating, marriage, and exogamy
Kin Ties	Limited by dispersal at adolescence	Maintained through sons and daughters

Universality, Generality, and Particularity

Anthropologists agree that cultural learning is uniquely elaborated among humans and that all humans have culture. Anthropologists also accept a doctrine termed in the 19th century "the psychic unity of man." This means that although *individuals* differ in their emotional and intellectual tendencies and capacities, all human *populations* have equivalent capacities for culture. Regardless of their genes or their physical appearance, people can learn *any* cultural tradition.

To understand this point, consider that contemporary Americans and Canadians are the genetically mixed descendants of people from all over the world. Our ancestors were biologically varied, lived in different countries and continents, and participated in hundreds of cultural traditions. However, early colonists, later immigrants, and their descendants all have become active participants in American and Canadian life. All now share a common national culture.

To recognize biopsychological equality is not to deny differences among populations. In studying human diversity in time and space, anthropologists distinguish among the universal, the generalized, and the particular. Certain biological, psychological, social, and cultural features are **universal,** found in every culture. Others are merely **generalities,** common to several but not all human groups. Still other traits are **particularities,** unique to certain cultural traditions.

Universals and Generalities

Biologically based universals include a long period of infant dependency, year-round (rather than seasonal) sexuality, and a complex brain that enables us to use symbols, languages, and tools. Among the social universals is life in groups and in some kind of family (see Brown 1991). Generalities occur in certain times and places but not in all cultures. They may be widespread, but they are not universal. One cultural generality that is present in many but not all societies is the *nuclear family,* a kinship group consisting of parents and children. Although many middle-class Americans ethnocentrically view the nuclear family as a proper and "natural" group, it is not universal. It was absent, for example, among the Nayars, who live on the Malabar Coast of India. Traditionally, the Nayars lived in female-headed households, and husbands and wives did not live together. In many other societies, the nuclear family is submerged in larger kin groups, such as extended families, lineages, and clans.

Societies can share the same beliefs and customs because of borrowing or through (cultural) inheritance from a common cultural ancestor. Speaking English is a generality shared by North Americans and Australians because both countries had English settlers. Another reason for generalities is domination, as in colonial rule, when customs and procedures are imposed on one culture by another one that is more powerful. In many countries, use of the English language reflects colonial history. More recently, English has spread through *diffusion* (cultural borrowing) to many other countries, as it has become the world's foremost language for business and travel.

Particularity: Patterns of Culture

A cultural particularity is a trait or feature of culture that is not generalized or widespread; rather it is confined to a single place, culture, or society. Yet because of cultural borrowing, which has accelerated through modern transportation and communication systems, traits that once were limited in their distribution have become more widespread. Traits that are useful, that have the capacity to please large audiences, and that don't clash with the cultural values of potential adopters are more likely to be borrowed than others are. Still, certain cultural particularities persist. One example would be a particular food dish (e.g., pork barbeque with a mustard-based sauce available only in South Carolina, or the pastie—beef stew baked in pie dough characteristic of Michigan's upper peninsula). Besides diffusion which, for example, has spread McDonald's food outlets, once confined to San Bernadino, California, across the globe, there are other reasons why cultural particularities are increasingly rare. Many cultural traits are shared as cultural universals and as a result of independent invention. Facing similar problems, people in different places have come up with similar solutions. Again and again, similar cultural causes have produced similar cultural results.

At the level of the individual cultural trait or element (e.g., bow and arrow, hot dog, MTV), particularities may be getting rarer. But at a higher level, particularity is more obvious. Different cultures emphasize different things. *Cultures are integrated and patterned differently and display tremendous variation and diversity.* When cultural traits are borrowed, they are modified to fit the culture that adopts them. They are reintegrated—patterned anew—to fit their new setting. MTV in Germany or Brazil isn't at all the same thing as MTV in the United States. As was stated in the earlier section "Culture Is Integrated," patterned beliefs, customs, and practices lend distinctiveness to particular cultural traditions.

Consider universal life-cycle events, such as birth, puberty, marriage, parenthood, and death, that many cultures observe and celebrate. The occasions (e.g., marriage, death) may be the same and universal, but the patterns of ceremonial observance may be dramatically different. Cultures vary in just which events merit special celebration. Americans, for example, regard expensive weddings as more socially appropriate than lavish funerals. The Betsileo of Madagascar take the opposite view. The marriage ceremony is a minor event that brings together just the couple and a few close relatives. However, a funeral is a measure of the deceased person's social position and lifetime achievement, and it may attract a thousand people. Why use money on a house, the Betsileo say, when one can use it on the tomb where one will spend eternity in the company of dead relatives? How unlike contemporary Americans' dreams of home ownership and preference for quick and inexpensive funerals. Cremation, an increasingly common option in the United States, would horrify the Betsileo, for whom ancestral bones and relics are important ritual objects.

Cultures vary tremendously in their beliefs, practices, integration, and patterning. By focusing on and trying to explain alternative customs, anthropology forces us to reappraise our familiar ways of thinking. In a world full of cultural diversity, contemporary American culture is just one cultural variant, more powerful perhaps, but no more natural, than the others.

Culture and the Individual: Agency and Practice

Generations of anthropologists have theorized about the relationship between the "system," on one hand, and the "person" or "individual" on the other. The system can refer to various concepts, including culture, society, social relations, or social structure.

Individual human beings always make up, or constitute, the system. But, living within that system, humans also are constrained (to some extent, at least) by its rules and by the actions of other individuals. Cultural rules provide guidance about what to do and how to do it, but people don't always do what the rules say should be done. People use their culture actively and creatively, rather than blindly following its dictates (see Handwerker 2009). Humans aren't passive beings doomed to follow their cultural traditions like programmed robots. Cultures are dynamic and constantly changing. People learn, interpret, and manipulate the same rule in different ways—or they emphasize different rules that better suit their interests. Culture is *contested:* Different groups in society struggle with one another over whose ideas, values, goals, and beliefs will prevail. Even common symbols may have radically different *meanings* to different individuals and groups in the same culture. Golden arches may cause one person to salivate while another plots a vegetarian protest. The same flag may be waved to support or oppose a given war.

Even when they agree about what should be done, people don't always do as their culture directs or as other people expect. Many rules are violated, some very often (for example, automobile speed limits). Some anthropologists find it useful to distinguish between ideal and real culture. The *ideal culture* consists of what people say they should do and what they say they do. *Real culture* refers to their actual behavior as observed by the anthropologist.

Culture is both public and individual, both in the world and in people's minds. Anthropologists are interested not only in public and collective behavior but also in how *individuals* think, feel, and act. The individual and culture are linked because human social life is a process in which individuals internalize the meanings of *public* (i.e., cultural) messages. Then, alone and in groups, people influence culture by converting their private (and often divergent) understandings into public expressions (D'Andrade 1984).

Conventionally, culture has been seen as social glue transmitted across the generations, binding people through their common past, rather than as something being continually created and reworked in the present. The tendency to view culture as an entity rather than as a process is changing. Contemporary anthropologists now emphasize how day-to-day action, practice, or resistance can make and remake culture (Gupta and Ferguson, eds. 1997b). *Agency* refers to the actions that individuals take, both alone and in groups, in forming and transforming cultural identities.

The approach to culture known as *practice theory* (Ortner 1984) recognizes that individuals within a society or culture have diverse motives and intentions and different degrees of power and influence. Such contrasts may be associated with gender, age, ethnicity, class, and other social variables. Practice theory focuses on how such varied individuals—through their ordinary and extraordinary actions and practices—manage to influence, create, and transform the world they live in. Practice theory appropriately recognizes a reciprocal relation between culture (the system—see above) and the individual. The system shapes how individuals experience and respond to external events, but individuals also play an active role in how society functions and changes. Practice theory recognizes both constraints on individuals and the flexibility and changeability of cultures and social systems.

Popular, Civic, and Public Culture

In the contemporary world, the *systems* in which we participate as individuals are not merely local or regional; they have national and international scope. The next section distinguishes between systems that are larger and smaller than nations. Here we focus on domains of national culture, which include popular, civic, and public culture. Any contemporary nation, such as the United States, Canada, Italy, Brazil, India, or Japan, has its national cultural traditions, its own media and popular culture; its own civic culture consisting of laws, institutions, and associations; and its own ways of doing things in public. To be sure, there are international spillovers. For example, the civic cultures of the United States, Canada, and India have been influenced by British law. The spillover is even greater in popular culture: American movies are watched worldwide; Simon Cowell is a powerful media figure both in England and the United States; you can take yoga or Bollywood classes in Los Angeles; Godzilla has visited New York. Despite its international spread, popular culture still varies and is patterned differently from country to country.

Today's consumption patterns both reflect and fuel *popular culture,* supplying widely shared images, information, narratives, products, events, and celebrations that have meaning for many or most people within the same national culture. American examples include Thanksgiving, Halloween, homecoming dances, reality shows, dinner-and-a-movie dates, and retirement parties. Although popular culture is available to us all, we use it selectively, and its meaning varies from one person to the next. In his book *Understanding Popular Culture* (1989), John Fiske argues that each individual's use of popular culture is a creative act. For example, *Glee,* Lady Gaga, the World Cup, the Superbowl, or *Avatar* mean something different to each of their fans. As Fiske puts it, "the meanings I make . . . [from popular culture] are pleasurable when I feel that they are *my* meanings and that they relate to *my* everyday life in a practical, direct way" (1989, p. 57). All of us creatively consume and interpret print media, music, television, films, theme parks, celebrities, politicians, and other popular culture products.

A nation's *civic culture* includes its citizens' compliance with the legal system, participation in formal elections, and membership in voluntary and faith-based associations. Fellow countrymen and women also share a *public culture:* generally accepted social behaviors, dress codes, speech, and other forms of expression that citizens enact in public spaces, including bars, parks, malls, and even grieving sites, such as Ground Zero (see Morrill, Snow, and White 2005; Shaffer 2008; and this chapter's "Anthropology Today").

Levels of Culture

Anthropologists also recognize cultural systems—levels of culture—that are larger and smaller than nation-states. **National culture,** examined in the previous section, embodies those beliefs, learned behavior patterns, values, and institutions that are shared by citizens of the same nation. **International culture** extends beyond and across national boundaries. Because culture is transmitted through learning rather than genetically, cultural traits can spread through borrowing or diffusion from one group to another.

Because of diffusion, migration, colonialism, and globalization, many cultural traits and patterns have acquired international scope. The contemporary United States, Canada, Great Britain, and Australia share cultural traits they have inherited from their common linguistic and cultural ancestors in Great Britain. Roman Catholics in many different countries share beliefs, symbols, experiences, and values transmitted by their church. The World Cup has become an international cultural event, as people in many countries know the rules of, play, and follow soccer.

Cultures also can be smaller than nations (see Jenks 2005). Although people who live in the same country share a national cultural tradition, all cultures also contain diversity. Individuals, families, communities, regions, classes, and other groups within a culture have different learning experiences as well as shared ones. **Subcultures** are different symbol-based patterns and traditions associated with particular groups in the same complex society. In large or diverse nations such as the United States or Canada, a variety of subcultures originate in region, ethnicity, language, class, and religion. The religious backgrounds of Jews, Baptists, and Roman Catholics create subcultural differences between them. While sharing a common national culture, U.S. northerners and southerners also differ in their beliefs, values, and customary behavior as a result of national and regional history. French-speaking Canadians sometimes pointedly contrast with English-speaking people in the same country. Italian Americans have ethnic traditions different from those of Irish, Polish, and African Americans.

Nowadays, many anthropologists are reluctant to use the term *subculture*. They feel that the prefix *sub-* is offensive because it means "below." Subcultures thus may be perceived as "less than" or somehow inferior to a dominant, elite, or national culture. In this discussion of levels of culture, I intend no such implication. My point is simply that nations may contain many different culturally defined groups. As mentioned earlier, culture is contested. Various groups may strive to promote the correctness and value of their own practices, values, and beliefs in comparison with those of other groups or the nation as a whole.

Ethnocentrism, Cultural Relativism, and Human Rights

Ethnocentrism is the tendency to view one's own culture as superior and to apply one's own cultural values in judging the behavior and beliefs of people raised in other cultures. We hear ethnocentric statements all the time. Ethnocentrism contributes to social solidarity, a sense of value and community, among people who share a cultural tradition. People everywhere think that the familiar explanations, opinions, and customs are true, right, proper, and moral. They regard different behavior as strange, immoral, or savage. Often other societies are not considered fully human. Their members may be castigated as cannibals, thieves, or people who do not bury their dead.

Among several tribes in the Trans-Fly region of Papua New Guinea homosexuality was valued over heterosexuality (see the chapter "Gender"). Men who grew up in the Etoro tribe (Kelly 1976) favored oral sex between men, while their neighbors the Marind-anim encouraged men to engage in anal sex. (In both groups heterosexual coitus was stigmatized and allowed only for reproduction.) Etoro men considered Marind-anim anal sex to be disgusting, while seeing nothing abnormal about their own oral homosexual practices.

Opposing ethnocentrism is **cultural relativism,** the viewpoint that behavior in one culture should not be judged by the standards of another culture. This position also can present problems. At its most extreme, cultural relativism argues that there is no superior, international, or universal morality, that the moral and ethical rules of all cultures deserve equal respect. In the extreme relativist view, Nazi Germany would be evaluated as nonjudgmentally as Athenian Greece.

In today's world, human rights advocates challenge many of the tenets of cultural relativism. For example, several societies in Africa and the Middle East have traditions of female genital modification (FGM). *Clitoridectomy* is the removal of a girl's clitoris. *Infibulation* involves sewing the lips (labia) of the vagina, to constrict the vaginal opening. Both procedures reduce female sexual pleasure, and, it is believed in some cultures, the likelihood of adultery. Such practices have been opposed by human rights advocates, especially women's rights groups. The idea is that the tradition infringes on a basic human right—disposition over one's body and one's sexuality. Some African countries have banned or otherwise discouraged the procedures, as have Western nations that receive immigration from such cultures. Similar issues arise with circumcision and other male genital operations. Is it right for a baby boy to be circumcised without his permission, as has been done routinely in the United States? Is it proper to require adolescent boys to undergo collective circumcision to fulfill cultural tradition, as has been done in parts of Africa and Australia?

Some would argue that the problems with relativism can be solved by distinguishing between methodological and moral relativism (see Kellenberger 2008). In anthropology, cultural relativism is not a moral position, but a methodological one. It states: To understand another culture fully, you must try to see how the people in that culture see things. What motivates them—what are they thinking—when they do those things? Such an approach does not preclude making moral judgments or taking action. When faced with Nazi atrocities, a methodological relativist would have a moral obligation to stop doing anthropology and take action to intervene. In the FGM example, one only can understand the *motivations* for the practice by looking at the situation from the point of view of those who engage in it. Having done this, one then faces the moral question of whether to intervene to stop it. We should recognize as well that different people and groups living in the same society—for example, women and men, old and you ng, the more and less powerful—can have widely different views about what is proper, necessary, and moral (see Hunt 2007).

The idea of **human rights** invokes a realm of justice and morality beyond and superior to the laws and customs of particular countries, cultures, and religions (see R. Wilson, ed. 1996). Human rights include the right to speak freely, to hold religious beliefs without persecution, and not to be murdered, injured, or enslaved or imprisoned without charge. Such rights are seen as *inalienable* (nations cannot abridge or terminate them) and international (larger than and superior to individual nations and cultures). Four United Nations documents describe nearly all the human rights that have been internationally recognized. Those documents are the U.N. Charter; the Universal Declaration of Human Rights; the Covenant on Economic, Social and Cultural Rights; and the Covenant on Civil and Political Rights.

Alongside the human rights movement has arisen an awareness of the need to preserve cultural rights. Unlike human rights, **cultural rights** are vested not in individuals

The notion of indigenous intellectual property rights (IPR) has arisen in an attempt to conserve each society's cultural base, including its medicinal plants, which may have commercial value. Shown here is the hoodia plant, a cactus that grows in the Kalahari Desert of southern Africa. Hoodia, which traditionally is used by the San people to stave off hunger, is used now in diet pills marketed on the Internet.

but in *groups,* such as religious and ethnic minorities and indigenous societies. Cultural rights include a group's ability to preserve its culture, to raise its children in the ways of its forebears, to continue its language, and not to be deprived of its economic base by the nation in which it is located (Greaves 1995). The related notion of indigenous **intellectual property rights (IPR)** has arisen in an attempt to conserve each society's cultural base—its core beliefs, knowledge, and practices (see Merry 2006). Much traditional cultural knowledge has commercial value. Examples include ethnomedicine (traditional medical knowledge and techniques), cosmetics, cultivated plants, foods, folklore, arts, crafts, songs, dances, costumes, and rituals (see Nazarea 2006). According to the IPR concept, a particular group may determine how indigenous knowledge and its products may be used and distributed and the level of compensation required.

The notion of cultural rights is related to the idea of cultural relativism, and the problem discussed previously arises again. What does one do about cultural rights that interfere with human rights? I believe that anthropology's main job is to present accurate accounts and explanations of cultural phenomena. The anthropologist doesn't have to approve infanticide, cannibalism, or torture to record their existence and determine their causes and the motivations behind them. However, each anthropologist has a choice about where he or she will do fieldwork. Some anthropologists choose not to study a particular culture because they discover in advance or early in fieldwork that behavior they consider morally repugnant is practiced there. Anthropologists respect human diversity. Most ethnographers try to be objective, accurate, and sensitive in their accounts of other cultures. However, objectivity, sensitivity, and a cross-cultural perspective don't mean that anthropologists have to ignore international standards of justice and morality. What do you think?

Mechanisms of Cultural Change

Why and how do cultures change? One way is **diffusion** or borrowing of traits between cultures. Such exchange of information and products has gone on throughout human history because cultures never have been truly isolated. Contact between neighboring groups has always existed and has extended over vast areas (Boas 1940/1966). Diffusion is *direct* when two cultures trade with, intermarry among, or wage war on one another. Diffusion is *forced* when one culture subjugates another and imposes its customs on the dominated group. Diffusion is *indirect* when items or traits move from group A to group C via group B without any firsthand contact between A and C. In this case, group B might consist of traders or merchants who take products from a variety of places to new markets. Or group B might be geographically situated between A and C, so that what it gets from A eventually winds up in C, and vice versa. In today's world, much international diffusion is indirect—culture spread by the mass media and advanced information technology.

Acculturation, a second mechanism of cultural change, is the ongoing exchange of cultural features that results when groups have continuous firsthand contact. The cultures of either or both groups may be changed by this contact (Redfield, Linton, and Herskovits 1936). With acculturation, parts of the cultures change, but each group remains distinct. One example of acculturation is a *pidgin,* a mixed language that develops to ease communication between members of different cultures in contact. This usually happens in situations of trade or colonialism. Pidgin English, for example, is a simplified form of English. It blends English grammar with the grammar of a native language. Pidgin English was first used for commerce in Chinese ports. Similar pidgins developed later in Papua New Guinea and West Africa. In situations of continuous contact, cultures have also exchanged and blended foods, recipes, music, dances, clothing, tools, and technologies.

Independent invention—the process by which humans innovate, creatively finding solutions to problems—is a third mechanism of cultural change. Faced with comparable problems and challenges, people in different societies have innovated and changed in similar ways, which is one reason cultural generalities exist. One example is the independent invention of agriculture in the Middle East and Mexico. Over the course of human history, major innovations have spread at the expense of earlier ones. Often a major invention, such as agriculture, triggers a series of subsequent interrelated changes. These economic revolutions have social and cultural repercussions. Thus in both Mexico and the Middle East, agriculture led to many social, political, and legal changes, including notions of property and distinctions in wealth, class, and power (see Naylor 1996).

Globalization

The term **globalization** encompasses a series of processes that work transnationally to promote change in a world in which nations and people are increasingly interlinked and mutually dependent. Promoting globalization are economic and political forces, along with modern systems of transportation and communication. The forces of globalization include international commerce and finance, travel and tourism, transnational migration, and the media—including the Internet and other high-tech information flows (see Appadurai, ed. 2001; Friedman and Friedman 2008; Kjaerulff 2010; Scholte 2000). New economic unions (which have met considerable resistance in their member nations) have been created through the World Trade Organization (WTO), the International Monetary Fund (IMF), and the European Union (EU).

The media, including the Internet, play a key role in globalization. Long-distance communication is faster and easier than ever, and now covers most of the globe. I can now e-mail or call families in Arembepe, Brazil, which lacked phones and even postal service when I first began to study the community. Information about Arembepe is now available to anyone, including potential tourists, on hundreds of websites. Anything can be Googled. The media help propel a transnational culture of consumption, as they spread information about products, services, rights, institutions, lifestyles, and the perceived costs and benefits of globalization. Emigrants transmit information and resources transnationally, as they maintain their ties with home (phoning, texting, e-mailing, visiting, sending money). In a sense such people live multilocally—in different places and cultures at once. They learn to play various social roles and to change behavior and identity depending on the situation (see Cresswell 2006).

The effects of globalization are broad and not always welcome. Local people must cope increasingly with forces generated by progressively larger systems—region, nation, and world. An army of outsiders and potential change agents now intrudes on people

Contemporary media play a key role in globalization. Here we see Egyptians using their cell phones to record–and potentially to transport globally–images from Cairo's Tahrir Square. This site was the epicenter of the popular revolt that drove President Hosni Mubarak from power in February, 2011.

Anthropology Today
Experiencing Culture: Personal Space and Displays of Affection

In winter 2008 I created and taught a course called "Experiencing Culture" to American college students in Italy. Students wrote biweekly journals reflecting on the cultural differences they observed between Europeans and Americans. One thing that really struck them was the greater frequency and intensity of PDAs—public displays of affection—between romantic couples in Italy, compared with the United States.

The world's nations and cultures have strikingly different notions about displays of affection and personal space. Cocktail parties in international meeting places such as the United Nations can resemble an elaborate insect mating ritual as diplomats from different countries advance, withdraw, and sidestep. When Americans talk, walk, and dance, they maintain a certain distance from others. Italians or Brazilians, who need less personal space, may interpret such "standoffishness" as a sign of coldness. In conversational pairs, the Italian or Brazilian typically moves in, while the American "instinctively" retreats from a "close talker." Such bodily movements illustrate not instinct, but culture—behavior programmed by years of exposure to a particular cultural tradition.

To what extent are you a product of your particular culture? How much does, and should, your cultural background influence your actions and decisions? Americans may not fully appreciate the power of culture because of the value their culture places on the individual. We have seen that individualism is a distinctive *shared* value, a feature of American culture, transmitted constantly in our daily lives. In the media, count how many stories focus on individuals versus groups. That we are individuals first and members of groups second is the opposite of this chapter's lesson about culture. Certainly we have distinctive features because we are individuals, but we have other distinct

In a public display of affection a young couple kisses on the steps outside a church in Via del Corso, Rome, Italy.

attributes because we belong to cultural groups.

To return to the cultural contrast that so impressed my American students in Italy, there are striking contrasts between a national culture (American) that tends to be reserved about displays of physical affection and national cultures in which the opposite is true. Brazilians approach, touch, and kiss one another much more frequently than North Americans do. Middle-class Brazilians teach their kids—both boys and girls—to kiss (on the cheek, two or three times, coming and going) every adult relative they ever see. Given the size of Brazilian extended families, this can mean hundreds of people. Women continue kissing all those people throughout their lives. Until they are adolescents, boys kiss all adult relatives. Men typically continue to kiss female relatives and friends, as well as their fathers and uncles throughout their lives.

Do you kiss your father? Your uncle? Your grandfather? How about your mother, aunt, or grandmother? The answer to these questions may differ between men and women, and for male and female relatives. Culture can help us to make sense of these differences. In America, a cultural homophobia (fear of homosexuality) may prevent American men from engaging in displays of affection with other men. Similarly, American girls typically are encouraged to show affection; this is less true for boys.

However, culture is not static. Sarah Kershaw (2009) describes a recent surge of teenage hugging behavior in American schools. Concerned about potential sexual harassment issues, parents and school officials remain suspicious of such PDAs, even if the younger generation is more tolerant. Even American boys appear to be more likely nowadays to share nonromantic hugs, as such expressions as "bromance" and "man crush" enter our vocabulary. Hugging also has migrated online, where Facebook applications allowing friends to send hugs have tens of thousands of fans.

It's important to note that cultural traits exist because they are learned, not because they are natural or inherently right. Ethnocentrism is the error of viewing one's own culture as superior and applying one's own cultural values in judging people from other cultures. How easy is it for you to see beyond the ethnocentric blinders of your own experience? Do you have an ethnocentric position regarding displays of affection?

everywhere. Tourism has become the world's number one industry (see Holden 2005). Economic development agents and the media promote the idea that work should be for cash rather than mainly for subsistence. Indigenous peoples and traditional societies have devised various strategies to deal with threats to their autonomy, identity, and livelihood (Maybury-Lewis 2002). New forms of cultural expression and political mobilization, including the rights movements discussed previously, are emerging from the interplay of local, regional, national, and international cultural forces (see Ong and Collier, eds. 2005).

Illustrating political mobilization against globalization are regular protests at the meetings of the main agencies concerned with international trade. One of the largest protests took place in December 1999 in Seattle, which witnessed a massive and violent demonstration against the WTO, which was meeting there. Protesters continue to show their disapproval of policies of the WTO, the IMF, and the World Bank. In November 2009 there were clashes with police during a march by demonstrators protesting the opening of a WTO meeting in Geneva. The WTO had called that meeting of its 153 members to find ways to revive world trade and get the global economy out of recession (*Huffington Post* 2009).

WTO opponents claim the agreements it produces foster the growth of wealth among corporations at the expense of farmers, workers, and others at the low end of the economy. Environmentalists seek tougher environmental impact assessments. Human rights groups contend that international development policies help only big business, not poor countries and their citizens. Trade unionists advocate for global labor standards. Are such protests valid, and are they likely to halt globalization? What's your opinion of globalization?

Summary

1. Culture, which is distinctive to humanity, refers to customary behavior and beliefs that are passed on through enculturation. Culture rests on the human capacity for cultural learning. Culture encompasses rules for conduct internalized in human beings, which lead them to think and act in characteristic ways.

2. Although other animals learn, only humans have cultural learning, dependent on symbols. Humans think symbolically—arbitrarily bestowing meaning on things and events. By convention, a symbol stands for something with which it has no necessary or natural relation. Symbols have special meaning for people who share memories, values, and beliefs because of common enculturation.

3. Cultural traditions mold biologically based desires and needs in particular directions. Everyone is cultured, not just people with elite educations. Cultures may be integrated and patterned through economic and social forces, key symbols, and core values. Cultural rules don't rigidly dictate our behavior. There is room for creativity, flexibility, diversity, and disagreement within societies. Cultural means of adaptation have been crucial in human evolution. Aspects of culture also can be maladaptive.

4. The human capacity for culture has an evolutionary basis that extends back at least 2.6 million years—to early toolmakers whose products survive in the archaeological record (and most probably even further back—based on observation of tool use and manufacture by apes). Humans share with monkeys and apes such traits as manual dexterity (especially opposable thumbs), depth and color vision, learning ability based on a large brain, substantial parental investment in a limited number of offspring, and tendencies toward sociality and cooperation.

5. Many hominin traits are foreshadowed in other primates, particularly in the African apes, which, like us, belong to the hominid family. The ability to learn, basic to culture, is an adaptive advantage available to monkeys and apes. Chimpanzees make tools for several purposes. They also hunt and share meat. Sharing and cooperation

are more developed among humans than among the apes, and only humans have systems of kinship and marriage that permit us to maintain lifelong ties with relatives in different local groups.

6. Using a comparative perspective, anthropology examines biological, psychological, social, and cultural universals and generalities. There also are unique and distinctive aspects of the human condition (cultural particularities). North American cultural traditions are no more natural than any others. Levels of culture can be larger or smaller than a nation. Cultural traits may be shared across national boundaries. Nations also include cultural differences associated with ethnicity, region, and social class.

7. Ethnocentrism describes judging other cultures by using one's own cultural standards. Cultural relativism, which anthropologists may use as a methodological position rather than a moral stance, is the idea of avoiding the use of outside standards to judge behavior in a given society. Human rights are those based on justice and morality beyond and superior to particular countries, cultures, and religions. Cultural rights are vested in religious and ethnic minorities and indigenous societies, and IPR, or intellectual property rights, apply to an indigenous group's collective knowledge and its applications.

8. Diffusion, migration, and colonialism have carried cultural traits and patterns to different world areas. Mechanisms of cultural change include diffusion, acculturation, and independent invention. Globalization describes a series of processes that promote change in a world in which nations and people are interlinked and mutually dependent.

Key Terms

acculturation, *34*
core values, *21*
cultural relativism, *32*
cultural rights, *32*
diffusion, *34*
enculturation, *18*
estrus, *26*
ethnocentrism, *31*
generality, *27*
globalization, *34*
hominids, *23*
hominins, *23*
human rights, *32*
independent invention, *34*
intellectual property rights (IPR), *33*
international culture, *30*
national culture, *30*
particularity, *27*
subcultures, *31*
symbol, *18*
universal, *27*

Go to our Online Learning Center website at **www.mhhe.com/kottak** for Internet resources directly related to the contents of this chapter.

Chapter  3

Doing Anthropology

Research Methods in Archaeology and Physical Anthropology

   Multidisciplinary Approaches

   Studying the Past

   Survey and Excavation

Kinds of Archaeology

Dating the Past

   Relative Dating

   Absolute Dating

   Molecular Anthropology

Kinds of Physical Anthropology

   Bone Biology

   Anthropometry

   Primatology

   Applying Anthropology to Popular Culture: Bones

Research Methods in Cultural Anthropology

Ethnography: Anthropology's Distinctive Strategy

Ethnographic Techniques

   Observation and Participant Observation

   Conversation, Interviewing, and Interview Schedules

   The Genealogical Method

   Key Cultural Consultants

   Life Histories

   Local Beliefs and Perceptions, and the Ethnographer's

   Problem-Oriented Ethnography

   Longitudinal Studies, Team Research, and Multisited Ethnography

Survey Research

Doing Anthropology Right and Wrong: Ethical Issues

   The Code of Ethics

   Anthropologists and Terrorism

   Anthropology Today: Archaeologist in New Orleans Finds a Way to Help the Living

"Been on any digs lately?" Ask your professor how many times she or he has been asked this question. Then ask how often he or she actually has been on a dig. Remember that anthropology has four subfields, only two of which (archaeology and biological anthropology) require much digging—in the ground at least. Even among biological anthropologists it's mainly paleoanthropologists (those concerned with the hominin fossil record) who must dig. Students of primate behavior in the wild, such as Jane Goodall, don't do it. Nor, most of the time, is it done by forensic anthropologists, such as the title character in the TV series *Bones*.

To be sure, cultural anthropologists "dig out" information about varied lifestyles, as linguistic anthropologists do about the features of language. Traditionally, cultural anthropologists have done a variant on the *Star Trek* theme of seeking out, if not new, at least different "life" and "civilizations," sometimes boldly going where no scientist has gone before.

Despite globalization, the cultural diversity under anthropological scrutiny right now may be as great as ever before, because the anthropological universe has expanded to modern nations. Today's cultural anthropologists are as likely to study artists in Miami or bankers in Beirut as Polynesians in outrigger canoes. Still, we can't forget that anthropology did originate in non-Western, nonindustrial societies. Its research techniques, especially those subsumed under the label "ethnography," were developed to deal with small populations. Even when working in modern nations, anthropologists still consider ethnography with small groups to be an excellent way of learning about how people live their lives and make decisions.

Before this course, did you know the names of any anthropologists? If so, which ones—real or fictional? For the general public, biological anthropologists and archaeologists tend to be better known than cultural anthropologists because of what they study and discover—making them attractive subjects for the Discovery channel. You're more likely to have watched *Bones* or seen film of Jane Goodall with chimps or a paleoanthropologist holding a skull than a linguistic or cultural anthropologist at work. Archaeologists occasionally appear in the media to describe a new discovery or to debunk pseudo-archaeological arguments about how visitors from space have left traces on Earth. One cultural anthropologist was an important public and media figure for much of the 20th century. Margaret Mead, famed for her work on teen sexuality in Samoa and gender roles in New Guinea, may well be the most famous anthropologist who ever lived. Mead, one of my own professors at Columbia University, appeared regularly on NBC's *Tonight Show*. In all her venues, including teaching, museum work, TV, anthropological films, popular books, and magazines, Mead helped Americans appreciate the relevance of anthropology to understanding their daily lives. That's a worthy goal that more contemporary anthropologists should emulate.

This chapter is about what anthropologists do. It focuses on archaeology, biological, and sociocultural anthropology. Linguistic methods are discussed in Chapter 10; and applied anthropology, in Chapter 18. (Given space limitations in a brief introductory textbook such as this, only some of the many methods and techniques employed by anthropologists can be covered here.)

Research Methods in Archaeology and Physical Anthropology

Recall from Chapter 1 that archaeology and biological or physical anthropology are two of anthropology's four subfields. Anthropological archaeology reconstructs human behavior, social patterns, and cultural features through the analysis of material remains (and other sources, including written records, if available). Biological anthropologists study living and recent humans (e.g., their genetics, growth, development, and physiological

At San Ignacio, archaeology students excavate a section of the Cahal Pech Maya site in western Belize. The students are volunteers, mostly from the United States. The work is under the direction of the Belize Valley Archaeological Reconnaissance Project.

Excavation

During an **excavation,** scientists dig through the layers of deposits that make up a site. These layers, or strata, are used to establish the time order of materials. This relative chronology is based on the principle of *superposition:* In an undisturbed sequence of strata, the oldest layer is on the bottom. Each successive layer above is younger than the one below. Thus, remains from lower strata are older than those recovered from higher strata in the same deposit. This relative time ordering of material lies at the heart of archaeological, paleoanthropological, and paleontological research.

The archaeological and fossil records are so rich, and excavation is so labor intensive and expensive, that nobody digs a site without a good reason. Sites are excavated because they are endangered, or because they answer specific research questions (see Sabloff 2008). Cultural resource management (CRM) focuses on managing the preservation of archaeological sites that are threatened by modern development. Many countries require archaeological impact studies before construction can take place. If a site is at risk and the development cannot be stopped, CRM archaeologists are called in to salvage what information they can from the site.

Another reason for choosing a particular site to excavate is that it is well suited to answer specific research questions. An archaeologist studying the origins of agriculture wouldn't want to excavate a large, fortified hilltop city with a series of buildings dating to a period well after the first appearance of farming communities. Rather, he or she would look for a small hamlet-size site located near good farmland and a water source. Such a site would have evidence of an early occupation dating to the period when farming communities first appeared in that region.

Kinds of Archaeology

Archaeologists pursue diverse research topics, using a wide variety of methods. Experimental archaeologists try to replicate ancient techniques and processes (e.g., tool making) under controlled conditions. Historical archaeologists use written records as guides and supplements to archaeological research. They work with remains more recent—often much more recent—than the advent of writing. (See this chapter's "Anthropology Today.") Colonial archaeologists are historical archaeologists who use written records as guides to locate and excavate postcontact sites in North and South America, and to verify or question the written accounts. Classical archaeologists usually are affiliated with university departments of classics or the history of art, rather than with anthropology departments. These classical scholars tend to focus on the literate civilizations of the Old World, such as Greece, Rome, and Egypt. Classical archaeologists often are more interested in styles of architecture and sculpture than in the social, economic, and political features that typically interest anthropological archaeologists. Underwater archaeology is a growing field that investigates submerged sites, most often shipwrecks. Special techniques, including remotely operated vehicles like the one shown in the movie *Titanic,* are used, but divers also do underwater survey and excavation.

Dating the Past

The archaeological record hasn't revealed every ancient society that has existed on Earth; nor is the fossil record a representative sample of all the plants and animals that ever have lived. Some species and body parts are better represented than others are, for many reasons. Hard parts, such as bones and teeth, preserve better than do soft parts, such as flesh and skin. The chances of fossilization increase when remains are buried in silt, gravel, or sand. Good places for bone preservation include swamps, floodplains, river deltas, lakes, and caves. The species that live in such areas have a better chance to be preserved than do animals that live in other habitats. Fossilization also is favored in areas with volcanic ash. Once remains do get buried, chemical conditions must be right for fossilization to occur. If the sediment is too acidic, even bones and teeth will dissolve. The study of the processes that affect the remains of dead animals is called **taphonomy,** from the Greek *taphos,* which means "tomb." Such processes include scattering by carnivores and scavengers, distortion by various forces, and the possible fossilization of the remains.

The conditions under which fossils are found also influence the fossil record. For example, fossils are more likely to be uncovered through erosion in arid areas than in wet areas. Sparse vegetation allows wind to scour the landscape and uncover fossils. The fossil record has been accumulating longer and is more extensive in Europe than in Africa because civil engineering projects and fossil hunting have been going on longer in Europe than in Africa. A world map showing where fossils have been found does not indicate the true range of ancient animals. Such a map tells us more about ancient geological activity, modern erosion, or recent human activity—such as paleontological research or road building. In considering the primate and hominin fossil records in later chapters, we'll see that certain areas provide more abundant fossil evidence for particular time periods. This doesn't necessarily mean that primates or hominins were only living in that area at that time. Nor does failure to find a fossil species in a particular place always mean the species didn't live there. In the words of paleoanthropologist Christopher Stringer, "absence of evidence does not necessarily prove evidence of absence" (quoted in Gugliotta 2005).

Relative Dating

Scientists use a variety of techniques to date fossils. These methods offer different degrees of precision and are applicable to different periods of the past. Dating may be relative or absolute. **Relative dating** provides a time frame in relation to other strata or materials rather than absolute dates in numbers. Many dating methods are based on the geological study of **stratigraphy,** the science that examines the ways in which earth sediments accumulate in layers known as strata (singular, stratum). Soil that erodes from a hillside into a valley covers, and is younger than, the soil already deposited there. Stratigraphy permits relative dating. That is, the fossils in a given stratum are younger than those below them and older than those above them. We may not know the exact or absolute dates of the fossils, but we can place them in time relative to remains in other layers. Remains of animals and plants that lived at the same time are found in the same stratum. When fossils are found in a particular stratum, the associated geological features (such as frost patterning) and remains of particular plants and animals offer clues about the climate at the time of deposition.

Absolute Dating

Fossils can be dated more precisely, with dates in numbers (**absolute dating**), by using several methods. For example, the ^{14}C, or carbon-14, technique is used to date organic remains. This is a *radiometric* technique (so called because it measures radioactive decay). ^{14}C is an unstable radioactive isotope of normal carbon, ^{12}C. Cosmic radiation entering the earth's atmosphere produces ^{14}C, and plants take in ^{14}C as they absorb carbon dioxide. ^{14}C moves up the food chain as animals eat plants and as predators eat other animals.

With death, the absorption of ^{14}C stops. This unstable isotope starts to break down into nitrogen (^{14}N). It takes 5,730 years for half the ^{14}C to change to nitrogen; this is the half-life of ^{14}C. After another 5,730 years one-quarter of the original ^{14}C will remain. After yet another 5,730 years one-eighth will be left. By measuring the proportion of ^{14}C in organic material, scientists can determine a fossil's date of death, or the date of an ancient campfire. However, because the half-life of ^{14}C is short, this dating technique is less dependable for specimens older than 40,000 years than it is for more recent remains.

Fortunately, other radiometric dating techniques are available for earlier periods. One of the most widely used is the potassium-argon (K/A) technique. ^{40}K is a radioactive isotope of potassium that breaks down into argon-40, a gas. The half-life of ^{40}K is far longer than that of ^{14}C—1.3 billion years. With this method, the older the specimen, the more reliable the dating. Furthermore, whereas ^{14}C dating can be done only on organic remains, K/A dating can be used only for inorganic substances: rocks and minerals. ^{40}K in rocks gradually breaks down into argon-40. That gas is trapped in the rock until the rock is heated intensely (as with volcanic activity), at which point it may escape. When the rock cools, the breakdown of potassium into argon resumes. Dating is done by reheating the rock and measuring the escaping gas.

In Africa's Great Rift Valley, which runs down eastern Africa and in which early hominin fossils abound, past volcanic activity permits K/A dating. In studies of strata containing fossils, scientists find out how much argon has accumulated in rocks since they were last heated. They then determine, using the standard ^{40}K deterioration rate (half-life), the date of that heating. Considering volcanic rocks at the top of a stratum with fossil remains, scientists establish that the fossils are older than, say, 1.8 million years. By dating the volcanic rocks below the fossil remains, they determine that the fossils are *younger than,* say, 2 million years. Thus, the age of the fossils is set at between 2 million and 1.8 million years. Note that absolute dating is that in name only; it may give ranges of numbers rather than exact dates.

Many fossils were discovered before the advent of modern stratigraphy. Often we can no longer determine their original stratigraphic placement. Furthermore, fossils aren't always discovered in volcanic layers. Like ^{14}C dating, the K/A technique applies to a limited period of the fossil record. Because the half-life of ^{40}K is so long, the technique cannot be used with materials less than 500,000 years old.

Other radiometric dating techniques can be used to cross-check K/A dates, again by using minerals surrounding the fossils. One such method, *uranium series dating,* measures fission tracks produced during the decay of radioactive uranium (^{238}U) into lead. Two other radiometric techniques are especially useful for fossils that can't be dated by ^{14}C (up to 40,000 B.P.—before the present) or ^{40}K (more than 500,000 B.P.). These methods are *thermoluminescence* (TL) and *electron spin resonance* (ESR). Both TL and ESR measure the electrons that are constantly being trapped in rocks and minerals (Shreeve 1992). Once a date is obtained for a rock found associated with a fossil, that date also can be applied to that fossil. Table 3.1 summarizes the time spans for which the various absolute dating techniques are applicable.

Molecular Anthropology

Molecular anthropology uses genetic analysis (of DNA sequences) to date, and to estimate evolutionary distance between, species. Molecular studies have been used to assess and date the origins of modern humans and to examine their relation to extinct human groups such as the Neandertals, which lived in Europe between 130,000 and 28,000 years ago.

TABLE 3.1 Absolute Dating Techniques

Technique	Abbreviation	Materials Dated	Effective Time Range
Carbon-14	^{14}C	Organic materials	Up to 40,000 years
Potassium-argon	K/A and ^{40}K	Volcanic rock	Older than 500,000 years
Uranium series	^{238}U	Minerals	Between 1,000 and 1,000,000 years
Thermoluminescence	TL	Rocks and minerals	Between 5,000 and 1,000,000 years
Electron spin resonance	ESR	Rocks and minerals	Between 1,000 and 1,000,000 years

Molecular anthropologists examine relationships among ancient and contemporary populations and among species. It's well established, for example, that humans and chimpanzees have more than 98 percent of their DNA in common. Molecular anthropologists also reconstruct waves and patterns of migration and settlement. A *haplogroup* is a biological lineage (a large group of related people) defined by a specific cluster of genetic traits that occur together. Native Americans have four major haplogroups, which also are linked to East Asia. Molecular anthropologists also use "genetic clocks" to estimate divergence time (date of most recent common ancestry) among species (e.g., humans, chimps, and gorillas—5 million to 8 million years ago) and of various human groups (e.g., Neandertals and modern humans).

Kinds of Physical Anthropology

Archaeologists study the very recent past when they do garbology—examining garbage to interpret behavior among contemporary humans. Besides fossils, physical anthropologists also study patterns of movement or growth and development among living people. The interests of physical anthropologists are varied and encompass recent and living as well as ancient and deceased humans and other primates. This chapter describes many, but far from all, of the topics and methods within contemporary physical anthropology.

Bone Biology

Central to biological or physical anthropology is **bone biology** (aka skeletal biology)—the study of bone as a biological tissue, including its genetics; cell structure; growth, development, and decay; and patterns of movement (biomechanics) (Katzenberg and Saunders, eds. 2000). Bone biologists study skeletal characteristics of living and deceased humans and hominins. Any scientific interpretation of fossil remains relies on understanding the structure and function of the skeleton. **Paleopathology** is the study of disease and injury in skeletons from archaeological sites. Some forms of cancer leave evidence in the bone. Breast cancer, for example, may spread (metastasize) skeletally, leaving holes or lesions in bones and skull. Certain infectious diseases (e.g., syphilis and

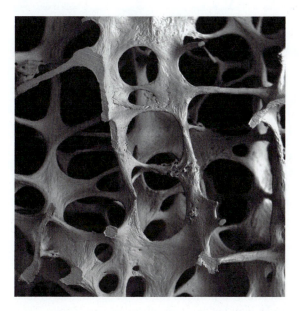

T Bone biology: Osteoporosis (shown here in an 89-year-old woman) is a disease in which bones become extremely porous. They fracture more easily and heal more slowly than firmer bones.

tuberculosis) also mark bone, as do injuries and nutritional deficiencies (e.g., rickets, a vitamin D deficiency that deforms the bones).

In *forensic anthropology,* physical anthropologists work in a legal context, assisting coroners, medical examiners, and law enforcement agencies in recovering, analyzing, and identifying human remains and determining the cause of death (Blau and Ubelaker 2008; Komar and Buikstra 2008). The television series *Bones* offers a view of such work through the character Temperance Brennan (aka "Bones" by her partner FBI agent Seeley Booth), whose creator is physical/forensic anthropologist Kathy Reichs.

Anthropometry

Physical anthropologists use various techniques to study nutrition, growth, and development. **Anthropometry** is the measurement of human body parts and dimensions, including skeletal parts (*osteometry*). Anthropometry is done on living people as well as on skeletal remains from sites. Body mass and composition provide measures of nutritional status in living people. Body mass is calculated from height and weight. The *body mass index* (kg/m^2) is the ratio of weight in kilograms divided by height in meters squared. An adult body mass above 30 is considered at risk of overweight, while one below 18 is at risk of underweight or malnutrition.

Primatology

Primatology is considered a subfield of biological anthropology, although primate studies also are useful to archaeologists attempting to understand the behavior and social life of ancient hominins. Primatology also links with sociocultural anthropology (especially ethnography) through its focus on behavior and social life. Primate behavior has been observed in zoos (e.g., de Waal 1998) and through experimentation (e.g., Harlow 1971), but the most significant studies have been done in natural settings, among free-ranging

Watch a few episodes of the Fox TV series *Bones*—based on characters created by Kathy Reichs, a physical and forensic anthropologist. *Bones* is one of the very few TV programs featuring a professional anthropologist, the character Temperance Brennan, aka "Bones" to her FBI agent partner, Seeley Booth. As you watch the program, pay attention to the following questions: How do Dr. Brennan's attitudes, beliefs, and opinions differ from those of other characters? How do her statements compare and contrast with anthropological perspectives as presented in this textbook? Ask your professor what she or he thinks about some of the statements you write down and quote from Dr. Brennan.

apes, monkeys, and lemurs. Since the 1950s, when primatologists began their shift from zoos to natural settings, numerous studies have been done of apes (chimps, gorillas, orangutans, and gibbons), monkeys (e.g., baboons, macaques), and lemurs (e.g., Madagascar's indrii, sifaka, and ring-tailed lemurs). Arboreal primates (those that spend most of their time in the trees) are difficult to see and follow, but they typically make a lot of noise. Their howls and calls can be studied and teach us about how primates communicate. Studies of primate social systems and behavior, including their mating patterns, infant care, and patterns of contact and dispersal, suggest hypotheses about behavior that humans do or do not share with our nearest relatives—and also with our hominin ancestors.

Research Methods in Cultural Anthropology

Cultural anthropology and sociology (like primatology) share an interest in social relations, organization, and behavior. Early students of society, such as the French scholar Émile Durkheim, were among the founders of both sociology and anthropology. Durkheim studied the religions of Native Australians (Durkheim 1912/2001), as well as mass phenomena, such as suicide rates, in modern nations (Durkheim 1897/1951). Key differences between anthropology and sociology eventually emerged from the kinds of societies each studied. Sociologists focused on the industrial West; anthropologists, on nonindustrial societies. Different methods of data collection and analysis were developed to deal with those different kinds of societies. To study large-scale, complex nations, sociologists came to rely on questionnaires and other means of gathering masses of quantifiable data. For many years sampling and statistical techniques have been basic to sociology, whereas statistical training has been less common in anthropology (although this is changing somewhat as anthropologists increasingly work in modern nations).

Traditional ethnographers studied small, nonliterate (without writing) populations and relied on ethnographic methods appropriate to that context. "Ethnography is a research process in which the anthropologist closely observes, records, and engages in the daily life of another culture—an experience labeled as the fieldwork method—and then writes accounts of this culture, emphasizing descriptive detail" (Marcus and Fischer

1986, p. 18). One key method described in this quote is **participant observation**—taking part in the events one is observing, describing, and analyzing.

Ethnography: Anthropology's Distinctive Strategy

Anthropology became a separate field as early scholars worked on Indian (Native American) reservations and traveled to distant lands to study small groups of foragers (hunters and gatherers) and cultivators. Traditionally, the process of becoming a cultural anthropologist has required a field experience in another society. Early ethnographers lived in small-scale, relatively isolated societies with simple technologies and economies.

Ethnography thus emerged as a research strategy in societies with greater cultural uniformity and less social differentiation than are found in large, modern nations. Traditionally, ethnographers have tried to understand the whole of a particular culture (or, more realistically, as much as they can, given limitations of time and perception). To pursue this goal, ethnographers adopt a free-ranging strategy for gathering information. In a given society or community, the ethnographer moves from setting to setting, person to person, and place to place to discover the totality and interconnectedness of social life. By expanding our knowledge of the range of human diversity, ethnography provides a foundation for generalizations about human behavior and social life. Ethnographers draw on varied techniques to piece together a picture of otherwise alien lifestyles. Anthropologists usually employ several (but rarely all) of the techniques discussed below (see also Bernard 2006; Wolcott 2008).

Ethnographic Techniques

The characteristic field techniques of the ethnographer include the following:

1. Direct, firsthand observation of behavior, including participant observation.
2. Conversation with varying degrees of formality, from the daily chitchat that helps maintain rapport and provides knowledge about what is going on, to prolonged interviews, which can be unstructured or structured.
3. The genealogical method.
4. Detailed work with key consultants, or informants, about particular areas of community life.
5. In-depth interviewing, often leading to the collection of life histories of particular people (narrators).
6. Discovery of local (native) beliefs and perceptions, which may be compared with the ethnographer's own observations and conclusions.
7. Problem-oriented research of many sorts.
8. Longitudinal research—the continuous long-term study of an area or site.
9. Team research—coordinated research by multiple ethnographers.
10. Multisited research that studies the various sites and systems in which people participate.

Observation and Participant Observation

Ethnographers must pay attention to hundreds of details of daily life, seasonal events, and unusual happenings. They should record what they see as they see it. Things never will seem quite as strange as they do during the first few weeks in the field. The ethnographer eventually gets used to, and accepts as normal, cultural patterns that initially were alien. Staying a bit more than a year in the field allows the ethnographer to repeat the season of his or her arrival, when certain events and processes may have been missed because of initial unfamiliarity and culture shock.

Many ethnographers record their impressions in a personal diary, which is kept separate from more formal field notes. Later, this record of early impressions will help point out some of the most basic aspects of cultural diversity. Such aspects include distinctive smells, noises people make, how they cover their mouths when they eat, and how they gaze at others. These patterns, which are so basic as to seem almost trivial, are part of what Bronislaw Malinowski called "the *imponderabilia* of native life and of typical behavior" (Malinowski 1922/1961, p. 20). These features of culture are so fundamental that natives take them for granted. They are too basic even to talk about, but the unaccustomed eye of the fledgling ethnographer picks them up. Thereafter, becoming familiar, they fade to the edge of consciousness. Initial impressions are valuable and should be recorded. First and foremost, ethnographers should try to be accurate observers, recorders, and reporters of what they see in the field.

Ethnographers strive to establish *rapport,* a good, friendly working relationship based on personal contact, with their hosts. One of ethnography's most characteristic procedures is participant observation, which means that we take part in community life as we study it. As human beings living among others, we cannot be totally impartial and

Bronislaw Malinowski (1884–1942), who was born in Poland but spent most of his professional life in England, did fieldwork in the Trobriand Islands from 1914 to 1918. Malinowski is generally considered to be the father of ethnography. Does this photo suggest anything about his relationship with Trobriand villagers?

detached observers. We take part in many events and processes we are observing and trying to comprehend. By participating, we may learn why people find such events meaningful, as we see how they are organized and conducted.

In Arembepe, Brazil, I learned about fishing by sailing on the Atlantic with local fishers. I gave Jeep rides to malnourished babies and their parents, to pregnant mothers, and once to a teenage girl possessed by a spirit. All those people needed to consult specialists outside the village. I danced on Arembepe's festive occasions, drank libations commemorating new births, and became a godfather to a village girl. Most anthropologists have similar field experiences. The common humanity of the student and the studied, the ethnographer and the research community, makes participant observation inevitable.

Conversation, Interviewing, and Interview Schedules

Participating in local life means that ethnographers constantly talk to people and ask questions. As their knowledge of the local language and culture increases, they understand more. There are several stages in learning a field language. First is the naming phase—asking name after name of the objects around us. Later we are able to pose more complex questions and understand the replies. We begin to understand simple conversations between two villagers. If our language expertise proceeds far enough, we eventually become able to comprehend rapid-fire public discussions and group conversations.

In Mozambique's Gaza province, the Dutch ethnographer Janine van Vugt (right center) sits on mats near reed houses, talking to local women.

One data-gathering technique I have used in both Arembepe and Madagascar involves an ethnographic survey that includes an interview schedule. Soon after I began research in Arembepe, my fellow field workers and I attempted to complete an interview schedule in each of Arembepe's (then) 160 households. We entered almost every household (fewer than 5 percent refused to participate) to ask a set of questions on a printed form. Our results provided us with a census and basic information about the village. We wrote down the name, age, and gender of each household member. We gathered data on family type, religion, present and previous jobs, income, expenditures, diet, possessions, and many other items on our eight-page form.

Although we were doing a survey, our approach differed from the survey research design routinely used by sociologists and other social scientists working in large, industrial nations. That survey research, discussed later in the chapter, involves sampling (choosing a **sample**—a small, manageable study group from a larger population). We did not select a partial sample from the total population. Instead, we tried to interview in all households in the community (that is, to have a total sample). We used an interview schedule rather than a questionnaire. With the **interview schedule,** the ethnographer talks face to face with people, asks the questions, and writes down the answers. Questionnaire procedures tend to be more indirect and impersonal; often the respondent fills in the form.

Our goal of getting a total sample allowed us to meet almost everyone in the village and helped us establish rapport. Decades later, Arembepeiros still talk warmly about how we were interested enough in them to visit their homes and ask them questions. We stood in sharp contrast to the other outsiders the villagers had known, who considered them too poor and backward to be taken seriously.

Like other survey research, however, our interview schedule did gather comparable quantifiable information. It gave us a basis for assessing patterns and exceptions in village life. Our schedules included a core set of questions that were posed to everyone. However, some interesting side issues often came up during the interview, which we would pursue then or later.

We followed such leads into many dimensions of village life. One woman, for instance, a midwife, became the key cultural consultant we sought out later when we wanted detailed information about local childbirth. Another woman had done an internship in an Afro-Brazilian cult (*candomblé*) in the city. She still went there regularly to study, dance, and get possessed. She became our *candomblé* expert.

Thus, our interview schedule provided a structure that directed but did not confine us as researchers. It enabled our ethnography to be both quantitative and qualitative. The quantitative part consisted of the basic information we gathered and later analyzed statistically. The qualitative dimension came from our follow-up questions, open-ended discussions, pauses for gossip, and work with key consultants.

The Genealogical Method

Many of us learn about our own ancestry and relatives by tracing our genealogies. Websites like ancestry.com allow us to trace our "family trees" and degrees of relationship. The **genealogical method** is a well-established ethnographic technique. Early ethnographers developed notation and symbols to deal with kinship, descent, and marriage. Genealogy is a prominent building block in the social organization of nonindustrial societies, where people live and work each day with their close kin. Anthropologists need to collect genealogical data to understand current social relations and to reconstruct history. Indeed, another term for such cultures is "kin-based societies," because everyone is related and spends most of his or her time with relatives. Rules of behavior attached to particular kin relations are basic to everyday life (see Carsten 2004). Marriage also is crucial in organizing nonindustrial societies because strategic marriages between villages, tribes, and clans create political alliances.

Key Cultural Consultants

Every community has people who by accident, experience, talent, or training can provide the most complete or useful information about particular aspects of life. These people are **key cultural consultants,** also called *key informants*. In Ivato, the Betsileo village in Madagascar where I spent most of my time, a man named Rakoto was particularly knowledgeable about village history. However, when I asked him to work with me on a genealogy of the 50 to 60 people buried in the village tomb, he called in his cousin Tuesdaysfather, who knew more about that subject. Tuesdaysfather had survived an epidemic of influenza that ravaged Madagascar, along with much of the world, around 1919. Immune to the disease himself, Tuesdaysfather had the grim job of burying his kin as they died. He kept track of everyone buried in the tomb. Tuesdaysfather helped me with the tomb genealogy. Rakoto joined him in telling me personal details about the deceased villagers.

Life Histories

In nonindustrial societies as in our own, individual personalities, interests, and abilities vary. Some villagers prove to be more interested in the ethnographer's work and are more helpful, interesting, and pleasant than others are. Anthropologists develop likes and dislikes in the field as we do at home. Often, when we find someone unusually interesting, we collect his or her **life history.** This recollection of a lifetime of experiences provides a more intimate and personal cultural portrait than would be possible otherwise. Life histories, which may be recorded or videotaped for later review and analysis, reveal how specific people perceive, react to, and contribute to changes that affect their lives. Many ethnographers include the collection of life histories as an important part of their research strategy.

Local Beliefs and Perceptions, and the Ethnographer's

One goal of ethnography is to discover local (native) views, beliefs, and perceptions, which may be compared with the ethnographer's own observations and conclusions. In the field, ethnographers typically combine two research strategies, the emic (local-oriented) and the etic (scientist-oriented). These terms, derived from linguistics, have been applied to ethnography by various anthropologists. Marvin Harris (1968/2001) popularized the following meanings of the terms: An **emic** approach investigates how local people think. How do they perceive and categorize the world? What are their rules for behavior? What has meaning for them? How do they imagine and explain things? Operating emically, the ethnographer relies on local people to explain things and to say whether something is significant or not. The term **cultural consultant,** or informant, refers to individuals the ethnographer gets to know in the field, the people who teach him or her about their culture, who provide the emic perspective.

The **etic** (scientist-oriented) approach shifts the focus from local observations, categories, explanations, and interpretations to those of the anthropologist. The etic approach realizes that members of a culture often are too involved in what they are doing to interpret their cultures impartially. Operating etically, the ethnographer emphasizes what he or she (the observer) notices and considers important. As a trained scientist, the ethnographer should try to bring an objective and comprehensive viewpoint to the study of other cultures. Of course, the ethnographer, like any other scientist, is also a human being with cultural blinders that prevent complete objectivity. As in other sciences, proper training can reduce, but not totally eliminate, the observer's bias. But anthropologists do have special training to compare behavior between different societies.

What are some examples of emic versus etic perspectives? Consider our holidays. For North Americans, Thanksgiving Day has special significance. In our view (emically) it is a unique cultural celebration that commemorates particular historical themes. But a wider, etic, perspective sees Thanksgiving as just one more example of the postharvest festivals held in many societies. Another example: Local people give folk explanations for illnesses caused by germs and other pathogens. Emic agents that cause illness include angry or envious spirits, ancestors, witches, and sorcerors. Illness refers to a culture's (emic) perception and explanation of bad health, whereas disease refers to the scientific (etic) explanation of poor health, involving known pathogens.

Ethnographers typically combine emic and etic strategies in their fieldwork. The statements, perceptions, categories, and opinions of local people help ethnographers understand how cultures work. Local beliefs are also interesting and valuable in themselves. However, people often fail to admit, or even recognize, certain causes and consequences of their behavior. This is as true of North Americans as it is of people in other societies.

Problem-Oriented Ethnography

Although anthropologists are interested in the whole context of human behavior, it's impossible to study everything. Most ethnographers now enter the field with a specific problem in mind, and they collect data relevant to that problem (see Chiseri-Strater and Sunstein 2001; Kutsche 1998). Local people's answers to questions aren't the only data source. Anthropologists also gather information on factors such as population density, environmental quality, climate, physical geography, diet, and land use. Sometimes this involves direct measurement—of rainfall, temperature, fields, yields, dietary quantities, or time allocation (Bailey 1990; Johnson 1978). Often it means that we consult government records or archives.

The information of interest to ethnographers isn't limited to what local people can and do tell us. In an increasingly interconnected and complicated world, local people lack knowledge about many factors that affect their lives. Our local consultants may be as mystified as we are by the exercise of power from regional, national, and international centers.

Longitudinal Studies, Team Research, and Multisited Ethnography

Geography limits anthropologists much less now than in the past, when it could take months to reach a field site, and return visits were rare. Modern systems of transportation allow anthropologists to widen the scope of their research and to return repeatedly. Ethnographic reports now routinely include data from two or more field stays. We can even follow the people we study as they move from village to city, cross the border, or travel internationally. **Longitudinal research** is the long-term study of an area or population, usually based on repeated visits.

One example is the longitudinal study of Gwembe District, Zambia. This study, planned in 1956 as a longitudinal project by Elizabeth Colson and Thayer Scudder, continues with Colson, Scudder, and their associates and successors of various nationalities. As is often the case with longitudinal research, the Gwembe study also illustrates *team research*—coordinated research by multiple ethnographers (Colson and Scudder 1975; Scudder and Colson 1980). Four villages in different areas have been followed for more than five decades. Periodic censuses provide basic data on population, economy, kinship, and religious behavior. Censused people who have moved are traced and interviewed to see how their lives compare with those of people who have stayed behind. The initial focus of study was the impact of a large hydroelectric dam, which subjected the Gwembe people to forced resettlement. Thereafter Scudder and Colson (1980) examined how education provided access to new opportunities as it also widened a social gap between people with different educational levels. They next focused on a change in brewing and drinking patterns, including a rise in alcoholism, in relation to changing markets, transportation, and exposure to town values (Colson and Scudder 1988).

As mentioned, longitudinal research often is team research. My own field site of Arembepe, Brazil, first entered the world of anthropology as a field-team village in the 1960s. It was one of four sites for the now defunct Columbia-Cornell-Harvard-Illinois Summer Field Studies Program in Anthropology. For at least three years, that program sent a total of about 20 undergraduates annually, the author included, to do summer research abroad. The teams were stationed in rural communities in four countries: Brazil, Ecuador, Mexico, and Peru. Since my wife, Isabel Wagley Kottak, and I began studying it in 1962, Arembepe has become a longitudinal field site. Three generations of researchers have monitored various aspects of change and development. The community has changed from a village into a town and illustrates the process of globalization at the local level. Its economy, religion, and social life have been transformed (see Kottak 2006).

Brazilian and American researchers worked with us on team research projects during the 1980s (on television's impact) and the 1990s (on ecological awareness and environmental risk perception). Graduate students from the University of Michigan have drawn on our baseline information from the 1960s in their recent studies in Arembepe. Their topics have included standards of physical attractiveness, family planning and changing female reproductive strategies, conversion to Protestantism, and changing food habits in relation to globalization. Arembepe is thus a site where various field workers have worked as members of a longitudinal team. The more recent researchers have built on prior contacts and findings to increase knowledge about how local people meet and manage new circumstances.

Traditional ethnographic research focused on a single community or "culture," treated as more or less isolated and unique in time and space. In recent years ethnography has shifted toward studies of change and of contemporary flows of people, technology, images, and information. Reflecting today's world, fieldwork must be more flexible and on a larger scale. Ethnography increasingly is *multitimed* and *multisited*.

Janet Dunn, one of many anthropologists who have worked in Arembepe. Where is Arembepe, and what kinds of research have been done there?

That is, it studies people through time and in multiple places. Malinowski could focus on Trobriand culture and spend most of his field time in a particular community. Nowadays we cannot afford to ignore, as Malinowski did, the outside forces that increasingly impinge on the places we study. Integral to our analyses now are the external entities (e.g., governments, corporations, nongovernmental organizations, new social movements) now laying claim to land, people, and resources throughout the world. Also important in contemporary ethnography is increased recognition of power differentials and how they affect cultures, and of the importance of diversity within cultures and societies.

Anthropologists increasingly study people in motion. Examples include people living on or near national borders, nomads, seasonal migrants, homeless and displaced people, immigrants, and refugees. As fieldwork changes, with less and less of a spatially set field, what can we take from traditional ethnography? Gupta and Ferguson correctly cite the "characteristically anthropological emphasis on daily routine and lived experience" (1997*a*, p. 5). The treatment of communities as discrete entities may be a thing of the past. However, "anthropology's traditional attention to the close observation of particular lives in particular places" has an enduring importance (Gupta and Ferguson 1997*b*, p. 25). The method of close observation helps distinguish cultural anthropology from sociology and survey research, to which we now turn.

Survey Research

Working increasingly in large-scale societies, anthropologists have developed innovative ways of blending ethnography and survey research (Fricke 1994). Before examining such mixed field methods, let's consider the main differences between survey research and ethnography. Sociologists have developed and refined the **survey research** design, which involves sampling, impersonal data collection, and statistical analysis. Survey research draws a sample (a manageable study group) from a much larger population. A properly selected and representative sample permits accurate inferences about the larger population.

In small communities, ethnographers can get to know almost everyone. Given the greater size and complexity of nations, survey research can't help being more impersonal. Survey researchers call the people they study *respondents*—those who respond to questions during a survey. Sometimes survey researchers interview their sample of respondents personally or by phone. Sometimes they ask them to fill out a questionnaire, nowadays often online.

Probably the most familiar example of survey research and sampling is the polling used to predict political races. The media hire agencies to estimate outcomes and do exit polls to find out what kinds of people voted for which candidates. During sampling, researchers gather information about age, gender, religion, occupation, income, and political party preference. These characteristics (**variables**—attributes that vary among members of a sample or population) are known to influence political decisions.

Many more variables affect social identities, experiences, and activities in a modern nation than in the small communities where ethnography grew up. In contemporary North America hundreds of factors influence our behavior and attitudes. These *social predictors* include our religion; the region of the country we grew up in; whether we come from a town, suburb, or city; and our parents' professions, ethnic origins, and income levels. In any large nation, many predictor variables (social indicators) influence behavior and opinions. Because we must be able to detect, measure, and compare the influence of social indicators, many contemporary anthropological studies have a statistical foundation. Even in rural fieldwork, more anthropologists now draw samples, gather quantitative data, and use statistics to interpret them (see Bernard 2006; Bernard, ed. 1998). Quantifiable information may permit a more precise assessment of similarities and differences among communities. Statistical analysis can support and round out an ethnographic account of local social life.

In the best studies, however, the hallmark of ethnography remains: Anthropologists enter the community and get to know the people. They participate in local activities, networks, and associations. They observe and experience social conditions and problems. They watch the effects of national policies and globalization on local life. The ethnographic method and the emphasis on personal relationships in social research are valuable gifts that cultural anthropology brings to the study of any society.

Doing Anthropology Right and Wrong: Ethical Issues

Science exists in society and in the context of law and ethics. Anthropologists can't study things simply because they happen to be interesting or of value to science. Ethical issues must be considered as well. Anthropologists typically have worked abroad, outside their own society. In the context of international contacts and cultural diversity, different ethical codes and value systems will meet, and often compete.

Archaeologists and physical anthropologists, in particular, often work as members of international teams (see Dalton 2006). These teams typically include researchers from several countries, including the host country—the place (e.g., Ethiopia) where the research takes place. Anthropologists must inform officials and colleagues in the host country about the purpose, funding, and likely results, products, and impacts of their research. They need to negotiate the matter of where the materials produced by the research will be analyzed and stored—in the host country or in the anthropologists' country—and for how long. To whom do research materials such as bones, artifacts, and blood samples belong? What kinds of restrictions will apply to their use?

Contemporary anthropologists recognize that **informed consent** (agreement to take part in the research—after having been informed about its nature, procedures, and possible impacts) should be obtained from anyone who provides information or who might be affected by the research. Although nonhuman primates can't give informed consent, primatologists still must take steps to ensure that their research doesn't endanger the animals they study. Either government agencies or nongovernmental organizations (NGOs) may be entrusted with protecting primates. If this is the case, the anthropologist will need their permission and informed consent to conduct research.

With living humans, informed consent is a necessity, not only in gathering information, but especially in obtaining biological samples, such as blood or urine. The research subjects must be told how the samples will be collected, used, and identified, and about the potential costs and benefits to them. Informed consent is needed from anyone providing data or information, owning materials being studied, or otherwise having an interest that might be affected by the research.

It is appropriate for North American anthropologists working in another country to (1) include host country colleagues in their research planning and requests for funding; (2) establish truly collaborative relationships with those colleagues and their institutions before, during, and after fieldwork; (3) include host country colleagues in dissemination, including publication, of the research results; and (4) ensure that something is "given back" to host country colleagues. For example, research equipment and technology are allowed to remain in the host country. Or funding is provided for host country colleagues to do research, attend international meetings, or visit foreign institutions—especially those where their international collaborators work.

Even with broad efforts to respect diverse value systems and acknowledge the contributions of the host country and its colleagues, ethical issues continue to arise. Lawsuits against museums by groups seeking the repatriation of remains and artifacts have become common (see Rothstein 2006). Peru, for instance, sued Yale University to recover objects removed during the exploration of Machu Picchu (an important Peruvian archaeological and touristic site) by Yale explorer Hiram Bingham in 1912. Native Australians have argued that images of native Australian fauna, such as the emu and kangaroo, belong exclusively to the Aboriginal people (Brown 2003). Michael F. Brown (2003) describes efforts by Hopi Indians to control and restrict historic photos of secret religious ceremonies.

The Code of Ethics

To guide its members in making decisions involving ethics and values, the American Anthropological Association (AAA) offers a Code of Ethics. The most recent code, approved in 2009, points out that anthropologists have obligations to their scholarly field, to the wider society and culture, and to the human species, other species, and the environment. Like physicians who take the Hippocratic oath, the anthropologist's first concern should be to *do no harm* to the people, animals, or artifacts being studied. The stated aim of the AAA code is to offer guidelines and to promote discussion and education, rather than to investigate possible misconduct. The code addresses several contexts in which anthropologists work. Some of its main points are highlighted here.

Anthropologists should be open and honest about their research projects with all parties affected by the research. These parties should be informed about the nature, procedures, purpose(s), potential impacts, and source(s) of support for the research. Researchers should pay attention to proper relations between themselves as guests and the host nations and communities where they work. The AAA does not advise anthropologists to avoid taking stands on issues. Indeed, seeking to shape actions and policies may be as ethically justifiable as inaction. The full Code of Ethics is available at the AAA website http://www.aaanet.org/issues/policy-advocacy/Code-of-Ethics.cfm.

Anthropologists and Terrorism

Anthropologists often complain that government officials ignore anthropological findings that are relevant to making informed policies. The AAA has deemed it of "paramount importance" that anthropologists study the roots of terrorism and violence. How should such studies be conducted? What ethical issues might arise?

Consider a Pentagon program, Project Minerva, initiated late in the George W. Bush administration, designed to draw on social science expertise to combat national security threats. Minerva sought scholars to translate original documents captured in Iraq, study China's shift to a more open political system, and explain the resurgence of the Taliban in Afghanistan (Cohen 2008). Project Minerva and related programs have raised serious concerns among anthropologists. Scholars worry that governments will use anthropological knowledge for goals, and in ways, that are ethically problematic. Government policies and military operations have the potential to harm the people anthropologists study.

Social scientists also object to the notion that the military should determine which research projects are worthy of funding. Rather, scholars favor a (peer review) system in which panels of their professional peers (other social scientists) judge the value and propriety of proposed research, including research that might help identify and deter threats to national security. One proposal was to have the National Science Foundation (because of its long experience with social science research), rather than the Pentagon, distribute Minerva money.

Anthropologists have been especially outspoken about the Pentagon's Human Terrain System (HTS) program. Launched in February 2007, HTS embeds anthropologists and other social scientists in military teams in Iraq and Afghanistan. The multimillion-dollar project planned to operate as many as 26 teams in those countries.

On October 31, 2007, the AAA Executive Board issued a statement of disapproval of HTS—outlining how HTS violates the AAA Code of Ethics (see http://www.aaanet.org/about/Policies/statements/Human-Terrain-System-Statement.cfm). The board noted that HTS places anthropologists, as contractors with the U.S. military, in war zones,

Anthropology Today *Archaeologist in New Orleans Finds a Way to Help the Living*

One role for anthropologists is to help communities preserve their culture in the face of threat or disaster. The following account describes the work of an anthropologist doing public archaeology in New Orleans in the wake of Hurricane Katrina. Cultural resource management, as discussed here, is one form of applied anthropology: the application of anthropological perspectives, theory, methods, and data to identify, assess, and solve social problems.

"That's a finger bone."

Shannon Lee Dawdy kneeled in the forlorn Holt graveyard to touch a thimble-size bone poking up out of the cracked dirt. She examined it without revulsion, with the fascination of a scientist and with the sadness of someone who loves New Orleans.

Dr. Dawdy, a 38-year-old assistant professor of anthropology at the University of Chicago, is one of the more unusual relief workers among the thousands who have come to the devastated expanses of Louisiana, Mississippi and Texas in the aftermath of Hurricanes Katrina and Rita. She is officially embedded with the Federal Emergency Management Agency [FEMA] as a liaison to the state's historic preservation office.

Her mission is to try to keep the rebuilding of New Orleans from destroying what is left of its past treasures and current culture.

While much of the restoration of the battered Gulf Coast is the effort of engineers and machines, the work of Dr. Dawdy, trained as an archaeologist, an anthropologist and a historian, shows that the social sciences have a role to play as well. "It's a way that archaeology can contribute back to the living," she said, "which it doesn't often get to do."

Holt cemetery, a final resting place for the city's poor, is just one example of what she wants to preserve and protect.

Other New Orleans graveyards have gleaming mausoleums that keep the coffins above the marshy soil. But the coffins of Holt are buried, and the ground covering many of them is bordered with wooden frames marked with makeshift headstones.

Mourners decorate the graves with votive objects: teddy bears for children and an agglomeration of objects, including ice chests, plastic jack-o'-lanterns and chairs, on the graves of adults. There is the occasional liquor bottle. . . .

Many of the objects on the graves were washed away by the storm, or shifted from one part of the graveyard to another. Dr. Dawdy has proposed treating the site as archaeologists would an ancient site in which objects have been exposed on the surface by erosion.

Before the hurricanes, the cemetery was often busy, a hub of activity on All Soul's Day, when people came to freshen the grave decorations.

"The saddest thing to me now was how few people we see," she said, looking at the empty expanse and the scarred live oaks. "I realize we're having enough trouble taking care of the living," she added, but the lack of activity in a city normally so close to the spirits of the past "drove home how far out of whack things are." . . .

Treating Holt as an archaeological site means the government should not treat the votive artifacts as debris, she said, but as the religious artifacts that they are, with some effort to restore the damaged site, to find the objects and at least record where they came from.

FEMA simply tries to clean up damaged areas, and its Disaster Mortuary

Archaelogist Shannon Lee Dawdy of the University of Chicago at work in New Orleans, post-Katrina.

Operational Response Teams—called Dmort—deal with the bodies of the dead and address problems in cemeteries that might lead to disease.

If such places are destroyed, Dr. Dawdy said, "then people don't feel as connected there." She added that they might be more willing to come back to a damaged city if they felt they were returning to a recognizable home.

Though she has deep emotional ties to New Orleans, Dr. Dawdy was born in Northern California. She came here in 1994 to write her master's thesis for the College of William & Mary, and, "I wrote it all day," she said. "If I had written a minimum of five pages, I could come out for a parade at night." Over the eight weeks it took to finish the project, she said: "I fell in love with New Orleans. I really consider it the home of my heart."

She started a pilot program at the University of New Orleans, working with city planners and grants for research projects that involved excavation, oral history and hands-on work with the city to safeguard its buried treasures.

She left that job to earn a double doctorate at the University of Michigan in anthropology and history that focused on French colonial times in New Orleans, then landed a coveted faculty position at the University of Chicago. . . .

Even before Hurricane Katrina, Dr. Dawdy had found ways to return to New Orleans. In 2004, she made an intriguing discovery while researching a possible archaeological site under an old French

continued

Anthropology Today   *continued*

Quarter parking garage slated for demolition. Property records and advertisements from the 1820s said that the site had been the location of a hotel with an enticing name: the Rising Sun Hotel.

Dr. Dawdy found a January 1821 newspaper advertisement for the hotel in which its owners promised to "maintain the character of giving the best entertainment, which this house has enjoyed for twenty years past."

It went on: "Gentlemen may here rely upon finding attentive Servants. The bar will be supplied with genuine good Liquors; and at the Table, the fare will be of the best the market or the season will afford." . . .

New Orleans, she noted, has always been known for its libertine lifestyle. The French all but abandoned the city as its colony around 1735 as being unworthy of the nation's support as a colony. Novels like "Manon Lescaut" portrayed the city as a den of iniquity and corruption, and across Europe, "they thought the locals were basically a bunch of rogues, immoral and corrupt," Dr. Dawdy said.

She added that she saw parallels to today, as some skepticism emerges about rebuilding the city. Dr. Dawdy characterized that posture as, "Those people in New Orleans aren't worth saving, because they're all criminals anyway." But even if the devastation makes it hard to envision the road back, the city, she said, is worth fighting for.

"The thing about New Orleans that gives me hope is they are so tied to family, place, history," Dr. Dawdy said. "If anyone is going to stick it out, out of a sense of history, out of a sense of tradition, it is New Orleans."

Source: John R. Schwartz, "Archaeologist in New Orleans Finds a Way to Help the Living," *New York Times,* January 3, 2006. Copyright © 2006 The New York Times. Reprinted by permission.

where they are charged with collecting cultural and social data for use by the military. The ethical concerns raised by these activities include the following:

1. It may be impossible for anthropologists in war zones to identify themselves as anthropologists, as distinct from military personnel. This constrains their ethical responsibility as anthropologists to disclose who they are and what they are doing.

2. HTS anthropologists are asked to negotiate relations among several groups, including local populations and the military units in which they are embedded. Their responsibilities to their units may conflict with their obligations to the local people they study or consult. This may interfere with the obligation, stipulated in the AAA Code of Ethics, to do no harm.

3. In an active war zone, it is difficult for local people to give "informed consent" without feeling coerced to provide information. As a result, "voluntary informed consent" (as stipulated by the AAA Code of Ethics, section III, A, 4) is compromised.

4. Information supplied by HTS anthropologists to military field commanders could help target specific groups for military action. Such use of fieldwork-derived information would violate the AAA Code of Ethics stipulation that those studied not be harmed.

5. The identification of anthropology and anthropologists with the U.S. military may indirectly (through suspicion of "guilt by association") endanger the research, and even the personal safety, of other anthropologists and their consultants throughout the world.

How should anthropologists study terrorism? What do you think about anthropologists' role in war?

Summary

1. As they study the past, archaeologists and physical anthropologists may share research topics and methods, and work together in multidisciplinary teams. Remote sensing may be used to locate ancient footpaths, roads, canals, and irrigation systems, which can then be investigated on the ground. Archaeologists combine both local (excavation) and regional (systematic survey) perspectives. Sites are excavated because they are in danger of being destroyed or because they address specific research interests. There are many kinds of archaeology, such as historical, classical, and underwater archaeology.

2. The fossil record is not a representative sample of all the plants and animals that have ever lived. Hard parts, such as bones and teeth, preserve better than soft parts, such as flesh and skin. Stratigraphy and radiometric techniques are used to date fossils. Carbon-14 (^{14}C) dating is most effective with fossils less than 40,000 years old. Potassium-argon (K/A) dating can be used for fossils older than 500,000 years. Molecular anthropology uses genetic analysis (of DNA sequences) to assess and date evolutionary relationships.

3. Within physical anthropology, bone biology is the study of bone genetics; cell structure; growth, development, and decay; and patterns of movement. Paleopathology is the study of disease and injury in skeletons from archaeological sites. Anthropometry, the measurement of human body parts and dimensions, is done on living people and on skeletal remains from sites. Studies of primates suggest hypotheses about behavior that humans do or do not share with our nearest relatives— and also with our hominid ancestors.

4. Ethnographic methods include firsthand and participant observation, rapport building, interviews, genealogies, work with key consultants or informants, collection of life histories, discovery of local beliefs and perceptions, problem-oriented and longitudinal research, and team research. Ethnographers work in communities and form personal relationships with local people as they study their lives.

5. An interview schedule is a form an ethnographer completes as he or she visits a series of households. Key consultants, or informants, teach us about particular areas of local life. Life histories document personal experiences with culture and culture change. Genealogical information is particularly useful in societies in which principles of kinship and marriage organize social and political life. Emic approaches focus on native perceptions and explanations. Etic approaches give priority to the ethnographer's own observations and conclusions. Longitudinal research

is the systematic study of an area or population over time. Longitudinal, team, and multisited ethnographic research are increasingly common.

6. Traditionally, anthropologists worked in small-scale societies; sociologists, in modern nations. Different techniques developed to study these different kinds of societies. Anthropologists do their fieldwork in communities and study the totality of social life. Sociologists use surveys and study samples to make inferences about a larger population. Anthropologists may employ ethnographic procedures to study cities, towns, or rural areas.

7. Because science exists in society, and in the context of law and ethics, anthropologists can't study things simply because they happen to be interesting or of scientific value. Anthropologists have obligations to their scholarly field, to the wider society and culture (including that of the host country), and to the human species, other species, and the environment. The AAA Code of Ethics offers ethical guidelines for anthropologists. Ethical problems often arise when anthropologists work for governments, especially the military.

Key Terms

absolute dating, *46*
anthropometry, *49*
bone biology, *48*
cultural
  consultant, *55*
emic, *55*
etic, *56*
excavation, *44*
fossils, *43*
genealogical
  method, *54*
informed
  consent, *60*

interview
  schedule, *54*
key cultural
  consultants, *55*
life history, *55*
longitudinal
  research, *57*
molecular
  anthropology, *47*
paleoanthropology,
  43
paleontology, *42*
paleopathology, *48*

participant
  observation, *51*
relative dating, *46*
sample, *54*
stratigraphy, *46*
survey
  research, *58*
systematic
  survey, *43*
taphonomy, *45*
variables, *59*

Go to our Online Learning Center website at **www.mhhe.com/kottak** for Internet resources directly related to the content of this chapter.

Chapter  4

Evolution, Genetics, and Human Variation

The Origin of Species

Theory and Fact

Genetics

Mendel's Experiments
Independent Assortment

Population Genetics

Mechanisms of Genetic Evolution

Natural Selection
Mutation
Random Genetic Drift
Gene Flow

Race: A Discredited Concept in Biology

Races Are Not
Biologically Distinct

Genetic Markers Don't
Correlate with Phenotype

Applying Anthropology to Popular
Culture: Oprah's DNA

Explaining Skin Color

Human Biological Adaptation

Genes and Disease

Anthropology Today: Genetic Study
Bolsters Columbus Link to Syphilis

Lactose Tolerance

Compared with other animals, humans have uniquely varied ways—cultural and biological—of evolving, of adapting to environmental stresses. Exemplifying *cultural* adaptation, we manipulate our artifacts and behavior in response to environmental conditions. We turn up thermostats or travel to Florida in the winter. We turn on fire hydrants, swim, or ride in air-conditioned cars to escape the summer's heat. Although such reliance on culture has increased in the course of human evolution, people haven't stopped adapting biologically. As in other species, human populations adapt genetically in response to environmental forces, and individuals react physiologically to stresses. Thus, when we work in the sun, sweating occurs spontaneously, cooling the skin and reducing the temperature of subsurface blood vessels.

We are ready now for a more detailed look at the principles that determine human biological adaptation, variation, and change.

The Origin of Species

During the 18th century, many scholars became interested in human origins, biological diversity, and our position within the classification of plants and animals. At that time, the commonly accepted explanation for the origin of species came from Genesis, the first book of the Bible: God had created all life during six days of Creation. According to **creationism,** biological similarities and differences originated at the Creation. Characteristics of life forms were seen as immutable; they could not change. Through calculations based on genealogies in the Bible, the biblical scholars James Ussher and John Lightfoot even purported to trace the Creation to a very specific time: October 23, 4004 B.C., at 9 A.M.

Carolus Linnaeus (1707–1778) developed the first comprehensive (and still influential) classification, or taxonomy, of plants and animals. He grouped life forms on the basis of similarities and differences in their physical characteristics. He used traits such as the presence of a backbone to distinguish vertebrates from invertebrates and the presence of mammary glands to distinguish mammals from birds. Linnaeus viewed the differences between life forms as part of the Creator's orderly plan. He thought that biological similarities and differences had been established at the time of Creation and had not changed.

According to creationism all life originated during the six days of Creation described in the Bible. Catastrophism proposed that fires and floods, including the biblical deluge involving Noah's ark (depicted in this painting by the American artist Edward Hicks), destroyed certain species.

Fossil discoveries during the 18th and 19th centuries raised doubts about creationism. Fossils showed that different kinds of life once had existed. If all life had originated at the same time, why weren't ancient species still around? Why weren't contemporary plants and animals found in the fossil record? A modified explanation combining creationism with **catastrophism** arose to replace the original doctrine. In this view, fires, floods, and other catastrophes, including the biblical flood involving Noah's ark, had destroyed ancient species. After each destructive event, God had created again, leading to contemporary species. How did the catastrophists explain certain clear similarities between fossils and modern animals? They argued that some ancient species had managed to survive in isolated areas. For example, after the biblical flood, the progeny of the animals saved on Noah's ark spread throughout the world.

Theory and Fact

The alternative to creationism and catastrophism was *transformism,* also called **evolution.** Evolutionists believe that species arise from others through a long and gradual process of transformation, or descent with modification. Charles Darwin became the best known of the evolutionists. However, he was influenced by earlier scholars, including his own grandfather. In a book called *Zoonomia* published in 1794, Erasmus Darwin had proclaimed the common ancestry of all animal species.

Charles Darwin also was influenced by Sir Charles Lyell, the father of geology. During Darwin's famous voyage to South America aboard the *Beagle,* he read Lyell's influential book *Principles of Geology* (1837/1969), which exposed him to Lyell's principle of **uniformitarianism.** Uniformitarianism states that the present is the key to the past. Explanations for past events should be sought in the long-term action of ordinary forces that still operate today. Thus, natural forces (rainfall, soil deposition, earthquakes, and volcanic action) gradually have built and modified geological features such as mountain ranges. The earth's structure has been transformed gradually through natural forces operating for millions of years (see Weiner 1994).

Uniformitarianism was a necessary building block for evolutionary theory. It cast serious doubt on the belief that the world was only 6,000 years old. It would take much longer for such ordinary forces as rain and wind to produce major geological changes. The longer time span also allowed enough time for the biological changes that fossil discoveries were revealing. Darwin applied the ideas of uniformitarianism and long-term transformation to living things. He argued that all life forms are ultimately related and that the number of species has increased over time. (For more on science, evolution, and creationism, see Futuyma 1995; Gould 1999; Wilson 2002.)

Charles Darwin provided a theoretical framework for understanding evolution. He offered natural selection as a powerful evolutionary mechanism that could explain the origin of species, biological diversity, and similarities among related life forms. Darwin proposed a *theory of evolution* in the strict sense. A **theory** is a set of ideas formulated (by reasoning from known facts) to explain something. The main value of a theory is to promote new understanding. A theory suggests patterns, connections, and relationships that may be confirmed by new research. The *fact* of evolution (that evolution has occurred) was known earlier, for example, by Erasmus Darwin. The *theory* of evolution, through natural selection (*how* evolution occurred), was Darwin's major contribution. Actually, natural selection wasn't Darwin's unique discovery. Working independently, the naturalist Alfred Russel Wallace had reached a similar conclusion (Shermer 2002). In a joint paper read to London's Linnaean Society in 1858, Darwin and Wallace made their discovery public. Darwin's book *On the Origin of Species* (1859/1958) offered much fuller documentation.

Natural selection is the process by which the forms most fit to survive and reproduce in a given environment do so in greater numbers than others in the same population. More than survival of the fittest, natural selection is differential reproductive success. Natural selection is a natural process that leads to a result. Natural selection operates when there is competition for strategic resources (those necessary for life) such as food and space between members of the population. There is also the matter of finding mates. You can win the competition for food and space and have no mate and thus have no impact on the future of the species. For natural selection to work on a particular population, there must be variety within that population, as there always is.

The giraffe's neck can illustrate how natural selection works on variety within a population. In any group of giraffes, there always is variation in neck length. When food is adequate, the animals have no problem feeding themselves. But when there is pressure on strategic resources, so that dietary foliage is not as abundant as usual, giraffes with longer necks have an advantage. They can feed off the higher branches. If this feeding advantage permits longer-necked giraffes to survive and reproduce even slightly more effectively than shorter-necked ones, giraffes with longer necks will transmit more of their genetic material to future generations than will giraffes with shorter necks.

An incorrect alternative to this (Darwinian) explanation would be the inheritance of acquired characteristics. That is the idea that in each generation, individual giraffes strain their necks to reach just a bit higher. This straining somehow modifies their genetic material. Over generations of strain, the average neck gradually gets longer through the accumulation of small increments of neck length acquired during the lifetime of each generation of giraffes. This is *not* how evolution works. If it did work in this way, weight lifters could expect to produce especially muscular babies. Workouts that promise no gain without the pain apply to the physical development of individuals, not species. Instead, evolution works as the process of natural selection takes advantage of the variety that already is present in a population. That's how giraffes got their necks.

Evolution through natural selection continues today. For example, in human populations there is differential resistance to disease, as we'll see in the discussion of sickle-cell anemia later in the chapter. One classic recent example of natural selection is the peppered moth, which can be light or dark (in either case with black speckles, thus the name "peppered"). A change in this species illustrates recent natural selection (in our own industrial age) through what has been called *industrial melanism*. Great Britain's industrialization changed the environment so as to favor darker moths (those with more melanin) rather than the lighter-colored ones that were favored previously. During the 1800s industrial pollution increased; soot coated buildings and trees, turning them a darker color. The previously typical peppered moth, which had a light color, now stood out against the dark backgrounds of sooty buildings and trees. Such light-colored moths were easily visible to their predators. Through mutations (discussed later), a new strain of peppered moth, with a darker phenotype, was favored. Because these darker moths were fitter—that is, harder to detect—in polluted environments, they survived and reproduced in greater numbers than lighter

A speckled peppered moth and a black one alight on a soot-blackened tree. Which phenotype is favored in this environment? How could this adaptive advantage change?

moths did. We see how natural selection may favor darker moths in polluted environments and lighter-colored moths in nonindustrial or less polluted environments because of their variant abilities to merge with their environmental colors and thus avoid predators.

Evolutionary theory is used to explain. The goal of science is to increase understanding through explanation: showing how and why the thing (or class of things) to be understood (e.g., the variation within species, the geographic distribution of species, the fossil record) depends on other things. Explanations rely on associations and theories. An association is an observed relationship between two or more variables, such as the length of a giraffe's neck and the number of its offspring, or an increase in the frequency of dark moths as industrial pollution spreads. A theory is more general, suggesting or implying associations and attempting to explain them. A thing or event, for example, the giraffe's long neck, is explained if it illustrates a general principle or association, such as the concept of adaptive advantage. The truth of a scientific statement (e.g., evolution occurs because of differential reproductive success due to variation within the population) is confirmed by repeated observations.

Genetics

Charles Darwin recognized that for natural selection to operate, there must be variety in the population undergoing selection. Documenting and explaining such variety among humans—human biological diversity—is one of anthropology's major concerns. Genetics, a science that emerged after Darwin, helps us understand the causes of biological variation. We now know that DNA (deoxyribonucleic acid) molecules make up genes and chromosomes, which are the basic hereditary units. Biochemical changes (mutations) in DNA provide much of the variety on which natural selection operates. Through sexual reproduction, recombination of the genetic traits of mother and father in each generation leads to new arrangements of the hereditary units received from each parent. Such genetic recombination also adds variety on which natural selection may operate.

Mendelian genetics studies the ways in which chromosomes transmit genes across the generations. *Biochemical genetics* examines structure, function, and changes in DNA. **Population genetics** investigates natural selection and other causes of genetic variation, stability, and change in breeding populations.

Mendel's Experiments

In 1856, in a monastery garden, the Austrian monk Gregor Mendel began a series of experiments that were to reveal the basic principles of genetics. Mendel studied the inheritance of seven contrasting traits in pea plants. For each trait there were only two forms. For example, plants were either tall (6 to 7 feet) or short (9 to 18 inches), with no intermediate forms. The ripe seeds could be either smooth and round or wrinkled. The peas could be either yellow or green, again with no intermediate colors.

When Mendel began his experiments, one of the prevailing beliefs about heredity was what has been called the "paint-pot" theory. According to this theory, the traits of the two parents blended in their children much as two pigments are blended in a can of paint. Children therefore were a unique mixture of their parents, and when these children married and reproduced, their traits would blend inextricably with those of their spouses. However, prevailing notions about heredity also recognized that occasionally the traits of one parent might swamp those of the other. If children looked far more like their mother than their father, people might say that her "blood" was stronger than his. Occasionally, too, there would be a "throwback," a child who was the image of his or her grandparent or who possessed a distinctive chin or nose characteristic of a whole line of descent.

Through his experiments with pea plants, Mendel discovered that heredity is determined by discrete particles or units. Although traits could disappear in one generation, they reemerged in their original form in later generations. For example, Mendel crossbred pure strains of tall and short plants. Their offspring were all tall. This was the first descending, or first filial, generation, designated F_1. Mendel then interbred the plants of the F_1 generation to produce a generation of grandchildren, the F_2 generation. In this generation, short plants reappeared. Among thousands of plants in the F_2 generation, there was approximately one short plant for every three tall ones.

From similar results with the other six traits, Mendel concluded that although a **dominant** form could mask the other form in *hybrid,* or mixed, individuals, the dominated trait—the **recessive**—was not destroyed; it wasn't even changed. Recessive traits would appear in unaltered form in later generations because genetic traits were inherited as discrete units.

These basic genetic units that Mendel described were factors (now called genes or alleles) located on **chromosomes.** Chromosomes are arranged in matching (homologous) pairs. Humans have 46 chromosomes, arranged in 23 pairs, one in each pair from the father and the other from the mother.

FIGURE 4.1

Simplified Representation of a Normal Chromosome Pair

Letters indicate genes; superscripts indicate alleles.

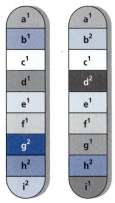

For simplicity, a chromosome may be pictured as a surface (see Figure 4.1) with several positions, to each of which we assign a lowercase letter. Each position is a **gene.** Each gene determines, wholly or partially, a particular biological trait, such as whether one's blood is type A, B, or O. **Alleles** (for example, b^1 and b^2 in Figure 4.1) are biochemically different forms of a given gene. In humans, A, B, AB, and O blood types reflect different combinations of alleles of a particular gene.

In Mendel's experiments, the seven contrasting traits were determined by genes located on seven different pairs of chromosomes. The gene for height occurred in one of the seven pairs. When Mendel crossbred pure tall and pure short plants to produce his F_1 generation, each of the offspring received an allele for tallness (T) from one parent and one for shortness (t) from the other. These offspring were mixed, or **heterozygous,** with respect to height; each had two dissimilar alleles of that gene. Their parents, in contrast, had been **homozygous,** possessing two identical alleles of that gene (see Hartl and Jones 2006).

In the next generation (F_2), after the mixed plants were interbred, short plants reappeared in the ratio of one short to three talls. Knowing that shorts produced only shorts, Mendel could assume that they were genetically pure. Another fourth of the F_2 plants produced only talls. The remaining half, like the F_1 generation, were heterozygous; when interbred, they produced three talls for each short (Figure 4.2).

Dominance produces a distinction between **genotype,** or hereditary makeup, and *phenotype,* or expressed physical characteristics. Genotype is what you really are genetically; phenotype is what you appear as. Mendel's peas had three genotypes—TT, Tt, and tt—but only two phenotypes—tall and short. Because of dominance, the heterozygous plants were just as tall as the genetically pure tall ones. How do Mendel's discoveries apply to humans? Although some of our genetic traits follow Mendelian laws, with only two forms—dominant and recessive—other traits are determined differently. For instance, three alleles determine whether our blood type is A, B, AB, or O. People with two alleles for type O have that blood type. However, if they received

FIGURE 4.2

Punnett Squares of a Homozygous Cross and a Heterozygous Cross

These squares show how phenotypic ratios of the F_1 and F_2 generation are generated. Colors show genotypes.

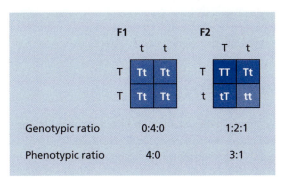

an allele for either A or B from one parent and one for O from the other, they will have blood type A or B. In other words, A and B are both dominant over O. A and B are said to be *codominant.* If people inherit an allele for A from one parent and one for B from the other, they will have type AB blood, which is chemically different from the other varieties, A, B, and O.

These three alleles produce four phenotypes—A, B, AB, and O—and six different genotypes—OO, AO, BO, AA, BB, and AB (Figure 4.3). There are fewer phenotypes than genotypes because O is recessive to both A and B.

FIGURE 4.3 **Determinants of Phenotypes (Blood Groups) in the ABO System**

The four phenotypes—A, B, AB, and O—are indicated in parentheses and by color.

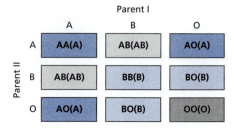

Independent Assortment

Through additional experiments, Mendel also formulated his law of **independent assortment.** He discovered that traits are inherited independently of one another. For example, he bred pure round yellow peas with pure wrinkled green ones. All the F_1 generation peas were round and yellow, the dominant forms. But when Mendel interbred the F_1 generation to produce the F_2, four phenotypes turned up. Round greens and wrinkled yellows had been added to the original round yellows and wrinkled greens. The independent assortment and recombination of genetic traits provide one of the main ways by which variety is produced in any population.

An organism develops from a fertilized egg, or *zygote,* created by the union of two sex cells, one from each parent. The zygote grows rapidly through **mitosis,** or ordinary cell division, which continues as the organism grows. The special process by which sex cells are produced is called **meiosis.** Unlike ordinary cell division, in which two cells emerge from one, in meiosis four cells are produced from one. Each has half the genetic material of the original cell. In human meiosis, four cells, each with 23 individual chromosomes, are produced from an original cell with 23 pairs.

With fertilization of egg by sperm, the father's 23 chromosomes combine with the mother's 23 to recreate the pairs in every generation. However, the chromosomes sort independently, so that a child's genotype is a random combination of the DNA of its four grandparents. It is conceivable that one grandparent will contribute very little to its grandchild's heredity. Independent assortment of chromosomes is a major source of variety because the parents' genotypes can be assorted in 2^{23}, or more than 8 million, different ways.

Population Genetics

Population genetics studies stable and changing populations in which most breeding normally takes place (see Gillespie 2004; Hartl 2000). The term **gene pool** refers to all the alleles, genes, chromosomes, and genotypes within a breeding population—the "pool" of genetic material available. When population geneticists use the term *evolution,* they have a more specific definition in mind than the one given earlier ("descent with modification over the generations"). For geneticists, **genetic evolution** is defined as change in gene frequency, that is, in the frequency of alleles in a breeding population from generation to generation. Any factor that contributes to such a change can be considered a *mechanism of genetic evolution.* Those mechanisms include natural selection, mutation, random genetic drift, and gene flow (see Mayr 2001).

Mechanisms of Genetic Evolution

Natural Selection

The first mechanism of genetic evolution is natural selection, which remains the best explanation for evolution. Essential to understanding evolution through natural selection is the distinction between genotype and phenotype. Genotype refers just to hereditary factors—genes and chromosomes. **Phenotype**—the organism's evident biological

This photo was taken at Hungary's ninth annual twins jamboree, held in 2008 in Szigethalom, Hungary, 25 kilometers south of Budapest. What factors other than genes influence phenotype?

characteristics—develops over the years as the organism is influenced by particular environmental forces. (See the photo of the identical twins on the preceding page). Identical twins have exactly the same genotype, but their actual biology, their phenotypes, may differ as a result of variation in the environments in which they have been raised. Also, because of dominance, individuals with different genotypes may have identical phenotypes (like Mendel's tall pea plants). Natural selection can operate only on phenotype—on what is exposed, not on what is hidden. For example, a harmful recessive gene can't be eliminated from the gene pool if it is masked by a favored dominant.

Phenotype includes not only outward physical appearance, but also internal organs, tissues, and cells and physiological processes and systems. Many biological reactions to foods, disease, heat, cold, sunlight, and other environmental factors are not automatic, genetically programmed responses but the product of years of exposure to particular environmental stresses. Human biology is not set at birth but has considerable *plasticity*. That is, it is changeable, being affected by the environmental forces, such as diet and altitude, that we experience as we grow up (see Bogin 2001).

The environment works on the genotype to build the phenotype, and certain phenotypes do better in some environments than other phenotypes do. However, remember that favored phenotypes can be produced by different genotypes. Because natural selection works only on genes that are expressed, maladaptive recessives can be removed only when they occur in homozygous form. When a heterozygote carries a maladaptive recessive, its effects are masked by the favored dominant. The process of perfecting the fit between organisms and their environment is gradual.

Directional Selection

After several generations of selection, gene frequencies will change. Adaptation through natural selection will have occurred. Once that happens, those traits that have proved to be the most **adaptive** (favored by natural selection) in that environment will be selected again and again from generation to generation. Given such *directional selection,* or long-term selection of the same trait(s), maladaptive recessive alleles will be removed from the gene pool.

Directional selection will continue as long as environmental forces stay the same. However, if the environment changes, new selective forces start working, favoring different phenotypes. This also happens when part of the population colonizes a new environment. Selection in the changed, or new, environment continues until a new equilibrium is reached. Then there is directional selection until another environmental change or migration takes place. Over millions of years, such a process of successive adaptation to a series of environments has led to biological modification and branching. The process of natural selection has led to the tremendous array of plant and animal forms found in the world today.

Selection also operates through competition for mates in a breeding population. Males may openly compete for females, or females may choose to mate with particular males because they have desirable traits. Obviously, such traits vary from species to species. Familiar examples include color in birds; male birds, such as cardinals, tend to be more brightly colored than females are. Colorful males have a selective advantage because females like them better. As, over the generations, females have opted for colorful mates, the alleles responsible for color have built up in the species. **Sexual selection,** based on differential success in mating, is the term for this process in which certain traits of one sex are selected because of advantages they confer in winning mates.

Selection operates *only* on traits that are present in a population. A favorable mutation *may* occur, but a population doesn't normally come up with a new genotype or phenotype just because one is needed or desirable. Many species have become extinct because they weren't sufficiently varied to adapt to environmental shifts.

Stabilizing Selection

We've seen that natural selection *reduces* variety in a population through directional selection—by favoring one trait or allele over another. Selective forces also can work to *maintain* variety through *stabilizing selection,* by favoring a **balanced polymorphism,** in which the frequencies of two or more alleles of a gene remain constant from generation to generation. This may be because the phenotypes they produce are neutral, or equally favored, or equally opposed, by selective forces. Sometimes a particular force favors (or opposes) one allele, while a different but equally effective force favors (or opposes) the other allele.

One well-studied example involves two alleles, Hb^A and Hb^S, that affect the production of the beta strain (Hb) of human hemoglobin. Hemoglobin, which is located in our red blood cells, carries oxygen from our lungs to the rest of the body via the circulatory system. The allele that produces normal hemoglobin is Hb^A. Another allele, Hb^S, produces a different hemoglobin. Individuals who are homozygous for Hb^S suffer from *sickle-cell anemia*. Such anemia, in which the red blood cells are shaped like crescents, or sickles, is associated with a disease that is usually fatal. This condition interferes with the blood's ability to store oxygen. It increases the heart's burden by clogging the small blood vessels.

Given the fatal disease associated with Hb^S, geneticists were surprised to discover that certain populations in Africa, India, and the Mediterranean had very high frequencies of Hb^S. In some West African populations, that frequency is around 20 percent. Researchers eventually discovered that both Hb^A and Hb^S are maintained because selective forces in certain environments favor the heterozygote over either homozygote.

Initially, scientists wondered why, if most Hb^S homozygotes died before they reached reproductive age, the harmful allele hadn't been eliminated. Why was its frequency so high? The answer turned out to lie in the heterozygote's greater fitness. Only people who were homozygous for Hb^S died from sickle-cell anemia. Heterozygotes suffered very mild anemia, if any. On the other hand, although people homozygous for Hb^A did not suffer from anemia, they were much more susceptible to *malaria*—a killer disease that continues to plague *Homo sapiens* in the tropics.

The heterozygote, with one sickle-cell allele and one normal one, was the fittest phenotype for a malarial environment. Heterozygotes have enough abnormal hemoglobin, in which malaria parasites cannot thrive, to protect against malaria. They also have enough normal hemoglobin to fend off sickle-cell anemia. The Hb^S allele has been maintained in these populations because the heterozygotes survived and reproduced in greater numbers than did people with any other phenotype.

The example of the sickle-cell allele demonstrates the relativity of evolution through natural selection: Adaptation and fitness are in relation to specific environments. Traits are not adaptive or maladaptive for all times and places. Even harmful alleles can be selected if heterozygotes have an advantage. Moreover, as the environment changes, favored phenotypes and gene frequencies can change. In malaria-free environments, normal-hemoglobin homozygotes reproduce more effectively than heterozygotes do. With no malaria, the frequency of Hb^S declines because Hb^S homozygotes can't compete in survival and reproduction with the other types. This has happened in areas of West Africa where malaria has been reduced through drainage programs and insecticides. Selection against Hb^S also has occurred in the United States among Americans descended from West Africans (Diamond 1997).

Mutation

The second mechanism of genetic evolution is mutation. Mutations, which occur spontaneously and regularly, provide new biochemical forms—variety—on which natural selection may operate. **Mutations** are changes in the DNA molecules of which genes and chromosomes are built. If a mutation occurs in a sex cell that combines with another as a fertilized egg, the new organism will carry the mutation in every cell. This may or may not, depending on dominance, result in a biochemical difference between the mutant child and the parent.

Random Genetic Drift

The third mechanism of genetic evolution is **random genetic drift.** This is a change in allele frequency that results not from natural selection but from chance. To understand why, compare the sorting of alleles to a game involving a bag of 12 marbles, 6 red and 6 blue. In step 1, you draw six marbles from the bag. Statistically, your chances of drawing three reds and three blues are less than those of getting four of one color and two of the other. Step 2 is to fill a new bag with 12 marbles on the basis of the ratio of marbles you drew in step 1. Assume that you drew four reds and two blues: The new bag will have eight red marbles and four blue ones. Step 3 is to draw six marbles from the new bag. Your chances of drawing blues in step 3 are lower than they were in step 1, and the probability of drawing all reds increases. If you do draw all reds, the next bag (step 4) will have only red marbles.

Although genetic drift can operate in any population, large or small, *fixation* due to drift is more rapid in small populations. Fixation refers to the total replacement of blue marbles by red marbles—or, to use a human example, of blue eyes by brown eyes. The history of the human line is characterized by a series of small populations, migrations, and fixation due to genetic drift. One cannot understand human origins, human genetic variation, and a host of other important anthropological topics without recognizing the importance of genetic drift.

This game is analogous to random genetic drift operating over the generations. The blue marbles were lost purely by chance. Alleles, too, can be lost by chance rather than because of any disadvantage they confer. Lost alleles can reappear in a gene pool only through mutation.

Gene Flow

The fourth mechanism of genetic evolution is **gene flow,** the exchange of genetic material between populations of the same species. Gene flow, like mutation, works in

FIGURE 4.4   Gene Flow between Local Populations

P_1–P_6 are six local populations of the same species. Each interbreeds (=) only with its neighbor(s). Although members of P_6 never interbreed with P_1, P_6 and P_1 are linked through gene flow. Genetic material that originates in P_1 eventually will reach P_6, and vice versa, as it is passed from one neighboring population to the next. Because they share genetic material in this way, P_1–P_6 remain members of the same species. In many species, local populations distributed throughout a larger territory than the 250 miles depicted here are linked through gene flow.

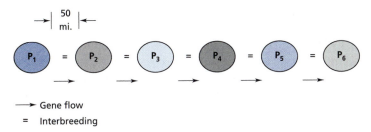

⟶ Gene flow

= Interbreeding

conjunction with natural selection by providing variety on which selection can work. Gene flow may consist of direct interbreeding between formerly separated populations of the same species (e.g., Europeans, Africans, and Native Americans in the United States), or it may be indirect.

Consider the following hypothetical case (Figure 4.4). In a certain part of the world live six local populations of a certain species. P_1 is the westernmost of these populations. P_2, which interbreeds with P_1, is located 50 miles to the east. P_2 also interbreeds with P_3, located 50 miles east of P_2. Assume that each population interbreeds with, and only with, the adjacent populations. P_6 is located 250 miles from P_1 and does not directly interbreed with P_1, but it is tied to P_1 through the chain of interbreeding that ultimately links all six populations.

Assume further that some allele exists in P_1 that isn't particularly advantageous in its environment. Because of gene flow, this allele may be passed on to P_2, by it to P_3, and so on, until it eventually reaches P_6. In P_6 or along the way, the allele may encounter an environment in which it does have a selective advantage. If this happens, it may serve, like a new mutation, as raw material on which natural selection can operate.

Alleles are spread through gene flow even when selection is not operating on the allele. In the long run, natural selection works on the variety within a population, whatever its source: mutation, drift, or gene flow. Selection and gene flow have worked together to spread the Hb^S allele in Central Africa. Frequencies of Hb^S in Africa reflect not only the intensity of malaria but also the length of time gene flow has been going on (Livingstone 1969).

Gene flow is important in the study of the origin of species. A **species** is a group of related organisms whose members can interbreed to produce offspring that can live and reproduce. A species has to be able to reproduce itself through time. We know that horses and donkeys belong to different species because their offspring cannot meet the test of long-term survival. A horse and a donkey may breed to produce a mule, but mules are sterile. So are the offspring of lions with tigers. Gene flow tends to prevent **speciation**—the formation of new species—unless subgroups of the same species are separated for a sufficient length of time.

When gene flow is interrupted, and isolated subgroups are maintained, new species may arise. Imagine that an environmental barrier arises between P_3 and P_4, so that they no longer interbreed. If over time, as a result of isolation, P_1, P_2, and P_3 become incapable of interbreeding with the other three populations, speciation will have occurred.

Race: A Discredited Concept in Biology

Historically, scientists have approached the study of human biological diversity in two main ways: (1) racial classification (now largely abandoned) versus (2) the current explanatory approach, which focuses on understanding specific differences. First we'll consider problems with **racial classification** (the attempt to assign humans to discrete categories [purportedly] based on common ancestry). Then we'll offer some explanations for specific aspects of human biological diversity. *Biological differences are real, important, and apparent to us all.* Modern scientists find it most productive to seek explanations for this diversity, rather than trying to pigeonhole people into categories called races. Certainly, human groups do vary biologically—for example, in their genetic attributes. But often we observe gradual, rather than abrupt, shifts in gene frequencies between neighboring groups. Such gradual genetic shifts are called **clines,** and they are incompatible with discrete and separate races.

What is race anyway? In theory, a biological race would be a geographically isolated subdivision of a species. Such a *subspecies* would be capable of interbreeding with other subspecies of the same species, but it would not actually do so because of its geographic isolation. Some biologists also use "race" to refer to "breeds," as of dogs or roses. Thus, a pit bull and a chihuahua would be different races of dogs. Such domesticated "races" have been bred by humans for generations. Humanity (*Homo sapiens*) lacks such races because human populations have not been isolated enough from one another to develop into such discrete groups. Nor have humans experienced controlled breeding like that which has created the various kinds of dogs and roses.

A race is supposed to reflect shared genetic material (inherited from a common ancestor), but early scholars instead used phenotypical traits (usually skin color) for racial classification. Phenotype refers to an organism's evident traits, its "manifest biology"—anatomy and physiology. Humans display hundreds of evident (detectable) physical traits. They range from skin color, hair form, eye color, and facial features (which are visible) to blood groups, color blindness, and enzyme production (which become evident through testing).

Racial classifications based on phenotype raise the problem of deciding which trait(s) should be primary. Should races be defined by height, weight, body shape, facial features, teeth, skull form, or skin color? Like their fellow citizens, early European and American scientists gave priority to skin color. Many schoolbooks and encyclopedias still proclaim the existence of three great races: the white, the black, and the yellow. This overly simplistic classification was compatible with the political use of race during the

The photos in this chapter illustrate only a small part of the range of human biological diversity. Shown above is a woman from Guangzhou province, People's Republic of China.

A young man from the Marquesas Islands in Polynesia.

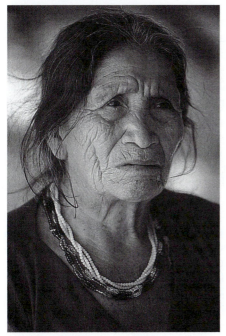

A Native American: a Chiquitanos Indian woman from Bolivia.

A Native Australian man from Cloncurry, Queensland, Australia.

colonial period of the late 19th and early 20th centuries. Such a tripartite scheme kept white Europeans neatly separate from their African, Asian, and Native American subjects. Colonial empires began to break up, and scientists began to question established racial categories, after World War II.

Races Are Not Biologically Distinct

History and politics aside, one obvious problem with "color-based" racial labels is that the terms don't accurately describe skin color. "White" people are more pink, beige, or tan than white. "Black" people are various shades of brown, and "yellow" people are tan or beige. But these terms have also been dignified by more scientific-*sounding* synonyms: Caucasoid, Negroid, and Mongoloid.

Another problem with the tripartite scheme is that many populations don't fit neatly into any one of the three "great races." For example, where would one put the Polynesians? *Polynesia* is a triangle of South Pacific islands formed by Hawaii to the north, Easter Island to the east, and New Zealand to the southwest. Does the "bronze" skin color of Polynesians connect them to the Caucasoids or to the Mongoloids? Some scientists, recognizing this problem, enlarged the original tripartite scheme to include the Polynesian "race." Native Americans presented a similar problem. Were they red or yellow? Some scientists added a fifth race—the "red," or Amerindian—to the major racial groups.

Many people in southern India have dark skins, but scientists have been reluctant to classify them with "black" Africans because of their Caucasoid facial features and hair form. Some, therefore, have created a separate race for these people. What about the Australian aborigines, hunters and gatherers native to what has been, throughout human history, the most isolated continent? By skin color, one might place some Native Australians in the same race as tropical Africans. However, similarities to Europeans in hair color (light or reddish) and facial features have led some scientists to classify them as Caucasoids. But there is no evidence that Australians are closer genetically or historically to either of these groups than they are to Asians. Recognizing this problem, scientists often regard Native Australians as a separate race.

Finally, consider the San ("Bushmen") of the Kalahari Desert in southern Africa. Scientists have perceived their skin color as varying from brown to yellow. Some who regard San skin as "yellow" have placed them in the same category as Asians. In theory, people of the same race share more recent common ancestry with each other than they do with any others. But there is no evidence for recent common ancestry between San and Asians. Somewhat more reasonably, some scholars assign the San to the Capoid race (from the Cape of Good Hope), which is seen as being different from other groups inhabiting tropical Africa.

Similar problems arise when any single trait is used as a basis for racial classification. An attempt to use facial features, height, weight, or any other phenotypical trait is fraught with difficulties. For example, consider the *Nilotes,* natives of the upper Nile region of Uganda and Sudan. Nilotes tend to be tall and to have long, narrow noses. Certain Scandinavians are also tall, with similar noses. Given the distance between their homelands, to classify them as members of the same race makes little sense. There is no reason to assume that Nilotes and Scandinavians are more closely related to each other than either is to shorter and nearer populations with different kinds of noses.

Would it be better to base racial classifications on a combination of physical traits? This would avoid some of the problems mentioned above, but others would arise. First, skin color, stature, skull form, and facial features (nose form, eye shape, lip thickness) don't go together as a unit. For example, people with dark skin may be tall or short and have hair ranging from straight to very curly. Dark-haired populations may have light or dark skin, along with various skull forms, facial features, and body sizes and shapes. The number of combinations is very large, and the amount that heredity (versus environment) contributes to such phenotypical traits is often unclear.

Genetic Markers Don't Correlate with Phenotype

The analysis of human DNA indicates that fully 94 percent of human genetic variation occurs within so-called "races." Considering conventional geographic "racial" groupings such as Africans, Asians, and Europeans, there is only about 6 percent variation in genes from one group to the other. In other words, there is much greater variation within each of the traditional "races" than between them. Humans are much more alike genetically than are any of the living apes. This suggests a recently shared common ancestor (perhaps as recent as 70,000 to 50,000 years) for all members of modern *Homo sapiens*. Sampling the mitochondrial DNA (mtDNA) of various populations, Rebecca Cann, Mark Stoneking, and Allan C. Wilson (1987) concluded that humans are genetically uniform overall, suggesting recent common ancestry. The fact that African populations are the most diverse genetically provides evidence that Africa was the site where the human diaspora originated.

Contemporary work in genomics has allowed scientists to construct regional and global phylogenetic trees based on shared genetic markers. Such trees are based on mitochondrial DNA (sampling females) and the Y chromosome (sampling males). As the human genome gets better known, molecular anthropologists refine their models of actual genetic relationships among humans and how they dispersed. A **haplogroup** is a lineage or branch of such a genetic tree marked by one or more specific genetic mutations. For example, the global mtDNA tree includes branches known as M and N (among others). The Y chromosome tree includes branches known as C and F (among others). Those four branches (either M or N for mtDNA and either C or F for the Y chromosome) are known to be associated with the spread of modern humans out of Africa between 70,000 and 50,000 B.P. Because Native Australians share those four branches, they are known to be part of that diaspora. The Americas were settled (from Asia) much later than Australia by multiple haplogroups, which probably arrived at different times and came by different routes.

Although long-term genetic markers do exist, they don't correlate neatly with phenotype. Phenotypical similarities and differences aren't precisely or even necessarily correlated with genetic relationships. Because of changes in the environment that affect individuals during growth and development, the range of phenotypes characteristic of a population may change without any genetic change whatsoever. There are several examples. In the early 20th century, the anthropologist Franz Boas (1940/1966) described changes in skull form (e.g., toward rounder heads) among the children of Europeans who had migrated to North America. The reason for this was not a change in genes, for the European immigrants tended to marry among themselves. Also, some of their children

Perhaps you've visited a website like ancestry .com or posted genealogical information on Facebook. North Americans have diverse ethnic and national roots, and many of us find it interesting to explore them. The website dnaancestryproject.com (DNA Ancestry Project), which arranges DNA testing, quotes the *Wall Street Journal,* which calls DNA testing the "hottest tool in genealogy." Oprah Winfrey made headlines in 2005 when she reported that a DNA test had discovered her (highly unlikely) Zulu ancestry. A more plausible result in 2006 linked Oprah to the Kpelle people of Liberia and Guinea, the Bamileke people of Cameroon, and the Nkoya people of Zambia. Ever the DNA explorer, Oprah in 2011 reported her discovery, confirmed by genetic testing, that she had a younger half sister whom her mother had placed for adoption while Oprah was living with her father in a different state. Why or why not would you want your DNA tested?

had been born in Europe and merely raised in the United States. Something in the environment, probably in the diet, was producing this change. We know now that changes in average height and weight produced by dietary differences in a few generations are common and may have nothing to do with race or genetics.

Explaining Skin Color

Traditional racial classification assumed that biological characteristics such as skin color were determined by heredity and that they were stable (immutable) over many generations. We now know that a biological similarity doesn't necessarily indicate recent common ancestry. Dark skin color, for example, can be shared by tropical Africans and indigenous Australians for reasons other than common heredity. Scientists have made considerable progress in explaining variation in human skin color, along with many other features of human biological diversity. We shift now from classification to explanation, in which natural selection plays a key role.

Natural selection is the process by which the forms most fit to survive and reproduce in a given environment do so. Over the generations, the less fit organisms die out, and the favored types survive by producing more offspring. The role of natural selection in producing variation in skin color will illustrate the explanatory approach to human biological diversity. Comparable explanations have been provided for many other aspects of human biological variation.

Skin color is a complex biological trait—influenced by several genes. Just how many genes is not known. **Melanin,** the primary determinant of human skin color, is a chemical substance manufactured in the epidermis, or outer skin layer. The melanin cells of darker-skinned people produce more and larger granules of melanin than do those of lighter-skinned people. By screening out ultraviolet (UV) radiation from the sun, melanin offers protection against a variety of maladies, including sunburn and skin cancer.

Prior to the 16th century, most of the world's very dark-skinned peoples lived in the *tropics,* a belt extending about 23 degrees north and south of the equator, between the Tropic of

How would you describe Prince Harry's phenotype?

Before the 16th century, almost all the very dark-skinned populations of the world lived in the tropics, as does this Samburu woman from Kenya.

Cancer and the Tropic of Capricorn. The association between dark skin color and a tropical habitat existed throughout the Old World, where humans and their ancestors have lived for millions of years. The darkest populations of Africa evolved not in shady equatorial forests but in sunny open grassland, or savanna, country.

Outside the tropics, skin color tends to be lighter. Moving north in Africa, for example, there is a gradual transition from dark brown to medium brown. Average skin color continues to lighten as one moves through the Middle East, into southern Europe, through central Europe, and to the north. South of the tropics skin color also is lighter. In the Americas, by contrast, tropical populations don't have very dark skin. This is the case because the settlement of the New World by light-skinned Asian ancestors of Native Americans was relatively recent, probably dating back no more than 20,000 years.

How, aside from migrations, can we explain the geographic distribution of human skin color? Natural selection provides an answer. In the tropics, intense UV radiation poses a series of threats, including severe sunburn, that make light skin color an adaptive disadvantage (Table 4.1 summarizes those threats). By damaging sweat glands sunburn reduces the body's ability to perspire and thus to regulate its own temperature (thermoregulation). Sunburn also can increase susceptibility to disease. Melanin, nature's own sunscreen, confers a selective advantage (i.e., a better chance to survive and reproduce) on darker-skinned people living in the tropics. (Today, light-skinned people manage to survive in the

TABLE 4.1 **Advantages and Disadvantages (Depending on Environment) of Dark and Light Skin Color**

Also shown are cultural alternatives that can make up for biological disadvantages and examples of natural selection (NS) operating today in relation to skin color

		Cultural Alternatives	NS in Action Today
DARK SKIN COLOR			
Advantage	Melanin is natural sunscreen		
	In tropics: screens out UV		
	Reduces susceptibility to folate destruction and thus to neural tube defects (NTDs), including spina bifida		
	Prevents sunburn and thus enhances sweating and thermoregulation		
	Reduces disease susceptibility		
	Reduces risk of skin cancer		
Disadvantage	Outside tropics: Reduces UV absorption		
	Increases susceptibility to rickets, osteoporosis	Foods, vitamin D supplements	East Asians in northern UK; Inuit with modern diets
LIGHT SKIN COLOR			
Advantage	No natural sunscreen		
	Outside tropics: Admits UV		
	Body manufactures vitamin D and thus prevents rickets and osteoporosis		
Disadvantage	Increases susceptibility to folate destruction and thus to NTDs, including spina bifida	Folic acid/folate supplements	Whites still have more NTDs
	Impaired spermatogenesis		
	Increases susceptibility to sunburn and thus to impaired sweating and poor thermoregulation	Shelter, sunscreens, lotions, etc.	
	Increases disease susceptibility		
	Increases susceptibility to skin cancer		

tropics by staying indoors and by using cultural products, such as umbrellas and lotions, to screen sunlight.) Yet another disadvantage of having light skin color in the tropics is that exposure to UV radiation can cause skin cancer (Blum 1961).

Years ago, W. F. Loomis (1967) focused on the role of UV radiation in stimulating the manufacture (synthesis) of vitamin D by the human body. The unclothed human body can produce its own vitamin D when exposed to sufficient sunlight. However, in a cloudy environment that also is so cold that people have to dress themselves much of the year (such as northern Europe, where very light skin color evolved), clothing interferes with the body's manufacture of vitamin D. The ensuing shortage of vitamin D diminishes the absorption of calcium in the intestines. A nutritional disease known as *rickets,* which softens and deforms the bones, may develop. In women, deformation of the pelvic bones from rickets can interfere with childbirth. In cold northern areas, light skin color maximizes the absorption of UV radiation and the synthesis of vitamin D by the few parts of the body that are exposed to direct sunlight. There has been selection against dark skin color in northern areas because melanin screens out UV radiation.

This natural selection continues today: East Asians who have migrated recently from India and Pakistan to northern areas of the United Kingdom have a higher incidence of rickets and osteoporosis (also related to vitamin D and calcium deficiency) than the general British population. A related illustration involves Eskimos (Inuit) and other indigenous inhabitants of northern Alaska and northern Canada. According to Nina Jablonski (quoted in Iqbal 2002), "Looking at Alaska, one would think that the native people should be pale as ghosts." One reason they aren't is that they haven't inhabited this region very long in terms of geological time. Even more important, their traditional diet, which is rich in seafood, including fish oils, supplies sufficient vitamin D so as to make a reduction in pigmentation unnecessary. However, and again illustrating natural selection at work today, "when these people don't eat their aboriginal diets of fish and marine mammals, they suffer tremendously high rates of vitamin D-deficiency diseases such as rickets in children and osteoporosis in adults" (Jablonski quoted in Iqbal 2002). Far from being immutable, skin color can become an evolutionary liability very quickly.

According to Jablonski and George Chaplin (2000), another key factor explaining the geographic distribution of skin color involves the effects of UV on folate, an essential nutrient that the human body manufactures from folic acid. Folate is needed for cell division and the production of new DNA. Pregnant women require large amounts of folate to support rapid cell division in the embryo, and there is a direct connection between folate and individual reproductive success. Folate deficiency causes neural tube defects (NTDs) in human embryos. NTDs are marked by the incomplete closure of the neural tube, so the spine and spinal cord fail to develop completely. One NTD, anencephaly (with the brain an exposed mass), results in stillbirth or death soon after delivery. With spina bifida, another NTD, survival rates are higher, but babies have severe disabilities, including paralysis. NTDs are the second-most-common human birth defect after cardiac abnormalities. Today, women of reproductive age are advised to take folate supplements to prevent serious birth defects such as spina bifida.

Natural sunlight and UV radiation destroy folate in the human body. Because melanin, as we have seen, protects against UV hazards, such as sunburn and its consequences, dark skin coloration is adaptive in the tropics. Now we see that melanin also is adaptive because it conserves folate in the human body and thus protects against NTDs, which are much more common in light-skinned than in darker-skinned populations (Jablonski and Chaplin 2000). Studies confirm that Africans and African Americans have a low incidence of severe folate deficiency, even among individuals with marginal nutritional status. Folate also plays a role in another process that is central to reproduction, spermatogenesis—the production of sperm. In mice and rats, folate deficiency can cause male sterility; it may well play a similar role in humans.

Today, of course, cultural alternatives to biological adaptation permit light-skinned people to survive in the tropics and darker-skinned people to live in the far north. People can clothe themselves and seek shelter from the sun; they can use artificial sunscreens if they lack the natural protection that melanin provides. Dark-skinned people living in the north can, indeed must, get vitamin D from their diet or take supplements. Today, pregnant women are routinely advised to take folic acid or folate supplements as a hedge against NTDs. Even so, light skin color still is correlated with a higher incidence of spina bifida.

Jablonski and Chaplin (2000) explain variation in human skin color as resulting from a balancing act between the evolutionary needs to (1) protect against all UV hazards (dark skin in the tropics) and (2) have an adequate supply of vitamin D (lighter skin outside the tropics). This discussion of skin color shows that common ancestry, the presumed basis of race, is not the only reason for biological similarities. Natural selection, still at work today, makes a major contribution to variations in human skin color, as well as to many other human biological differences and similarities.

Human Biological Adaptation

This section considers additional examples of human biological diversity that reflect adaptation to environmental stresses, such as disease and diet. There is abundant evidence for human genetic adaptation and thus for evolution (change in gene frequency) through selection working in specific environments. One example is the adaptive value of the Hb^S heterozygote and its spread in malarial environments, which was discussed previously.

Genes and Disease

Microbes have been major selective agents for humans, particularly before the arrival of modern medicine. Some people are genetically more susceptible to certain diseases than others are, and the distribution of human blood types continues to change in response to natural selection.

After food production emerged around 10,000 years ago, infectious diseases posed a mounting risk and eventually became the foremost cause of human mortality. Food production favors infection for several reasons. Cultivation sustains larger, denser populations and a more sedentary lifestyle than does hunting and gathering. People live closer to each other and to their own wastes, making it easier for microbes to survive and to find hosts. Domesticated animals also transmit diseases to people.

In New York City in 1947, the appearance of nine cases of smallpox, including two deaths, spurred a very successful mass vaccination program. Shown here, lines of people wait to be vaccinated at the New York Health Department on April 14, 1947. The smallpox threat made the cover of *Cosmopolitan* magazine.

Until 1977, when the last case of smallpox was reported, smallpox had been a major threat to humans and a determinant of blood group frequencies (Diamond 1990, 1997). The smallpox virus is a mutation from one of the pox viruses that plague such domesticated animals as cows, sheep, goats, horses, and pigs. Smallpox appeared in human beings after people and animals started living together. Smallpox epidemics have played important roles in world history, often killing one-fourth to one-half of the affected populations. Smallpox contributed to Sparta's defeat of Athens in 430 B.C.E. and to the decline of the Roman empire after 160 C.E.

The ABO blood groups have figured in human resistance to smallpox. Blood is typed according to the protein and sugar compounds on the surface of the red blood cells. Different substances (compounds) distinguish between type A and type B blood. Type A cells trigger the production of *antibodies* in B blood, so that A cells clot in B blood. The different substances work like chemical passwords; they help us distinguish our own cells from invading cells, including microbes, we ought to destroy. The surfaces of some microbes have substances similar to ABO blood group substances. We don't produce antibodies to substances similar to those on our own blood cells. We can think of this as a clever evolutionary trick by the microbes to deceive their hosts, because we don't normally develop antibodies against our own biochemistry.

People with A or AB blood are more susceptible to smallpox than are people with type B or type O. Presumably this is because a substance on the smallpox virus mimics the type A substance, permitting the virus to slip by the defenses of the type A individual. By contrast, type B and type O individuals produce antibodies against smallpox because they recognize it as a foreign substance.

The relation between type A blood and susceptibility to smallpox was first suggested by the low frequencies of the A allele in areas of India and Africa where smallpox had been endemic. A comparative study done in rural India in 1965–1966, during a virulent smallpox epidemic, did much to confirm this relationship. Drs. F. Vogel and M. R. Chakravartti analyzed blood samples from smallpox victims and their uninfected siblings (Diamond 1990). The researchers found 415 infected children, none ever vaccinated against smallpox. All but 8 of the infected children had an uninfected (also unvaccinated) sibling.

The results of the study were clear: Susceptibility to smallpox varied with ABO type. Of the 415 infected children, 261 had the A allele; 154 lacked it. Among their 407 uninfected siblings, the ratio was reversed. Only 80 had the A allele; 327 lacked it. The researchers calculated that a type A or type AB person had a seven times greater chance of getting smallpox than did an O or B person.

In most human populations, the O allele is more common than A and B combined. A is most common in Europe; B frequencies are highest in Asia. Since smallpox was once widespread in the Old World, we might wonder why natural selection didn't eliminate the A allele entirely. The answer appears to be this: Other diseases spared the type A people and penalized those with other blood groups.

For example, type O people seem to be especially susceptible to the bubonic plague— the "Black Death" that killed a third of the population of medieval Europe. Type O people are also more likely to get cholera, which has killed as many people in India as smallpox continued

Anthropology Today *Genetic Study Bolsters Columbus Link to Syphilis*

This box reports on a recent comparative genetic study investigating the origin of syphilis. Known to us as a dreaded venereal, aka sexually transmitted, disease (STD), syphilis apparently originated in the Americas as a nonvenereal bacterium. It spread to the Old World as part of the Columbian exchange, an early form of globalization, in which products, populations, and pathogens of the Old World and the New World became forever linked after 1492. Once in Europe the bacterium mutated into venereal syphilis, which became a major killer during the Renaissance. Globalization remains an important factor in the spread and mutation of diseases in today's world.

Columbus, it seems, made another discovery of something that he was not looking for.

In a comprehensive genetic study, scientists have found what they say is the strongest evidence yet linking the first European explorers of the New World to the origin of sexually transmitted syphilis.

The research, they say, supports the hypothesis that returning explorers introduced organisms leading, in probably modified forms, to the first recorded syphilis epidemic, beginning in Europe in 1493.

The so-called Columbus hypothesis had previously rested on circumstantial evidence, mainly the timing of the epidemic. . . .

Earlier traces of syphilis or related diseases had been few and inconclusive in Europe. Yet nonvenereal forms of the diseases were widespread in the American tropics.

Leaders of the new study said the most telling results were that the bacterium causing sexually transmitted syphilis arose relatively recently in humans and was closely related to a strain responsible for the nonvenereal infection known as yaws. The similarity was especially evident, the researchers said, in a variation of the yaws pathogen isolated recently among afflicted children in a remote region of Guyana in South America. . . .

The findings suggested Columbus and his men could have carried the nonvenereal tropical bacteria home, where the organisms may have mutated into a more deadly form in the different conditions of Europe.

In the New World, the infecting organisms for nonvenereal syphilis, known as bejel, and yaws were transmitted by skin-to-skin and oral contact, more often in children. The symptoms are lesions primarily on the legs, not on or near the genitals.

Kristin N. Harper, a researcher in molecular genetics at Emory University who was the principal investigator in the study, said the findings supported "the hypothesis that syphilis, or some progenitor, came from the New World." . . . Her co-authors included George J. Armelagos, an Emory anthropologist who has studied the origins of syphilis for more than 30 years, and Dr. Michael S. Silverman, a Canadian infectious diseases physician who collected and tested specimens from yaws lesions in Guyana, the only known site today of yaws infections in the Western Hemisphere. The researchers said their study "represents the first attempt to address the problem of the origin of syphilis using molecular genetics, as well as the first source of information regarding the genetic makeup of nonvenereal strains from the Western Hemisphere."

They applied phylogenetics, the study of evolutionary relationships between organisms, in examining 26 geographically disparate strains in the family of

continued

Anthropology Today *continued*

Treponema bacteria. Treponema pallidum subspecies pallidum is the agent for the scourge of venereal syphilis. The subspecies endemicum causes bejel, usually in hot, arid climates. . . .

John W. Verano, an anthropologist at Tulane, said the findings would "probably not settle the debate" over the origins of venereal syphilis, though most scientists had become convinced that the disease was not transmitted sexually before Europeans made contact with the New World.

Donald J. Ortner, an anthropologist at the Smithsonian Institution, questioned whether the organisms causing the first European epidemic were actually distinct from others in the treponemal family. "What we are seeing is an organism with a long history, and it is very adaptable to different modes of transmission that produce different manifestations," Dr. Ortner said.

Paleopathologists . . . have for years analyzed skeletons for the bone scars from lesions produced by treponemal diseases, except for the mild form called pinta. In this way, they traced the existence of these infections in the New World back at least 7,000 years. But it has often been difficult to determine the age of the bones and distinguish the different diseases that share symptoms but have different modes of transmission. . . .

In her investigation, Ms. Harper studied 22 human Treponemal pallidum strains. The DNA in their genes was sequenced in nearly all cases, examined for changes and

eventually used in constructing phylogenetic trees incorporating all variations in the strains.

An Old World yaws subspecies was found to occupy the base of the tree, indicating its ancestral position in the treponemal family, she said. The terminal position of the venereal syphilis subspecies on the tree showed it had diverged most recently from the rest of the bacterial family.

Specimens from two Guyana yaws cases were included in the study, after they were collected and processed by Dr. Silverman. Genetic analysis showed that this yaws strain was the closest known relative to venereal syphilis.

If this seemed to solidify the Columbus hypothesis, the researchers cautioned that a "transfer agent between humans and non-human primates cannot be ruled out. . . ."

Dr. Armelagos said research into the origins of syphilis would continue, because "understanding its evolution is important not just for biology, but for understanding social and political history."

Noting that the disease was a major killer in Renaissance Europe, he said, "It could be argued that syphilis is one of the important early examples of globalization and disease, and globalization remains an important factor in emerging diseases."

Source: John Noble Wilford, "Genetic Study Bolsters Columbus Link to Syphilis" from *New York Times*, January 15, 2008. Copyright © 2008 The New York Times. Reprinted by permission.

has. On the other hand, blood group O may increase resistance to syphilis. The ravages of that sexually transmitted disease, which may have originated in the New World, may explain the very high frequency of type O blood among the native populations of Central and South America. The distribution of human blood groups appears to represent a compromise among the selective effects of many diseases.

Lactose Tolerance

Many biological traits that illustrate human adaptation are not under simple genetic control. Genetic determination of such traits may be likely but unconfirmed, or several genes may interact to influence the trait in question. Sometimes there is a genetic component, but the trait also responds to stresses encountered during growth. We speak of **phenotypical adaptation** when adaptive changes occur during an individual's lifetime. Phenotypical adaptation is made possible by biological plasticity—our ability to change in response to the environments we encounter as we grow (see Bogin 2001; Frisancho 1993).

Genes and phenotypical adaptation work together to produce a biochemical difference between human groups in the ability to digest large amounts of milk—an adaptive advantage when other foods are scarce and milk is available, as it is in dairying societies. All milk, whatever its source, contains a complex sugar called *lactose.* The digestion of milk depends on an enzyme called *lactase,* which works in the small intestine. Among all mammals except humans and some of their pets, lactase production ceases after weaning, so that these animals can no longer digest milk.

Lactase production and the ability to tolerate milk vary between populations. About 90 percent of northern Europeans and their descendants are lactose tolerant; they can digest several glasses of milk with no difficulty. Similarly, about 80 percent of two African populations, the Tutsi of Rwanda and Burundi in East Africa and the Fulani of Nigeria in West Africa, produce lactase and digest milk easily. Both of these groups traditionally have been herders. However, such nonherders as the Yoruba and the Igbo in Nigeria, the Baganda in Uganda, the Japanese and other Asians, Eskimos, South American Indians, and many Israelis cannot digest lactose (Kretchmer 1972/1975).

The variable human ability to digest milk seems to be a difference of degree. Some populations can tolerate very little or no milk, but others are able to metabolize much greater quantities. Studies show that people who move from no-milk or low-milk diets to high-milk diets increase their lactose tolerance; this suggests some phenotypical adaptation. We can conclude that no simple genetic trait accounts for the ability to digest milk. Lactose tolerance appears to be one of many aspects of human biology governed both by genes and by phenotypical adaptation to environmental conditions.

Summary

1. In the 18th century, Carolus Linnaeus developed biological taxonomy. He viewed differences and similarities among organisms as part of God's orderly plan rather than as evidence for evolution. In the mid-19th century, Charles Darwin and Alfred Russel Wallace proposed that natural selection could explain the origin of species, biological diversity, and similarities among related life forms. Natural selection requires variety in the population undergoing selection.

2. Through breeding experiments with peas in 1856, Gregor Mendel discovered that genetic traits pass on as units. These are now known to be chromosomes, which occur in homologous pairs. Alleles, some dominant, some recessive, are the chemically different forms that occur at a given genetic locus. Mendel also formulated the law of independent assortment. Each of the seven traits he studied in peas was inherited independently of all the others. Independent assortment of chromosomes and their recombination provide some of the variety needed for natural selection. But the major source of such variety is mutation, a chemical change in the DNA molecules of which genes are made.

3. Population genetics studies gene frequencies in stable and changing populations. Natural selection is the most important mechanism of evolutionary change. Others are mutation, random genetic drift, and gene flow. Given environmental change, nature selects traits already present in the population. If variety is insufficient to permit adaptation to the change, extinction is likely. New types don't appear just because they are needed.

4. One well-documented case of natural selection in contemporary human populations is that of the sickle-cell allele. In homozygous form, the sickle-cell allele, Hb^S, produces an abnormal hemoglobin. This clogs the small blood vessels, impairing the blood's capacity to store oxygen. The result is sickle-cell anemia, which is usually fatal. Homozygotes for normal hemoglobin are susceptible to malaria and die in great numbers. Heterozygotes get only mild anemia and are resistant to malaria. In a malarial environment, the heterozygote has the advantage.

5. Other mechanisms of genetic evolution complement natural selection. Random genetic drift operates most obviously in small populations, where pure chance can easily change allele frequencies. Gene flow and interbreeding keep subgroups of the same species genetically connected and thus impede speciation.

6. How do scientists approach the study of human biological diversity? Because of a range of problems involved in classifying humans into racial categories, contemporary biologists focus on specific differences and try to explain them. Because of extensive gene flow and interbreeding, *Homo sapiens* has not evolved subspecies or distinct races. The genetic breaks that do exist among human populations have not led to the formation of discrete races. Biological similarities between groups may reflect—rather than common ancestry—similar but independent adaptations to similar natural selective forces, such as degrees of ultraviolet radiation from the sun in the case of skin color.

7. Differential resistance to infectious diseases such as smallpox has influenced the distribution of human blood groups. There are genetic antimalarials, such as the sickle-cell allele. Phenotypical adaptation refers to adaptive changes that occur in an individual's lifetime in response to the environment the organism encounters as it grows. Lactose tolerance is due partly to phenotypical adaptation. Biological similarities between geographically distant populations may be due to similar but independent genetic changes rather than to common ancestry. Or they may reflect similar physiological responses to common stresses during growth.

Key Terms

adaptive, *76*
alleles, *73*
balanced
    polymorphism, *77*
catastrophism, *69*
chromosomes, *72*
cline, *80*
creationism, *68*
dominant, *72*
evolution, *69*
gene, *73*
gene flow, *78*
gene pool, *74*
genetic
    evolution, *75*
genotype, *73*

haplogroup, *83*
heterozygous, *73*
homozygous, *73*
independent
    assortment, *74*
meiosis, *74*
melanin, *84*
Mendelian
    genetics, *72*
mitosis, *74*
mutations, *78*
natural
    selection, *70*
phenotype, *75*
phenotypical
    adaptation, *93*

population
    genetics, *72*
racial
    classification, *80*
random genetic
    drift, *78*
recessive, *72*
sexual
    selection, *77*
speciation, *80*
species, *79*
theory, *69*
uniformitarianism,
    69

Go to our Online Learning Center website at **www.mhhe.com/kottak** for Internet resources directly related to the content of this chapter.

Chapter 5

The Primates

Our Place among Primates
  *Applying Anthropology to Popular
    Culture: Planet of the Apes*
Homologies and Analogies
Primate Tendencies
Prosimians
Monkeys
  New World Monkeys
  Old World Monkeys
Apes
  Gibbons
  Orangutans
  Gorillas

Chimpanzees
Bonobos
Endangered Primates
Primate Evolution
Chronology
Early Primates
  Early Cenozoic Primates
  Oligocene Anthropoids
Miocene Hominoids
  Proconsul
  Later Miocene Apes
  Pierolapithecus catalaunicus
  *Anthropology Today: Global Economy
    Threatens Orangutans*

Primatology is the study of nonhuman **primates**—fossil and living apes, monkeys, and prosimians—including their behavior and social life. Primatology is fascinating in itself, but it also helps anthropologists make inferences about the early social organization of *hominids* (members of the zoological family that includes fossil and living humans). Of particular relevance to humans are two kinds of primates:

1. Those whose ecological adaptations are similar to our own: **terrestrial** monkeys and apes—that is, primates that live on the ground rather than in the trees.
2. Those that are most closely related to us: the great apes, specifically the chimpanzees and gorillas.

Our Place among Primates

Similarities between humans and apes are evident in anatomy, brain structure, genetics, and biochemistry. The physical similarities between humans and apes are recognized in zoological **taxonomy**—the assignment of organisms to categories (*taxa;* singular,

FIGURE 5.1

The Principal Classificatory Units of Zoological Taxonomy. Moving down the figure, the classificatory units become more exclusive, so that "Kingdom" at the top is the most inclusive unit and "Subspecies" at the bottom is the most exclusive.

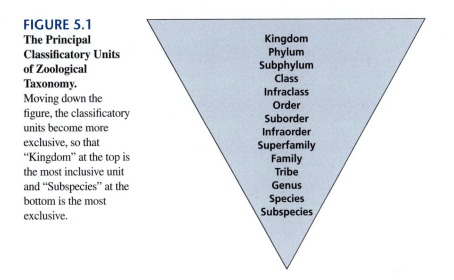

Kingdom
Phylum
Subphylum
Class
Infraclass
Order
Suborder
Infraorder
Superfamily
Family
Tribe
Genus
Species
Subspecies

taxon) according to their relationship and resemblance. Many similarities between organisms reflect their common *phylogeny*—their genetic relatedness based on common ancestry. In other words, organisms share features they have inherited from the same ancestor. Humans and apes belong to the same taxonomic superfamily Hominoidea (hominoids). Monkeys are placed in two others (Ceboidea and Cercopithecoidea). This means that humans and apes are more closely related to each other than either is to monkeys.

Figure 5.1 summarizes the various levels of classification used in zoological taxonomy. Each lower-level unit belongs to the higher-level unit above it. Thus, looking toward the bottom of Figure 5.1, similar species belong to the same genus (plural, *genera*). Similar genera make up the same family, and so on through the top of Figure 5.1, where similar phyla (plural of *phylum*) are included in the same kingdom. The highest (most inclusive) taxonomic level is the *kingdom*. At that level, animals are distinguished from plants.

At the lowest level of taxonomy, a species may have subspecies. These are its more or less—but not yet totally—isolated subgroups. Subspecies can coexist in time and space. For example, the Neandertals, who thrived between 130,000 and 28,000 years ago, often are assigned not to a separate species but merely to a different subspecies of *Homo sapiens*. Just one subspecies of *Homo sapiens* survives today.

The similarities used to assign organisms to the same taxon are called **homologies,** similarities they have jointly inherited from a common ancestor. Table 5.1 summarizes the place of humans in zoological taxonomy. We see in Table 5.1 that we are mammals, members of the class Mammalia. This is a major subdivision of the kingdom Animalia. Mammals share certain traits, including mammary glands, that set them apart from other taxa, such as birds, reptiles, amphibians, and insects. Mammalian homologies indicate that all mammals share more recent common ancestry with each other than they do with any bird, reptile, or insect.

Applying Anthropology to Popular Culture

PLANET OF THE APES

Apes are much more like people than they are like monkeys. Why is it then that at zoos parents tell kids to "look at the monkey" when they are talking about a chimp, gorilla, or orangutan? Despite this confusion, apes do fascinate us, precisely because of their humanlike qualities. Zoo gorillas are especially popular when named and shown in "family" groups. Ape antics have enlivened movies and TV shows. The film *Planet of the Apes* is a movie that does acknowledge the close relation between apes and humans, and its human actors easily play ape roles. Imagine, however, a live-action film called *Planet of the Monkeys*. Could human actors locomote on four legs for an entire movie?

Humans are mammals that, at a lower taxonomic level, belong to the *order* Primates. Another mammalian order is Carnivora: the carnivores (dogs, cats, foxes, wolves, badgers, weasels). Rodentia (rats, mice, beavers, squirrels) form yet another mammalian order. The primates share structural and biochemical homologies that distinguish them from other mammals. These resemblances were inherited from their common early primate ancestors after those early primates became reproductively isolated from the ancestors of the other mammals.

TABLE 5.1 **The Place of Humans (*Homo sapiens*) in Zoological Taxonomy**

Homo sapiens is an Animal, Chordate, Vertebrate, Mammal, Eutherian, Primate, Anthropoid, Catarrhine, Hominoid, Hominid, and Hominin. (Table 5.2 shows the taxonomic placement of the other primates.)

Taxon	Scientific (Latin) Name	Common (English) Name
Kingdom	Animalia	Animals
Phylum	Chordata	Chordates
Subphylum	Vertebrata	Vertebrates
Class	Mammalia	Mammals
Infraclass	Eutheria	Eutherians
Order	Primates	Primates
Suborder	Anthropoidea	Anthropoids
Infraorder	Catarrhini	Catarrhines
Superfamily	Hominoidea	Hominoids
Family	Hominidae	Hominids
Tribe	Hominini	Hominins
Genus	*Homo*	Humans
Species	*Homo sapiens*	Recent humans
Subspecies	*Homo sapiens sapiens*	Anatomically modern humans

Homologies and Analogies

Organisms should be assigned to the same taxon on the basis of homologies. The extensive biochemical homologies between apes and humans confirm our common ancestry and support our traditional joint classification as hominoids (see Table 5.2). For example, it is estimated that humans, chimpanzees, and gorillas have more than 98 percent of their DNA in common.

However, common ancestry isn't the only reason for similarities between species. Similar traits also can arise if species experience similar selective forces and adapt to them in similar ways. We call such similarities **analogies.** The process by which analogies are produced is called **convergent evolution.** For example, fish and porpoises share many analogies resulting from convergent evolution to life in the water. Like fish, porpoises, which are mammals, have fins. They are also hairless and streamlined for efficient locomotion. Analogies between birds and bats (wings, small size, light bones) illustrate convergent evolution to flying (see Angier 1998).

In theory, only homologies should be used in taxonomy. With reference to the hominoids, there is no doubt that humans, gorillas, and chimpanzees are more closely related to each other than any of the three is to orangutans, which are Asiatic apes (Ciochon 1983). As discussed, *Hominidae* is the name of the zoological family that includes

TABLE 5.2 Primate Taxonomy
The major subdivisions of the two primate suborders are *Prosimii* and *Anthropoidea.* Humans are anthropoids who belong to the superfamily *Hominoidea,* along with the apes.

Source: R. Martin, "Classification of Primates" from *The Cambridge Encyclopedia of Human Evolution,* ed. by S. Jones, R. Martin and D. Pilbeam, pp. 20–21. Reprinted by permission of Cambridge University Press.

Suborder	Infraorder	Superfamily	Family
Prosimii (Prosimians)	Lemuriformes (Lemurs)	Lemuroidea	Daubentoniidae (Aye-ayes), Indridae (Indri), Lemuridae (Lemurs)
	Lorisiformes (Lorises)	Lorisoidea	Lorisidae
	Tarsiiformes (Tarsiers)	Tarsioidea	Tarsiidae
Anthropoidea (Anthropoids)	Platyrrhini (Platyrrhines—New World monkeys)	Ceboidea	Callitrichidae (Tamarins and marmosets), Cebidae
	Catarrhini (Catarrhines—Old World monkeys, apes, and humans)	Cercopithecoidea	Cercopithecidae (Old World monkeys)
		Hominoidea (Hominoids)	Hylobatidae (Gibbons and siamangs), Pongidae (Pongids—orangutans), Hominidae (Hominids—Gorillas, chimpanzees, and humans)

FIGURE 5.2   Primate Family Tree

When did the common ancestors of all the primates live?

Source: Roger Lewin, *Human Evolution: An Illustrated Introduction*, 3rd ed., p. 44. Copyright © 1993. Reprinted by permission of Blackwell Publishing Ltd.

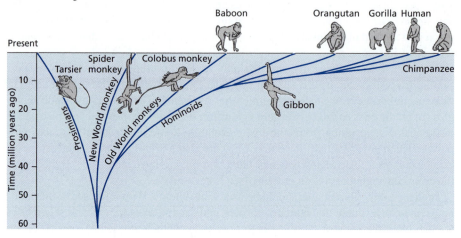

hominids—fossil and living humans. Because chimps and gorillas share a more recent common ancestor with humans than they do with the orangutan, many scientists now also place gorillas and chimps in the hominid family. *Hominid* would then refer to the zoological family that includes fossil and living humans, chimpanzees, gorillas, and their common ancestors. This leaves the orangutan (genus *Pongo*) as the only member of the pongid family (*Pongidae*). If chimps and gorillas are classified as hominids, what do we call the group that leads to humans but not to chimps and gorillas? For that, some scientists insert a taxonomic level called *tribe* between family and genus. The tribe *hominini* describes all the human species that ever have existed (including the extinct ones) and excludes chimps and gorillas. When scientists use the word *hominin* today, they mean pretty much the same thing as when they used the word *hominid* 20 years ago (Greiner 2003). Table 5.2 and Figure 5.2 illustrate our degree of relatedness to other primates.

Primate Tendencies

Primates are varied because they have adapted to diverse ecological niches. Some primates are active during the day; others, at night. Some eat insects; others, fruits; others, shoots, leaves, and bulk vegetation; and others, seeds or roots. Some primates live on the ground, others live in trees, and there are intermediate adaptations (see Campbell, ed. 2011; Potocki and Krasinski, eds. 2009). However, because the earliest primates were tree dwellers, modern primates share homologies reflecting their common **arboreal** heritage.

Many trends in primate evolution are best exemplified by the **anthropoids:** monkeys, apes, and humans, which constitute the suborder *Anthropoidea*. The other primate suborder, *Prosimii,* includes lemurs, lorises, and tarsiers. These **prosimians** are more distant relatives of humans than are monkeys and apes. The primate trends—most developed in the anthropoids—can be summarized briefly. Together they constitute an anthropoid heritage that humans share with monkeys and apes.

1. **Grasping.** Primates have five-digited feet and hands that are suited for grasping. Certain features of hands and feet that were originally adaptive for arboreal life have been transmitted across the generations to contemporary primates. Flexible hands and feet that could encircle branches were important features in the early primates' arboreal life. Thumb opposability might have been favored by the inclusion of insects in the early primate diet. Manual dexterity makes it easier to catch insects attracted to abundant arboreal flowers and fruits. Humans and many other primates have **opposable thumbs:** The thumb can touch the other fingers. Some primates also have grasping feet. However, in adapting to **bipedal** (two-footed) locomotion, humans eliminated most of the foot's grasping ability.

2. **Smell to Sight.** Several anatomical changes reflect the shift from smell to sight as the primates' most important means of obtaining information. Monkeys, apes, and humans have excellent *stereoscopic* (able to see in depth) and color vision. The portion of the brain devoted to vision expanded, while the area concerned with smell shrank.

Primates have five-digited feet and hands, well suited for grasping. Flexible hands and feet that could encircle branches were important features in the early primates' arboreal life. In adapting to bipedal (two-footed) locomotion, hominids eliminated most of the foot's grasping ability—illustrated here by the chimpanzee.

3. **Nose to Hand.** Sensations of touch, conveyed by *tactile organs,* also provide information. The tactile skin on a dog's or cat's nose transmits information. Cats' tactile hairs, or whiskers, also serve this function. In primates, however, the main touch organ is the hand, specifically the sensitive pads of the "fingerprint" region.

4. **Brain Complexity.** The proportion of brain tissue concerned with memory, thought, and association has increased in primates. The primate ratio of brain size to body size exceeds that of most mammals.

5. **Parental Investment.** Most primates give birth to a single offspring rather than a litter. Because of this, growing primates receive more attention and have more learning opportunities than do other mammals. Learned behavior is an important part of primate adaptation.

6. **Sociality.** Primates tend to be social animals that live with others of their species. The need for longer and more attentive care of offspring places a selective value on support by a social group.

Prosimians

The primate order has two suborders: prosimians and anthropoids. The early history of the primates is limited to prosimianlike animals known through the fossil record. The first anthropoids, ancestral to monkeys, apes, and humans, appeared more than 40 million years ago. Some prosimians managed to survive in Africa and Asia because they were adapted to nocturnal life. As such, they did not compete with anthropoids, which are active during the day. Prosimians (lemurs) in Madagascar had no anthropoid competitors until people colonized that island some 1,500 years ago.

In their behavior and biology, Madagascar's *lemurs,* with 33 species, show adaptations to an array of environments or ecological niches. Their diets and times of activity differ. Lemurs eat fruits, other plant foods, eggs, and insects. Some are nocturnal; others are active during the day. Some are totally arboreal; others spend some time in the trees and some on the ground. Another kind of prosimian is the *tarsier,* today confined to Indonesia, Malaysia, and the Philippines. From the fossil record, we know that 50 million years ago, several genera of tarsierlike prosimians lived in North America and Europe, which were much warmer then than they are now (Boaz 1997). The one genus of tarsier that survived is totally nocturnal. Active at night, tarsiers don't directly compete with anthropoids, which are active during the day. Lorises are other nocturnal prosimians found in Africa and Asia.

Monkeys

All anthropoids share resemblances that can be considered trends in primate evolution in the sense that these traits are fully developed neither in the fossils of primates that lived prior to 50 million years ago nor among contemporary prosimians.

The anthropoid suborder has two infraorders: *platyrrhines* (New World monkeys) and *catarrhines* (Old World monkeys, apes, and humans). The catarrhines (sharp-nosed) and platyrrhines (flat-nosed) take their names from Latin terms that describe the placement of the nostrils. Old World monkeys, apes, and humans are all catarrhines. Being placed in the same taxon (infraorder in this case) means that Old World monkeys, apes, and humans are more closely related to each other than to New World monkeys. In other words, one kind of monkey (Old World) is more like a human than it is like another kind of monkey (New World). The New World monkeys were reproductively isolated from the catarrhines before the latter diverged into the Old World monkeys, apes, and humans. This is why New World monkeys are assigned to a different infraorder.

All New World monkeys and many Old World monkeys are arboreal. Whether in the trees or on the ground, however, monkeys move differently from apes and humans. Their arms and legs move parallel to one another, as dogs' legs do. This contrasts with the tendency toward *orthograde posture,* the straight and upright stance of apes and humans. Unlike apes, which have longer arms than legs, and humans, who have longer legs than arms, monkeys have arms and legs of about the same length. Most monkeys also have tails, which help them maintain balance in the trees. Apes and humans lack tails. The apes' tendency toward orthograde posture is most evident when they sit down. When they move about, chimps, gorillas, and orangutans habitually use all four limbs.

New World Monkeys

New World monkeys live in the forests of Central and South America (see Strier 2011). Unlike Old World monkeys, many New World monkeys have *prehensile,* or

A woolly spider monkey, aka muriqui, with infant, in Brazil's Atlantic forest. The long arms and elongated prehensile tail create a spiderlike image for this New World monkey.

lesser apes separated from those of the great apes some 16–14 m.y.a. Then, around 11–10 m.y.a., the orangutan line diverged from that leading to the African apes and humans. Yet another split took place when the gorilla line branched off from the line leading to chimpanzees and hominins. Around 7–6 m.y.a., another split in the lineage led to the various early hominins, to be examined in the next chapter.

Summary

1. Humans, apes, monkeys, and prosimians are primates. The primate order is subdivided into suborders, superfamilies, families, tribes, genera, species, and subspecies. Organisms in any subdivision (taxon) of a taxonomy are assumed to share more recent ancestry with each other than they do with organisms in other taxa. But it's sometimes hard to tell the difference between homologies, which reflect common ancestry, and analogies, biological similarities that develop through convergent evolution.

2. Prosimians are the older of the two primate suborders. Some 40 million years ago, anthropoids displaced prosimians from niches their ancestors once occupied. Tarsiers and lorises are prosimians that survived by adapting to nocturnal life. Lemurs survived on the island of Madagascar.

3. Anthropoids include humans, apes, and monkeys. All share fully developed primate trends, such as depth and color vision. Other anthropoid traits include a shift in tactile areas to the fingers. The New World monkeys are all arboreal. Old World monkeys include both terrestrial species (e.g., baboons and macaques) and arboreal ones. The great apes are orangutans, gorillas, chimpanzees, and bonobos. The lesser apes are gibbons and siamangs.

4. Gibbons and siamangs live in Southeast Asian forests. These apes are slight, arboreal animals whose mode of locomotion is brachiation. Sexual dimorphism, slight among gibbons, is marked among orangutans, which are confined to two Indonesian islands. Sexually dimorphic gorillas, the most terrestrial apes, are vegetarians confined to equatorial Africa. Two species of chimpanzees live in the forests and woodlands of tropical Africa. Chimps are less sexually dimorphic, more numerous, and more omnivorous than gorillas are.

5. Primates have lived during the past 65 million years, the Cenozoic era, with seven epochs: Paleocene, Eocene, Oligocene, Miocene, Pliocene, Pleistocene, and Holocene, or Recent. The arboreal theory states that primates evolved by adapting to life high up in the trees.

6. The first (prosimianlike) fossils clearly identified as primates lived during the Eocene (54–34 m.y.a.), mainly in North America and Europe. During the Oligocene (34–23 m.y.a.), anthropoids became the most numerous primates. During the Oligocene the ancestors of the New World monkeys diverged from the line leading to the catarrhines—Old World monkeys, apes, and humans.

7. The earliest hominoid fossils are from the Miocene (23–5 m.y.a.). Africa's *Proconsul* group contained the last common ancestor shared by the Old World monkeys and the apes. Since the middle Miocene (16–10 m.y.a.), Africa, Europe, and Asia

have been connected. Protoapes spread beyond Africa and became the most common primates of the middle Miocene. Asia's *Gigantopithecus,* the largest primate ever to live, persisted for millions of years, finally coexisting with *Homo erectus.* *Pierolapithecus catalaunicus,* which lived around 13 million years ago, could be the last common ancestor of humans, chimpanzees, gorillas, and orangutans.

Key Terms

analogies, *99*	hominoid, *105*	prosimians, *100*
anthropoids, *100*	homologies, *97*	taxonomy, *96*
arboreal, *100*	m.y.a., *111*	terrestrial, *96*
bipedal, *101*	opposable	
brachiation, *105*	thumb, *101*	
convergent	primates, *96*	
evolution, *99*	primatology, *96*	

Go to our Online Learning Center website at **www.mhhe.com/kottak** for Internet resources directly related to the content of this chapter.

Chapter 6

Early Hominins

What Makes Us Human?

Bipedalism

Applying Anthropology to Popular Culture: Monkey Bars

Brains, Skulls, and Childhood Dependency

Tools

Teeth

Chronology of Hominin Evolution

Who Were the Earliest Hominins?

Sahelanthropus tchadensis

Orrorin tugenensis

Ardipithecus

The Varied Australopithecines

Australopithecus anamensis

Australopithecus afarensis

Gracile and Robust Australopithecines

The Australopithecines and Early *Homo*

Oldowan Tools

Anthropology Today: Anthropologist's Son Finds New Species of Australopithecus

A. garhi and Early Stone Tools

What Makes Us Human?

In trying to determine whether a fossil is a human ancestor, should we look for traits that make us human today? Sometimes yes; sometimes no. We do look for similarities in DNA, including mutations shared by certain lineages but not others. But what about such key human attributes as bipedal locomotion, a long period of childhood dependency, big brains, and the use of tools and language? Some of these key markers of humanity are fairly recent—or have origins that are impossible to date. And ironically, some of the physical markers that have led scientists to identify certain fossils as early hominins rather than apes are features that have been lost during subsequent human evolution.

Bipedalism

As is true of all subsequent hominins, postcranial material from *Ardipithecus,* the earliest widely accepted hominin genus (5.8–4.4 m.y.a.), indicates a capacity—albeit an imperfect one—for upright bipedal locomotion. The *Ardipithecus* pelvis appears to be transitional between one suited for arboreal climbing and one modified for bipedalism.

Reliance on bipedalism—upright two-legged locomotion—is the key feature differentiating early hominins from the apes. This way of moving around eventually led to the distinctive hominin way of life. Based on African fossil discoveries, such as Ethiopia's *Ardipithecus,* hominin bipedalism is more than five million years old. Some scientists see even earlier evidence of bipedalism in two other fossil finds described later in the chapter—one from Chad (*Sahelanthropus tchadensis*) and one from Kenya (*Orrorin tugenensis*).

Bipedalism traditionally has been viewed as an adaptation to open grassland or savanna country, although *Ardipithecus* appears to have lived in a humid woodland habitat. Adaptation to the savanna occurred later in hominin evolution. Perhaps bipedalism developed in the woodlands but became even more adaptive in a savanna habitat. Scientists have suggested several advantages of bipedalism: the ability to see over long grass and scrub, to carry items back to a home base, and to reduce the body's exposure to solar radiation. Studies with scale models of primates suggest that quadrupedalism exposes the body to 60 percent more solar radiation than does bipedalism. The fossil and archaeological records confirm that upright bipedal locomotion preceded stone tool manufacture and the expansion of the hominin brain. However, although early hominins could move bipedally on the ground, they also preserved enough of an apelike anatomy to make them good climbers (see the description of *Ardipithecus* on pp. 126–128 as well as of "Lucy's baby" on pp. 130–131). They could take to the trees to sleep and to escape terrestrial predators.

Reconstruction of *Australopithecus* running bipedally with a pebble tool in hand. Along with tool use and manufacture, bipedalism is a key part of being human.

Remember the "monkey bars" in your playground? When children use monkey bars, they hang and move hand over hand rather than getting on top and running across, as a monkey would do. Proficiency on the monkey bars isn't something we typically take into adulthood. Bipedal locomotion, on the other hand, is an ability we rely on every day and can't easily do without. Only when we lose it do we fully appreciate its supreme significance. Think of someone who has broken a leg or had hip surgery and how limiting it is. Images of the future in the movie *Wall-E* notwithstanding, humans today are no less bipedal than our ancestors were five million years ago. From mambo to marathons, bipedalism remains an integral and enduring feature of human adaptation.

Brains, Skulls, and Childhood Dependency

Compared with contemporary humans, early hominins had very small brains. *Australopithecus afarensis,* a bipedal hominin that lived more than three million years ago, had a cranial capacity (430 cm^3—cubic centimeters) that barely surpassed the chimp average (390 cm^3). The form of the *afarensis* skull also is like that of the chimpanzee, although the brain-to-body size ratio may have been larger. Brain size has increased during hominin evolution, especially with the advent of the genus *Homo.* But this increase had to overcome some obstacles. Compared with the young of other primates, human children have a long period of childhood dependency, during which their brains and skulls grow dramatically. Larger skulls demand larger birth canals, but the requirements of upright bipedalism impose limits on the expansion of the human pelvic opening. If the opening is too large, the pelvis doesn't provide sufficient support for the trunk. Locomotion suffers, and posture problems develop. If, by contrast, the birth canal is too narrow, mother and child (without the modern option of Caesarean section) may die. Natural selection has struck a balance between the structural demands of upright posture and the tendency toward increased brain size—the birth of immature and dependent children whose brains and skulls grow dramatically after birth.

Tools

Given what is known about tool use and manufacture by the great apes, it is likely that early hominins shared this ability as a homology with the apes. We'll see later that the first firm evidence for hominin stone tool manufacture is dated to 2.6 m.y.a. Upright bipedalism would have permitted the use of tools and weapons against predators and competitors. Bipedal locomotion also allowed early hominins to carry things, perhaps including scavenged parts of carnivore kills. We know that primates have generalized abilities to adapt through learning. It would be amazing if early hominins, who are much more closely related to us than the apes are, didn't have even greater cultural abilities than contemporary apes have.

Teeth

One example of an early hominin trait that has been lost during subsequent human evolution is big back teeth. (Indeed a pattern of overall dental reduction has characterized human evolution.) Once they adapted to the savanna, with its gritty, tough, and fibrous vegetation, it was adaptively advantageous for early hominins to have large back teeth and thick tooth enamel. This permitted thorough chewing of tough, fibrous vegetation and mixture with salivary enzymes to permit digestion of foods that otherwise would not have been digestible. The churning, rotary motion associated with such chewing also favored reduction of the canines and first premolars (bicuspids). These front teeth are much sharper and longer in the apes than in early hominins. The apes use their sharp, self-honing teeth to pierce fruits. Males also flash their big sharp canines to intimidate and impress others, including potential mates. Although bipedalism seems to have characterized the human lineage since it split from the line leading to the African apes, many other "human" features came later. Yet other early hominin features, such as large back teeth and thick enamel—which we don't have now—offer clues about who was a human ancestor back then.

Chronology of Hominin Evolution

Recall that the term *hominin* is used to designate the human line after its split from ancestral chimps. *Hominid* refers to the taxonomic family that includes humans and the African apes and their immediate ancestors. In this book *hominid* is used when there is doubt about the hominin status of the fossil (e.g., with Toumai, as described on pp. 124–126). Although recent fossil discoveries have pushed the hominin lineage back to almost six million years, humans actually haven't been around too long when the age of the Earth is considered. If we compare Earth's history to a 24-hour day (with one second equaling 50,000 years),

> Earth originates at midnight.
> The earliest fossils were deposited at 5:45 A.M.
> The first vertebrates appeared at 9:02 P.M.
> The earliest mammals, at 10:45 P.M.
> The earliest primates, at 11:43 P.M.
> The earliest hominins, at 11:57 P.M.
> And *Homo sapiens* arrives 36 seconds before midnight. (Wolpoff, 1999, p. 10)

Although the first hominins appeared late in the Miocene epoch, for the study of hominin evolution, the Pliocene (5–2 m.y.a.), Pleistocene (2 m.y.a.–10,000 B.P.), and Recent (10,000 B.P.–present) epochs are most important. Until the end of the Pliocene, the main hominin genus was *Australopithecus,* which lived in sub-Saharan Africa. By the start of the Pleistocene, *Australopithecus* had evolved into *Homo*.

Who Were the Earliest Hominins?

Recent discoveries of fossils and tools have increased our knowledge of hominid and hominin evolution. The most significant recent discoveries have been made in Africa—Kenya, Tanzania, Ethiopia, and Chad. These finds come from different sites and may be

TABLE 6.1   Dates and Geographic Distribution of Major Hominoid, Hominid, and Hominin Fossil Groups

Fossil Group	Dates, m.y.a.	Known Distribution
Hominoid		
Pierolapithecus catalaunicus	13	Spain
Hominid		
Common ancestor of hominids	8?	East Africa
Sahelanthropus tchadensis	7–6	Chad
Orrorin tugenensis	6	Kenya
Hominins		
Ardipithecus kadabba	5.8–5.5	Ethiopia
Ardipithecus ramidus	4.4	Ethiopia
Australopithecines		
A. anamensis	4.2–3.9	Kenya
A. afarensis	3.8–3.0	East Africa (Laetoli, Hadar)
A. garhi	2.5	Ethiopia
Robusts	2.6–1.2	East and South Africa
A. robustus (aka *Paranthropus*)	2.0?–1.0?	South Africa
A. boisei	2.6?–1.2	East Africa
Graciles		
A. africanus	3.0?–2.0?	South Africa
Homo		
H. habilis/H. rudolfensis	2.4?–1.4?	East Africa
H. erectus	1.9?–0.3?	Africa, Asia, Europe
Homo sapiens	0.3–present	
Archaic *H. sapiens*	0.3–0.28 (300,000–28,000)	Africa, Asia, Europe
Neandertals	0.13–0.28 (130,000–28,000)	Europe, Middle East, North Africa
Anatomically Modern Humans (AMHs)	0.15?–present (150,000–present)	Worldwide (after 20,000 B.P.)

the remains of individuals that lived hundreds of thousands of years apart. Furthermore, geological processes operating over thousands or millions of years inevitably distort fossil remains. Table 6.1 summarizes the major events in hominid and hominin evolution. You should consult it throughout this chapter and the next one.

Sahelanthropus tchadensis

In July 2001 anthropologists working in Central Africa—in northern Chad's Djurab Desert—unearthed the 6-to-7-million-year-old skull of the oldest possible human ancestor yet found. This discovery consists of a nearly complete skull, two lower jaw fragments, and three teeth. It dates to the time period when humans and chimps would have been diverging from a common ancestor. "It takes us into another world, of creatures

On July 10, 2002, in N'Djamena, Chad, the French paleontologist Michel Brunet holds Toumai's skull along with Ahounta Djimdoumalbaye (left), who discovered the skull. Toumai is a possible hominin ancestor.

that include the common ancestor, the ancestral human and the ancestral chimp," George Washington University paleobiologist Bernard Wood said (quoted in Gugliotta 2002). The discovery was made by a 40-member multinational team led by the French paleoanthropologist Michel Brunet. The actual discoverer was the university undergraduate Ahounta Djimdoumalbaye, who spied the skull embedded in sandstone. The new fossil was dubbed *Sahelanthropus tchadensis,* referring to the northern Sahel region of Chad where it was found. The fossil is also known as "Toumai," a local name meaning "hope of life."

The discovery team identified the skull as that of an adult male with a chimp-sized brain (320–380 cubic centimeters), heavy brow ridges, and a relatively flat, humanlike face. Toumai's habitat included savanna, forests, rivers, and lakes—and abundant animal life such as elephants, antelope, horses, giraffes, hyenas, hippopotamuses, wild boars, crocodiles, fish, and rodents. The animal species enabled the team to date the site where Toumai was found (by comparison with radiometrically dated sites with similar fauna).

Toumai blends apelike and human characteristics. Although the brain was chimp-sized, the tooth enamel was thicker than a chimp's enamel, suggesting a diet that included not just fruits but also tougher vegetation of a sort typically found in the savanna. Also, Toumai's snout did not protrude as far as a chimp's, making it more humanlike, and the canine tooth was shorter than those of other apes. "The fossil is showing the first glimmerings of evolution in our direction," according to University of California at Berkeley anthropologist Tim White (quoted in Gugliotta 2002).

Sahelanthropus is a nearly complete, although distorted, skull. The placement of its *foramen magnum* (the "big hole" through which the spinal cord joins the brain) farther forward than in apes suggests that *Sahelanthropus* moved bipedally. Its discovery in Chad indicates that early hominid (and possibly hominin) evolution was not confined to East Africa's Rift Valley. The Rift Valley's abundant early hominin fossil record may well reflect geology, preservation, and modern exposure of fossils rather than the actual geographic distribution of species in the past. The discovery of *Sahelanthropus* in Chad is the first proof of a more widespread distribution of early hominids.

Orrorin tugenensis

In January 2001 Brigitte Senut, Martin Pickford, and others reported the discovery, near the village of Tugen in Kenya's Baringo district, of possible early hominin fossils they called *Orrorin tugenensis* (Aiello and Collard 2001; Senut et al. 2001). The find consisted of 13 fossils from at least five individuals. The fossils include pieces of jaw with teeth, isolated upper and lower teeth, arm bones, and a finger bone. *Orrorin* appears to have been a chimp-sized creature that climbed easily and walked on two legs when on the ground. Its date of six million years is close to the time of the common ancestor of humans and chimps. The fossilized left femur (thigh bone) suggests upright bipedalism (walking with two feet), while the thick right humerus (upper arm bone) suggests tree-climbing skills. Animal fossils found in the same rocks indicate *Orrorin* lived in a wooded environment.

Orrorin's upper incisor, upper canine, and lower premolar are more like the teeth of a female chimpanzee than like human teeth. But other dental and skeletal features, especially bipedalism, led the discoverers to assign *Orrorin* to the hominin lineage. *Orrorin* lived after *Sahelanthropus tchadensis* but before *Ardipithecus kadabba,* discovered in Ethiopia, also in 2001, and dated to 5.8–5.5 m.y.a. The hominin status of *Ardipithecus* is more generally accepted than is that of either *Sahelanthropus tchadensis* or *Orrorin tugenensis.*

Ardipithecus

Early hominins assigned to *Ardipithecus kadabba* lived during the late Miocene, between 5.8 and 5.5 million years ago. *Ardipithecus (ramidus)* fossils were first discovered at Aramis in Ethiopia by Berhane Asfaw, Gen Suwa, and Tim White. Dating to 4.4 m.y.a., these *Ardipithecus ramidus* fossils consisted of the remains of some 17 individuals, with cranial, facial, dental, and

In October 2009, a newly reported *Ardipithecus* find—a fairly complete skeleton of *Ardipithecus ramidus,* dubbed "Ardi," was heralded throughout the media.

upper limb bones. Subsequently, much older *Ardipithecus (kadabba)* fossils, dating back to 5.8 m.y.a., were found in Ethiopia. The *kadabba* find consists of 11 specimens, including a jawbone with teeth, hand and foot bones, fragments of arm bones, and a piece of collarbone. At least five individuals are represented. These creatures were apelike in size, anatomy, and habitat. They lived in a wooded area rather than the open grassland or savanna habitat where later hominins proliferated. As of this writing, because of its probable bipedalism, *Ardipithecus kadabba* is recognized as the earliest known hominin, with the *Sahelanthropus tchadensis* find from Chad, dated to 7–6 m.y.a., and *Orrorin tugenensis* from Kenya, dated to 6 m.y.a. possibly even older hominins.

In October 2009, a newly reported *Ardipithecus* find—a fairly complete skeleton of *Ardipithecus ramidus,* dubbed "Ardi"—was heralded on the front page of the *New York Times* and throughout the media (Wilford 2009*b*). Ardi (4.4 m.y.a.) replaces Lucy (3.2 m.y.a.—see later in the chapter) as the earliest known hominin skeleton. The Ethiopian discovery site lies on what is now an arid floodplain of the Awash River, 45 miles south of Hadar, where Lucy was found. Scientists infer that Ardi was female, based on its small and lightly built (gracile) skull and its small canine teeth compared with others at the site. At 4 feet tall and 120 pounds, Ardi stood about a foot taller and weighed twice as much as Lucy.

The *Ardipithecus* pelvis appears to be transitional between one suited for arboreal climbing and one modified for bipedal locomotion. The pelvis of later hominins such as Lucy shows nearly all the adaptations needed for full bipedalism. Although Ardi's lower pelvis remains primitive, the structure of her upper pelvis allowed her to walk on two legs

Shown here are members of the international team responsible for Ardi's discovery and reconstruction. Meet Ethiopian paleoanthropologists Johannes Haile-Selassie and Berhane Asfaw.

with a straightened hip. Still, she probably could neither walk nor run as well as later hominins. Her feet lacked the archlike structure of later hominin feet. Ardi's apelike lower pelvis indicates retention of powerful hamstring muscles for climbing. Her hands, very long arms, and short legs all recall those of extinct apes, and her brain was no larger than that of a modern chimp.

Based on associated animal and plant remains, *Ardipithecus* lived in a humid wood-land habitat. More than 145 teeth have been collected at the site. Their size, shape, and wear patterns suggest an omnivorous diet of plants, nuts, and small mammals. Although *Ardipithecus* probably fed both in trees and on the ground, the canines suggest less of a fruit diet than is characteristic of living apes. With reduced sexual dimorphism, *Ardipithecus* canines resemble modern human canines more than the tusklike piercing upper canines of chimps and gorillas.

The first comprehensive reports describing Ardi and related findings, the result of 17 years of study, were published on October 2, 2009, in the journal *Science,* including 11 papers by 47 authors from 10 countries. They analyzed more than 110 *Ardipithecus* specimens from at least 36 different individuals, including Ardi. The ancestral relationship of *Ardipithecus* to *Australopithecus* has not been determined, but Ardi has been called a plausible ancestor for *Australopithecus* (see Wilford 2009*b*).

The Varied Australopithecines

Some Miocene hominins eventually evolved into a varied group of Pliocene–Pleistocene hominins known as the **australopithecines**—for which we have an abundant fossil record. This term reflects their one-time classification as members of a distinct taxonomic subfamily, the "Australopithecinae." We now know that the various species of *Australopithecus* discussed in this chapter do not form a distinct subfamily within the order Primates, but the name "australopithecine" has stuck to describe them. Today the distinction between the australopithecines and later hominins is made on the genus level. The australopithecines are assigned to the genus *Australopithecus (A.);* later humans, to *Homo (H.).*

In the scheme followed here, *Australopithecus* had at least six species:

1. *A. anamensis* (4.2 to 3.9 m.y.a.)
2. *A. afarensis* (3.8 to 3.0 m.y.a.)
3. *A. africanus* (3.0? to 2.0? m.y.a.)
4. *A. garhi* (2.5 m.y.a.)
5. *A. robustus* (2.0? to 1.0? m.y.a.)
6. *A. boisei* (2.6? to 1.2 m.y.a.)

The dates given for each species are approximate because an organism isn't a member of one species one day and a member of another species the next day. Nor could the same dating techniques be used for all the finds. The South African australopithecine fossils (*A. africanus* and *A. robustus*), for example, come from a nonvolcanic area where radiometric dating could not be done. Dating of those fossils has been based mainly on stratigraphy. The hominin fossils from the volcanic regions of East Africa usually have radiometric dates. (See "Anthropology Today" for the most recent *Australopithecus* find from South Africa.)

Australopithecus anamensis

Ardipithecus ramidus may (or may not) have evolved into *A. anamensis,* a bipedal hominin from northern Kenya, whose fossil remains were reported first by Maeve Leakey and Alan Walker in 1995 (Leakey et al. 1995; Rice 2002). *A. anamensis* consists of 78 fragments from two sites: Kanapoi and Allia Bay. The fossils include upper and lower jaws, cranial fragments, and the upper and lower parts of a leg bone (tibia). The Kanapoi fossils date to 4.2 m.y.a., and those at Allia Bay to 3.9 m.y.a. The molars have thick enamel, and the apelike canines are large. Based on the tibia, *anamensis* weighed about 110 pounds (50 kilograms). This would have made it larger than either the earlier *Ardipithecus* or the later *A. afarensis*. Its anatomy implies that *anamensis* was bipedal. Because of its date and its location in the East African Rift valley, *A. anamensis* may be ancestral to *A. afarensis* (3.8–3.0 m.y.a.) which usually is considered ancestral to all the later australopithecines (*garhi, africanus, robustus,* and *boisei*) as well as to *Homo* (Figure 6.1).

Australopithecus afarensis

The hominin species known as *A. afarensis* includes fossils found at two sites, Laetoli in northern Tanzania and Hadar in the Afar region of Ethiopia. Laetoli is earlier (3.8–3.6 m.y.a.). The Hadar fossils probably date to between 3.3 and 3.0 m.y.a. Thus, based on the current evidence, *A. afarensis* lived between about 3.8 and 3.0 m.y.a. Research directed by Mary Leakey was responsible for the Laetoli finds. The Hadar discoveries resulted from an international expedition directed by D. C. Johanson and M. Taieb. The two sites have yielded significant samples of early hominin fossils. There are two dozen specimens from Laetoli, and the Hadar finds include the remains of between 35 and 65 individuals. The Laetoli remains are mainly teeth and jaw fragments, along with some very informative fossilized footprints. The Hadar sample includes skull fragments and postcranial material, most notably 40 percent of the complete skeleton of a tiny hominin female, dubbed "Lucy," who lived around 3 m.y.a.

Although the hominin remains at Laetoli and Hadar were deposited half a million years apart, their many resemblances explain their placement in the same species, *A. afarensis*. These fossils forced a reinterpretation of the early hominin fossil record. *A. afarensis*, although clearly a hominin, was so similar in many ways to chimps and gorillas that our common ancestry with the African apes must be very recent, certainly no more than 8 m.y.a. *Ardipithecus* and *A. anamensis* are even more apelike.

Discussion of hominin fossils requires a brief review of dentition. Moving from front to back, on either side of the upper or lower jaw, humans (and apes) have two incisors, one canine, two premolars, and three molars. Our dental formula is 2.1.2.3, for a total of 8 teeth on each side, upper and lower—32 teeth in all—if we have all our "wisdom teeth" (our third molars). Now back to the australopithecines.

From the same general area of northern Ethiopia as Lucy comes another important member of *A. afarensis* (Owen 2006). This toddler, the world's oldest fossil child, soon

FIGURE 6.1 **Phylogenetic Tree for African Apes, Hominids, and Hominins**
The presumed divergence date for ancestral chimps and hominins was between 8 and
6 m.y.a. Branching in later hominin evolution is also shown. For more exact dates,
see the text and Table 6.1.

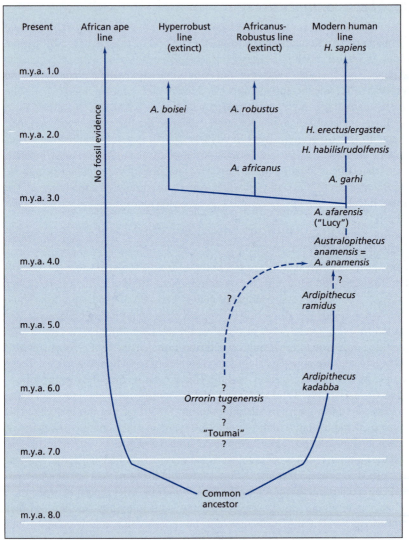

was dubbed "Lucy's Baby"—despite having lived a hundred thousand years before Lucy
(3.3 m.y.a. for the child versus 3.2 for Lucy). The child is an amazingly complete find,
with a more intact skull and much more skeletal material than exists for Lucy. Not surprisingly, given what we already know about *A. afarensis,* the skull and upper body are
apelike, while the lower body confirms bipedalism. Despite bipedalism, the skeleton's

An ancient trail of hominin footprints fossilized in volcanic ash. Mary Leakey found this 230-foot (70-meter) trail at Laetoli, Tanzania, in 1979. It dates from 3.6 m.y.a. and confirms that *A. afarensis* was a striding biped.

upper body includes two complete shoulder blades similar to a gorilla's, so it probably was better at climbing than humans are.

Unearthed in 2000, the child probably was female and about three years old when she died. The remains include a well-preserved skull, milk teeth, tiny fingers, a torso, a foot, and a kneecap. Although Lucy doesn't have much of a head, her "baby" has a complete skull, a mandible (jaw bone), and a monkey-sized face with a smooth brow.

Lucy's baby sheds light on the growth process in early humans. A prolonged, dependent childhood allowed later human species to grow larger brains, which need several years to develop after birth. Such a long period of brain growth apparently did not characterize *A. afarensis*. While the adult *A. afarensis* brain is thought to have been slightly larger than a chimp's, Lucy's "baby's" brain was smaller than that of a chimp of comparable age.

The *A. afarensis* fossils show that as recently as 3.0 m.y.a., our ancestors had a mixture of apelike and hominin features. Canines, premolars, and skulls were much more apelike than most scholars had imagined would exist in such a recent ancestor. Compared with *Homo, A. afarensis* had larger and sharper canine teeth that projected beyond the other teeth. The canines, however, were reduced compared with an ape's tusklike canines. The *afarensis* lower premolar was pointed and projecting to sharpen the upper canine. It had one long cusp and one tiny bump that hints at the bicuspid premolar that eventually developed in hominin evolution. On the other hand, the molars, chewing apparatus, and cheekbones foreshadowed later hominin trends.

FIGURE 6.2 **Comparison of Dentition in Ape, Human, and *A. afarensis* Palates**

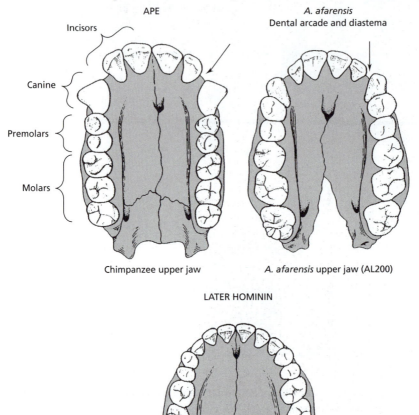

APE

A. afarensis
Dental arcade and diastema

Incisors

Canine

Premolars

Molars

Chimpanzee upper jaw

A. afarensis upper jaw (AL200)

LATER HOMININ

Human upper jaw

When the coarse, gritty, fibrous vegetation of grasslands and semidesert enters the diet, the back teeth change to accommodate heavy chewing stresses. Massive back teeth, jaws, and facial and cranial structures suggest a diet demanding extensive grinding and powerful crushing. *A. afarensis* molars are large (see Figure 6.2). The lower jaw (mandible) is thick and is buttressed with a bony ridge behind the front teeth. The cheekbones are large and flare out to the side for the attachment of powerful chewing muscles.

The skull of *A. afarensis* contrasts with those of later hominins. The cranial capacity barely surpasses the chimp average. Below the neck, however—particularly in regard to locomotion—*A. afarensis* was unquestionably human. Early evidence of striding bipedalism comes from Laetoli, where volcanic ash, which can be dated directly by the K/A technique, covered a trail of footprints of two or three hominins walking to a water hole.

These prints leave no doubt that a small striding biped lived in Tanzania by 3.6 m.y.a. The structure of the pelvic, hip, leg, and foot bones also confirms that upright bipedalism was *A. afarensis*'s mode of locomotion. As we have seen, more recent finds show that bipedalism predated *A. afarensis*. *A. anamensis* (4.2 m.y.a.) was bipedal, as was the even older *Ardipithecus* (5.8–4.4 m.y.a.).

Although bidepal, *A. afarensis* still contrasts in many ways with later hominins. Sexual dimorphism is especially marked. The male–female contrast in jaw size in *A. afarensis* was more marked than in the orangutan. There was a similar contrast in body size. *A. afarensis* females, such as Lucy, stood between 3 and 4 feet (.9 and 1.2 meters) tall; males might have reached 5 feet (1.5 meters). *A. afarensis* males weighed perhaps twice as much as the females did (Wolpoff 1999). Table 6.2 summarizes data on the various australopithecines, including mid-sex body weight and brain size. *Mid-sex* means midway between the male average and the female average.

Lucy and her kind were far from dainty. Lucy's muscle-engraved bones are much more robust than ours are. With only rudimentary tools and weapons, early hominins needed powerful and resistant bones and muscles. Lucy's arms are longer relative to her legs than are those of later hominins. Here again her proportions are more apelike than ours are. Although Lucy neither brachiated nor knuckle-walked, she was probably a much better climber than modern people are, and she spent some of her day in the trees.

The pelvis, the lower spine, the hip joint, and the thigh bone change in accordance with the stresses of bipedal locomotion. With bipedalism, the pelvis forms a sort of basket that balances the weight of the trunk and supports this weight with less stress.

TABLE 6.2 **Facts about the Australopithecines Compared with Chimps and *Homo***

Species	Dates (m.y.a.)	Known Distribution	Important Sites	Body Weight (Mid-Sex)	Brain Size (Mid-Sex) (cm³)
Anatomically modern humans (AMHs)	195,000 to present			132 lb/60 kg	1,350
Pan troglodytes (chimpanzee)	Modern			93 lb/42 kg	390
A. boisei	2.6? to 1.2	E. Africa	Olduvai, East Turkana	86 lb/39 kg	490
A. robustus	2.0? to 1.0?	S. Africa	Kromdraai, Swartkrans	81 lb/37 kg	540
A. africanus	3.0? to 2.0?	S. Africa	Taung, Sterkfontein, Makapansqat	79 lb/36 kg	490
A. afarensis	3.8 to 3.0	E. Africa	Hadar, Laetoli	77 lb/35 kg	430
A. anamensis	4.2 to 3.9	Kenya	Kanapoi Allia Bay	Not enough data	No published skulls
Ardipithecus	5.8 to 4.4	Ethiopia	Aramis	Not enough data	Not enough data

Fossilized spinal bones (vertebrae) show that the australopithecine spine had the lower spine (lumbar) curve characteristic of *Homo*. This curvature helps transmit the weight of the upper body to the pelvis and the legs. The pelvises of the australopithecines were similar but not identical to those of *Homo*. The most significant contrast is a narrower australopithecine birth canal (Tague and Lovejoy 1986). Expansion of the birth canal is a trend in hominin evolution. The width of the birth canal is related to the size of the skull and brain. *A. afarensis* had a small cranial capacity. Even in later australopithecines, brain size did not exceed 600 cubic centimeters. Undoubtedly, the australopithecine skull grew after birth to accommodate a growing brain, as it does (much more) in *Homo*. However, the brains of the australopithecines expanded less than ours do. In the australopithecines, the cranial sutures (the lines where the bones of the skull eventually come together) fused relatively earlier in life. Young australopithecines must have depended on their parents and kin for nurturance and protection. Those years of childhood dependency would have provided time for observation, teaching, and learning. This may provide indirect evidence for a rudimentary cultural life.

Gracile and Robust Australopithecines

The fossils of *A. africanus* and *A. robustus* come from South Africa. In 1924, the anatomist Raymond Dart coined the term ***Australopithecus africanus*** to describe the first fossil representative of this species, the skull of a juvenile that was found accidentally in a quarry at Taung, South Africa. Radiometric dates are lacking for this nonvolcanic region, but the fossil hominins found at the five main South African sites appear (from stratigraphy) to have lived between 3 and 1 m.y.a.

There were two groups of South African australopithecines: **gracile** (*A. africanus*) and **robust** (*A. robustus*). "Gracile" indicates that members of *A. africanus* were smaller and slighter, less robust, than were members of *A. robustus*. There also were very robust—*hyperrobust*—australopithecines in East Africa. In the classification scheme used here, these have been assigned to *A. boisei*. However, some scholars consider *A. robustus* and *A. boisei* to be regional variants of just one species, usually called *robustus* (sometimes given its own genus, *Paranthropus*).

(Left) Profile view of an *A. africanus* (gracile) skull (Sterkfontein 5). The cranium, discovered by Dr. Robert Broom and J. T. Robinson in April 1947, dates back to 2.9–2.4 m.y.a. (Right) Profile view of an *A. boisei* skull—Olduvai Hominid (OH) 5, originally called *Zinjanthropus boisei*. This skull of a young male, discovered by Mary Leakey in 1959 at Olduvai Gorge, Tanzania, dates back 1.8 million years.

Graciles and robusts probably descend from *A. afarensis,* which itself was gracile in form, or from a South African version of *A. afarensis.* Some scholars have argued that the graciles lived before (3.0?–2.0? m.y.a.) and were ancestral to the robusts (2.0?–1.0? m.y.a.). Others contend that the graciles and the robusts were separate species that may have overlapped in time. (Classifying them as members of different species implies they were reproductively isolated from each other in time or space.) Other paleoanthropologists view the gracile and robust australopithecines as different ends of a continuum of variation in a single *polytypic species*—one with considerable phenotypic variation.

The trend toward enlarged back teeth, chewing muscles, and facial buttressing, which already is noticeable in *A. afarensis,* continues in the South African australopithecines. However, the canines are reduced, and the premolars are fully bicuspid. Dental form and function changed as dietary needs shifted from cutting and slashing to chewing and grinding. The mainstay of the australopithecine diet was the vegetation of the savanna grasslands.

In the South African australopithecines, both deciduous ("baby") and permanent molars and premolars are massive, with multiple cusps. The later australopithecines had bigger back teeth than did the earlier ones. However, this evolutionary trend ended with early *Homo,* which had much smaller back teeth, reflecting a dietary change that will be described later.

Contrasts with *Homo* in the front teeth are less marked. But they are still of interest because of what they tell us about sexual dimorphism. *A. africanus*'s canines were more pointed, with larger roots, than *Homo*'s are. Still, the *A. africanus* canines were only 75 percent the size of the canines of *A. afarensis.* Despite this canine reduction, there was just as much canine sexual dimorphism in *A. africanus* as there had been in *A. afarensis* (Wolpoff 1999). Sexual dimorphism in general was much more pronounced among the early hominins than it is among *Homo sapiens. A. africanus* females were about 4 feet (1.2 meters), and males 5 feet (1.5 meters), tall. The average female probably had no more than 60 percent the weight of the average male (Wolpoff 1980a). (That figure contrasts with today's average female-to-male weight ratio of about 88 percent.)

Teeth, jaw, face, and skull changed to fit a diet based on tough, gritty, fibrous grasslands vegetation. A massive face housed large upper teeth and provided a base for the attachment of powerful chewing muscles. Australopithecine cheekbones were elongated and massive structures that anchored large chewing muscles running up the jaw. Another set of robust chewing muscles extended from the back of the jaw to the sides of the skull. In the more robust australopithecines (*A. robustus* in South Africa and *A. boisei* in East Africa), these muscles were strong enough to produce a *sagittal crest,* a bony ridge on the top of the skull. Such a crest forms as the bone grows. It develops from the pull of the chewing muscles as they meet at the midline of the skull (see Figure 6.3).

Overall robustness, especially in the chewing apparatus, increased through time among the australopithecines. This trend was most striking in *A. boisei,* which survived through 1.2 m.y.a in East Africa. Compared with their predecessors, the later australopithecines tended to have larger overall size, skulls, and back teeth. They also had thicker faces, more prominent crests, and more rugged muscle markings on the skeleton. By contrast, the front teeth stayed the same size.

FIGURE 6.3
Four Types of Early Hominins
What are the main differences you notice?

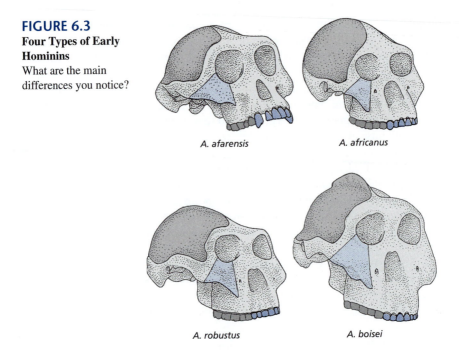

A. afarensis

A. africanus

A. robustus

A. boisei

Brain size (measured as cranial capacity, in cubic centimeters—cm^3) increased only slightly between *A. afarensis* (430 cm^3), *A. africanus* (490 cm^3), and *A. robustus* (540 cm^3) (Wolpoff 1999). These figures can be compared with an average cranial capacity of 1,350 cm^3 in *Homo sapiens.* The modern range goes from less than 1,000 cm^3 to more than 2,000 cm^3 in normal adults. The cranial capacity of chimps (*Pan troglodytes*) averages 390 cm^3 (see Table 6.2). The brains of gorillas (*Gorilla gorilla*) average around 500 cm^3, which is within the australopithecine range, but gorilla body weight is much greater.

The Australopithecines and Early *Homo*

Between 3 and 2 m.y.a., the ancestors of *Homo* became reproductively isolated from the later australopithecines, such as *A. robustus* and *A. boisei.* The earliest (very fragmentary) evidence for the genus *Homo* (2.5 m.y.a.) comes from the Chemeron formation in Kenya's Baringo Basin (Sherwood, Ward, and Hill 2002). This is a skull fragment, an isolated right temporal bone, known as the Chemeron temporal. By 2 m.y.a. the fossil sample of hominin teeth from East Africa has two clearly different sizes. One set is huge, the largest molars and premolars in hominin evolution; those teeth belonged to *A. boisei.* The other group of (smaller) teeth belonged to members of the genus *Homo.*

By 1.9 m.y.a., there is fossil evidence that different hominin groups occupied different ecological niches in Africa. One of them, *Homo*—by then *Homo erectus*—had a larger brain and a reproportioned skull; it had increased the areas of the brain that regulate higher mental functions. These were our ancestors, hominins with greater capacities for culture than the australopithecines had. *H. erectus* hunted and gathered, made sophisticated tools, and eventually displaced its cousin species, *A. boisei.*

A. boisei of East Africa, the hyperrobust australopithecines, had mammoth back teeth. Their females had bigger back teeth than did earlier australopithecine males. *A. boisei* became ever more specialized with respect to one part of the traditional australopithecine diet, concentrating on coarse vegetation with a high grit content.

We still don't know why, how, and exactly when the split between *Australopithecus* and *Homo* took place. Scholars have defended many different models, or theoretical schemes, to interpret the early hominin fossil record. Because new finds so often have forced reappraisals, most scientists are willing to modify their interpretation when given new evidence.

The model of Johanson and White (1979), who coined the term *A. afarensis,* proposes that *A. afarensis* split into two groups. One group, the ancestors of *Homo,* became reproductively isolated from the australopithecines between 3 and 2 m.y.a. Within this group was **Homo habilis,** a term coined by L. S. B. and Mary Leakey to describe the earliest members of the genus *Homo.* Another form of early *Homo* was *H. erectus,* which appears to have lived contemporaneously with *H. habilis* between around 1.9 and 1.4 m.y.a. (Spoor et al. 2007). Other members of *A. afarensis* evolved into the various kinds of later australopithecines (*A. africanus, A. robustus,* and hyperrobust *A. boisei,* the last member to become extinct).

There is good fossil evidence that *Homo* and *A. boisei* coexisted in East Africa. *A. boisei* seems to have lived in very arid areas, feeding on harder-to-chew vegetation than had any previous hominin. This diet would explain the hyperrobusts' huge back teeth, jaws, and associated areas of the face and skull.

"Anthropology Today" describes the most recent find, in South Africa, of a late gracile australopithecine boy, which was given the name *A. sediba.* Its date of 1.95 to 1.78 m.y.a. and its mosaic of primitive and modern features spurred a debate among scientists about whether it should be considered *Homo* or *Australopithecus.* Species of *Homo* were coexisting with the late gracile australopithecines and the early robust australopithecines by this time.

Oldowan Tools

The simplest obviously manufactured tools were discovered in 1931 by L. S. B. and Mary Leakey at Olduvai Gorge, Tanzania. That locale gave the tools their name—Oldowan pebble tools. The oldest tools from Olduvai are about 1.8 million years old. Still older (2.6–2.0 m.y.a.) Oldowan implements have been found in Ethiopia, Congo, and Malawi.

Stone tools consist of flakes and cores. The *core* is the piece of rock, in the Oldowan case about the size of a tennis ball, from which flakes are struck. Once flakes have been removed, the core can become a tool itself. A *chopper* is a tool made by flaking the edge of such a core on one side and thus forming a cutting edge.

Oldowan pebble tools represent the world's oldest formally recognized stone tools. Core tools are not the most common Oldowan tools; flakes are. The purpose of flaking

Oldowan core tools or choppers are the most common stone tools found at early African tool sites. Some may have been used for food processing, by pounding, breaking, or bashing. Other "choppers" may have been only cores from which flakes, used for cutting or scraping, were removed. Above, a chopper core tool; below, a flake tool.

stone in the Oldowan tradition was not to create pebble tools or choppers but to create the sharp stone flakes that made up the mainstay of the Oldowan tool kit (Toth 1985). Choppers were a convenient by-product of flaking and were used as well. However, hominins most likely did not have a preconceived tool form in mind while making them.

Oldowan choppers could have been used for food processing—by pounding, breaking, or bashing. Flakes probably were used mainly as cutters, for example, to dismember game carcasses. Crushed fossil animal bones indicate that stones were used to break open marrow cavities. Also, Oldowan deposits include pieces of bone or horn with scratch marks suggesting they were used to dig up tubers or insects. Oldowan core and flake tools are shown in the photos above. The flake tool in the lower photo is made of chert. Most Oldowan tools at Olduvai Gorge were made from basalt, which is locally more common and coarser.

For decades anthropologists have debated the identity of the earliest stone toolmakers. The first *Homo habilis* find got its name (*habilis* is Latin for "able") for its presumed

Anthropology Today *Anthropologist's Son Finds New Species of Australopithecus*

Luck is a factor in fossil hunting. Described here is a recent South African find in an area where fossil hunters had looked for years. Many anthropologists, your author included, take their children with them to the field, where they sometimes aid in fieldwork. Few, however, are as helpful as Matthew Berger, whose discovery of a new species of gracile australopithecine, called A. sediba, *is described here.*

CRADLE OF HUMANKIND, South Africa—Nine-year-old Matthew Berger dashed after his dog, Tau, into the high grass here one sunny morning, tripped over a log and stumbled onto . . . the bones of a new hominid species that lived almost two million years ago. . . .

"Dad, I found a fossil!" Matthew . . . cried out to his father, Lee R. Berger, an American paleoanthropologist, who had been searching for hominid bones just a hill and a half away for almost two decades. . . .

Matthew held the ancient remains of a 4-foot-2 boy who had been just a few years older than Matthew himself. Dr. Berger . . . and his fellow researchers have since found much more of the boy's skeleton, including his extraordinarily well-preserved skull, and three other individuals. . . .

The fossils . . . were a surprising and distinctive mixture of primitive and advanced anatomy and thus qualified as a new species . . . *Australopithecus sediba.*

The species *sediba*, which means fountain or wellspring in Sotho, strode upright on long legs, with human-shaped hips and pelvis, but still climbed through trees on apelike arms. It had the small teeth and more modern face of *Homo* . . . but the relatively primitive feet . . . of *Australopithecus*. . . .

Geologists estimated that the individuals lived 1.78 million to 1.95 million years ago, probably closer to the older date, when australopithecines and early species of *Homo* were contemporaries.

Dr. Berger's team said that the new species probably descended from *Australopithecus africanus*. . . . He described the species as a possible ancestor of *Homo erectus* . . . or a close "side branch" that did not lead to modern humans.

Scientists not involved in the research are debating whether the bones belong to the *Homo* or *Australopithecus* genus, but most agree that the discovery of the skeletons . . . is a major advance. . . .

"They are a fascinating mosaic of features," said Rick Potts, director of the Human Origins Program at the Smithsonian. "It reminds us of the combining and recombining of characteristics, the

Dr. Lee R. Berger, an American paleoanthropologist, with his son Matthew, 11, and dog Tau, at South Africa's Malapa site, where they discovered the new hominin species, *Australopithecus sediba*, on April 1, 2009.

continued

Anthropology Today *continued*

tinkering and experimentation, that go on in evolution."

Dr. Berger said the path to the discovery began over the Christmas holidays in 2007 when he began using Google Earth to map caves in the Cradle of Humankind. . . . Shadows and distortions of the earth . . . gave clues to the location of caves. . . .

On Aug. 15, 2008, when Matthew called his father to look at the bones he had found . . . from 15 feet, Dr. Berger, who had done his Ph.D. thesis on hominid shoulder bones, among them the clavicle, was astounded to see that his son had in his hands a clavicle with the unmistakable shape of a hominid.

"I couldn't believe it," Dr. Berger giddily recalled. "I took the rock, and I turned it" and "sticking out of the back of the rock was a mandible with a tooth, a canine, sticking out. And I almost died," he said, adding, "What are the odds?"

In March 2009 he found the remarkably intact cranium of the *sediba* boy whose clavicle Matthew had picked up. . . .

As the taxonomic debate continues, so, too, does fossil hunting. . . . "Every time we sift anything or pick up a rock, it has something in it," Dr. Berger said. . . .

Source: Celia W. Dugger and John Noble Wilford, "New Hominid Species Discovered in South Africa," *New York Times,* April 8, 2010.

status as the first hominin toolmaker. Recently the story has grown more complicated, with a discovery making it very likely that one kind of australopithecine also made and habitually used stone tools.

A. garhi and Early Stone Tools

In 1999 an international team reported the discovery, in Ethiopia, of a new species of hominin, along with the earliest traces of animal butchery (Asfaw, White, and Lovejoy 1999). These new fossils, dating to 2.5 m.y.a., may be the remains of a direct human ancestor and an evolutionary link between *Australopithecus* and the genus *Homo*. At the same site was evidence that antelopes and horses had been butchered with the world's earliest stone tools. When scientists excavated these hominin fossils, they were shocked to find a combination of unforeseen skeletal and dental features. They named the specimen *Australopithecus garhi*. The word *garhi* means "surprise" in the Afar language. Evidence that large mammals were being butchered shows that early stone technologies were aimed at getting meat and marrow from big game. This signals a dietary revolution that eventually may have allowed an invasion of new habitats and continents (Berkleyan 1999).

In 1997 the Ethiopian archaeologist Sileshi Semaw announced he had found the world's earliest stone tools, dating to 2.6 m.y.a., at the nearby Ethiopian site of Gona. But which human ancestor had made these tools, he wondered, and what were they used for? The 1999 discoveries by Asfaw, White, and their colleagues provided answers, identifying *A. garhi* as the best candidate for toolmaker (Berkleyan 1999).

The association, in the same area at the same time, of *A. garhi,* animal butchery, and the earliest stone tools suggests that the australopithecines were toolmakers, with some capacity for culture. Nevertheless, cultural abilities developed exponentially with *Homo*'s appearance and expansion. With increasing reliance on hunting, tool making, and other cultural abilities, *Homo* eventually became the most efficient exploiter of the savanna niche. The last surviving members of *A. boisei* may have been forced into ever-more-marginal areas. They eventually became extinct. By 1 m.y.a., a single species of hominin, *H. erectus,* not only had rendered other hominin forms extinct but also had expanded the hominin range to Asia and Europe. An essentially human strategy of adaptation, incorporating hunting as a fundamental ingredient of a generalized foraging economy, had emerged. Despite regional variation, it was to be the basic economy for our genus until 11,000 years ago.

Summary

1. A skull found in 2001 in northern Chad, dated at 6–7 million years old, officially named *Sahelanthropus tchadensis,* more commonly called "Toumai," may or may not be the earliest hominin yet known, as may the somewhat less ancient *Orrorin tugenensis,* found in Kenya in 2001.

2. Hominins lived during the late Miocene, Pliocene (5.0–2.0 m.y.a.), and Pleistocene (2.0 m.y.a.–10,000 B.P.) epochs. The australopithecines had appeared by 4.2 m.y.a. The six species of *Australopithecus* were *A. anamensis* (4.2–3.9 m.y.a.), *A. afarensis* (3.8–3.0 m.y.a.), *A. africanus* (3.0?–2.0? m.y.a.), *A. garhi* (2.5 m.y.a.), *A. robustus* (2.0?–1.0? m.y.a.), and *A. boisei* (2.6?–1.2 m.y.a.). The earliest generally accepted hominin remains are classified as *Ardipithecus kadabba* (5.8–5.5 m.y.a.) and *ramidus* (4.4 m.y.a.). Next comes *A. anamensis,* then a group of fossils from Hadar, Ethiopia, and Laetoli, Tanzania, classified as *A. afarensis.*

3. These earliest hominins shared many primitive features, including slashing canines, elongated premolars, a small apelike skull, and marked sexual dimorphism. Still, *A. afarensis* and its recently discovered predecessors were definite hominins. In *A. afarensis* this is confirmed by large molars and, more important, by skeletal evidence (e.g., in Lucy) for upright bipedalism.

4. Remains of two later groups, *A. africanus* (graciles) and *A. robustus* (robusts), were found in South Africa. Both groups show the australopithecine trend toward a powerful chewing apparatus. They had large molars and premolars and large and robust faces, skulls, and muscle markings. All these features are more pronounced in the robusts than they are in the graciles. The basis of the australopithecine diet was savanna vegetation.

5. By 2.0 m.y.a. there is ample evidence for two distinct hominin groups: early *Homo* and *A. boisei,* the hyperrobust australopithecines. The latter eventually became extinct around 1.2 m.y.a. *A. boisei* became increasingly specialized, dependent on tough, coarse, gritty, fibrous savanna vegetation. The australopithecine trend toward dental, facial, and cranial robustness continued with *A. boisei,* but these structures were reduced in *H. habilis* (2.4?–1.4? m.y.a.) and *H. erectus.* (1.9–0.37? m.y.a.).

6. Pebble tools dating to between 2.6 and 2.0 m.y.a. have been found in Ethiopia, Congo, and Malawi. Scientists have disagreed about their maker, some arguing that only early *Homo* could have made them. Evidence has been presented that *A. garhi* made pebble tools around 2.6 m.y.a. Cultural abilities developed exponentially with *Homo*'s appearance and evolution.

Key Terms

A. afarensis, 129
A. africanus, 134
A. anamensis, 129
A. boisei, 137
A. garhi, 140

A. robustus, 134
Ardipithecus, 120
australopithecines, *128*
gracile, *134*

Homo habilis, 137
Oldowan pebble tools, *137*
robust, *134*

Go to our Online Learning Center website at **www.mhhe.com/kottak** for Internet resources directly related to the content of this chapter.

Chapter 7

The Genus *Homo*

Early *Homo*
    H. rudolfensis *and* H. habilis
    H. habilis *and* H. erectus
Out of Africa I: *H. erectus*
    Paleolithic Tools
    Adaptive Strategies of H. erectus
    The Evolution and Expansion of
        H. erectus
Archaic *H. Sapiens*
    Ice Ages of the Pleistocene
    H. antecessor *and* H. heidelbergensis
The Neandertals
    Cold-Adapted Neandertals
    The Neandertals and Modern People

Modern Humans
    Out of Africa II
    Genetic Evidence for Out of Africa II
    The Denisovans
The Advent of Behavioral Modernity
Advances in Technology
    *Applying Anthropology to Popular
        Culture: So Easy a Caveman Can Do It*
Glacial Retreat
Settling The Americas
Homo floresiensis
    *Anthropology Today: Neandertal
        Cannibalism*

Early *Homo*

As we saw in Chapter 6, at two million years ago, there is East African evidence for two distinct hominin groups: early *Homo* and *A. boisei,* the hyperrobust australopithecines, which became extinct around 1.2 m.y.a. *A. boisei* became increasingly specialized, dependent on tough, coarse, gritty, fibrous savanna vegetation. The australopithecine trend toward dental, facial, and cranial robustness continued with *A. boisei.* However, these structures were reduced as early forms of *Homo* evolved into early *H. erectus* by 1.9 m.y.a. By that date *Homo* was generalizing the subsistence quest to the hunting of large animals to supplement the gathering of vegetation and scavenging.

H. rudolfensis **and** H. habilis

In 1972, in an expedition led by Richard Leakey, Bernard Ngeneo unearthed a skull designated KNM-ER 1470. The name comes from its catalog number in the Kenya National Museum (KNM) and its discovery location (East Rudolph—ER)—east of Lake

Rudolph, at a site called Koobi Fora. The 1470 skull attracted immediate attention because of its unusual combination of a large brain (775 cm^3) and very large molars. Its brain size was more human than that of the australopithecines, but its molars recalled those of the hyperrobust australopithecines. Some paleoanthropologists attributed the large skull and teeth to a very large body, assuming that this had been one *big hominin*. But no postcranial remains were found with 1470, nor have they been found with any later discovery of a 1470-like specimen.

How to interpret KNM-ER 1470? On the basis of its brain size, it seemed to belong in *Homo*. On the basis of its back teeth, it seemed more like *Australopithecus*. There also are problems with dating. The best dating guess is 1.8 m.y.a., but another estimate suggests that 1470 may be as old as 2.4 m.y.a. Originally, some paleoanthropologists assigned 1470 to *H. habilis*, while others saw it as an unusual australopithecine. In 1986, it received its own species name, *Homo rudolfensis*, from the lake near which it was found. This label has stuck—although it isn't accepted by all paleoanthropologists. Those who find *H. rudolfensis* to be a valid species emphasize its contrasts with *H. habilis*. Note the contrasts in the two skulls in the photo below. KNM-ER 1813, on the left, is considered *H. habilis*; KNM-ER 1470, on the right, is *H. rudolfensis*. The *habilis* skull has a more marked brow ridge and a depression behind it, whereas 1470 has a less pronounced brow ridge and a longer, flatter face. Some think that *rudolfensis* lived earlier than and is ancestral to *habilis*. Some think that *rudolfensis* and *habilis* are simply male and female members of the same species—*H. habilis*. Some think they are separate species that coexisted in time and space (from about 2.4 m.y.a. to about 1.7 m.y.a.). Some think that one or the other gave rise to *H. erectus*. The debate continues. The only sure conclusion is that several different kinds of hominin lived in Africa before and after the advent of *Homo*.

H. habilis and *H. erectus*

A team headed by L. S. B. and Mary Leakey found the first representative of *Homo habilis* (OH7—Olduvai Hominid 7) at Olduvai Gorge in Tanzania in 1960. Olduvai's

Meet two kinds of early *Homo*: On the left KNM-ER 1813; On the right KNM-ER 1470. The latter (1470) has been classified as *H. rudolfensis*. What's the classification of 1813?

oldest layer, Bed I, dates to 1.8 m.y.a. This layer has yielded both small-brained *A. boisei* (average 490 cm^3) fossils and *H. habilis* skulls, with cranial capacities between 600 and 700 cm^3.

Another important *habilis* find was made in 1986 by Tim White of the University of California, Berkeley. OH62 is the partial skeleton of a female *H. habilis* from Oldu-vai Bed I. This was the first find of an *H. habilis* skull with a significant amount of skeletal material. OH62, dating to 1.8 m.y.a., consists of parts of the skull, the right arm, and both legs. Because scientists had assumed that *H. habilis* would be taller than tiny Lucy (*A. afarensis*), OH62 was surprising because of its small size and apelike limb bones. Not only was OH62 just as tiny as Lucy (3 feet, or 0.9 meter), its arms were longer and more apelike than expected. The limb proportions suggested greater tree-climbing ability than later hominins had. *H. habilis* may still have sought occa-sional refuge in the trees.

The small size and primitive proportions of *H. habilis* were unexpected given what was known about early **_H. erectus_** in East Africa. In deposits near Lake Turkana, Kenya, Richard Leakey had uncovered two *H. erectus* skulls dating to 1.6 m.y.a. By that date, *H. erectus* (males at least) had already attained a cranial capacity of 900 cm^3, along with a modern body shape and height. An amazingly complete young male *H. erectus* fossil (WT15,000) found at West Turkana in 1984 by Kimoya Kimeu, a collaborator of the Leakeys, has confirmed this. WT15,000, also known as the Nariokotome boy, was a

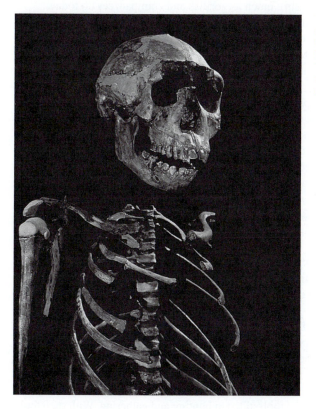

This photo shows the early (1.6 m.y.a.) *Homo erectus* WT15,000, or Nariokotome boy, found in 1984 near Lake Turkana, Kenya. This is the most complete *Homo erectus* ever found.

12-year-old male who had already reached 5 feet 5 inches (1.67 meters). He might have grown to 6 feet had he lived.

Sister Species

Two recent hominin fossil finds from Ileret, Kenya (east of Lake Turkana), are very significant for two main reasons; they show that (1) *H. habilis* and *H. erectus* overlapped in time rather than being ancestor and descendant, as had been thought; (2) sexual dimorphism in *H. erectus* was much greater than expected (see Spoor et al. 2007; Wilford 2007*a*).

One of these finds (KNM-ER 42703) is the upper jawbone of a 1.44-million-year-old *H. habilis*. The other (KNM-ER 42700) is the almost complete but faceless skull of a 1.55-million-year-old *H. erectus*. Their names come from their catalog numbers in the Kenya National Museum–East Rudolph, and their dates were determined from volcanic ash deposits.

These Ileret finds negated the conventional view (held since the Leakeys described the first *habilis* in 1960) that *habilis* and then *erectus* evolved one after the other. Instead, they apparently split from a common ancestor prior to 2 m.y.a. Then they lived side by side in eastern Africa for perhaps half a million years. According to Maeve Leakey, one of the authors of the report (Spoor et al. 2007), the fact that they remained separate species for so long "suggests that they had their own ecological niche, thus avoiding direct competition" (quoted in Wilford 2007*a*, p. A6). They lived in the same general area (an ancient lake basin), much as gorillas and chimpanzees do today.

Given these finds, the fossil record for early *Homo* in East Africa can be revised as follows: *H. habilis* (1.9–1.44 m.y.a.) and *H. erectus* (1.9–1.0 m.y.a.). The oldest definite *H. habilis* (OH24) dates to 1.9 m.y.a. although some fossil fragments with *habilis* attributes have been dated as early as 2.33 m.y.a. The oldest *erectus* may date back to 1.9 m.y.a. as well.

What about sexual dimorphism in *H. erectus*? As the smallest *erectus* find ever, KNM-ER 42700 appears to be one of the rare female representatives of *erectus* found so far, most probably a young adult or late subadult. The small skull suggests that the range in overall body size among *H. erectus* was much greater than previously had been imagined, with greater sexual dimorphism than among chimps or contemporary humans. Human and chimp males are about 15 percent larger than females, but dimorphism is much greater in gorillas, and apparently also in *erectus*. Another possibility is that the (as yet undiscovered) *H. erectus* males that inhabited this lake basin along with this female at that time also were smaller than the typical *erectus* male.

The Significance of Hunting

The ecological niche that separated *H. erectus* from both *H. habilis* and *A. boisei* probably involved greater reliance on hunting, along with improved cultural means of adaptation, including better tools. Significant changes in technology occurred during the 200,000-year period between Bed I (1.8 m.y.a.) and Lower Bed II (1.6 m.y.a.) at Olduvai. Tool making got more sophisticated soon after the advent of *H. erectus*. Out of the crude tools in Bed I evolved better-made and more varied tools. Edges were straighter, for example, and differences in form suggest functional differentiation—that is, the tools were being made and used for different jobs, such as smashing bones or digging for tubers. The more sophisticated tools aided in hunting and gathering. With such tools,

Homo could obtain meat on a more regular basis and dig and process tubers, roots, nuts, and seeds more efficiently. New tools that could batter, crush, and pulp coarse vegetation also reduced chewing demands.

With changes in the types of foods consumed, the burden on the chewing apparatus eased. Chewing muscles developed less, and supporting structures, such as jaws and cranial crests, also were reduced. With less chewing, jaws developed less, and so there was no place to put large teeth. The size of teeth, which form before they erupt, is under stricter genetic control than jaw size and bone size are. Natural selection began to operate against the genes that caused large teeth. In smaller jaws, large teeth now caused dental crowding, impaction, pain, sickness, fever, and sometimes death (there were no dentists). *H. erectus* back teeth are smaller, and the front teeth are relatively larger than australopithecine teeth. *H. erectus* used its front teeth to pull, twist, and grip objects. A massive ridge over the eyebrows (a superorbital torus) provided buttressing against the forces exerted in these activities.

As hunting became more important, encounters with large animals increased. Individuals with stronger skulls had better-protected brains and better survival rates. Given the dangers associated with larger prey, and without sophisticated spear or arrow technology, which developed later, natural selection favored the thickening of certain areas for better protection against blows and falls. The base of the skull expanded dramatically, with a ridge of spongy bone (an occipital bun) across the back, for the attachment of massive neck muscles. The frontal and parietal (side) areas of the skull also increased, indicating expansion in those areas of the brain. Finally, average cranial capacity expanded from about 500 cm^3 in the australopithecines to 1,000 cm^3 in *H. erectus,* which is within the modern range of variation.

Out of Africa I: *H. erectus*

Biological and cultural changes enabled *H. erectus* to exploit a new adaptive strategy— gathering and hunting. *H. erectus* pushed the hominin range beyond Africa—to Asia and Europe. Small groups broke off from larger ones and moved a few miles away. They foraged new tracts of edible vegetation and carved out new hunting territories. Through population growth and dispersal, *H. erectus* gradually spread and changed. Hominins were following an essentially human lifestyle based on hunting and gathering. This basic pattern survived until recently in marginal areas of the world, although it is now fading rapidly. We focus in this chapter on the biological and cultural changes that led from early *Homo,* through intermediate forms, to anatomically modern humans (AMHs).

Paleolithic Tools

The stone-tool-making techniques that evolved out of the Oldowan, or pebble tool, tradition and that lasted until about 15,000 years ago are described by the term **Paleolithic** (from Greek roots meaning "old" and "stone"). The Paleolithic has three divisions: Lower (early), Middle, and Upper (late). Each part is roughly associated with a particular stage in human evolution. The Lower Paleolithic is roughly associated with *H. erectus;* the Middle Paleolithic with archaic *H. sapiens,* including the Neandertals of Western Europe and the Middle East; and the Upper Paleolithic with anatomically modern humans.

The best stone tools are made from rocks such as flint that fracture sharply and in predictable ways when hammered. Quartz, quartzite, chert, and obsidian also are suitable. Each of the three main divisions of the Paleolithic had its typical *tool-making traditions*—coherent patterns of tool manufacture. The main Lower Paleolithic tool-making tradition used by *H. erectus* was the **Acheulian,** named after the French village of St. Acheul, where it was first identified.

As we saw in Chapter 6, Oldowan flaking wasn't done to make choppers (according to a predetermined form). It was done simply to produce sharp flakes. A fundamental difference shows up in the Acheulian tool-making tradition. The Acheulian technique involved chipping the core bilaterally and symmetrically. The core was converted from a round piece of rock into a flattish oval hand ax about 6 inches (15 centimeters) long. Its cutting edge was far superior to that of the Oldowan chopper (see Figure 7.1). The Acheulian hand ax, shaped like a tear drop, represents a predetermined shape based on a template in the mind of the toolmaker. Evidence for such a mental template in the archaeological record suggests a cognitive leap between earlier hominins and *H. erectus*.

Acheulian hand axes, routinely carried over long distances, were used in varied cutting and butchering tasks, including gutting, skinning, and dismembering animals. Analysis of their wear patterns suggests that hand axes were versatile tools used for many tasks, including wood working and vegetable preparation. Cleavers—core tools with a straight edge at one end—were used for heavy chopping and hacking at the sinews of larger animals. Stone picks, which were heavier than the hand ax, probably were used for digging. Hand axes, cleavers, and picks were heavy-duty tools, used for cutting and digging. Acheulian toolmakers also used flakes, with finer edges, for light-duty

FIGURE 7.1 **Evolution in Tool Making**
Finds at Olduvai Gorge and elsewhere show how pebble tools (the first tool at the left) evolved into the Acheulian hand ax of *H. erectus*. This drawing begins with an Oldowan pebble tool and moves through crude hand axes to fully developed Acheulian tools associated with *H. erectus*.

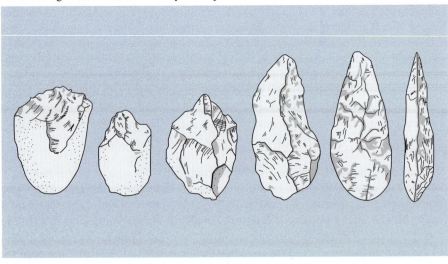

tools—to make incisions and for finer work. Flakes became progressively more important in human evolution, particularly in Middle and Upper Paleolithic tool making.

The Acheulian tradition illustrates trends in the evolution of technology: greater efficiency, manufacture of tools with predetermined forms and for specific tasks, and an increasingly complex technology. These trends became even more obvious with the advent of *H. sapiens.*

Adaptive Strategies of *H. erectus*

Interrelated changes in biology and culture have increased human adaptability—the capacity to live in and modify an ever-wider range of environments. Improved tools helped *H. erectus* increase its range. Biological changes also increased hunting efficiency. *H. erectus* had a rugged but essentially modern skeleton that permitted long-distance stalking and endurance during the hunt. The *H. erectus* body was much larger and longer-legged than those of previous hominins, permitting longer-distance hunting of large prey. There is archaeological evidence of *H. erectus*'s success in hunting elephants, horses, rhinos, and giant baboons.

An increase in cranial capacity has been a trend in human evolution. The average *H. erectus* brain (about 1,000 cm^3) doubled the australopithecine average. The capacities of *H. erectus* skulls range from 800 to 1,250 cm^3, well above the modern minimum.

H. erectus had an essentially modern, though very robust, skeleton with a brain and body closer in size to *H. sapiens* than to *Australopithecus.* Still, several anatomical contrasts, particularly in the cranium, distinguish *H. erectus* from modern humans. Compared with moderns, *H. erectus* had a lower and more sloping forehead accentuated by a large brow ridge above the eyes. Skull bones were thicker, and, as noted, average cranial capacity was smaller. The brain case was lower and flatter than in *H. sapiens,* with spongy bone development at the lower rear of the skull. Seen from behind, the *H. erectus* skull has a broad-based angular shape that has been compared to a half-inflated football and a hamburger bun (Figure 7.2). The *H. erectus* face, teeth, and jaws were larger than those in contemporary humans but smaller than those in *Australopithecus.* The front teeth were especially large, but molar size was well below the australopithecine average. Presumably, this reduction reflected changes in diet or food processing.

Taken together, the *H. erectus* skeleton and chewing apparatus provide biological evidence of a fuller commitment to hunting and gathering, which was *Homo*'s only adaptive strategy until plant cultivation and animal domestication emerged some 10,000 to 12,000 years ago. Archaeologists have found and studied several sites of *H. erectus* activity, including cooperative hunting.

Hearths at various sites confirm that fire was part of the human adaptive kit by this time. Earlier evidence for human control over fire has been found in Israel, dating back to almost 800,000 years ago (Gugliotta 2004). Sites with even earlier claims for fire (around 1.5 m.y.a.) include Koobi Fora, Kenya; Baringo, Kenya; and Middle Awash, Ethiopia. However, none of these early claims has unequivocal evidence for the controlled use of fire. Definitive evidence of human control of fire by 500,000 B.P. has been demonstrated at Cave of Hearths, South Africa; Montagu Cave, South Africa; Kalambo Falls, Zambia; and Kabwe in Zimbabwe. Fire provided protection against cave bears and saber-toothed tigers. It permitted *H. erectus* to occupy cave sites, including Zhoukoudian,

FIGURE 7.2

Rear Views of Three Skulls of *H. erectus* and One of "Archaic" *Homo sapiens* (a Neandertal)

Note the more angular shape of the *H. erectus* skulls, with the maximum breadth low down, near the base.

Source: C. J. Jolly and R. White, *Physical Anthropology and Archaeology*, 5th ed., p. 271. Copyright © 1995. Reprinted by permission of The McGraw-Hill Companies.

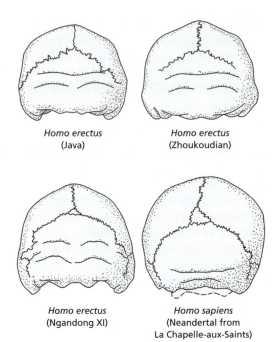

Homo erectus
(Java)

Homo erectus
(Zhoukoudian)

Homo erectus
(Ngandong XI)

Homo sapiens
(Neandertal from
La Chapelle-aux-Saints)

near Beijing, in China, which has yielded the remains of more than 40 specimens of *H. erectus*. Fire widened the range of climates open to human colonization. It may have played a role in the expansion out of Africa. Its warmth enabled people to survive winter cold in temperate regions. Human control over fire offered other advantages, such as cooking, which breaks down vegetable fibers and tenderizes meat. Cooking kills parasites and makes meat more digestible, thus reducing strain on the chewing apparatus.

The Evolution and Expansion of *H. erectus*

The archaeological record of *H. erectus* activities can be combined with the fossil evidence to provide a more complete picture of our Lower Paleolithic ancestors. We now consider some of the fossil data, whose geographic distribution is shown in Figure 7.3. Early *H. erectus* remains, found by Richard Leakey's team at East and West Turkana, Kenya, and dated to around 1.6 m.y.a., including the Nariokotome boy, were discussed previously.

One fairly complete skull, one large mandible, and two partial skulls—one of a young adult male (780 cm^3) and one of an apparent adolescent female (650 cm^3)—were found in the 1990s at the Dmanisi site in the former Soviet Republic of Georgia. They have been assigned a date of 1.7–1.77 m.y.a. There are notable similarities between the two partial skulls and that of the Nariokotome boy from Kenya (1.6 m.y.a.). Chopping tools of comparable age associated with the Kenyan and Georgian fossils also are similar. The most complete skull find is more primitive, with a stronger resemblance to *H. habilis* than is the case with the other Dmanisi fossils. Primitive characteristics of this skull include its large canine teeth and small cranial capacity (Vekua, Lordkipanidze,

FIGURE 7.3 The Sites of Discovery of *Homo erectus* and Its
Probable Maximum Distribution

Source: C. J. Jolly and R. White, *Physical Anthropology and Archaeology,* 5th ed., p. 268. Copyright ©
1995. Reprinted by permission of The McGraw-Hill Companies.

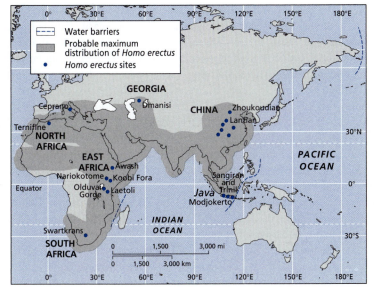

and Rightmire 2002). This specimen may be that of a teenage girl whose skull had not
yet reached full size, but whose canines had. The simplest explanation for the anatomical diversity observed at Dmanisi is that *H. erectus* was at least as variable a species as
is *H. sapiens*. The Dmanisi finds suggest a rapid spread, by 1.77 m.y.a., of early *Homo*
out of Africa and into Eurasia (see Figure 7.3).

The Dmanisi fossils are the most ancient undisputed human fossils outside Africa.
How did those hominins get to Georgia? The most probable answer is in pursuit of meat.
As hominins became more carnivorous, they expanded their home ranges in accordance
with those of the animals they hunted. Meat-rich diets provided higher-quality protein
as fuel. The australopithecines, with smaller bodies and brains, could survive mainly on
plants. They probably used a limited range at the edge of forests, not too deep in or too
exposed far out on the savanna. Once hominins developed stronger bodies and high-
protein meat diets, they could—indeed had to—spread out. They ranged farther to find
meat, and this expansion eventually led them out of Africa, into Eurasia (Georgia) and
eventually Asia (see Wilford 2000).

More recent skeletal finds from Dmanisi suggest how this expansion might have
taken place (Wilford 2007*b*). (Previously only skulls had been found there.) Four new
fossil skeletons show that the ancient Dmanisi population combined primitive skulls and
upper bodies with more advanced spines and lower limbs for greater mobility. These
evolved limb proportions enabled early *Homo* to expand beyond Africa.

In 1891, the Indonesian island of Java yielded the first *H. erectus* fossil find, popu-
larly known as "Java man." Eugene Dubois, a Dutch army surgeon, had gone to Java to

discover a transitional form between apes and humans. Of course, we now know that the transition to hominin had taken place much earlier than the *H. erectus* period and occurred in Africa. However, Dubois's good luck did lead him to the most ancient human fossils discovered at that time. Excavating near the village of Trinil, Dubois found parts of an *H. erectus* skull and a thigh bone. During the 1930s and 1940s, excavations in Java uncovered additional remains. The various Indonesian *H. erectus* fossils date back at least 700,000, and perhaps as much as 1.6 million, years. Fragments of a skull and a lower jaw found in northern China at Lantian may be as old as the oldest Indonesian fossils. Other *H. erectus* remains, of uncertain date, have been found in Algeria and Morocco in North Africa.

H. erectus remains also have been found in Upper Bed II at Olduvai, Tanzania, in association with Acheulian tools. One such find, OH9, dates back perhaps 1.4 million years. African *H. erectus* fossils also have been found in Ethiopia, Eritrea, and South Africa (in addition to Kenya and Tanzania). The time span of *H. erectus* in East Africa was long. *H. erectus* fossils have been found in Bed IV at Olduvai, dating to 500,000 B.P., about the same age as the Beijing fossils.

The largest group of *H. erectus* fossils was found in the Zhoukoudian cave in China. The Zhoukoudian ("Peking"—now Beijing—"man") site, excavated from the late 1920s to the late 1930s, was a major find for the human fossil record. Zhoukoudian yielded remains of tools, hearths, animal bones, and more than 40 hominins, including five skulls. The analysis of these remains led to the conclusion that the Java and Zhoukoudian fossils were examples of the same broad stage of human evolution. Today they are commonly classified together as *H. erectus.*

The Zhoukoudian individuals lived more recently than did the Javanese *H. erectus,* between 670,000 and 410,000 years ago, when the climate in China was colder and moister than it is today. The inference about the climate has been made on the basis of the animal remains found with the human fossils. The people at Zhoukoudian ate venison, and seed and plant remains suggest they were both gatherers and hunters.

What about Europe? A cranial fragment found at Ceprano, Italy, in 1994 has been assigned a date of 800,000 B.P. Other probable *H. erectus* remains have been found in Europe, but their dates are uncertain. All are later than the Ceprano skull, and they usually are classified as late *H. erectus,* or transitional between *H. erectus* and early *H. sapiens.*

Archaic *H. sapiens*

Africa, which was center stage during the australopithecine period, is joined by Asia and Europe during the *H. erectus* and *H. sapiens* periods of hominin evolution. European fossils and tools have contributed disproportionately to our knowledge and interpretation of early (archaic) *H. sapiens.* This doesn't mean that *H. sapiens* evolved in Europe or that most early *H. sapiens* lived in Europe. Indeed, the fossil evidence suggests that *H. sapiens,* like *H. erectus* before it, originated in Africa. *H. sapiens* lived in Africa for more than 100,000 years before starting the settlement of Europe around 50,000 B.P. There were probably many more humans in the tropics than in Europe during the ice

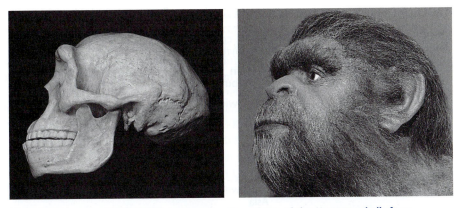

Meet *Homo erectus*. On the left is a reconstruction of one of the *H. erectus* skulls from Zhoukoudian, China. On the right, an attempt to render *H. erectus* in the flesh.

ages. We merely *know more* about recent human evolution in Europe because archaeology and fossil hunting—not human evolution—have been going on longer there than in Africa and Asia.

Recent discoveries, along with reinterpretation of the dating and the anatomical relevance of some earlier finds, are filling in the gap between *H. erectus* and archaic *H. sapiens*. **Archaic *H. sapiens*** (300,000? to 28,000 B.P.) encompasses the earliest members of our species, along with the **Neandertals** (*H. sapiens neanderthalensis*—130,000 to 28,000 B.P.) of Europe and the Middle East and their Neandertal-like contemporaries in Africa and Asia. Brain size in archaic *H. sapiens* was within the modern human range. (The modern average, remember, is about 1,350 cm^3.) (See Table 7.1 and Figure 7.4 for a summary of the major groups.) A rounding out of the brain case was associated with the increased brain size. As Jolly and White (1995) put it, evolution was pumping more brain into the *H. sapiens* cranium—like filling a football with air.

Ice Ages of the Pleistocene

Traditionally and correctly, the geological epoch known as the **Pleistocene** has been considered the epoch of early human life. Its subdivisions are the Lower Pleistocene (2 to 1 m.y.a.), the Middle Pleistocene (1 m.y.a. to 130,000 B.P.), and the Upper Pleistocene (130,000 to 11,000 B.P.). These subdivisions refer to the placement of geological strata containing, respectively, older, intermediate, and younger fossils. The Lower Pleistocene extends from the start of the Pleistocene to the advent of the ice ages in the Northern Hemisphere around one million years ago.

Each subdivision of the Pleistocene is associated with a particular group of hominins. Late *Australopithecus* and early *Homo* lived during the Lower Pleistocene. *Homo erectus* spanned most of the Middle Pleistocene. *Homo sapiens* appeared late in the Middle Pleistocene and was the sole hominin of the Upper Pleistocene.

During the second million years of the Pleistocene, there were several ice ages, or **glacials,** major advances of continental ice sheets in Europe and North America. These periods were separated by **interglacials,** long warm periods between the major glacials.

The Denisovans

In late 2010, based on ancient DNA evidence, scientists identified a hominin group known as the Denisovans as distant cousins to Neandertals (Callaway 2010; Zimmer 2010). The research was led by Svante Pääbo, who in May 2010 had published a complete Neandertal genome. Analyzing the Neandertal genome, Paabo and his colleagues concluded that humans and Neandertals descend from common ancestors that lived in Africa 600,000 years ago. They also found 2.5 percent of the Neandertal genome to be more similar to the DNA of living Europeans and Asians than to African DNA. This finding suggests that Neandertals interbred with AMHs soon after the latter emerged from Africa around 50,000 years ago.

The Denisovans get their name from Denisova, a cave in southern Siberia where their traces (so far only a finger fragment and a wisdom tooth) were found. The Denisovans apparently lived in Asia from roughly 400,000 to 50,000 years ago. Remarkably, scientists have managed to extract the entire Denisovan genome from the finger and the tooth. The common ancestors of Neandertals and Denisovans may have left Africa around half a million years ago. The DNA suggests that the split between ancestral Neandertals and Denisovans happened around 400,000 years ago. The Neandertals spread to the west, eventually reaching the Middle East and Europe. The Denisovans headed east.

Comparison of the Denisovan genome with a spectrum of modern human populations revealed a striking relationship. Melanesians, who inhabit Papua New Guinea and islands northeast of Australia, have inherited about one-20th of their DNA from Denisovan roots. This suggests that after the ancestors of today's Papuans split from other AMHs and migrated east, they interbred with Denisovans (see Callaway 2010). Precisely when, where, and to what extent is unclear.

If the Denisovan range extended from Siberia to South Asia, they must have been a very successful kind of hominin. The wisdom tooth offers the only clues as to what they looked like. It resembles the teeth of neither AMHs nor Neandertals. It has bulging sides and large flaring roots. Only when someone finds the same kind of tooth in a fossil skull, or perhaps even a complete skeleton, will we be able to see what the Denisovans really looked like.

The Advent of Behavioral Modernity

Scientists agree that (1) around six million years ago, our hominin ancestors originated in Africa, and as apelike creatures they became habitual bipeds; (2) by 2.6 million years ago, still in Africa, hominins were making crude stone tools; (3) by 1.7 million years ago, hominins had spread from Africa to Asia and eventually Europe; and (4) sometime around 200,000 years ago, anatomically modern humans (AMHs) evolved from ancestors who had remained in Africa. Like earlier hominins (*Homo erectus*), AMHs spread out from Africa. Eventually they replaced nonmodern human types, such as the Neandertals in Europe and the successors of *Homo erectus* in the Far East.

There is disagreement, however, about when, where, and how early AMHs achieved **behavioral modernity**—relying on symbolic thought, elaborating cultural creativity, and as a result becoming fully human in behavior as well as in anatomy. Was it as much

Body ornamentation, a sign of behavioral modernity. On the left, a man from Papua Barat, Indonesia (island of New Guinea). On the right, a man photographed at Finsbury Park, England. What are the social functions of such ornamentation?

as 165,000 or as little as 45,000 years ago? Was it in Africa, the Middle East, or Europe? What triggered the change: a genetic mutation, population increase, competition with nonmodern humans, or some other cause? The traditional view has been that modern behavior originated fairly recently, perhaps 45,000–40,000 years ago, and only after *Homo sapiens* pushed into Europe. This theory of a "creative explosion" is based on finds such as the impressive cave paintings at Lascaux, Chauvet Cave, and other sites in France and Spain (Wilford 2002). However, recent discoveries outside Europe suggest a much older, more gradual evolution of modern behavior.

Discoveries made in Africa and the Middle East during the last 30 years provide substantial evidence for earlier (than in Europe) modern behavior, in the form of finely made stone and bone tools, self-ornamentation, and abstract carvings. Surveying African archaeological sites dating to between 300,000 and 30,000 years ago, Sally McBrearty and Alison Brooks (2000) conclude that what might appear to be a sudden event in Europe actually rested on a slow process of cultural accumulation within Africa, where *Homo sapiens* became fully human long before 40,000 years ago. At South Africa's Blombos Cave, for example, an archaeological team led by Christopher Henshilwood found evidence that AMHs were making bone awls and weapon points more than 70,000 years ago. Three points had been shaped with a stone blade and then finely polished. Henshilwood thinks these artifacts indicate symbolic behavior and artistic creativity—people trying to make beautiful objects (Wilford 2002).

Earlier excavations in Congo's Katanda region had uncovered barbed bone harpoon points dating back 90,000 to 80,000 years (Yellen, Brooks, and Cornelissen 1995). Anthropologists Alison Brooks and John Yellen contend that these ancient people "not only possessed considerable technological capabilities at this time, but also incorporated symbolic or stylistic content into their projectile forms" (quoted in Wilford 2002).

In 2007 anthropologists reported the discovery of even earlier evidence (dating back to 164,000 B.P.) for behavioral modernity in a cave site at Pinnacle Point, South Africa. The cave yielded small stone bladelets, which could be attached to wood to make spears, as well as red ochre, a pigment often used for body paint. Also significant is the ancient diet revealed by remains from this seaside site. For the first time, we see early representatives of *H. sapiens* subsisting on a variety of shellfish and other marine resources. According to paleoanthropologist Curtis Marean, who led the discovery team, once early humans knew how to make a living from the sea, they could use coastlines as productive home ranges and move long distances (Guyot and Hughes 2007).

Cultural advances would have facilitated the spread of AMHs out of Africa. Such advances had reached the Middle East by 43,000 years ago, where, in Turkey and Lebanon, Steven Kuhn, Mary Stiner, and David Reese (2001) found evidence that coastal people made and wore beads and shell ornaments (see also Mayell 2004*b*). Some of the shells were rare varieties, white or brightly colored. These authors suggest that population increase could have caused changes in the living conditions of these AMHs—putting pressure on their resources and forcing experimentation with new strategies for survival (Kuhn, Stiner, and Reese 2001).

Even a modest increase in the population growth rate could double or triple the numbers and populations of small AMH bands. People would be living nearer to one another with more opportunities to interact. Body ornaments could have been part of a system of communication, signaling group identity and social status. Such communication through ornamentation implies "the existence of certain [modern] cognitive capacities" (Stiner and Kuhn, quoted in Wilford 2002; Kuhn, Stiner, and Reese 2001).

The origin of behavioral modernity continues to be debated. We see, however, that archaeological work in many world areas suggests strongly that neither anatomical modernity nor behavioral modernity was a European invention. Africa's role in the origin and development of humanity has been prominent for millions of years of hominin evolution.

Advances in Technology

In Europe, Upper Paleolithic tool making is associated with AMHs. In Africa, earlier AMHs made varied tools. The terms *Lower, Middle,* and *Upper Paleolithic* are applied to stone tools from Europe. The terms *Early, Middle,* and *Late Stone Age* are applied to materials from Africa. The people who lived at the Klasies River Mouth cave sites in South Africa made Middle Stone Age tools. However, some of the early African tool finds at Blombos Cave and in Katanda are reminiscent of the European Upper Paleolithic. AMHs in Europe made tools in a variety of traditions, collectively known as Upper Paleolithic because of the tools' location in the upper, or more recent, layers of

FIGURE 7.7 **Upper Paleolithic Blade-Tool Making**
Blades are flakes that are detached from a specially prepared core. A punch (usually a piece of bone or antler) and a hammerstone (not shown here) were used to knock the blade off the core.

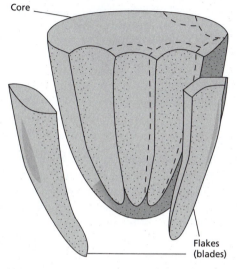

Core

Flakes (blades)

sedimentary deposits. Some cave deposits have Middle Paleolithic Mousterian tools (made by Neandertals) at lower levels and increasing numbers of Upper Paleolithic tools at higher levels.

The **Upper Paleolithic** traditions all emphasized **blade tools.** Blades were hammered off a prepared core, as in Mousterian technology, but a blade is longer than a flake—its length is more than twice its width. Blades were chipped off cores 4 to 6 inches (10 to 15 centimeters) high by hitting a punch made of bone or antler with a hammerstone (Figure 7.7). Blades were then modified to produce a variety of special-purpose implements. Some were composite tools that were made by joining reworked blades to other materials.

The blade-core method was faster than the Mousterian and produced 15 times as much cutting edge from the same amount of material. More efficient tool production might have been especially valued by people whose economy depended on cooperative hunting of mammoths, woolly rhinoceroses, bison, wild horses, bears, wild cattle, wild boars, and—principally—reindeer. It has been estimated that approximately 90 percent of the meat eaten by Western Europeans between 25,000 and 15,000 B.P. came from reindeer.

Trends observable throughout the archaeological record also mark the changeover from the Mousterian to the Upper Paleolithic. First, the number of distinct tool types increased. This trend reflected functional specialization—the manufacture of special tools for particular jobs. A second trend was increasing standardization in tool manufacture. The form and inventory of tools reflect several factors: the jobs tools are intended to perform, the physical properties of the raw materials from which they are made, and distinctive cultural traditions about how to make tools (Isaac 1972).

Other trends include growth in *Homo*'s total population and geographic range and increasing local cultural diversity as people specialized in particular economic activities. Illustrating increasing economic diversity are the varied special-purpose tools made by Upper Paleolithic populations. Scrapers were used to hollow out wood and bone, scrape animal hides, and remove bark from trees. Burins, the first chisels, were used to make slots in bone and wood and to engrave designs on bone. Awls, which were drills with sharp points, were used to make holes in wood, bone, shell, and skin. Upper Paleolithic bone tools have survived: knives, pins, needles with eyes, and fishhooks. The needles suggest that clothes sewn with thread—made from the sinews of animals—were being worn. Fishhooks and harpoons confirm an increased emphasis on fishing.

Different tool types may represent culturally distinct populations that made their tools differently because of different ancestral traditions. Archaeological sites also may represent different activities carried out at different times of the year by a single population. Some sites, for example, are obviously butchering stations, where prehistoric people hunted, made their kills, and carved them up. Others are residential sites, where a wider range of activities was carried out.

With increasing technological differentiation, specialization, and efficiency, humans have become increasingly adaptable. Through heavy reliance on cultural means of adaptation, *Homo* has become (in numbers and range) the most successful primate by far. The hominin range expanded significantly in Upper Paleolithic times.

Glacial Retreat

Consider now one regional example, Western Europe, of the consequences of glacial retreat. The Würm glacial ended in Europe between 17,000 and 12,000 years ago, with the melting of the ice sheet in northern Europe (Scotland, Scandinavia, northern Germany, and Russia). As the ice retreated, the tundra and steppe vegetation grazed by reindeer and other large herbivores gradually moved north. Some people moved north, too, following their prey.

Shrubs, forests, and more solitary animals appeared in southwestern Europe. With most of the big-game animals gone, Western Europeans were forced to use a greater variety of foods. To replace specialized economies based on big game, more generalized adaptations developed during the 5,000 years of glacial retreat.

As water flowed from melting glacial ice, sea levels all over the world started rising. Today, off most coasts, there is a shallow-water zone called the *continental shelf*, over which the sea gradually deepens until the abrupt fall to deep water, which is known as the *continental slope*. During the ice ages, so much water was frozen in glaciers that most continental shelves were exposed. Dry land extended right up to the slope's edge.

The waters right offshore were deep, cold, and dark. Few species of marine life could thrive in this environment.

How did people adapt to the postglacial environment? As seas rose, conditions more encouraging to marine life developed in the shallower, warmer offshore waters. The quantity and variety of edible species increased tremendously in waters over the shelf. Furthermore, because rivers now flowed more gently into the oceans, fish such as salmon could ascend rivers to spawn. Flocks of birds that nested in seaside marshes migrated across Europe during the winter. Even inland Europeans could take advantage of new resources, such as migratory birds and springtime fish runs, which filled the rivers of southwestern France.

Although hunting remained important, southwestern European economies became less specialized. A wider range, or broader spectrum, of plant and animal life was being hunted, gathered, collected, caught, and fished. This was the beginning of what anthropologist Kent Flannery (1969) has called the *broad-spectrum revolution*. It was revolutionary because, in the Middle East, it led to food production—human control over the reproduction of plants and animals, a process to be examined in Chapter 8. In a mere 10,000 years—after more than a million years during which hominins had subsisted by foraging for natural resources—food production based on plant cultivation and animal domestication would replace hunting and gathering in most areas.

Settling the Americas

Another effect of continental glaciation was to expose—during several periods of glacial advance—*Beringia,* the Bering land bridge that once connected North America and Siberia. Submerged today under the Bering Sea, Beringia was once a vast area of dry land, several hundred miles wide. The original settlers of the Americas came from Northeast Asia. Living in Beringia thousands of years ago, these ancestors of Native Americans didn't realize they were embarking on the colonization of a new continent. They were merely big-game hunters who, over the generations, moved gradually eastward as they spread their camps and followed their prey—woolly mammoths and other tundra-adapted herbivores. Other ancient hunters entered North America along the shore by boat, fishing and hunting sea animals.

This was truly a "new world" to its earliest colonists, as it would be to the European voyagers who rediscovered it thousands of years later. Its natural resources, particularly its big game, never before had been exploited by humans. Early bands followed the game south. Although ice sheets covered most of what is now Canada, colonization gradually penetrated the heartland of what is now the United States. Successive generations of hunters followed game through unglaciated corridors, breaks in the continental ice sheets. Other colonists spread by boat down the Pacific coast.

On North America's rolling grasslands, early American Indians, *Paleoindians,* hunted horses, camels, bison, elephants, mammoths, and giant sloths. The **Clovis tradition**—a sophisticated stone technology based on a point that was fastened to the end of a hunting spear (Figure 7.8)—flourished, widely but very briefly, in the Central Plains, on their western margins, and in what is now the eastern United States (Green 2006; Largent

FIGURE 7.8

A Clovis Spear Point
Such points were attached to spears used by Paleoindians of the North American plains between 12,000 and 11,000 B.P. Are there sites with comparable ages in South America?

2007*a*, 2007*b*). Non-Clovis sites dating to the Clovis period also exist, in both North and South America.

Using C^{14} (radiocarbon) dates, where available, for all known Clovis sites, Michael Waters and Thomas Stafford (2007) conclude that the Clovis tradition lasted no more than 450 years (13,250–12,800 B.P.) and perhaps only 200 years (13,125–12,925 B.P.). During this short time span, Clovis technology originated and spread throughout North America. Unknown is whether this spread involved the actual movement of big-game hunters, or the very rapid diffusion of a superior technology from group to group (Largent 2007*b*). Waters and Stafford (2007) also calculate that it would have taken from 600 to 1,000 years for the first Americans and their descendants to travel by land from the southern part of the Canadian ice-free corridor to Tierra del Fuego at the southern tip of South America—a distance of more than 8,680 miles (14,000 km). At least four sites in southern South America have C^{14} dates about the same as the Clovis C^{14} dates. No more than 350 years separate the youngest possible date of those sites from the oldest possible date for Clovis. This would be insufficient time (10–18 human generations) for people to enter North America; adapt to environments ranging from arctic tundra to grasslands, deserts, and rain forests; increase in population; and reach southern South America.

Waters and Stafford conclude there must have been people in the Americas before Clovis. Indeed, an emerging archaeological record supports a pre-Clovis occupation of the New World. For example, non-Clovis tools and butchered mammoth remains dating to 13,500 B.P. and 12,500 B.P. have been found at sites in Wisconsin. People also appear to have been living in South America as much as 1,500 years before Clovis at Monte Verde, Chile (Largent 2007*a*).

Thus, the Clovis people were not the first settlers of the Americas. Evidence for the early occupation of southern South America (along with other lines of evidence) suggests that the first migration(s) of people into the Americas may date back 18,000 years. Analysis of DNA—bolstered, some anthropologists believe, by anatomical evidence—suggests that the Americas were settled by more than one haplogroup—a lineage marked by one or more specific genetic mutations. The various early colonists (as many as four or five haplogroups, according to some anthropologists) came at different times, perhaps by different routes, and had different physiques and genetic markers, which continue to be discovered and debated (see Bonnichsen and Schneider 2000).

Homo floresiensis

In 2004 news reports trumpeted the discovery of bones and tools of a group of tiny humans who inhabited Flores, an Indonesian island 370 miles east of Bali, until fairly recent times (see Roach 2007; Wade 2004). Early in hominin evolution, it wasn't unusual for different species, even genera, of hominins, to live at the same time. But until the 2003–2004 discoveries on Flores, few scientists imagined that a different human species had survived through 12,000 B.P., and possibly even later. These tiny people (fancifully dubbed "hobbits" in the popular press) lived, hunted, and gathered on Flores from about 95,000 B.P. until at least 12,000 B.P. One of their most surprising features is the very small skull, about 370 cm^3—slightly smaller than the chimpanzee average.

A skull and several skeletons of these miniature people were found in a limestone cave on Flores by a team of Australian and Indonesian archaeologists, who assigned them to a new human species, *H. floresiensis.* (Additional specimens have been found and described subsequently; see Gugliotta 2005; Roach 2007.) The discovery of *H. floresiensis,* described as a downsized version of *H. erectus,* shows that archaic humans survived much later than had been thought. Before modern people reached Flores, which is very isolated, the island was inhabited only by a select group of animals that had managed to reach it. These animals, including *H. floresiensis,* faced unusual evolutionary forces that pushed some toward gigantism and some toward dwarfism. The carnivorous lizards that reached Flores, perhaps on natural rafts, became giants. These Komodo dragons now are confined mainly to the nearby island of Komodo. Elephants, which are excellent swimmers, reached Flores, where they evolved to a dwarf form the size of an ox.

Previous excavations by Michael Morwood, one of the discoverers of *H. floresiensis,* estimated that *H. erectus* had reached Flores by 840,000 years ago, based on crude stone tools found there. This *H. erectus* population and its descendants are assumed to have been influenced by the same evolutionary forces that reduced the size of the elephants. The first specimen of *H. floresiensis,* an adult female, was uncovered in 2003, from beneath 20 feet (6.1 meters) of silt coating the floor of a cave. Paleoanthropologists identified her as a very small but otherwise normal individual—a diminutive version of *H. erectus.* Because the downsizing was so extreme, smaller than that in modern human pygmies, she and her fellows were assigned to a new species. Her skeleton is estimated to date back some 18,000 years. Remains of six additional individuals found in the cave date from 95,000 to 12,000 B.P. The cave also has yielded bones of giant lizards, giant rats, pygmy elephants, fish, and birds.

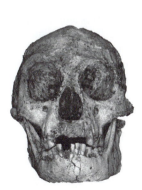
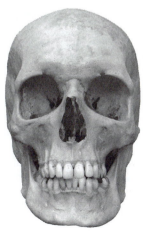

The skull of *Homo floresiensis* (left; modern human, right), a miniature hominid that inhabited Middle Earth, or at least the Indonesian island of Flores, between 95,000 and 12,000 years ago.

Anthropology Today *Neandertal Cannibalism*

Described here is a Spanish cave site where remains of Neandertal bones and tools have allowed scientists to reconstruct ancient social structure and behavior—including cannibalism. This discovery and other recent ones described in this chapter show how anthropologists now routinely use a combination of fossil, archaeological, and DNA evidence to unravel the mysteries of the hominin past.

Deep in a cave in the forests of northern Spain are the remains of a gruesome massacre. The first clues came to light in 1994, when explorers came across a pair of what they thought were human jawbones in the cave, called El Sidrón. . . . The police discovered more bone fragments . . . which they sent to forensic scientists, who determined that the bones . . . were the remains of Neanderthals who died 50,000 years ago.

Today, El Sidrón is one of the most important sites on Earth for learning about Neanderthals. . . . Scientists have found 1,800 more Neanderthal bone fragments in the cave, some of which have yielded snippets of DNA.

But the mystery has lingered on for 16 years. What happened to the El Sidrón victims? . . . Spanish scientists who analyzed the bones and DNA report the gruesome answer. The victims were a dozen members of an extended family, slaughtered by cannibals.

"It's an amazing find," said Todd Disotell, an anthropologist at New York University. Chris Stringer of the Natural History Museum of London said the report "gives us the first glimpse of Neanderthal social structures."

All of the bones were located in a room-size space the scientists dubbed the Tunnel of Bones. They were mixed into a jumble of gravel and mud, which suggests that the Neanderthals did not die in the chamber. Instead, they died on the surface above the cave. . . .

"The bones haven't been scavenged or worn out by erosion," said Carles Lalueza-Fox of Pompeu Fabra University in Barcelona, a co-author of the new paper. Part of the ceiling . . . most likely collapsed during a storm, and the bones fell into the cave. . . .

The only other things scientists have found there are fragments of Neanderthal stone blades. And when the scientists closely examined the Neanderthal bones, they found cut marks—signs that the blades had been used to slice muscle from bone. The long bones had been snapped open. From these clues, the scientists concluded that the Neanderthals were victims of cannibalism. Scientists have found hints of cannibalism among Neanderthals at other sites, but El Sidrón is exceptional for the scale of evidence. . . .

Dr. Lalueza-Fox and his colleagues could identify 12 individuals. The shape of the bones allowed the scientists to estimate their age and sex. The bones belonged to three men, three women, three teenage boys and three children, including one infant.

Once the scientists knew who they were dealing with, they looked for DNA in the bones. The cold, damp darkness of El Sidrón has made it an excellent storehouse for ancient DNA. . . . In two individuals . . . they found a gene variant that may have given them red hair. . . . They were able to identify a Y chromosome in four [individuals]. The scientists had already identified all four of them as males—the three men and one teenage boy—based on their bones.

The scientists then hunted for mitochondrial DNA, which is passed from mothers to their children. . . . The scientists found that seven of them belonged to the same mitochondrial lineage, four to a second, and one to a third.

Dr. Lalueza-Fox argues that the Neanderthals must have been closely related. "If you go to the street and sample 12 individuals at random, there's no way you're going to find seven out of 12 with the same mitochondrial lineage," he said. "But if you go to the birthday party for a grandmother, chances are you'll find brothers and sisters and first cousins. You'd easily find seven with the same mitochondrial lineage."

All three men had the same mitochondrial DNA, which could mean they were brothers, cousins, or uncles. The females, however, all came from different lineages. Dr. Lalueza-Fox suggests that Neanderthals lived in small bands of close relatives. When two bands met, they sometimes exchanged daughters.

"I cannot help but suppose that Neanderthal girls wept as bitterly as modern girls faced by the prospect of leaving closest family behind on their 'wedding' day," said Mary Stiner, an anthropologist at the University of Arizona. . . .

Dr. Lalueza-Fox thinks it may be possible to draw a detailed genealogy of the El Sidrón Neanderthals in the next few years. He also hopes to get a better idea of how they died. The stone blades may provide a clue. They were made from rocks located just a few miles away from the cave. The victims might have wandered into the territory of another band of Neanderthals. For their act of trespass, they paid the ultimate price.

Source: Carl Zimmer, "Bones Give Peek into the Lives of Neanderthals," *New York Times,* December 20, 2010.

H. floresiensis apparently controlled fire, and the stone tools found with them are more sophisticated than any known to have been made by *H. erectus.* Among the tools were small blades that might have been mounted on wooden shafts. Hunting elephants—probably cooperatively—and making complex tools, the Floresians may (or may not) have had some form of language. The suggestion of such cultural abilities is surprising for a hominin with a chimplike brain. The small cranium has raised some doubt that *H. floresiensis* actually made the tools. The ancestors of the anatomically modern people who colonized Australia more than 40,000 years ago may have traveled through this area, and it is possible that they made the stone tools. On the other hand, there is no evidence that modern humans reached Flores prior to 11,000 years ago.

The *H. floresiensis* population at the cave site appears to have been wiped out by a volcanic eruption around 12,000 B.P., but they may have survived until much later elsewhere on Flores. The Ngadha people of central Flores and the Manggarai people of West Flores still tell stories about little people who lived in caves until the arrival of the Dutch traders in the 16th century (Wade 2004).

As reported in 2009, an analysis of the lower limbs and especially an almost complete left foot and parts of the right shows that *H. floresiensis* walked upright, but possessed apelike features (Wilford 2009*a*). The big toe, for example, was stubby, like a chimp's. The feet were large, more than seven and a half inches long, out of proportion to the short lower limbs. These proportions, similar to those of some African apes, have never before been seen in hominins. The feet were flat. The navicular bone, which helps form the arch in modern human feet, was more like one in the great apes. Without a strong arch *H. floresiensis* could have walked but not run like humans.

William Jungers (2009), the anthropologist who led the analytic team, raised the possibility that the ancestor of *H. floresiensis* was not *H. erectus,* as originally had been assumed, but possibly another, more primitive, hominin ancestor (see Wilford 2009*a*).

Summary

1. Compared with late *Australopithecus,* dental, facial, and cranial robustness was reduced in early *Homo, habilis* (1.9–1.44 m.y.a.) and *erectus* (1.9–0.3 m.y.a.). *H. erectus* extended the hominin food quest to the hunting of large animals. *H. erectus,* with a much larger body, had smaller back teeth than *Australopithecus* but larger front teeth and supporting structures, including a massive eyebrow ridge. The Lower Paleolithic Acheulian tradition provided *H. erectus* with better tools. *H. erectus*'s average cranial capacity doubled the australopithecine average. *H. erectus* extended the hominin range beyond Africa to Asia and Europe.

2. Ancient *H. erectus* skulls have been found in Kenya and Georgia (in Eurasia), dating back some 1.77–1.6 million years. At Olduvai Gorge, Tanzania, geological strata spanning more than a million years demonstrate a transition from Oldowan tools to the Acheulian implements of *H. erectus. H. erectus* persisted for more than a million years, evolving into archaic *H. sapiens* by the Middle Pleistocene epoch, some 300,000 years ago. Fire allowed *H. erectus* to expand into cooler areas, to cook, and to live in caves.

3. The classic Neandertals, who inhabited Western Europe during the early part of the Würm glacial, were among the first hominin fossils found. With no examples of *Australopithecus* or *H. erectus* yet discovered, the differences between them and modern humans were accentuated. Even today, anthropologists tend to exclude the Neandertals from the ancestry of Western Europeans.

4. The classic Neandertals adapted physically and culturally to bitter cold. Their front teeth were among the largest to appear in human evolution. The Neandertals manufactured Mousterian flake tools. The changeover from Neandertal to modern appears to have occurred in Western Europe by 28,000 B.P.

5. The ancestors of AMHs (anatomically modern humans) were archaic *H. sapiens* groups, most probably those in Africa. Early AMH fossil finds include Skhül (100,000 B.P.), Qafzeh (92,000 B.P.), Herto (160,000–154,000 B.P.), Omo Kibish (195,000 B.P.), and various South African sites. The Neandertals (130,000–28,000 B.P.) and AMHs were contemporaries, rather than ancestor and descendant. AMHs made Upper Paleolithic blade tools in Europe and Middle and Late Stone Age flake tools in Africa.

6. As glacial ice melted, foraging patterns were generalized, adding fish, fowl, and plant foods to the diminishing big-game supply. During the major glacial phases, land bridges formed, aiding human colonization of new areas, including the Americas.

7. Humans probably entered the Americas no more than 18,000 years ago. Pursuing big game or moving by boat along the North Pacific Coast, they gradually moved into North America. Adapting to different environments, Native Americans developed a variety of cultures. Some continued to rely on big game. Others became broad-spectrum foragers.

8. In 2004 and 2005 scientists reported discoveries of bones and tools of a new hominin species they called *H. floresiensis.* This population of tiny humans lived on the isolated island of Flores in Indonesia. A probable descendant of *H. erectus,* which had settled Flores by 840,000 B.P., *H. floresiensis* is marked by the unusually small size of its body and its chimp-sized skull. There is debate about whether *H. floresiensis* was smart enough to have made the stone tools found in association with the skeletal remains, though there is no evidence that AMHs reached Flores before 11,000 B.P. The *H. floresiensis* remains have been assigned dates ranging from 95,000 to 12,000 B.P.

Key Terms

Acheulian, *148*
anatomically
   modern humans
   (AMHs), *158*
archaic
   H. sapiens, 153
behavioral
   modernity, *162*
blade tool, *165*

Clovis
   tradition, *167*
Cro-Magnon, *158*
glacials, *153*
H. (Homo)
   erectus, 145
Herto, *159*
interglacials, *153*
Mousterian, *156*

Neandertals, *153*
Paleolithic, *147*
Pleistocene, *153*
Upper
   Paleolithic, *165*

Go to our Online Learning Center website at **www.mhhe.com/kottak** for Internet resources directly related to the content of this chapter.

Chapter 8

The First Farmers

The Mesolithic

The Neolithic

The First Farmers and Herders in the
Middle East

Genetic Changes and Domestication

Food Production and the State

Other Old World Farmers

The First American Farmers

*Applying Anthropology to Popular
Culture: McDonald's*

*The Tropical Origins of New World
Domestication*

The Mexican Highlands

Explaining the Neolithic

*Geography and the Spread of
Food Production*

*Anthropology Today: The Early Origin of
New World Domestication*

In Chapter 7, we considered some of the economic implications of the end of the Ice Age in Europe. With glacial retreat, foragers pursued a more generalized economy, focusing less on large animals. This was the beginning of what Kent Flannery (1969) has called the **broad-spectrum revolution.** This refers to the period beginning around 15,000 B.P. in the Middle East and 12,000 B.P. in Europe, during which a wider range, or broader spectrum, of plant and animal life was hunted, gathered, collected, caught, and fished. It was revolutionary because, in the Middle East, it led to food production—human control over the reproduction of plants and animals.

The Mesolithic

The broad-spectrum revolution in Europe includes the late Upper Paleolithic and the **Mesolithic,** which followed it. Again, because of the long history of European archaeology, our knowledge of the Mesolithic (particularly in southwestern Europe and the British Isles) is extensive. The Mesolithic had a characteristic tool type—the *microlith* (Greek for "small stone"). Of interest to anthropologists is what an abundant inventory of small and delicately shaped stone tools can tell us about the total economy and way of life of the people who made them.

By 10,000 B.P. the glaciers had retreated to such a point that the human range in Europe extended to the formerly glaciated British Isles and Scandinavia. The reindeer herds had gradually retreated to the far north, with some human groups following (and ultimately domesticating) them. Europe around 10,000 B.P. was forest rather than treeless steppe and tundra—as it had been during the Upper Paleolithic. Europeans were exploiting a much wider variety of resources and gearing their lives to the seasonal appearance of particular plants and animals. People still hunted, but they stalked solitary forest animals rather than herd species. The coasts and lakes of Europe and the Middle East were fished intensively. Some important Mesolithic sites are Scandinavian shell mounds—the garbage dumps of prehistoric oyster collectors. Microliths were used as fishhooks and in harpoons. Dugout canoes were used for fishing and travel. The process of preserving meat and fish by smoking and salting grew increasingly important. (Meat preservation had been less of a problem previously, in a subarctic environment.) The bow and arrow became essential for hunting water fowl in swamps and marshes, and dogs were domesticated as retrievers (Champion and Gamble 1984). For woodworking, Mesolithic carpenters used new kinds of axes, chisels, and gouges.

Such generalized, broad-spectrum economies lasted about 5,000 years longer in Europe than in the Middle East. Whereas Middle Easterners had begun to cultivate plants and breed animals by 10,000 B.P., food production reached Western Europe only around 6000 B.P. (4000 B.C.E.) and northern Europe 500 years later.

After 15,000 B.P., throughout the inhabited world, as the big-game supply diminished, people had to pursue new resources. Human attention shifted from large-bodied, slow reproducers (such as mammoths) to such species as fish, mollusks, and rabbits that reproduce quickly and prolifically (Hayden 1981). This happened with the European Mesolithic. It also happened at the Japanese site of Nittano (Akazawa 1980), located on an inlet near Tokyo. Nittano was occupied several times between 6000 and 5000 B.P. by members of the *Jomon* culture, for which 30,000 sites are known in Japan. The Jomon people hunted deer, pigs, bears, and antelope and ate fish, shellfish, and plants. Their sites have yielded the remains of 300 species of shellfish and 180 species of edible plants (including berries, nuts, and tubers) (Akazawa and Aikens 1986).

The Neolithic

The archaeologist V. Gordon Childe (1951) used the term "Neolithic Revolution" to describe the origin and impact of food production—plant cultivation and animal domestication. **Neolithic** was coined to refer to new techniques of grinding and polishing stone tools. However, the primary significance of the Neolithic was the new total economy rather than just its characteristic artifacts, which also included pottery.

The transition from Mesolithic to Neolithic occurs when groups become dependent on domesticated foods for more than 50 percent of their diet. Usually this happens after a very long period of experimenting with and using domesticates as supplements to broad-spectrum foraging. The archaeological signature of Neolithic cultures (which are called *Formative* in the Americas) includes dependence on cultivation, sedentary (settled) life, and the use of ceramic vessels.

Neolithic economies based on food production were associated with substantial changes in human lifestyles. By 12,000 B.P., the shift toward the Neolithic was under

"Neolithic" was coined to refer to techniques of grinding and polishing stone tools, like these axes and hammers from Austria, Hungary, and the Czech Republic. Was the new tool-making style the most significant thing about the Neolithic?

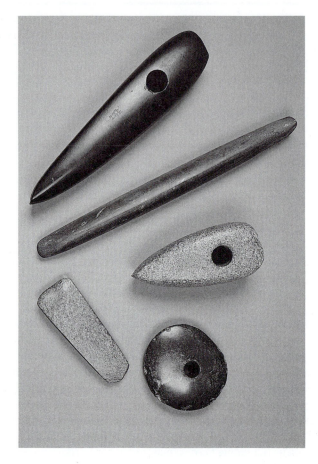

way in the Middle East (Turkey, Iraq, Iran, Syria, Jordan, and Israel). People started intervening in the reproductive cycles of plants and animals. No longer simply harvesting nature's bounty, they modified the biological characteristics of plants and animals as they began to grow their own food. By 10,000 B.P., domesticated plants and animals were part of the broad spectrum of resources used by Middle Easterners. By 7500 B.P., most Middle Easterners had abandoned broad-spectrum foraging for more specialized, Neolithic economies based on fewer species, which were domesticates.

They had become committed farmers and herders. Kent Flannery (1969) has proposed a series of eras during which the Middle Eastern transition to farming and herding took place. The era of seminomadic hunting and gathering (12,000–10,000 B.P.) encompasses the last stages of broad-spectrum foraging. This was the period just before the first domesticated plants (wheat and barley) and animals (goats and sheep) were added to the diet. Next came the era of early dry farming (of wheat and barley) and caprine domestication (10,000–7500 B.P.). *Dry farming* refers to farming without irrigation; such farming depended on rainfall. *Caprine* (from *capra,* Latin for "goat") refers to goats and sheep, which were domesticated during this era.

FIGURE 8.1   The Vertical Economy of the Ancient Middle East

Geographically close but contrasting environments were linked by seasonal movements and trade patterns of broad-spectrum foragers. Traded resources included copper, obsidian, and asphalt, located in particular zones. As people traveled and traded, they removed plants from the zones where they grew wild in the Hilly Flanks into adjacent zones where humans became agents of selection.

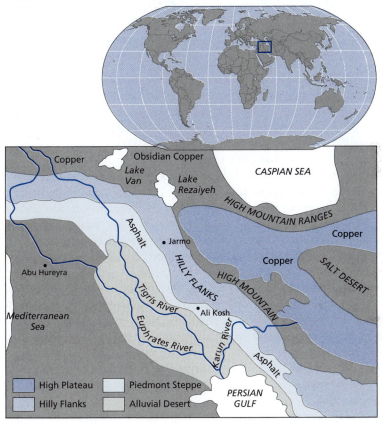

During the era of increased specialization in food production (7500–5500 B.P.), new crops were added to the diet, along with more productive varieties of wheat and barley. Cattle and pigs were domesticated. By 5500 B.P., agriculture extended to the alluvial plain of the Tigris and Euphrates rivers (Figure 8.1), where early Mesopotamians lived in walled towns, some of which grew into cities. (Table 8.1 highlights these stages or eras in the transition to food production in the ancient Middle East.) After more than two million years of stone-tool making, the genus *Homo* was living in the Bronze Age, when metallurgy and the wheel were invented.

TABLE 8.1   The Transition to Food Production in the Middle East

Era	Dates (B.P.)
Origin of state (Sumer)	5500
Increasing specialization in food production	7500–5500
Early dry farming and caprine domestication	10,000–7500
Seminomadic hunting and gathering (e.g., Natufians)	12,000–10,000

The First Farmers and Herders in the Middle East

Middle Eastern food production arose in the context of four environmental zones. From highest to lowest, they are high plateau (5,000 feet, or 1,500 meters), Hilly Flanks, piedmont steppe (treeless plain), and alluvial desert—the area watered by the Tigris and Euphrates rivers (100 to 500 feet, or 30 to 150 meters). The **Hilly Flanks** is a subtropical woodland zone that flanks those rivers to the north (Figure 8.1).

It once was thought that food production began in oases in the alluvial desert. (*Alluvial* describes rich, fertile soil deposited by rivers and streams.) This arid region was where Mesopotamian civilization arose later. Today, we know that although the world's first civilization (Mesopotamian) did indeed develop in this zone, irrigation, a late invention (7000 B.P.), was necessary to farm the alluvial desert. Plant cultivation and animal domestication started not in the dry river zone but in areas with reliable rainfall.

The archaeologist Robert J. Braidwood (1975) proposed instead that food production started in the Hilly Flanks, or subtropical woodland, zone, where wild wheat and barley would have been most abundant (see Figure 8.1). In 1948, a team headed by Braidwood started excavations at Jarmo, an early food-producing village inhabited between 9000 and 8500 B.P., located in the Hilly Flanks. We now know, however, that there were farming villages earlier than Jarmo (Figure 8.1) in zones adjacent to the Hilly Flanks. One example is Ali Kosh, a village in the foothills (piedmont steppe) of the Zagros Mountains. By 9000 B.P., the people of Ali Kosh were herding goats, intensively collecting various wild plants, and harvesting wheat during the late winter and early spring (Hole, Flannery, and Neely 1969).

Climate change played a role in the origin of food production (Smith 1995). The end of the Ice Age brought greater regional and local variation in climatic conditions. Lewis Binford (1968) proposed that in certain areas of the Middle East (such as the Hilly Flanks), local environments were so rich in resources that foragers could adopt **sedentism**—sedentary (settled) life in villages. Binford's prime example is the widespread Natufian culture (12,500 to 10,500 B.P.), based on broad-spectrum foraging. The **Natufians,** who collected wild cereals and hunted gazelles, had year-round villages. They were able to stay in the same place (early villages) because they could harvest nearby wild cereals for six months.

Donald Henry (1989, 1995) documented a climate change toward warmer, more humid, conditions just before the Natufian period. This expanded the altitude range of wild wheat and barley, thus enlarging the available foraging area and allowing a longer harvest season. Wheat and barley ripened in the spring at low altitudes, in the summer at middle altitudes, and in the fall at high altitudes. As locations for their villages, the Natufians chose central places where they could harvest wild cereals in all three zones.

Around 11,000 B.P., this favorable foraging pattern was threatened by a second climate change—to drier conditions. Many wild cereal habitats dried up, and the optimal zone for foraging shrank. Natufian villages were now restricted to areas with permanent water. As population continued to grow, some Natufians attempted to maintain productivity by transferring wild cereals to well-watered areas, where they started cultivating.

In the view of many scholars, the people most likely to adopt a new subsistence strategy, such as food production, would be those having the most trouble in following their traditional subsistence strategy (Binford 1968; Flannery 1973; Wenke and Olszewski 2007). Thus, those ancient Middle Easterners living outside the area where wild foods were most abundant would be the most likely to experiment and to adopt new subsistence strategies. This would have been especially true as the climate dried up. Recent archaeological finds support this hypothesis that food production began in *marginal areas*, such as the piedmont steppe, rather than in the optimal zones, such as the Hilly Flanks, where traditional foods were most abundant.

People would have had no reason to invent cultivation when wild grain was ample to feed them. Wild wheat ripens rapidly and can be harvested over a three-week period. According to Flannery, over that time period a family of experienced plant collectors could harvest enough grain—2,200 pounds (1,000 kilograms)—to feed themselves for a year. But after harvesting all that wheat, they'd need a place to put it. They could no longer maintain a nomadic lifestyle, since they'd need to stay close to their grain.

In the Middle East, sedentary village life developed before farming and herding did. The Natufians had no choice but to build villages near the densest stands of wild grains. They needed a place to keep their grain. Furthermore, sheep and goats came to graze on the stubble that remained after humans had harvested the grain. The fact that basic plants and animals were available in the same area also favored village life. Hilly Flanks foragers built houses, dug storage pits for grain, and made ovens to roast it.

Natufian settlements, occupied year-round, show permanent architectural features and evidence for the processing and storage of wild grains. One such site is Abu Hureyra, Syria (see Figure 8.1), which initially was occupied by Natufian foragers around 11,000 to 10,500 B.P. Then it was abandoned—to be reoccupied later by food producers, between 9500 and 8000 B.P. From the Natufian period, Abu Hureyra has yielded the remains of grinding stones, wild plants, and gazelle bones (Jolly and White 1995).

Prior to domestication, the favored Hilly Flanks zone had the densest human population. Eventually, its excess population started to spill over into adjacent areas. Colonists from the Flanks tried to maintain their traditional broad-spectrum foraging in these marginal zones. But with sparser wild foods available, they had to experiment with new subsistence strategies. Eventually, population pressure forced people in the marginal zones to become the first food producers (Binford 1968; Flannery 1969). *Early cultivation began as an attempt to copy, in a less favorable environment, the dense stands of wheat and barley that grew wild in the Hilly Flanks.*

The Middle East is a region that for thousands of years has had a *vertical economy*. (Other examples include Peru and **Mesoamerica**—Middle America, including Mexico, Guatemala, and Belize.) A vertical economy exploits environmental zones that, although close together in space, contrast with one another in altitude, rainfall, overall climate, and vegetation (Figure 8.1). Such a close juxtaposition of varied environments allowed broad-spectrum foragers to use different resources in different seasons.

Early seminomadic foragers in the Middle East had followed game from zone to zone. In winter they hunted in the piedmont steppe region, which had winter rains rather than snow and provided winter pasture for game animals 12,000 years ago. (Indeed it is still used for winter grazing by herders today.) When winter ended, the steppe dried up. Game moved up to the Hilly Flanks and high plateau country as the snow melted. Pasture land became available at higher elevations. Foragers gathered as they climbed, harvesting wild grains that ripened later at higher altitudes. Sheep and goats followed the stubble in the wheat and barley fields after people had harvested the grain.

The four Middle Eastern environmental zones shown in Figure 8.1 also were tied together through trade. Certain resources were confined to specific zones. Asphalt, used as an adhesive in the manufacture of sickles, came from the steppe. Copper and turquoise sources were located in the high plateau. Contrasting environments were therefore linked in two ways: by foragers' seasonal migration and by trade.

The movement of people, animals, and products between zones—plus population increase supported by highly productive broad-spectrum foraging—was a precondition for the emergence of food production. As they traveled between zones, people carried seeds into new habitats. Mutations, genetic recombinations, and human selection led to new kinds of wheat and barley. Some of the new varieties were better adapted to the steppe and, eventually, the alluvial desert than the wild forms had been.

Genetic Changes and Domestication

What are the main differences between wild and domesticated plants? The seeds of domesticated cereals, and often the entire plant, are larger. Compared with wild plants, crops produce a higher yield per unit of area. Domesticated plants also lose their natural seed dispersal mechanisms. Cultivated beans, for example, have pods that hold together, rather than shattering as they do in the wild. Domesticated cereals have tougher connective tissue holding the seedpods to the stem.

Grains of wheat, barley, and other cereals occur in bunches at the end of a stalk (Figure 8.2). The grains are attached to the stalk by an *axis,* plural *axes.* In wild cereals, this axis is brittle. Sections of the axis break off one by one, and a seed attached to each section falls to the ground.

FIGURE 8.2

A Head of Wheat or Barley
In the wild, the axis comes apart as its parts fall off one by one. The connecting parts (interstices) are tough and don't come apart in domesticated grains. In wild grains, the husks are hard. In domestic plants, they are brittle, which permits easy access to the grain. How did people deal with hard husks before domestication?

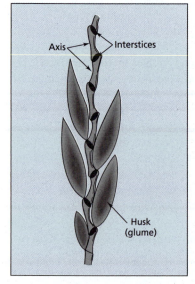

Axis

Interstices

Husk
(glume)

This is how wild cereals spread their seeds and propagate their species. But a brittle axis is a problem for people. Imagine the annoyance experienced by broad-spectrum foragers as they tried to harvest wild wheat, only to have the grain fall off or be blown away.

In very dry weather, wild wheat and barley ripen—their axes totally disintegrating—in just three days (Flannery 1973). The brittle axis must have been even more irritating to people who planted the seeds and waited for the harvest. But fortunately, certain stalks of wild wheat and barley happened to have tough axes. These were the ones whose seeds people saved to plant the following year.

Another problem with wild cereals is that the edible portion is enclosed in a tough husk. This husk was too tough to remove with a pounding stone. Foragers had to roast the grain to make the husk brittle enough to come off. However, some wild plants happened to have genes for brittle husks. Humans chose the seeds of these plants (which would have germinated prematurely in nature) because they could be more effectively prepared for eating.

People also selected certain features in animals (Diamond 1997; Smith 1995). Wild sheep aren't woolly; wool coats were products of domestication. Although it's hard to imagine, a wool coat offers protection against extreme heat. Skin temperatures of sheep living in very hot areas are much lower than temperatures on the surface of their wool. Woolly sheep, but not their wild ancestors, could survive in hot, dry alluvial lowlands. Wool had an additional advantage: its use for clothing.

What are some of the differences between wild and domesticated animals? Plants got larger with domestication, while animals got smaller, probably because smaller animals are easier to control. Middle Eastern sites document changes in the horns of domesticated goats. Such change may have been genetically linked to some other desirable trait that has left no skeletal evidence behind.

Food Production and the State

The shift from foraging to food production was gradual. The knowledge of how to grow crops and breed livestock didn't immediately convert Middle Easterners into full-time farmers and herders. Domesticated plants and animals began as minor parts of a broad-spectrum economy. Foraging for fruits, nuts, grasses, grains, snails, and insects continued.

Over time, Middle Eastern economies grew more specialized, geared more exclusively toward crops and herds. The former marginal zones became centers of the new economy and of population increase and emigration. Some of the increasing population spilled back into the Hilly Flanks, where people eventually had to intensify production by cultivating. Domesticated crops could now provide a bigger harvest than could the grains that grew wild there. Thus, in the Hilly Flanks, too, farming eventually replaced foraging as the economic mainstay.

Farming colonies spread down into drier areas. By 7000 B.P., simple irrigation systems had developed, tapping springs in the foothills. By 6000 B.P., more complex irrigation techniques made agriculture possible in the arid lowlands of southern Mesopotamia. In the alluvial desert plain of the Tigris and Euphrates rivers, a new economy based on irrigation and trade fueled the growth of an entirely new form of society. This was the *state,* a social and political unit featuring a central government, extreme contrasts of wealth, and social classes. The process of state formation is examined in the next chapter.

Around 8000 B.P., communities on Europe's Mediterranean shores, in Greece, Italy, and France, started shifting from foraging to farming, using imported species. By 7000 B.P., there were fully sedentary farming villages in Greece and Italy. By 6000 B.P., there were thousands of farming villages as far east as Russia and as far west as northern France (see Bogaard 2004).

In Pakistan's Indus River Valley, ancient cities (Harappa and Mohenjo-daro) emerged slightly later than did the first Mesopotamian city-states. Domestication and state formation in the Indus Valley probably were influenced by developments in, and trade with, the Middle East. Still, archaeological research confirms the early (8000 B.P.) presence of domesticated goats, sheep, cattle, wheat, and barley in Pakistan (Meadow 1991).

China also was one of the first world areas to develop farming, based on millet and rice. Millet is a tall, coarse cereal grass still grown in northern China. This grain, which today feeds a third of the world's population, is used in contemporary North America mainly as birdseed. By 7500 B.P., two kinds of millet supported early farming communities in northern China, along the Yellow River. Millet cultivation paved the way for widespread village life and eventually for Shang dynasty civilization, based on irrigated agriculture, between 3600 and 3100 B.P. (See Chapter 9.) The northern Chinese also had domesticated dogs, pigs, and possibly cattle, goats, and sheep by 7000 B.P. (Chang 1977).

Discoveries by Chinese archaeologists suggest that rice was domesticated in the Yangtze River corridor of southern China as early as 8400 B.P. (Smith 1995). Other early rice comes from the 7,000-year-old site Hemudu in southern China. The people of Hemudu used both wild and domesticated rice, along with domesticated water buffalo, dogs, and pigs. They also hunted wild game (Jolly and White 1995).

As mentioned, it appears that food production arose independently at least seven times in different world areas. Figure 8.3 highlights those seven areas: the Middle East, north

FIGURE 8.3 **Seven World Areas Where Food Production Was Independently Invented**
Do any of these areas surprise you?

Source: Bruce D. Smith, "Seven World Areas Where Food Production Was Independently Invented," in *The Emergence of Agriculture*, p. 12. W. H. Freeman & Co; New Edition (February 1999). Reprinted by permission of Bruce D. Smith.

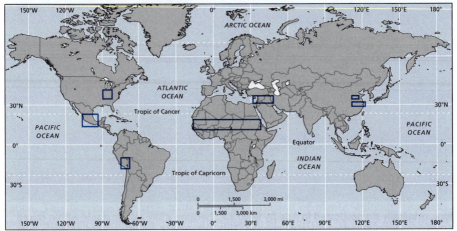

TABLE 8.2   Seven World Areas Where Food Production Was Independently Invented

Source: Bruce D. Smith, "Seven World Areas Where Food Production Was Independently Invented," in *The Emergence of Agriculture*, p. 12. W. H. Freeman & Co; New Ed edition (February 1999). Reprinted by permission of Bruce D. Smith.

World Area	Major Domesticated Plants/Animals	Earliest Date (B.P.)
Middle East	Wheat, barley Sheep, goats, cattle, pigs	10,000
Andean region	Squash, potato, quinoa, beans Camelids (llama, alpaca), guinea pigs	10,000–5000
Southern China (Yangtze River corridor)	Rice Water buffalo, dogs, pigs	8500–6500
Mesoamerica	Maize, beans, squash Dogs, turkeys	8000–4700
Northern China (Yellow River)	Millet Dogs, pigs, chickens	7500
Sub-Saharan Africa	Sorghum, pearl millet, African rice	4000
Eastern United States	Goosefoot, marsh elder, sunflower, squash	4500

China, south China, sub-Saharan Africa, central Mexico, the south central Andes, and the eastern United States. A different set of major foods was domesticated, at different times, in each area, as we see in Table 8.2. Some grains, such as millet and rice, were domesticated more than once. Millet grows wild in China and Africa, where it became an important food crop, as well as in Mexico, where it did not. Indigenous African rice, grown only in West Africa, belongs to the same genus as Asian rice. Pigs and probably cattle were independently domesticated in the Middle East, China, and sub-Saharan Africa. Independent domestication of the dog was virtually a worldwide phenomenon, including the Western Hemisphere. We turn now to archaeological sequences in the Americas.

The First American Farmers

Homo did not, of course, originate in the Western Hemisphere. Never have fossils of Neandertals or earlier hominins been found in North or South America. The settlement of the Americas was one of the major achievements of anatomically modern humans. This colonization continued the trends toward population increase and expansion of geographic range that have marked human evolution generally.

Spreading gradually through the Americas, early Native Americans occupied a variety of environments. Their descendants would independently invent food production, paving the way for the emergence of states based on agriculture and trade in Mexico and Peru. The most significant contrast between Old and New World food production involved animal domestication, which was much more important in the Old World than in the New World. The animals that had been hunted during the early American big-game tradition either became extinct before people could domesticate them or were not domesticable. The largest animal ever domesticated in the New World (in Peru, around like the piedmont steppe. In such marginal zones people started cultivating plants. They were trying to duplicate the dense wild grains of the Hilly Flanks.

4. After the harvest, sheep and goats fed off the stubble of these wild plants. Animal domestication occurred as people started selecting certain features and behavior and guiding the reproduction of goats, sheep, cattle, and pigs. Gradually, food production spread into the Hilly Flanks. Later, with irrigation it spread down into Mesopotamia's alluvial desert, where the first cities, states, and civilizations developed by 5500 B.P. Food production then spread west from the Middle East into North Africa and Europe and east to India and Pakistan.

5. There were at least seven independent inventions of food production: in the Middle East, sub-Saharan Africa, northern and southern China, Mesoamerica, the south central Andes, and the eastern United States.

6. In the New World, the most important domesticates were maize, potatoes, and manioc. The llama of the central Andes was the largest animal domesticated in the New World, where herding traditions analogous to those of the Old World did not develop. Economic similarities between the hemispheres must be sought in foraging and farming.

7. New World farming started in the lowlands of South America, then spread to Central America, Mexico, and the Caribbean islands. Tropical lowland cultivation in Central and South America began at about the same time as food production arose in the Middle East—around 10,000 years ago. By 7000 B.P., farming was diffusing from tropical lowlands into drier regions at higher elevations. The specific ancestor of maize, teosinte, grows wild in tropical southwestern Mexico, where maize probably was domesticated around 8000 B.P. At Oaxaca, in Mexico's southern highlands, maize was gradually added to a broad-spectrum diet by 4000 B.P. Permanent villages supported by maize cultivation arose in the lowlands and in a few frost-free areas of the highlands.

8. Several factors, including a diversity of useful plant and animal species and early sedentism, combined to promote early domestication in the ancient Middle East. The first domesticates spread rapidly across Eurasia, facilitated by climatic similarities across a broad territorial expanse. In the Americas, food production spread less rapidly because of north–south contrasts. Another factor that slowed the Neolithic transition in the Americas was the lack of large animals suitable for domestication.

Key Terms

broad-spectrum revolution, *174*
Hilly Flanks, *178*
maize, *186*
manioc, *186*
Mesoamerica, *179*
Mesolithic, *174*
Natufians, *178*
Neolithic, *175*
sedentism, *178*
teosinte, *188*

Go to our Online Learning Center website at **www.mhhe.com/kottak** for Internet resources directly related to the content of this chapter.

Chapter 9

The First Cities and States

The Origin of the State
Hydraulic Systems
Long-Distance Trade Routes
Population, War, and Circumscription
The Urban Revolution
Attributes of States
Applying Anthropology to Popular
Culture: Royalty Today
State Formation in the Middle East
Urban Life
The Elite Level
Social Ranking and Chiefdoms

Advanced Chiefdoms
The Rise of the State
Other Early States
State Formation in Mesoamerica
Early Chiefdoms and Elites
Warfare and State Formation:
  The Zapotec Case
States in the Valley of Mexico
Why States Collapse
The Mayan Decline
Anthropology Today: The Fantastic
  Claims of Pseudo-Archaeology

The Origin of the State

As food-producing economies spread and became more productive, chiefdoms, and eventually states, developed in many parts of the world. A **state** is a form of social and political organization that has a formal, central government and a division of society into classes. The first states developed in Mesopotamia by 5500 B.P. and in Mesoamerica some 3,000 years later. Chiefdoms were precursors to states, with privileged and effective leaders—chiefs—but lacking the sharp class divisions that characterize states. By 7000 B.P. in the Middle East and 3200 B.P. in Mesoamerica, there is evidence for what archaeologists call the elite level, indicating a chiefdom or a state.

How and why did chiefdoms and states originate? Compared with foraging, food production could support larger and denser populations. Also, the complexity of the division of social and economic labor tended to grow as food production spread and intensified. Systems of political authority and control typically develop to handle regulatory problems encountered as the population grows or the economy increases in scale and diversity. Anthropologists have identified the causes of state formation and reconstructed the rise of several states. A systemic perspective recognizes that multiple factors always contribute to state formation, with the effects of one magnifying those of the others. Although some contributing factors have appeared again and again, no single one is always present. In other words, state formation has generalized rather than universal causes.

Hydraulic Systems

One suggested cause of state formation is the need to regulate *hydraulic* (water-based) agricultural economies (Wittfogel 1957). In certain arid areas, such as ancient Egypt and Mesopotamia, states have emerged to manage systems of irrigation, drainage, and flood control. However, hydraulic agriculture is neither a sufficient nor a necessary condition for the rise of the state. That is, many societies with irrigation never experienced state formation, and states have developed without hydraulic systems.

But hydraulic agriculture does have certain implications. Water control increases production in arid lands. Because of its labor demands and its ability to feed more people, irrigated agriculture fuels population growth. This in turn leads to enlargement of the system. The expanding hydraulic system supports larger and denser concentrations of people. Conflicts over access to water and irrigated land become more frequent. Political authorities may arise to regulate production, as well as interpersonal and intergroup relations. Large hydraulic works can sustain towns and cities and become essential to their subsistence. Regulators protect the economy by mobilizing crews to maintain and repair the hydraulic system. These life-and-death functions enhance the authority of state officials. Thus, growth in hydraulic systems is often (as in Mesopotamia, Egypt, and the Valley of Mexico), but not always, associated with state formation.

Long-Distance Trade Routes

Another theory is that states arise at strategic locations in regional trade networks. These sites include points of supply or exchange, such as crossroads of caravan routes, and places (e.g., mountain passes and river narrows) situated to threaten or halt trade between centers. Here again, however, the cause is generalized but neither necessary nor sufficient. Long-distance trade has been important in the evolution of many states, including those of Mesopotamia and Mesoamerica. Such exchange does develop eventually in all states, but it can follow rather than precede state formation. Furthermore, long-distance trade also occurs in societies where no states developed, such as those of Papua New Guinea.

Population, War, and Circumscription

Robert Carneiro (1970) put forth an influential theory that incorporates three factors working together instead of a single cause of state formation. (We call a theory involving multiple factors or variables a **multivariate** theory.) Wherever and whenever *environmental circumscription* (or *resource concentration*), *increasing population,* and *warfare* exist, suggested Carneiro, state formation will begin. Environmental circumscription may be physical or social. Physically circumscribed environments include small islands and, in arid areas, river plains, oases, and valleys with streams. Social circumscription exists when neighboring societies block expansion, emigration, or access to resources. When strategic resources are concentrated in limited areas—even when no obstacles to migration exist—the effects are similar to those of circumscription.

Coastal Peru, one of the world's most arid areas, illustrates the interaction of environmental circumscription, warfare, and population increase. The earliest cultivation there was limited to valleys with springs. Each valley was circumscribed by the Andes Mountains to the east, the Pacific Ocean to the west, and desert regions to the north and south. The advent of food production triggered population increase, leading to bigger villages in each valley. Colonists split off from the old villages and founded new ones. With more villages and people, a scarcity of land developed. Rivalries and raiding developed among villages in the same valley.

Because the valleys were circumscribed, when one village conquered another, the losers had to submit to the winners—they had nowhere else to go. Conquered villagers could keep their land only if they agreed to pay tribute to their conquerors. To do this, they had to intensify production, using new techniques to produce more food. By working harder, they managed to pay tribute while meeting their own subsistence needs. Villagers brought new areas under cultivation by means of irrigation and terracing.

Those early inhabitants of the Andes didn't work harder because they chose to do so. They were *forced* to pay tribute, accept political domination, and intensify production by factors beyond their control. Once established, all these trends accelerated. Population grew, warfare intensified, and villages eventually were united in chiefdoms. The first states developed when one chiefdom in a valley conquered the others (Carneiro 1990). Eventually, different valleys began to fight. The winners brought the losers into growing states and empires, which eventually expanded from the coast to the highlands. By the 16th century, from their capital, Cuzco, in the high Andes, the Inca ruled one of the major empires of the tropics.

Carneiro's theory is very useful, but again, the association between population density and state organization is generalized rather than universal. States do tend to have large and dense populations (Stevenson 1968). However, population increase and warfare within a circumscribed environment did not trigger state formation in highland Papua New Guinea. Certain valleys there are socially or physically circumscribed and have population densities similar to those of many states. Warfare also was present, but no states emerged. Again, we are dealing with an important theory that explains many but not all cases of state formation.

Early states arose in different places, and for many reasons. In each case, interacting causes (often comparable ones) magnified each other's effects. To explain any instance of state formation, we must search for the specific changes in access to resources and in regulatory problems that fostered stratification and state machinery. We must remember also that chiefdoms and states don't inevitably arise from food production. Anthropologists know of, and have studied, many societies that maintained Neolithic economies without ever developing chiefdoms or states. Similarly there are chiefdoms that never developed into states, just as there are foragers who never adopted food production, even when they knew about it. Recall from the previous chapter those early food producers in what is now the eastern United States who had to keep on hunting and gathering for the bulk of their subsistence because the foods they had domesticated (e.g., sunflower, marsh elder) could not provide a complete diet.

The Urban Revolution

The previous chapter cited V. Gordon Childe's (1951) phrase "Neolithic Revolution" to describe the origin and impact of food production. Childe, probably the most influential archaeologist of the 20th century, chose the term "revolution" deliberately. He wanted to compare the major social transformations of prehistory (food production and the state) to the Industrial Revolution (Smith 2009). He used the term "Urban Revolution" (1950) to describe the major transformation of human life and social institutions examined in this chapter. Key features were that institutions of government, including rulers with real power, emerged for the first time, along with social stratification. As a result of the Urban Revolution, economic activity of all sorts expanded greatly, and the first cities were built. On the downside, former freedoms and independence were replaced by servitude, taxes, rules, and regulations (Smith 2009).

Childe listed 10 key attributes of early cities and states—all revealed by archaeological evidence. They may be paraphrased as follows:

1. The first cities were larger, more extensive, and more densely populated than any previous settlements.
2. Early cities differed from villages in composition and function; within the city were full-time specialist craftsmen, transport workers, merchants, officials, and priests.
3. Each primary producer (e.g., farmer) had to pay a tithe or tax to a deity or a divine king, who concentrated these contributions in a central place, such as a temple or treasury.
4. Monumental buildings distinguished cities from villages, while also symbolizing the right of rulers to draw on the treasury and to command a labor force.
5. Supported by the treasury, priests, civil officials, and military leaders made up a ruling class.
6. Writing was used for record keeping.
7. Predictive sciences developed, including arithmetic, geometry, and astronomy.
8. Sophisticated art styles developed, expressed in sculpture, painting, and architecture.
9. There was long-distance and foreign trade.
10. Society was reorganized on the basis of territorial divisions (where one lived) rather than kinship groups.

Cities and writing were key features of Childe's Urban Revolution. In and after the 1960s, however, anthropologists shifted to such phrases as "the origin of the state," "the rise of the state," and "state formation" for this process. Use of such terms, which continues today, recognizes that some instances of state formation lack writing and significant urbanism (see Peregrine, Ember, and Ember 2007; Spencer and Redmond 2004).

Attributes of States

Childe's list of 10 defining attributes of the Urban Revolution aptly describes the first states in Mesopotamia and Egypt. Something a bit less specific, however, is needed to characterize all states, including those without writing. Most anthropologists today

Early states had hereditary rulers and a military, with the rulers often playing a military role. Rulers stayed in power by combining personal ability, religious authority, economic control, and the privileged use of force. Shown here is a detail from the painted casket of Egypt's Tutankhamun, the famous "King Tut," who ruled between 1347 and 1337 B.C.E.

probably would agree that the following attributes (from Fagan 1996; some shared with Childe's list) distinguish states from earlier forms of society:

1. A state controls a specific territory, such as the Nile Valley or the Valley of Mexico. The state's large expanse contrasts with the much smaller territories controlled by kin groups and villages in prestate societies.

2. Early states had productive farming economies, supporting dense populations, often including cities. The agricultural economies of early states often depended on some form of water control or irrigation.

3. Early states used tribute and taxation to accumulate, at a central place or treasury, resources needed to support hundreds, or thousands, of specialists. These states had rulers, a military, and control over human labor.

4. States are stratified into social classes. In the first states, the non-food-producing population consisted of a tiny elite, plus artisans, officials, priests, and other specialists. Most people were commoners. Slaves and prisoners constituted the lowest rung of the social ladder. Rulers stayed in power by combining personal ability, religious authority, economic control, and force.

5. Early states had imposing public buildings and monumental architecture, including temples, palaces, and storehouses.

6. Early states developed some form of record-keeping system, frequently a written script.

The founders of the United States wanted no king to rule us, and Americans tend to be suspicious of elected officials who act too much like royals. Nevertheless, we share with much of the world a certain fascination with royalty that is expressed in popular culture. What would a girl's imagination or a Disney film be without a princess? Princess Di was one of the 20th century's foremost celebrities. In 2011 millions tuned in to the nuptials of England's Prince William and Kate Middleton, as they did a generation earlier for the wedding of Charles and Diana—whose funeral also was a world event. English actors routinely win Oscar nominations, and frequently the actual award, for portraying kings and queens. Michael Jackson claimed to be the "King of Pop" and named his children accordingly. How do you imagine ancient monarchs were regarded by their people? Do media today treat certain commoners as if they were royalty?

State Formation in the Middle East

In the previous chapter we saw that food production arose around 10,000 B.P. In the Middle East, in the ensuing process of change, the center of population growth shifted from the zone where wheat and barley grew wild (Hilly Flanks) to adjacent areas (piedmont steppe) where those grains were first domesticated. By 6000 B.P., population was increasing most rapidly in the alluvial plain of southern Mesopotamia. (**Mesopotamia** refers to the area between the Tigris and Euphrates rivers in what is now southern Iraq and southwestern Iran.) This growing population supported itself through irrigation and intensive river valley agriculture. By 5500 B.P. towns had grown into cities (Gates 2003). The earliest city-states were Sumer (southern Iraq) and Elam (southwestern Iran), with their capitals at Uruk (Warka) and Susa, respectively.

Urban Life

The first towns arose around 10,000 years ago in the Middle East. Over the generations houses of mud brick were built and rebuilt in the same place. Substantial *tells* or mounds arose from the debris of a succession of such houses. The Middle East and Asia have thousands of such mounds, only a few of which have been excavated. These sites have yielded remains of ancient community life, including streets, buildings, terraces, courtyards, wells, and other artifacts.

The earliest known town was Jericho, located in what now is Israel, below sea level at a well-watered oasis (Figure 9.1). From the lowest (oldest) level, we know that around 11,000 years ago, Jericho was first settled by Natufian foragers. Occupation continued thereafter, through and beyond biblical times, when "Joshua fit the battle of Jericho, and the walls came tumbling down" (Laughlin 2006).

During the phase just after the Natufians, the earliest known town appeared. It was an unplanned, densely populated settlement with round houses and some 2,000 people. At this time, well before the invention of pottery, Jericho was surrounded by a sturdy wall,

FIGURE 9.1   Sites in Middle Eastern State Formation

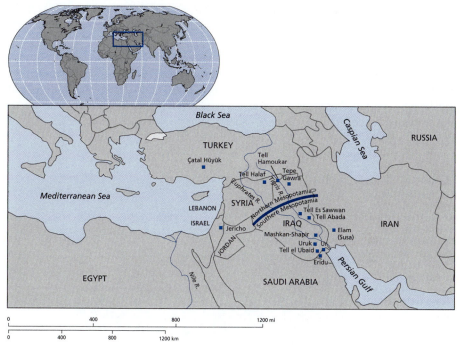

with a massive tower. The wall may have been built initially as a flood barrier rather than for defense. Around 9000 B.P. Jericho was destroyed, to be rebuilt later. The new occupants lived in square houses with finished plaster floors. They buried their dead beneath their homes, a pattern seen at other sites, such as Çatal Hüyük in Turkey (see below). Pottery reached Jericho around 8000 B.P. (Gowlett 1993).

Long-distance trade, especially of obsidian, a volcanic glass used to make tools and ornaments, became important in the Middle East between 9500 and 7000 B.P. One town that prospered from this trade was Çatal Hüyük in Anatolia, Turkey (DeMarco 1997). A grassy mound 65 feet (20 meters) high holds the remains of this 9,000-year-old town, probably the largest settlement of the Neolithic age. Çatal Hüyük was located on a river, which deposited rich soil for crops, created a lush environment for animals, and was harnessed for irrigation by 7000 B.P. Over the mound's 32 acres (12.9 hectares), up to 10,000 people once lived in crowded mud-brick houses packed so tight that residents entered from their roofs.

Shielded by a defensive wall, Çatal Hüyük flourished between 8000 and 7000 B.P. Its individual mud-brick dwellings, rarely larger than a suburban American bedroom, had separate areas reserved for ritual and secular uses. In a given house, the ritual images (wall paintings) were placed along the walls that faced north, east, or west, but never south. That area was reserved for cooking and other domestic tasks. The dwellings at Çatal Hüyük were entered through the roof, and people had to crawl through holes from room to room, somewhat like moving between chambers of a cave.

Two or three generations of a family were buried beneath their homes. In one dwelling, archaeologists found remains of 17 individuals, mostly children. After two or three generations of family burials, the dwelling was burned. The site was then covered with fine dirt, and a floor laid for a new dwelling.

Çatal Hüyük's residents, though living in a town, acted independently in family groups without any apparent control by a priestly or political elite. The town never became a full-fledged city with centralized organization. Just as it lacked priests, Çatal Hüyük never had leaders who controlled or managed trade and production (Fagan 1996). Food was stored and processed not collectively, but on a smaller, domestic scale (DeMarco 1997).

The world's earliest known town was Jericho, located in what is now Israel. Jericho was first settled by Natufian foragers around 11,000 B.P. The round tower in the lower half of this photo dates back 8,000 years.

The Elite Level

The first pottery (ceramics) dates back a bit more than 8,000 years, when it first reached Jericho. Before that date, the Neolithic is called the prepottery Neolithic. By 7000 B.P., pottery had become widespread in the Middle East. Archaeologists consider pottery shape, finishing, decoration, and type of clay as features used for dating. The geographic distribution of a given pottery style may indicate trade or alliance spanning a large area at a particular time.

An early and widespread pottery style, the **Halafian,** was first found at Tell Halaf in the mountains of northern Syria. Halafian (7500–6500 B.P.) refers to a delicate ceramic style. It also describes the period during which the elite level and the first chiefdoms emerged. The low number of Halafian ceramics suggests they were luxury goods associated with a social hierarchy.

By 7000 B.P. chiefdoms had emerged in the Middle East. The Ubaid period (7000–6000 B.P.) is named for a southern Mesopotamian pottery type first discovered at a small site, Tell el-Ubaid, located near the major city of Ur in southern Iraq. Similar pottery has been discovered in the deep levels of the Mesopotamian cities of Ur, Uruk, and Eridu. Ubaid pottery is associated with advanced chiefdoms and perhaps the earliest states. It diffused rapidly over a large area, becoming more widespread than earlier ceramic styles such as the Halafian.

Social Ranking and Chiefdoms

It is easy for archaeologists to identify early states. Evidence for state organization includes monumental architecture, central storehouses, irrigation systems, and written records. In Mesoamerica, chiefdoms also are easily detected archaeologically. Ancient Mexican chiefdoms left behind stone works, such as temple complexes and the huge carved Olmec heads. Mesoamericans also had a penchant for marking their elites with durable ornaments and prestige goods, including those buried with chiefs and their families. Early Middle Eastern chiefs were less ostentatious in their use of material markers of prestige, making their chiefdoms somewhat harder to detect archaeologically (Flannery 1999).

On the basis of the kinds of status distinctions within society, the anthropologist Morton Fried (1960) divided societies into three types: egalitarian, ranked, and stratified. An **egalitarian society,** most typically found among foragers, lacks status distinctions except for those based on age, gender, and individual qualities, talents, and achievements. Thus, depending on the society, adult men, elder women, talented musicians, or ritual specialists might receive special respect for their activities or knowledge. In egalitarian societies, status distinctions usually are not inherited. The child of a respected person will not receive special recognition because of his or her parent, but must earn such respect.

Ranked societies, in contrast, do have hereditary inequality. But they lack **stratification** (sharp social divisions—*strata*—based on unequal access to wealth and power) into noble and commoner classes. In ranked societies, individuals tend to be ranked in terms of their genealogical distance from the chief. Closer relatives of the chief have higher rank or social status than more distant ones do. But there is a continuum of status, with many individuals and kin groups ranked about equally, which can lead to competition for positions of leadership.

Not all ranked societies are chiefdoms. Robert Carneiro (1991) has distinguished between two kinds of ranked societies, only the second of which is a chiefdom. In the first type, exemplified by some Indians of North America's Pacific Northwest, there were hereditary differences in rank among individuals, but villages were independent of one another and not ranked in relation to each other. Exemplifying the second type were the Cauca of Colombia and the Natchez of the southeastern United States. These ranked societies had become **chiefdoms,** societies in which relations among villages as well as among individuals were unequal. The smaller villages had lost their autonomy and were under the authority of leaders who lived at larger villages. According to Kent Flannery (1999), *only those ranked societies with such loss of village autonomy should be called chiefdoms.* In chiefdoms, there always is inequality—differences in rank—among both individuals and communities.

In Mesopotamia, Mesoamerica, and Peru, chiefdoms were precursors to **primary states** (states that arose on their own, and not through contact with other state societies—see Wright 1994). Primary states emerged from competition among chiefdoms, as one chiefdom managed to conquer its neighbors and to make them part of a larger political unit (Flannery 1995).

Archaeological evidence for chiefdoms in Mesoamerica dates back more than 3,000 years. Mesoamerican chiefdoms are easy to detect archaeologically because they were flamboyant in the way they marked their aristocracy. High-status families deformed the heads of their infants and buried them with special symbols and grave goods. In burials, prestige goods show a continuum from graves with many, to less, to none, of precious materials, such as jade and turquoise (Flannery 1999).

The first Middle Eastern states developed between 6000 and 5500 B.P. The first societies based on rank, including the first chiefdoms, emerged during the preceding 1,500 years. In the Middle East, the archaeological record of the period after 7300 B.P. reveals behavior typical of chiefdoms, including exotic goods used as markers of status, along with raiding and political instability. Early Middle Eastern chiefdoms included both the Halafian culture of northern Iraq and the Ubaid culture of southern Iraq, which eventually spread north.

As in Mesoamerica, ancient Middle Eastern chiefdoms had cemeteries where chiefly relatives were buried with distinctive items: vessels, statuettes, necklaces, and high-quality ceramics. Such goods were buried with children too young to have earned prestige on their own, but who happened to be born into elite families. In the ancient village of Tell es-Sawwan, infant graves show a continuum of richness from six statuettes, to three statuettes, to one statuette, to none. Such signs of slight gradations in social status are exactly what one expects in ranked societies (Flannery 1999).

Such burials convince Flannery (1999) that hereditary status differences were present in the Middle East by 7000 B.P. But had the leaders of large villages extended their authority to the smaller villages nearby? Is there evidence for the loss of village autonomy, converting simple ranked societies into chiefdoms? One clue that villages were linked in political units is the use of a common canal to irrigate several villages. This suggests a way of resolving disputes among farmers over access to water, for example, by appeal to a strong leader. By later Halafian times in northern Mesopotamia, there is evidence for such multivillage alliances (Flannery 1999). Another clue to the loss of village autonomy is the emergence of a two-tier settlement hierarchy, with small villages clustering around a large village, especially one with public buildings. There is evidence for this pattern in northern Mesopotamia during the Halafian period (Watson 1983).

Advanced Chiefdoms

In northeastern Syria, near the border with Iraq, archaeologists have been excavating an ancient settlement that once lay on a major trade route. This large site, Tell Hamoukar, dates back more than 5,500 years (Wilford 2000). Its remains suggest that advanced chiefdoms arose in northern areas of the Middle East independently of the better-known city-states of southern Mesopotamia, in southern Iraq (Wilford 2000).

The oldest layer yet uncovered at Tell Hamoukar contains traces of villages dating back 6,000 years. By 5700 B.P. the settlement was a prosperous town of 32 acres (13 hectares) enclosed by a defensive wall 10 feet (3 meters) high . The site had fine pottery and large ovens—evidence of food preparation on an institutional scale. The site has yielded pieces of large cooking pots, animal bones, and traces of wheat, barley, and oats for baking and brewing. The archaeologist McGuire Gibson, one of the excavators, believes that food preparation on this scale is evidence of a ranked society in which elites were organizing people and resources (Wilford 2000). Most likely they were hosting and entertaining in a chiefly manner.

The Rise of the State

In southern Mesopotamia at this time (5700 B.P.), an expanding population and increased food production from irrigation were changing the social landscape even more drastically than in the north. Irrigation had allowed Ubaid communities to spread along the Euphrates River. Travel and trade were expanding, with water serving as the highway system. Such raw materials as hardwood and stone, which southern Mesopotamia lacked, were imported via river routes. Population density increased as new settlements appeared. Social and economic networks now linked communities on the rivers in the south and in the foothills to the north. Settlements spread north into what is now Syria. Social differentials also increased. Priests and political leaders joined expert potters and other specialists. These non-food-producers were supported by the larger population of farmers and herders (Gilmore-Lehne 2000).

Economies were being managed by central leadership. Agricultural villages had grown into cities, some of which were ruled by local kings. The Uruk period (6000–5200 B.P.), which succeeded the Ubaid period, takes its name from a prominent southern city-state located more than 400 miles (644 kilometers) south of Tell Hamoukar (Table 9.1). The Uruk period established Mesopotamia as "the cradle of civilization" (see Pollock 1999).

There is no evidence of Uruk influence at Tell Hamoukar until 5200 B.P., when some Uruk pottery showed up. When southern Mesopotamians expanded north, they found advanced chiefdoms, which were not yet states. The fact that writing originated in Sumer, in southern Mesopotamia, indicates a more advanced, state-organized society there. The first writing presumably developed to handle record keeping for a centralized economy.

Writing initially was used to keep accounts, reflecting the needs of trade. Rulers, nobles, priests, and merchants were the first to benefit from it. Writing spread from

TABLE 9.1 Archaeological Periods in Middle Eastern State Formation

Dates	Period	Age
3000–2539 B.P.	Neo-Babylonian	Iron Age
3600–3000 B.P.	Kassite	
4000–3600 B.P.	Old Babylonian	Bronze Age
4150–4000 B.P.	Third Dynasty of Ur	
4350–4150 B.P.	Akkadian	
4600–4350 B.P.	Early Dynastic III	
4750–4600 B.P.	Early Dynastic II	
5000–4750 B.P.	Early Dynastic I	
5200–5000 B.P.	Jemdet Nasr	
6000–5200 B.P.	Uruk	Chalcolithic
7500–6000 B.P.	Ubaid (southern Mesopotamia)–Halaf (northern Mesopotamia)	
10,000–7000 B.P.		Neolithic

Mesopotamia to Egypt by 5000 B.P. The earliest writing was pictographic, for example, with pictorial symbols of horses used to represent them. Early Mesopotamian scribes used a stylus (writing implement) to scrawl symbols on raw clay. This writing left a wedge-shaped impression on the clay, called **cuneiform** writing, from the Latin word for "wedge." Both the Sumerian (southern Mesopotamia) and Akkadian (northern Mesopotamia) languages were written in cuneiform (Gowlett 1993).

Writing and temples played key roles in the Mesopotamian economy. For the historic period after 5600 B.P., when writing was invented, there are temple records of economic activities. States can exist without writing, but literacy facilitates the flow and storage of information. As the economy expanded, trade, manufacture, herding, and grain storage were centrally managed. Temples collected and distributed meat, dairy products, crops, fish, clothing, tools, and trade items. Potters, metalworkers, weavers, sculptors, and other artisans perfected their crafts.

Prior to the invention of **metallurgy** (knowledge of the properties of metals, including their extraction and processing and the manufacture of metal tools), raw copper was shaped by hammering. If copper is hammered too long, it hardens and becomes brittle, with a risk of cracking. But once heated (annealed) in a fire, copper becomes malleable again. Such annealing of copper was an early form of metallurgy. A vital step for metallurgy was the discovery of **smelting,** the high-temperature process by which pure metal is produced from an ore. Ores, including copper ore, have a much wider distribution than does native copper, which initially was traded as a luxury good because of its rarity (Gowlett 1993).

When and how smelting was discovered is unknown. But after 5000 B.P., metallurgy evolved rapidly. The Bronze Age began when alloys of arsenic and copper, or tin and copper (in both cases known as **bronze**), became common and greatly extended the use of metals. Bronze flows more easily than copper does when heated to a similar temperature, so bronze was more convenient for metal casting. Early molds were carved in stone, as shaped depressions to be filled with molten metal. A copper ax cast from such a mold

Early Mesopotamian scribes used a stylus to scrawl symbols on raw clay. This writing, called *cuneiform*, left a wedge-shaped impression on the clay. What languages were written in cuneiform?

has been found in northern Mesopotamia and predates 5000 B.P. Thereafter, other metals came into common use. By 4500 B.P. golden objects were found in royal burials at Ur.

Iron ore is distributed more widely than is copper ore. Iron, when smelted, can be used on its own; there is no need for tin or arsenic to make a metal alloy (bronze). The Iron Age began once high-temperature iron smelting was mastered. In the Old World after 3200 B.P. iron spread rapidly. Formerly valued as highly as gold, iron crashed in value when it became plentiful (Gowlett 1993).

The Mesopotamian economy, based on craft production, trade, and intensive agriculture, spurred population growth and an increase in urbanism. Sumerian cities were protected by a fortress wall and surrounded by a farming area. By 4800 B.P., Uruk, the largest early Mesopotamian city, had a population of 50,000. As irrigation and the population expanded, communities fought over water. People sought protection in the fortified cities (Adams 1981), which defended themselves when neighbors or invaders threatened.

By 4600 B.P., secular authority had replaced temple rule. The office of military coordinator developed into kingship. This change shows up architecturally in palaces and royal tombs. The palace raised armies and supplied them with armor, chariots, and metal armaments. At Ur's royal cemetery, by 4600 B.P. monarchs were being buried with soldiers, charioteers, and ladies in waiting. These subordinates were killed at the time of royal burial to accompany the monarch to the afterworld.

Agricultural intensification made it possible for the number of people supported by a given area to increase. Population pressure on irrigated fields helped create a stratified society. Land became scarce private property that was bought and sold. Some people amassed large estates, and their wealth set them off from ordinary farmers. These landlords joined the urban elite, while sharecroppers and serfs toiled in the fields. By 4600 B.P., Mesopotamia had a well-defined class structure, with complex stratification into nobles, commoners, and slaves.

Other Early States

In northwestern India and Pakistan, the Indus River Valley (or *Harappan*) state, with major cities at Harappa and Mohenjo-daro, takes its name from the river valley along which it extended. (Figure 9.2 maps the four great early river-valley states of the Old World: Mesopotamia, Egypt, India/Pakistan, and northern China.) Trade and the spread of writing from Mesopotamia may have played a role in the emergence of the Harappan

FIGURE 9.2   **The Four Great Early River-Valley States of the Old World**
By approximately 4000 B.P. urban life had been established along the Tigris and Euphrates rivers in Mesopotamia, the Nile River in Egypt, the Indus and Ganges rivers in India/Pakistan, and the Yellow River in China.

Source: A. M. Craig, W. A. Graham, D. M. Kagan, S. Ozment, and F. M. Turner, *Heritage of World Civilizations, Volume 1 to 1650,* 4th ed., map 1-1. Copyright © 1997. Adapted by permission of Pearson Education, Inc., Upper Saddle River, NJ.

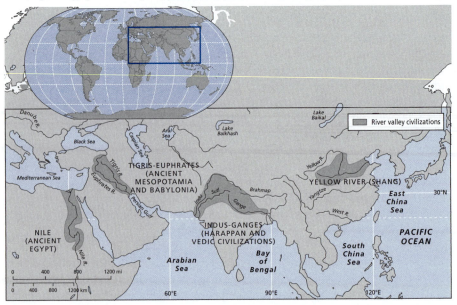

state around 4600 B.P. Located in Pakistan's Punjab Province, the ruins of Harappa were the first to be identified as part of the Indus River Valley civilization. At its peak, the Indus River Valley state incorporated 1,000 cities, towns, and villages, spanning 280,000 square miles (725,000 square kilometers). This state flourished between 4600 and 3900 B.P. It displayed such features of state organization as urban planning, social stratification, and an early writing system, which remains undeciphered. The Harappans maintained a uniform system of weights, and their cities had carefully planned residential areas with wastewater systems. An array of products from sophisticated craft industries included ceramic vessels made on potter's wheels (Meadow and Kenoyer 2000).

The Indus River Valley state collapsed, apparently through warfare, around 3900 B.P. Its cities became largely depopulated. Skeletons of massacre victims have been found in the streets of Mohenjo-daro. Harappa continued to be occupied, but on a much smaller scale than previously (Meadow and Kenoyer 2000).

The first Chinese state, dating to 3750 B.P., was that of the Shang dynasty. It arose in the Huang He (Yellow) River area of northern China, where wheat was the dietary staple. This state was characterized by urbanism, palatial (as well as domestic) architecture, human sacrifice, and a sharp division between social classes. Burials of the aristocracy were marked by ornaments of stone, including jade. The Shang had bronze metallurgy and an elaborate writing system. In warfare they used chariots and took prisoners (Gowlett 1993; Trigger 2003).

Do you detect evidence for urban planning in this photo of Mohenjo-Daro, now in Pakistan? Mohenjo-Daro and Harappa were the two major cities of the ancient Indus Valley civilization that flourished between 4600 and 3900 B.P.

Like Mesopotamia and China, many early civilizations came to rely on metallurgy. At Nok Nok Tha in northern Thailand, metalworking goes back 6,000 years. In Peru's Andes metalworking appeared around 4000 B.P. The ancient inhabitants of the Andes were skilled workers of bronze, copper, and gold. They also are well known for their techniques of pottery manufacture. Their arts, crafts, and agricultural knowledge compared well with those of Mesoamerica at its height, to which we now turn. Note that both Mesoamerican and Andean state formation were truncated by Spanish conquest. The Aztecs of Mexico were conquered in 1519 C.E. (formerly A.D.); and the Inca of Peru, in 1532.

State Formation in Mesoamerica

In the previous chapter we examined the independent inventions of farming in the Middle East and Mesoamerica. The processes of state formation that took place in these areas also were comparable, beginning with ranked societies and chiefdoms, and ending with fully formed states and empires. The first monumental buildings (temple complexes) in the Western Hemisphere were constructed by Mesoamerican chiefdoms in many areas, from the Valley of Mexico to Guatemala. These chiefdoms influenced one another as they traded materials, such as obsidian, shells, jade, and pottery. (Figure 9.3 maps major sites in the emergence of Mesoamerican food production, chiefdoms, and states.)

Early Chiefdoms and Elites

The Olmec built a series of ritual centers on Mexico's southern Gulf Coast between 3,200 and 2,500 years ago. Three of these centers, each from a different century, are known. Earthen mounds were grouped into plaza complexes, presumably for religious use. Such centers show that Olmec chiefs could marshal human labor to construct such mounds. The Olmec also were master sculptors; they carved massive stone heads, perhaps as images of their chiefs or their ancestors.

The Olmec are famous for those carved images, but other early Mexican chiefdoms also had accomplished artists and builders, who used adobes and lime plaster and constructed stone buildings, precisely oriented 8 degrees north of east. The period between 3200 and 3000 B.P. was one of rapid social change in Mexico. Mesoamerica's chiefdoms were linked by trade and exchange. Many competing chiefly centers were intensifying agriculture, exchanging trade goods, and borrowing ideas, including art motifs and styles, from each other. Archaeologists now believe it was the *intensity of competitive interaction*—rather than the supremacy of any one chiefdom—that made social change so rapid. The social and political landscape of Mexico around 3000 B.P. was one in which 25 or so chiefly centers were (1) sufficiently separate and autonomous to adapt to local zones and conditions; and (2) sufficiently interacting and competitive to borrow and incorporate new ideas and innovations as they arose in other regions (Flannery and Marcus 2000).

It used to be thought that a single chiefdom could become a state on its own. Archaeologists know now that state formation involves one chiefdom incorporating several others into the emerging state it controls, and making changes in its own infrastructure

FIGURE 9.3   **Major Sites in the Emergence of Food Production and the State in Mesoamerica**

Source: C. J. Jolly and R. White, *Physical Anthropology and Archaeology*, 5th ed., p. 115. Copyright © 1995. Reprinted by permission of the McGraw-Hill Companies.

as it acquires and holds on to new territories, followers, and goods. Warfare and attracting followers are two key elements in state formation.

Many chiefdoms have dense populations, intensive agriculture, and settlement hierarchies that include hamlets, villages, and perhaps towns. These factors pave the way for greater social and political complexity. Political leaders emerge, and military success (in raiding) often solidifies their position. Such figures attract lots of followers, who are loyal to their leader. Success in warfare leads to states becoming even more densely occupied and in control of new lands. States, unlike chiefdoms, can acquire labor and land

and hold on to them. States have armies, warfare, developed political hierarchies, law codes, and military force, which can be used in fact or as a threat.

The Olmec and Oaxaca were just two of many flamboyant early Mexican chiefdoms. Oaxaca and other highland areas eventually came to overshadow the Olmec area and the Mesoamerican lowlands in general. The first Mesoamerican state, **Zapotec,** had developed from a chiefdom in Mexico's Valley of Oaxaca by about 2100 B.P. The Zapotecs developed a distinctive art style, perfected at the capital city of Monte Alban. The Zapotec state lasted until it—along with the rest of Mexico—was conquered by Spain (see Blanton 1999; Marcus and Flannery 1996). Warfare played a key role in its formation.

Warfare and State Formation: The Zapotec Case

The city of Monte Alban served as capital of the Zapotec *polity* (political unit, such as a chiefdom or a state) for *twelve hundred years,* between 500 B.C.E. and 700 C.E. (The Zapotec polity was a chiefdom from ca. 500 B.C.E. to 100 B.C.E., and after that a state.) Kent Flannery and Joyce Marcus (2003*b*) describe the archaeological evidence for changing warfare patterns in Oaxaca—from early raiding among sedentary villages to warfare aimed at conquest between 330 and 20 B.C.E. (formerly B.C.).

The oldest defensive palisade in the Valley of Oaxaca dates back to over 3,000 years, just a few centuries after village life had been established there. Over the next millennium, raiding evolved into war, with homes and temples burned, captives killed, and populations relocating to defensible hills. A monument from the site of San José Mogote, dating no later than 2500 B.P. (500 B.C.E.), is the earliest reliably dated monument with writing in Mesoamerica. It depicts a named, sacrificed captive, likely a rival chief and a probable victim of intervillage raiding. Armed conflict in Oaxaca began as raiding, with killing, burning, and captive taking but no permanent acquisition of territory. By the time the Spanish conquistadors arrived in the 16th century, the Zapotec-speaking inhabitants of the Valley of Oaxaca (no longer centered at Monte Alban) had armies with noble officers and commoner foot soldiers. They waged wars that exacted tribute from conquered territories (Flannery and Marcus 2003*b*).

The shift from raiding to warfare aimed at territorial conquest occurred prior to 300 B.C.E. This shift is documented not only by hieroglyphs but also by survey and excavation in areas that were targets of Monte Alban's expansionistic designs. As Charles Spencer (2003) notes of Oaxaca, evidence for the earliest conquest warfare occurs simultaneously with evidence for emerging state organization. This co-occurrence supports the idea of a causal link between conquest warfare and state formation.

Long ago, Henry Wright (1977) described the state as a society with not only a centralized but also an internally specialized, administrative organization—a bureaucracy. Chiefdoms, by contrast, lack administrative specialization. States have at least four levels of decision making (Wright 1977). The center or capital establishes subsidiary administrative centers. The result is a nested lattice of secondary, tertiary, and even quaternary centers. Population size tends to follow this administrative structure: States typically have at least a four-level hierarchy of settlements according to both administrative functions and population size. Chiefdoms have no more than three levels (Spencer 2003).

To expand, a state must send delegates, such as soldiers, governors, and other officials, to subjugate and rule in distant territories. Lacking a group of bureaucrats, chiefdoms

Three of more than 300 carved stones depicting slain war captives at the important archaeological site of Monte Alban, Oaxaca, Mexico. Dated to 500–400 B.C.E., these images originally were set in the Prisoner Gallery of Monte Alban's Building L. This huge display of slain enemies was a form of political and military propaganda. The carved stones warned potential rivals what would happen if they defied Monte Alban.

can't do this, which means that the geographic range of chiefly authority is smaller than in a state. According to Spencer (2003), the limit of a chiefdom's range is half a day's travel from its center. States, however, can transcend such limits and carry out long-distance conquests. Archaeological evidence for conquest warfare includes burned and abandoned villages, specialized forts and administrative outposts, and forced changes in the economic, social, and religious behaviors of subjugated peoples.

Expansion through conquest can play a key role in the formation of a primary state by building the administrative hierarchy. Subjugation of polities in other regions, coupled with regularized tribute exaction, can bring about a transition from chiefdom to state (Spencer 2003). For such a strategy to succeed (especially when the conquered polities lie more than a half-day's trip away), the leadership will have to dispatch agents to the conquered areas. Generals and bureaucrats are needed not only to carry out the subjugation but also to maintain long-term control and to manage tribute collection. Given its need to rely on distant representatives, the central leadership promotes internal administrative specialization and loyalty (and thus bureaucratic proliferation). Tribute provides new resources to support this administrative transformation. Archaeological data from Oaxaca confirm that the conquest of distant polities and bureaucratic growth were integral parts of the process of Zapotec primary state formation.

Typically, state bureaucracies occupy a group of administrative buildings, especially at the capital. Surrounding the Main Plaza at Monte Alban were specialized buildings, including palaces, temples, and ball courts. Of these, the palace is an especially useful diagnostic of state organization. Hieroglyphs on a building in Monte Alban's Main Plaza record the bringing of outlying areas under Monte Alban's control, often by conquest. There is archaeological evidence at Cañada de Cuicatlán (a two-day walk north of Monte Alban) for Zapotec conquest around 300 B.C.E. Evidence of outright colonization has been found in the Sola Valley, a two-day walk southwest of Monte Alban. The Zapotec also claimed control of the Tututepec area on Oaxaca's Pacific coast.

Monte Alban did not expand its rule in a gradual, concentric fashion. Although it managed to subjugate distant regions to the north, west, and southwest by approximately

300 B.C.E., certain areas to the east and south managed to resist for centuries. For example, Monte Alban attacked and burned its chief local rival, San Martín Tilcajete, only a day's travel to the south, around 330 B.C.E., but the local inhabitants refused to capitulate. They rebuilt their community and constructed defensive walls at a higher location, El Palenque. These people continued to resist Monte Alban until roughly 20 B.C.E., when they finally were conquered.

Evidence for co-occurrence of Monte Alban's conquest strategy with the emerging Zapotec state offers strong support for the expansionist model of primary state formation. That state had formed by 30–20 B.C.E., with a four-tier, site-size settlement hierarchy: royal palaces and two-room state temples. Monte Alban built its own secondary administrative center on a hilltop above the ruins of El Palenque (Elson 2007). After centuries of dominating the region, Monte Alban eventually lost its central role as capital. After 700 C.E., the Zapotec state dissolved into a series of smaller centers or principalities—alternately vying for supremacy through continued warfare and forming peaceful alliances through marriage (Flannery and Marcus 2003a; Marcus 1989).

States in the Valley of Mexico

During the first century C.E., the Valley of Mexico, located in the highlands where Mexico City now stands, came to prominence in Mesoamerican state formation. In this large valley, **Teotihuacan** flourished between 1900 and 1300 B.P. (100 and 700 C.E.).

The Valley of Mexico is a large basin surrounded by mountains. The valley has rich volcanic soils, but rainfall isn't always reliable. The northern part of the valley, where the huge city and state of Teotihuacan eventually arose, is colder and drier than the south. Frosts there limited farming until quick-growing varieties of maize were developed. Until 2500 B.P., most people lived in the warmer and wetter southern part of the valley, where rainfall made farming possible. After 2500 B.P., new maize varieties and small-scale irrigation appeared. Population increased and began to spread north.

By 1 C.E. Teotihuacan was a town of 10,000 people. It governed a territory of a few thousand square kilometers and perhaps 50,000 people (Parsons 1974). Teotihuacan's growth reflected its agricultural potential. Perpetual springs permitted irrigation of a large alluvial plain. Rural farmers supplied food for the growing urban population. By this time, a clear **settlement hierarchy** had emerged. This is a ranked series of communities that differ in size, function, and building types. The settlements at the top of the hierarchy were political and religious centers. Those at the bottom were rural villages.

Along with state organization went large-scale irrigation, status differentiation, and complex architecture. Teotihuacan thrived between 100 and 700 C.E. It grew as a planned city built on a grid pattern, with the Pyramid of the Sun at its center. By 500 C.E., the population of Teotihuacan had reached 130,000, making it larger than imperial Rome. Farmers were one of its diverse specialized groups, along with artisans, merchants, and political, religious, and military personnel.

After 700 C.E. Teotihuacan declined in size and power. By 900 C.E. its population had shrunk to 30,000. Between 900 and 1200 C.E., the Toltec period, the population scattered, and small cities and towns sprang up throughout the valley. People also left the Valley of Mexico to live in larger cities—like Tula, the Toltec capital—on its edge (see Figure 9.3).

Population increase (including immigration by the ancestors of the Aztecs) and urban growth returned to the Valley of Mexico between 1200 and 1520 C.E. During the **Aztec** period (1325 to 1520 C.E.) there were several cities, the largest of which—Tenochtitlan, the capital—may have surpassed Teotihuacan at its height. A dozen Aztec towns had more than 10,000 people. Fueling this population growth was intensification of agriculture, particularly in the southern part of the valley, where the drainage of lake bottoms and swamps added new cultivable land (Parsons 1976).

Another factor in the renaissance of the Valley of Mexico was trade. Local manufacture created products for a series of markets. The major towns and markets were located on the lake shores, with easy access to canoe traffic. The Aztec capital stood on an island in the lake. In Tenochtitlan, the production of luxury goods was more prestigious and more highly organized than that of pottery, basket making, and weaving. Luxury producers, such as stone workers, feather workers, and gold- and silversmiths, occupied a special position in Aztec society. The manufacture of luxury goods for export was an important part of the economy of the Aztec capital (Hassig 1985; Santley 1985).

Why States Collapse

States can be fragile and decomposable, falling apart along the same cleavage lines (e.g., regional political units) that were forged together to form the state originally. Various factors could threaten their economies and political institutions. Invasion, disease, famine, or prolonged drought could upset the balance. A state's citizens might harm the environment, usually with economic costs. For example, farmers and smelters might cut down trees. Such deforestation promotes erosion and leads to a decline in the water supply. Overuse of land may deplete the soil of the nutrients needed to grow crops.

The Mayan Decline

Generations of scholars have debated the decline of classic Mayan civilization around 900 C.E. Classic Mayan culture, featuring several competing states, flourished between 300 and 900 C.E. in parts of what are now Mexico, Honduras, El Salvador, Guatemala, and Belize. The ancient Maya are known for their monuments (temples and pyramids), calendars, mathematics, and hieroglyphic writing.

Archaeological clues to Mayan decline have been found at Copán, in western Honduras. This classic Mayan royal center, the largest site in the southeastern part of the Mayan area, covered 29 acres. It was built on an artificial terrace overlooking the Copán River. Its rulers inscribed their monuments with accounts of their coronation, their lineage history, and reports of important battles. The Maya dated their monuments with the names of kings and when they reigned. One monument at Copán was intended to be the ruler's throne platform, but only one side had been finished. The monument bears a date, 822 C.E., in a section of unfinished text. Copán has no monuments with later dates. The site probably was abandoned by 830 C.E.

Environmental factors implicated in Copán's demise may have included erosion and soil exhaustion due to overpopulation and overfarming. Overfarming contributes to deforestation and erosion. Hillside farmhouses in particular had debris from

The major archaeological site of Tikal in Guatemala.

erosion—erosion probably caused by overfarming of the hillsides that began as early as 750 C.E.—that caused many farm sites to be abandoned, with some eventually buried by erosion debris. Food stress and malnutrition were clearly present at Copán, where 80 percent of the buried skeletons display signs of anemia, due to iron deficiency. One skull shows anemia severe enough to have been the cause of death. Even the nobility were malnourished. One noble skull, known to be such from its carved teeth and cosmetic deformation, also has telltale signs of anemia: spongy areas at its rear (Annenberg/CPB Exhibits 2000).

Just as the origins of states, and their causes, are diverse, so are the reasons for state decline. The Mayan state was not as powerful as once was assumed; it was fragile and vulnerable. Increased warfare and political competition destabilized many of its dynasties and governments. Archaeologists now stress the role of warfare in Mayan state decline. Hieroglyphic texts document increased warfare among many Mayan cities. From the period just before the collapse, there is archaeological evidence for increased concern with fortifications (moats, ditches, walls, and palisades) and moving to defensible locations. Archaeologists have evidence of the burning of structures, the projectile points from spears, and some of the bodies of those killed. Some sites were abandoned, with the people fleeing into the forests to occupy perishable huts. (Copán, as we have seen, was depopulated soon after 822 C.E.) Archaeologists now believe that social, political, and military upheaval and competition had as much as or more to do with the Mayan decline and abandonment of cities than did natural environmental factors (Marcus, personal communication).

Anthropology Today *The Fantastic Claims of Pseudo-Archeology*

Interest in prehistory has spawned numerous popular-culture creations, including movies, TV programs, and books. In fictional works, the anthropologists don't bear much resemblance to their real-life counterparts. Unlike Indiana Jones, normal and reputable archaeologists don't go around fighting Nazis, lashing whips, or seizing antiquities. The archaeologist's profession isn't a matter of raiding lost arks, going on crusades, or finding crystal skulls, but of reconstructing ancient lifeways through the careful and systematic analysis of material remains.

Over the generations the media have exposed us to the pseudoscientific theories of such popular writers as Thor Heyerdahl (1971), Erich von Daniken (1971), and Graham Hancock (2011)—none of them a professional archaeologist. Heyerdahl argued that developments in one world area (e.g., Mesoamerica) were based on ideas borrowed from somewhere else (e.g., Egypt). Von Daniken carried diffusionism several steps further, proposing that major human achievements were created or assisted by extraterrestrials. These writers share a degree of contempt for human inventiveness. They assume that major features of the ancient human landscape were beyond the capabilities of people actually living in the places where the achievements occurred.

In *The Ra Expeditions*, world traveler and adventurer Heyerdahl (1971) argued that his voyage in a papyrus boat from the Mediterranean to the Caribbean demonstrated that ancient Egyptians could have navigated to the New World. (The boat was modeled on an ancient Egyptian vessel, but Heyerdahl and his crew had with them such modern conveniences as a radio and canned goods.) Heyerdahl maintained that given the possibility of ancient transatlantic travel, Old World people could have influenced the emergence of civilization in the Americas. In *Fingerprints of the Gods* (2011) and other books aimed at popular audiences, writer-journalist Graham Hancock has advanced a series of fantastic claims, including that Africans influenced the Olmecs (because of, in his opinion, African-looking faces in Olmec sculpture).

The University of Michigan offers a popular undergraduate class titled Frauds and Fantastic Claims in Archaeology. The course examines and debunks popular media theories that archaeologists view as fringe or pseudoscientific. Especially problematic are claims that cultural

Sarajevo-born American Semir Osmanagic claims to have discovered a giant pyramid built by an ancient civilization under Visocica Hill, Bosnia. Most scientists doubt his claim.

continued

Anthropology Today *continued*

achievements by indigenous peoples result from contact with superior beings. The course exposes the logical flaws and questionable evidence used to support such claims. Its textbook is Kenneth L. Feder's *Frauds, Myths, and Mysteries: Science and Pseudoscience in Archaeology* (2011)—a must for any reader wanting to pursue this topic further.

Pseudo-archaeologists often have trouble with chronology. We've seen in this chapter that, around 2,000 years ago, states fully comparable to those of Mesopotamia and Egypt began to rise and fall in the Mexican highlands. This occurred about 1,500 years after the major period of Egyptian pyramid building. If Egypt did contribute to Mesoamerican civilization, we would expect this influence to have been exerted during Egypt's heyday as an ancient power—not 1,500 years later. There is, however, no archaeological evidence for trans-Atlantic contact at either time.

There is, on the other hand, abundant archaeological evidence for the gradual emergence of food production and the state in the Middle East, in Mesoamerica, and in Peru. This evidence effectively counters the diffusionist theories and other fantastic claims about how and why human achievements, including farming and the state, began. Popular theories to the contrary, changes, advances, and setbacks in ancient American social life were the products of the ideas and activities of Native Americans themselves.

Neither Mexico nor Peru has yielded a shred of accepted archaeological evidence for Old World interference prior to the European Age of Discovery, which began late in the 15th century. Francisco Pizarro conquered Peru's Inca state in 1532, 11 years after its Mesoamerican counterpart, Tenochtitlan, the Aztec capital, fell to Spanish conquistadors. (We do have abundant archaeological, as well as written, evidence for this contact between Europeans and Native Americans.)

The archaeological record also casts doubt on contentions that the advances of earthlings came with extraterrestrial help. Abundant, well-analyzed archaeological data from the Middle East, Mesoamerica, and Peru tell a clear story. Food production and the state were not brilliant secrets, discoveries, or inventions that humans needed to learn or borrow from outsiders. They were long-term developments, gradual processes with down-to-earth causes and effects. They required thousands of years of orderly change, not some chance meeting in the high Andes between an ancient Inca chief and a beneficent Johnny Appleseed from Aldebaran.

Occasionally, fantastic claims about prehistory *exaggerate*, rather than deny, the abilities of ancient humans. One example is when pseudo-archaeologists claim that Paleolithic societies could have constructed monumental structures. Writer-journalist Graham Hancock, for example, has suggested that an Upper Paleolithic civilization, rather than ancient Egyptians, built Egypt's great Sphinx, some 7,000 years earlier than its actual construction date (Hancock and Bauval 1996). Semir Osmanagic is a Bosnian amateur archaeologist who has been dubbed the Indiana Jones of the Balkans because of his favored flat-crowned Navajo hat. Osmanagic claims to have identified in Bosnia the world's largest ancient pyramid, which he thinks is "older than the last ice age" (Smith 2006). Archaeologists and geologists, however, say that his "pyramid" is actually a large symmetrical hill formed by buckling of the earth's crust millions of years ago. Zilka Kujundzic-Vejzagic, a trained prehistoric archaeologist at Bosnia's National Museum, points out the lack of any evidence for a

Paleolithic civilization in Bosnia. (Were there Paleolithic civilizations anywhere in the world?) Indeed, archaeologists working in Bosnia have found little more than flint tools from the end of the last ice age and only simple Neolithic settlements that appeared thousands of years after that. The country's most substantial ancient monument is a modest stone city in southern Bosnia built during the third century B.C.E. Nevertheless, uncritical media coverage has popularized Osmanagic's theories, and volunteers have flocked to the site to help him excavate (Smith 2006).

Responding to his claims, the European Association of Archaeologists issued an official statement signed by the heads of the official archaeological organizations of seven European countries (Parzinger et al. 2006). Their statement called Osmanagic's so-called "pyramid" project "a cruel hoax on an unsuspecting public" that "has no place in the world of genuine science" (Parzinger el al. 2006). When and where have you heard a fantastic claim about prehistory?

Formerly archaeologists tended to explain state origin and decline mainly in terms of natural environmental factors, such as climate change, habitat destruction, and demographic pressure (see Weiss 2005). Archaeologists now see state origins and declines more fully—in social and political terms—because we can read the texts. The Mayan texts document competition and warfare between dynasties jockeying for position and power. Warfare was indeed a creator and a destroyer of ancient chiefdoms and states. What's its role in our own?

Summary

1. States develop to handle regulatory problems as the population grows and the economy gets more complex. Multiple factors contribute to state formation. Some appear repeatedly, but no single factor is always present.

2. A state is a society with a formal, central government and a division of society into classes. The first cities and states, supported by irrigated farming, developed in southern Mesopotamia between 6000 and 5500 B.P. Evidence for early state organization includes monumental architecture, central storehouses, irrigation systems, and written records.

3. Towns predate pottery in the Middle East. The first towns grew up 10,000 to 9,000 years ago. The first pottery dates back just over 8,000 years. Halafian (7500–6500 B.P.) refers to a pottery style and to the period when the first chiefdoms emerged. Ubaid pottery (7000–6000 B.P.) is associated with advanced chiefdoms and perhaps the earliest states. Most state formation occurred during the Uruk period (6100–5100 B.P.).

4. Based on the status distinctions they include, societies may be divided into egalitarian, ranked, and stratified. In egalitarian societies, status distinctions are not usually inherited. Ranked societies have hereditary inequality, but they lack stratification.

Stratified societies have sharp social divisions—social classes or strata—based on unequal access to wealth and power. Ranked societies with loss of village autonomy are chiefdoms.

5. Mesopotamia's economy was based on craft production, trade, and intensive agriculture. Writing, invented by 5600 B.P., was first used to keep accounts for trade. With the invention of smelting, the Bronze Age began just after 5000 B.P.

6. In northwestern India and Pakistan, the Indus River Valley state flourished from 4600 to 3900 B.P. The first Chinese state, dating to 3750 B.P., was that of the Shang dynasty in northern China. The major early states of the Western Hemisphere were in Mesoamerica and Peru.

7. Between 3200 and 3000 B.P., intense competitive interaction among the many chiefdoms in Mesoamerica at that time fueled rapid social change. Some chiefdoms would develop into states (e.g., Oaxaca, Valley of Mexico). Others (e.g., Olmec) would not. In the Valley of Oaxaca, changing patterns of warfare—from village raiding to conquest warfare to gain territory and tribute—played a prominent role in the formation of Mesoamerica's earliest state, the Zapotec state, whose capital was Monte Alban. This city served as the Zapotec capital for one thousand years, from 300 B.C.E. to 700 C.E. After that, the Zapotec state continued, but in the form of small principalities that fought among themselves until Spanish conquest in the early 16th century C.E. By 1 C.E. (2000 B.P.), the Valley of Mexico had come to prominence. In this large valley in the highlands, Teotihuacan thrived between 100 and 700 C.E. Tenochtitlan, the capital of the Aztec state (1325 to 1520 C.E.), may have surpassed Teotihuacan at its height.

8. States may collapse when they fail to keep social and economic order or to protect themselves against outsiders. The Mayan state fell in the face of increased warfare among competing dynasties.

Key Terms

Aztec, *215*
bronze, *206*
chiefdoms, *204*
cuneiform, *206*
egalitarian society, *203*
Halafian, *203*
Mesopotamia, *200*
metallurgy, *206*
multivariate, *196*
primary states, *204*
ranked societies, *203*
settlement hierarchy, *214*
smelting, *206*
state, *195*
stratification, *203*
Teotihuacan, *214*
Zapotec, *212*

Go to our Online Learning Center website at **www.mhhe.com/kottak** for Internet resources directly related to the content of this chapter.

Chapter 10

Language and Communication

Language

Nonhuman Primate Communication

Call Systems

Sign Language

The Origin of Language

Nonverbal Communication

*Applying Anthropology to Popular
Culture: Facebook and Twitter*

The Structure of Language

Speech Sounds

Language, Thought, and Culture

The Sapir-Whorf Hypothesis

Focal Vocabulary

Sociolinguistics

Social and Linguistic Variation

Linguistic Diversity within Nations

Gender Speech Contrasts

Stratification and Symbolic Domination

Black English Vernacular (BEV)

Historical Linguistics

Language Loss

*Anthropology Today: Linguistic Diversity
and the Internet*

North Americans have certain stereotypes about how people in other regions talk. Some stereotypes, spread by the mass media, are more generalized than others are. Most Americans think they can imitate a "Southern accent." We also stereotype speech in New York City (the pronunciation of *coffee,* for example), Boston ("I pahked the kah in Hahvahd Yahd"), and Canada ("oot" for "out").

It's sometimes thought that midwesterners don't have accents. This belief stems from the fact that midwestern dialects don't have many stigmatized linguistic variants—speech patterns that people in other regions recognize and look down on, such as *r*lessness and *dem, dese,* and *dere* (instead of *them, these,* and *there*).

Far from having no accents, midwesterners, even in the same high school, exhibit linguistic diversity (see Eckert 1989, 2000). One of the best examples of variable midwestern speech, involving vowels, is pronunciation of the *e* sound (called the /e/ phoneme), in such words as *ten, rent, section, lecture, effect, best,* and *test.* In southeastern Michigan, there are four different ways of pronouncing this *e* sound. Speakers of Black

English and immigrants from Appalachia often pronounce *ten* as "tin," just as Southerners habitually do. Some Michiganders say "ten," the correct pronunciation in Standard English. However, two other pronunciations also are common. Instead of "ten," many Michiganders say "tan," or "tun" (as though they were using the word *ton*, a unit of weight).

My students often astound me with their pronunciation. One day I met one of my Michigan-raised teaching assistants in the hall. She was deliriously happy. When I asked why, she replied, "I've just had the best suction."

"What?" I said.

She finally spoke more precisely. "I've just had the best saction." She considered this a clearer pronunciation of the word *section*.

Another TA complimented me, "You luctured to great effuct today." After an exam a student lamented that she had not done her "bust on the tust" (i.e., "best on the test").

The truth is, regional patterns affect the way we all speak.

Language

Linguistic anthropology illustrates anthropology's characteristic interests in diversity, comparison, and change—but here the focus is on language. Language, spoken (*speech*) and written (*writing*—which has existed for about 6,000 years), is our primary means of communication. Like culture in general, of which language is a part, language is transmitted through learning. Language is based on arbitrary, learned associations between words and the things they stand for. Unlike the communication systems of other animals, language allows us to discuss the past and future, share our experiences with others, and benefit from their experiences.

Anthropologists study language in its social and cultural context (see Bonvillain 2010; Salzmann 2007). Some linguistic anthropologists reconstruct ancient languages by comparing their contemporary descendants and in doing so make discoveries about history. Others study linguistic differences to discover the varied worldviews and patterns of thought in a multitude of cultures. Sociolinguists examine dialects and styles in a single language to show how speech reflects social differences, as in the above discussion of regional speech contrasts. Linguistic anthropologists also explore the role of language in colonization and globalization (Blommaert 2010; Geis 1987; Thomas 1999).

Nonhuman Primate Communication

Call Systems

Only humans speak. No other animal has anything approaching the complexity of language. The natural communication systems of other primates (monkeys and apes) are **call systems.** These vocal systems consist of a limited number of sounds—*calls*—that are produced only when particular environmental stimuli are encountered. Such calls may be varied in intensity and duration, but they are much less flexible than language because they are automatic and can't be combined. When primates encounter food and danger simultaneously, they can make only one call. They can't combine the calls for food and danger into a single utterance, indicating that both are present. At some point in human evolution, however, our ancestors began to combine calls and to understand the combinations. The number of calls also expanded, eventually becoming too great to be transmitted even partly through the genes. Communication came to rely almost totally on learning.

Although wild primates use call systems, the vocal tract of apes is not suitable for speech. Until the 1960s, attempts to teach spoken language to apes suggested that they lack linguistic abilities. In the 1950s, a couple raised a chimpanzee, Viki, as a member of their family and systematically tried to teach her to speak. However, Viki learned only four words ("mama," "papa," "up," and "cup").

Sign Language

More recent experiments have shown that apes can learn to use, if not speak, true language (Fouts 1997; Miles 1983). Several apes have learned to converse with people through means other than speech. One such communication system is American Sign Language, or ASL, which is widely used by hearing-impaired Americans. ASL employs a limited number of basic gesture units that are analogous to sounds in spoken language. These units combine to form words and larger units of meaning.

Apes, such as these Congo chimpanzees, use call systems to communicate in the wild. Their vocal systems consist of a limited number of sounds—calls—that are produced only when particular environmental stimuli are encountered.

The first chimpanzee to learn ASL was Washoe, a female, who died in 2007 at the age of 42. Captured in West Africa, Washoe was acquired by R. Allen Gardner and Beatrice Gardner, scientists at the University of Nevada in Reno, in 1966, when she was a year old. Four years later, she moved to Norman, Oklahoma, to a converted farm that had become the Institute for Primate Studies. Washoe revolutionized the discussion of the language-learning abilities of apes (Carey 2007). At first she lived in a trailer and heard no spoken language. The researchers always used ASL to communicate with each other in her presence. The chimp gradually acquired a vocabulary of more than 100 signs representing English words (Gardner, Gardner, and Van Cantfort, eds. 1989). At the age of two, Washoe began to combine as many as five signs into rudimentary sentences such as "you, me, go out, hurry."

The second chimp to learn ASL was Lucy, Washoe's junior by one year. Lucy died, or was murdered by poachers, in 1986, after having been introduced to "the wild" in Africa in 1979 (Carter 1988). From her second day of life until her move to Africa, Lucy lived with a family in Norman, Oklahoma. Roger Fouts, a researcher from the nearby Institute for Primate Studies, came two days a week to test and improve Lucy's knowledge of ASL. During the rest of the week, Lucy used ASL to converse with her foster parents. After acquiring language, Washoe and Lucy exhibited several human traits: swearing, joking, telling lies, and trying to teach language to others (Fouts 1997).

When irritated, Washoe called her monkey neighbors at the institute "dirty monkeys." Lucy insulted her "dirty cat." On arrival at Lucy's place, Fouts once found a pile of excrement on the floor. When he asked the chimp what it was, she replied, "dirty, dirty," her expression for feces. Asked whose "dirty, dirty" it was, Lucy named Fouts's coworker, Sue. When Fouts refused to believe her about Sue, the chimp blamed the excrement on Fouts himself.

Cultural transmission of a communication system through learning is a fundamental attribute of language. Washoe, Lucy, and other chimps have tried to teach ASL to other animals, including their own offspring. Washoe taught gestures to other institute chimps, including her son Sequoia, who died in infancy (Fouts, Fouts, and Van Cantfort 1989).

Because of their size and strength as adults, gorillas are less likely subjects than chimps for such experiments. Lean adult male gorillas in the wild weigh 400 pounds (180 kilograms), and full-grown females can easily reach 250 pounds (110 kilograms). Because of this, psychologist Penny Patterson's work with gorillas at Stanford University seems more daring than the chimp experiments. Patterson raised her now full-grown female gorilla, Koko, in a trailer next to a Stanford museum. Koko's vocabulary surpasses that of any chimp. She regularly employs 400 ASL signs and has used about 700 at least once.

Koko and the chimps also show that apes share still another linguistic ability with humans: **productivity.** Speakers routinely use the rules of their language to produce entirely new expressions that are comprehensible to other native speakers. I can, for example, create "baboonlet" to refer to a baboon infant. I do this by analogy with English words in which the suffix *-let* designates the young of a species. Anyone who speaks English immediately understands the meaning of my new word. Koko, Washoe, Lucy, and others have shown that apes also are able to use language productively. Lucy used gestures she already knew to create "drinkfruit" for watermelon. Washoe, seeing a swan for the first time, coined "waterbird." Koko, who knew the gestures for "finger" and "bracelet," formed "finger bracelet" when she was given a ring.

Chimps and gorillas have a rudimentary capacity for language. They may never have invented a meaningful gesture system in the wild. However, given such a system, they show many humanlike abilities in learning and using it. Of course, language use by apes is a product of human intervention and teaching. The experiments mentioned here do not suggest that apes can invent language (nor are human children ever faced with that task). However, young apes have managed to learn the basics of gestural language. They can employ it productively and creatively, although not with the sophistication of human ASL users.

Apes also have demonstrated linguistic **displacement.** Absent in call systems, this is a key ingredient in language. Normally, each call is tied to an environmental stimulus such as food. Calls are uttered only when that stimulus is present. Displacement means that humans can talk about things that are not present. We don't have to see the objects before we say the words. Human conversations are not limited by place. We can discuss the past and future, share our experiences with others, and benefit from theirs.

Patterson (1978) has described several examples of Koko's capacity for displacement. The gorilla once expressed sorrow about having bitten Penny three days earlier. Koko has used the sign "later" to postpone doing things she doesn't want to do. Table 10.1 summarizes the contrasts between language, whether sign or spoken, and call systems.

Certain scholars doubt the linguistic abilities of chimps and gorillas (Sebeok and Umiker-Sebeok, eds. 1980; Terrace 1979). These people contend that Koko and the chimps are comparable to trained circus animals and don't really have linguistic ability. However, in defense of Patterson and the other researchers (Hill 1978; Van Cantfort and Rimpau 1982), only one of their critics has worked with an ape. This was Herbert Terrace, whose experience teaching a chimp sign language lacked the continuity and personal involvement that have contributed so much to Patterson's success with Koko.

No one denies the huge difference between human language and gorilla signs. There is a major gap between the ability to write a book or say a prayer and the few hundred gestures employed by a well-trained chimp. Apes aren't people, but they aren't just animals either. Let Koko express it: When asked by a reporter whether she was a person or

TABLE 10.1   Language Contrasted with Call Systems

Human Language	Primate Call Systems
Has the capacity to speak of things and events that are not present (displacement).	Are stimuli-dependent; the food call will be made only in the presence of food; it cannot be faked.
Has the capacity to generate new expressions by combining other expressions (productivity).	Consist of a limited number of calls that cannot be combined to produce new calls.
Is group specific in that all humans have the capacity for language, but each linguistic community has its own language, which is culturally transmitted.	Tend to be species specific, with little variation among communities of the same species for each call.

an animal, Koko signed "fine animal gorilla" (Patterson 1978). For the latest on Koko, see http://koko.org.

The Origin of Language

Although the capacity to remember and combine linguistic symbols may be latent in the apes (Miles 1983), human evolution was needed for this seed to flower into language. A mutated gene known as FOXP2 helps explain why humans speak and chimps don't (Paulson 2005). The key role of FOXP2 in speech came to light in a study of a British family, identified only as KE, half of whose members had an inherited, severe deficit in speech (Trivedi 2001). The same variant form of FOXP2 that is found in chimpanzees causes this disorder. Those who have the nonspeech version of the gene cannot make the fine tongue and lip movements that are necessary for clear speech, and their speech is unintelligible—even to other members of the KE family (Trivedi 2001). Chimps have the same (genetic) sequence as the KE family members with the speech deficit. Comparing chimp and human genomes, it appears that the speech-friendly form of FOXP2 took hold in humans around 150,000 years ago. This mutation conferred selective advantages (linguistic and cultural abilities) that allowed those who had it to spread at the expense of those who did not (Paulson 2005).

Language offered a tremendous adaptive advantage to *Homo sapiens*. Language permits the information stored by a human society to exceed by far that of any nonhuman group. Language is a uniquely effective vehicle for learning. Because we can speak of things we have never experienced, we can anticipate responses before we encounter the stimuli. Adaptation can occur more rapidly in *Homo* than in the other primates because our adaptive means are more flexible.

Nonverbal Communication

Language is our principal means of communicating, but it isn't the only one we use. We *communicate* when we transmit information about ourselves to others and receive such information from them. Our expressions, stances, gestures, and movements, even if unconscious, convey information and are part of our communication styles. Deborah Tannen (1990) discusses differences in the communication styles of American men and women, and her comments go beyond language. She notes that American girls and women tend to look directly at each other when they talk, whereas American boys and men do not. Males are more likely to look straight ahead rather than turn and make eye contact with someone, especially another man, seated beside them. Also, in conversational groups, American men tend to relax and sprawl out. American women may adopt a similar relaxed posture in all-female groups, but when they are with men, they tend to draw in their limbs and adopt a tighter stance.

Kinesics is the study of communication through body movements, stances, gestures, and expressions. Linguists pay attention not only to what is said but to how it is said, and to features besides language itself that convey meaning. A speaker's enthusiasm is conveyed not only through words, but also through facial expressions, gestures, and other signs of animation. We use gestures, such as a jab of the hand, for emphasis. We vary

Imagine life without Twitter, Facebook, and texting—modern current means of communication that allow people to stay in almost constant contact with others. Facebook, created in 2004, enables people to send public posts and private messages, share photos, organize events, and remember birthdays. Twitter, launched in 2006, was developed as a way of sending text messages to multiple people. People now use it to keep track of their friends and celebrity favorites (e.g., Ashton Kutcher, Sarah Palin). People emit "tweets" to update people who "follow" them. According to Mashable: The Social Media Guide (mashable .com), Twitter helps people get to know new sides of other people. How does online communication change the quality and quantity of friendships and family ties? How does it affect your awareness of world, national, and local events? Try going a day or even a week without any form of communication that is not absolutely necessary.

our intonation and the pitch or loudness of our voices. We communicate through strategic pauses, and even by being silent. An effective communication strategy may be to alter pitch, voice level, and grammatical forms, such as declaratives ("I am . . ."), imperatives ("Go forth . . ."), and questions ("Are you . . . ?"). Culture teaches us that certain manners and styles should accompany certain kinds of speech. Our demeanor, verbal and nonverbal, when our favorite team is winning would be out of place at a funeral, or when a somber subject is being discussed.

Much of what we communicate is nonverbal and reflects our emotional states and intentions. This can create problems when we use contemporary means of communication such as texting and online messaging. People can use emoticons (☺,☹, :~/ [confused], :~0 ['hah!' no way!]) and abbreviations (lol—laugh out loud; lmao—laugh my a** off; wtf—what the f**; omg—oh my god) to fill in what would otherwise be communicated by tone of voice, laughter, and facial expression.

Culture always plays a role in shaping the "natural." Cross-culturally, nodding does not always mean affirmative, nor does head shaking from side to side always mean negative. Brazilians wag a finger to mean no. Americans say "uh huh" to affirm, whereas in Madagascar a similar sound is made to deny. Americans point with their fingers; the people of Madagascar point with their lips.

Body movements communicate social differences. In Japan, bowing is a regular part of social interaction, but different bows are used depending on the social status of the people who are interacting. In Madagascar and Polynesia, people of lower status should not hold their heads above those of people of higher status. When one approaches someone older or of higher status, one bends one's knees and lowers one's head as a sign of respect. In Madagascar, one always does this, for politeness, when passing between two people. Although our gestures, facial expressions, and body stances have roots in our primate heritage, and can be seen in the monkeys and the apes, they have not escaped cultural shaping. Language, which is so highly dependent on the use of symbols, is the domain of communication in which culture plays the strongest role.

Does any etiquette govern the public use of hand-held electronic devices? Is texting appropriate at a college graduation? Whom do you think they're texting?

The Structure of Language

The scientific study of a spoken language (**descriptive linguistics**) involves several inter-related areas of analysis: phonology, morphology, lexicon, and syntax. **Phonology,** the study of speech sounds, considers which sounds are present and meaningful in a given language. **Morphology** studies the forms in which sounds combine to form *morphemes—* words and their meaningful parts. Thus, the word *cats* would be analyzed as containing two morphemes—*cat,* the name for a kind of animal, and *-s,* a morpheme indicating plurality. A language's **lexicon** is a dictionary containing all its morphemes and their meanings. **Syntax** refers to the arrangement and order of words in phrases and sentences. For example, do nouns usually come before or after verbs? Do adjectives normally precede or follow the nouns they modify?

Speech Sounds

From the movies and TV, and from meeting foreigners, we know something about foreign accents and mispronunciations. We know that someone with a marked French accent doesn't pronounce *r* like an American does. But at least someone from France can distinguish between "craw" and "claw," which someone from Japan may not be able to do. The difference between *r* and *l* makes a difference in English and in French, but it doesn't in Japanese. In linguistics we say that the difference between *r* and *l* is *phonemic*

Syntax refers to the arrangement and order of words in phrases and sentences. A photo of Yoda from *Star Wars* (*Revenge of the Sith*) this is. What's odd about Yoda's syntax?

in English and French but not in Japanese. In English and French *r* and *l* are phonemes but not in Japanese. A **phoneme** is a sound contrast that makes a difference, that differentiates meaning.

We find the phonemes in a given language by comparing *minimal pairs,* words that resemble each other in all but one sound. The words have different meanings, but they differ in just one sound. The contrasting sounds therefore are phonemes in that language. An example in English is the minimal pair *pit/bit*. These two words are distinguished by a single sound contrast between /p/ and /b/ (we enclose phonemes in slashes). Thus /p/ and /b/ are phonemes in English. Another example is the different vowel sound of *bit* and *beat* (Figure 10.1). This contrast serves to distinguish these two words and the two vowel phonemes written /I/ and /i/ in English.

Standard (American) English (SE), the "region-free" dialect of TV network newscasters, has about 35 phonemes—at least 11 vowels and 24 consonants. The number of phonemes varies from language to language—from 15 to 60, averaging between 30 and 40. The number of phonemes also varies between dialects of a given language. In North American English, for example, vowel phonemes vary noticeably from dialect to dialect. Readers should pronounce the words in Figure 10.1, paying attention to (or asking someone else) whether they distinguish each of the vowel sounds. Most North Americans don't pronounce them all.

Phonetics is the study of speech sounds in general, what people actually say in various languages, like the differences in vowel pronunciation described in the discussion of midwestern speech at the beginning of the chapter. **Phonemics** studies only the *significant* sound contrasts (phonemes) of a given language. In English, like /r/ and /l/ (remember *craw* and *claw*), /b/ and /v/ also are phonemes, occurring in minimal pairs like *bat* and *vat*. In Spanish, however, the contrast between [b] and [v] doesn't distinguish meaning, and they therefore are not phonemes (we enclose sounds that are not phonemic in

FIGURE 10.1 Vowel phonemes in Standard American English

They are shown according to height of tongue and tongue position at front, center, or back of mouth. Phonetic symbols are identified by English words that include them; note that most are minimal pairs.

Source: Dwight Bolinger, *Aspects of Language,* 3rd ed., fig. 2.1. Copyright © 1981 Heinle/Arts & Sciences, a part of Cengage Learning, Inc. Reproduced by permission. www.cengage.com/permissions.

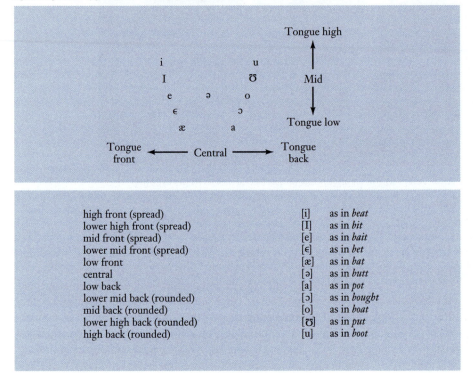

high front (spread)	[i]	as in *beat*
lower high front (spread)	[I]	as in *bit*
mid front (spread)	[e]	as in *bait*
lower mid front (spread)	[ɛ]	as in *bet*
low front	[æ]	as in *bat*
central	[ə]	as in *butt*
low back	[a]	as in *pot*
lower mid back (rounded)	[ɔ]	as in *bought*
mid back (rounded)	[o]	as in *boat*
lower high back (rounded)	[ʊ]	as in *put*
high back (rounded)	[u]	as in *boot*

brackets). Spanish speakers normally use the [b] sound to pronounce words spelled with either *b* or *v*.

In any language a given phoneme extends over a phonetic range. In English the phoneme /p/ ignores the phonetic contrast between the [pʰ] in *pin* and the [p] in *spin*. Most English speakers don't even notice that there is a phonetic difference. The [pʰ] is aspirated, so that a puff of air follows the [p]. The [p] in *spin* is not. (To see the difference, light a match, hold it in front of your mouth, and watch the flame as you pronounce the two words.) The contrast between [pʰ] and [p] *is* phonemic in some languages, such as Hindi (spoken in India). That is, there are words whose meaning is distinguished only by the contrast between an aspirated and an unaspirated [p].

Native speakers vary in their pronunciation of certain phonemes, such as the /e/ phoneme in the midwestern United States. This variation is important in the evolution of language. Without shifts in pronunciation, there could be no linguistic change. The section on sociolinguistics later in this chapter considers phonetic variation and its relationship to social divisions and the evolution of language.

Language, Thought, and Culture

The well-known linguist Noam Chomsky (1957) has argued that the human brain contains a limited set of rules for organizing language, so that all languages have a common structural basis. (Chomsky calls this set of rules *universal grammar.*) That people can learn foreign languages and that words and ideas translate from one language to another supports Chomsky's position that all humans have similar linguistic abilities and thought processes. Another line of support comes from creole languages. Such languages develop from *pidgins,* languages that form in situations of acculturation, when different societies come into contact and must devise a system of communication. Pidgins based on English and native languages developed through trade and colonialism in many world areas, including China, Papua New Guinea, and West Africa. Eventually, after generations of being spoken, pidgins may develop into *creole languages.* These are more mature languages, with developed grammatical rules and native speakers (people who learn the language as their primary one during enculturation).

Creoles are spoken in several Caribbean societies. Gullah, which is spoken by African Americans on coastal islands in South Carolina and Georgia, is a creole language. Supporting the idea that creoles are based on universal grammar is the fact that such languages all share certain features. Syntactically, all use particles (e.g., will, was) to form future and past tenses and multiple negation to deny or negate (e.g., he don't got none). Also, all form questions by changing inflection rather than by changing word order. For example, "You're going home for the holidays?" (with a rising tone at the end) rather than "Are you going home for the holidays?"

The Sapir-Whorf Hypothesis

Other linguists and anthropologists take a different approach to the relation between language and thought. Rather than seeking universal linguistic structures and processes, they believe that different languages produce different ways of thinking. This position sometimes is known as the **Sapir-Whorf hypothesis** after Edward Sapir (1931) and his student Benjamin Lee Whorf (1956), its prominent early advocates. Sapir and Whorf argued that the grammatical categories of particular languages lead their speakers to think about things in different ways. For example, English divides time into past, present, and future. Hopi, a language of the Pueblo region of the Native American Southwest, does not. Rather, Hopi distinguishes between events that exist or have existed (what we use present and past to discuss) and those that don't or don't yet (our future events, along with imaginary and hypothetical events). Whorf argued that this difference leads Hopi speakers to think about time and reality in different ways than English speakers do.

A similar example comes from Portuguese, which employs a future subjunctive verb form, introducing a degree of uncertainty into discussions of the future. In English we routinely use the future tense to talk about something we think will happen. We don't feel the need to qualify "The sun'll come out tomorrow," by adding "if it doesn't go supernova." We don't hesitate to proclaim "I'll see you next year," even when we can't be absolutely sure we will. The Portuguese future subjunctive qualifies the future event, recognizing that the future can't be certain. Our way of expressing the future as certain is so ingrained that we don't even think about it, just as the Hopi don't see the need to distinguish between present and past, both of which are real, while the future remains hypothetical. It seems, however, that language does not tightly restrict thought, because cultural changes can produce changes in thought and in language, as we'll see in the next section (see also Gumperz and Levinson, eds. 1996).

Focal Vocabulary

A lexicon (or vocabulary) is a language's dictionary, its set of names for things, events, and ideas. Lexicon influences perception. Thus, Eskimos (or Inuit) have several distinct words for different types of snow that in English are all called *snow*. Most English speakers never notice the differences between these types of snow and might have trouble seeing them even if someone pointed them out. Eskimos recognize and think about differences in snow that English speakers don't see because our language gives us just one word.

Similarly, the Nuer of South Sudan have an elaborate vocabulary to describe cattle. Eskimos have several words for snow and Nuer have dozens for cattle because of their particular histories, economies, and environments (Brown 1958; Eastman 1975). When the need arises, English speakers can also elaborate their snow and cattle vocabularies. For example, skiers name varieties of snow with words that are missing from the lexicons of Florida retirees. Similarly, the cattle vocabulary of a Texas rancher is much more ample than that of a salesperson in a New York City department store. Such specialized sets of terms and distinctions that are particularly important to certain groups (those with particular *foci* of experience or activity) are known as **focal vocabulary.**

Shown here (in 1995) is Leigh Jenkins, who was or is director of Cultural Preservation for the Hopi tribal council. The Hopi language would not distinguish between *was* and *is* in the previous sentence. For the Hopi, present and past are real and are expressed grammatically in the same way, while the future remains hypothetical and has a different grammatical expression.

Vocabulary is the area of language that changes most readily. New words and distinctions, when needed, appear and spread. For example, who would have "texted" someone a generation ago? Names for items get simpler as they become common and important. A television has become a *TV,* an automobile a *car,* and an application for a smartphone an *app*.

Language, culture, and thought are interrelated. Opposing the Sapir-Whorf hypothesis, however, it might be more accurate to say that changes in culture produce changes in language and thought than to say the reverse. Consider differences between female and male Americans regarding the color terms they use (Lakoff 2004). Distinctions implied by such terms as *salmon, rust, peach, beige, teal, mauve, cranberry,* and *dusky orange* aren't in the vocabularies of most American men. However, many of them weren't even in American women's lexicons 50 years ago. These changes reflect changes in American economy, society, and culture. Color terms and distinctions have increased with the growth of the fashion and cosmetic industries. A similar contrast (and growth) in Americans' lexicons shows up in football, basketball, and hockey vocabularies. Sports fans, more often males than females, use more terms concerning, and make more elaborate distinctions between, the games they watch, such as hockey (see Table 10.2). Thus, cultural contrasts and changes affect lexical distinctions (for instance, *peach*

April 13, 2011–Pittsburgh Penguins goalie Marc-Andre Fleury makes a save against Tampa Bay Lightning's Marty St. Louis (26). Pittsburgh went on to defeat the Lightning 3 to 0 in this game one of the 2011 Stanley Cup playoffs. How might an avid fan describe this photo?

TABLE 10.2
Focal Vocabulary for Hockey
Insiders have special terms for the major elements of the game

Elements of Hockey	Insiders' Term
puck	biscuit
goal/net	pipes
penalty box	sin bin
hockey stick	twig
helmet	bucket
space between a goalie's leg pads	five hole

versus *salmon*) within semantic domains (for instance, color terminology). **Semantics** refers to a language's meaning system.

The ways in which people divide the world—the lexical contrasts they perceive as meaningful or significant—reflect their experiences (see Bicker, Sillitoe, and Pottier, eds. 2004). Anthropologists have discovered that certain sets of vocabulary items evolve in a determined order. For example, after studying more than 100 languages, Berlin and Kay (1969/1992) discovered 10 basic color terms: *white, black, red, yellow, blue, green, brown, pink, orange,* and *purple* (they evolved in more or less that order). The number of terms varied with cultural complexity. Representing one extreme were Papua New Guinea cultivators and Australian hunters and gatherers, who used only two basic terms, which translate as *black* and *white* or *dark* and *light*. At the other end of the continuum were European and Asian languages with all the color terms. Color terminology was most developed in areas with a history of using dyes and artificial coloring.

Sociolinguistics

Social and Linguistic Variation

Do you think there's anything distinctive or unusual about the way you talk? If you're from Canada, Virginia, or Savannah, you may say "oot" instead of "out." A southerner might request a "soft drink" rather than a New Yorker's "soda" or someone else's "pop." Can you imitate how a "Valley Girl" or "surfer dude" might talk? Usually when we pay attention to how we talk, it's because someone comments on our speech. It may be only when students move from one state or region to another that they realize how much of a regional accent they have. I moved as a teenager from Atlanta to New York City. Previously I hadn't realized I had a southern accent, but some guardian of linguistic correctness in my new high school did. They put me in a speech class, pointing out linguistic flaws I never knew I had. One was my "dull *s*," particularly in terminal consonant clusters, as in the words *tusks* and *breakfasts*. Apparently I didn't pronounce all three consonants at the ends of those words. Later it occurred to me that these weren't words I used very often. As far as I know, I've never had a conversation about tusks or proclaimed "I ate seven breakfasts last week."

Unlike grammarians, linguists and anthropologists are interested in what people do say, rather than what they should say. Speech differences are associated with, and tell us a lot about, social variation, such as region, education, ethnic background, and gender. Men and women talk differently. I'm sure you can think of examples based on your own experience, although you probably never realized that women tend to peripheralize their vowels (think of the sounds in *weasel* and *whee*), whereas men tend to centralize them (think of *rough* and *ugh*). Men are more likely to speak "ungrammatically" than women are. Men and women also show differences in their sports and color terminologies. Men typically know more terms related to sports, make more distinctions among them (e.g., *runs* versus *points*), and try to use the terms more precisely than women do. Correspondingly, influenced more by the fashion and cosmetics industries than men are, women use more color terms and attempt to use them more specifically than men do. To make this point when I lecture, I bring an off-purple shirt to class. Holding it up, I first ask women to say aloud what color the shirt is. The women rarely answer with a uniform voice, as they try to distinguish the actual shade (mauve, lilac, lavender, wisteria, or some other purplish hue). I then ask the men, who consistently answer as one, "PURPLE." Rare is the man who on the spur of the moment can imagine the difference between fuchsia and magenta or grape and aubergine.

No language is a uniform system in which everyone talks just like everyone else. The field of **sociolinguistics** investigates relationships between social and linguistic variation (Romaine 2000; Spencer 2010; Trudgill 2000). How do different speakers use a given language? How do linguistic features correlate with social diversity and stratification, including class, ethnic, and gender differences (Tannen 1990; Tannen, ed. 1993)? How is language used to express, reinforce, or resist power (Geis 1987; G. Lakoff 2008)?

Sociolinguists focus on features that vary systematically with social position and situation. To study variation, sociolinguists must observe, define, and measure variable use of language in real-world situations. To show that linguistic features correlate with social, economic, and political differences, the social attributes of speakers also must be measured and related to speech (Fasold 1990; Labov 1972*a*).

Variation within a language at a given time is historical change in progress. The same forces that, working gradually, have produced large-scale linguistic change over the centuries are still at work today. Linguistic change doesn't occur in a vacuum but in society. When new ways of speaking are associated with social factors, they are imitated, and they spread (see Blommaert 2010). In this way, a language changes.

Linguistic Diversity within Nations

As an illustration of the linguistic variation encountered in all nations, consider the contemporary United States. Ethnic diversity is revealed by the fact that millions of Americans learn first languages other than English. Spanish is the most common. Most of those people eventually become bilinguals, adding English as a second language. In many multilingual (including colonized) nations, people use two languages on different occasions—one in the home, for example, and the other on the job or in public (see this chapter's "Anthropology Today").

Whether bilingual or not, we all vary our speech in different contexts; we engage in **style shifts.** In certain parts of Europe, people regularly switch dialects. This phenomenon, known as **diglossia,** applies to "high" and "low" variants of the same language, for example, in German and Flemish (spoken in Belgium). People employ the high variant at universities and in writing, professions, and the mass media. They use the low variant for ordinary conversation with family members and friends. (See Tannen, Kendall, and Gordon [2007] and Tannen [2005] for analysis of communication among American families and friends.)

Ethnic and linguistic diversity characterize many nations, especially in big cities, as illustrated by this California sign written in seven languages: Chinese, Korean, Spanish, Vietnamese, Japanese, Tagalog, and English.

Just as social situations influence our speech, so do geographical, cultural, and socio-economic differences. Many dialects coexist in the United States with Standard (American) English (SE). SE itself is a dialect that differs, say, from "BBC English," which is the preferred dialect in Great Britain. Different dialects are equally effective as systems of communication, which is language's main job. Our tendency to think of particular dialects as cruder or more sophisticated than others is a social rather than a linguistic judgment. We rank certain speech patterns as better or worse because we recognize that they are used by groups that we also rank. People who say *dese, dem,* and *dere* instead of *these, them,* and *there* communicate perfectly well with anyone who recognizes that the *d* sound systematically replaces the *th* sound in their speech. However, this form of speech has become an indicator of low social rank. We call it, like the use of *ain't,* "uneducated speech." The use of *dem, dese,* and *dere* is one of many phonological differences that Americans recognize and look down on.

Gender Speech Contrasts

Comparing men and women, there are differences in phonology, grammar, and vocabulary, and in the body stances and movements that accompany speech (Eckert and McConnell-Ginet 2003; R. Lakoff 2004; Tannen 1990). In public contexts, Japanese women tend to adopt an artificially high voice, for the sake of politeness, according to their traditional culture. Women tend to be more careful about uneducated speech. This trend shows up in both the United States and England. Men may adopt working-class speech because they associate it with masculinity. Perhaps women pay more attention to the media, in which standard dialects are employed.

According to Robin Lakoff (2004), the use of certain types of words and expressions has been associated with women's traditional lesser power in American society (see also Coates 1986; Romaine 1999; Tannen 1990; Tannen, ed. 1993). For example, *Oh dear, Oh fudge,* and *Goodness!* are less forceful than *Hell* and *Damn.* Watch the lips of a disgruntled athlete in a televised competition, such as a football game. What's the likelihood he's saying "Phooey on you"? Women are more likely to use such adjectives as *adorable, charming, sweet, cute, lovely,* and *divine* than men are.

Differences in the linguistic strategies and behavior of men and women are examined in several books by the well-known sociolinguist Deborah Tannen (1990; ed. 1993). Tannen uses the terms "rapport" and "report" to contrast women's and men's overall linguistic styles. Women, says Tannen, typically use language and the body movements that accompany it to build rapport, social connections with others. Men, on the other hand, tend to make reports, reciting information that serves to establish a place for themselves in a hierarchy, as they also attempt to determine the relative ranks of their conversation mates.

Stratification and Symbolic Domination

We use and evaluate speech in the context of *extralinguistic* forces—social, political, and economic. Mainstream Americans evaluate the speech of low-status groups negatively, calling it "uneducated." This is not because these ways of speaking are bad in themselves but because they have come to symbolize low status. Consider variation in the pronunciation of *r*. In some parts of the United States *r* is regularly pronounced, and in other (*r*less) areas it is not. Originally, American *r*less speech was modeled on the fashionable speech of England. Because of its prestige, *r*lessness was adopted in many areas and continues as the norm around Boston and in the South.

New Yorkers sought prestige by dropping their *r*'s in the 19th century, after having pronounced them in the 18th. However, contemporary New Yorkers are going back to the 18th-century pattern of pronouncing *r*'s. What matters, and what governs linguistic change, is not the reverberation of a strong midwestern *r* but *social* evaluation, whether *r*'s happen to be "in" or "out."

Studies of *r* pronunciation in New York City have clarified the mechanisms of phonological change. William Labov (1972*b*) focused on whether *r* was pronounced after vowels in such words as *car, floor, card,* and *fourth*. To get data on how this linguistic variation correlated with social class, he used a series of rapid encounters with employees in three New York City department stores, each of whose prices and locations attracted a different socioeconomic group. Saks Fifth Avenue (68 encounters) catered to the upper middle class, Macy's (125) attracted middle-class shoppers, and S. Klein's (71) had predominantly lower-middle-class and working-class customers. The class origins of store personnel reflected those of their customers.

Having already determined that a certain department was on the fourth floor, Labov approached ground-floor salespeople and asked where that department was. After the

Knowledge of linguistic relationships often is valuable to anthropologists interested in history, particularly events during the past 5,000 years. Cultural features may (or may not) correlate with the distribution of language families. Groups that speak related languages may (or may not) be more culturally similar to each other than they are to groups whose speech derives from different linguistic ancestors. Of course, cultural similarities aren't limited to speakers of related languages. Even groups whose members speak unrelated languages have contact through trade, intermarriage, and warfare. Ideas and inventions diffuse widely among human groups. Many items of vocabulary in contemporary English, particularly food items such as "beef" and "pork," come from French. Even without written documentation of France's influence after the Norman Conquest of England in 1066, linguistic evidence in contemporary English would reveal a long period of important firsthand contact with France. Similarly, linguistic evidence may confirm cultural contact and borrowing when written history is lacking. By considering which words have been borrowed, we also can make inferences about the nature of the contact.

Language Loss

One aspect of linguistic history is language loss. When languages disappear, cultural diversity is reduced as well. According to linguist K. David Harrison, "When we lose a language, we lose centuries of thinking about time, seasons, sea creatures, reindeer, edible flowers, mathematics, landscapes, myths, music, the unknown and the everyday" (quoted in Maugh 2007). Harrison's book *When Languages Die* (2007) notes that an indigenous language goes extinct every two weeks, as its last speakers die. The world's linguistic diversity has been cut in half (measured by number of distinct languages) in the past 500 years, and half of the remaining languages are predicted to disappear during this century. Colonial languages (e.g., English, Spanish, Portuguese, French, Dutch, Russian) have expanded at the expense of indigenous ones. Of approximately 7,000 remaining languages, about 20 percent are endangered, compared with 18 percent of mammals, 8 percent of plants, and 5 percent of birds (Maugh 2007).

Harrison, who teaches at Swarthmore College, is director of research for the Living Tongues Institute for Endangered Languages (http://www.livingtongues.org), which works to maintain, preserve, and revitalize endangered languages through multimedia documentation projects. Researchers from the institute use digital audio and video equipment to record the last speakers of the most endangered languages. *National Geographic*'s Enduring Voices Project (http://www.nationalgeographic.com/mission/enduringvoices/) strives to preserve endangered languages by identifying the geographic areas with unique, poorly understood, or threatened languages and by documenting those languages and cultures.

The website shows various language hot spots where the endangerment rate ranges from low to severe. The rate is high in an area encompassing Oklahoma, Texas, and New Mexico, where 40 Native American languages are at risk. The top hot spot is northern Australia, where 153 Aboriginal languages are endangered (Maugh 2007). Other hot spots are in central South America, the Pacific Northwest of North America, and eastern Siberia. In all these areas indigenous tongues have yielded, either voluntarily or through coercion, to a colonial language.

Anthropology Today *Linguistic Diversity and the Internet*

Despite language loss, linguistic diversity is alive and well in many countries, including India, as described below. Despite that nation's colonial history, only about a tenth of the Indian population speaks English. However, even many of those English speakers prefer to read, and to seek out Internet content, in their own regional languages. In this story we see how local entrepreneurs and international companies such as Google, Yahoo, and Microsoft are rushing to meet the demand for Web content in local languages. This example illustrates one of the main lessons of applied anthropology, that external inputs fit in best when they are tailored properly to local settings. We see also how Indians shift their linguistic styles—even languages—as they interact with friends, family, coworkers, and Internet sources in their daily lives.

Asia already has twice as many Internet users as North America, and by 2012 it will have three times as many. Already, more than half of the search queries on Google come from outside the United States.

The globalization of the Web has inspired entrepreneurs like Ram Prakash Hanumanthappa, an engineer from outside Bangalore, India. Mr. Ram Prakash learned English as a teenager, but he still prefers to express himself to friends and family members in his native Kannada. But using Kannada on the Web involves computer keyboard maps that even Mr. Ram Prakash finds challenging to learn.

So in 2006 he developed Quillpad, an online service for typing in 10 South Asian languages. Users spell out words of local languages phonetically in Roman letters, and Quillpad's predictive engine converts them into local-language script. Bloggers and authors rave about the service, which has attracted interest from the cellphone maker Nokia and the attention of Google Inc., which has since introduced its own transliteration tool.

Mr. Ram Prakash said Western technology companies have misunderstood the linguistic landscape of India, where English is spoken proficiently by only about a tenth of the population and even many college-educated Indians prefer the contours of their native tongues for everyday speech. "You've got to give them an opportunity to express themselves correctly, rather than make a fool out of themselves and forcing them to use English," he said.

Only there is a shortage of non-English content and applications. So, American technology giants are spending hundreds of millions of dollars each year to build and develop foreign-language Web sites and services— before local companies like Quillpad beat them to the punch and the profits. . . .

Nowhere are the obstacles, or the potential rewards, more apparent than in India, whose online population . . . is poised to become the third-largest in the world after China and the United States by 2012. Indians may speak one language to their boss, another to their spouse and a third to a parent. In casual speech, words can be drawn from a grab bag of tongues. . . .

Yahoo and Google have introduced more than a dozen services to encourage India's Web users to search, blog, chat and learn in their mother tongues. Microsoft has built its Windows Live bundle of online consumer services in seven Indian languages. Facebook has enlisted hundreds of volunteers to translate its social networking site into Hindi and other regional languages, and Wikipedia now has more entries in Indian local languages than in Korean. Google's search service has lagged behind the local competition in

continued

Anthropology Today *continued*

China, and that has made providing locally flavored services a priority for the company in India. Google's initiatives in India are aimed at opening the country's historically slow-growing personal computer market, and at developing expertise that Google will be able to apply to building services for emerging markets worldwide.

"India is a microcosm of the world," said Dr. Prasad Bhaarat Ram, Google India's head of research and development. "Having 22 languages creates a new level of complexity in which you can't take the same approach that you would if you had one predominant language and applied it 22 times."

Global businesses are spending hundreds of millions of dollars a year working their way down a list of languages into which to translate their Web sites, said Donald A. DePalma, the chief research officer of Common Sense Advisory, a consulting business in Lowell, Mass., that specializes in localizing Web sites. India—with relatively undeveloped e-commerce and online advertising markets—is actually lower on the list than Russia, Brazil and South Korea, Mr. DePalma said. . . .

English simply will not suffice for connecting with India's growing online market, a lesson already learned by Western television producers and consumer products makers. . . .

Even among the largely English-speaking base of around 50 million Web users in

India today, nearly three-quarters prefer to read in a local language, according to a survey by JuxtConsult, an Indian market research company. Many cannot find the content they are seeking. "There is a huge shortage of local language content," said Sanjay Tiwari, the chief executive of JuxtConsult. A Microsoft initiative, Project Bhasha, coordinates the efforts of Indian academics, local businesses and solo software developers to expand computing in regional languages. The project's Web site, which counts thousands of registered members, refers to language as "one of the main contributors to the digital divide" in India.

The company is also seeing growing demand from Indian government agencies and companies creating online public services in local languages.

"As many of these companies want to push their services into rural India or tier-two towns or smaller towns, then it becomes essential they communicate with their customers in the local language," said Pradeep Parappil, a Microsoft program manager.

"Localization is the key to success in countries like India," said Gopal Krishna, who oversees consumer services at Yahoo India.

Source: Daniel Sorid, "Writing the Web's Future in Numerous Languages," *New York Times,* December 31, 2008. Copyright © 2008 The New York Times. Reprinted by permission.

Summary

1. Wild primates use call systems to communicate. Environmental stimuli trigger calls, which cannot be combined when multiple stimuli are present. Contrasts between language and call systems include displacement, productivity, and cultural transmission. Over time, our ancestral call systems grew too complex for genetic transmission, and hominin communication began to rely on learning. Humans still use nonverbal communication, such as facial expressions, gestures, and body stances

and movements. But language is the main system humans use to communicate. Chimps and gorillas can understand and manipulate nonverbal symbols based on language.

2. No language uses all the sounds the human vocal tract can make. Phonology—the study of speech sounds—focuses on sound contrasts (phonemes) that distinguish meaning. The grammars and lexicons of particular languages can lead their speakers to perceive and think in certain ways.

3. Linguistic anthropologists share anthropology's general interest in diversity in time and space. Sociolinguistics investigates relationships between social and linguistic variation by focusing on the actual use of language. Only when features of speech acquire social meaning are they imitated. If they are valued, they will spread. People vary their speech, shifting styles, dialects, and languages.

4. As linguistic systems, all languages and dialects are equally complex, rule-governed, and effective for communication. However, speech is used, is evaluated, and changes in the context of political, economic, and social forces. Often the linguistic traits of a low-status group are negatively evaluated. This devaluation is not because of linguistic features per se. Rather, it reflects the association of such features with low social status. One dialect, supported by the dominant institutions of the state, exercises symbolic domination over the others.

5. Historical linguistics is useful for anthropologists interested in historical relationships among populations. Cultural similarities and differences often correlate with linguistic ones. Linguistic clues can suggest past contacts between cultures. Related languages—members of the same language family—descend from an original protolanguage. Relationships between languages don't necessarily mean there are biological ties between their speakers, because people can learn new languages.

6. One aspect of linguistic history is language loss. The world's linguistic diversity has been cut in half in the past 500 years, and half of the remaining 7,000 languages are predicted to disappear during this century.

Key Terms

Black English Vernacular (BEV), *239*
call systems, *222*
cultural transmission, *224*
daughter languages, *240*
descriptive linguistics, *228*
diglossia, *235*

displacement, *225*
focal vocabulary, *232*
historical linguistics, *240*
kinesics, *226*
lexicon, *228*
morphology, *228*
phoneme, *229*
phonemics, *229*
phonetics, *229*

phonology, *228*
productivity, *224*
protolanguage, *240*
Sapir-Whorf hypothesis, *231*
semantics, *234*
sociolinguistics, *235*
style shifts, *235*
subgroups, *240*
syntax, *228*

Go to our Online Learning Center website at **www.mhhe.com/kottak** for Internet resources directly related to the content of this chapter.

Chapter 11

Making a Living

Adaptive Strategies
  Foraging
Adaptive Strategies Based on Food
  Production
  Horticulture
  Agriculture
  *Agricultural Intensification: People and
    the Environment*
  Pastoralism
Economic Systems
  Production in Nonindustrial Societies
  Means of Production
  Alienation in Industrial Economies

Economizing and Maximization
  Alternative Ends
Distribution, Exchange
  The Market Principle
  *Applying Anthropology to Popular
    Culture: Hip-Hop Lyrics*
  Redistribution
  Reciprocity
  Coexistence of Exchange Principles
    Potlatching
  *Anthropology Today: Scarcity and the
    Betsileo*

In today's globalizing world, communities and societies are being incorporated, at an accelerating rate, into larger systems. The origin (around 10,000 years ago) and spread of food production (plant cultivation and animal domestication) led to the formation of larger and more powerful social and political systems. Food production led to major changes in human life. The pace of cultural transformation increased enormously. This chapter provides a framework for understanding a variety of human adaptive strategies and economic systems.

Adaptive Strategies

The anthropologist Yehudi Cohen (1974) used the term *adaptive strategy* to describe a society's system of economic production. Cohen argued that the most important reason for similarities between two (or more) unrelated societies is their possession of a similar adaptive strategy. In other words, similar economic causes have similar sociocultural effects. For example, there are clear similarities among societies that have a foraging (hunting and gathering) strategy. Cohen developed a typology of societies based on correlations between their economies and their social features. His typology includes these five adaptive strategies: foraging, horticulture, agriculture, pastoralism, and industrialism. Industrialism is discussed in the chapter, "The World System and Colonialism." The present chapter focuses on the first four adaptive strategies.

Foraging

Until 10,000 years ago all humans were foragers (see Barnard 2004). However, environmental differences did create substantial contrasts among the world's foragers. Some, like the people who lived in Europe during the ice ages, were big-game hunters. Today, hunters in the Arctic still focus on large animals and herd animals; they have much less vegetation and variety in their diets than do tropical foragers. Moving from colder to hotter areas, the number of species increases. The tropics contain tremendous biodiversity, and tropical foragers typically hunt and gather a wide range of plant and animal species. The same may be true in temperate areas. For example, on the North Pacific Coast of North America, foragers could draw on varied sea, river, and land species, such as salmon and other fish, sea mammals, berries, and mountain goats. Despite differences caused by such environmental variation, all foraging economies have shared one essential feature: People rely on nature to make their living.

Animal domestication (initially of sheep and goats) and plant cultivation (of wheat and barley) began 10,000 to 12,000 years ago in the Middle East. Cultivation based on different crops, such as corn (maize), manioc (cassava), and potatoes, arose independently in the Americas. In both hemispheres most foragers eventually turned to food production. Today most foragers have at least some dependence on food production or on food producers (Kent 1992; 2002).

The foraging way of life survived into modern times in certain forests, deserts, islands, and very cold areas—places where food production was not practicable with simple technology (see Lee and Daly 1999). In many areas, foragers were exposed to the "idea" of food production but never adopted it because their own economies provided a perfectly adequate and nutritious diet—with a lot less work. In some places, people reverted to foraging after trying food production and abandoning it. In most areas where hunter-gatherers did survive, foraging should be described as "recent" rather than "contemporary." *All modern foragers live in nation-states and depend to some extent on government assistance.* They are in contact with food-producing neighbors as well as with missionaries and other outsiders. We should not view contemporary foragers as isolated or pristine survivors of the Stone Age. Modern foragers are influenced by national and international policies and political and economic events in the world system.

Although foraging is disappearing rapidly as a way of life, we can trace the outlines of Africa's two broad belts of recent foraging. One is the Kalahari Desert of southern Africa. This is the home of the San ("Bushmen"), who include the Ju/'hoansi (see Kent 1996; Lee 2003). The other main African foraging area is the equatorial forest of central and eastern Africa, home of the Mbuti, Efe, and other "pygmies" (Bailey et al. 1989; Turnbull 1965).

People still do, or until recently did, subsistence foraging in certain remote forests in Madagascar, Southeast Asia, Malaysia, the Philippines, and on certain islands off the Indian coast. Some of the best-known recent foragers are the aborigines of Australia. Those Native Australians lived on their island continent for more than 60,000 years without developing food production.

The Western Hemisphere also had recent foragers. The Eskimos, or Inuit, of Alaska and Canada are well-known hunters. These (and other) northern foragers now use modern technology, including rifles and snowmobiles, in their subsistence activities (Pelto 1973). The native populations of California, Oregon, Washington, and British Columbia all were foragers, as were those of inland subarctic Canada and the Great Lakes. For many Native Americans, fishing, hunting, and gathering remain important subsistence (and sometimes commercial) activities.

Coastal foragers also lived near the southern tip of South America, in Patagonia. On the grassy plains of Argentina, southern Brazil, Uruguay, and Paraguay, there were other hunter-gatherers. The contemporary Aché of Paraguay usually are called "hunter-gatherers" although they now get just a third of their livelihood from foraging. The Aché also grow crops, have domesticated animals, and live in or near mission posts, where they receive food from missionaries (Hawkes, O'Connell, and Hill 1982; Hill et al. 1987).

Throughout the world, foraging survived in environments that posed major obstacles to food production. (Some foragers took refuge in such areas after the rise of food production, the state, colonialism, or the modern world system.) The difficulties of cultivating at the North Pole are obvious. In southern Africa the Dobe Ju/'hoansi San area studied by Richard Lee and others is surrounded by a waterless belt 43 to 124 miles (70 to 200 kilometers) in breadth (Solway and Lee 1990).

Environmental obstacles to food production aren't the only reason foragers survived. See Figure 11.1 and Table 11.1 for the distribution of recent hunter-gatherers. Their

FIGURE 11.1   Worldwide Distribution of Recent Hunter-Gatherers

Source: Adapted from a map by Ray Sim, in Göran Burenhult, ed., *Encyclopedia of Humankind: People of the Stone Age*, p. 193. Copyright © 1993. Reprinted by permission of Weldon Owen Pty Ltd.

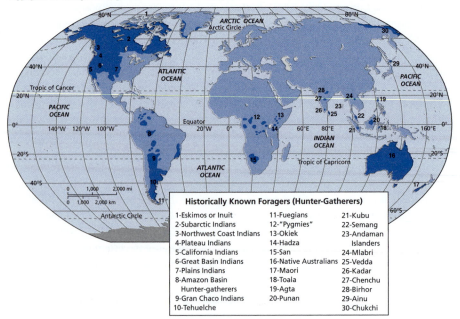

Historically Known Foragers (Hunter-Gatherers)

1-Eskimos or Inuit	11-Fuegians	21-Kubu
2-Subarctic Indians	12-"Pygmies"	22-Semang
3-Northwest Coast Indians	13-Okiek	23-Andaman
4-Plateau Indians	14-Hadza	Islanders
5-California Indians	15-San	24-Mlabri
6-Great Basin Indians	16-Native Australians	25-Vedda
7-Plains Indians	17-Maori	26-Kadar
8-Amazon Basin	18-Toala	27-Chenchu
Hunter-gatherers	19-Agta	28-Birhor
9-Gran Chaco Indians	20-Punan	29-Ainu
10-Tehuelche		30-Chukchi

TABLE 11.1   Foragers Then and Now

Geographic Locations	
Archaeologically Known	Europe: Paleolithic big game hunters
	Europe, Japan, Middle East, elsewhere: Mesolithic broad-spectrum foragers
	Africa: Stone Age hunters and gatherers
Recent (Ethnographically Known) Old World	Africa:
	Kalahari Desert, southern Africa: *San* ("Bushmen")
	Equatorial forest, central & eastern Africa: Mbuti, Efe ("pygmies")
	Madagascar, remote forests: Mikea
	Southeast Asia—Malaysia and Philippines: Tasaday
	Islands off India's coast: Andaman Islanders
	Australia: entire continent—Native Australians ("aborigines")
Western Hemisphere	Eskimos, or Inuit: Alaska and Canada
	N. Pacific coast: California, Oregon, Washington, British Columbia, and Alaska
	Inland subarctic Canada and U.S. Great Lakes
	South America:
	coastal Patagonia
	pampas: Argentina, southern Brazil, Uruguay, Paraguay
Generalizations About Foragers	
	Not pristine "survivors of the Stone Age."
	Recent rather than contemporary.
	Rely on natural resources for subsistence.
	Don't control plant and animal reproduction.
	Environments posed major obstacles to food production.
	Live on or in islands, forests, deserts, very cold areas.
	Some knew about food production but rejected it.
	Some fled food production, states, or colonial rule.
All Foragers Today	Live in nation-states.
	Depend on outside assistance.
	Have significant contact with outsiders.
	Are influenced by:
	food-producing economies
	regional forces (e.g., trade and war)
	national and international policies
	political and economic events in the world system

Means of Production

In nonindustrial societies the relationship between the worker and the means of production is more intimate than it is in industrial nations. **Means, or factors, of production** include land (territory), labor, and technology.

Land as a Means of Production

Among foragers, ties between people and land were less permanent than among food producers. Although many bands had territories, the boundaries usually were not marked, and there was no way they could be enforced. The hunter's stake in an animal was more important than where the animal finally died. A person acquired the rights to use a band's territory by being born in the band or by joining it through a tie of kinship, marriage, or fictive kinship. In Botswana in southern Africa, Ju/'hoansi San women habitually used specific tracts of berry-bearing trees. When a woman changed bands, she immediately acquired a new gathering area.

Among food producers, rights to the means of production also come through kinship and marriage. Descent groups (groups whose members claim common ancestry) are common among nonindustrial food producers. Those who descend from the founder share the group's territory and resources. If the adaptive strategy is horticulture, the estate includes gardens and fallow land for shifting cultivation. As members of a descent group, pastoralists have access to animals to start their own herds, to grazing land, to garden land, and to other means of production.

Labor, Tools, and Specialization

Like land, labor is a means of production. In nonindustrial societies, access to both land and labor comes through social links such as kinship, marriage, and descent. Mutual aid in production is merely one aspect of ongoing social relations that are expressed on many other occasions.

Nonindustrial societies contrast with industrial nations regarding another means of production—technology. Manufacturing often is linked to age and gender. Women may weave and men may make pottery, or vice versa. Most people of a particular age and gender share the technical knowledge associated with that age and gender. If married women customarily make baskets, most married women know how to make baskets. Neither technology nor technical knowledge is very specialized.

Some tribal societies, however, do promote specialization. Among the Yanomami of Venezuela and Brazil, for instance, certain villages manufacture clay pots and others make hammocks. They don't specialize, as one might suppose, because certain raw materials happen to be available near particular villages. Clay suitable for pots is widely available. Everyone knows how to make pots, but not everybody does so. Craft specialization reflects the social and political environment rather than the natural environment. Such specialization promotes trade, which is the first step in creating an alliance with enemy villages (Chagnon 1997).

Alienation in Industrial Economies

There are significant contrasts between nonindustrial economies and industrial ones. In the former, economic relations are just one part of a larger, multidimensional, social matrix. People don't just work for and with others; they live with those same people; they pray with, feast with, and care about them. One works for and with people with whom one has long-term personal and social bonds (e.g., kin or in-laws).

In industrial societies, by contrast, workers sell their labor to bosses who can fire them. Work and the workplace are separated—*alienated*—from one's social essence. Rather than expressing an ongoing, mutual social relationship, labor becomes a thing (commodity) to be paid for, bought, and sold—and from which the boss can generate an individual profit. Furthermore, industrial workers usually don't work with their relatives and neighbors. If coworkers are friends, the personal relationship often develops out of their common employment rather than being based on a previous social tie.

In nonindustrial societies, an individual who makes something can use or dispose of it as he or she sees fit. The maker may feel pride in such a personal product, and, if it is given away, a renewed commitment to the social relationship that is reinforced by the gift. On the other hand, when factory workers produce for their employer's profit, their products as well as their labor are alienated. Their bosses have use or disposal rights. Human labor and its products belong to someone other than the individual producer. Unlike assembly-line workers, producers in nonindustrial societies typically see their work through from start to finish and feel a sense of accomplishment.

Thus, industrial workers have impersonal relations with their employers, coworkers, and products. People sell their labor for cash in a market economy, and work stands apart from family life. In nonindustrial societies, by contrast, the relations of production, distribution, and consumption are social relations with economic aspects. Economy is not a separate entity but is *embedded* in the society.

A Case of Industrial Alienation

For decades, the government of Malaysia has promoted export-oriented industry, allowing transnational companies to install manufacturing operations in rural Malaysia. In search of cheaper labor, corporations headquartered in Japan, Western Europe, and the United States have moved labor-intensive factories to developing countries. Malaysia has hundreds of Japanese and American subsidiaries, which produce garments, foodstuffs, and electronics components. Thousands of young Malaysian women from peasant families now assemble microchips and microcomponents for transistors and capacitors. Aihwa Ong (1987) did a study of electronics assembly workers in an area where 85 percent of the workers were young unmarried females from nearby villages.

Ong found that, unlike village women, female factory workers had to cope with a rigid work routine and constant supervision by men. The discipline that factories value was being taught in local schools, where uniforms helped prepare girls for the factory dress code. Village women wear loose, flowing tunics, sarongs, and sandals, but factory workers had to don tight overalls and heavy rubber gloves, in which they felt constrained. Assembling electronics components requires precise, concentrated labor. Labor in these factories illustrates the separation of intellectual and manual activity—the alienation that Karl Marx considered the defining feature of industrial work. One woman said about her bosses, "They exhaust us very much, as if they do not think that we too are human beings" (Ong 1987, p. 202). Nor does factory work bring women a substantial financial reward, given low wages, job uncertainty, and family claims on wages. Although young

Large numbers of young Asian women now work in factories, producing garments, foodstuffs, and electronics components. Unlike village women, factory workers often face a rigid work schedule and constant supervision by men. Shown here, factory women make garments in Jian city, in east China's Jiangxi Province.

women typically work just a few years, production quotas, three daily shifts, overtime, and surveillance take their toll in mental and physical exhaustion.

One response to factory relations of production has been spirit possession (factory women are possessed by spirits). Ong interprets this phenomenon as the women's unconscious protest against labor discipline and male control of the industrial setting. Sometimes possession takes the form of mass hysteria. Spirits have simultaneously invaded as many as 120 factory workers. Weretigers (the Malay equivalent of the werewolf) arrive to avenge the construction of a factory on aboriginal burial grounds. Disturbed earth and grave spirits swarm on the shop floor. First the women see the spirits; then their bodies are invaded. The weretigers send the women into sobbing, laughing, and shrieking fits. To deal with possession, factories employ local medicine men, who sacrifice chickens and goats to fend off the spirits. This solution works only some of the time; possession still goes on. Ong argues that spirit possession expresses anguish at, and resistance to, capitalist relations of production. By engaging in this form of rebellion, however, factory women avoid a direct confrontation with the source of their distress. Ong concludes that spirit possession, while expressing repressed resentment, doesn't do much to modify factory conditions. (Other tactics, such as unionization, would do more.) Spirit possession may even help maintain the current system by operating as a safety valve for accumulated tensions.

Economizing and Maximization

Economic anthropologists have been concerned with two main questions:

1. How are production, distribution, and consumption organized in different societies? This question focuses on *systems* of human behavior and their organization.
2. What motivates people in different societies to produce, distribute or exchange, and consume? Here the focus is not on systems of behavior but on the *individuals* who participate in those systems.

Anthropologists view economic systems and motivations in a cross-cultural perspective. Motivation is a concern of psychologists, but it also has been a concern of economists and anthropologists. American economists assume that producers and distributors make decisions rationally, using the *profit motive,* as do consumers when they shop around for the best value. Although anthropologists know that the profit motive is not universal, the assumption that individuals try to maximize profits is basic to capitalism and to Western economic theory. In fact, the subject matter of economics often is defined as economizing, or the rational allocation of scarce means (or resources) to alternative ends (or uses).

What does that mean? Classical economic theory assumes that our wants are infinite while our means are limited. People must make choices about how to use their scarce resources—their time, labor, money, and capital. (The "Anthropology Today" at the end of this chapter disputes the idea that people always make economic choices based on scarcity.) Western economists assume that when confronted with choices and decisions, people tend to make the one that maximizes profit. This is assumed to be the most rational choice.

The idea that individuals choose to maximize profits was a basic assumption of the classical economists of the 19th century and one held by many contemporary economists. However, certain economists now recognize that individuals may be motivated by many other goals. Depending on the society and the situation, people may try to maximize profit, wealth, prestige, pleasure, comfort, or social harmony. Individuals may want to realize their personal or family ambitions or those of another group to which they belong (see Sahlins 2004).

Alternative Ends

To what uses do people put their scarce resources? Throughout the world, people devote some of their time and energy to building up a *subsistence fund* (Wolf 1966). In other words, they have to work to eat, to replace the calories they use in daily activity. People also must invest in a *replacement fund.* They must maintain their technology and other items essential to production. If a hoe or plow breaks, they must repair or replace it. They also must obtain and replace items that are essential not to production but to everyday life, such as clothing and shelter.

People everywhere also have to invest in a *social fund.* They must help their friends, relatives, in-laws, and neighbors. It is useful to distinguish between a social fund and a *ceremonial fund.* The latter term refers to expenditures on ceremonies or rituals. To prepare a festival honoring one's ancestors, for example, requires time and the outlay of wealth.

Citizens of nonindustrial states also must allocate scarce resources to a *rent fund*. We think of rent as payment for the use of property. Rent fund, however, has a wider meaning. It refers to resources that people must render to an individual or agency that is superior politically or economically. Tenant farmers and sharecroppers, for example, either pay rent or give some of their produce to their landlords, as peasants did under feudalism.

Peasants are small-scale agriculturists who live in nonindustrial states and have rent fund obligations (see Kearney 1996). They produce to feed themselves, to sell their produce, and to pay rent. All peasants have two things in common:

1. They live in state-organized societies.
2. They produce food without the elaborate technology—chemical fertilizers, tractors, airplanes to spray crops, and so on—of modern farming or agribusiness.

Besides paying rent to landlords, peasants must satisfy government obligations, paying taxes in the form of money, produce, or labor. The rent fund is not simply an *additional* obligation for peasants. Often it becomes their foremost and unavoidable duty. Sometimes their own diets suffer as a result. The demands of social superiors may divert resources from subsistence, replacement, social, and ceremonial funds.

Motivations vary from society to society, and people often lack freedom of choice in allocating their resources. Because of obligations to pay rent, peasants may allocate their scarce means toward ends that are not their own but those of government officials. Thus, even in societies in which there is a profit motive, people often are prevented from rationally maximizing self-interest by factors beyond their control.

Distribution, Exchange

The economist Karl Polanyi (1968) stimulated the comparative study of exchange, and several anthropologists followed his lead. Polanyi defined three principles that guide exchanges: the market principle, redistribution, and reciprocity. These principles all can be present in the same society, but in that case they govern different kinds of transactions. In any society, one of them usually dominates. The principle of exchange that dominates in a given society is the one that allocates the means of production.

The Market Principle

In today's world capitalist economy, the **market principle** dominates. It governs the distribution of the means of production—land, labor, natural resources, technology, and capital. With market exchange, items are bought and sold, using money, with an eye to maximizing profit, and value is determined by the *law of supply and demand* (things cost more the scarcer they are and the more people want them). Bargaining is characteristic of market-principle exchanges. The buyer and seller strive to maximize—to get their "money's worth." Bargaining doesn't require that the buyer and seller meet. Consumers bargain whenever they shop around or use advertisements or the Internet in their decision making (see Madra 2004).

Many hip-hop lyrics are centered around how much money the performers have in comparison to others, how much more they have than before their music career took off, and how this money often leads to problems. Locate and read over the lyrics to these songs: "Beamer, Benz, or Bentley," "Mo Money Mo Problems," and "It's All about the Benjamins." What do they say about the music industry and the artist? Do you believe that these musicians have as much money as they say they have, or is their bragging a technique to place themselves above others, a lesson in bravado? Might these lyrics entice you into beginning a seemingly lucrative music career? Why or why not? What does this say about our culture?

Redistribution

Redistribution operates when goods, services, or their equivalent move from the local level to a center. The center may be a capital, a regional collection point, or a storehouse near a chief's residence. Products often move through a hierarchy of officials for storage at the center. Along the way officials and their dependents may consume some of them, but the exchange principle here is *re*distribution. The flow of goods eventually reverses direction—out from the center, down through the hierarchy, and back to the common people.

One example of a redistributive system comes from the Cherokee, the original owners of the Tennessee Valley. Productive farmers who subsisted on maize, beans, and squash, supplemented by hunting and fishing, the Cherokee had chiefs. Each of their main villages had a central plaza, where meetings of the chief's council took place and where redistributive feasts were held. According to Cherokee custom, each family farm had an area where the family could set aside part of their annual harvest for the chief. This supply of corn was used to feed the needy, as well as travelers and warriors journeying through friendly territory. This store of food was available to all who needed it, with the understanding that it "belonged" to the chief and was available through his generosity. The chief also hosted the redistributive feasts held in the main settlements (Harris 1978).

Reciprocity

Reciprocity is exchange between social equals, who normally are related by kinship, marriage, or another close personal tie. Because it occurs between social equals, it is dominant in the more egalitarian societies—among foragers, cultivators, and pastoralists. There are three degrees of reciprocity: *generalized, balanced,* and *negative* (Sahlins 1968, 2004; Service 1966). These may be imagined as areas of a continuum defined by these questions:

1. How closely related are the parties to the exchange?
2. How quickly and unselfishly are gifts reciprocated?

Generalized reciprocity, the purest form of reciprocity, is characteristic of exchanges between closely related people. In balanced reciprocity, social distance increases, as does the need to reciprocate. In negative reciprocity, social distance is greatest and re-ciprocation is most calculated. This range, from generalized to negative, is called the **reciprocity continuum.**

With **generalized reciprocity,** someone gives to another person and expects nothing immediate in return. Such exchanges are not primarily economic transactions but expres-sions of personal relationships. Most parents don't keep accounts of every penny they spend on their children. They merely hope their children will respect their culture's cus-toms involving obligations to parents.

Among foragers, generalized reciprocity usually has governed exchanges. People routinely have shared with other band members (Bird-David 1992; Kent 1992). So strong is the ethic of sharing that most foragers have lacked an expression for "thank you." To offer thanks would be impolite because it would imply that a particular act of sharing, which is the keystone of egalitarian society, was unusual. Among the Semai, foragers of central Malaysia (Dentan 1979), to express gratitude would suggest surprise at the hunter's success (Harris 1974).

Balanced reciprocity applies to exchanges between people who are more distantly related than are members of the same band or household. In a horticultural society, for example, a man presents a gift to someone in another village. The recipient may be a cousin, a trading partner, or a brother's fictive kinsman. The giver expects something in return. This may not come immediately, but the social relationship will be strained if there is no reciprocation.

Exchanges in nonindustrial societies also may illustrate **negative reciprocity,** mainly in dealing with people on the fringes of or outside their social systems. To people who live in a world of close personal relations, exchanges with outsiders are full of ambiguity and distrust. Exchange is one way of establishing friendly relations, but when trade begins, the relationship is still tentative. Often the initial exchange is close to being purely economic; people want to get something back immediately. Just as in market economies, but without using money, they try to get the best possible immediate return for their investment.

Generalized reciprocity and balanced reciprocity are based on trust and a social tie. Negative reciprocity involves the attempt to get something for as little as possible, even if it means being cagey or deceitful or cheating. Among the most extreme and "nega-tive" examples of negative reciprocity was 19th-century horse thievery by North Ameri-can Plains Indians. Men would sneak into camps and villages of neighboring tribes to steal horses. A similar pattern of livestock (cattle) raiding continues today in East Africa, among tribes such as the Kuria (Fleisher 2000). In these cases, the party that starts the raiding can expect reciprocity—a raid on their own village—or worse. The Kuria hunt down cattle thieves and kill them. It's still reciprocity, governed by "Do unto others as they have done unto you."

One way of reducing the tension in situations of potential negative reciprocity is to engage in "silent trade." One example was the silent trade of the Mbuti pygmy foragers of the African equatorial forest and their neighboring horticultural villagers. There was no personal contact during their exchanges. A Mbuti hunter left game, honey, or another forest product at a customary site. Villagers collected it and left crops in exchange. Of-ten the parties bargained silently. If one felt the return was insufficient, he or she simply left it at the trading site. If the other party wanted to continue trade, it was increased.

Coexistence of Exchange Principles

In today's North America, the market principle governs most exchanges, from the sale of the means of production to the sale of consumer goods. We also have redistribution. Some of our tax money goes to support the government, but some of it also comes back to us in the form of social services, education, health care, and road building. We also have reciprocal exchanges. Generalized reciprocity characterizes the relationship between parents and children. However, even here the dominant market mentality surfaces in comments about the high cost of raising children and in the stereotypical statement of the disappointed parent: "We gave you everything money could buy."

Exchanges of gifts, cards, and invitations exemplify reciprocity, usually balanced. Everyone has heard remarks like "They invited us to their daughter's wedding, so when ours gets married, we'll have to invite them" and "They've been here for dinner three times and haven't invited us yet. I don't think we should ask them back until they do." Such precise balancing of reciprocity would be out of place in a foraging band, where resources are communal (common to all) and daily sharing based on generalized reciprocity is an essential ingredient of social life and survival.

Potlatching

One of the most famous cultural practices studied by ethnographers is the **potlatch.** This is a festive event within a regional exchange system among tribes of the North Pacific Coast of North America, including the Salish and Kwakiutl of Washington and British

The historic photo shows the amassing of blankets to be given away at a Kwakiutl potlatch. The man in the foreground is making a speech praising the generosity of the potlatch host.

Columbia. Some tribes still practice the potlatch, sometimes as a memorial to the dead (Kan 1986, 1989). At each such event, assisted by members of their communities, potlatch sponsors traditionally gave away food, blankets, pieces of copper, or other items. In return for this, they got prestige. To give a potlatch enhanced one's reputation. Prestige increased with the lavishness of the potlatch, the value of the goods given away in it.

The potlatching tribes were foragers, but atypical ones for relatively recent times. They were sedentary and had chiefs. They had access to a wide variety of land and sea resources. Among their most important foods were salmon, herring, candlefish, berries, mountain goats, seals, and porpoises (Piddocke 1969).

According to classical economic theory, the profit motive is universal, with the goal of maximizing material benefits. How then does one explain the potlatch, in which substantial wealth is given away (and even destroyed—see below)? Christian missionaries considered potlatching to be wasteful and antithetical to the Protestant work ethic. By 1885, under pressure from Indian agents, missionaries, and Indian converts to Christianity, both Canada and the United States had outlawed potlatching. Between 1885 and 1951 the custom went underground. By 1951, however, both countries had discreetly dropped the antipotlatching laws from the books (Miller n.d.).

Some scholars seized on this view of the potlatch as a classic case of economically wasteful behavior. The economist and social commentator Thorstein Veblen cited potlatching as an example of conspicuous consumption in his influential book *Theory of the Leisure Class* (1899/1992), claiming that potlatching was based on an economically irrational drive for prestige. This interpretation stressed the lavishness and supposed wastefulness, especially of the Kwakiutl displays, to support the contention that in some societies people strive to maximize prestige at the expense of their material well-being. This interpretation has been challenged.

Ecological anthropology, also known as *cultural ecology,* is a theoretical school that attempts to interpret cultural practices, such as the potlatch, in terms of their long-term role in helping humans adapt to their environments. Wayne Suttles (1960) and Andrew Vayda (1961/1968) saw potlatching not in terms of its immediate wastefulness, but in terms of its long-term role as a cultural adaptive mechanism. This view also helps us understand similar patterns of lavish feasting throughout the world. Here is the ecological interpretation: *Customs such as the potlatch are cultural adaptations to alternating periods of local abundance and shortage.*

How does this work? Although the natural environment of the North Pacific Coast is favorable, resources do fluctuate from year to year and place to place. Salmon and herring aren't equally abundant every year in a given locality. One village can have a good year while another is experiencing a bad one. Later their fortunes reverse. In this context, the potlatch cycle had adaptive value, and the potlatch was not a competitive display that brought no material benefit.

A village enjoying an especially good year had a surplus of subsistence items, which it could trade for more durable wealth items, such as blankets, canoes, or pieces of copper. Wealth, in turn, by being distributed, could be converted into prestige. Members of several villages were invited to any potlatch and got to take home the resources that were given away. In this way, potlatching linked villages together in a regional economy—an exchange system that distributed food and wealth from wealthy to needy communities. In return, the potlatch sponsors and their villages got prestige. The decision to potlatch

Anthropology Today *Scarcity and the Betsileo*

In the late 1960s my wife and I lived among the Betsileo people of Madagascar, studying their economy and social life (Kottak 1980). Soon after our arrival we met two well-educated schoolteachers (first cousins) who were interested in our research. The woman's father was a congressional representative who became a cabinet minister during our stay. Their family came from a historically important and typical Betsileo village called Ivato, which they invited us to visit with them.

We had traveled to many other Betsileo villages, where often we were displeased with our reception. As we drove up, children would run away screaming. Women would hurry inside. Men would retreat to doorways, where they lurked bashfully. This behavior expressed the Betsileo's great fear of the *mpakafo*. Believed to cut out and devour his victim's heart and liver, the mpakafo is the Malagasy vampire. These cannibals are said to have fair skin and to be very tall. Because I have light skin and stand over six feet tall, I was a natural suspect. The fact that such creatures were not known to travel with their wives helped convince the Betsileo that I wasn't really a mpakafo.

When we visited Ivato, its people were different—friendly and hospitable. Our very first day there we did a brief census and found out who lived in which households. We learned people's names and their relationships to our schoolteacher friends and to each other. We met an excellent informant who knew all about the local history. In a few afternoons I learned much more than I had in the other villages in several sessions.

Ivatans were so willing to talk because we had powerful sponsors, village natives who had made it in the outside world, people the Ivatans knew would protect them. The schoolteachers vouched for us,

but even more significant was the cabinet minister, who was like a grandfather and benefactor to everyone in town. The Ivatans had no reason to fear us because their more influential native son had asked them to answer our questions.

Once we moved to Ivato, the elders established a pattern of visiting us every evening. They came to talk, attracted by the inquisitive foreigners but also by the wine, tobacco, and food we offered. I asked questions about their customs and beliefs. I eventually developed interview schedules about various subjects, including rice production. I used these forms in Ivato and in two other villages I was studying less intensively. Never have I interviewed as easily as I did in Ivato.

As our stay neared its end, our Ivatan friends lamented, saying, "We'll miss you. When you leave, there won't be any more cigarettes, any more wine, or any more questions." They wondered what it would be like for us back in the United States. They knew we had an automobile and that we regularly purchased things, including the wine, cigarettes, and food we shared with them. We could afford to buy products they never would have. They commented, "When you go back to your country, you'll need a lot of money for things like cars, clothes, and food. We don't need to buy those things. We make almost everything we use. We don't need as much money as you, because we produce for ourselves."

The Betsileo weren't unusual for nonindustrial people. Strange as it may seem to an American consumer, those rice farmers actually believed *they had all they needed*. The lesson from the Betsileo of the 1960s is that scarcity, which economists view as universal, is variable. Although shortages do arise in nonindustrial societies, the concept of scarcity (insufficient means) is much less developed in stable subsistence-oriented

continued

Anthropology Today *continued*

societies than in the societies characterized by industrialism, particularly as the reliance on consumer goods increases.

But, with globalization over the past few decades, significant changes have affected the Betsileo—and most nonindustrial peoples (Kottak 2004). On my last visit to Ivato, in 2006, the effects of cash and of population increase were evident there—and throughout Madagascar—where the national growth rate has been about 3 percent per year. Madagascar's population doubled between 1966 and 1991—from 6 to 12 million people. Today it approaches 20 million. One result of population pressure has been agricultural intensification. In Ivato, farmers who formerly had grown only rice in their rice fields now use the same land for commercial crops, such as carrots, after the annual rice harvest. A more tragic change affecting Ivato has been the breakdown of social and political order, fueled by increasing demand for cash.

Cattle rustling has become a growing threat. Cattle thieves (sometimes from neighboring villages) have terrorized peasants who previously felt secure in their villages. Some of the rustled cattle are driven to the coasts for commercial export to nearby islands. Prominent among the rustlers are relatively well-educated young men who have studied long enough to be comfortable negotiating with outsiders, but who have been unable to find formal work, and who are unwilling to work the rice fields like their peasant ancestors. The formal education system has familiarized them with external institutions and norms, including the need for cash. The concepts of scarcity, commerce, and negative reciprocity now thrive among the Betsileo.

I have witnessed other striking evidence of the new addiction to cash during my most recent visits to Betsileo country. Near Ivato's county seat, people now sell precious stones—tourmalines, which were found by chance in local rice fields. We

Women hull rice in a Betsileo village. In the village of Ivato, farmers who traditionally grew only rice in their fields now use the same land for commercial crops, such as carrots, after the annual rice harvest.

saw an amazing sight: dozens of villagers destroying an ancestral resource, digging up a large rice field, seeking tourmalines—clear evidence of the encroachment of cash on the local subsistence economy.

Throughout the Betsileo homeland, population growth and density are propelling emigration. Locally, land, jobs, and money are all scarce. One woman with ancestors from Ivato, herself now a resident of the national capital (Antanana-

rivo), remarked that half the children of Ivato now lived in that city. Although she was exaggerating, a census of all the descendants of Ivato reveals a substantial emigrant and urban population.

Ivato's recent history is one of increasing participation in a cash economy. That history, combined with the pressure of a growing population on local resources, has made scarcity not just a concept but a reality for Ivatans and their neighbors.

was determined by the health of the local economy. If there had been subsistence surpluses, and thus a buildup of wealth over several good years, a village could afford a potlatch to convert its surplus food and wealth into prestige.

The long-term adaptive value of intercommunity feasting becomes clear when a formerly prosperous village had a run of bad luck. Its people started accepting invitations to potlatches in villages that were doing better. The tables were turned as the temporarily rich became temporarily poor and vice versa. The newly needy accepted food and wealth items. They were willing to receive rather than bestow gifts and thus to relinquish some of their stored-up prestige. They hoped their luck would eventually improve so that resources could be recouped and prestige regained.

The potlatch linked local groups along the North Pacific Coast into a regional alliance and exchange network. Potlatching and intervillage exchange had adaptive functions, regardless of the motivations of the individual participants. The anthropologists who stressed rivalry for prestige were not wrong. They were merely emphasizing *motivations* at the expense of an analysis of economic and ecological *systems*.

The use of feasts to enhance individual and community reputations and to redistribute wealth is not peculiar to populations of the North Pacific Coast. Competitive feasting is widely characteristic of nonindustrial food producers. But among most surviving foragers, who live in marginal areas, resources are too meager to support feasting on such a level. In such societies, sharing rather than competition prevails.

Summary

1. Cohen's adaptive strategies include foraging (hunting and gathering), horticulture, agriculture, pastoralism, and industrialism. Foraging was the only human adaptive strategy until the advent of food production (farming and herding) 10,000 years ago. Food production eventually replaced foraging in most places. Almost all modern foragers have some dependence on food production or food producers.

2. Horticulture doesn't use land or labor intensively. Horticulturalists cultivate a plot for one or two years (sometimes longer) and then abandon it. There is always a

fallow period. Agriculturists farm the same plot of land continuously and use labor intensively. They use one or more of the following: irrigation, terracing, domesticated animals as means of production, and manuring.

3. The pastoral strategy is mixed. Nomadic pastoralists trade with cultivators. Part of a transhumant pastoral population cultivates while another part takes the herds to pasture. Except for some Peruvians and the Navajo, who are recent herders, the New World lacks native pastoralists.

4. Economic anthropology is the cross-cultural study of systems of production, distribution, and consumption. In nonindustrial societies, a kin-based mode of production prevails. One acquires rights to resources and labor through membership in social groups, not impersonally through purchase and sale. Work is just one aspect of social relations expressed in varied contexts.

5. Economics has been defined as the science of allocating scarce means to alternative ends. Western economists assume the notion of scarcity is universal—which it isn't—and that in making choices, people strive to maximize personal profit. In nonindustrial societies, indeed as in our own, people often maximize values other than individual profit.

6. In nonindustrial societies, people invest in subsistence, replacement, social, and ceremonial funds. States add a rent fund: People must share their output with their social superiors. In states, the obligation to pay rent often becomes primary.

7. Besides studying production, economic anthropologists study and compare exchange systems. The three principles of exchange are the market principle, redistribution, and reciprocity, which may coexist in a given society. The primary exchange mode is the one that allocates the means of production.

8. Patterns of feasting and exchanges of wealth among villages are common among nonindustrial food producers, as among the potlatching societies of North America's North Pacific Coast. Such systems help even out the availability of resources over time.

Key Terms

agriculture, 253
balanced
  reciprocity, 264
band, 250
correlation, 250
economy, 256
generalized
  reciprocity, 264
horticulture, 251
market
  principle, 262

means (or factors)
  of production,
  258
mode of
  production, 257
negative
  reciprocity, 264
pastoral
  nomadism, 256
pastoralists, 255
peasants, 262

potlatch, 265
reciprocity, 263
reciprocity
  continuum, 264
redistribution, 263
transhumance, 256

Go to our Online Learning Center website at **www.mhhe.com/kottak** for Internet resources directly related to the content of this chapter.

Chapter 12

Political Systems

What Is "The Political"?

Types and Trends

Bands and Tribes

Foraging Bands

Tribal Cultivators

The Village Head

The "Big Man"

Applying Anthropology
to Popular Culture: Superheroes

Pantribal Sodalities

Nomadic Politics

Chiefdoms

Political and Economic Systems

Status Systems

The Emergence of Stratification

State Systems

Population Control

Judiciary

Enforcement

Fiscal Support

Social Control

Hegemony and Resistance

Weapons of the Weak

Shame and Gossip

The Igbo Women's War

Anthropology Today: Yanomami
Update: Venezuela Takes Charge,
Problems Arise

Anthropologists share an interest in political systems and organization with political scientists. Here again, however, the anthropological approach is global and comparative and includes nonstates, while political scientists tend to focus on contemporary and recent nation-states. Anthropological studies have revealed substantial variation in power, authority, and legal systems in different societies. (**Power** is the ability to exercise one's will over others; **authority** is the formal, socially approved use of power, e.g., by government officials.) (See Gledhill 2000; Kurtz 2001; Lewellen 2003; Nugent and Vincent, eds. 2004; Wolf with Silverman 2001.)

What Is "The Political"?

Morton Fried offered the following definition of political organization:

> Political organization comprises those portions of social organization that specifically relate to the individuals or groups that manage the affairs of public policy or seek to control the appointment or activities of those individuals or groups. (Fried 1967, pp. 20–21)

Seeking to influence public policy are these participants in an Immigrant Rights Rally in Union Square Park, New York City. They urged Congress to offer a path to citizenship for millions of illegal/undocumented immigrants in the United States.

This definition certainly fits contemporary North America. Under "individuals or groups that manage the affairs of public policy" come various agencies and levels of government. Those who seek to influence public policy include political parties, unions, corporations, consumers, lobbyists, activists, action committees, religious groups, and nongovernmental organizations (NGOs).

Fried's definition is less applicable to nonstates, where it's often difficult to detect any "public policy." For this reason, I prefer to speak of *socio*political organization in discussing the exercise of power and the regulation of relations among groups and their representatives. Political regulation includes such processes as decision making, dispute management, and conflict resolution. The study of political regulation draws our attention to those who make decisions and resolve conflicts (are there formal leaders?).

Types and Trends

Ethnographic and archaeological studies in hundreds of places have revealed many correlations between the economy and social and political organization. Decades ago, the anthropologist Elman Service (1962) listed four types, or levels, of political organization: band, tribe, chiefdom, and state. Today, none of the first three types can be studied as a self-contained form of political organization, because all now exist within the context of nation-states and are subject to state control (see Ferguson 2002 and this chapter's "Anthropology Today"). There is archaeological evidence for early bands, tribes, and chiefdoms that existed before the first states appeared. However, because anthropology came into being long after the origin of the state, anthropologists never have been able to observe "in the flesh" a band, tribe, or chiefdom outside the influence of some state. There still may be local political leaders (e.g., village heads) and regional figures

Kent (1§
and space ;
1950s and
Richard B. l
Lee and otł
1981; Tana
work in mỉ
contrasts w
and Vierich
San groups
Dobe Ju/'h
have retain

To the eː
can illustra
culture. Fo
emphasize
tics. A soc
economy v
get it; othei
age permaı

In the p
seasonally
vary from
bands. Trac
such an *eg*
or made d
spread of ş
phers to fiı

The Inuit

The aborị
good exam
ies. All so
cultural ru
dards or gı
propriate
cultural uı
mal laws t

Forage
ment, but
sence of l
classic etł
Inuit span
cant sociạ
linked the

(e.g., chiefs) of the sort discussed in this chapter, but all now exist and function within the context of state organization.

A band is a small kin-based group (all its members are related by kinship or marriage) found among foragers. **Tribes** have economies based on nonintensive food production (horticulture and pastoralism). Living in villages and organized into kin groups based on common descent (clans and lineages—see the next chapter), tribes have no formal government and no reliable means of enforcing political decisions. **Chiefdom** refers to a form of sociopolitical organization intermediate between the tribe and the state. In chiefdoms, social relations were based mainly on kinship, marriage, descent, age, generation, and gender—just as in bands and tribes. However, although chiefdoms were kin-based, they featured **differential access** to resources (some people had more wealth, prestige, and power than others did) and a permanent political structure. The **state** is a form of sociopolitical organization based on a formal government structure and socioeconomic stratification.

The four labels in Service's typology are much too simple to account for the full range of political diversity and complexity known to archaeology and ethnography. We'll see, for instance, that tribes have varied widely in their political systems and institutions. Nevertheless, Service's typology does highlight some significant contrasts in political organization, especially those between states and nonstates. For example, in bands and tribes—unlike states, which have clearly visible governments—political organization did not stand out as separate and distinct from the total social order. In bands and tribes, it was difficult to characterize an act or event as political rather than merely social.

Service's labels "band," "tribe," "chiefdom," and "state" are categories or types within a **sociopolitical typology.** These types are correlated with the adaptive strategies (an *economic typology*) discussed in the previous chapter. Thus, foragers (an economic type) tended to have band organization (a sociopolitical type). Similarly, many horticulturalists and pastoralists lived in tribes. Although most chiefdoms had farming economies, herding was important in some Middle Eastern chiefdoms. Nonindustrial states usually had an agricultural base.

With food production came larger, denser populations and more complex economies than was the case among foragers. These features posed new regulatory problems, which gave rise to more complex relations and linkages. Many sociopolitical trends reflect the increased regulatory demands associated with food production. Archaeologists have studied these trends through time, and cultural anthropologists have observed them among more contemporary groups.

Bands and Tribes

This chapter examines a series of societies with different political systems. A common set of questions will be addressed for each one. What kinds of social groups does the society have? How do those groups represent themselves to each other? How are their internal and external relations regulated? To answer these questions, we begin with bands and tribes and then consider chiefdoms and states.

Foragir

Modern h
ties they r
different f
interlinke
social wo
agers now
rely on go

The San

In the pre
the gover
into a wi
southern .
years and
scend fro
the San t
by Europ
for wealt
ticated ar

Susan
all as ali
Age. A r
groups f

Among t
contribu
Namibia
foragers

(part-time religious specialists). However, these positions conferred little power on those who occupied them.

Hunting and fishing by men were the primary Inuit subsistence activities. The diverse and abundant plant foods available in warmer areas, where female labor in gathering is important, were absent in the Arctic. Traveling on land and sea in a bitter environment, Inuit men faced more dangers than women did. The traditional male role took its toll in lives, so that adult women outnumbered men. This permitted some men to have two or three wives. The ability to support more than one wife conferred a certain amount of prestige, but it also encouraged envy. (*Prestige* is social esteem, respect, or approval.) If a man seemed to be taking additional wives just to enhance his reputation, a rival was likely to steal one of them. Most Inuit disputes were between men and originated over women, caused by wife stealing or adultery.

A jilted husband had several options. He could try to kill the wife stealer. However, if he succeeded, one of his rival's kinsmen surely would try to kill him in retaliation. One dispute might escalate into several deaths as relatives avenged a succession of murders. No government existed to intervene and stop such a *blood feud* (a murderous feud between families). However, one also could challenge a rival to a song battle. In a public setting, contestants made up insulting songs about each other. At the end of the match, the audience proclaimed the winner. However, if the winner was the man whose wife had been stolen, there was no guarantee she would return. Often she stayed with her abductor.

Thefts are common in societies with marked property differentials, like our own, but thefts are uncommon among foragers. Each Inuit had access to the resources he or she needed to sustain life. Every man could hunt, fish, and make the tools necessary for subsistence. Every woman could obtain the materials needed to make clothing, prepare food, and do domestic work. Inuit men could even hunt and fish in the territories of other local groups. There was no notion of private ownership of territory or animals.

Tribal Cultivators

As is true of foraging bands, there are no totally autonomous tribes in today's world. Still, there are societies, for example, in Papua New Guinea and in South America's tropical forests, in which tribal principles continue to operate. Tribes typically have a horticultural or pastoral economy and are organized into villages and/or *descent groups* (kin groups whose members trace descent from a common ancestor). Tribes lack socioeconomic stratification (i.e., a class structure) and a formal government of their own. A few tribes still conduct small-scale warfare, in the form of intervillage raiding. Tribes have more effective regulatory mechanisms than foragers do, but tribal societies have no sure means of enforcing political decisions. The main regulatory officials are village heads, "big men," descent-group leaders, village councils, and leaders of pantribal associations (see later in the chapter). All these figures and groups have limited authority.

Like foragers, horticulturalists tend to be egalitarian, although some have marked *gender stratification:* an unequal distribution of resources, power, prestige, and personal freedom between men and women (see the chapter "Gender"). Horticultural villages usually are small, with low population density and open access to strategic resources. Age, gender, and personal traits determine how much respect people receive and how much support they get from others. Egalitarianism diminishes, however, as village size and population density increase. Horticultural villages usually have headmen—rarely, if ever, headwomen.

The Village Head

The Yanomami (Chagnon 1997; Ferguson 1995; Ramos 1995) are Native Americans who live in southern Venezuela and the adjacent part of Brazil. (See this chapter's "Anthropology Today" for an update on the Yanomami.) Their tribal society has about 26,000 people living in 200 to 250 widely scattered villages, each with a population between 40 and 250. The Yanomami are horticulturalists who also hunt and gather. Their staple crops are bananas and plantains (a bananalike crop). There are more significant social groups among the Yanomami than exist in a foraging society. The Yanomami have families, villages, and descent groups. Their descent groups, which span more than one village, are *patrilineal* (ancestry is traced back through males only) and *exogamous* (people must marry outside their own descent group). However, branches of two different descent groups may live in the same village and intermarry.

Traditionally among the Yanomami the only leadership position has been that of **village head** (always a man). His authority, like that of a foraging band's leader, is severely limited. If a headman wants something done, he must lead by example and persuasion. The headman lacks the right to issue orders. He can only persuade, harangue, and try to influence public opinion. For example, if he wants people to clean up the central plaza in preparation for a feast, he must start sweeping it himself, hoping his covillagers will take the hint and relieve him.

When conflict erupts within the village, the headman may be called on as a mediator who listens to both sides. He will give an opinion and advice. If a disputant is unsatisfied, the headman has no power to back his decisions and no way to impose punishments. Like the band leader, he is first among equals.

A Yanomami village headman also must lead in generosity. Expected to be more generous than any other villager, he cultivates more land. His garden provides much of the food consumed when his village hosts a feast for another village. The headman represents the village in its dealings with outsiders, including Venezuelan and Brazilian government agents.

The way someone acts as headman depends on his personal traits and the number of supporters he can muster. Napoleon Chagnon (1983/1992) describes how one village headman, Kaobawa, guaranteed safety to a delegation from a village with which a covillager of his wanted to start a war. Kaobawa was a particularly effective headman. He had demonstrated his fierceness in battle, but he also knew how to use diplomacy to avoid offending other villagers. No one in his village had a better personality for the headmanship. Nor (because Kaobawa had many brothers) did anyone have more supporters. Among the Yanomami, when a village is dissatisfied with its headman, its members can leave and found a new village. This happens from time to time and is called *village fissioning*.

With its many villages and descent groups, Yanomami sociopolitical organization is more complicated than that of a band-organized society. The Yanomami face more problems in regulating relations between groups and individuals. Although a headman sometimes can prevent a specific violent act, intervillage raiding has been a feature of some areas of Yanomami territory, particularly those studied by Chagnon (1997).

It's important to recognize as well that the Yanomami are not isolated from outside events. They live in two nation-states, Venezuela and Brazil, and attacks by outsiders, especially Brazilian ranchers and miners, have plagued them (Chagnon 1997; *Cultural Survival Quarterly* 1989; Ferguson 1995). During a Brazilian gold rush between 1987 and 1991, one Yanomami died each day, on average, from such attacks. By 1991, there were some 40,000 miners in the Brazilian Yanomami homeland. Some Indians were killed outright. The miners introduced new diseases, and the swollen population ensured that old diseases became epidemic. In 1991, the American Anthropological Association reported on the plight of the Yanomami (*Anthropology Newsletter,* September 1991). Brazilian Yanomami were dying at a rate of 10 percent annually, and their fertility rate had dropped to zero. Since then, one Brazilian president declared a huge Yanomami territory off-limits to outsiders. Unfortunately, local politicians, miners, and ranchers have managed to evade the ban. The future of the Yanomami remains uncertain (see "Anthropology Today").

The "Big Man"

Many societies of the South Pacific, particularly on the Melanesian Islands and in Papua New Guinea, had a kind of political leader that we call the big man. The **big man** (almost always a male) was an elaborate version of the village head, but with one significant difference. Unlike the village head, whose leadership is limited to one village, the big man had supporters in several villages. The big man thus was a regulator of *regional* political organization.

Consider the Kapauku Papuans, who live in Irian Jaya, Indonesia (which is on the island of New Guinea). Anthropologist Leopold Pospisil (1963) studied the Kapauku (then 45,000 people), who grow crops (with the sweet potato as their staple) and raise pigs. Their economy is too complex to be described as simple horticulture. Labor-intensive cultivation requires mutual aid in turning the soil before planting. The digging of long drainage ditches, which a big man often helped organize, is even more complex. Kapauku cultivation supports a larger and denser population than does the simpler horticulture of the Yanomami. The Kapauku economy required collective cultivation and political regulation of the more complex tasks.

The key political figure among the Kapauku was the big man. Known as a *tonowi,* he achieved his status through hard work, amassing wealth in the form of pigs and other native riches. Consider the term *status,* which often is used as a synonym for prestige. Thus, "she's got a lot of status" means she's got a lot of prestige; people look up to her. Among social scientists, however, that's not the primary meaning of "status." Social scientists use **status** more neutrally—for any social position, no matter what its prestige. In this sense, status encompasses all the positions that people occupy in society, such as spouse, parent, trading partner, teacher, student, salesperson, big man, and many others. People always occupy multiple statuses (e.g., son, brother, father, big man). Among the statuses we occupy, particular ones dominate in particular settings, such as son or daughter at home and student in the classroom.

Some statuses are **ascribed:** People have little or no choice about occupying them. Age is an ascribed status; we can't choose not to age. One's status as a member of the nobility, or as a male or a female, usually is ascribed; people are born members of a

The big man persuades people to organize feasts, which distribute pork and wealth. Shown here is such a regional event, drawing on several villages, in Papua New Guinea. Big men owe their status to their individual personalities rather than to inherited wealth or position. Does our society have equivalents of big men?

certain social category and remain so all their lives. **Achieved statuses,** by contrast, aren't automatic; they are based on choices, actions, efforts, or circumstances, and may be positive or negative. Examples of achieved statuses include big man, healer, senator, convicted felon, terrorist, salesperson, union member, father, and college student.

The achieved status of the big man rested on certain characteristics that distinguished the big man from his fellows. Key attributes included wealth, generosity, eloquence, physical fitness, bravery, supernatural powers, and the ability to gain the support and loyalty of others. Men became big men because they had certain personalities; they did not inherit their status but created it through hard work and good judgment. Wealth resulted from successful pig breeding and trading. As a man's pig herd and prestige grew, he attracted supporters. He sponsored pig feasts in which pork (provided by the big man and his supporters) was distributed to guests, bringing him more prestige and widening his network of support.

The big man's supporters, recognizing his past favors and anticipating future rewards, recognized him as a leader and accepted his decisions as binding. The tonowi was an important regulator of regional events in Kapauku life. He helped determine the dates for feasts and markets. He initiated economic projects requiring the cooperation of a regional community.

The Kapauku big man again exemplifies a generalization about leadership in tribal societies: If someone achieves wealth and widespread respect and support, he or she must be generous. The big man worked hard not to hoard wealth but to be able to give away the fruits of his labor, to convert wealth into prestige and gratitude. A stingy big man would lose his support. Selfish and greedy big men sometimes were murdered by their fellows (Zimmer-Tamakoshi 1997).

How similar are contemporary politicians to the big man? Big men get their loyalists to produce and deliver pigs, just as modern politicians persuade their supporters to make campaign contributions. And, like big men, successful American politicians try to be generous with their supporters. Payback may take the form of a night in the Lincoln bedroom, a strategic dinner invitation, an ambassadorship, or largesse to a place that was particularly supportive. Big men amass wealth, and then distribute pigs and their

Superhero films celebrate differences in power between those heroes and ordinary people. Power differentials also are key interests in political anthropology. Some superheroes (e.g., Superman and the X-Men) have their special powers from infancy on. Others (e.g., Iron Man and Batman) use technology to become superhuman. Still others (e.g., Spiderman and the Fantastic Four) get their powers accidentally. In each case, is superherodom an ascribed status or an achieved status?

meat. Successful American politicians also give away "pork." As with the big man, eloquence and communication skills contribute to political success (e.g., Ronald Reagan, Bill Clinton, Barack Obama), although lack of such skills isn't necessarily fatal (e.g., either President Bush). What about physical fitness? Hair, height, and health are still political advantages. Bravery, in the form of military service, also helps political careers (e.g., Wesley Clark and John McCain), but it certainly isn't required, nor does it guarantee success. Supernatural powers? Candidates who proclaim themselves atheists are even rarer than self-identified witches. Almost all political candidates claim to belong to a mainstream religion. Some even present their candidacies as promoting God's will.

On the other hand, contemporary politics isn't just about personality, as it is in big man systems. We live in a state-organized, stratified society with inherited wealth, power, and privilege, all of which have political implications. As is typical of states, inheritance and kin connections play a role in political success. Just think of Kennedys, Bushes, Gores, Clintons, and Gandhis.

Pantribal Sodalities

Big men could forge regional political organization, albeit temporarily, by mobilizing supporters from several villages. Other principles in tribal societies—such as a belief in common ancestry, kinship, or descent—could be used to link local groups within a region. The same descent group, for example, might span several villages, and its dispersed members might recognize the same leader.

Principles other than kinship also can link local groups, especially in modern societies. People who live in different parts of the same nation may belong to the same labor union, sorority or fraternity, political party, or religious denomination. In tribes, nonkin groups called *associations* or *sodalities* may serve a similar linking function. Often, sodalities are based on common age or gender, with all-male sodalities more common than all-female ones.

Pantribal sodalities are groups that extend across the whole tribe, spanning several villages. Such sodalities were especially likely to develop in situations of warfare with a neighboring tribe. Mobilizing their members from multiple villages within the same tribe, pantribal sodalities could assemble a force to attack or retaliate against another tribe.

The best examples of pantribal sodalities come from the Central Plains of North America and from tropical Africa. During the 18th and 19th centuries, Native American populations of the Great Plains of the United States and Canada experienced a rapid growth of pantribal sodalities. This development reflected an economic change that followed the spread of horses, which had been reintroduced to the Americas by the Spanish, to the area between the Rocky Mountains and the Mississippi River. Many Plains Indian societies changed their adaptive strategies because of the horse. At first they had been foragers who hunted bison (buffalo) on foot. Later they adopted a mixed economy based on hunting, gathering, and horticulture. Finally they changed to a much more specialized economy based on horseback hunting of bison (eventually with rifles).

As the Plains tribes were undergoing these changes, other Indians also adopted horseback hunting and moved into the Plains. Attempting to occupy the same area, groups came into conflict. A pattern of warfare developed in which the members of one tribe raided another, usually for horses. The economy demanded that people follow the movement of the bison herds. During the winter, when the bison dispersed, a tribe fragmented into small bands and families. In the summer, when huge herds assembled on the Plains, the tribe reunited. They camped together for social, political, and religious activities, but mainly for communal bison hunting.

Two activities demanded strong leadership: organizing and carrying out raids on enemy camps (to capture horses) and managing the summer bison hunt. All the Plains societies developed pantribal sodalities, and leadership roles within them, to police the summer hunt. Leaders coordinated hunting efforts, making sure that people did not cause a stampede with an early shot or an ill-advised action. Leaders imposed severe penalties, including seizure of a culprit's wealth, for disobedience.

Many tribes that adopted this Plains strategy of adaptation had once been foragers for whom hunting and gathering had been individual or small-group affairs. They never had come together previously as a single social unit. Age and gender were available as social principles that could quickly and efficiently forge unrelated people into pantribal sodalities.

Raiding of one tribe by another, this time for cattle rather than horses, also was common in eastern and southeastern Africa, where pantribal sodalities also developed. Among the pastoral Masai of Kenya, men born during the same four-year period were circumcised together and belonged to the same named group, an age set, throughout their lives. The sets moved through *age grades,* the most important of which was the warrior grade. Members of a set felt a strong allegiance to one another. Masai women lacked comparable set organization, but they also passed through culturally recognized age grades: the initiate, the married woman, and the female elder.

In certain parts of western and central Africa, pantribal sodalities are secret societies, made up exclusively of men or women. Like our college fraternities and sororities, these associations have secret initiation ceremonies. Among the Mende of Sierra Leone, men's and women's secret societies were very influential. The men's group, the Poro, trained boys in social conduct, ethics, and religion and supervised political and economic activities. Leadership roles in the Poro often overshadowed village headship and played an important part in social control, dispute management, and tribal political regulation. Age, gender, and ritual can link members of different local groups into a single social collectivity in a tribe and thus create a sense of ethnic identity, of belonging to the same cultural tradition.

Nomadic Politics

Herders have varied political systems. Unlike the Masai (just discussed) and other tribal herders, some pastoralists have chiefs and live in nation-states. The scope of political authority among pastoralists expands considerably as regulatory problems increase in densely populated regions (see Salzman 2008). Consider two Iranian pastoral nomadic tribes—the Basseri and the Qashqai (Salzman 1974). Starting each year from a plateau near the coast, these groups took their animals to grazing land 17,000 feet (5,400 meters) above sea level. The Basseri and the Qashqai shared this route with one another and with several other ethnic groups.

Use of the same pasture land at different times of year was carefully scheduled. Ethnic-group movements were tightly coordinated. Expressing this schedule is *il-rah,* a concept common to all Iranian nomads. A group's il-rah is its customary path in time and space. It is the schedule, different for each group, of when specific areas can be used in the annual trek.

Each tribe had its own leader, known as the *khan* or *il-khan*. The Basseri khan, because he dealt with a smaller population, faced fewer problems in coordinating its movements than did the leaders of the Qashqai. Correspondingly, his rights, privileges, duties, and authority were weaker. Nevertheless, his authority exceeded that of any political figure discussed so far. The khan's authority still came from his personal traits rather than from his office. That is, the Basseri followed a particular khan not because of a political position he happened to fill but because of their personal allegiance and loyalty to him as a man. The khan relied on the support of the heads of the descent groups into which Basseri society was divided.

Among the Qashqai, however, allegiance shifted from the person to the office. The Qashqai had multiple levels of authority and more powerful chiefs or khans. Managing 400,000 people required a complex hierarchy. Heading it was the il-khan, helped by a deputy, under whom were the heads of constituent tribes, under each of whom were descent-group heads.

A case illustrates just how developed the Qashqai authority structure was. A hailstorm prevented some nomads from joining the annual migration at the appointed time. Although everyone recognized that they were not responsible for their delay, the il-khan assigned them less favorable grazing land, for that year only, in place of their usual pasture. The tardy herders and other Qashqai considered the judgment fair and didn't question it. Thus, Qashqai authorities regulated the annual migration. They also adjudicated disputes between people, tribes, and descent groups.

These Iranian cases illustrate the fact that pastoralism often is just one among many specialized economic activities within a nation-state. As part of a larger whole, pastoral tribes are constantly pitted against other ethnic groups. In these nations, the state becomes a final authority, a higher-level regulator that attempts to limit conflict between ethnic groups. State organization arose not just to manage agricultural economies but also to regulate the activities of ethnic groups within expanding social and economic systems (see Das and Poole, eds. 2004).

Chiefdoms

The first states emerged in the Old World around 5,500 years ago. The first chiefdoms developed perhaps a thousand years earlier, but few survive today. In many parts of the world, the chiefdom was a transitional form of organization that emerged during the evolution of tribes into states. State formation began in Mesopotamia (currently Iran and Iraq). It next occurred in Egypt, the Indus Valley of Pakistan and India, and northern China. A few thousand years later states arose in two parts of the Western Hemisphere— Mesoamerica (Mexico, Guatemala, Belize) and the central Andes (Peru and Bolivia). Early states are known as *archaic,* or *nonindustrial,* states, in contrast to modern industrial nation-states. Robert Carneiro defines the state as "an autonomous political unit encompassing many communities within its territory, having a centralized government with the power to collect taxes, draft men for work or war, and decree and enforce laws" (Carneiro 1970, p. 733).

The chiefdom and the state, like many categories used by social scientists, are *ideal types.* That is, they are labels that make social contrasts seem sharper than they really are. In reality there is a continuum from tribe to chiefdom to state. Some societies had many attributes of chiefdoms but retained tribal features. Some advanced chiefdoms had many attributes of archaic states and thus are difficult to assign to either category. Recognizing this "continuous change" (Johnson and Earle 2000), some anthropologists speak of "complex chiefdoms" (Earle 1987, 1997), which are almost states.

Political and Economic Systems

Geographic areas with chiefdoms included the circum-Caribbean (e.g., Caribbean islands, Panama, Colombia), lowland Amazonia, what is now the southeastern United States, and Polynesia. Chiefdoms created the megalithic cultures of Europe, including the one that built Stonehenge. Bear in mind that chiefdoms and states can fall (disintegrate) as well as rise. Before Rome's expansion, much of Europe was organized at the chiefdom level, to which it reverted for centuries after the fall of Rome in the 5th century C.E.

Much of our ethnographic knowledge about chiefdoms comes from Polynesia, where they were common at the time of European exploration. In chiefdoms, social relations are based mainly on kinship, marriage, descent, age, generation, and gender—just as in bands and tribes. This is a fundamental difference between chiefdoms and states. States bring nonrelatives together and oblige them all to pledge allegiance to a government.

Unlike bands and tribes, however, chiefdoms administer a clear-cut and permanent regional political system. Chiefdoms may include thousands of people living in many villages or hamlets. Regulation is carried out by the chief and his or her assistants, who occupy political offices. An **office** is a permanent position, which must be refilled when it is vacated by death or retirement. Because official vacancies are filled systematically, the political system that is the chiefdom endures across the generations, thus ensuring permanent political regulation.

Polynesian chiefs were full-time specialists whose duties included managing the economy. They regulated production by commanding or prohibiting (using religious taboos) the cultivation of certain lands and crops. Chiefs also regulated distribution

Stonehenge, England, and an educational display designed for tourists and visitors. Chiefdoms created the megalithic cultures of Europe, such as the one that built Stonehenge over 5,000 years ago. Between the emergence and spread of food production and the expansion of the Roman empire, much of Europe was organized at the chiefdom level, to which it reverted after the fall of Rome.

PERIOD IIIc
From c.1550 BC

Bluestones rearranged into circle and horseshoe in positions as seen today. Both settings now very ruined.

and consumption. At certain seasons—often on a ritual occasion such as a first-fruit ceremony—people would offer part of their harvest to the chief through his or her representatives. Products moved up the hierarchy, eventually reaching the chief. Conversely, illustrating obligatory sharing with kin, chiefs sponsored feasts at which they gave back some of what they had received. Unlike big men, chiefs were exempt from ordinary work and had rights and privileges unavailable to the masses. Like big men, however, they still returned a portion of the wealth they took in.

Such a flow of resources to and then from a central place is known as *chiefly redistribution,* which offers economic advantages. If different parts of the chiefdom specialized in particular products, chiefly redistribution made those products available to the entire society. Chiefly redistribution also helped stimulate production beyond the basic subsistence level and provided a central storehouse for goods that might become scarce in times of famine (Earle 1987, 1997).

Status Systems

Social status in chiefdoms was based on seniority of descent. Polynesian chiefs kept extremely long genealogies. Some chiefs (without writing) managed to trace their ancestry back 50 generations. All the people in the chiefdom were thought to be related to each other. Presumably, all were descended from a group of founding ancestors.

The status of chief was ascribed, based on seniority of descent. The chief would be the oldest child (usually son) of the oldest child of the oldest child, and so on. Degrees of seniority were calculated so intricately on some islands that there were as many ranks as people. For example, the third son would rank below the second, who in turn would rank below the first. The children of an eldest brother, however, would all rank above the children of the next brother, whose children in turn would outrank those of younger brothers. However, even the lowest-ranking man or woman in a chiefdom was still the chief's relative. In such a kin-based context, everyone, even a chief, had to share with his or her relatives. Because everyone had a slightly different status, it was difficult to draw a line between elites and common people. Other chiefdoms calculated seniority differently and had shorter genealogies than did those in Polynesia. Still, the concern for seniority and the lack of sharp gaps between elites and commoners are features of all chiefdoms.

The status systems of chiefdoms, as of states, were associated with differential access to resources. Some men and women had privileged access to power, prestige, and wealth. They controlled strategic resources such as land and water. Earle characterizes chiefs as "an incipient aristocracy with advantages in wealth and lifestyle" (1987, p. 290).

Compared with chiefdoms, archaic states drew a much firmer line between elites and masses, distinguishing at least between nobles and commoners. Kinship ties did not extend from the nobles to the commoners because of *stratum endogamy*—marriage within one's own group. Commoners married commoners; elites married elites.

The Emergence of Stratification

The status system of a chiefdom differed from that of a state because of the chiefdom's kinship basis. In the context of differential wealth and power, the chiefly type of status system didn't last very long. Chiefs would start acting like kings and try to erode the kinship basis of the chiefdom. In Madagascar they would do this by demoting their more distant relatives to commoner status and banning marriage between nobles and commoners (Kottak 1980). Such moves, if accepted by the society, created separate *social strata*—unrelated groups that differ in their access to wealth, prestige, and power. (A *stratum* is

Winning a lottery confers wealth, but not necessarily prestige or power. Shown here is a winner of $1 million in New York state's scratch-off lottery.

TABLE 12.1
Max Weber's Three Dimensions of Stratification

wealth	economic status
power	political status
prestige	social status

one of two or more groups that contrast in social status and access to strategic resources. Each stratum includes people of both sexes and all ages.) The creation of separate social strata is called *stratification,* and its emergence signified the transition from chiefdom to state. The presence of stratification is one of the key distinguishing features of a state.

The influential sociologist Max Weber (1922/1968) defined three related dimensions of social stratification: (1) Economic status, or **wealth,** encompasses all a person's material assets, including income, land, and other types of property. (2) Power, the ability to exercise one's will over others—to get what one wants—is the basis of political status. (3) **Prestige**—the basis of social status—refers to esteem, respect, or approval for acts, deeds, or qualities considered exemplary. Prestige, or "cultural capital" (Bourdieu 1984), gives people a sense of worth and respect, which they may often convert into economic advantage (Table 12.1).

In archaic states—for the first time in human evolution—there were contrasts in wealth, power, and prestige between entire groups (social strata) of men and women. Each stratum included people of both genders and all ages. The **superordinate** (the higher or elite) stratum had privileged access to valued resources. Access to those resources by members of the **subordinate** (lower or underprivileged) stratum was limited by the privileged group.

State Systems

Table 12.2 summarizes the information presented so far on bands, tribes, chiefdoms, and states. States, remember, are autonomous political units with social strata and a formal government. States tend to be large and populous, and certain statuses, systems,

TABLE 12.2 Economic Basis of and Political Regulation in Bands, Tribes, Chiefdoms, and States

Sociopolitical Type	Economic Type	Examples	Type of Regulation
Band	Foraging	Inuit, San	Local
Tribe	Horticulture, pastoralism	Yanomami, Masai, Kapauku	Local, temporary, regional
Chiefdom	Intensive horticulture, pastoral nomadism, agriculture	Qashqai, Polynesia, Cherokee	Permanent, regional
State	Agriculture, industrialism	Ancient Mesopotamia, contemporary U.S., and Canada	Permanent, regional

and subsystems with specialized functions are found in all states (see Sharma and Gupta, eds. 2006). They include the following:

- Population control: fixing of boundaries, establishment of citizenship categories, and censusing
- Judiciary: laws, legal procedure, and judges
- Enforcement: permanent military and police forces
- Fiscal: taxation

In archaic states, these subsystems were integrated by a ruling system or government composed of civil, military, and religious officials (Fried 1960). Let's look at the four subsystems one by one.

Population Control

To keep track of whom they govern, states conduct censuses. States demarcate boundaries to separate that state from other societies. Customs agents, immigration officers, navies, and coast guards patrol frontiers. States also regulate population through administrative subdivision: provinces, districts, "states," counties, subcounties, and parishes. Lower-level officials manage the populations and territories of the subdivisions.

States often promote geographic mobility and resettlement, severing longstanding ties among people, land, and kin (Smith 2003). Population displacements have increased with globalization and as war, famine, and job seeking churn up migratory currents. People in states come to identify themselves by new statuses, both ascribed and achieved—including residence, ethnicity, occupation, political party, religion, and team or club affiliation—rather than only as members of a descent group or extended family.

States also manage their populations by granting different rights and obligations to citizens and noncitizens. Status distinctions among citizens also are common. Archaic states granted different rights to nobles, commoners, and slaves. In American history before the Emancipation Proclamation, there were different laws for enslaved and free people. In European colonies, separate courts judged cases involving only natives and cases involving Europeans. In contemporary America, a military judiciary coexists alongside the civil system.

Judiciary

All states have laws based on precedent and legislative proclamations. Without writing, laws may be preserved in oral tradition. *Crimes* are violations of the legal code ("breaking the law"), with specified types of punishment. To handle crimes and disputes, all states have courts and judges.

A striking contrast between states and nonstates is intervention in family affairs. Governments step in to halt blood feuds and regulate previously private disputes. States attempt to curb *internal* conflict, but they aren't always successful. About 85 percent of the world's armed conflicts since 1945 have begun within states—in efforts to overthrow a ruling regime or as disputes over ethnic, religious, or human rights issues (see Barnaby, ed. 1984; Chatterjee 2004; Nordstrom 2004; Tishkov 2004).

Enforcement

All states have agents to enforce judicial decisions, for example, to mete out punishment and collect fines. Confinement requires jailers. If there is a death penalty, executioners are needed. Government officials have the power to collect fines and confiscate property. The government attempts to suppress internal disorder (with police) and to guard against external threats (with the military and border officials).

Armies help states subdue and conquer neighboring nonstates, but this isn't the only reason why state organization has spread. Although states impose hardships, they also offer advantages. They have formal mechanisms designed to protect against external threats and to preserve internal order. When they are successful in promoting internal peace, states enhance production. Their economies can support massive, dense populations, which supply armies and colonists to promote expansion.

Fiscal Support

States need financial or **fiscal** mechanisms (e.g., taxation) to support government officials and numerous other specialists. As in the chiefdom, the state intervenes in production, distribution, and consumption. The state may require a certain area to produce specific things, or ban certain activities in particular places. Although, like chiefdoms, states have redistribution (aka "spreading the wealth around"), less of what comes in from the people actually goes back to the people.

In nonstates, people customarily share with their relatives, but citizens also have to turn over a substantial portion of what they produce to the state. Markets and trade usually are under at least some state oversight, with officials overseeing distribution and exchange, standardizing weights and measures, and collecting taxes on goods passing into or through the state. Of the revenues the state collects, it reallocates part for the general good and keeps another part (often larger) for itself—its agents and agencies. State organization doesn't bring more freedom or leisure to the common people, who may be conscripted to build monumental public works. Some projects, such as dams and irrigation systems, may be economically necessary, but residents of archaic states also had to build temples, palaces, and tombs for the elites. Those elites reveled in the consumption of sumptuary goods—jewelry, exotic food and drink, and stylish clothing reserved for, or affordable only by, the rich. Peasants' diets suffered as they struggled to meet government demands. Commoners perished in territorial wars that had little relevance to their own needs. Are any of these observations true of contemporary states?

Social Control

In studying political systems, anthropologists pay attention not only to the formal institutions but to other forms of social control as well. The concept of social control is broader than "the political." **Social control** refers to "those fields of the social system (beliefs, practices, and institutions) that are most actively involved in the maintenance of any norms and the regulation of any conflict" (N. Kottak 2002, p. 290). *Norms,* as defined earlier in this chapter, are cultural standards or guidelines that enable individuals to distinguish between appropriate and inappropriate behavior.

Previous sections of this chapter have focused more on formal political organization than on sociopolitical process. We've seen how the scale and strength of political systems have expanded in relation to economic changes. We've examined means of conflict resolution, or their absence, in various types of society. We've looked at political decision making, including leaders and their limits. We've also recognized that all contemporary humans have been affected by states, colonialism, and the spread of the modern world system.

Sociopolitical was introduced as a key concept at the beginning of this chapter. So far, we've focused mainly on the *political* part of sociopolitical; now we focus on the *social* part. In this section we'll see that political systems have their informal, social, and subtle aspects along with their formal, governmental, and public dimensions.

Hegemony and Resistance

Antonio Gramsci (1971) developed the concept of **hegemony** for a stratified social order in which subordinates comply with domination by internalizing their rulers' values and accepting the "naturalness" of domination (this is the way things were meant to be). According to Pierre Bourdieu (1977, p. 164), every social order tries to make its own arbitrariness (including its mechanisms of control and domination) seem natural and in everyone's interest. Often promises are made (things will get better if you're patient).

Both Bourdieu (1977) and Michel Foucault (1979) argue that it is easier and more effective to dominate people in their minds than to try to control their bodies. Nonphysical forms of social control include various techniques of persuading and managing people and of monitoring and recording their beliefs, activities, and contacts.

Hegemony, the internalization of a dominant ideology, is one way in which elites curb resistance and maintain power. Another way is to make subordinates believe they eventually will gain power—as young people usually foresee when they let their elders dominate them. Another way of curbing resistance is to separate or isolate people while supervising them closely, as is done in prisons (Foucault 1979).

Popular resistance is most likely to be expressed openly when people are allowed to assemble. The oppressed may draw courage from their common sentiments and the anonymity of the crowd. Sensing danger, the elites often discourage public gatherings. They try to limit and control holidays, funerals, dances, festivals, and other occasions that might unite the oppressed. For example, in the American South before the Civil War, gatherings of five or more slaves were prohibited unless a white person was present.

Factors that interfere with community formation—such as geographic, linguistic, and ethnic separation—also work to curb resistance. Consequently, southern U.S. plantation owners sought slaves with diverse cultural and linguistic backgrounds. Despite the measures used to divide them, the slaves resisted, developing their own popular culture, linguistic codes, and religious vision. The masters stressed portions of the Bible that stressed compliance, such as the book of Job. The slaves, however, preferred the story of Moses and deliverance. The cornerstone of slave religion became the idea of a reversal in the conditions of whites and blacks. Slaves also resisted directly, through sabotage and flight. In many New World areas, slaves managed to establish free communities in the hills and other isolated areas (Price, ed. 1973).

Weapons of the Weak

The study of sociopolitical systems also should consider the sentiments and activity that may lurk beneath the surface of evident, public behavior. In public, the oppressed may seem to accept their own domination, even as they question it in private. James Scott (1990) uses "public transcript" to describe the open, public interactions between superordinates and subordinates—the outer shell of power relations. He uses "hidden transcript" to describe the critique of power that proceeds out of sight of the power holders. In public, the elites and the oppressed may observe the etiquette of power relations. The dominants act like masters while their subordinates show humility and defer.

Often, situations that seem to be hegemonic do have active resistance, but it is individual and disguised rather than collective and defiant. James Scott (1985) uses Malay peasants, among whom he did fieldwork, to illustrate small-scale acts of resistance—which he calls "weapons of the weak." The Malay peasants used an indirect strategy to resist an Islamic tithe (religious tax). Peasants were expected to pay the tithe, usually in the form of rice, which was sent to the provincial capital. In theory, the tithe would come back as charity, but it never did. Peasants didn't resist the tithe by rioting, demonstrating, or protesting. Instead they used a "nibbling" strategy, based on small acts of resistance. For example, they failed to declare their land or lied about the amount they farmed. They underpaid, or delivered rice contaminated with water, rocks, or mud, to add weight. Because of this resistance, only 15 percent of what was due actually was paid (Scott 1990, p. 89).

Hidden transcripts tend to be expressed publicly at certain times (festivals and Carnavals) and in certain places (such as markets). Because of its costumed anonymity, Carnaval (aka Mardi Gras in New Orleans) is an excellent arena for expressing normally suppressed feelings. Carnavals celebrate freedom through immodesty, dancing, gluttony, and sexuality (DaMatta 1991). Carnaval may begin as a playful outlet for frustrations built up during the year. Over time, it may evolve into a powerful annual critique of stratification and domination and thus a threat to the established order (Gilmore 1987). (Recognizing that ceremonial license could turn into political defiance, the Spanish dictator Francisco Franco outlawed Carnaval.)

Shame and Gossip

Many anthropologists have cited the importance of "informal" processes of social control, such as stigma, shame, and gossip, especially in small-scale societies (see Freilich, Raybeck, and Savishinsky 1991). Gossip, which can lead to shame, sometimes is used when a direct or formal sanction is risky or impossible (Herskovits 1937). Margaret Mead (1937) and Ruth Benedict (1946) distinguished between *shame* as an external sanction (i.e., forces set in motion by others) and *guilt* as an internal sanction, psychologically generated by the individual. They regarded shame as a more prominent form of social control in non-Western societies and guilt as a more dominant emotional sanction in Western societies. Of course, to be effective as a sanction, the prospect of being shamed or of shaming oneself must be internalized by the individual. In small-scale societies, in a social environment where everyone knows everyone else, most people try to avoid behavior that might spoil their reputations and alienate them from their social network (N. Kottak 2002).

Bronislaw Malinowski (1927) described how Trobriand Islanders might climb to the top of a palm tree and dive to their deaths because they couldn't tolerate the shame associated with public knowledge of some stigmatizing action. Nicholas Kottak (2002) heard Makua villagers in northern Mozambique tell the story of a man rumored to have fathered a child with his stepdaughter. The political authorities imposed no formal sanctions (e.g., a fine or jail time) on this man, but gossip about the affair circulated widely. The gossip crystallized in the lyrics of a song that groups of young women would perform. After the man heard his name and alleged incestuous behavior mentioned in that song, he hanged himself by the neck from a tree. (Previously we saw the role of song in the social control system of the Inuit. We'll see it again in the case of the Igbo women's war, discussed below.)

Although it isn't part of any formal or official authority structure, shame can be a powerful social sanction. People aren't just citizens of governments, they are members of society, and social sanctions exist alongside governmental ones. Such sanctions exemplify other "weapons of the weak," because they often are wielded most effectively by people, such as women or young people, who have limited access to the formal authority structure.

The Igbo Women's War

Shame and ridicule—used by women against men—played a key role in a decisive protest movement that took place in southeastern Nigeria in late 1929. This is remembered as the "Aba Women's Riots of 1929" in British colonial history, and as the "Women's War" in Igbo history (see Dorward, ed. 1983; Martin 1988; Mba 1982; Oriji 2000; Van Allen 1971). During this two-month "war," at least 25,000 Igbo women joined protests against British officials, their agents, and their colonial policies. This massive revolt touched off the most serious challenge to British rule in the history of what was then the British colony of Nigeria.

A book cover photograph of Funmilayo Ransome Kuti (1900-1978), a prominent Nigerian leader, who fought for Nigerian women's right to vote. Kuti, mother of Fela Kuti, an internationally known musician, was the first woman in Nigeria to drive a car and to ride a bike.

Anthropology Today   *Yanomami Update: Venezuela Takes Charge, Problems Arise*

Never have people lived in isolation from other human beings. People have been linked through cultural practices including marriage, religion (e.g., the missionization described here), trade, travel, exploration, warfare, and conquest. As described below, local people today must heed not only their own customs but also laws, policies, and decisions made by outsiders. As you read this account, pay attention to the various interest groups involved and how their goals and wishes might clash. Also consider the levels of political regulation (local, regional, national, and international) that determine how contemporary people such as the Yanomami live their lives and maintain their health, autonomy, and cultural traditions. Consider as well the effectiveness of Yanomami leaders in dealing with agents of the Venezuelan state.

PUERTO AYACUCHO, Venezuela—Three years after President Hugo Chávez expelled American missionaries from the Venezuelan Amazon, accusing them of using proselytism of remote tribes as a cover for espionage, resentment is festering here over what some tribal leaders say was official negligence. . . .

Some leaders of the Yanomami, one of South America's largest forest-dwelling tribes, say that 50 people in their communities in the southern rain forest have died since the expulsion of the missionaries in 2005 because of recurring shortages of medicine and fuel, and unreliable transportation out of the jungle to medical facilities.

Mr. Chávez's government disputes the claims and points to more spending than ever on social welfare programs for the Yanomami. The spending is part of a broader plan to assert greater military and social control over expanses of rain forest that are viewed as essential for Venezuela's sovereignty. . . .

In recent interviews here, government officials contended that the Yanomami could be exaggerating their claims to win more resources from the government and undercut its authority in the Amazon. . . .

The Yanomami claims come amid growing concern in Venezuela over indigenous health care after a scandal erupted . . . over a tepid official response to a mystery disease that killed 38 Warao Indians in the country's northeast.

"This government makes a big show of helping the Yanomami, but rhetoric is one thing and reality another," said Ramón González, 49, a Yanomami leader from the village of Yajanamateli who traveled recently to Puerto Ayacucho, the capital of Amazonas State, to ask military officials and civilian doctors for improved health care.

"The truth is that Yanomami lives are still considered worthless," said Mr. González. "The boats, the planes, the money, it's all for the criollos, not for us," he said, using a term for nonindigenous Venezuelans. . . .

There are about 26,000 Yanomami in the Amazon rain forest, in Venezuela and Brazil, where they subsist as seminomadic hunters and cultivators of crops like manioc and bananas.

They remain susceptible to ailments for which they have weak defenses, including respiratory diseases and drug-resistant strains of malaria. In Puerto Ayacucho, they can be seen wandering through the traffic-clogged streets, clad in the modern uniform of T-shirts and baggy pants, toting cellphones. . . .

Mr. González and other Yanomami leaders provided the names of 50 people, including 22 children, who they said died from ailments like malaria and pneumonia after the military limited civilian and missionary flights to their villages in 2005.

The military replaced the missionaries' operations with its own fleet of small planes and helicopters, but critics say the missions were infrequent or unresponsive.

The Yanomami leaders said they made the list public after showing it to health and military officials and receiving a cold response. "They told us we should be grateful for the help we're already being given," said Eduardo Mejía, 24, a Yanomami leader from the village of El Cejal.

"The missionaries were in Amazonas for 50 years, creating dependent indigenous populations in some places, so their withdrawal was bound to have positive and negative effects," said Carlos Botto, a senior official with Caicet, a government research institute that focuses on tropical diseases.

"But one cannot forget that the Yanomami and other indigenous groups have learned how to exert pressure on the government in order to receive food or other benefits," he said. "This does not mean there aren't challenges in providing them with health care, but caution is necessary with claims like these."

The dispute has also focused attention on an innovative government project created in late 2005, the Yanomami Health Plan. With a staff of 46, it trains some Yanomami to be health workers in their villages while sending doctors into the jungle to provide health care to remote communities.

"We have 14 doctors in our team, with 11 trained in Cuba for work in jungle areas,"

Yanomami leader Davi Yanomami, a shaman and winner of the UN Global 500 award, on a 2007 visit to London to draw attention to health conditions among indigenous peoples.

continued

Anthropology Today *continued*

said Meydell Simancas, 32, a tropical disease specialist who directs the project from a compound here once owned by New Tribes Mission.

Dr. Simancas said that more than 20 Yanomami had been trained as paramedics, and that statistics showed that doctors had increased immunizations and programs to control malaria and river blindness across Amazonas.

The Yanomami leaders . . . acknowledged Dr. Simancas's good intentions. But they said serious problems persisted in co-ordinating access to doctors and medicine with the military, which the Yanomami and government doctors both rely on for travel in and out of the rain forest. . . .

Yanomami leaders point to what they consider to be a broad pattern of neglect and condescension from public officials. . . .

Source: Simon Romero, "Rain Forest Tribe's Charge of Neglect Is Shrouded by Religion and Politics," *New York Times*, October 7, 2008. Copyright © 2008 The New York Times. Reprinted by permission.

In 1914, the British had implemented a policy of indirect rule by appointing local Nigerian men as their agents—known as "warrant chiefs." These chiefs became increasingly oppressive, seizing property, imposing arbitrary regulations, and imprisoning people who criticized them. Colonial administrators further stoked local outrage when they announced plans to impose taxes on Igbo market women. These women were key suppliers of food for Nigeria's growing urban population; they feared being forced out of business by the new tax. Market women were key organizers of the protests.

After hearing about the tax in November 1929, thousands of Igbo women assembled in various towns to protest both the warrant chiefs and the taxes on market women. They used a traditional practice of censoring and shaming men through all-night song and dance ridicule (often called "sitting on a man"). This process entailed constant singing and dancing around the houses and offices of the warrant chiefs. The women also would follow the chiefs' every move, forcing the men to pay attention by invading their space. Disturbed by the whole process, wives of the warrant chiefs also pressured their husbands to listen to the protesters' demands.

The protests were remarkably effective. The tax was abandoned, and many of the warrant chiefs resigned, some to be replaced by women. Other women were appointed to the Native courts as judges. The position of women improved in Nigeria, where market women especially remain a powerful political force to this day. Many Nigerian political events in the 1930s, 1940s, and 1950s were inspired by the Women's War, including additional tax protests. This women's war inspired many other protests in regions all over Africa. The Igbo uprising is seen as the first major challenge to British authority in Nigeria and West Africa during the colonial period.

At the beginning of this chapter, *power* was defined as the ability to exercise one's will over others. It was contrasted with *authority*—the formal, socially approved use of power by government officials and others. The case of the Igbo women's war shows how women effectively used their social power (through song, dance, noise, and "in-your-face" behavior) to subvert the formal authority structure and, in so doing, gained greater influence within that structure. Can you think of other, perhaps recent, examples?

Summary

1. Although no ethnographer has been able to observe a polity uninfluenced by some state, many anthropologists use a sociopolitical typology that classifies societies as bands, tribes, chiefdoms, or states. Foragers tended to live in egalitarian, band-organized societies. Personal networks linked individuals, families, and bands. Band leaders were first among equals, with no sure way to enforce decisions. Disputes rarely arose over strategic resources, which were open to all.

2. Political authority increased with growth in population size and density and in the scale of regulatory problems. More people mean more relations among individuals and groups to regulate. Increasingly complex economies pose further regulatory problems.

3. Heads of horticultural villages are local leaders with limited authority. They lead by example and persuasion. Big men have support and authority beyond a single village. They are regional regulators, but temporary ones. In organizing a feast, they mobilize labor from several villages. Sponsoring such events leaves them with little wealth but with prestige and a reputation for generosity.

4. Age and gender also can be used for regional political integration. Among North America's Plains Indians, men's associations (pantribal sodalities) organized raiding and buffalo hunting. Such sodalities provide offense and defense when there is intertribal raiding for animals. Among pastoralists, the degree of authority and political organization reflects population size and density, interethnic relations, and pressure on resources.

5. The state is an autonomous political unit that encompasses many communities. Its government collects taxes, drafts people for work and war, and decrees and enforces laws. The state is a form of sociopolitical organization based on central government and social stratification. Early states are known as archaic, or nonindustrial, states, in contrast to modern industrial nation-states.

6. Unlike tribes, but like states, chiefdoms had permanent regional regulation and differential access to resources. But chiefdoms lacked stratification. Unlike states, but like bands and tribes, chiefdoms were organized by kinship, descent, and marriage. Chiefdoms emerged in several areas, including the circum-Caribbean, lowland Amazonia, the southeastern United States, and Polynesia.

7. Weber's three dimensions of stratification are wealth, power, and prestige. In early states—for the first time in human history—contrasts in wealth, power, and prestige between entire groups of men and women came into being. A socioeconomic stratum includes people of both sexes and all ages. The superordinate—higher or elite—stratum enjoys privileged access to resources.

8. Certain systems are found in all states: population control, judiciary, enforcement, and fiscal. These are integrated by a ruling system or government composed of

civil, military, and religious officials. States conduct censuses and demarcate boundaries. Laws are based on precedent and legislative proclamations. Courts and judges handle disputes and crimes. A police force maintains internal order, as a military defends against external threats. A financial or fiscal system supports rulers, officials, judges, and other specialists and government agencies.

9. *Hegemony* describes a stratified social order in which subordinates comply with domination by internalizing its values and accepting its "naturalness." Situations that appear hegemonic may have resistance that is individual and disguised rather than collective and defiant. "Public transcript" refers to the open, public interactions between the dominators and the oppressed. "Hidden transcript" describes the critique of power that goes on where the power holders can't see it. Discontent also may be expressed in public rituals such as Carnaval.

10. Broader than the political is the concept of social control—those fields of the social system most actively involved in the maintenance of norms and the regulation of conflict. Sanctions are social as well as governmental. Shame and gossip can be effective social sanctions. In the Igbo women's war, women effectively used their social power (through song, dance, noise, and "in-your-face" behavior) to subvert the formal authority structure and, in so doing, gained greater influence within that structure.

Key Terms

achieved status, *279*
ascribed status, *278*
authority, *271*
big man, *278*
chiefdom, *273*
conflict
   resolution, *275*
differential
   access, *273*
fiscal, *288*

hegemony, *289*
law, *275*
norms, *275*
office, *283*
pantribal
   sodality, *280*
power, *271*
prestige, *286*
social
   control, *288*

sociopolitical
   typology, *273*
state, *273*
status, *278*
subordinate, *286*
superordinate, *286*
tribe, *273*
village head, *277*
wealth, *286*

Go to our Online Learning Center website at **www.mhhe.com/kottak** for Internet resources directly related to the content of this chapter.

Chapter  13

Families, Kinship, and Marriage

Families

   Nuclear and Extended Families

   Industrialism and Family Organization

   Changes in North American Kinship

   Applying Anthropology to Popular
     Cultures: TV Families

   The Family among Foragers

Descent

   Descent Groups

   Lineages, Clans, and Residence Rules

Marriage

   Exogamy and Incest

   Incest Happens

   Endogamy

Marital Rights and Same-Sex Marriage

Marriage across Cultures

   Bridewealth and Dowry

   Durable Alliances

Divorce

Plural Marriages

   Polygyny

   Anthropology Today: Five Wives and
     55 Children

   Polyandry

Although it still is something of an ideal in our culture, the nuclear family (parents and their children) now accounts for fewer than one-fourth of all American households. Such phrases as "love and marriage," "marriage and the family," and "mom and pop" no longer apply to a majority of American households. What kind of family raised you? Perhaps it was a nuclear family. Or maybe you were raised by a single parent, with or without the help of extended kin. Perhaps your extended kin acted as your parents. Or maybe you had a stepparent and/or step or half siblings in a blended family. Maybe you had two moms or two dads. Given the diversity of families in contemporary North America, your family may not have fit any of these descriptions, or perhaps it varied over time.

Although contemporary American family types are diverse, other cultures offer family alternatives that Americans might have trouble understanding. Imagine a society in which someone doesn't know for sure, and doesn't care much about, who his actual mother was. Consider Joseph Rabe, a Betsileo man who was my field assistant in Madagascar. Rabe, who had been raised by his aunt—his father's sister—told me about two sisters, one of whom was his mother and the other his mother's sister. He knew their names, but he didn't know which was which. Illustrating an adoptive pattern common among the Betsileo, Rabe was given as a toddler to his childless aunt. His mother and her sister lived far away and died in his childhood (as did his father), and so he didn't really know them. But he was very close to his father's sister, for whom he used the term for mother. Indeed, he had to call her that, because the Betsileo have only one kin term, *reny,* for mother, mother's sister, and father's sister. (They also use a single term, *ray,* for father and all uncles.) The difference between "real" (biologically based) and socially constructed kinship didn't matter to Rabe.

Contrast the Betsileo case with Americans' attitudes about kinship and adoption. On family-oriented radio talk shows, I've heard hosts distinguish between "birth mothers" and adoptive mothers, and between "sperm daddies" and "daddies of the heart." The latter may be adoptive fathers, or stepfathers who have "been like fathers" to someone. American culture tends to promote the idea that kinship is, and should be, biological. It's increasingly common for adopted children to seek out their birth mothers or sperm donors (which used to be discouraged as disruptive), even after a perfectly satisfactory upbringing in an adoptive family. The American emphasis on biology for kinship is seen also in the recent proliferation of DNA testing. Viewing our beliefs through the lens of cross-cultural comparison helps us appreciate that kinship and biology don't always converge, nor do they need to.

The societies anthropologists traditionally have studied have stimulated a strong interest in families, along with larger systems of kinship and marriage. The wide web of kinship—as vitally important in daily life in nonindustrial societies as work outside the home is in our own—has become an essential part of anthropology because of its importance to the people we study. We are ready to take a closer look at the systems of kinship and marriage that have organized human life for much of our history.

Ethnographers quickly recognize social divisions, or groups, within any society they study. They learn about significant groups by observing their activities and membership. Often people live in the same village or neighborhood, or work, socialize, or celebrate together because they are related in some way. A significant kin group might consist of descendants of the same grandfather. These people live in neighboring houses, farm adjoining fields, and help each other in daily tasks. Groups based on other kin links get together less often in that society (see Strathern and Stewart 2010).

The nuclear family is one kind of kin group that is widespread in human societies. Other kin groups include extended families (families consisting of three or more generations) and descent groups—lineages and clans. Much of kinship is *culturally constructed,* that is, based on learning and variable from culture to culture (McKinnon 2005; Schneider 1967). Different societies have different kinds of families, households, kin groups, marriage customs, and living arrangements.

Families

Consider the term *family,* which is basic, familiar (so much so it even shares its root with *familiar*), and difficult to define in a way that applies to all cultures. A **family** is a group of people (e.g., parents, children, siblings, grandparents, grandchildren, uncles, aunts, nephews, nieces, cousins, spouses, siblings-in-law, parents-in-law, children-in-law) who are considered to be related in some way, for example, by "blood" (common ancestry or descent) or marriage. Some families, such as the nuclear family, are residentially based; its members live together. Others are not; they live apart but come together for family reunions of various sorts from time to time.

Consider a striking contrast between the United States and Brazil, the two most populous countries of the Western Hemisphere, in the meaning and role of family. American adults usually define their family as consisting of their spouse and children. However, when middle-class Brazilians talk about their family (*família*), they mean their parents, siblings, aunts, uncles, grandparents, and cousins. Later they add their children, but rarely the husband or wife, who has his or her own family. The children are shared by the two families. Because middle-class Americans typically lack an extended family support system, marriage assumes more importance. The husband–wife relationship is supposed to take precedence over either spouse's relationship with his or her own parents. This places a significant strain on North American marriages.

Living in a less mobile society, Brazilians stay in closer face-to-face contact with their relatives, including members of the extended family, than North Americans do. Residents of Rio de Janeiro and São Paulo, two of South America's largest cities, are reluctant to leave those urban centers to live away from family and friends. Brazilians find it hard to imagine, and unpleasant to live in, social worlds without relatives. Contrast this with a characteristic American theme: learning to live with strangers.

Nuclear and Extended Families

A nuclear family is *impermanent;* it lasts only as long as the parents and children remain together. Most people belong to at least two nuclear families at different times in their lives. They are born into a family consisting of their parents and siblings. When they reach adulthood, they may marry and establish a nuclear family that includes the spouse and eventually children. Since most societies permit divorce, some people establish more than one family through marriage.

Anthropologists distinguish between the **family of orientation** (the family in which one is born and grows up) and the **family of procreation** (formed when one marries and has children). From the individual's point of view, the critical relationships are with parents and siblings in the family of orientation and with spouse and children in the family of procreation. In Brazil, as we just saw, the family of orientation predominates, whereas in the United States it is the family of procreation.

In most societies, relations with nuclear family members (parents, siblings, and children) take precedence over relations with other kin. Nuclear family organization is very widespread but not universal, and its significance in society differs greatly from one place to another. In a few societies, such as the classic Nayar case described below, nuclear families are rare or nonexistent. In others, the nuclear family plays no special role in social life. Other social units—most notably descent groups and extended families— can assume many of the functions otherwise associated with the nuclear family.

Consider an example from the former Yugoslavia. Traditionally, among the Muslims of western Bosnia (Lockwood 1975), nuclear families lacked autonomy. Several such families lived in an extended family household called a *zadruga*. The zadruga was

Many married couples live hundreds of miles from their parents. Their jobs have determined where they live. Such a postmarital residence pattern is **neolocality:** Married couples are expected to establish a new place of residence—a "home of their own." Among middle-class North Americans, neolocal residence is both a cultural preference and a statistical norm. Most middle-class Americans eventually establish households and nuclear families of their own.

There are significant differences between middle-class and poorer North Americans. For example, in the lower class the incidence of *expanded family households* (those that include nonnuclear relatives) is greater than it is in the middle class. When an expanded family household includes three or more generations, it is an **extended family household,** such as the zadruga. Another type of expanded family is the *collateral household,* which includes siblings and their spouses and children.

The higher proportion of expanded family households among poorer Americans has been explained as an adaptation to poverty (Stack 1975). Unable to survive economically as nuclear family units, relatives band together in an expanded household and pool their resources. Adaptation to poverty causes kinship values and attitudes to diverge from middle-class norms. Thus, when North Americans raised in poverty achieve financial success, they often feel obligated to provide financial help to a wide circle of less fortunate relatives (see Willie 2003).

Changes in North American Kinship

Although the nuclear family remains a cultural ideal for many Americans, Table 13.1 and Figure 13.1 show that nuclear families accounted for just 21 percent of American households in 2009. Other domestic arrangements now outnumber the "traditional" American household almost five to one. There are several reasons for this changing household composition. Women increasingly are joining men in the cash workforce. This often

TABLE 13.1   **Changes in Family and Household Organization in the United States, 1970 versus 2009**

Sources: From U.S. Census data in J. M. Fields, "America's Families and Living Arrangements: 2003," *Current Population Reports,* P20-553, November 2004, http://www.census.gov/prod/2004pubs/p20-553.pdf, p. 4; *Statistical Abstract of the United States,* 2011, Tables 59, 61, 62.

	1970	2009
Numbers:		
Total number of households	63 million	117 million
Number of people per household	3.1	2.6
Percentages:		
Married couples living with children	40%	21%
Family households	81%	67%
Households with five or more people	21%	11%
People living alone	17%	27%
Percentage of single-mother families	5%	12%
Percentage of single-father families	0%	4%
Households with own children under 18	45%	30%

FIGURE 13.1   Households by Type: Selected Years, 1970 to 2009 (percent distribution).

Sources: J. M. Fields, "America's Families and Living Arrangements: 2003," *Current Population Reports,* P20-553, November 2004, http://www.census.gov/prod/2004pubs/p20-553.pdf, p. 4; *Statistical Abstract of the United States* 2011, Tables 59, 61.

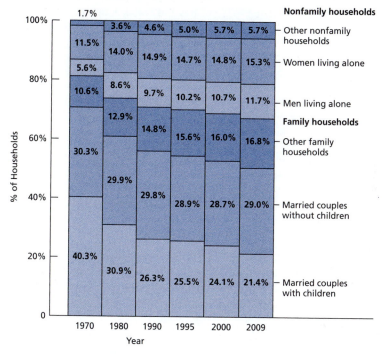

removes them from their family of orientation while making it economically feasible to delay marriage. Furthermore, job demands compete with romantic attachments. The median age at first marriage for American women rose from 21 years in 1970 to 26 in 2009. For men the comparable ages were 23 and 28 (U.S. Census Bureau 2011).

Also, the U.S. divorce rate has risen, making divorced Americans much more common today than they were in 1970. U.S. Census Bureau figures show that between 1970 and 2009 the number of divorced Americans more than quintupled—some 23.2 million in 2009 versus 4.3 million in 1970. (Note, however, that each divorce creates two divorced people.) Table 13.2 shows the ratio of divorces to marriages in the United

TABLE 13.2   Ratio of Divorces to Marriages per 1,000 U.S. Population, Selected Years, 1950–2007

Source: *Statistical Abstract of the United States* 2011, Table 78.

1950	1960	1970	1980	1990	2000	2007
23%	26%	35%	49%	48%	49%	49%

In their 2009 book *Media and Middle-Class Moms: Images and Realities of Work and Family,* Lara Descartes and Conrad Kottak point out that, contrary to popular belief, it is the 1980s—not the 1950s—that best qualifies as the golden decade of the TV family. Not only did such family-oriented programs as *The Cosby Show* and *Family Ties* dominate Nielsen's top 10, there also was a revival of interest in earlier family shows. The now iconic series *Leave It to Beaver,* for example, never made it into even the Nielsen top 30 during its original broadcast years, 1957–1963. However, in the mid-1980s, *Beaver* reappeared in syndication, a reunion telemovie, and a sequel series (see Descartes and Kottak 2009). Idealized media representations of traditional nuclear families increased in tandem with the subversion of that structure by socioeconomic fact, as more and more women joined the workforce. To be sure, 1980s shows had working women like Claire Huxtable and Elyze Keaton. And they, too, were idealized in their ability to blend professional success with exemplary motherhood. Watch a few episodes, and evaluate Claire or Elyze as role models compared with the reality of your own family life.

States for selected years between 1950 and 2007. The major jump in the American divorce rate took place between 1960 and 1980. During that period the ratio of divorces to marriage almost doubled. Since 1980 the ratio has stayed the same, slightly below 50 percent. That is, each year there are about half as many new divorces as there are new marriages.

The rate of growth in single-parent families also has outstripped population growth, quintupling from fewer than 4 million in 1970 to 20 million in 2009. (The overall American population in 2009 was 1.5 times its size in 1970.) The percentage (22.8 percent) of children living in fatherless (mother-headed, no resident dad) households in 2009 was more than twice the 1970 rate, while the percentage (3.4 percent) in motherless (father-headed, no resident mom) homes increased fourfold. About 56 percent of American women and 59 percent of American men were currently married in 2009, versus 60 and 65 percent, respectively, in 1970 (Fields 2004; Fields and Casper 2001; *Statistical Abstract of the United States 2011*). Recent census data also reveal that more American women are now living without a husband than with one.

Table 13.3 documents similar changes in family and household size in the United States and Canada between 1980 and 2009. Those figures confirm a general trend toward smaller families and living units in North America. This trend is also detectable in Western Europe and other industrial nations.

Immigrants often are shocked by what they perceive as weak kinship bonds and lack of proper respect for family in contemporary North America. In fact, most of the people whom middle-class North Americans see every day are either nonrelatives or members of the nuclear family. On the other hand, Stack's (1975) study of welfare-dependent families in a ghetto area of a midwestern city shows that regular sharing with nonnuclear relatives is an important strategy that the urban poor use to adapt to poverty.

TABLE 13.3   Household and Family Size in the United States and Canada, 1980 versus 2009

Sources: J. M. Fields, "America's Families and Living Arrangements: 2003," *Current Population Reports,* P20-553, November 2004, http://www.census.gov/prod/2004pubs/p20-553.pdf, pp. 3–4; U.S. Census Bureau, *Statistical Abstract of the United States,* 2011, Table 59; *Statistics Canada,* 2006 Census, http://www12.statcan.ca/english/census06/data/topics/, http://www40.statcan.ca/101/cst01/famil532.

	1980	2009
Average family size:		
United States	3.3	3.2
Canada	3.4	3.0
Average household size:		
United States	2.9	2.6
Canada	2.9	2.6

The Family among Foragers

Foraging societies are far removed from industrial nations in terms of social complexity, but they do feature geographic mobility, which is associated with nomadic or seminomadic hunting and gathering. Here again, the nuclear family often is the most significant kin group, although in no foraging society is it the only group based on kinship. The two basic social units of traditional foraging societies are the nuclear family and the band.

Unlike middle-class couples in industrial nations, foragers don't usually reside neolocally. Instead, they join a band in which either the husband or the wife has relatives. However, couples and families may move from one band to another several times. Although nuclear families are ultimately as impermanent among foragers as they are in any other society, they usually are more stable than bands are.

Many foraging societies lacked year-round band organization. The Native American Shoshone of Utah and Nevada provide an example. The resources available to the Shoshone were so meager that for most of the year families traveled alone through the countryside hunting and gathering. In certain seasons families assembled to hunt cooperatively as a band, but after just a few months together they dispersed.

In neither industrial nor foraging economies are people permanently tied to the land. The mobility and the emphasis on small, economically self-sufficient family units promote the nuclear family as a basic kin group in both types of societies.

Descent

We've seen that the nuclear family is important in industrial nations and among foragers. The analogous group among nonindustrial food producers is the descent group. A **descent group** is a *permanent* social unit whose members claim common ancestry. Descent group members believe they all descend from those common ancestors. The group endures even though its membership changes, as members are born and die, move in and move out. Often, descent-group membership is determined at birth and is life-long. In this case, it is an ascribed status.

Descent Groups

Descent groups frequently are exogamous (members seek their mates from other descent groups). Two common rules serve to admit certain people as descent-group members while excluding others. With a rule of **patrilineal descent,** people automatically have lifetime membership in their father's group. The children of the group's men join the group, but the children of the group's women are excluded. With **matrilineal descent,** people join the mother's group automatically at birth and stay members throughout life. Matrilineal descent groups therefore include only the children of the group's women. (In Figures 13.2 and 13.3, which show patrilineal and matrilineal descent groups, respectively, the triangles stand for males and the circles for females.) Matrilineal and patrilineal descent are types of **unilineal descent.** This means the descent rule uses one line only, either the male or the female line. Patrilineal descent is much more common than matrilineal descent is. In a sample of 564 societies (Murdock 1957), about three times as many were found to be patrilineal (247 to 84).

Descent groups may be **lineages** or **clans.** Common to both is the belief that members descend from the same *apical ancestor,* the person who stands at the apex, or top, of the common genealogy. For example, Adam and Eve are the apical ancestors of the biblical Jews, and, according to the Bible, of all humanity. Since Eve is said to have come from Adam's rib, Adam stands as the original apical ancestor for the patrilineal genealogy laid out in the Bible.

FIGURE 13.2 **A Patrilineage Five Generations Deep**

Lineages are based on demonstrated descent from an apical ancestor. With patrilineal descent, children of the group's men (shaded) are included as descent-group members. Children of the group's women are excluded; they belong to *their* father's patrilineage.

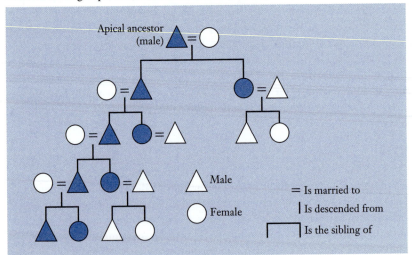

FIGURE 13.3   **A Matrilineage Five Generations Deep**

Matrilineages are based on demonstrated descent from a female ancestor. Only the children of the group's women (shaded) belong to the matrilineage. The children of the group's men are excluded; they belong to *their* mother's matrilineage.

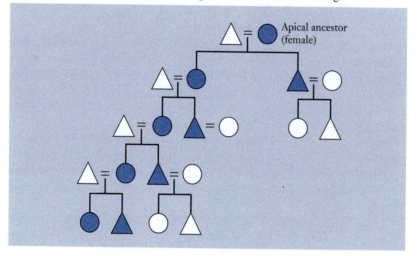

How do lineages and clans differ? A lineage uses *demonstrated descent*. Members recite the names of their forebears from the apical ancestor through the present. (This doesn't mean their recitations are accurate, only that lineage members think they are.) In the Bible the litany of men who "begat" other men is a demonstration of genealogical descent for a large patrilineage that ultimately includes Jews and Arabs (who share Abraham as their last common apical ancestor).

Unlike lineages, clans use *stipulated descent*. Clan members merely say they descend from the apical ancestor, without trying to trace the actual genealogical links. The Betsileo of Madagascar have both clans and lineages. Descent may be demonstrated for the most recent 8–10 generations, then stipulated for the more remote past—sometimes with mermaids and vaguely defined foreign royalty mentioned among the founders (Kottak 1980). Like the Betsileo, many societies have both lineages and clans. In such a case, clans have more members and cover a larger geographical area than lineages do. Sometimes a clan's apical ancestor is not a human at all but an animal or plant (called a *totem*).

The economic types that usually have descent group organization are horticulture, pastoralism, and agriculture. Such societies tend to have several descent groups. Any one of them may be confined to a single village, but usually they span more than one village. Two or more local branches of different descent groups may live in the same village. Descent groups in the same village or different villages may establish alliances through frequent intermarriage.

Lineages, Clans, and Residence Rules

As we've seen, descent groups, unlike families, are permanent and enduring units, with new members added in every generation. Members have access to the lineage estate, where some of them must live, in order to benefit from and manage that estate across the generations. An easy way to keep members at home is to have a rule about who belongs to the descent group and where they should live after they get married. Patrilineal and matrilineal descent, and the postmarital residence rules that usually accompany them, ensure that about half the people born in each generation will spend their lives on the ancestral estate.

Patrilocality is the rule that when a couple marries, it moves to the husband's community, so that their children will grow up in their father's village. Patrilocality is associated with patrilineal descent. This makes sense. If the group's male members are expected to exercise their rights in the ancestral estate, it's a good idea to raise them on that estate and to keep them there after they marry. This can be done by having wives move to the husband's village, rather than vice versa.

A less common postmarital residence rule, often associated with matrilineal descent, is **matrilocality:** Married couples live in the wife's community, and their children grow up in their mother's village. This rule keeps related women together (see Stone 2010). Together, patrilocality and matrilocality are known as *unilocal* rules of postmarital residence.

Marriage

"Love and marriage," "marriage and the family": These familiar phrases show how we link the romantic love of two individuals to marriage, and how we link marriage to reproduction and family creation. But marriage is an institution with significant roles and functions in addition to reproduction. What is marriage, anyway?

No definition of marriage is broad enough to apply easily to all societies and situations. A commonly quoted definition comes from *Notes and Queries on Anthropology:*

> Marriage is a union between a man and a woman such that the children born to the woman are recognized as legitimate offspring of both partners. (Royal Anthropological Institute 1951, p. 111)

This definition isn't valid universally for several reasons. In many societies, marriages unite more than two spouses. Here we speak of *plural marriages,* as when a man weds two (or more) women, or a woman weds a group of brothers—an arrangement called *fraternal polyandry* that is characteristic of certain Himalayan cultures. In the Brazilian community of Arembepe, people can choose among various forms of marital union. Most people live in long-term "common-law" domestic partnerships that are not legally sanctioned. Some have civil marriages, which are licensed and legalized by a justice of the peace. Still others go through religious ceremonies, so they are united in "holy matrimony," although not legally. And some have both civil and religious ties. The different forms of union permit someone to have multiple spouses (e.g., one common-law, one civil, one religious) without ever getting divorced.

Some societies recognize various kinds of same-sex marriages. In Sudan, a Nuer woman could marry a woman if her father had only daughters but no male heirs, who are necessary if his patrilineage is to survive. He might ask his daughter to stand as a son in order to take a bride. This daughter would become the socially recognized husband of another woman (the wife). This was a symbolic and social relationship rather than a sexual one. The "wife" had sex with a man or men (whom her female "husband" had to approve) until she got pregnant. The children born to the wife were accepted as the off-spring of both the female husband and the wife. Although the female husband was not the actual *genitor*, the biological father, of the children, she was their *pater*, or socially recognized father. What's important in this Nuer case is *social* rather than *biological paternity*. We see again how kinship is socially constructed. The bride's children were considered the legitimate offspring of her female husband, who was biologically a woman but socially a man, and the descent line continued.

Exogamy and Incest

In nonindustrial societies, a person's social world includes two main categories—friends and strangers. Strangers are potential or actual enemies. Marriage is one of the primary ways of converting strangers into friends, of creating and maintaining personal and po-litical alliances, relationships of affinity. **Exogamy,** the custom and practice of seeking a mate outside one's own group, has adaptive value because it links people into a wider social network that nurtures, helps, and protects them in times of need. Incest restric-tions (prohibitions on sex with relatives) reinforce exogamy by pushing people to seek their mates outside the local group. Most societies discourage sexual contact involving close relatives, especially members of the same nuclear family.

Incest refers to sexual contact with a relative, but cultures define their kin, and thus incest, differently. In other words, incest, like kinship, is socially constructed. Marriage entails sex, so one can marry only someone with whom sex is permitted. Besides kin-ship, other factors that restrict sexual access include age and the range of sexual acts that are socially tolerated. In the United States the age of consent for sexual activity varies by state between 16 and 18. It is 16 in Canada and 14 in Italy. Cultures and governments routinely try to regulate sexual activity. Until 2003, when the Supreme Court struck down sodomy laws, several states used them mainly against gay men who engaged in nonreproductive sex. Most people probably don't know what is legal and what isn't in a given state or country and can get in trouble as a result (e.g., when an 18-year-old has sex with a 17-year-old).

Sex is contested. That is, people in the same culture can disagree and argue about the definition and propriety of particular sexual acts. President Bill Clinton famously as-serted, "I did not have sexual relations with that woman." Should sexual practices other than heterosexual coitus (oral sex, for example) be considered "sexual relations"? With respect to incest restrictions, what, if any, kind of sexual contact is permissible between a teenager and his or her same-sex or opposite-sex cousin of comparable age? How about step siblings, half siblings, and siblings? Some U.S. states permit marriage, and therefore sex, with first cousins, while others ban it. The social construction of kinship, and of incest, is far from simple.

Let's turn from the United States to nonindustrial societies. When unilineal descent is very strongly developed, the parent who belongs to a different descent group than your own isn't considered a relative. Thus, with strict patrilineality, the mother is not a relative but a kind of in-law who has married a member of your own group—your father.

FIGURE 13.4   **Patrilineal Descent-Group Identity and Incest among the Lakher**

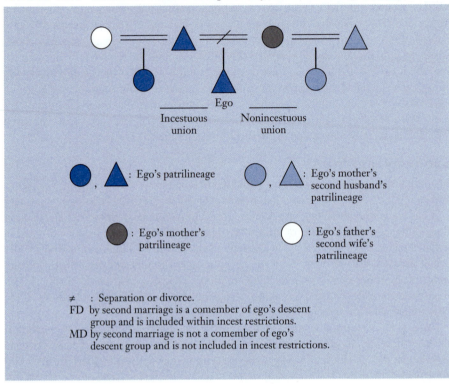

With strict matrilineality, the father isn't a relative because he belongs to a different descent group.

The Lakher of Southeast Asia are strictly patrilineal (Leach 1961). Using the male ego (the reference point, the person in question) in Figure 13.4, let's suppose that ego's father and mother get divorced. Each remarries and has a daughter by a second marriage. A Lakher always belongs to his or her father's group, all of whose members (one's *agnates,* or *patrikin*) are considered relatives, because they belong to the same descent group. Ego can't have sex with or marry his father's daughter by the second marriage, just as in contemporary North America it's illegal for half siblings to have sex and marry. However, unlike our society, where all half siblings are restricted, sex between our Lakher ego and his maternal half sister would be nonincestuous. She isn't ego's relative because she belongs to her own father's descent group rather than ego's. The Lakher illustrate very well that definitions of relatives, and therefore of incest, vary from culture to culture.

Incest Happens

We know from primate research that adolescent males (among monkeys) or females (among apes) often move away from the group in which they were born (Rodseth et al. 1991). This emigration reduces the frequency of incestuous unions, but it doesn't eliminate them. DNA testing of wild chimps has confirmed incestuous unions between adult sons and their mothers, who reside in the same group. Human behavior with respect to mating with close relatives may express a generalized primate tendency, in which we see both urges and avoidance.

A cross-cultural study of 87 societies (Meigs and Barlow 2002) suggested that incest occurred in several of them. It's not clear, however, whether the authors of the study controlled for the social construction of incest. They report, for example, that incest occurs among the Yanomami, but they may be considering cross-cousin marriage to be incestuous, when it is not so considered by the Yanomami. Indeed it is the preferred form of marriage, not just for the Yanomami but in many tribal societies. Another society in their sample is the Ashanti, for whom the ethnographer Meyer Fortes reports "In the old days it [incest] was punished by death. Nowadays the culprits are heavily fined" (Fortes 1950, p. 257). This suggests that there really were violations of Ashanti incest restrictions, and that such violations were, and still are, punished. More strikingly, among 24 Ojibwa individuals from whom he obtained information about incest, A. Irving Hallowell found 8 cases of parent–child incest and 10 cases of brother–sister incest (Hallowell 1955, pp. 294–95). Because reported cases of actual parent–child and sibling incest are rare in the ethnographic literature, questions about the possibility of social construction arise here, too. In many cultures, including the Ojibwa, people use the same terms for their mother and their aunt, their father and their uncle, and their cousins and siblings. Could the siblings in the Ojibwa case actually have been cousins; and the parents and children, uncles and nieces?

In ancient Egypt, sibling marriage apparently was allowed both for royalty and commoners, in some districts at least. Based on official census records from Roman Egypt (first to third centuries C.E.), 24 percent of all documented marriages in the Arsinoites district were between "brothers" and "sisters." The rates were 37 percent for the city of Arsinoe and 19 percent for the surrounding villages. These figures are much higher than any other documented levels of inbreeding among humans (Scheidel 1997). Again one wonders if the relatives involved were actually as close biologically as the kin terms would imply.

According to Anna Meigs and Kathleen Barlow (2002), for Western societies with nuclear family organization, "father–daughter incest" is much more common with stepfathers than with biological fathers. But is it really incest if they aren't biological relatives? American culture is unclear on this matter. Incest also happens with biological fathers, especially those who were absent or did little caretaking of their daughters in childhood (Williams and Finkelhor 1995). In a carefully designed study, Linda M. Williams and David Finkelhor (1995) found father–daughter incest to be least likely when there was substantial paternal parenting of daughters. This experience enhanced the father's parenting skills and his feelings of nurturance, protectiveness, and identification with his daughter, thus reducing the chance of incest.

A century ago, early anthropologists speculated that incest restrictions reflect an instinctive horror of mating with close relatives (Hobhouse 1915; Lowie 1920/1961). But why, one wonders, if humans really do have an instinctive aversion to incest, would formal restrictions be necessary? No one would want to have sexual contact with a relative. Yet, as social workers, judges, psychiatrists, and psychologists are well aware, incest is more common than we might suppose.

Endogamy

The practice of exogamy pushes social organization outward, establishing and preserving alliances among groups. In contrast, rules of **endogamy** dictate mating or marriage within a group to which one belongs. Endogamic rules are less common but are still familiar to anthropologists. Indeed, most cultures *are* endogamous units, although they usually do not need a formal rule requiring people to marry someone from their own society. In our own society, classes and ethnic groups are quasi-endogamous groups. Members of an ethnic or religious group often want their children to marry within that group, although many of them do not do so. The outmarriage rate varies among such groups, with some more committed to endogamy than others.

Caste

An extreme example of endogamy is India's **caste system,** which was formally abolished in 1949, although its structure and effects linger. Castes are stratified groups in which membership is ascribed at birth and is lifelong. Indian castes are grouped into five major categories, or *varna*. Each is ranked relative to the other four, and these categories extend throughout India. Each varna includes a large number of castes (*jati*), each of which includes people within a region who may intermarry. All the jati in a single varna in a given region are ranked, just as the varna themselves are ranked.

Occupational specialization often sets off one caste from another. A community may include castes of agricultural workers, merchants, artisans, priests, and sweepers. The untouchable varna, found throughout India, includes castes whose ancestry, ritual status, and occupations are considered so impure that higher-caste people consider even casual contact with untouchables to be defiling.

The belief that intercaste sexual unions lead to ritual impurity for the higher-caste partner has been important in maintaining endogamy. A man who has sex with a lower-caste woman can restore his purity with a bath and a prayer. However, a woman who has intercourse with a man of a lower caste has no such recourse. Her defilement cannot be undone. Because the women have the babies, these differences protect the purity of the caste line, ensuring the pure ancestry of high-caste children. Although Indian castes are endogamous groups, many of them are internally subdivided into exogamous lineages. Traditionally this meant that Indians had to marry a member of another descent group from the same caste. This shows that rules of exogamy and endogamy can coexist in the same society.

Marital Rights and Same-Sex Marriage

The British anthropologist Edmund Leach (1955) observed that, depending on the society, several kinds of rights are allocated by marriage. According to Leach, marriage can, but doesn't always, accomplish the following:

1. Establish the legal father of a woman's children and the legal mother of a man's.
2. Give either or both spouses a monopoly in the sexuality of the other.
3. Give either or both spouses rights to the labor of the other.

4. Give either or both spouses rights over the other's property.
5. Establish a joint fund of property—a partnership—for the benefit of the children.
6. Establish a socially significant "relationship of affinity" between spouses and their relatives.

The discussion of same-sex marriage that follows will serve to illustrate the six rights just listed by seeing what happens in their absence (see also Stone 2004). What if same-sex marriages, which by and large remain illegal in the United States, were legal? Could a same-sex marriage establish legal parentage of children born to one or both partners after the partnership is formed? In the case of a different-sex marriage, children born to the wife after the marriage takes place usually are defined legally as her husband's regardless of whether he is the genitor.

Nowadays, of course, DNA testing makes it possible to establish paternity, just as modern reproductive technology makes it possible for a lesbian couple to have one or both partners artificially inseminated (see Levine 2008 and the 2010 movie *The Kids Are All Right*). When same-sex marriage is legal, the social construction of kinship easily can make both partners parents. If a Nuer woman married to a woman can be the pater of a child she did not father, why can't two lesbians be the *maters* (socially recognized mothers) of a child one of them did not give birth to? And if a married different-sex couple can adopt a child and have it be theirs through the social and legal construction of kinship, the same logic could be applied to a gay male or lesbian couple.

Same sex couples can marry legally in the District of Columbia. Shown here, a marriage ceremony uniting two women in March 2010.

Continuing with Leach's list of the rights transmitted by marriage, same-sex marriage certainly could give each spouse rights to the sexuality of the other. Same-sex marriages, as forms of monogamous commitment, have been endorsed by representatives of many religions, including Unitarians, Quakers (the Society of Friends), and reform Jewish synagogues (Eskridge 1996). In June 2003 a court ruling established same-sex marriages as legal in the province of Ontario, Canada. On June 28, 2005, Canada's House of Commons voted to guarantee full marriage rights to same-sex couples throughout that nation. In the United States, the District of Columbia and six states—Massachusetts, Connecticut, Iowa, Vermont, New Hampshire, and New York—allowed same-sex marriage as of 2011. Civil unions for same-sex couples are legal in New Jersey. In reaction to same-sex marriage, voters in at least 19 U.S. states have approved measures in their state constitutions defining marriage as an exclusively heterosexual union. On November 4, 2008, Californians voted 52 percent to 48 percent to override the right to same-sex marriage, which the courts had approved earlier that year. Currently that ban is under judicial review.

Legal same-sex marriages can easily give each spouse rights to the other spouse's labor and its products. Some societies do allow marriage between members of the same biological sex. Several Native American groups had figures known as *berdaches*. These were biological men who assumed many of the mannerisms, behavior patterns, and tasks of women. Sometimes berdaches married men, who shared the products of their labor from hunting and traditional male roles, as the berdache fulfilled the traditional wifely role. Also, in some Native American cultures, a marriage of a "manly-hearted woman" to another woman brought the traditional male–female division of labor to their household. The manly woman hunted and did other male tasks, while the wife played the traditional female role.

There's no logical reason why same-sex marriage cannot give spouses rights over the other's property. But in the United States, the same inheritance rights that apply to male–female couples usually do not apply to same-sex couples. For instance, even in the absence of a will, property can pass to a widow or a widower without going through probate. The wife or husband pays no inheritance tax. This benefit is not available to gay men and lesbians (Weston 1991).

What about Leach's fifth right—to establish a joint fund of property—to benefit the children? Here again, gay and lesbian couples are at a disadvantage. If there are children, property is separately, rather than jointly, transmitted. Some organizations do make staff benefits, such as health and dental insurance, available to same-sex domestic partners.

Finally, there is the matter of establishing a socially significant "relationship of affinity" between spouses and their relatives. In many societies, one of the main roles of marriage is to establish an alliance between groups, in addition to the individual bond. *Affinals* are relatives through marriage, such as a brother-in-law or mother-in-law. For same-sex couples in contemporary North America, affinal relations are problematic. In an unofficial union, terms like "daughter-in-law" and "mother-in-law" may sound strange. Many parents are suspicious of their children's sexuality and lifestyle choices and may not recognize a relationship of affinity with a child's partner of the same sex.

This discussion of same-sex marriage has been intended to illustrate the different kinds of rights that typically accompany marriage, by seeing what may happen when there is a permanent pair bond without legal sanction. In just six of the United States are such unions fully legal. As we have seen, same-sex unions have been recognized in different historical and cultural settings. In certain African cultures, including the Igbo of Nigeria and the Lovedu of South Africa, women could marry other women. In situations in which women, such as prominent market women in West Africa, are able to amass property and other forms of wealth, they may take a wife. Such marriage allows the prominent woman to strengthen her social status and the economic importance of her household (Amadiume 1987).

Marriage across Cultures

Outside industrial societies, marriage often is more a relationship between groups than one between individuals. We think of marriage as an individual matter. Although the bride and groom usually seek their parents' approval, the final choice (to live together, to marry, to divorce) lies with the couple. The idea of romantic love symbolizes this individual relationship.

In nonindustrial societies, although there can be romantic love (Goleman 1992), marriage is a group concern. People don't just take a spouse; they assume obligations to a group of in-laws. When residence is patrilocal, for example, a woman must leave the community where she was born. She faces the prospect of spending the rest of her life in her husband's village, with his relatives.

Bridewealth and Dowry

In societies with descent groups, people enter marriage not alone but with the help of the descent group. Descent-group members often contribute to the **bridewealth,** a customary gift before, at, or after the marriage from the husband and his kin to the wife and her kin. Another word for bridewealth is *brideprice,* but this term is inaccurate because people with the custom don't usually think of marriage as a commercial relationship between a man and an object to be bought and sold.

Bridewealth compensates the bride's group for the loss of her companionship and labor. More important, it makes the children born to the woman full members of her husband's descent group. For this reason, the institution also is called **progeny price.** Rather than the woman herself, it is her children who are permanently transferred to the husband's group. Whatever we call it, such a transfer of wealth at marriage is common in patrilineal groups. In matrilineal societies, children are members of the mother's group, and there is no reason to pay a progeny price.

Dowry is a marital exchange in which the bride's family or kin group provides substantial gifts when their daughter marries. For rural Greece, Ernestine Friedl (1962) has described a form of dowry in which the bride gets a wealth transfer from her mother, to serve as a kind of trust fund during her marriage. Usually, however, the dowry goes to the husband's family, and the custom is correlated with low female status. In this form of dowry, best known from India, women are perceived as burdens. When a man and his family take a wife, they expect to be compensated for the added responsibility.

Bridewealth exists in many more cultures than dowry does, but the nature and quantity of transferred items differ. In many African societies, cattle constitute bridewealth, but the number of cattle given varies from society to society. As the value of bridewealth increases, marriages become more stable. Bridewealth is insurance against divorce.

Imagine a patrilineal society in which a marriage requires the transfer of about 25 cattle from the groom's descent group to the bride's. Michael, a member of descent group A, marries Sarah from group B. His relatives help him assemble the bridewealth. He gets the most help from his close agnates—his older brother, father, father's brother, and closest patrilineal cousins.

The distribution of the cattle once they reach Sarah's group mirrors the manner in which they were assembled. Sarah's father, or her oldest brother if the father is dead, receives her bridewealth. He keeps most of the cattle to use as bridewealth for his sons' marriages. However, a share also goes to everyone who will be expected to help when Sarah's brothers marry.

When Sarah's brother David gets married, many of the cattle go to a third group—C, which is David's wife's group. Thereafter, they may serve as bridewealth to still other groups. Men constantly use their sisters' bridewealth cattle to acquire their own wives. In a decade, the cattle given when Michael married Sarah will have been exchanged widely.

In such societies marriage entails an agreement between descent groups. If Sarah and Michael try to make their marriage succeed but fail to do so, both groups may conclude that the marriage can't last. Here it becomes especially obvious that marriages are relationships between groups as well as between individuals. If Sarah has a younger sister or niece (her older brother's daughter, for example), the concerned parties may agree to Sarah's replacement by a kinswoman.

However, incompatibility isn't the main problem that threatens marriage in societies with bridewealth. Infertility is a more important concern. If Sarah has no children, she and her group have not fulfilled their part of the marriage agreement. If the relationship is to endure, Sarah's group must furnish another woman, perhaps her younger sister, who can have children. If this happens, Sarah may choose to stay in her husband's village. Perhaps she will someday have a child. If she does stay on, her husband will have established a plural marriage.

Most nonindustrial food-producing societies, unlike most industrial nations, allow **plural marriages,** or **polygamy.** There are two varieties; one is common and the other is very rare. The more common variant is **polygyny,** in which a man has more than one wife. The rare variant is **polyandry,** in which a woman has more than one husband. If the infertile wife remains married to her husband after he has taken a substitute wife provided by her descent group, this is polygyny.

Durable Alliances

It is possible to exemplify the group-alliance nature of marriage by examining still another common practice—continuation of marital alliances when one spouse dies.

Sororate

What happens if Sarah dies young? Michael's group will ask Sarah's group for a substitute, often her sister. This custom is known as the **sororate** (Figure 13.5). If Sarah has no sister, or if all her sisters already are married, another woman from her group may be available. Michael marries her, there is no need to return the bridewealth, and the alliance continues.

FIGURE 13.5

Sororate and
Levirate

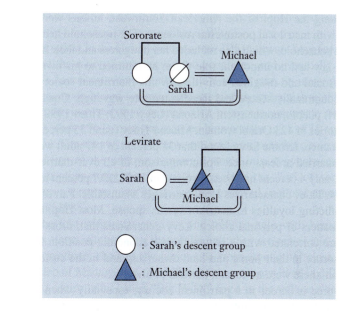

The sororate exists in both matrilineal and patrilineal societies. In a matrilineal society with matrilocal postmarital residence, a widower may remain with his wife's group
by marrying her sister or another female member of her matrilineage (Figure 13.5).

Levirate

What happens if the husband dies? In many societies, the widow may marry his brother.
This custom is known as the **levirate** (Figure 13.5). Like the sororate, it is a continuation
marriage that maintains the alliance between descent groups, in this case by replacing
the husband with another member of his group. The implications of the levirate vary
with age. One study found that in African societies the levirate, although widely permitted, rarely involves cohabitation of the widow and her new husband. Furthermore, widows don't automatically marry the husband's brother just because they are allowed to.
Often they prefer to make other arrangements (Potash 1986).

Divorce

In some societies marriages may seem to go on forever, but in our own they are fairly
brittle. Ease of divorce varies across cultures. What factors work for and against divorce? As we've seen, marriages that are political alliances between groups are more
difficult to dissolve than are marriages that are more individual affairs, of concern
mainly to the married couple and their children. Substantial bridewealth may decrease
the divorce rate for individuals; replacement marriages (levirate and sororate) also
work to preserve group alliances. Divorce tends to be more common in matrilineal
than in patrilineal societies. When residence is matrilocal (in the wife's home village),
the wife may simply send off a man with whom she's incompatible.

Anthropology Today *Five Wives and 55 Children*

Many societies, including Turkey, as described here, that once permitted plural marriage have outlawed it. This story reports on polygyny, the form of polygamy (plural marriage) in which a man has more than one wife. Marriage usually is a domestic partnership, but secondary wives may or may not reside near the first wife. In this Turkish case the five wives have their own homes. Polygamy, although formally outlawed, has survived in Turkey since the Ottoman period, when having several wives was viewed as a symbol of power, wealth, and sexual prowess. Unlike the past, when the practice was customary (for men who could afford it) and not illegal, polygamy can put contemporary women at risk. Because their marriages have no official status, secondary wives who are abused or mistreated have no legal recourse. Like all institutions studied by anthropologists, customs involving plural marriage are changing in the contemporary world and in the context of nation-states and globalization.

ISIKLAR, Turkey, July 6—With his 5 wives, 55 children and 80 grandchildren, 400 sheep, 1,200 acres of land and a small army of servants, Aga Mehmet Arslan would seem an unlikely defender of monogamy.

Though banned, polygamy is widespread in the Isiklar region. Yet if he were young again, said Mr. Arslan, a sprightly, potbellied, 64-year-old Kurdish village chieftain, he would happily trade in his five wives for one.

"Marrying five wives is not sinful, and I did so because to have many wives is a sign of power," he said, perched on a divan in a large cushion-filled room at his house, where a portrait of Turkey's first president, Mustafa Kemal Ataturk, who outlawed polygamy in 1926, is prominently displayed.

"But I wouldn't do it again," he added, listing the challenges of having so many kin—like the need to build each wife a house away from the others to prevent friction and his struggle to remember all of his children's names. "I was uneducated back then, and God commands us to be fruitful and multiply."

Though banned by Ataturk as part of an effort to modernize the Turkish republic and empower women, polygamy remains widespread in this deeply religious and rural Kurdish region of southeastern Anatolia, home to one-third of Turkey's 71 million people. The practice is generally accepted under the Koran.

Polygamy is creating cultural clashes in a country struggling to reconcile the secularism of the republic with its Muslim traditions.

Because polygamous marriages are not recognized by the state—imams who conduct them are subject to punishment—the wives have no legal status, making them vulnerable when marriages turn violent. Yet the local authorities here typically turn a blind eye because the practice is viewed as a tradition. . . .

In Turkey, polygamy experts explain the practice as a hangover from the Ottoman period, when harem culture abounded and having several wives was viewed as a symbol of influence, sexual prowess and wealth.

Remzi Otto, a sociology professor at Dicle University in Diyarbakir, who conducted a survey of 50 polygamous families, said some men took second wives if their first wives could not conceive sons. Some also take widowed women and orphan girls as second wives to give them a social safety net. Love, he added, can also play a role.

"Many men in this region are forced into marriages when they are as young as 13, so finding their own wife is a way to rebel and express their independence," he said.

Isiklar, the remote village where Mr. Arslan is the aga, or chief, can be found at the end of a long dirt road, surrounded by sweeping verdant fields. Most of the local residents share the surname Arslan, which means lion in Turkish and connotes virility.

Mr. Arslan said he regretted his multiple marriages and had forbidden his sons to take more than one wife. He is also educating his daughters. "I have done nothing shameful," he said. "I don't drink. I treat everyone with respect. But having so many wives can create problems."

His biggest headache, he said, stems from jealousy among the wives, the first of whom he married out of love. "My rule is to behave equally toward all of my wives," he said. "But the first wife was very, very jealous when the second wife came. When the third arrived, the first two created an alliance against her. So I have to be a good diplomat.". . .

Source: Dan Bilefsky, "Polygamy Fosters Culture Clashes (and Regrets) in Turkey," *New York Times,* July 10, 2006. Copyright © 2006 The New York Times. Reprinted by permission.

Plural wives can play important political roles in nonindustrial states. The king of the Merina, a populous society in the highlands of Madagascar, had palaces for each of his 12 wives in different provinces. He stayed with them when he traveled through the kingdom. They were his local agents, overseeing and reporting on provincial matters. The king of Buganda, the major precolonial state of Uganda, took hundreds of wives, representing all the clans in his nation. Everyone in the kingdom became the king's in-law, and all the clans had a chance to provide the next ruler. This was a way of giving the common people a stake in the government.

These examples show there is no single explanation for polygyny. Its context and function vary from society to society and even within the same society. Some men are polygynous because they have inherited a widow from a brother. Others have plural wives because they seek prestige or want to increase household productivity. Men and women with political and economic ambitions cultivate marital alliances that serve their aims. In many societies, including the Betsileo of Madagascar and the Igbo of Nigeria, women arrange the marriages.

Polyandry

Polyandry is rare and is practiced under very specific conditions. Most of the world's polyandrous peoples live in South Asia—Tibet, Nepal, India, and Sri Lanka. In some of these areas, polyandry seems to be a cultural adaptation to mobility associated with customary male travel for trade, commerce, and military operations. Polyandry ensures there will be at least one man at home to accomplish male activities within a gender-based division of labor. Fraternal polyandry is also an effective strategy when resources are scarce. Brothers with limited resources (in land) pool their resources in expanded (polyandrous) households. They take just one wife. Polyandry restricts the number of wives and heirs. Less competition among heirs means that land can be transmitted with minimal fragmentation.

Summary

1. Kinship and marriage organize social and political life in nonindustrial societies. One widespread kin group is the nuclear family, consisting of a married couple and their children. Other groups, such as extended families and descent groups, may assume functions usually associated with the nuclear family. Nuclear families tend to be especially important in foraging and industrial societies.

2. In contemporary North America, the nuclear family is the characteristic kin group for the middle class. Expanded households and sharing with extended family kin occur more frequently among the poor, who may pool their resources in dealing with poverty. Today, however, even in the American middle class, nuclear family households are declining as single-person households and other domestic arrangements increase.

3. The descent group is a basic kin group among nonindustrial food producers (farmers and herders). Unlike families, descent groups have perpetuity, lasting for generations. Descent-group members share and manage an estate. Lineages are based on demonstrated descent; clans, on stipulated descent. Unilineal (patrilineal and matrilineal) descent is associated with unilocal (patrilocal and matrilocal, respectively) postmarital residence.

4. Most societies have incest restrictions. Because kinship is socially constructed, such restrictions apply to different relatives in different societies. Human behavior with respect to mating with close relatives may express a generalized primate tendency, illustrating both urges and avoidance. But types, risks, and avoidance of incest also reflect specific kinship structures. Exogamy extends social and political ties outward; endogamy does the reverse. Endogamic rules are common in stratified societies. One extreme example is India, where castes are the endogamous units.

5. The discussion of same-sex marriage, which, by and large, is illegal in the United States, illustrates the various rights that go along with marriage. Marriage establishes the legal parents of children. It gives spouses rights to the sexuality, labor, and property of the other. And it establishes a socially significant "relationship of affinity" between spouses and each other's relatives.

6. In societies with descent groups, marriages are relationships between groups as well as between spouses. With bridewealth, the groom and his relatives transfer wealth to the bride and her relatives. As the bridewealth's value increases, the divorce rate declines. Bridewealth customs show that marriages among nonindustrial food producers create and maintain group alliances. So do the sororate, by which a man marries the sister of his deceased wife, and the levirate, by which a woman marries the brother of her deceased husband.

7. The ease and frequency of divorce vary across cultures. When marriage is a matter of intergroup alliance, as is typically true in societies with descent groups, divorce is less common. A large fund of joint property also complicates divorce.

8. Many societies permit plural marriages. The two kinds of polygamy are polygyny and polyandry. The former involves multiple wives; the latter, multiple husbands. Polygyny is much more common than polyandry.

Key Terms

bridewealth, *315*
caste system, *312*
clan, *306*
descent group, *305*
dowry, *315*
endogamy, *312*
exogamy, *309*
extended family
    household, *302*
family, *298*
family of
    orientation, *299*

family of
    procreation, *299*
incest, *309*
levirate, *317*
lineage, *306*
matrilineal
    descent, *306*
matrilocality, *308*
neolocality, *302*
patrilineal
    descent, *306*
patrilocality, *308*

plural
    marriages, *316*
polyandry, *316*
polygamy, *316*
polygyny, *316*
progeny price, *315*
sororate, *316*
unilineal
    descent, *306*

Go to our Online Learning Center website at **www.mhhe.com/kottak** for
Internet resources directly related to the content of this chapter.

Chapter  14

Gender

Sex and Gender

Recurrent Gender Patterns

Gender Roles and Gender Stratification

Reduced Gender Stratification—
Matrilineal–Matrilocal Societies

Matriarchy

Increased Gender Stratification—
Patrilineal–Patrilocal Societies

Patriarchy and Violence

Gender in Industrial Societies

Applying Anthropology to Popular
Culture: Lisa vs. Malibu Stacy

The Feminization of Poverty

Work and Happiness

Beyond Male and Female

Sexual Orientation

Anthropology Today: Changing Images
of Masculinity

Because anthropologists study biology, society, and culture, they are in a unique position to comment on nature (biological predispositions) and nurture (environment) as determinants of human behavior. Human attitudes, values, and behavior are limited not only by our genetic predispositions—which often are difficult to identify—but also by our experiences during enculturation. Our attributes as adults are determined both by our genes and by our environment during growth and development.

Sex and Gender

Questions about nature and nurture emerge in the discussion of human sex–gender roles and sexuality. Men and women differ genetically. Women have two X chromosomes, and men have an X and a Y. The father determines a baby's sex because only he has the Y chromosome to transmit. The mother always provides an X chromosome.

The chromosomal difference is expressed in hormonal and physiological contrasts. Humans are sexually dimorphic, more so than some primates, such as gibbons (small tree-living Asiatic apes) and less so than others, such as gorillas and orangutans. **Sexual dimorphism** refers to differences in male and female biology besides the contrasts in breasts and genitals. Women and men differ not just in primary (genitalia and reproductive organs) and secondary (breasts, voice, hair distribution) sexual characteristics, but in average weight, height, strength, and longevity. Women tend to live longer than men and have excellent endurance capabilities. In a given population, men tend to be taller and to weigh more than women do. Of course, there is a considerable overlap between the sexes in terms of height, weight, and physical strength, and there has been a pronounced reduction in sexual dimorphism during human biological evolution.

Just how far, however, do such genetically and physiologically determined differences go? What effects do they have on the way men and women act and are treated in different societies? Anthropologists have discovered both similarities and differences in the roles of men and women in different cultures. The predominant anthropological position on sex–gender roles and biology may be stated as follows:

> The biological nature of men and women [should be seen] not as a narrow enclosure limiting the human organism, but rather as a broad base upon which a variety of structures can be built. (Friedl 1975, p. 6)

Although in most societies men tend to be somewhat more aggressive than women are, many of the behavioral and attitudinal differences between the sexes emerge from culture rather than biology. Sex differences are biological, but gender encompasses all the traits that a culture assigns to and inculcates in males and females. "Gender," in other words, refers to the cultural construction of whether one is female, male, or something else.

Given the "rich and various constructions of gender" within the realm of cultural diversity, Susan Bourque and Kay Warren (1987) note that the same images of masculinity and femininity do not always apply. Anthropologists have gathered systematic

The realm of cultural diversity contains richly different social constructions and expressions of gender roles, as illustrated by these Wodaabe male celebrants in Niger. (Look closely for suggestions of diffusion.) For what reasons do men decorate their bodies in our society?

ethnographic data about similarities and differences involving gender in many cultural settings (Bonvillain 2007; Brettell and Sargent, eds. 2009; Gilmore 2001; Kimmel 2007; Mascia-Lees and Black 2000; Nanda 2000; Ward and Edelstein 2009). Before we examine the cross-cultural data, some definitions are in order.

Gender roles are the tasks and activities a culture assigns to the sexes. Related to gender roles are **gender stereotypes,** which are oversimplified but strongly held ideas about the characteristics of males and females. **Gender stratification** describes an unequal distribution of rewards (socially valued resources, power, prestige, human rights, and personal freedom) between men and women, reflecting their different positions in a social hierarchy. According to Ann Stoler (1977), the economic determinants of gender status include freedom or autonomy (in disposing of one's labor and its fruits) and social power (control over the lives, labor, and produce of others).

In stateless societies, gender stratification often is more obvious in regard to prestige than it is in regard to wealth. In her study of the Ilongots of northern Luzon in the Philippines, Michelle Rosaldo (1980*a*) described gender differences related to the positive cultural value placed on adventure, travel, and knowledge of the external world. More often than women, Ilongot men, as headhunters, visited distant places. They acquired knowledge of the external world, amassed experiences there, and returned to express their knowledge, adventures, and feelings in public oratory. They received acclaim as a result. Ilongot women had inferior prestige because they lacked external experiences on which to base knowledge and dramatic expression. On the basis of Rosaldo's study and findings in other stateless societies, Ong (1989) argues that we must distinguish between prestige systems and actual power in a given society. High male prestige may not entail economic or political power held by men over their families.

Recurrent Gender Patterns

You probably had chores when you were growing up. Was there any gender bias in what you were asked to do compared with your brother or sister? If you were raised by two parents, did any tension arise over your parental division of labor? Based on cross-cultural data from societies worldwide, Table 14.1 lists activities that are generally male, generally female, or swing (either male or female). Before you look at that table, see if you can assign the following to one gender or the other (M or F): hunting large animals ( ), gathering wild vegetable foods ( ), tending crops ( ), fishing ( ), cooking ( ), fetching water ( ), making baskets ( ), making drinks ( ). Now consult Table 14.1 and see how you did. Reflect on your results. Is what's true cross-culturally still true of the division of labor by gender in today's world, including the United States?

Even if we still think in terms of "men's work" and "women's work," ideas about gender are changing along with the employment patterns of men and women. But old beliefs, cultural expectations and challenges, and gender stereotypes linger. As of this writing, only 17 out of 100 United States senators are women. Only three women have ever served on the U.S. Supreme Court. Women, in general, remain less powerful than men. The lingering American expectation that proper female behavior should be polite, restrained, or meek poses a challenge for women, because American culture also values

TABLE 14.1   **Generalities in the Division of Labor by Gender, Based on Data from 185 Societies**

Source: Murdock and Provost 1973.

Generally Male Activities	Swing (Male or Female) Activities	Generally Female Activities
Hunting of large aquatic animals (e.g., whales, walrus)	Making fire	Gathering fuel (e.g., firewood)
Smelting of ores	Body mutilation	Making drinks
Metalworking	Preparing skins	Gathering wild vegetal foods
Lumbering	Gathering small land animals	Dairy production (e.g., churning)
Hunting large land animals	Planting crops	Spinning
Working wood	Making leather products	Doing the laundry
Hunting fowl	Harvesting	Fetching water
Making musical instruments	Tending crops	Cooking
Trapping	Milking	Preparing vegetal food (e.g., processing cereal grains)
Building boats	Making baskets	
Working stone	Carrying burdens	
Working bone, horn, and shell	Making mats	
Mining and quarrying	Caring for small animals	
Setting bones	Preserving meat and fish	
Butchering*	Loom weaving	
Collecting wild honey	Gathering small aquatic animals	
Clearing land	Clothing manufacture	
Fishing	Making pottery	
Tending large herd animals		
Building houses		
Preparing the soil		
Making nets		
Making rope		

*All the activities above "butchering" are almost always done by men; those from "butchering" through "making rope" usually are done by men.

decisiveness and "standing up for your beliefs." When American men and women display certain behavior—speaking up for their ideas, for example—they are judged differently. A man's assertive behavior may be admired and rewarded, but a woman's similar behavior may be labeled "aggressive"—or worse.

Both men and women are constrained by their cultural training, stereotypes, and expectations. For example, American men are told they should "be decisive"—make decisions and stick to them. In our stereotypes, changing one's mind is more associated with women than men and may be perceived as a sign of weakness. Politicians routinely criticize their opponents for being indecisive, for waffling or "flip-flopping" on issues. What a strange idea—that people shouldn't change their positions if they've discovered there's a better way. Males, females, and humanity may be equally victimized by aspects of cultural training.

Data relevant to the cross-cultural study of gender can be drawn from the domains of economics, politics, domestic activity, kinship, and marriage. Table 14.1 shows cross-cultural data from 185 randomly selected societies on the division of labor by gender.

Remembering the discussion in Chapter 2 of universals, generalities, and particularities, the findings in Table 14.1 about the division of labor by gender illustrate generalities rather than universals. That is, among the societies known to ethnography, there is a very strong tendency for men to build boats, but there are exceptions. One was the Hidatsa, a Native American group in which the women made the boats used to cross the Missouri River. (Traditionally, the Hidatsa were village farmers and bison hunters on the North American Plains; they now live in North Dakota.) Another exception: Pawnee women worked wood; this is the only Native American group that assigned this activity to women. (The Pawnee, also traditionally Plains farmers and bison hunters, originally lived in what is now central Nebraska and central Kansas; they now live on a reservation in north central Oklahoma.)

Exceptions to cross-cultural generalizations may involve societies or individuals. That is, a society like the Hidatsa can contradict the cross-cultural generalization that men build boats by assigning that task to women. Or, in a society where the cultural expectation is that only men build boats, a particular woman or women can contradict that expectation by doing the male activity. Table 14.1 shows that in a sample of 185 societies, certain activities ("swing activities") are assigned to either or both men and women. Among the most important of such activities are planting, tending, and harvesting crops. Some societies customarily assign more farming chores to women, whereas others call on men to be the main farm laborers. Among the tasks almost always assigned to men (Table 14.1), some (e.g., hunting large animals on land and sea) seem clearly related to the greater average size and strength of males. Others, such as working wood and making musical instruments, seem more culturally arbitrary. And women, of course, are not exempt from arduous and time-consuming physical labor, such as gathering firewood and fetching water. In Arembepe, Bahia, Brazil, women routinely transported water in five-gallon tins, balanced on their heads, from wells and lagoons located long distances from their homes.

Both women and men have to fit their activities into 24-hour days. Based on cross-cultural data, Table 14.2 shows that the time and effort spent in subsistence activities by men and women tend to be about equal. If anything, men do slightly less subsistence work than women do. Think about how female domestic activities could have been

TABLE 14.2   **Time and Effort Expended on Subsistence Activities by Men and Women***

Source: Whyte 1978.

More by men	16
Roughly equal	61
More by women	23

*Percentage of 88 randomly selected societies for which information was available on this variable.

TABLE 14.3   Who Does the Domestic Work?*

Source: Whyte 1978.

Males do virtually none	51
Males do some, but mostly done by females	49

*Percentage of 92 randomly selected societies for which information was available on this variable.

TABLE 14.4   Who Has Final Authority over the Care, Handling, and Discipline of Infant Children (under Four Years Old)?*

Source: Whyte 1978.

Males have more say	18
Roughly equal	16
Females have more say	66

*Percentage of 67 randomly selected societies for which information was available on this variable.

specified in greater detail in Table 14.1. The original coding of the data in Table 14.1 probably illustrates a male bias in that extradomestic activities received much more prominence than domestic activities did. For example, is collecting wild honey (listed in Table 14.1) more necessary or time-consuming than cleaning a baby's bottom (absent from Table 14.1)? Also, notice that Table 14.1 does not mention trade and market activity, in which either or both men and women are active.

Cross-culturally the subsistence contributions of men and women are roughly equal (Table 14.2). But in domestic activities and child care, female labor predominates, as we see in Tables 14.3 and 14.4. Table 14.3 shows that in about half the societies studied, men did virtually no domestic work. Even in societies where men did some domestic chores, the bulk of such work was done by women. Adding together their subsistence activities and their domestic work, women tend to work more hours than men do. Has this changed in the contemporary world?

What about child care? Women tend to be the main caregivers in most societies, but men often play a role. Table 14.4 uses cross-cultural data to answer the question, "Who—men or women—has final authority over the care, handling, and discipline of children younger than four years?" Women have primary authority over infants in two-thirds of the societies. Given the critical role of breast-feeding in ensuring infant survival, it makes sense, for infants especially, for the mother to be the primary caregiver.

There are differences in male and female reproductive strategies. Women work to ensure their progeny will survive by establishing a close bond with each baby. It's also advantageous for a woman to have a reliable mate to ease the child-rearing process and ensure the survival of her children. (Again, there are exceptions, for example, the matrilineal Nayars discussed in the previous chapter.) Women can have only so many babies during their reproductive years, which begin after menarche (the advent of first menstruation) and end with menopause (cessation of menstruation). Men, in contrast, have a longer reproductive period, which can last into the elder years. If they choose to do so,

After 1900, European immigration produced a male labor force willing to work for wages lower than those of American-born men. Those immigrant men moved into factory jobs that previously had gone to women. As machine tools and mass production further reduced the need for female labor, the notion that women were biologically unfit for factory work began to gain ground (Martin and Voorhies 1975).

Maxine Margolis (1984, 2000) has shown how gendered work, attitudes, and beliefs have varied in response to American economic needs. For example, wartime shortages of men have promoted the idea that work outside the home is women's patriotic duty. During the world wars the notion that women are unfit for hard physical labor faded. Inflation and the culture of consumption also have spurred female employment. When prices or demand rise, multiple paychecks help maintain family living standards.

The steady increase in female paid employment since World War II also reflects the baby boom and industrial expansion. American culture traditionally has defined clerical work, teaching, and nursing as female occupations. With rapid population growth and business expansion after World War II, the demand for women to fill such jobs grew steadily. Employers also found they could increase their profits by paying women lower wages than they would have to pay returning male war veterans.

Margolis (1984, 2000) contends that changes in the economy lead to changes in attitudes toward and about women. Economic changes paved the way for the contemporary women's movement, which also was spurred by the publication of Betty Friedan's book *The Feminine Mystique* in 1963 and the founding of NOW, the National Organization of Women, in 1966. The movement in turn promoted expanded work opportunities for women, including the goal of equal pay for equal work. Between 1970 and 2009, the female percentage of the American workforce rose from 38 to 47 percent. In other words, almost half of all Americans who work outside the home are women. Over 72 million women now have paid jobs, compared with 82 million men. Women fill more than half (58 percent) of all professional jobs (*Statistical Abstract of the United States 2011*, Tables 585, 615). And it's not mainly single women working, as once was the case. Table 14.8 presents figures on the ever-increasing cash employment of American wives and mothers, including those with children under 6 years old.

TABLE 14.8 Cash Employment of American Mothers, Wives, and Husbands, 1960–2009[*]

Source: *Statistical Abstract of the United States 2011*, Table 596, 598. http://www.census.gov/compendia/statab/2011edition.html.

Year	Percentage of Married Women, Husband Present with Children under six	Percentage of All Married Women[†]	Percentage of All Married Men[‡]
1960	19	32	89
1970	30	40	86
1980	45	50	81
1990	59	58	79
2009	62	62	76

[*]Civilian population 16 years of age and older.
[†]Husband present.
[‡]Wife present.

In an episode of *The Simpsons* titled "Lisa vs. Malibu Stacy," eight-year-old Lisa is outraged when her talking doll (Stacy) says things like, "Let's buy makeup so boys will like us." The doll's statement, and Lisa's reaction to it, reveal American cultural values reflecting consumerism, gender roles, and gender stereotypes. Watch a few episodes of *The Simpsons, South Park,* or *Family Guy.* What can we learn about gender roles and stereotypes (and about culture and society more generally) by analyzing such popular culture products?

Note in Table 14.8 that the cash employment of American married men has been falling while that of American married women has been rising. There has been a dramatic change in behavior and attitudes since 1960, when 89 percent of all married men worked, compared with just 32 percent of married women. The comparable figures in 2009 were 76 percent and 62 percent. Ideas about the gender roles of males and females have changed. Compare your grandparents and your parents. Chances are you have a working mother, but your grandmother was more likely a stay-at-home mom. Your grandfather is more likely than your father to have worked in manufacturing and to have belonged to a union. Your father is more likely than your grandfather to have shared child care and domestic responsibilities. Age at marriage has been delayed for both men and women. College educations and professional degrees have increased. What other changes do you associate with the increase in female employment outside the home?

The Feminization of Poverty

Alongside the economic gains of many American women stands an opposite extreme: the feminization of poverty, or the increasing representation of women (and their children) among America's poorest people. Women head over half of U.S. households with incomes below the poverty line. In 1959 female-headed households accounted for just one-fourth of the American poor. Since then that figure has more than doubled.

Married couples are much more secure economically than single mothers are. The average income for married-couple families is more than twice that of families maintained by a single woman. The median one-earner family maintained by a single woman had an annual income of $33,073 in 2008. This was less than one-half the median income ($73,010) of a married-couple household. (*Statistical Abstract of the United States 2011,* Tables 691).

The feminization of poverty isn't just a North American trend. The percentage of single-parent (usually female-headed) households has been increasing worldwide. The figure ranges from about 10 percent in Japan, to below 20 percent in certain South Asian and Southeast Asian countries, to almost 50 percent in certain African countries and the Caribbean (Buvinic 1995, *Statistical Abstract of the United States 2011,* Table 1336). The percentage of single-parent households rose in every nation listed in Table 14.9 between 1980–1981 and 2009. The United States maintains the largest percentage of single-parent households (29.5 percent in 2009), followed by the United Kingdom

TABLE 14.9
Percentage of Single-Parent Households, Selected Countries, 1980–1981 and 2009

Country	1980–1981	2009
United States	19.5%	29.5%
United Kingdom	13.9	25.0
Canada	12.7	24.6
Ireland	7.2	22.6
Denmark	13.4	21.7
France	10.2	19.8
Japan	4.9	10.2

(25 percent), Canada (24.6 percent), Ireland (22.6 percent), and Denmark (21.7 percent). The rate of increase in single-parent households over the past 30 years has been highest in Ireland, where it tripled, from 7.2 to 22.6 percent.

Globally, households headed by women tend to be poorer than those headed by men. In one study, the percentage of single-parent families considered poor was 18 percent in Britain, 20 percent in Italy, 25 percent in Switzerland, 40 percent in Ireland, 52 percent in Canada, and 63 percent in the United States.

It is widely believed that one way to improve the situation of poor women is to encourage them to organize. New women's groups can in some cases revive or replace traditional forms of social organization that have been disrupted. Membership in a group can help women to mobilize resources, to rationalize production, and to reduce the risks and costs associated with credit. Organization also allows women to develop self-confidence and to decrease dependence on others. Through such organization, poor women throughout the world are working to determine their own needs and priorities and to change things so as to improve their social and economic situation (Buvinic 1995).

Work and Happiness

Table 14.10 shows female labor force participation in various countries—condensed from 30 countries for which data were available—in 2008. The United States, with 69.3 percent of its women employed, ranked 13th, while Canada (74.4 percent) ranked 6th. Iceland topped the list, with 82.5 percent of its women in the workforce. Turkey was lowest; only 26.7 percent of its women were employed.

In 2010, Gallup conducted a survey of the world's 132 happiest countries, based on various measures, including the percentages of people in that country who were thriving—and suffering. Respondents also were asked to rate their own lives on a scale from zero (worst possible) to 10 (best possible). Denmark was the world's happiest nation; Canada came in 6th; the United States, 12th.

Denmark, which has a high rate of workplace women, a rising birthrate, and readily available child care, is rated the world's happiest country. The genetics researcher shown here is the mother of a toddler.

TABLE 14.10
Female Labor Force Participation by Country, 2008

Source: *Statistical Abstract of the United States* 2010, Table 1330; Huffington Post, http://www.huffingtonpost.com/2010/07/03/worlds-happiest-countries_n_633814.

Country	Percentage of Women in Labor Force	Rank among World's 15 "Happiest Countries"
Iceland	82.5	*
Sweden	78.2	9
Norway	77.4	3
Denmark	77.3	1
Switzerland	76.6	7
Canada	74.4	6
Finland	74.0	2
New Zealand	72.0	8
Netherlands	72.6	4
United Kingdom	70.2	*
Australia	69.9	11
Germany	69.7	*
United States	69.3	12
Turkey (lowest in table)	26.7	*

*These countries were not among the 15 "happiest countries."

Interestingly, we can detect a correlation between the two rankings—of happiness and of women's work outside the home. We see in Table 14.10 that of the 13 countries with greatest female labor force participation, 10 ranked among the world's happiest (see Levy 2010). What factors might explain this correlation? Why, as more women work outside the home, might a country's population achieve a greater sense of well-being? More money? More taxes? More social services? More personal freedom? We report; you decide!

Beyond Male and Female

Gender is socially constructed, and societies may recognize more than two genders. The contemporary United States, for example, includes individuals who self-identify using such labels as "transgender," "intersex," "third gender," and "transsexual." Such persons contradict dominant male/female gender distinctions by being part male and female, or neither male nor female. Because people who self-identify as "transgender" are increasingly visible, we must be careful about seeing "masculine " and "feminine" as absolute and binary categories.

Sex, we have seen, is biological, whereas gender is socially constructed. Transgender is a social category that includes individuals who *may or may not* contrast biologically with ordinary males and females. Within the transgender category, intersex people (see below) usually contrast biologically with ordinary males and females, but *transgender also includes people whose gender identity has no apparent biological roots.*

The term **intersex** encompasses a group of conditions involving a discrepancy between the external genitals (penis, vagina, etc.) and the internal genitals (testes, ovaries, etc.).

The older term for this condition, *hermaphroditism,* combined the names of a Greek god and goddess. Hermes was a god of male sexuality (among other things) and Aphrodite a goddess of female sexuality, love, and beauty.

The causes of intersex are varied and complex (Kaneshiro 2009): (1) An XX Intersex person has the chromosomes of a woman (XX) and normal ovaries, uterus, and Fallopian tubes, but the external genitals appear male. Usually this results from a female fetus having been exposed to an excess of male hormones before birth. (2) An XY Intersex person has the chromosomes of a man (XY), but the external genitals are incompletely formed, ambiguous, or female. The testes may be normal, malformed, or absent. (3) A True Gonadal Intersex person has both ovarian and testicular tissue. The external genitals may be ambiguous or may appear to be female or male. (4) Intersex also can result from an unusual chromosome combination, such as X0 (only one X chromosome), XXY, XYY, and XXX. In the last three cases there is an extra sex chromosome, either an X or a Y. These chromosomal combinations don't typically produce a discrepancy between internal and external genitalia, but there may be problems with sex hormone levels and overall sexual development.

The XXY configuration, known as *Klinefelter's syndrome,* is the most common unusual sex chromosome combination and the second most common condition (after Down syndrome) caused by the presence of extra chromosomes in humans. Effects of Klinefelter's occur in about 1 of every 1,000 males. One in every 500 males has an extra X chromosome but lacks the main symptoms—small testicles and reduced fertility. With XXX, aka *triple X syndrome,* there is an extra X chromosome in each cell of a human female. Triple X occurs in about 1 of every 1,000 female births. There usually is no physically distinguishable difference between triple X women and other women. The same is true of XYY compared with other males.

Turner syndrome encompasses several conditions, of which X0 (absence of one sex chromosome) is most common. In this case, all or part of one of the sex chromosomes is absent. Typical females have two X chromosomes, but in Turner syndrome, one of those chromosomes is missing or abnormal. Girls with Turner syndrome typically are sterile because of nonworking ovaries and amenorrhea (absence of a menstrual cycle).

Biology isn't destiny; people construct their identities in society. Many individuals affected by one of the biological conditions just described see themselves simply as male or female, rather than transgender. Self-identified **transgender** people tend to be individuals whose gender identity contradicts their biological sex at birth and the gender identity that society assigned to them in infancy. The transgender category is diverse; it includes individuals with varied perceptions of self and manner of gender performance. Some lean toward male; some, female, and some toward neither of the dominant genders.

Fear and ignorance related to diversity in gender fuels discrimination, principally because outsiders perceive transgender as a homogeneous and stigmatized category. In fact, there is nothing new or abnormal about diverse gender roles and identities, as the anthropological record attests. Gender variance is a human phenomenon that has taken many forms across societies and cultures.

The historical and ethnographic records reveal the malleability of gender categories and roles (Herdt 1994). Consider, for example, the *eunuch,* or "perfect servant" (a castrated man who served as a safe attendant to harems in Byzantium [Tougher 2008]).

Neither man nor woman, hijras constitute India's third gender. Many hijras get their income from performing at ceremonies, begging, or prostitution. The beauty contest shown here was organized by an AIDS prevention and relief organization that works with the local hijra community.

Acknowledgment and accommodation of *hijras* as a third sex/gender in Indian society indicates that certain societal requirements necessitated the castration of some men who then filled special social roles (Nanda 1998). Roscoe writes of the "Zuni man-woman," or *berdache* in the 19th century. As described in the previous chapter, a berdache was a male who adopted social roles traditionally assigned to women, and through performance of a third gender contributed to the social and spiritual well-being of the community as a whole (1991; 1998). Some Balkan societies included "sworn virgins," born females who assumed male gender roles and activities to meet societal needs when there was a shortage of men (Gremaux 1993).

Among the Gheg tribes of North Albania, "virginal transvestites" were biologically female, but locals consider them "honorary men" (Shryock 1988). Albanian adolescent girls have chosen to become men, remain celibate, and live among men, with the support of their families and villagers (Young 2000). And consider Polynesia. In Tonga the term *fakaleitis* describes males who behave like women, thereby contrasting with mainstream Tongan men who display masculine characteristics. Similar to the *fakaleitis* of Tonga, Samoan *fa'afafine* and Hawaiian *mahu* refer to men who adopt feminine attributes, behaviors, and visual markers.

In the contemporary West, the umbrella category *transgender* encompasses a similar variety of persons whose gender performance and identity contradict or defy a binary gender structure. Transgender people are productive and contributing members of society, at least in those sectors to which they have access and relative protection to live as who they are. In recent years, the gay and lesbian rights movement has achieved many successes, including the legalization of same-sex marriage in a few states and the repeal of the "Don't Ask Don't Tell" (DADT) policy of the U. S. armed services. The gay and lesbian rights movement has expanded to include the lesbian, gay, bisexual, and transgender community (LGBT), which works to promote government policies and social practices that protect its members' civil and human rights.

Sexual Orientation

Sexual orientation refers to a person's habitual sexual attraction to, and sexual activities with, persons of the opposite sex (*heterosexuality*), the same sex (*homosexuality*), or both sexes (*bisexuality*). *Asexuality,* indifference toward, or lack of attraction to either sex, also is a sexual orientation. All four of these forms are found in contemporary North America, and throughout the world. But each type of desire and experience holds different meanings for individuals and groups. For example, an asexual disposition may be acceptable in some places but may be perceived as a character flaw in others. Male–male sexual activity may be a private affair in Mexico, rather than public, socially sanctioned, and encouraged as among the Etoro (see below) of Papua New Guinea (see also Blackwood and Wieringa, eds. 1999; Boellstorff 2007; Kimmel and Plante 2004; Kottak and Kozaitis 2011; Nanda 2000).

Recently in the United States there has been a tendency to see sexual orientation as fixed and biologically based. There is not enough information at this time to determine the exact extent to which sexual orientation is based on biology. What we can say is that all human activities and preferences, including erotic expression, are at least partially culturally constructed.

In any society, individuals will differ in the nature, range, and intensity of their sexual interests and urges. No one knows for sure why such individual sexual differences exist. Part of the answer probably is biological, reflecting genes or hormones (Wade 2005). Another part may have to do with experiences during growth and development. But whatever the reasons for individual variation, culture always plays a role in molding individual sexual urges toward a collective norm. And such sexual norms vary from culture to culture.

What do we know about variation in sexual norms from society to society, and over time? A classic cross-cultural study (Ford and Beach 1951) found wide variation in attitudes about masturbation, bestiality (sex with animals), and homosexuality. In a single society, such as the United States, attitudes about sex differ over time and with socioeconomic status, region, and rural versus urban residence. However, even in the 1950s, prior to the "age of sexual permissiveness" (the pre-HIV period from the mid-1960s through the 1970s), research showed that almost all American men (92 percent) and more than half of American women (54 percent) admitted to masturbation. In the famous Kinsey report (Kinsey, Pomeroy, and Martin 1948), 37 percent of the men surveyed admitted having had at least one sexual experience leading to orgasm with another male. In a later study of 1,200 unmarried women, 26 percent reported same-sex sexual activities. (Because Kinsey's research relied on nonrandom samples, it should be considered merely illustrative, rather than a statistically accurate representation, of sexual behavior at the time.)

Sex acts with people of the same sex were absent, rare, or secret in only 37 percent of 76 societies for which data were available in the Ford and Beach study (1951). In the others, various forms of same-sex sexual activity were acceptable. Sometimes sexual relations between people of the same sex involved transvestism on the part of one of the partners (see Kulick 1998). Transvestism did not characterize male–male sex among the Sudanese Azande, who valued the warrior role (Evans-Pritchard 1970). Prospective warriors—young men aged 12 to 20—left their families and shared quarters with adult fighting men, who paid bridewealth for, and had sex with, them. During this apprenticeship, the young men did the domestic duties of women. Upon reaching warrior status, these young men took their own younger male brides. Later, retiring from the warrior role, Azande men married women. Flexible in their sexual expression, Azande males had no difficulty shifting from sex with older men (as male brides), to sex with younger men (as warriors), to sex with women (as husbands) (see Murray and Roscoe, eds. 1998).

Consider also the Etoro (Kelly 1976), a group of 400 people who subsist by hunting and horticulture in the Trans-Fly region of Papua New Guinea. The Etoro illustrate the power of culture in molding human sexuality. The following account, based on ethnographic fieldwork by Raymond C. Kelly in the late 1960s, applies only to Etoro males and their beliefs. Etoro cultural norms prevented the male anthropologist who studied them from gathering comparable information about female attitudes. Note, also, that the activities described have been discouraged by missionaries. Because there has been no restudy of the Etoro specifically focusing on these activities, the extent to which these practices continue today is unknown. For this reason, I'll use the past tense in describing them.

Etoro opinions about sexuality were linked to their beliefs about the cycle of birth, physical growth, maturity, old age, and death. Etoro men believed that semen was necessary to give life force to a fetus, which was, they believed, implanted in a woman by an ancestral spirit. Sexual intercourse during pregnancy nourished the growing fetus. The Etoro believed that men had a limited lifetime supply of semen. Any sex act leading to ejaculation was seen as draining that supply, and as sapping a man's virility and vitality. The birth of children, nurtured by semen, symbolized a necessary sacrifice that would lead to the husband's eventual death. Heterosexual intercourse, required only for reproduction, was discouraged. Women who wanted too much sex were viewed as witches, hazardous to their husbands' health. Etoro culture allowed heterosexual intercourse only about 100 days a year. The rest of the time it was tabooed. Seasonal birth clustering shows the taboo was respected.

So objectionable was male–female sex that it was removed from community life. It could occur neither in sleeping quarters nor in the fields. Coitus could happen only in the woods, where it was risky because poisonous snakes, the Etoro claimed, were attracted by the sounds and smells of male–female sex.

Although coitus was discouraged, sex acts between men were viewed as essential. Etoro believed that boys could not produce semen on their own. To grow into men and

Anthropology Today *Changing Images of Masculinity*

Some have argued that the anthropological study of gender has focused too much on women and alternative genders, forgetting that men are gendered, too. That is, the social construction of masculinity varies across space and time, from culture to culture, and from one historical period to another. This story argues that in times of prosperity, male gender images can be less serious and more playful, tending toward youth and androgyny—blurred gender lines. But when times get tough, images of masculinity revert to the celebration of traditional male roles, including the values of age, experience, and hard work. Also highlighted is the extent to which the international fashion industry, and its reflections throughout the media, influences images of gender. Examine some recent fashion magazines to see if the comments here about changing gender images might also apply to female models.

Has anyone seen the Dior man . . . that scrawny rocker dude with a chicken chest, a size 36 suit and a face that seems to be sprouting its first crop of peach fuzz?

It has been almost a decade since Hedi Slimane, then the designer for Dior men's wear, jump-started an aesthetic shift away from stiffly traditional male images that long dominated men's fashion. . . . The image of the Dior man was so influential that it . . . exiled a generation of conventionally handsome and mature models from runways into the gulag of catalogs.

On catwalks and in advertising campaigns the prevalent male image [became] . . . that of skinny skate-rat, a juvenile with pipe-cleaner proportions. Designers . . . developed so pronounced an appetite for the jailbait type that at some model castings in Milan and Paris the new faces often showed up chaperoned by Mom.

"Men have always been defined by their jobs—always," said Joe Levy, the edi-

A recent American advertising trend has been to use mature, masculine, muscular men rather than younger, thinner male models.

tor in chief of Maxim. When the economy was flush, consumers were content to indulge designer subversions of age and gender expectations, he added. That was before the recession. . . . "Suddenly the notion of having a job or a career is in doubt," Mr. Levy said. "So you fall back on old notions of what it meant to be a man or to look like one."

You lose the T-shirt and the skateboard. You buy an interview suit and a package of Gillette Mach 3 blades. You grow up, in other words. Suddenly evidence of a new phase in the cycle of evolving masculine imagery was all over the catwalks in the runway season that recently ended. Just as suddenly it can be seen splashed across the covers of magazines, where the boys of recent memory have been transformed overnight into men. . . .

"It's not just models, it's actors, it's advertising, it's the movies," said Sam Shahid, creative director of Shahid & Company and a force behind campaigns that first helped put Calvin Klein's name on half the world's backsides. "It's trendy to do this, and everyone's suddenly jumping on it," Mr. Shahid said, referring to the abrupt rejiggering of masculine ideals.

"It's also, like comfort food, about the economy," he said. "Look back to movies during the Depression, and all you saw was real guys like James Cagney. In tough times, people want a strong man."

Or, at the very least, they want images of men who look old enough to vote. "The twink thing seems over," said Jim Nelson, the editor of GQ. "When people open GQ, I don't want them to feel like they're looking at clothes on 16-year-olds."

It is not merely a matter of body type, Mr. Nelson noted. "When we cast, we want a model with some heft to him and a few years on him," he said. "Someone who has aged a little bit and who feels like he's a man."

What they want, in short, is Jon Hamm. That Mr. Hamm's square-jawed Don Draper so persuasively resembles an archetypal father on a time-travel visa from an era of postwar expansion and fixed gender roles can hardly be incidental to the success of "Mad Men."

"At a time of underemployment . . . people want to be reminded" through images from pop culture, Mr. Nelson said, "that we as men do work, we do labor. . . ."

Designers . . . have responded with a wholesale revival of so-called "heritage" labels and work wear. And they are casting their runway shows and ad campaigns with increasingly hirsute, well-built, mature types—men who certainly look as if they've never been waxed or had a manicure. . . .

When casting a recent fashion pictorial, the editors of Details were aware that in seeking a "real man" type they were looking for a nonexistent ideal. There is of course no such thing as a "real" man, Dan Peres, the magazine's editor in chief, remarked. "But we have a product to produce that . . . has to be relatable to a reader . . . who wants to be able to see some vision of himself in the pages of a magazine." Especially in a depressed economy, the editors concluded, the Details man was not well represented by the boys so fashionable a moment ago. . . .

"It's about what connection a reader is going to make with some waify 17-year-old versus a 34-year-old man."

Source: Guy Trebay, "From Boys to Men," *New York Times,* October 15, 2010, http://www.nytimes.com/2010/10/17/fashion/17MANLY.html?sq=men%20and%20boys&st=cse&scp=3&pagewanted=print.

eventually give life force to their children, boys had to acquire semen orally from older men. From the age of 10 until adulthood, boys were inseminated by older men. No taboos were attached to this. Such oral insemination could proceed in the sleeping area or garden. Every three years, a group of boys around the age of 20 was formally initiated into manhood. They went to a secluded mountain lodge, where they were visited and inseminated by several older men.

Male–male sex among the Etoro was governed by a code of propriety. Although sexual relations between older and younger males were considered culturally essential, those between boys of the same age were discouraged. A boy who took semen from other youths was believed to be sapping their life force and stunting their growth. A boy's rapid physical development might suggest he was getting semen from other boys. Like a sex-hungry wife, he might be shunned as a witch.

These sexual practices among the Etoro rested not on hormones or genes but on cultural beliefs and traditions. The Etoro shared a cultural pattern, which Gilbert Herdt (1984) calls "ritualized homosexuality," with some 50 other tribes in Papua New Guinea, especially in that country's Trans-Fly region. These societies illustrate one extreme of a male–female avoidance pattern that is widespread in Papua New Guinea and indeed in many patrilineal–patrilocal societies.

Flexibility in sexual expression seems to be an aspect of our primate heritage. Both masturbation and same-sex sexual activity exist among chimpanzees and other primates. Male bonobos (pygmy chimps) regularly engage in a form of mutual masturbation known as "penis fencing." Females get sexual pleasure from rubbing their genitals against those of other females (de Waal 1997). Our primate sexual potential is molded by culture, the environment, and reproductive necessity. Heterosexual coitus is practiced in all human societies—which, after all, must reproduce themselves—but alternatives also are widespread (Rathus, Nevid, and Fichner-Rathus 2008). Like gender roles and attitudes more generally, the sexual component of human personality and identity— just how we express our "natural" sexual urges—is a matter that culture and environment determine and limit.

Summary

1. Gender roles are the tasks and activities that a culture assigns to each sex and to the genders it recognizes. Gender stereotypes are oversimplified ideas about attributes of males and females. Gender stratification describes an unequal distribution of rewards by gender, reflecting different positions in a social hierarchy.

2. Cross-cultural comparison reveals some recurrent patterns involving the division of labor by gender, as well as gender-based differences in reproductive strategies. Gender roles and gender stratification vary with environment, economy, adaptive strategy, system of kinship and descent, level of social complexity, and degree of participation in the world economy.

3. When gathering is prominent, gender status is more equal than when hunting or fishing dominates a foraging economy. Gender status also is more equal when the domestic and public spheres aren't sharply separated.

4. Gender stratification also is linked to descent and residence. Women's status in matrilineal societies tends to be high because overall social identity comes through female links. Women in many societies, especially matrilineal ones, wield power and make decisions. Scarcity of resources promotes intervillage warfare, patriliny, and patrilocality. The localization of related males is adaptive for military solidarity. Men may use their warrior role to symbolize and reinforce the social devaluation and oppression of women. Patriarchy describes a political system ruled by men in which women have inferior social and political status, including basic human rights.

5. Americans' attitudes about gender roles has varied with class and region, and historically. A declining need for female labor promotes the idea that women are unfit for many jobs, and vice versa. Countering the economic gains of many American women is the feminization of poverty. This has become a global phenomenon as impoverished female-headed households have increased worldwide. A cross-national

survey revealed a correlation between degree of happiness and women's work outside the home.

6. Societies may recognize more than two genders. The term *intersex* describes a group of conditions, including chromosomal configurations, that may produce a discrepancy between external and internal genitals. Transgender individuals may or may not contrast biologically with ordinary males and females. Self-identified transgender people tend to be individuals whose gender identity contradicts their biological sex at birth and the gender identity that society assigned to them in infancy.

7. There has been a recent tendency to see sexual orientation as fixed and biologically based. But, to some extent at least, all human activities and preferences, including erotic expression, are influenced by culture. Sexual orientation stands for a person's habitual sexual attraction to, and activities with, persons of the opposite sex (heterosexuality), the same sex (homosexuality), or both sexes (bisexuality). Sexual norms vary widely from culture to culture.

Key Terms

domestic, *331*
domestic–public dichotomy, *331*
gender roles, *326*
gender stereotypes, *326*
gender stratification, *326*
intersex, *339*
patriarchy, *334*
patrilineal–patrilocal complex, *333*
sexual dimorphism, *324*
sexual orientation, *342*
transgender, *340*

Go to our Online Learning Center website at **www.mhhe.com/kottak** for Internet resources directly related to the content of this chapter.

Chapter 15

Religion

Expressions of Religion
  Spiritual Beings
  Powers and Forces
  Magic and Religion
  Uncertainty, Anxiety, Solace
  Rituals
  Rites of Passage
  Totemism
Social Control
Kinds of Religion

World Religions
  *Applying Anthropology to Popular
    Culture: Muslims and Media*
Religion and Change
  Revitalization Movements
  Cargo Cults
  New and Alternative Religious Movements
Secular Rituals
  *Anthropology Today: Hinduism Takes
    Back Yoga*

Given the varied and worldwide scope of beliefs and behavior labeled "religious," anthropologists know how difficult it is to define **religion.** In his book *Religion: An Anthropological View,* Anthony F. C. Wallace offered this definition: "belief and ritual concerned with supernatural beings, powers, and forces" (1966, p. 5). By "supernatural" he referred to a nonmaterial realm beyond (but believed to impinge on) the observable world. This realm cannot be verified or falsified empirically and is inexplicable in ordinary terms. It must be accepted "on faith." Supernatural beings—deities, ghosts, demons, souls, and spirits—make their homes outside our material world, although they may visit it from time to time. There also are supernatural or sacred forces, some of them wielded by deities and spirits, others that simply exist. In many societies, people believe they can benefit from, become imbued with, or manipulate supernatural forces (see Bowie 2006; Bowen 2008; Crapo 2006; Lambek 2008; Stein and Stein 2008; Warms, Garber, and McGee, eds. 2009).

Wallace's definition of religion focuses on presumably universal categories (beings, powers, and forces) within the supernatural realm. For Emile Durkheim (1912/2001), one of the founders of the anthropology of religion, the key distinction was between the sacred and the profane. Like the supernatural for Wallace, Durkheim's "sacred" was the domain set off from the ordinary or the mundane (he used the word "profane"). For Durkheim, every society had its sacred, but that domain was socially constructed; it varied from society to society. Durkheim focused on Native Australian societies, which he believed had preserved the most elementary or basic forms of religion. He noted that their most sacred objects, including plants and animals that served as totems, were not supernatural at all. Rather they were "real world" entities (e.g., kangaroos, grubs) that, over the generations, had acquired special meaning for the social groups that had made them sacred and continued to "worship" them.

Many definitions of religion focus on groups of people who gather together regularly for worship (see Reese 1999). These congregants or adherents internalize common beliefs and a shared system of meaning. They accept a set of doctrines involving the relationship between the individual and divinity, the sacred, or whatever is taken to be the ultimate nature of reality. Anthropologists like Durkheim have stressed the collective, social, shared, and enacted nature of religion, the emotions it generates, and the meanings it embodies. As Michael Lambek (2008, p. 5) remarks, "good anthropology understands that religious worlds are real, vivid, and significant to those who construct and inhabit them." Durkheim (1912/2001) highlighted religious effervescence, the bubbling up of collective emotional intensity generated by worship. Victor Turner (1969/1995) updated Durkheim's notion, using the term **communitas,** an intense community spirit, a feeling of great social solidarity, equality, and togetherness.

The word *religion* derives from the Latin *religare*—"to tie, to bind," but it is not necessary for all members of a given religion to meet together as a common body. Subgroups meet regularly at local congregation sites. They may attend occasional meetings with adherents representing a wider region. And they may form an imagined community with people of similar faith throughout the world.

In studying religion cross-culturally, anthropologists pay attention to religion as a social phenomenon as well as to the meanings of religious doctrines, settings, acts, and events. Verbal manifestations of religious beliefs include prayers, chants, myths, texts, and statements about, including rules of, ethics and morality (see Cunningham 1999; Klass 2003; Lehmann, Meyers, and Moro 2005; Stein and Stein 2008). The anthropological study of religion also encompasses notions about purity and pollution (including taboos involving diet and physical contact), sacrifice, initiation, rites of passage, vision quests, pilgrimages, spirit possession, prophecy, study, devotion, and moral actions (Lambek 2008, p. 9).

Like ethnicity and language, religion is associated with social divisions within and between societies and nations. Religion both unites and divides. Participation in common rites may affirm, and thus maintain, the solidarity of a group of adherents. As we know from daily headlines, however, religious difference also may be associated with bitter enmity. In today's world, contacts and confrontations have increased between so-called world religions, such as Christianity and Islam, and the more localized forms of religion that missionaries typically lump together under the disparaging term "paganism." Increasingly, world religions compete for adherents and global power, and ethnic, regional, and class conflicts come to be framed in religious terms. Recent and contemporary examples of religion as a social and political force include the Iranian revolution, the rise of the religious right in the United States, and the spread of Pentecostalism in Korea, Africa, and Latin America.

Long ago, Edward Sapir (1928/1956) argued for a distinction between "a religion" and "religion." The former term would apply only to a formally organized religion, such as the world religions just mentioned. The latter—religion—is universal; it refers to religious beliefs and behavior, which exist in all societies, even if they don't stand out as a separate and clearly demarcated sphere. Indeed, many anthropologists (e.g., Asad 1983/2008) argue that such categories as "religion," "politics," and "the economy" are arbitrary constructs that apply best, and perhaps only, to Western, Christian, and modern societies. In such contexts religion can be seen as a specific domain, separate from politics and the economy. By contrast, in nonindustrial societies, religion typically is more embedded in society. Religious beliefs may help regulate the economy (e.g., astrologers determine when to plant) or permeate politics (e.g., divine right of kings). (Although religion also spills over into politics in the contemporary United States, it isn't supposed to. That is, the legal system views religion and politics as spheres that should be kept separate.)

Anthropologists agree that religion exists in all human societies; it is a cultural universal. However, we'll see that it isn't always easy to distinguish the sacred from the profane and that different societies conceptualize divinity, the sacred, the supernatural, and ultimate realities very differently.

Expressions of Religion

When did religion begin? No one knows for sure. There are suggestions of religion in Neandertal burials and on European cave walls, where painted stick figures may represent **shamans,** early religious specialists. Nevertheless, any statement about when, where, why, and how religion arose, or any description of its original nature, can only be speculative. Although such speculations are inconclusive, many have revealed important functions and effects of religious behavior. Several theories will be examined now.

Spiritual Beings

Another founder of the anthropology of religion was the Englishman Sir Edward Burnett Tylor (1871/1958). Religion arose, Tylor thought, as people tried to understand conditions and events they could not explain by reference to daily experience. Tylor believed that ancient humans—and contemporary nonindustrial peoples—were particularly intrigued with death, dreaming, and trance. People see images they may remember when they wake up or come out of a trance state. Tylor concluded that attempts to explain dreams and trances led early humans to believe that two entities inhabit the body. One is active during the day, and the other—a double or soul—is active during sleep and trance states. Although they never meet, they are vital to each other. When the double permanently leaves the body, the person dies. Death is departure of the soul. From the Latin for soul, *anima,* Tylor named this belief **animism.** The soul was one sort of spiritual entity; people remembered various images from their dreams and trances—other spirits. For Tylor, animism, the earliest form of religion, was a belief in spiritual beings.

Tylor proposed that religion evolved through stages, beginning with animism. **Polytheism** (the belief in multiple gods) and then **monotheism** (the belief in a single, all-powerful deity) developed later. Because religion originated to explain things, Tylor thought it would decline as science offered better explanations. To an extent, he was right. We now have scientific explanations for many things that religion once elucidated.

Participation in a collective religious act, such as singing in this choir, can strengthen social bonds among congregants, while promoting feelings of spiritual effervescence.

Nevertheless, because religion persists, it must do something more than explain. It must, and does, have other functions and meanings.

Powers and Forces

In addition to animism—and sometimes coexisting with it in the same society—is a view of the supernatural as a domain of impersonal power, or force, which people can control under certain conditions. (You'd be right to think of *Star Wars.*) Such a conception is particularly prominent in Melanesia, the area of the South Pacific that includes Papua New Guinea and adjacent islands. Melanesians believed in **mana,** a sacred impersonal force existing in the universe. Mana can reside in people, animals, plants, and objects.

Melanesian mana was similar to our notion of good luck. Objects with mana could change someone's luck. For example, a charm or amulet belonging to a successful hunter might transmit the hunter's mana to the next person who held or wore it. A woman might put a rock in her garden, see her yields improve, and attribute the change to the force contained in the rock.

Beliefs in manalike forces are widespread, although the specifics of the religious doctrines vary. Consider the contrast between mana in Melanesia and Polynesia (the islands included in a triangular area marked by Hawaii to the north, Easter Island to the east, and New Zealand to the southwest). In Melanesia, anyone could acquire mana by chance, or by working hard to get it. In Polynesia, however, mana wasn't potentially available to everyone but was attached to political offices. Chiefs and nobles had more mana than ordinary people did.

So charged with mana were the highest chiefs that contact with them was dangerous to commoners. The mana of chiefs flowed out of their bodies. It could infect the ground, making it dangerous for others to walk in the chief's footsteps. It could permeate the containers and utensils chiefs used in eating. Because high chiefs had so much mana, their bodies and possessions were **taboo** (set apart as sacred and off-limits to ordinary people). Because ordinary people couldn't bear as much sacred current as royalty could, when commoners were accidentally exposed, purification rites were necessary.

One function of religion is to explain. As Horton (1993) and Lambek (2008) point out, there are universals in human thought and experience, common conditions and situations that call out for explanation. What happens in sleep and trance, and with death?—The soul leaves the body. Why do some people prosper while others fail?—Blame it on such nonmaterial factors as luck, mana, sorcery, or being one of "God's chosen."

The beliefs in spiritual beings (e.g., animism) and supernatural forces (e.g., mana) fit within Wallace's definition of religion given at the beginning of this chapter. Most religions include both spirits and impersonal forces. Likewise the supernatural beliefs of contemporary North Americans include beings (gods, saints, souls, demons) and forces (charms, talismans, crystals, and sacred objects).

Magic and Religion

Magic refers to supernatural techniques intended to accomplish specific aims. These techniques include magical actions, offerings, spells, formulas, and incantations used with deities or with impersonal forces. Magicians employ *imitative magic* to produce a desired effect by imitating it. If magicians wish to harm someone, they may imitate that effect on an image of the victim. Sticking pins in "voodoo dolls" is an example. With *contagious magic,* whatever is done to an object is believed to affect a person who once had contact with it. Sometimes practitioners of contagious magic use body products from prospective victims—their nails or hair, for example. The spell performed on the body product is believed eventually to reach the person (see Stein and Stein 2008). Magic exists in societies with diverse religious beliefs, including animism, mana, polytheism, or monotheism.

Uncertainty, Anxiety, Solace

Religion and magic don't just explain things. They serve emotional needs as well as cognitive (e.g., explanatory) ones. Religion helps people face death and endure life crises. Magical techniques can dispel doubts that arise when outcomes are beyond human control. According to Malinowski, when people face uncertainty and danger, they often turn to magic. He observed that the Trobriand Islanders he studied used magic when sailing—a hazardous activity in which people lacked control over wind and weather (Malinowski 1931/1978). Only in situations they could not control did Trobrianders, out of psychological stress, turn from technology to magic.

Despite our improving technical skills, we still can't control every outcome, and magic persists in contemporary societies. Magic is particularly evident in baseball, where George Gmelch (1978, 2001) describes a series of rituals, taboos, and sacred objects. Like Trobriand sailing magic, these behaviors serve to reduce psychological stress, creating an illusion of (magical) control when real control is lacking. Examples of pitchers' magic include tugging one's cap between pitches, touching the resin bag after each bad pitch, and talking to the ball. Gmelch's conclusions confirm Malinowski's finding that magic is most prevalent in situations of chance and uncertainty. All sorts of magical behavior surround pitching and batting, where uncertainty is rampant, but few rituals involve fielding, where players have much more control. (Batting averages of .350 or higher are very rare after a full season, but a fielding percentage below .900 is a disgrace.)

Baseball magic: Relief pitcher Cla Meredith jumps over the third base line on his way back to the dugout after pitching a scoreless eighth inning in his team's eventual victory. Baseball magic is most common in pitching and batting. Why is that?

Rituals

Several features distinguish **rituals** from other kinds of behavior (Rappaport 1974, 1999). Rituals are formal—stylized, repetitive, and stereotyped. People perform them in special (sacred) places and at set times. Rituals include liturgical orders—sequences of words and actions invented prior to the current performance of the ritual in which they occur.

These features link rituals to plays, but there are important differences. Actors merely portray something, but ritual performers—who make up congregations—are in earnest.

Rituals convey information about the participants and their traditions. Repeated year after year, generation after generation, rituals translate enduring messages, values, and sentiments into action.

Rituals are social acts. Inevitably, some participants are more committed than others are to the beliefs that lie behind the rites. However, just by taking part in a joint public act, the performers signal that they accept a common social and moral order, one that transcends their status as individuals.

Rites of Passage

Magic and religion, as Malinowski noted, can reduce anxiety and allay fears. Ironically, beliefs and rituals also can create anxiety and a sense of insecurity and danger (Radcliffe-Brown 1962/1965). Anxiety may arise because a rite exists. Indeed, participation in a collective ritual (e.g., circumcision of early teen boys, common among East African pastoralists) may produce stress, whose common reduction, once the ritual is completed, enhances the solidarity of the participants.

Rites of passage can be individual or collective. The traditional vision quests of Native Americans, particularly the Plains Indians, illustrate individual rites of passage (customs associated with the transition from one place or stage of life to another). To move from boyhood to manhood, a youth temporarily separated from his community. After a period of isolation in the wilderness, often featuring fasting and drug consumption, the young man would see a vision, which would become his guardian spirit. He would return then to his community as an adult.

Contemporary rites of passage include confirmations, baptisms, bar and bat mitzvahs, initiations, weddings, and applying for Medicare. Passage rites involve changes in social status, such as from boyhood to manhood and from nonmember to sorority sister. More generally, a rite of passage may mark any change in place, condition, social position, or age.

All rites of passage have three phases: separation, liminality, and incorporation. In the first phase, people withdraw from ordinary society. In the third phase, they reenter society, having completed a rite that changes their status. The second, or liminal, phase is the most interesting. It is the limbo or "time out" during which people have left one status but haven't yet entered or joined the next (Turner 1967/1974).

Liminality always has certain characteristics. Liminal people exist apart from ordinary distinctions and expectations, living in a time out of time. A series of contrasts demarcate liminality from normal social life. For example, among the Ndembu of Zambia, a chief underwent a rite of passage before taking office. During the liminal period, his past and future positions in society were ignored, even reversed. He was subjected to a variety of insults, orders, and humiliations.

Passage rites often are collective. Several individuals—boys being circumcised, fraternity or sorority initiates, men at military boot camps, football players in summer training camps, women becoming nuns—pass through the rites together as a group. Table 15.1 summarizes the contrasts or oppositions between liminality and normal social life. Most notable is a social aspect of collective liminality called communitas (Turner 1967/1974), an intense community spirit, a feeling of great social solidarity, equality, and togetherness. Liminal people experience the same treatment and conditions and must act alike.

TABLE 15.1   Oppositions between Liminality and Normal Social Life

Source: Victor Turner, *The Ritual Process.* Copyright © 1969 by Aldine Publishers. Reprinted by permission of Aldine Transaction, a division of Transaction Publishers.

Liminality	Normal Social Structure
transition	state
homogeneity	heterogeneity
communitas	structure
equality	inequality
anonymity	names
absence of property	property
absence of status	status
nakedness or uniform dress	dress distinctions
sexual continence or excess	sexuality
minimization of sex distinctions	maximization of sex distinctions
absence of rank	rank
humility	pride
disregard of personal appearance	care for personal appearance
unselfishness	selfishness
total obedience	obedience only to superior rank
sacredness	secularity
sacred instruction	technical knowledge
silence	speech
simplicity	complexity
acceptance of pain and suffering	avoidance of pain and suffering

Liminality may be marked ritually and symbolically by reversals of ordinary behavior. For example, sexual taboos may be intensified, or conversely, sexual excess may be encouraged. Liminal symbols, such as special clothing or body paint, mark the condition as extraordinary—outside and beyond ordinary society and everyday life.

Liminality is basic to all passage rites. Furthermore, in certain societies, including our own, liminal symbols may be used to set off one (religious) group from another, and from society as a whole. Such "permanent liminal groups" (e.g., sects, brotherhoods, and cults) are found most characteristically in nation-states. Such liminal features as humility, poverty, equality, obedience, sexual abstinence, and silence (see Table 15.1) may be required for all sect or cult members. Those who join such a group agree to its rules. As if they were undergoing a passage rite—but in this case a never-ending one— they may have to abandon their previous possessions and social ties, including those with family members. Is liminality compatible with Facebook?

Members of a sect or cult often wear uniform clothing. Often they adopt a common hair style (shaved head, short hair, or long hair). Liminal groups submerge the individual in the collective. This may be one reason why Americans, whose core values include individuality and individualism, are so fearful and suspicious of "cults."

Not all collective rites are rites of passage. Most societies observe occasions on which people come together to worship or celebrate and, in doing so, affirm and reinforce their solidarity. Rituals such as the totemic ceremonies described below are *rites*

Passage rites are often collective. A group—such as these initiates in Togo or these Navy trainees in San Diego—passes through the rites as a unit. Such liminal people experience the same treatment and conditions and must act alike. They share communitas, an intense community spirit, a feeling of great social solidarity or togetherness.

of intensification: They intensify social solidarity. The ritual creates communitas and produces emotions (the collective spiritual effervescence described by Durkheim 1912/2001) that enhance social solidarity.

Totemism

Totemism was a key ingredient in the religions of the Native Australians. **Totems** could be animals, plants, or geographical features. In each tribe, groups of people had particular totems. Members of each totemic group believed themselves to be descendants of their totem. They customarily neither killed nor ate it, but this taboo was lifted once a year, when people assembled for ceremonies dedicated to the totem. These annual rites were believed to be necessary for the totem's survival and reproduction.

Totemism uses nature as a model for society. The totems usually are animals and plants, which are part of nature. People relate to nature through their totemic association with natural species. Because each group has a different totem, social differences mirror natural contrasts. Diversity in the natural order becomes a model for diversity in the social order. However, although totemic plants and animals occupy different niches in nature, on another level they are united because they all are part of nature. The unity of the human social order is enhanced by symbolic association with and imitation of the natural order (Durkheim 1912/2001; Lévi-Strauss 1963; Radcliffe-Brown 1962/1965).

Totemic principles continue to demarcate groups, including clubs, teams, and universities, in modern societies. Badgers and Wolverines are animals, and (it is said in Michigan) Buckeyes are some kind of nut (more precisely, buckeye nuts come from the buckeye tree). Differences between natural species (e.g., lions, and tigers, and bears) serve to distinguish sports teams, and even political parties (donkeys and elephants). Although the modern context is more secular, one can still witness, in intense college football rivalries, some of the effervescence Durkheim noted in Australian totemic religion and other rites of intensification.

Totems are sacred emblems symbolizing common identity. This is true not just among Native Australians, but also among Native American groups of the North Pacific Coast of North America, whose totem poles are well known. Their totemic carvings, which commemorated, and told visual stories about, ancestors, animals, and spirits, were also associated with ceremonies. In totemic rites, people gather together to honor their totem. In so doing, they use ritual to maintain the social oneness that the totem symbolizes.

Social Control

Religion means a lot to people. It helps them cope with uncertainty, adversity, fear, and tragedy. It offers hope that things will get better. Lives can be transformed through spiritual healing. Sinners can repent and be saved—or they can go on sinning and be damned. If the faithful truly internalize a system of religious rewards and punishments, their religion becomes a powerful influence on their attitudes and behavior, and what they teach their children.

Many people engage in religious activity because it works for them. Prayers get answered. Faith healers heal. Many American Indian people in southwestern Oklahoma use faith healers at high monetary costs, not just because it makes them feel better about the uncertain, but because it works (Lassiter 1998). Each year legions of Brazilians visit a church, Nosso Senhor do Bomfim, in the city of Salvador, Bahia. They vow to repay "Our Lord" (Nosso Senhor) if healing happens. Showing that the vows work, and are repaid, are the thousands of *ex votos,* plastic impressions of every conceivable body part, that adorn the church, along with photos of people who have been cured.

Religion can work by getting inside people and mobilizing their emotions—their joy, their wrath, their certainty, their righteousness. People can feel a deep sense of shared joy, meaning, experience, communion, belonging, and commitment to their religion. The power of religion affects action. When religions meet, they can coexist peacefully, or their differences can be a basis for enmity and disharmony, even battle. Religious fervor has inspired Christians on crusades against the infidel and has led Muslims to wage holy wars against non-Islamic peoples. Throughout history, political leaders have used religion to promote and justify their views and policies.

How may leaders mobilize communities and, in so doing, gain support for their own policies? One way is by persuasion; another is by instilling hatred or fear. Consider witchcraft accusations. Witch hunts can be powerful means of social control by creating a climate of danger and insecurity that affects everyone, not just the people who are likely targets. No one wants to seem deviant, to be accused of being a witch. Witch hunts often take aim at people who can be accused and punished with least chance of retaliation. During the great European witch craze of the 15th, 16th, and 17th centuries (Harris 1974), most accusations and convictions were against poor women with little social support.

Witchcraft accusations often are directed at socially marginal or anomalous individuals. Consider the Betsileo of Madagascar, who believe that married men should live in their father's village. Marcel contradicts this rule by residing in his mother's village. People like Marcel who violate cultural norms have to be particularly careful about how they act. Just a bit of unusual behavior (e.g., staying up late at night) can fuel suspicion that they are engaging in witchcraft; they may be avoided or ostracized as a result. In peasant communities, people who stand out economically, especially if they seem to be benefiting at the expense of others, often face witchcraft accusations, leading to social ostracism or punishment. In this case witchcraft accusation becomes a **leveling mechanism,** a custom or social action that operates to reduce status differences and thus to bring standouts in line with community norms—another form of social control.

To ensure proper behavior, religions offer rewards (e.g., the fellowship of the religious community) and punishments (e.g., the threat of being cast out or excommunicated). Religions, especially the formal organized ones

This 19th century woodcut depicts the trial of Anne Hutchinson, an outspoken woman who was tried as a heretic and banished from the Massachusetts Bay Colony in 1637.

typically found in state societies, often prescribe a code of ethics and morality to guide behavior. The Judaic Ten Commandments laid down a set of prohibitions against killing, stealing, adultery, and other misdeeds. Crimes are breaches of secular laws, as sins are breaches of religious strictures. Some rules (e.g., the Ten Commandments) proscribe or prohibit behavior; others prescribe behavior. The Golden Rule, for instance, is a religious guide to do unto others as you would have them do unto you. Moral codes are ways of maintaining order and stability. Codes of morality and ethics are constantly reinforced in religious sermons, catechisms, and the like. They become internalized psychologically. They guide behavior and produce regret, guilt, shame, and the need for forgiveness, expiation, and absolution when they are not followed.

Kinds of Religion

Religion is a cultural universal. But religions exist in particular societies, and cultural differences show up systematically in religious beliefs and practices. For example, the religions of stratified, state societies differ from those of societies with less marked social contrasts—societies without kings, lords, and subjects. What can a given society afford in terms of religion? Churches, temples, and other full-time religious establishments, with their monumental structures and hierarchies of officials, must be supported in some consistent way, such as by tithes and taxes. What kinds of societies can support such hierarchies and architecture?

All societies have religious figures—those believed capable of mediating between humans and the supernatural. More generally, all societies have medico-magico-religious specialists. Modern societies can support both priesthoods and health care professionals. Lacking the resources for such specialization, foraging societies typically have only part-time specialists, who often have both religious and healing roles. Shaman is the general term encompassing curers ("witch doctors"), mediums, spiritualists, astrologers, palm readers, and other independent diviners. In foraging societies, shamans are usually part-time; that is, they also hunt or gather.

The annual totemic ceremonies of Native Australians temporarily brought together foragers who had to disperse most of the year to hunt and gather for subsistence. Given seasonal harvests of fish and other resources in a rich natural environment, foraging tribes on the North Pacific Coast of North America could host ceremonies like the potlatch described in the chapter "Making a Living." However, community rituals including harvest ceremonies and collective rites of passage are much more common in farming and herding societies than among foragers.

Societies with productive economies (based on agriculture and trade) and large, dense populations (nation-states) can support full-time religious specialists—professional priesthoods. Like the state itself, priesthoods are hierarchically and bureaucratically organized. Anthony Wallace (1966) describes the religions of such stratified societies as "ecclesiastical" (pertaining to an established church and its hierarchy of officials) and "Olympian," after Mount Olympus, home of the classical Greek gods. In such religions, powerful anthropomorphic gods have specialized functions, for example, gods of love, war, the sea, and death. Such *pantheons* (collections of deities) were prominent in the religions of many nonindustrial nation-states, including the Aztecs of Mexico, several African and Asian kingdoms, and classical Greece and Rome.

Greco-Roman religions were polytheistic, featuring many deities. In monotheism, all supernatural phenomena are believed to be manifestations of, or under the control of, a single eternal, omniscient, omnipotent, and omnipresent being. In the ecclesiastical monotheistic religion known as Christianity, a single supreme being is manifest in a trinity. Robert Bellah (1978) viewed most forms of Christianity as examples of "world-rejecting religion." According to Bellah, the first world-rejecting religions arose in ancient civilizations, along with literacy and a specialized priesthood. These religions are so named because of their tendency to reject the natural (mundane, ordinary, material, secular) world and to focus instead on a higher (sacred, transcendent) realm of reality. The divine is a domain of exalted morality to which humans can only aspire. Salvation through fusion with the supernatural is the main goal of such religions.

World Religions

Information on the world's major religions today is provided in Figure 15.1 and Table 15.2 (number of adherents). Based on people's claimed religions, Christianity is the world's largest, with some 2.1 billion adherents. Islam, with some 1.5 billion practitioners, is next, followed by Hinduism, then Chinese traditional religion (also known as Chinese

FIGURE 15.1 **Major World Religions by Percentage of World Population, 2005**

Source: www.adherents.com. Reprinted by permission.

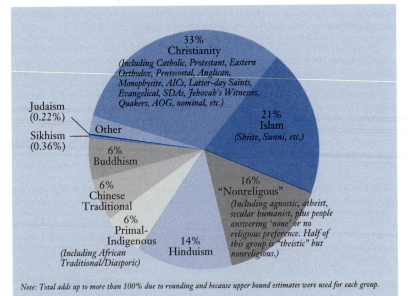

Note: Total adds up to more than 100% due to rounding and because upper bound estimates were used for each group.

TABLE 15.2   Religions of the World, by Estimated Number of Adherents, 2005

Source: Reprinted by permission of Ontario Consultants on Religious Tolerance, www.religioustolerance.org.

Christianity	2.1 billion
Islam	1.5 billion
Secular/nonreligious/agnostic/atheist	1.1 billion
Hinduism	900 million
Chinese traditional religion	394 million
Buddhism	376 million
Primal-indigenous	300 million
African traditional and diasporic	100 million
Sikhism	23 million
Juche	19 million
Spiritism	15 million
Judaism	14 million
Baha'i	7 million
Jainism	4.2 million
Shinto	4 million
Cao Dai	4 million
Zoroastrianism	2.6 million
Tenrikyo	2 million
Neo-Paganism	1 million
Unitarian-Universalism	800 thousand
Rastafarianism	600 thousand
Scientology	500 thousand

folk religion or Confucianism), and Buddhism. More than a billion people claim no official religion, but only about a fifth of them are self-proclaimed atheists.

Worldwide, Islam is growing at a rate of about 2.9 percent annually, versus 2.3 percent for Christianity, whose overall growth rate is the same as the rate of world population increase (Ontario Consultants 2001; adherents.com 2002). Within Christianity, the growth rate varies. There were an estimated 680 million "born-again" Christians (e.g., Pentecostals

Evangelical Christianity has an annual growth rate three times that of Christianity as a whole. Shown here are worshipers at the Church of Jesus Christ is Love in Buenos Aires, Argentina. Throughout Latin America, the Catholic Church is finding it increasingly hard to compete with evangelical churches like this one.

In an analysis of more than a thousand films, Jack Shaheen (2006, 2009) found that only 5 percent of Arab and Muslim characters were presented in a positive light. Arabs repeatedly were caricatured as villains, buffoons, lechers, incompetents, and terrorists. Watch a film or TV show featuring Arab or Islamic characters (e.g., *Babel, Syriana, 24*). How are those characters portrayed? Is religion an important part of the portrayal? Do characters with other ethnic backgrounds (e.g., Latinos, African Americans, non-Hispanic whites) have as many religious markers? How do you account for the differences you note in these portrayals?

and Evangelicals) in the world in 2001, with an annual worldwide growth rate of 7 percent, versus just 2.3 percent for Christianity overall. (This would translate into 1.4 billion Pentecostals/Evangelicals by 2012.) The global growth rate of Roman Catholics has been estimated at only 1.3 percent, compared with a Protestant growth rate of 3.3 percent per year (Winter 2001). Much of this explosive growth, especially in Africa, is of a type of Protestantism that would be scarcely recognizable to most Americans, given its incorporation of many animistic elements.

Religion and Change

Religious fundamentalists seek order based on strict adherence to purportedly traditional standards, beliefs, rules, and customs. Christian and Islamic fundamentalists recognize, decry, and attempt to redress change, yet they also contribute to change (Antoun 2008). In a worldwide process, new religions challenge established churches. In the United States, for example, conservative Christian TV hosts have become influential broadcasters and opinion shapers. In Latin America evangelical Protestantism is winning millions of converts from Roman Catholicism.

Like political organization, religion helps maintain social order. And like political mobilization, religious energy can be harnessed not just for change but also for revolution. Reacting to conquest or to actual or perceived foreign domination, for instance, religious leaders may seek to alter or revitalize their society. In an "Islamic Revolution," for example, Iranian ayatollahs marshaled religious fervor to create national solidarity and radical change. We call such movements *nativistic movements* (Linton 1943) or *revitalization movements* (Wallace 1956).

Revitalization Movements

Revitalization movements are social movements that occur in times of change, in which religious leaders emerge and undertake to alter or revitalize a society. Christianity originated as a revitalization movement. Jesus was one of several prophets who preached new religious doctrines while the Middle East was under Roman rule. It was a time of social unrest, when a foreign power ruled the land. Jesus inspired a new, enduring, and major religion. His contemporaries were not so successful.

The Handsome Lake religion arose around 1800 among the Iroquois of New York State (Wallace 1969). Handsome Lake, the founder of this revitalization movement, was a leader of one of the Iroquois tribes. The Iroquois had suffered because of their support of the British against the American colonials. After the colonial victory and a wave of immigration to their homeland, the Iroquois were dispersed on small reservations. Unable to pursue traditional horticulture and hunting in their homeland, the Iroquois became heavy drinkers and quarreled among themselves.

Handsome Lake was a heavy drinker who started having visions from heavenly messengers. The spirits warned him that unless the Iroquois changed their ways, they would be destroyed. His visions offered a plan for coping with the new order. Witchcraft, quarreling, and drinking would end. The Iroquois would copy European farming techniques, which, unlike traditional Iroquois horticulture, stressed male rather than female labor. Handsome Lake preached that the Iroquois should also abandon their communal long houses and matrilineal descent groups for more permanent marriages and individual family households. The teachings of Handsome Lake produced a new church and religion, one that still has members in New York and Ontario. This revitalization movement helped the Iroquois adapt to and survive in a modified environment. They eventually gained a reputation among their non-Indian neighbors as sober family farmers.

Cargo Cults

Like the Handsome Lake religion, **cargo cults** are revitalization movements. Such movements may emerge when natives have regular contact with industrial societies but lack their wealth, technology, and living standards. Some such movements attempt to explain European domination and wealth and to achieve similar success magically by mimicking European behavior and manipulating symbols of the desired lifestyle. The cargo cults of Melanesia and Papua New Guinea weave Christian doctrine with aboriginal beliefs. They take their name from their focus on cargo—European goods of the sort natives have seen unloaded from the cargo holds of ships and airplanes.

In one early cult, members believed that the spirits of the dead would arrive in a ship. These ghosts would bring manufactured goods for the natives and would kill all the whites. More recent cults replaced ships with airplanes (Worsley 1959/1985). Many cults have used elements of European culture as sacred objects. The rationale is that Europeans use these objects, have wealth, and therefore must know the "secret of cargo." By mimicking how Europeans use or treat objects, natives hope also to come upon the secret knowledge needed to gain cargo.

For example, having seen Europeans' reverent treatment of flags and flagpoles, the members of one cult began to worship flagpoles. They believed the flagpoles were sacred towers that could transmit messages between the living and the dead. Other natives built airstrips to entice planes bearing canned goods, portable radios, clothing, wristwatches, and motorcycles. Near the airstrips they made effigies of towers, airplanes, and radios. They talked into the cans in a magical attempt to establish radio contact with the gods.

Some cargo cult prophets proclaimed that success would come through a reversal of European domination and native subjugation. The day was near, they preached, when

A cargo cult in Vanuatu, a country in Melanesia. Boys and men march with spears, imitating British colonial soldiers. Does anything in your own society remind you of a cargo cult?

natives, aided by God, Jesus, or native ancestors, would turn the tables. Native skins would turn white, and those of Europeans would turn brown; Europeans would die or be killed.

Cargo cults blend aboriginal and Christian beliefs. Melanesian myths told of ancestors shedding their skins and changing into powerful beings and of dead people returning to life. Christian missionaries, who had been in Melanesia since the late 19th century, also spoke of resurrection. The cults' preoccupation with cargo is related to traditional Melanesian big-man systems. In the chapter "Political Systems," we saw that a Melanesian big man had to be generous. People worked for the big man, helping him amass wealth, but eventually he had to give a feast and give away all that wealth.

Because of their experience with big-man systems, Melanesians believed that all wealthy people eventually had to give their wealth away. For decades they had attended Christian missions and worked on plantations. All the while they expected Europeans to return the fruits of their labor as their own big men did. When the Europeans refused to distribute the wealth or even to let natives know the secret of its production and distribution, cargo cults developed.

Like arrogant big men, Europeans would be leveled, by death if necessary. However, natives lacked the physical means of doing what their traditions said they should do. Thwarted by well-armed colonial forces, natives resorted to magical leveling. They called on supernatural beings to intercede, to kill or otherwise deflate the European big men and redistribute their wealth.

Cargo cults are religious responses to the expansion of the world capitalist economy. However, this religious mobilization had political and economic results. Cult participation gave Melanesians a basis for common interests and activities and thus helped pave the way for political parties and economic interest organizations. Previously separated by geography, language, and customs, Melanesians started forming larger groups as members of the same cults and followers of the same prophets. The cargo cults paved the way for political action through which the indigenous peoples eventually regained their autonomy.

New and Alternative Religious Movements

The New Age movement, which emerged in the 1980s, draws on and blends cultural elements from multiple traditions. It advocates change through individual personal transformation. In the United States and Australia, respectively, some people who are not Native Americans or Native Australians have appropriated the symbols, settings, and purported religious practices of Native Americans and Native Australians, for New Age religions. Native American activists decry the appropriation and commercialization of their spiritual beliefs and rituals, as when "sweat lodge" ceremonies are held on cruise ships, with wine and cheese served. They see the appropriation of their ceremonies and traditions as theft.

New religious movements have varied origins. Some have been influenced by Christianity, others by Eastern (Asian) religions, still others by mysticism and spiritualism. Religion also evolves in tandem with science and technology. For example, the Raelian movement, a religious group centered in Switzerland and Montreal, promotes cloning as a way of achieving eternal life (Palmer 2001).

Many contemporary nations contain unofficial religions. One example is "Yoruba religion," a term applied to perhaps 15 million adherents in Africa, as well as to millions of practitioners of *syncretic,* or blended, religions (with elements of Catholicism and spiritism) in the Western Hemisphere. Forms of Yoruba religion include *santeria* (in the Spanish Caribbean and the United States), *candomblé* (in Brazil), and *vodoun* (in the French Caribbean). Yoruba religion, with roots in precolonial nation-states of West Africa, has spread far beyond its religion of origin, as part of the African diaspora. It remains an influential, identifiable religion today, despite suppression, such as by Cuba's communist government. There are perhaps 3 million practitioners of santeria in Cuba, plus another 800,000 in the United States. At least 1 million Brazilians participate in candomblé, also known as macumba. Voodoo (or *vodoun*) has between 2.8 and 3.2 million practitioners (Ontario Consultants 2002), many (perhaps most) of whom would name something else, such as Catholicism, as their religion.

Secular Rituals

In concluding this discussion of religion, we may recognize some problems with the definitions of religion given at the beginning of this chapter. The first problem: If we define religion with reference to the sacred and/or supernatural beings, powers, and forces, how do we classify ritual-like behaviors that occur in secular contexts? Some

Anthropology Today   *Hinduism Takes Back Yoga*

As long as Homo sapiens *has existed, shamans have played both religious and healing roles. The spillover of religion into health continues today. Fitness is a major industry in contemporary North America and western Europe. Yoga classes are routine offerings in gyms and fitness centers. But what of yoga's origins, its religious underpinnings? Here we learn of a growing movement, abetted by print media and the Internet, to foster awareness of yoga's roots in Hinduism. Raised here are issues of commercialism and IPR (intellectual property rights): Who has the right to the yoga "brand"?*

Yoga is practiced by about 15 million people in the United States, for reasons almost as numerous—from the physical benefits mapped in brain scans to the less tangible rewards that New Age journals call spiritual centering. Religion, for the most part, has nothing to do with it.

But a group of Indian-Americans has ignited a surprisingly fierce debate in the gentle world of yoga by mounting a campaign to acquaint Westerners with the faith that it says underlies every single yoga style: Hinduism.

The campaign, labeled "Take Back Yoga," does not ask yoga devotees to become Hindu, or instructors to teach more about Hinduism. The . . . group behind it, the Hindu American Foundation, suggests only that people become more aware of yoga's debt to the faith's ancient traditions.

That suggestion . . . has drawn a flurry of strong reactions from figures far apart on the religious spectrum. Dr. Deepak Chopra, the New Age writer, has dismissed the campaign as a jumble of faulty history and Hindu nationalism. R. Albert Mohler Jr., president of the Southern Baptist Theological Seminary, . . . agrees that yoga is Hindu—and cited that as evidence that the practice imperiled the souls of Christians who engage in it.

The question at the core of the debate—who owns yoga?—has become an enduring topic of chatter in yoga Web forums, Hindu American newspapers and journals catering to the many consumers of what is now a multibillion-dollar yoga industry. . . .

Organizers of the Take Back Yoga effort point out that the philosophy of yoga was first described in Hinduism's seminal texts and remains at the core of Hindu teaching. Yet, because the religion has been stereotyped in the West as a polytheistic faith of "castes, cows and curry," they say, most Americans prefer to see yoga as the legacy of a more timeless, spiritual "Indian wisdom."

"In a way," said Dr. Aseem Shukla, the foundation's co-founder, "our issue is that yoga has thrived, but Hinduism has lost control of the brand."

For many practitioners, including Debbie Desmond, 27, a yoga instructor in Williamsburg, Brooklyn, the talk of branding and ownership is bewildering. "Nobody owns yoga," she said, sitting cross-legged in her studio, Namaste Yoga. . . . "Yoga is not a religion. It is a way of life, a method of becoming. We were taught that the roots of yoga go back further than Hinduism itself."

Like Dr. Chopra and some religious historians, Ms. Desmond believes that yoga originated in the Vedic culture of Indo-Europeans who settled in India in the third millennium B.C., long before the tradition now called Hinduism emerged. Other historians trace the first written description of yoga to the Bhagavad Gita, the sacred Hindu scripture believed to have been written between the fifth and second centuries B.C.

The effort to "take back" yoga began . . . with a scholarly essay . . . on the Web site of the Hindu American Foundation, a Minneapolis-based group that promotes human rights for Hindu minorities worldwide. The essay lamented a perceived snub in modern yoga culture, saying that yoga magazines and studios had assiduously decoupled the practice "from the Hinduism that gave forth this immense contribution to humanity."

Dr. Shukla put a sharper point on his case . . . in a column on the On Faith blog of *The Washington Post*. Hinduism, he wrote, had become a victim of "overt intellectual property theft," made possible by generations of Hindu yoga teachers who had "offered up a religion's spiritual wealth at the altar of crass commercialism."

That drew the attention of Dr. Chopra, an Indian-American who has done much to popularize Indian traditions like alternative medicine and yoga. He posted a reply saying that Hinduism was too "tribal" and "self-enclosed" to claim ownership of yoga. . . .

The debate . . . raised important issues about a spectrum of Hindu concepts permeating American culture, including meditation, belief in karma and reincarnation, and even cremation. . . .

The effort [to "take back yoga"] has been received most favorably by Indian-American community leaders like Dr. Uma V. Mysorekar, the president of the Hindu Temple Society of North America, in Flushing, Queens, which helps groups across the country build temples.

A naturalized immigrant, she said Take Back Yoga represented a coming-of-age for Indians in the United States. "My generation was too busy establishing itself in business and the professions," she said. "Now, the second and third generation is looking around and finding its voice, saying, 'Our civilization has made contributions to the world, and these should be acknowledged.'"

In the basement of the society's Ganesha Temple, an hourlong yoga class ended one recent Sunday morning with a long exhalation of the sacred syllable "om." Via the lung power of 60 students, it sounded as deeply as a blast from the organ at St. Patrick's Cathedral.

Source: Paul Vitello, "Hindu Group Stirs a Debate over Yoga's Soul," *New York Times*, November 27, 2010.

anthropologists believe there are both sacred and secular rituals. Secular rituals include formal, invariant, stereotyped, earnest, repetitive behavior and rites of passage that take place in nonreligious settings.

A second problem: If the distinction between the supernatural and the natural is not consistently made in a society, how can we tell what is religion and what isn't? The Betsileo of Madagascar, for example, view witches and dead ancestors as real people who play roles in ordinary life. However, their occult powers are not empirically demonstrable.

A third problem: The behavior considered appropriate for religious occasions varies tremendously from culture to culture. One society may consider drunken frenzy the surest sign of faith, whereas another may inculcate quiet reverence. Who is to say which is "more religious"?

It is possible for apparently secular settings, things, and events to acquire intense meaning for individuals who have grown up in their presence. For example, identities and loyalties based on fandom, football, baseball, and soccer can be powerful indeed. Rock stars and bands can mobilize many. A World Series win led to celebrations across a "Red Sox nation." Italians and Brazilians are rarely if ever as nationally focused and emotionally unified as they are when their teams are competing in the World Cup. The collective effervescence that Durkheim found so characteristic of religion can equally well describe what Brazilians experience when their country wins a World Cup.

In the context of comparative religion, the idea that the secular can become sacred isn't surprising. Long ago, Durkheim (1912/2001) pointed out that almost everything, from the sublime to the ridiculous, has in some societies been treated as sacred. The distinction between sacred and profane doesn't depend on the intrinsic qualities of the sacred symbol. In Australian totemic religion, for example, sacred beings include such humble creatures as ducks, frogs, rabbits, and grubs, whose inherent qualities could hardly have given rise to the religious sentiment they inspire.

Madagascar's tomb-centered ceremonies are times when the living and the dead are joyously reunited, when people get drunk, gorge themselves, and have sexual license. Perhaps the gray, sober, ascetic, and moralistic aspects of many official religious events, in taking the fun out of religion, force us to find religion (i.e., truth, beauty, meaning, passionate involvement) in fun.

Summary

1. Given the varied and worldwide scope of beliefs and behavior labeled "religious," anthropologists recognize the difficulty of defining religion. Religion, a cultural universal, describes beliefs and behavior concerned with supernatural beings, powers, and forces. Religion also encompasses the feelings, meanings, and congregations associated with such beliefs and behavior. Religious worlds are real, vivid, and significant to those who construct and inhabit them. Anthropological studies have revealed many forms, expressions, and functions of religion.

2. Tylor considered animism—the belief in spirits or souls—to be religion's earliest and most basic form. He focused on religion's explanatory role, arguing that religion would eventually disappear as science provided better explanations. Besides animism, another view of the supernatural also occurs in nonindustrial societies, seeing the supernatural as a domain of raw, impersonal power or force (called *mana* in Polynesia and Melanesia). People can manipulate and control mana under certain conditions.

3. When ordinary technical and rational means of doing things fail, people may turn to magic. Often they use magic when they lack control over outcomes. Religion offers comfort and psychological security at times of crisis. On the other hand, rites can also create anxiety. Rituals are formal, invariant, stylized, earnest acts in which people subordinate their particular beliefs to a social collectivity. Rites of passage have three stages: separation, liminality, and incorporation. Such rites can mark any change in social status, age, place, or social condition. Collective rites are often cemented by communitas, a feeling of intense solidarity.

4. Religion establishes and maintains social control through a series of moral and ethical beliefs and real and imagined rewards and punishments, internalized in individuals. Religion also achieves social control by mobilizing its members for collective action.

5. Religions exist in particular societies, and cultural differences show up systematically in religious beliefs and practices. The Olympian, ecclesiastical, and monotheistic religions of stratified, state societies, for example, differ from those of societies with less marked social contrasts—societies without hierarchies and specialized officials. The world's major religions vary in their growth rates, with Islam expanding more rapidly than Christianity.

6. Religion helps maintain social order, but it also can promote change. Revitalization movements blend old and new beliefs and have helped people adapt to changing conditions. Among contemporary, "new" religious movements, some have been influenced by Christianity, others by Eastern (Asian) religions, still others by mysticism and spiritualism, or by science and technology. There are secular as well as religious rituals. It is possible for apparently secular settings, things, and events to acquire intense meaning for individuals who have grown up in their presence.

Key Terms

animism, *350*
cargo cults, *363*
communitas, *349*
leveling
   mechanism, *358*
liminality, *354*
magic, *352*

mana, *351*
monotheism, *350*
polytheism, *350*
religion, *348*
revitalization
   movements, *362*
rites of passage, *354*

rituals, *353*
shaman, *350*
taboo, *351*
totem, *357*

Go to our Online Learning Center website at **www.mhhe.com/kottak** for Internet resources directly related to the content of this chapter.

Chapter 16

The World System and Colonialism

The World System

   The Emergence of the World System

Industrialization

   Causes of the Industrial Revolution

Socioeconomic Effects of Industrialization

   Industrial Stratification

Colonialism

   British Colonialism

   French Colonialism

   Colonialism and Identity

   Postcolonial Studies

Development

   Neoliberalism

The Second World

   Communism

   Postsocialist Transitions

The World System Today

   Energy Consumption and Industrial Degradation

   Applying Anthropology to Popular Culture: Avatar

   Anthropology Today: Mining Giant Compatible with Sustainability Institute?

Although fieldwork in small communities has been anthropology's hallmark, isolated groups are impossible to find today. Truly isolated societies probably never have existed. For thousands of years, human groups have been in contact with one another. Local societies always have participated in a larger system, which today has global dimensions—we call it the *modern world system,* by which we mean a world in which nations are economically and politically interdependent.

The World System

The world system and the relations among the countries within it are shaped by the capitalist world economy. A huge increase in international trade during and after the 15th century led to the **capitalist world economy** (Wallerstein 1982, 2004*b*), a single world system committed to production for sale or exchange, with the object of maximizing

Illustrating the contemporary global spread of capitalism are these shoppers inside the Kowloon Tong Festival Walk shopping center in Hong Kong.

profits, rather than supplying domestic needs. **Capital** refers to wealth or resources invested in business, with the intent of using the means of production to make a profit.

World-system theory can be traced to the French social historian Fernand Braudel. In his three-volume work *Civilization and Capitalism, 15th–18th Century* (1981, 1982, 1992), Braudel argued that society consists of interrelated parts assembled into a system. Societies are subsystems of larger systems, with the world system the largest. The key claim of **world-system theory** is that an identifiable social system, based on wealth and power differentials, extends beyond individual countries. That system is formed by a set of economic and political relations that has characterized much of the globe since the 16th century, when the Old World established regular contact with the New World (see Bodley 2008).

According to Wallerstein (1982, 2004*b*), countries within the world system occupy three different positions of economic and political power: core, periphery, and semiperiphery. The geographic center, or **core,** the dominant position in the world system, includes the strongest, most powerful, and technically most advanced industrial nations. In core nations, "the complexity of economic activities and the level of capital accumulation is the greatest" (Thompson 1983, p. 12). According to Arrighi (1994), the core monopolizes the most profitable activities, especially the control of world finance.

Semiperiphery and periphery countries have less power, wealth, and influence than the core does. The **semiperiphery** is intermediate between the core and the periphery. Contemporary nations of the semiperiphery are industrialized. Like core nations, they export both industrial goods and commodities, but they lack the power and economic dominance of core nations. Thus Brazil, a semiperiphery nation, exports automobiles to Nigeria (a periphery nation) and auto engines, orange juice extract, coffee, and shrimp to the United States (a core nation). The **periphery** includes the world's least privileged

Technological advances, including the Internet and telecommunications technology, allow jobs to be outsourced from core nations to cities in the semiperiphery, such Bangalore, India, where call center workers are shown in this photo.

and powerful countries. Economic activities there are less mechanized than are those in the core and semiperiphery, although some degree of industrialization has reached even peripheral nations. The periphery produces raw materials, agricultural commodities, and, increasingly, human labor for export to the core and the semiperiphery (Shannon 1996).

In the United States and Western Europe today, immigration—legal and illegal—from the periphery and semiperiphery supplies cheap labor, especially for agriculture, construction, and paid domestic labor in core countries. U.S. states as distant as California, Michigan, and South Carolina make significant use of farm labor from Mexico. The availability of relatively cheap workers from noncore nations such as Mexico (in the United States) and Turkey (in Germany) benefits farmers and business owners in core countries, while also supplying remittances to families in the semiperiphery and periphery. As a result of 21st-century telecommunications technology, cheap labor doesn't even need to migrate to the United States. Thousands of families in India are being supported as American companies "outsource" jobs—from telephone assistance to software engineering—to nations outside the core (see Nadeem 2011).

The Emergence of the World System

By the 15th century, Europeans were profiting from a transoceanic trade-oriented economy, and people worldwide entered Europe's sphere of influence. What was new was the transatlantic component of a long history of Old World sailing and commerce. As early as 600 B.C.E., the Phoenicians/Carthaginians sailed around Britain on regular trade routes and circumnavigated Africa. Likewise, Indonesia and Africa have been linked in Indian Ocean trade for at least 2,000 years. In the 15th century Europe established regular contact with Asia, Africa, and eventually the New World (the Caribbean and the Americas). Christopher Columbus's first voyage from Spain to the Bahamas and the Caribbean in 1492 was soon followed by additional voyages. These journeys opened the way for a major exchange of people, resources, products, ideas, and diseases, as the Old and New Worlds were forever linked (Crosby 2003; Diamond 1997; Fagan 1998). Led by Spain and Portugal, Europeans extracted silver and gold, conquered the natives (taking some as slaves), and colonized their lands.

Previously in Europe as throughout the world, rural people had produced mainly for their own needs, growing their own food and making clothing, furniture, and tools from local products. Production beyond immediate needs was undertaken to pay taxes and to purchase trade items such as salt and iron. As late as 1650 the English diet was based on locally grown starches (Mintz 1985). In the 200 years that followed, however, the English became extraordinary consumers of imported goods. One of the earliest and most popular of those goods was sugar (Mintz 1985).

Sugarcane originally was domesticated in Papua New Guinea, and sugar was first processed in India. Reaching Europe via the Middle East and the eastern Mediterranean, it was carried to the New World by Columbus (Mintz 1985). The climate of Brazil and the Caribbean proved ideal for growing sugarcane, and Europeans built plantations there to supply the growing demand for sugar. This led to the development in the 17th century of a plantation economy based on a single cash crop—a system known as *monocrop* production.

The demand for sugar in a growing international market spurred the development of the transatlantic slave trade and New World plantation economies based on slave labor. By the 18th century, an increased English demand for raw cotton led to rapid settlement of what is now the southeastern United States and the emergence there of another slave-based monocrop production system. Like sugar, cotton was a key trade item that fueled the growth of the world system.

Industrialization

By the 18th century the stage had been set for the **Industrial Revolution**—the historical transformation (in Europe, after 1750) of "traditional" into "modern" societies through industrialization of the economy. The seeds of industrial society were planted well before the 18th century (Gimpel 1988). For example, a knitting machine invented in England in 1589 was so far ahead of its time that it played a profitable role in factories two and three centuries later. The appearance of cloth mills late in the Middle Ages foreshadowed the search for new sources of wind and water power that characterized the Industrial Revolution. Industrialization required capital for investment. The established system of transoceanic trade and commerce supplied this capital from the profits it generated. Wealthy people sought investment opportunities and eventually found them in machines and engines to drive machines. Capital and scientific innovation fueled invention. Industrialization increased production in both farming and manufacturing.

European industrialization developed from (and eventually replaced) the *domestic system* of manufacture (or home-handicraft system). In this system, an organizer-entrepreneur supplied the raw materials to workers in their homes and collected the finished products from them. The entrepreneur, whose sphere of operations might span several villages, owned the materials, paid for the work, and arranged the marketing.

Causes of the Industrial Revolution

The Industrial Revolution began with cotton products, iron, and pottery. These were widely used goods whose manufacture could be broken down into simple routine motions that machines could perform. When manufacturing moved from homes to factories, where machinery replaced handwork, agrarian societies evolved into industrial ones. As factories produced cheap staple goods, the Industrial Revolution led to a dramatic increase in production. Industrialization fueled urban growth and created a new kind of city, with factories crowded together in places where coal and labor were cheap.

The Art of STOCKING-FRAME-WORK-KNITTING.

Engrav'd for the Universal Magazine 1750, for J. Hinton at the Kings Arms in St. Pauls Church Yard LONDON.

In the home-handicraft, or domestic, system of production, an organizer supplied raw materials to workers in their homes and collected their products. Family life and work were intertwined, as in this English scene. Is there a modern equivalent to the domestic system of production?

The Industrial Revolution began in England, and, as its industrialization proceeded, Britain's population began to increase dramatically. It doubled during the 18th century (especially after 1750) and did so again between 1800 and 1850. This demographic explosion fueled consumption, but British entrepreneurs couldn't meet the increased demand with the traditional production methods. This spurred further experimentation, innovation, and rapid technological change.

English industrialization drew on national advantages in natural resources. Britain was rich in coal and iron ore, and had navigable waterways and easily negotiated coasts. It was a seafaring island-nation located at the crossroads of international trade. These features gave Britain a favored position for importing raw materials and exporting manufactured goods. Another factor in England's industrial growth was the fact that much of its 18th-century colonial empire was occupied by English settler families who looked to the mother country as they tried to replicate European civilization in the New World. These colonies bought large quantities of English staples.

It also has been argued that particular cultural values and religion contributed to industrialization. Many members of the emerging English middle class were Protestant nonconformists. Their beliefs and values encouraged industry, thrift, the dissemination of new knowledge, inventiveness, and willingness to accept change (Weber 1904/1958).

Socioeconomic Effects of Industrialization

The socioeconomic effects of industrialization were mixed. English national income tripled between 1700 and 1815 and increased 30 times more by 1939. Standards of comfort rose, but prosperity was uneven. At first, factory workers got wages higher than those available in the domestic system. Later, owners started recruiting labor in places where living standards were low and labor (including that of women and children) was cheap.

Social ills worsened with the growth of factory towns and industrial cities, amid conditions like those Charles Dickens described in *Hard Times*. Filth and smoke polluted the 19th-century cities. Housing was crowded and unsanitary, with insufficient water and sewage disposal facilities. People experienced rampant disease and rising death rates. This was the world of Ebenezer Scrooge, Bob Cratchit, Tiny Tim—and Karl Marx.

Industrial Stratification

The social theorists Karl Marx and Max Weber focused on the stratification systems associated with industrialization. From his observations in England and his analysis of 19th-century industrial capitalism, Marx (Marx and Engels 1848/1976) saw socioeconomic stratification as a sharp and simple division between two opposed classes: the bourgeoisie (capitalists) and the proletariat (propertyless workers). The bourgeoisie traced its origins to overseas ventures and the world capitalist economy, which had created a wealthy commercial class.

Industrialization shifted production from farms and cottages to mills and factories, where mechanical power was available and where workers could be assembled to operate heavy machinery. The **bourgeoisie** were the owners of the factories, mines, large farms, and other means of production. The **working class, or proletariat,** was made up of people who had to sell their labor to survive. With the decline of subsistence production and with the rise of urban migration and the possibility of unemployment, the bourgeoisie came to stand between workers and the means of production.

Industrialization hastened the process of *proletarianization*—the separation of workers from the means of production. The bourgeoisie also came to dominate the means of communication, the schools, and other key institutions. *Class consciousness* (recognition of collective interests and personal identification with one's economic group) was a vital part of Marx's view of class. He saw bourgeoisie and proletariat as socioeconomic divisions with radically opposed interests. Marx viewed classes as powerful collective forces that could mobilize human energies to influence the course of history. On the basis of their common experience, workers would develop class consciousness, which could lead to revolutionary change. Although no proletarian revolution was to occur in England, workers did develop organizations to protect their interests and increase their share of industrial profits. During the 19th century, trade unions and socialist parties emerged to express a rising anticapitalist spirit. The concerns of the English labor movement were to remove young children from factories and limit the hours during which women and children could work. The profile of stratification in industrial core nations gradually took shape. Capitalists controlled production, but labor was organizing for better wages and working conditions. By 1900 many governments had factory legislation and social-welfare programs. Mass living standards in core nations improved as population grew.

In today's capitalist world system the class division between owners and workers is now worldwide. However, publicly traded companies complicate the division between capitalists and workers in industrial nations. Through pension plans and personal investments, some American workers now have a proprietary interest in the means of production. They are part-owners rather than propertyless workers. The key difference is that the wealthy have *control* over these means. The key capitalist now is not the factory owner, who may have been replaced by thousands of stockholders, but the CEO or the chair of the board of directors, neither of whom may actually own the corporation.

Modern stratification systems aren't simple and dichotomous. They include (particularly in core and semiperiphery nations) a middle class of skilled and professional workers. Gerhard Lenski (1966) argues that social equality tends to increase in advanced industrial societies. The masses improve their access to economic benefits and political power. In Lenski's scheme, the shift of political power to the masses reflects the growth of the middle class, which reduces the polarization between owning and working classes. The proliferation of middle-class occupations creates opportunities for social mobility. The stratification system grows more complex (Giddens 1973).

In the United States this complex stratification system has gone largely unnoticed by many Americans. Most contemporary Americans, for example, think they belong to, and claim identity with, the middle class, which they tend to perceive as a vast undifferentiated group. However, there are substantial differences in income and wealth between the richest and the poorest Americans, and the gap is widening. According to U.S. Census data from 1967 to 2000, the top (richest) fifth, or quintile, of American households increased their share of national income by 13.5 percent, while all other quintiles fell. The percentage share of the lowest fifth fell most dramatically—17.6 percent. The divergence continues: In 2009 the highest quintile of households got 50.3 percent (versus 49.7 percent in 2000) of all national income, while the lowest fifth got only 3.4 percent (versus 3.6 in 2000). Comparable figures in 1967 were 43.8 percent and 4.0 percent. The 2009 ratio was 15:1, versus 14:1 in 2000 and 11:1 in 1967. In other words, the richest fifth of American households, with a mean annual income of $170,844, is now 15 times wealthier than the poorest fifth, with a mean annual income of $11,552 (DeNavas-Walt, Proctor, and Smith 2010). When we consider wealth (investments, property, possessions, etc.) rather than income, the contrast is even more striking: 1 percent of American families hold just over one-third of the nation's wealth (Council on International and Public Affairs 2006). Figure 16.1 shows that, in 2007, the top 1 percent owned 33.8 percent of all wealth in the United States. By contrast, the bottom 50 percent owned just 2.5 percent. In fact, the top 1 percent owns more than the bottom 90 percent combined (Witt 2011, p. 229).

FIGURE 16.1

Percentage of Wealth Owned by Percentile of U.S. Population

Source: Witt 2011.

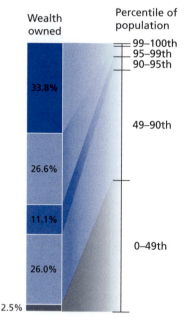

Weber faulted Marx for an overly simple and exclusively economic view of stratification. As we saw in the chapter "Political Systems," Weber (1922/1968) defined three dimensions of social stratification: wealth, power, and prestige. Although, as Weber showed, wealth, power, and prestige are separate components of social ranking, they tend to be correlated. Weber also believed that social identities based on ethnicity, religion, race, nationality, and other attributes could take priority over class (social identity based on economic status). In addition to class contrasts, the modern world system *is* cross-cut by collective identities based on ethnicity, religion, and nationality (Shannon 1996). Class conflicts tend to occur within nations, and nationalism has prevented global class solidarity, particularly of proletarians.

Although the capitalist class dominates politically in most countries, growing wealth made it easier for core nations to grant higher wages (Hopkins and Wallerstein 1982). However, the improvement in core workers' living standards wouldn't have occurred without the world system. Without the periphery, core capitalists would have trouble maintaining their profits and also satisfying the demands of core workers. In the periphery, wages and living standards are much lower. The current *world stratification system* features a substantial contrast between both capitalists and workers in the core nations and workers on the periphery (see Kerbo 2006).

Colonialism

World-system theory stresses the existence of a global culture and economy. It emphasizes historical contacts, linkages, and power differentials between local people and international forces. The major forces influencing cultural interaction during the past 500 years have been commercial expansion, industrial capitalism, and the dominance of colonial and core nations (Wallerstein 1982, 2004b; Wolf 1982). As state formation had done previously, industrialization accelerated local participation in larger networks. According to Bodley (2007), perpetual expansion is a distinguishing feature of industrial economic systems. Bands and tribes were small, self-sufficient, subsistence-based systems. Industrial economies, by contrast, are large, highly specialized systems in which market exchanges occur with profit as the primary motive (Bodley 2007).

During the 19th century European business interests initiated a concerted search for markets. This process led to European imperialism in Africa, Asia, and Oceania. **Imperialism** refers to a policy of extending the rule of a country or empire over foreign nations and of taking and holding foreign colonies. Imperialism goes back to early states, including Egypt in the Old World and the Incas in the New. A Greek empire was forged by Alexander the Great, and Julius Caesar and his successors spread the Roman empire. More recent examples include the British, French, and Soviet empires (Scheinman 1980).

After 1850, European imperial expansion was aided by improved transportation, which facilitated the colonization of vast areas of sparsely settled lands in the interior of North and South America and Australia. The new colonies purchased masses of goods from the industrial centers and shipped back wheat, cotton, wool, mutton, beef, and leather. The first phase of European colonialism had been the exploration and exploitation of the Americas and the Caribbean after Columbus. A new second phase began as European nations competed for colonies between 1875 and 1914, setting the stage for World War I.

Colonialism is the political, social, economic, and cultural domination of a territory and its people by a foreign power for an extended time (see Bremen and Shimizu, eds. 1999; Cooper and Stoler, eds. 1997). If imperialism is almost as old as the state, colonialism can be traced back to the Phoenicians, who established colonies along the eastern Mediterranean 3,000 years ago. The ancient Greeks and Romans were avid colonizers, as well as empire builders.

The first phase of modern colonialism began with the European "Age of Discovery"—of the Americas and of a sea route to the Far East. After 1492, the Spanish, the original conquerors of the Aztecs and the Incas, explored and colonized widely in the New World—the Caribbean, Mexico, the southern portions of what was to become the United States, and Central and South America. In South America, Portugal ruled over Brazil. Rebellions and wars aimed at independence ended the first phase of European colonialism by the early 19th century. Brazil declared independence from Portugal in 1822. By 1825 most of Spain's colonies were politically independent. Spain held onto Cuba and the Philippines until 1898, but otherwise withdrew from the colonial field. During the first phase of colonialism, Spain and Portugal, along with Britain and France, were major colonizing nations. The latter two (Britain and France) dominated the second phase.

British Colonialism

At its peak about 1914, the British empire covered a fifth of the world's land surface and ruled a fourth of its population (see Figure 16.2). Like several other European nations, Britain had two stages of colonialism. The first began with the Elizabethan voyages of the 16th century. During the 17th century, Britain acquired most of the eastern coast of North America, Canada's St. Lawrence basin, islands in the Caribbean, slave stations in Africa, and interests in India.

The British shared the exploration of the New World with the Spanish, Portuguese, French, and Dutch. The British by and large left Mexico, along with Central and South America, to the Spanish and the Portuguese. The end of the Seven Years' War in 1763 forced a French retreat from most of Canada and India, where France previously had competed with Britain (Cody 1998; Farr 1980).

The American revolution ended the first stage of British colonialism. A second colonial empire, on which the "sun never set," rose from the ashes of the first. Beginning in 1788, but intensifying after 1815, the British settled Australia. Britain had acquired Dutch South Africa by 1815. The establishment of Singapore in 1819 provided a base for a British trade network that extended to much of South Asia and along the coast of

FIGURE 16.2 Map of British Empire in 1765 and 1914

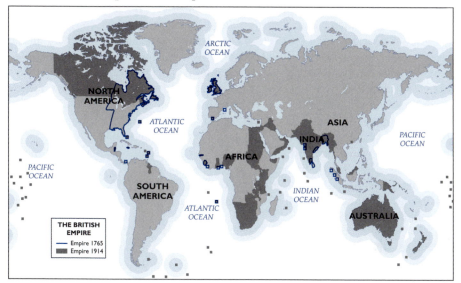

On January 1, 1900, a British officer in India receives a pedicure from a servant. What does this photo say to you about colonialism? Who gives pedicures in your society?

China. By this time, the empires of Britain's traditional rivals, particularly Spain, had been severely diminished in scope. Britain's position as imperial power and the world's leading industrial nation was unchallenged (Cody 1998; Farr 1980).

During the Victorian Era (1837–1901), as Britain's acquisition of territory and of further trading concessions continued, Prime Minister Benjamin Disraeli implemented a foreign policy justified by a view of imperialism as shouldering "the white man's burden"—a phrase coined by the poet Rudyard Kipling. People in the empire were seen as unable to govern themselves, so that British guidance was needed to civilize and Christianize them. This paternalistic and racist doctrine served to legitimize Britain's acquisition and control of parts of central Africa and Asia (Cody 1998).

After World War II, the British empire began to fall apart, with nationalist movements for independence. India became independent in 1947, as did Ireland in 1949. Decolonization in Africa and Asia accelerated during the late 1950s. Today, the ties that remain between Britain and its former colonies are mainly linguistic or cultural rather than political (Cody 1998).

French Colonialism

French colonialism also had two phases. The first began with the explorations of the early 1600s. Prior to the French revolution in 1789, missionaries, explorers, and traders carved out niches for France in Canada, the Louisiana territory, several Caribbean islands, and parts of India, which were lost along with Canada to Great Britain in 1763 (Harvey 1980).

The foundations of the second French empire were established between 1830 and 1870. In Great Britain the sheer drive for profit led expansion, but French colonialism was spurred more by the state, church, and armed forces than by pure business interests. France acquired Algeria and part of what eventually became Indochina (Cambodia, Laos, and Vietnam). By 1914 the French empire covered 4 million square miles and included some 60 million people (see Figure 16.3). By 1893 French rule had been fully established in Indochina. Tunisia and Morocco became French protectorates in 1883 and 1912, respectively (Harvey 1980).

To be sure, the French, like the British, had substantial business interests in their colonies, but they also sought, again like the British, international glory and prestige. The French promulgated a *mission civilisatrice,* their equivalent of Britain's "white man's burden." The goal was to implant French culture, language, and religion, Roman Catholicism, throughout the colonies (Harvey 1980).

The French used two forms of colonial rule: *indirect rule,* governing through native leaders and established political structures, in areas with long histories of state organization, such as Morocco and Tunisia; and *direct rule* by French officials in many areas of Africa, where the French imposed new government structures to control diverse societies, many of them previously stateless. Like the British empire, the French empire began to disintegrate after World War II. France fought long—and ultimately futile—wars to keep its empire intact in Indochina and Algeria (Harvey 1980).

Colonialism and Identity

Many geopolitical labels in the news today had no equivalent meaning before colonialism. Whole countries, along with social groups and divisions within them, were colonial

FIGURE 16.3   Map of the French Empire at Its Height around 1914

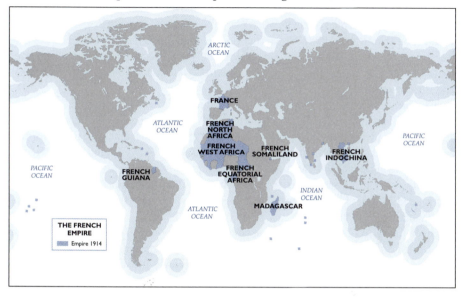

inventions. In West Africa, for example, by geographic logic, several adjacent countries could be one (Togo, Ghana, Ivory Coast, Guinea, Guinea-Bissau, Sierra Leone, Liberia). Instead, they are separated by linguistic, political, and economic contrasts promoted under colonialism.

Hundreds of ethnic groups and "tribes" are colonial constructions (see Ranger 1996). The Sukuma of Tanzania, for instance, were first registered as a single tribe by the colonial administration. Then missionaries standardized a series of dialects into a single Sukuma language into which they translated the Bible and other religious texts. Thereafter, those texts were taught in missionary schools and to European foreigners and other non-Sukuma speakers. Over time this standardized the Sukuma language and ethnicity (Finnstrom 1997).

As in most of East Africa, in Rwanda and Burundi farmers and herders live in the same areas and speak the same language. Historically they have shared the same social world, although their social organization is "extremely hierarchical," almost "castelike" (Malkki 1995, p. 24). There has been a tendency to see the pastoral Tutsis as superior to the agricultural Hutus. Tutsis have been presented as nobles, Hutus as commoners. Yet when distributing identity cards in Rwanda, the Belgian colonizers simply identified all people with more than 10 head of cattle as Tutsi. Owners of fewer cattle were registered as Hutus (Bjuremalm 1997). Years later, these arbitrary colonial registers were used systematically for "ethnic" identification during the mass killings (genocide) that took place in Rwanda in 1994 (as portrayed vividly in the film *Hotel Rwanda*).

Postcolonial Studies

In anthropology, history, and literature, the field of postcolonial studies has gained prominence since the 1970s (see Ashcroft, Griffiths, and Tiffin 1989; Chakrabarty 2007;

Cooper and Stoler, eds. 1997). **Postcolonial** refers to the study of the interactions between European nations and the societies they colonized (mainly after 1800). In 1914, European empires, which broke up after World War II, ruled more than 85 percent of the world (Petraglia-Bahri 1996). The term "postcolonial" also has been used to describe the second half of the 20th century in general, the period succeeding colonialism. Even more generically, "postcolonial" may be used to signify a position against imperialism and Eurocentrism (Petraglia-Bahri 1996).

The former colonies (*postcolonies*) can be divided into settler, nonsettler, and mixed (Petraglia-Bahri 1996). The settler countries, with large numbers of European colonists and sparser native populations, include Australia and Canada. Examples of nonsettler countries include India, Pakistan, Bangladash, Sri Lanka, Malaysia, Indonesia, Nigeria, Senegal, Madagascar, and Jamaica. All these had substantial native populations and relatively few European settlers. Mixed countries include South Africa, Zimbabwe, Kenya, and Algeria. Such countries had significant European settlement despite having sizable native populations.

Given the varied experiences of such countries, "postcolonial" has to be a loose term. The United States, for instance, was colonized by Europeans and fought a war for independence from Britain. Is the United States a postcolony? It usually isn't perceived as such, given its current world power position, its treatment of native Americans (sometimes called internal colonization), and its annexation of other parts of the world (Petraglia-Bahri 1996). Research in postcolonial studies is growing, permitting a wide-ranging investigation of power relations in varied contexts. Broad topics in the field include the formation of an empire, the impact of colonization, and the state of the postcolony today.

Development

During the Industrial Revolution, a strong current of thought viewed industrialization as a beneficial process of organic development and progress. Many economists still assume that industrialization increases production and income. They seek to create in Third World ("developing") countries a process like the one that first occurred spontaneously in 18th-century Great Britain.

We have seen that Britain used the notion of a white man's burden to justify its imperialist expansion and that France claimed to be engaged in a *mission civilisatrice,* a civilizing mission, in its colonies. Both these ideas illustrate an **intervention philosophy,** an ideological justification for outsiders to guide native peoples in specific directions. Economic development plans also have intervention philosophies. John Bodley (2008) argues that the basic belief behind interventions—whether by colonialists, missionaries, governments, or development planners—has been the same for more than one hundred years. This belief is that industrialization, modernization, Westernization, and individualism are desirable evolutionary advances and that development schemes that promote them will bring long-term benefits to local people. In a more extreme form, intervention philosophy may pit the assumed wisdom of enlightened colonial or other First World planners against the purported conservatism, ignorance, or "obsolescence" of "inferior" or "backward" local people.

Neoliberalism

One currently influential intervention philosophy is neoliberalism. This term encompasses a set of assumptions that have become widespread during the last 30 years. Neoliberal policies are being implemented in developing nations, including postsocialist societies (e.g., those of the former Soviet Union). **Neoliberalism** is the current form of the classic economic liberalism laid out in Adam Smith's famous capitalist manifesto, *The Wealth of Nations,* published in 1776, soon after the Industrial Revolution. Smith advocated laissez-faire (hands-off) economics as the basis of capitalism: The government should stay out of its nation's economic affairs. Free trade, Smith thought, was the best way for a nation's economy to develop. There should be no restrictions on manufacturing, no barriers to commerce, and no tariffs. This philosophy is called "liberalism" because it aimed at liberating or freeing the economy from government controls. Economic liberalism encouraged "free" enterprise and competition, with the goal of generating profits. (Note the difference between this meaning of *liberal* and the one that has been popularized on American talk radio, in which "liberal" is used—usually as a derogatory term—as the opposite of "conservative." Ironically, Adam Smith's liberalism is today's capitalist "conservatism.")

Economic liberalism prevailed in the United States until President Franklin Roosevelt's New Deal during the 1930s. The Great Depression produced a turn to Keynesian economics, which challenged liberalism. John Maynard Keynes (1927, 1936) insisted that full employment was necessary for capitalism to grow, that governments and central banks should intervene to increase employment, and that government should promote the common good.

Especially since the fall of Communism (1989–1991), there has been a revival of economic liberalism, now known as neoliberalism, which has been spreading globally. Around the world, neoliberal policies have been imposed by powerful financial institutions such as the International Monetary Fund (IMF), the World Bank, and the Inter-American Development Bank (see Edelman and Haugerud 2004). Neoliberalism entails open (tariff- and barrier-free) international trade and investment. Profits are sought through lowering of costs, whether through improving productivity, laying off workers, or seeking workers who accept lower wages. In exchange for loans, the governments of postsocialist and developing nations have been required to accept the neoliberal premise that deregulation leads to economic growth, which will eventually benefit everyone through a process sometimes called "trickle down." Accompanying the belief in free markets and the idea of cutting costs is a tendency to impose austerity measures that cut government expenses. This can entail reduced public spending on education, health care, and other social services (Martinez and Garcia 2000).

The Second World

The labels "First World," "Second World," and "Third World" represent a common, although ethnocentric, way of categorizing nations. The *First World* refers to the "democratic West"—traditionally conceived in opposition to a "Second World" ruled by "Communism." The *Second World* refers to the former Soviet Union and the socialist and once-socialist countries of Eastern Europe and Asia. Proceeding with this classification, the "less-developed countries" or "developing nations" make up the *Third World*.

Communism

The two meanings of communism involve how it is written, whether with a lowercase (small) or an uppercase (large) *c*. Small-*c* **communism** describes a social system in which property is owned by the community and in which people work for the common good. Large-*C* **Communism** was a political movement and doctrine seeking to overthrow capitalism and to establish a form of communism such as that which prevailed in the Soviet Union (USSR) from 1917 to 1991. The heyday of Communism was a 40-year period from 1949 to 1989, when more Communist regimes existed than at any time before or after. Today only five Communist states remain—China, Cuba, Laos, North Korea, and Vietnam, compared with 23 in 1985.

Communism, which originated with Russia's Bolshevik Revolution in 1917, and took its inspiration from Karl Marx and Friedrich Engels, was not uniform over time or among countries. All Communist systems were *authoritarian* (promoting obedience to authority rather than individual freedom). Many were *totalitarian* (banning rival parties and demanding total submission of the individual to the state). Several features distinguished Communist societies from other authoritarian regimes (e.g., Spain under Franco) and from socialism of a social democratic type. First, the Communist Party monopolized power in every Communist state. Second, relations within the party were highly centralized and strictly disciplined. Third, Communist nations had state ownership, rather than private ownership, of the means of production. Finally, all Communist regimes, with the goal of advancing communism, cultivated a sense of belonging to an international movement (Brown 2001).

Postsocialist Transitions

Social scientists have tended to refer to "Second World" societies as socialist rather than Communist. Today research by anthropologists is thriving in *postsocialist* societies—those that once emphasized bureaucratic redistribution of wealth according to a central plan (Verdery 2001). In the postsocialist period, states that once had planned economies have been following the neoliberal agenda, by divesting themselves of state-owned resources in favor of privatization. Some of them have moved toward formal liberal democracy, with political parties, elections, and a balance of powers (Grekova 2001).

Neoliberal economists assumed that dismantling the Soviet Union's planned economy would raise gross domestic product (GDP) and living standards. The goal was to enhance production by substituting a decentralized market system and providing incentives through privatization. In October 1991, Boris Yeltsin, who had been elected president of Russia that June, announced a program of radical market-oriented reform, pursuing a changeover to capitalism. Yeltsin's program of "shock therapy" cut subsidies to farms and industries and ended price controls. Since then, postsocialist Russia has faced many problems. The anticipated gains in productivity did not materialize. After the fall of the Soviet Union, Russia's GDP fell by half. Life expectancy and the birth rate declined. Poverty increased, with a quarter of the population now living below the poverty line.

The World System Today

The spread of industrialization continues today, although nations have shifted their positions within the world system. By 1900, the United States had become a core nation, having overtaken Great Britain in iron, coal, and cotton production. In a few decades (1868–1900), Japan changed from a medieval handicraft economy to an industrial one, joining the semiperiphery by 1900 and moving to the core between 1945 and 1970. India and China have joined Brazil as leaders of the semiperiphery. The map in Figure 16.4 shows the world system today.

Twentieth-century industrialization added hundreds of new industries and millions of new jobs. Production increased, often beyond immediate demand, spurring strategies, such as advertising, to sell everything industry could churn out. Mass production gave rise to a culture of consumption, which valued acquisitiveness and conspicuous consumption.

How do things stand in the 21st century? Worldwide, young people are abandoning traditional subsistence pursuits and seeking cash. A popular song once queried "How're you gonna keep 'em down on the farm after they've seen Paree." Nowadays most people *have* seen Paree—Paris, that is—along with other world capitals, maybe not in person, but in print or on-screen images. Young people today are better educated and wiser in the ways of the world than ever before. Increasingly they are exposed to the material and cultural promises of a better life away from the farm. They seek paying jobs, but work is scarce, spurring migration within and across national boundaries. If they can't get cash legally, they seek it illegally.

FIGURE 16.4   **The World System Today**

Source: Conrad Kottak, *Anthropology,* 10th ed., fig 23.5, p. 660. Reprinted by permission of The McGraw-Hill Companies.

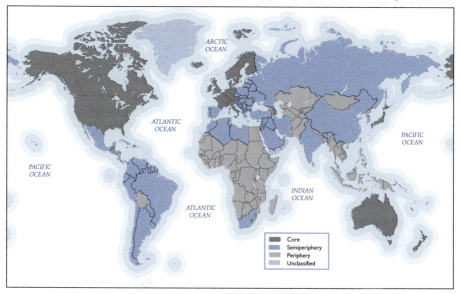

Recently work has been scarce as well in the industrial world, including the United States and western Europe. As the United States struggled to emerge from the recession of 2008–2009, its stock market rose 80 percent between March 2009 and January 2011. In what many saw as a "jobless recovery," increasingly profitable corporations held onto their cash, rather than using it to hire new workers. The goal of capitalism, remember, is to generate profits and to maintain profitability. In a global economy, profitability doesn't necessarily result from hiring workers who are fellow citizens. Jobs continue being outsourced. Machines and information technology continue to replace people. Corporations, such as airlines and banks, offer their customers incentives to by-pass humans. Even outside the industrial world, but especially within it, the Internet allows an increasing number of people to buy plane tickets, print boarding passes, rent cars, reserve hotel rooms, move money, or pay bills online. Amazon as a virtual bookstore and, increasingly a department store as well, threatens to send not only "mom and pop" shops but even national chains such as Sears and Radio Shack into oblivion. Borders bit the dust in 2011. Nowadays, when one does manage to speak by phone to an actual human, that person is as likely to be in Mumbai or Manila as Minneapolis or Miami.

Companies claim, with some justification, that labor unions limit their flexibility, adaptability, and profitability in the global economy. American corporations have become more ideologically opposed to unions and more aggressive in discouraging organizing drives. Unions still bring benefits to their workers. Median weekly earnings for union members—$917 in 2010—remain higher than those of nonunion workers—$717 (Greenhouse 2011). Still, union membership in the United States has fallen to its lowest point in more than seventy years. The unionized percentage of the American workforce fell to 11.9 percent in 2010, compared with 20.1 percent in 1983, and a high of 35 percent during the mid-1950s. The number of unionized private sector workers stood at 7.1 million in 2010, versus a larger share—7.6 million workers—in the public sector (Greenhouse 2011). What jobs do you know that are unionized? How likely is it that you will join a union?

Energy Consumption and Industrial Degradation

Industrialization entailed a shift from reliance on renewable resources to the use of fossil fuels. Stored over millions of years, fossil fuel energy (oil, gas, coal, etc.) is being depleted rapidly to support a previously unknown level of consumption. The population of the United States is the world's foremost consumer of nonrenewable energy. The average American consumes about 35 times more energy than the average forager or tribesperson (Bodley 1985, 2008).

Table 16.1 compares energy consumption, per capita and total, in the United States and selected other countries. The United States represents 21.1 percent of the world's annual energy consumption, compared with China's 15.6 percent, but the average American consumes 6 times the energy used by the average Chinese and 21 times the energy used by the average inhabitant of India.

Industrialization and factory labor now characterize many societies in Latin America, Africa, the Pacific, and Asia. One effect of the spread of industrialization has been the destruction of indigenous economies, ecologies, and populations. Two centuries ago, as industrialization was developing, 50 million people still lived in politically independent

The hugely popular film *Avatar* is about what it means to be human—and not human, while still cultured in the anthropological sense. *Avatar* also raises ethical questions involving humanoid rights and proper loyalties for humans—to nature, indigenous "peoples," science, and commerce. Although set on a distant moon, far beyond the modern world system, *Avatar* portrays the familiar struggle that local cultures face in resisting and surviving powerful external forces. The movie also features a quasi-anthropologist, Dr. Grace Augustine, played by Sigourney Weaver, whose prime loyalty is to the natives she seeks to understand, as they confront commercially driven marauders in their homeland.

bands, tribes, and chiefdoms. Occupying vast areas, those nonstate societies, although not totally isolated, were only marginally affected by nation-states and the world capitalist economy. In 1800, bands, tribes, and chiefdoms controlled half the globe and 20 percent of its population (Bodley 2008). Industrialization tipped the balance in favor of states (see Hornborg and Crumley, eds. 2007).

As industrial states have conquered, annexed, and "developed" nonstates, there has been genocide on a grand scale. *Genocide* refers to a deliberate policy of exterminating a group through warfare or murder. Examples include the Holocaust, Rwanda in 1994, and Bosnia in the early 1990s. Bodley (2008) estimates that an average of 250,000 indigenous people perished annually between 1800 and 1950. Besides warfare, the causes included foreign diseases (to which natives lacked resistance), slavery, land grabbing, and other forms of dispossession and impoverishment.

Many native groups have been incorporated into nation-states, where they now live as ethnic minorities. Such groups maintain an ethnic identity, despite having lost their ancestral cultures to varying degrees (partial ethnocide). Also, many descendants of tribespeople live on as culturally distinct and self-conscious colonized peoples within contemporary nation-states. Many such groups aspire to autonomy. As the original inhabitants of their territories, they are called **indigenous peoples** (see Maybury-Lewis 2002).

TABLE 16.1

Energy Consumption in Selected Countries, 2007

Source: Based on data in *Statistical Abstract of the United States,* 2011 (Table 1381).

	Total	Per Capita
World	483.6[*]	73[†]
United States	101.6	337
China	77.8	59
Russia	30.4	215
India	19.1	17
Germany	14.2	172
Canada	13.8	418
France	11.2	176
United Kingdom	9.5	156

[*]483.6 quadrillion (483,600,000,000,000,000) Btu.
[†]73 million Btu.

Anthropology Today Mining Giant Compatible with Sustainability Institute?

The spread of industrialization, illustrated by the mining described here, has contributed to the destruction of indigenous economies, ecologies, and populations. Today, multinational conglomerates, along with nations such as Papua New Guinea as described here, are repeating—at an accelerated rate—the process of resource depletion that started in Europe and the United States during the Industrial Revolution. Fortunately, however, today's world has some environmental watchdogs, including anthropologists, that did not exist during the first centuries of the Industrial Revolution. Described here is a conundrum confronting a major university. Is a firm whose operations have destroyed the landscapes and livelihoods of indigenous peoples a proper advisor for an institute devoted to ecological sustainability?

In the 1990s, the giant mining company now known as BHP Billiton drew worldwide condemnation for the environmental damage caused by its copper and gold mine in Papua New Guinea. Its mining practices destroyed the way of life of thousands of farming and fishing families who lived along and subsisted on the rivers polluted by the mine, and it was only after being sued in a landmark class-action case that the company agreed to compensate them.

Today several activists and academics who work on behalf of indigenous people around the world say the company continues to dodge responsibility for the problems its mines create for communities in undeveloped parts of the world.

Yet at the University of Michigan at Ann Arbor, BHP Billiton enjoys a loftier reputation: It is one of 14 corporate members of an External Advisory Board for the university's new Graham Environmental Sustainability Institute.

Critics at and outside the university contend that Michigan's decision to enlist BHP Billiton as an adviser to an institute devoted to sustainability reflects badly on the institution and allows the company to claim a mantle of environmental and social responsibility that it does not deserve.

The institute's director says he is satisfied that the company is serious about operating in a more sustainable way. . . .

The arguments echo the discussions about corporate "greenwashing" that have arisen at Stanford University and the University of California at Berkeley over major research grants from ExxonMobil and BP, respectively, and more recently, the debate at the Smithsonian Institution among its trustees over whether to accept a gift from the American Petroleum Institute for a museum exhibition about oceans. (The gift was withdrawn in November.)

For one BHP Billiton critic at Michigan, the issue is personal. Stuart Kirsch, an associate professor of anthropology, has spent most of his academic career documenting the damage caused by BHP Billiton's Ok Tedi mine in Papua New Guinea. . . .

Mr. Kirsch, who first visited some of the affected communities as a young ethnographer in 1987, became involved in the class-action lawsuit brought against the company and helped villagers participate in the 1996 legal settlement. "I put my career on hold while being an activist," he says.

He subsequently published several papers related to his work with the Yonggom people as they fought for recognition and compensation from mine operators—scholarship that helped him win tenure this year—and he remains involved with the network of activists and academics who follow mining and its impact on undeveloped communities around the world. . . .

This photo of the Ok Tedi copper mine, taken February 10, 2002, shows the ecological devastation of the native landscape.

The company's practices polluted the Ok Tedi and Fly Rivers and caused thousands of people to leave their homes because the mining-induced flooding made it impossible for them to grow food to feed themselves, says Mr. Kirsch.

BHP Billiton, based in Australia, later acknowledged that the mine was "not compatible with our environmental values," and spun it off to an independent company that pays all of its mining royalties to the government of Papua New Guinea.

But Mr. Kirsch says that in doing so, the company skirted responsibility for ameliorating the damage it caused. BHP Billiton says it would have preferred to close the mine, but the Papua New Guinea government, in need of the mine revenues, pressed to keep it open. The deal freed BHP Billiton from any future liabilities for environmental damage.

"They didn't clean it up; they didn't take responsibility for the damage they had done," Mr. Kirsch says of the company. With that record, "it's supposed to provide education to the University of Michigan?". . .

Illtud Harri, a BHP Billiton spokesman, says the company regrets its past with Ok Tedi but considers its pullout from the mine "a responsible exit" that left in place a system that supports educational, agricultural, and social programs for the people of the community.

He says the company also aims for the most ethical standards in its projects. The company mines only when it can fully comply with the host country's environmental laws. In places where those regulatory requirements fall below the company's, "we will always be guided by our higher standards," he says.

continued

Anthropology Today *continued*

Mr. Talbot, the interim director of the two-year-old sustainability institute, says . . . "We intentionally selected a cross-sector group of organizations" for the advisory board from a list of about 140 nominees, . . . and several companies that "weren't making any serious efforts" toward sustainability were rejected. . . .

BHP Billiton, a company formed from the 2001 merger of the Australian mining enterprise Broken Hill Proprietary Company with London-based Billiton, is now the world's largest mining company, with more than 100 operations in 25 countries. . . .

The BHP Billiton charter includes a statement that the company has "an overriding commitment to health, safety, environmental responsibility, and sustainable development." But its critics say the company continues to play a key role in mining projects with questionable records on environmental and human rights, even though in many of those cases, it is not directly responsible. . . .

Mr. Kirsch, who is now on leave from Michigan to write a book, says he is planning to press for an open forum at the university that includes environmental scientists, indigenous people affected by the Ok Tedi mine, and company officials themselves.

BHP Billiton has the resources to present itself as the "golden boy," but, says Mr. Kirsch, "it's much harder to see the people on the Ok Tedi and Fly rivers."

A forum could help to right that imbalance, he says. "Let the students and faculty decide whether this is an appropriate company to advise the University of Michigan," says Mr. Kirsch. "It would be an educational process for everyone involved."

Source: Goldie Blumenstyk, "Mining Company Involved in Environmental Disaster Now Advises Sustainability Institute at U. of Michigan," *Chronicle of Higher Education,* December 7, 2007. Copyright © 2007, The Chronicle of Higher Education. Reprinted with permission.

Globally many contemporary nations are repeating—at an accelerated rate—the process of resource depletion that started in Europe and the United States during the Industrial Revolution. Fortunately, however, today's world has some environmental watchdogs that did not exist during the first centuries of the Industrial Revolution. Given national and international cooperation and sanctions, the modern world may benefit from the lessons of the past (see Hornborg, McNeill, and Martinez-Alier, eds. 2007 and "Anthropology Today" above).

Summary

1. Local societies increasingly participate in wider systems—regional, national, and global. The capitalist world economy depends on production for sale, with the goal of maximizing profits. The key claim of world-system theory is that an identifiable social system, based on wealth and power differentials, extends beyond individual countries. That system is formed by a set of economic and political relations that has characterized much of the globe since the 16th century. World capitalism has political and economic specialization at the core, semiperiphery, and periphery.

2. Columbus's voyages opened the way for a major exchange between the Old and New Worlds. Seventeenth-century plantation economies in the Caribbean and Brazil were based on sugar. In the 18th century, plantation economies based on cotton arose in the southeastern United States.

3. The Industrial Revolution began in England around 1760. Transoceanic commerce supplied capital for industrial investment. Industrialization hastened the separation of workers from the means of production. Marx saw a sharp division between the bourgeoisie and the proletariat. Class consciousness was a key feature of Marx's view of this stratification. Weber believed that social solidarity based on ethnicity, religion, race, or nationality could take priority over class. Today's capitalist world economy maintains the contrast between those who own the means of production and those who don't, but the division is now worldwide. There is a substantial contrast between not only capitalists but workers in the core nations and workers on the periphery.

4. Imperialism is the policy of extending the rule of a nation or empire over other nations and of taking and holding foreign colonies. Colonialism is the domination of a territory and its people by a foreign power for an extended time. European colonialism had two main phases. The first started in 1492 and lasted through 1825. For Britain this phase ended with the American Revolution. For France it ended when Britain won the Seven Years' War, forcing the French to abandon Canada and India. For Spain, it ended with Latin American independence. The second phase of European colonialism extended approximately from 1850 to 1950. The British and French empires were at their height around 1914, when European empires controlled 85 percent of the world. Britain and France had colonies in Africa, Asia, Oceania, and the New World.

5. Many geopolitical labels and identities were created under colonialism that had little or nothing to do with existing social demarcations. The new ethnic or national divisions were colonial inventions, sometimes aggravating conflicts.

6. Like colonialism, economic development has an intervention philosophy that provides a justification for outsiders to guide native peoples toward particular goals. Development usually is justified by the idea that industrialization and modernization are desirable evolutionary advances. Neoliberalism revives and extends classic economic liberalism: the idea that governments should not regulate private enterprise and that free market forces should rule. This intervention philosophy currently dominates aid agreements with postsocialist and developing nations.

7. Spelled with a lowercase c, communism describes a social system in which property is owned by the community and in which people work for the common good. Spelled with an uppercase C, Communism indicates a political movement and doctrine seeking to overthrow capitalism and to establish a form of communism such as that which prevailed in the Soviet Union from 1917 to 1991. The heyday of Communism was between 1949 and 1989. The fall of Communism can be traced to 1989–1990 in eastern Europe and 1991 in the Soviet Union. Postsocialist states have followed the neoliberal agenda, through privatization, deregulation, and democratization.

8. By 1900 the United States had become a core nation. Mass production gave rise to a culture that valued acquisitiveness and conspicuous consumption. As subsistence economies yield increasingly to cash, job seeking and unemployment have become global problems. One effect of industrialization has been an accelerated rate of resource depletion.

Key Terms

bourgeoisie, *375*
capital, *371*
capitalist world
   economy, *370*
colonialism, *378*
communism, *384*
Communism, *384*
core, *371*

imperialism, *377*
indigenous
   peoples, *387*
Industrial
   Revolution, *373*
intervention
   philosophy, *382*
neoliberalism, *383*

periphery, *371*
postcolonial, *382*
semiperiphery, *371*
working class, or
   proletariat, *375*
world-system
   theory, *371*

Go to our Online Learning Center website at **www.mhhe.com/kottak** for Internet resources directly related to the content of this chapter.

Chapter 17

Ethnicity and Race

Ethnic Groups and Ethnicity
  Shifting Status
Race and Ethnicity
The Social Construction of Race
  Hypodescent: Race in the
    United States
  Race in the Census
  Not Us: Race in Japan
  Phenotype and Fluidity: Race in Brazil
Ethnic Groups, Nations, and
  Nationalities
  Nationalities and Imagined Communities

Ethnic Tolerance and Accommodation
  Assimilation
  The Plural Society
  Multiculturalism and Ethnic Identity
  Applying Anthropology to Popular
    Culture: Diversity on TV
Roots of Ethnic Conflict
  Prejudice and Discrimination
  Chips in the Mosaic
  Aftermaths of Oppression
  Anthropology Today: From Saturday
    Night Fever *to* Jersey Shore

Ethnicity is based on cultural similarities and differences in a society or nation. The similarities are with members of the same ethnic group; the differences are between that group and others. Ethnic groups must deal with other such groups in the nation or region they inhabit, so that interethnic relations are important in the study of that nation or region. (Table 17.1 lists American ethnic groups, based on the 2010 U.S. census.)

Ethnic Groups and Ethnicity

As with any culture, members of an **ethnic group** *share* certain beliefs, values, habits, customs, and norms because of their common background. They define themselves as different and special because of cultural features. This distinction may arise from language, religion, historical experience, geographic placement, kinship, or "race" (see Spickard, ed. 2004). Markers of an ethnic group may include a collective name, belief in common descent, a sense of solidarity, and an association with a specific territory, which the group may or may not hold (Ryan 1990, pp. xiii, xiv).

According to Fredrik Barth (1969), ethnicity can be said to exist when people claim a certain ethnic identity for themselves and are defined by others as having that identity.

and the newspaper were "two forms of imagining" communities (consisting of all the people who read the same sources and thus witnessed the same events) that flowered in the 18th century (Anderson 1991, pp. 24–25).

Over time, political upheavals, wars, and migration have divided many imagined national communities that arose in the 18th and 19th centuries. The German and Korean homelands were artificially divided after wars, according to communist and capitalist ideologies. World War I split the Kurds, who remain an imagined community, forming a majority in no state. Kurds are a minority group in Turkey, Iran, Iraq, and Syria.

In creating multitribal and multiethnic states, colonialism often erected boundaries that corresponded poorly with preexisting cultural divisions. But colonial institutions also helped create new "imagined communities" beyond nations. A good example is the idea of *négritude* ("Black identity") developed by African intellectuals in Francophone (French-speaking) West Africa. Négritude can be traced to the association and common experience in colonial times of youths from Guinea, Mali, Ivory Coast, and Senegal at the William Ponty school in Dakar, Senegal (Anderson 1991, pp. 123–124).

Ethnic Tolerance and Accommodation

Ethnic diversity may be associated with positive group interaction and coexistence or with conflict (discussed shortly). There are nation-states in which multiple cultural groups live together in reasonable harmony, including some less developed countries.

Assimilation

Assimilation describes the process of change that a minority ethnic group may experience when it moves to a country where another culture dominates. By assimilating, the minority adopts the patterns and norms of its host culture. It is incorporated into the dominant culture to the point that it no longer exists as a separate cultural unit. Some countries, such as Brazil, are more assimilationist than others. Germans, Italians, Japanese, Middle Easterners, and East Europeans started migrating to Brazil late in the 19th century. These immigrants have assimilated to a common Brazilian culture, which has Portuguese, African, and Native American roots. The descendants of these immigrants speak the national language (Portuguese) and participate in the national culture. (During World War II, Brazil, which was on the Allied side, forced assimilation by banning instruction in any language other than Portuguese—especially in German.)

The Plural Society

Assimilation isn't inevitable, and there can be ethnic harmony without it. Ethnic distinctions can persist despite generations of interethnic contact. Through a study of three ethnic groups in Swat, Pakistan, Fredrik Barth (1958/1968) challenged an old idea that interaction always leads to assimilation. He showed that ethnic groups can be in contact for generations without assimilating. Barth (1958/1968, p. 324) defines **plural society** (an idea he extended from Pakistan to the Middle East) as a society combining ethnic contrasts, ecological specialization (i.e., use of different environmental resources by each ethnic group), and the economic interdependence of those groups.

In Barth's view, ethnic boundaries are most stable and enduring when the groups occupy different ecological niches. That is, they make their living in different ways and don't compete. Ideally, they should depend on each other's activities and exchange with one another. When different ethnic groups exploit the *same* ecological niche, the militarily more powerful group will normally replace the weaker one. If they exploit more or less the same niche, but the weaker group is better able to use marginal environments, they also may coexist (Barth 1958/1968, p. 331). Given niche specialization, ethnic boundaries and interdependence can be maintained, although the specific cultural features of each group may change. By shifting the analytic focus from individual cultures or ethnic groups to *relationships* between cultures or ethnic groups, Barth (1958/1968, 1969) has made important contributions to ethnic studies.

Multiculturalism and Ethnic Identity

The view of cultural diversity in a country as something good and desirable is called **multiculturalism** (see Kottak and Kozaitis 2011). The multicultural model is the opposite of the assimilationist model, in which minorities are expected to abandon their cultural traditions and values, replacing them with those of the majority population. The multicultural view encourages the practice of cultural–ethnic traditions. A multicultural society socializes individuals not only into the dominant (national) culture but also into an ethnic culture. Thus in the United States millions of people speak both English and another language, eat both "American" (apple pie, steak, hamburgers) and "ethnic" foods, and celebrate both national (July 4, Thanksgiving) and ethnic–religious holidays.

In the United States and Canada multiculturalism is of growing importance. This reflects an awareness that the number and size of ethnic groups have grown dramatically in recent years. If this trend continues, the ethnic composition of the United States will change dramatically. (See Figure 17.4.)

Even now, because of immigration and differential population growth, whites are outnumbered by minorities in many urban areas. For example, of the 8,302,659 people residing in New York City in 2009, 25 percent were black, 27 percent Hispanic, 12 percent Asian, and 36 percent other—including non-Hispanic whites. The comparable percentages for Los Angeles county in 2010 were 9 percent black, 48 percent Hispanic, 14 percent Asian, and 29 percent other, including non-Hispanic whites (U.S. Census Bureau 2010).

In October 2006, the population of the United States reached 300 million people, just 39 years after reaching 200 million and 91 years after reaching the 100 million mark (in 1915). The country's ethnic composition has changed dramatically in the past 40 years, most notably involving Hispanics. The 1970 census, the first to attempt an official count of Hispanics, found they represented no more than 4.7 percent of the American population, compared with 16.3 percent in 2010. In 1967 fewer than 10 million people in the United States (5 percent of the population) had been born elsewhere, compared with more than 38 million immigrants (over 12 percent) today (Ohlemacher 2006).

In 1973, 78 percent of the students in American public schools were white, and 22 percent were minorities: blacks, Hispanics, Asians, Pacific Islanders, and "others." By 2004, only 57 percent of public school students were white, and 43 percent were minorities. If current trends continue, minority students will outnumber (non-Hispanic) white students

FIGURE 17.4 *Ethnic Composition of the United States* The proportion of the American population that is white and non-Hispanic is declining. The projection for 2050 shown here comes from a U.S. Census Bureau report issued in March 2004. Note especially the dramatic rise in the Hispanic portion of the American population between 2010 and 2050.

Source: Based on data from U.S. Census Bureau, International Data Base, Table 094, http://www.census.gov/ipc /www.idbprint.html; Files 2005 and U. S. Census Bureau, 2010 census.

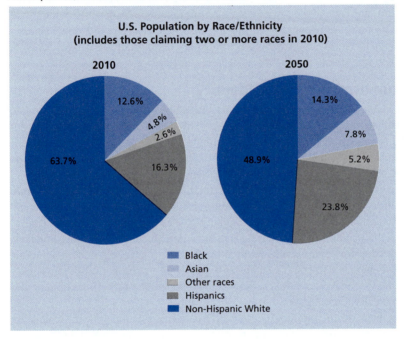

by 2015. They already do in California, Hawaii, Mississippi, New Mexico, and Texas (Dillon 2006).

Immigration, mainly from southern and eastern Europe, had a similar effect on class-room diversity, at least in the largest American cities, a century ago. A study of American public schools in 1908–09 found that only 42 percent of those urban students were na-tive-born, while 58 percent were immigrants. In a very different (multicultural now ver-sus assimilationist then) context, today's American classrooms have regained the ethnic diversity they demonstrated in the early 1900s, when this author's German-speaking Austro-Hungarian-born father and grandparents immigrated to the United States.

One response to ethnic diversification and awareness has been for many whites to reclaim ethnic identities (Italian, Albanian, Serbian, Lithuanian, etc.) and to join ethnic associations (clubs, gangs). Some such groups are new. Others have existed for de-cades, although they lost members during the assimilationist years of the 1920s through the 1950s.

Multiculturalism seeks ways for people to understand and interact that don't depend on sameness but rather on respect for differences. Multiculturalism stresses the interaction of

Despite the increasing diversity of American society, some recently popular TV shows (e.g., *Seinfeld, Sex and the City, Entourage, Curb Your Enthusiasm, Jersey Shore*) have principal characters who are ethnically homogeneous. Other programs, from *Glee,* which is fictional, to MTV's *The Real World* and CBS's *Survivor,* which are classified as "reality shows," make diversity a key part of their cast of characters. What kinds of diversity are shown on *Glee* and *The Real World*? How might you explain the presence or absence of diversity in the eight shows mentioned here?

ethnic groups and their contribution to the country. It assumes that each group has something to offer to and learn from the others. Several forces have propelled North America away from the assimilationist model toward multiculturalism. First, multiculturalism reflects the fact of recent large-scale migration, particularly from the "less developed countries" to the "developed" nations of North America and Western Europe. The global scale of modern migration introduces unparalleled ethnic variety to host nations. Multiculturalism is related to globalization: People use modern means of transportation to migrate to nations whose lifestyles they learn about through the media and from tourists who increasingly visit their own countries (see Inda and Rosaldo, eds. 2008).

Migration also is fueled by rapid population growth, coupled with insufficient jobs (both for educated and uneducated people), in the less developed countries. As traditional rural economies decline or mechanize, displaced farmers move to cities, where they and their children often are unable to find jobs. As people in the less developed countries get better educations, they seek more skilled employment. They hope to partake of an international culture of consumption that includes such modern amenities as refrigerators, televisions, and automobiles (Ahmed 2004).

In the face of globalization, much of the world, including the entire "democratic West," is experiencing an "ethnic revival." The new assertiveness of long-resident ethnic groups extends to the Basques and Catalans in Spain, the Bretons and Corsicans in France, and the Welsh and Scots in the United Kingdom. The United States and Canada are becoming increasingly multicultural, focusing on their internal diversity (see Laguerre 1999). "Melting pots" no longer, they are better described as ethnic "salads" (each ingredient remains distinct, although in the same bowl, with the same dressing).

Roots of Ethnic Conflict

Ethnicity, based on perceived cultural similarities and differences in a society or nation, can be expressed in peaceful multiculturalism or in discrimination or violent interethnic confrontation. The roots of ethnic differentiation—and therefore, potentially, of ethnic conflict—can be political, economic, religious, linguistic, cultural, or racial (see Kuper 2006). Why do ethnic differences often lead to conflict and violence? The causes include a sense of injustice because of resource distribution, economic or political competition, and reaction to discrimination, prejudice, and other expressions of devalued identity (see Friedman 2003; Ryan 1990, p. xxvii).

In Iraq, under the dictator Saddam Hussein, there was discrimination by one Muslim group (Sunnis) against others (Shiites and Kurds). Sunnis, although a numeric minority within Iraq's population, enjoyed privileged access to power, prestige, and position. After the elections of 2005, which many Sunnis chose to boycott, Shiites gained political control. A civil war developed out of "sectarian violence" (conflicts among sects of the same religion) as Sunnis (and their foreign supporters) fueled an insurgency against the new government and its foreign supporters, including the United States. Shiites retaliated against Sunni attacks and a history of Sunni privilege and perceived discrimination against Shiites, as Shiite militias engaged in ethnic (sectarian) cleansing of their own.

Prejudice and Discrimination

Ethnic conflict often arises in reaction to prejudice (attitudes and judgments) or discrimination (action). **Prejudice** means devaluing (looking down on) a group because of its assumed behavior, values, capabilities, or attributes. People are prejudiced when they hold stereotypes about groups and apply them to individuals. (**Stereotypes** are fixed ideas— often unfavorable—about what the members of a group are like.) Prejudiced people assume that members of the group will act as they are "supposed to act" (according to the stereotype) and interpret a wide range of individual behaviors as evidence of the stereotype. They use this behavior to confirm their stereotype (and low opinion) of the group.

Discrimination refers to policies and practices that harm a group and its members. Discrimination may be *de facto* (practiced, but not legally sanctioned) or *de jure* (part of the law). An example of de facto discrimination is the harsher treatment that American minorities (compared with other Americans) tend to get from the police and the judicial system. This unequal treatment isn't legal, but it happens anyway. Segregation in the southern United States and *apartheid* in South Africa provide two examples of de jure discrimination, which no longer are in existence. In both systems, by law, blacks and whites had different rights and privileges. Their social interaction ("mixing") was legally curtailed.

Chips in the Mosaic

Although the multicultural model is increasingly prominent in North America, ethnic competition and conflict also are evident. There is conflict between newer arrivals, for instance, Central Americans and Koreans, and longer-established ethnic groups, such as African Americans. Ethnic antagonism flared in South-Central Los Angeles in spring 1992 in rioting that followed the acquittal of four white police officers who were tried for the videotaped beating of Rodney King (see Abelmann and Lie 1995).

Angry blacks attacked whites, Koreans, and Latinos. This violence expressed frustration by African Americans about their prospects in an increasingly multicultural society. A *New York Times* CBS News Poll conducted just after the Los Angeles riots found that blacks had a bleaker outlook than whites about the effects of immigration on their lives. Only 23 percent of the blacks felt they had more opportunities than recent immigrants, compared with twice that many whites (Toner 1992).

Aftermaths of Oppression

Fueling ethnic conflict are such forms of discrimination as genocide, forced assimilation, ethnocide, and cultural colonialism. The most extreme form of ethnic discrimination is **genocide,** the deliberate elimination of a group (such as Jews in Nazi Germany, Muslims in Bosnia, or Tutsi in Rwanda) through mass murder. A dominant group may try to destroy the cultures of certain ethnic groups (**ethnocide**) or force them to adopt the dominant culture (*forced assimilation*). Many countries have penalized or banned the language and customs of an ethnic group (including its religious observances). One example of forced assimilation is the anti-Basque campaign that the dictator Francisco Franco (who ruled between 1939 and 1975) waged in Spain. Franco banned Basque books, journals, newspapers, signs, sermons, and tombstones and imposed fines for using the Basque language in schools (Ryan 1990). His policies led to the formation of a Basque terrorist group and spurred strong nationalist sentiment in the Basque region.

A policy of *ethnic expulsion* aims at removing groups who are culturally different from a country. There are many examples, including Bosnia-Herzegovina in the 1990s. Uganda expelled 74,000 Asians in 1972. The neofascist parties of contemporary Western Europe advocate repatriation (expulsion) of immigrant workers (West Indians in England, Algerians in France, and Turks in Germany) (see Friedman 2003; Ryan 1990, p. 9). A policy of expulsion may create **refugees**—people who have been forced (involuntary refugees) or who have chosen (voluntary refugees) to flee a country, to escape persecution or war.

In many countries, colonial nation-building left ethnic strife in its wake. Thus, over a million Hindus and Muslims were killed in the violence that accompanied the division of the Indian subcontinent into India and Pakistan. Problems between Arabs and Jews in Palestine began during the British mandate period.

Multiculturalism may be growing in the United States and Canada, but the opposite is happening in the former Soviet Union, where ethnic groups (nationalities) want their own nation-states. The flowering of ethnic feeling and conflict as the Soviet empire disintegrated illustrates that years of political repression and ideology provide insufficient common ground for lasting unity. **Cultural colonialism** refers to internal domination—by one group and its culture or ideology over others. One example is the domination over the former Soviet empire by Russian people, language, and culture, and by communist ideology. The dominant culture makes itself the official culture. This is reflected in schools, the media, and public interaction. Under Soviet rule ethnic minorities had very limited self-rule in republics and regions controlled by Moscow. All the republics and their peoples were to be united by the oneness of "socialist internationalism." One common technique in cultural colonialism is to flood ethnic areas with members of the dominant ethnic group. Thus, in the former Soviet Union, ethnic Russian colonists were sent to many areas, to diminish the cohesion and clout of the local people.

The Commonwealth of Independent States (CIS), founded in 1991 and headquartered in Minsk, Belarus, is what remains of the once-powerful Soviet Union (see Yurchak 2005). In Russia and other formerly Soviet nations, ethnic groups (nationalities) have sought, and continue to seek, to forge separate and viable nation-states based on cultural boundaries. This celebration of ethnic autonomy is part of an ethnic florescence that—as surely as globalization and transnationalism—is a trend of the late 20th and early 21st centuries.

Anthropology Today *continued*

and redefine it their own way. Young African-Americans did that with the "n word," he added, much to the consternation of their elders, and gay people did the same by proudly using the word "queer.". . .

As for "Jersey Shore," what Ms. Savino—and pretty much everyone else who spoke—objected to is the way the subculture has "been exploited by MTV." . . . Joseph Sciame, the president of the Italian Heritage & Culture Committee, said the problem was that no matter how many other positive depictions of Italian-Americans there are, "one showing of a program like 'Jersey Shore,' and that's what people think all Italian-Americans are like." . . . As another speaker said, "We have a responsibility to make sure people know that's not us."

Mr. DeCarlo, who turns 29 this year, auditioned for "Jersey Shore" and made it to the final tryouts. He wore a black leather jacket, large gold cross around his neck and a pinky ring. His hair was spiked with gel. As the audition process went along, he said it became clear that MTV was more interested in "shocking reality TV mayhem instead of a family culture.". . .

To Mr. DeCarlo, Guido refers to a culture of family, food, wine, cigars, coffee, gold chains, Cadillacs and a dialect that gives "fuhgeddaboudit" some panache. Neither his style nor his fondness for clubbing means that "I'm looking for a fight," he said.

"A true Guido is someone with dreams, aspirations and goals," he said. Tony Manero "was very flawed, but you rooted for him because you knew he wanted to do something with his life.". . .

Source: Patricia Cohen, "Discussing That Word That Prompts Either a Fist Pump or a Scowl," *New York Times,* January 23, 2010. http://www.nytimes.com/2010/01/23/arts/television/23shore.html?_r=1&sq=&st=cse&%2334;=&%2334;Discussing%20that%20word%20that%20prompts=&scp=1&pagewanted=print.

Summary

1. An ethnic group refers to members of a particular culture in a nation or region that contains others. Ethnicity is based on actual, perceived, or assumed cultural similarities (among members of the same ethnic group) and differences (between that group and others). Ethnic distinctions can be based on language, religion, history, geography, kinship, or race. A race is an ethnic group assumed to have a biological basis. Usually race and ethnicity are ascribed statuses; people are born members of a group and remain so all their lives.

2. Human races are cultural rather than biological categories. Such races derive from contrasts perceived in particular societies, rather than from scientific classifications based on common genes. In the United States, racial labels such as "white" and "black" designate socially constructed categories defined by American culture. American racial classification, governed by the rule of hypodescent, is based neither on phenotype nor on genes. Children of mixed unions, no matter what their appearance, are classified with the minority group parent.

3. Racial attitudes in Japan illustrate intrinsic racism—the belief that a perceived racial difference is a sufficient reason to value one person less than another. The

valued group is majority (pure) Japanese, who are believed to share the same blood. Majority Japanese define themselves by opposition to others, such as Koreans and burakumin. These may be minority groups in Japan or outsiders—anyone who is "not us."

4. Such exclusionary racial systems are not inevitable. Although Brazil shares a history of slavery with the United States, it lacks the hypodescent rule. Brazilian racial identity is more of an achieved status. It can change during someone's lifetime, reflecting phenotypical changes.

5. The term *nation* once was synonymous with *ethnic group*. Now nation has come to mean a state—a centrally organized political unit. Because of migration, conquest, and colonialism, most nation-states are not ethnically homogeneous. Ethnic groups that seek autonomous political status (their own country) are nationalities. Political upheavals, wars, and migrations have divided many imagined national communities.

6. Assimilation describes the process of change an ethnic group may experience when it moves to a country where another culture dominates. By assimilating, the minority adopts the patterns and norms of its host culture. Assimilation isn't inevitable, and there can be ethnic harmony without it. A plural society combines ethnic contrasts and economic interdependence between ethnic groups. The view of cultural diversity in a nation-state as good and desirable is multiculturalism. A multicultural society socializes individuals not only into the dominant (national) culture but also into an ethnic one.

7. Ethnicity can be expressed in peaceful multiculturalism, or in discrimination or violent confrontation. Ethnic conflict often arises in reaction to prejudice (attitudes and judgments) or discrimination (action). The most extreme form of ethnic discrimination is genocide, the deliberate elimination of a group through mass murder. A dominant group may try to destroy certain ethnic practices (ethnocide), or to force ethnic group members to adopt the dominant culture (forced assimilation). A policy of ethnic expulsion may create refugees. Cultural colonialism refers to internal domination—by one group and its culture or ideology over others.

Key Terms

assimilation, *406*
cultural colonialism, *411*
descent, *398*
discrimination, *410*
ethnic group, *393*
ethnicity, *394*
ethnocide, *411*
genocide, *411*

hypodescent, *398*
majority groups, *396*
minority groups, *395*
multiculturalism, *407*
nation, *404*
nation-state, *404*

nationalities, *405*
plural society, *406*
prejudice, *410*
race, *396*
racism, *396*
refugees, *411*
stereotypes, *410*

Go to our Online Learning Center website at **www.mhhe.com/kottak** for Internet resources directly related to the content of this chapter.

Chapter  18

Applying Anthropology

The Role of the Applied Anthropologist
  Early Applications
  Academic and Applied Anthropology
  Applied Anthropology Today
Development Anthropology
  Equity
Strategies for Innovation
  Overinnovation
  *Applying Anthropology to Popular
    Culture: Coca-Cola*

Underdifferentiation
Indigenous Models
Anthropology and Education
Urban Anthropology
  Urban versus Rural
Medical Anthropology
Anthropology and Business
Careers and Anthropology
  *Anthropology Today:
    Culturally Appropriate Marketing*

As we learned in Chapter 1, applied anthropology is the use of anthropological data, perspectives, theory, and methods to identify, assess, and solve contemporary problems (see Ervin 2005). Applied anthropologists help make anthropology relevant and useful to the world beyond anthropology. Medical anthropologists, for example, have worked as cultural interpreters in public health programs, helping such programs fit into local culture. Development anthropologists work for or with international development agencies, such as the World Bank and the U.S. Agency for International Development (USAID). The findings of garbology, the archaeological study of waste, are relevant to the Environmental Protection Agency, the paper industry, and packaging and trade associations. Archaeology also is applied in cultural resource management and historic preservation. Biological anthropologists apply their expertise in programs aimed at public health, nutrition, genetic counseling, aging, substance abuse, and mental health. Forensic anthropologists work with the police, medical examiners, the courts, and international organizations to identify victims of crimes, accidents, wars, and terrorism. Linguistic anthropologists study physician–patient communication and show how dialect differences influence classroom learning. Most applied anthropologists seek humane and effective ways of helping local people.

The ethnographic method is a particularly valuable tool in applying anthropology. Remember that ethnographers study societies firsthand, living with, observing, and learning from ordinary people. Nonanthropologists working in social-change programs often are content to converse with officials, read reports, and copy statistics. However, the applied anthropologist's likely early request is some variant of "take me to the local people." Anthropologists know that people must play an active role in the changes that affect them and that "the people" have information that "the experts" lack.

Anthropological *theory,* the body of findings and generalizations of the four sub-fields, also guides applied anthropology. Just as theory aids practice, application fuels theory (see Rylko-Bauer, Singer, and Van Willigen 2006). As we compare social-change programs, our understanding of cause and effect increases. We add new generalizations about culture change to those discovered in traditional and ancient cultures.

The Role of the Applied Anthropologist

Early Applications

Application was a central concern of early anthropology in Great Britain (in the context of colonialism) and the United States (in the context of Native American policy). Before turning to the new, we should consider some deficiencies and dangers of the old. For the British empire, specifically its African colonies, Bronislaw Malinowski (1929) proposed that "practical anthropology" (his term for colonial applied anthropology) should focus on Westernization, the diffusion of European culture into tribal societies. Malinowski questioned neither the legitimacy of colonialism nor the anthropologist's role in making it work. He saw nothing wrong with aiding colonial regimes by studying land tenure and land use, to recommend how much of their land local people should be allowed to keep and how much Europeans should be permitted to take. Malinowski's views exemplify a historical association between early anthropology, particularly in Europe (especially England, France, and Portugal), and colonialism (see also Duffield and Hewitt, eds. 2009; Lange 2009; Maquet 1964; Rylko-Bauer, Singer, and Van Willigen 2006).

During World War II, American anthropologists studied Japanese and German "culture at a distance" in an attempt to predict the behavior of the enemies of the United States. After that war, applied anthropologists worked on Pacific islands to promote local-level cooperation with American policies in various trust territories. The American Anthropological Association (AAA) has raised strong ethical objections to applying anthropology in war zones and for military intelligence. Such concerns were voiced during the Vietnam War. More recently they have emerged in criticisms of anthropologists' participation in the Human Terrains System (HTS) project in Iraq and Afghanistan, as discussed in Chapter 3. Anthropological research should not be applied to the potential detriment of the people anthropologists study.

Academic and Applied Anthropology

After World War II, the baby boom, which began in 1946 and peaked in 1957, fueled a tremendous expansion of the American educational system. New junior, community, and four-year colleges opened, and anthropology became a standard part of the college curriculum. During the 1950s and 1960s, most American anthropologists were college professors, although some still worked in agencies and museums.

The growth of academic anthropology continued through the early 1970s. Especially during the Vietnam War, undergraduates flocked to anthropology classes to learn about other cultures. Students were especially interested in Southeast Asia, whose indigenous societies were being disrupted by war. Many anthropologists protested the superpowers' apparent disregard for non-Western lives, values, customs, and social systems.

Most anthropologists still worked in colleges and museums during the 1970s and 1980s. However, an increasing number of anthropologists were employed by international organizations, governments, businesses, hospitals, and schools. The AAA estimates that nowadays more than half of anthropology PhDs seek nonacademic employment. This shift toward application has benefited the profession. It has forced anthropologists to consider the wider social value and implications of their research.

Applied Anthropology Today

Most contemporary applied anthropologists see their work as radically removed from the colonial enterprise. Modern applied anthropology usually is seen as a helping profession, devoted to assisting local people, as anthropologists speak up for the disenfranchised. However, applied anthropologists also have clients that are neither poor nor powerless. An applied anthropologist working as a market researcher for a business is concerned with discovering how to expand profits for his or her employer or client. Such goals can pose ethical dilemmas, as can work in cultural resource management (CRM). The CRM anthropologist helps decide how to preserve significant remains when sites are threatened by development or public works. A CRM firm typically is hired by someone seeking to build a road or a factory. That client may have a strong interest in an outcome in which no sites are found that need protecting. Even if they don't work for colonial powers or the military, applied anthropologists still face ethical questions: To whom does the researcher owe loyalty? What problems are involved in holding firm to the truth? What happens when applied anthropologists don't make the policies they are required to implement? How does one criticize programs in which one has participated (see Escobar 1991, 1994)? Anthropology's professional organizations have addressed such questions by establishing codes of ethics and ethics committees. As Karen Tice (1997) notes, attention to ethical issues has become paramount in the teaching of applied anthropology today.

Anthropologists are experts on human problems and social change who study, understand, and respect diverse cultural values. Given this background, anthropologists are highly qualified to suggest, plan, and implement social policy affecting people. Proper roles for applied anthropologists include (1) identifying needs for change that local people perceive, (2) working with those people to design culturally appropriate and socially sensitive change, and (3) protecting local people from harmful policies and projects that may threaten them.

Development Anthropology

Development anthropology is the branch of applied anthropology that focuses on social issues in, and the cultural dimension of, economic development. Development anthropologists don't just carry out development policies planned by others; they also plan and guide policy. (For more detailed discussions of issues in development anthropology, see Edelman and Haugerud 2005; Escobar 1995; Ferguson 1995; Nolan 2002.)

Still, ethical dilemmas often confront development anthropologists (Escobar 1991, 1995). Foreign aid, including funds for economic development, usually doesn't go where need and suffering are greatest. Rather, such funds are spent on political, economic, and strategic priorities as international donors, political leaders, and powerful interest groups perceive them. Planners' interests don't always coincide with the best interests of the local people. Although the stated aim of most development projects is to enhance the quality of life, living standards often decline in the affected area (Bodley, ed. 1988).

Equity

A commonly stated goal of recent development policy is to promote equity. **Increased equity** means reduced poverty and a more even distribution of wealth. However, if projects are to increase equity, they must have the support of reform-minded governments. Wealthy and powerful people typically resist projects that threaten their vested interests.

Some development projects actually widen wealth disparities; that is, they have a negative equity impact. An initial uneven distribution of resources often becomes the basis for even greater socioeconomic inequality after the project. In Bahia, Brazil (Kottak 2006), for example, sailboat owners (but not nonowners) got loans to buy motors for their boats. To repay the loans, the owners increased the percentage of the catch they took from the men who fished in their boats. Over the years, they used their rising profits to buy larger and more expensive boats. The result was stratification—the creation of a group of wealthy people within a formerly more egalitarian community. These events hampered individual initiative and interfered with further development of the fishing industry. New boats became so expensive that ambitious young men, who once would have sought careers in fishing, no longer could afford to buy a boat of their own. They sought wage labor on land instead. To avoid such results, credit-granting agencies must seek out and invest in enterprising young fishers, rather than giving loans only to owners and established businesspeople.

Strategies for Innovation

Development anthropologists should work closely with local people to assess, and help them realize, their own wishes and needs for change. Funding development projects in area A that are inappropriate there but needed in area B, or that are unnecessary anywhere, is a waste of money when so many true local needs cry out for a solution. Development anthropology can help sort out the needs of the As and Bs and fit projects accordingly. Projects that put people first by consulting with them and responding to their expressed needs must be identified (Cernea, ed. 1991). Thereafter, development anthropologists can work to ensure socially compatible ways of implementing a good project.

In a comparative study of 68 rural development projects from around the world, I found the culturally compatible economic development projects to be twice as successful financially as the incompatible ones (Kottak 1990*b*, 1991). This finding suggests that

To maximize benefits, development projects should respond to locally perceived needs. Shown here (foreground) is the president of a Nicaraguan cooperative that makes and markets hammocks. This cooperative has been assisted by an NGO whose goals include increasing the benefits that women derive from economic development. What's an NGO?

using anthropological expertise in planning, to ensure cultural compatibility, is cost effective. To maximize social and economic benefits, projects must (1) be culturally compatible, (2) respond to locally perceived needs, (3) involve men and women in planning and carrying out the changes that affect them, (4) harness traditional organizations, and (5) be flexible.

Overinnovation

In my comparative study, the compatible and successful projects avoided the fallacy of **overinnovation** (too much change). People usually are willing to change just enough to maintain, or slightly improve on, what they already have. Motives for modifying behavior come from the traditional culture and the small concerns of ordinary life. Peasants' values are not such abstract ones as "learning a better way," "progressing," "increasing technical know-how," "improving efficiency," or "adopting modern techniques." (Those phrases exemplify intervention philosophy.)

Instead, their objectives are down-to-earth and specific. People want to guarantee the productivity of their crops, amass resources for a ceremony, get a child through school, or have enough cash to pay the tax bill. The goals and values of subsistence producers differ from those of people who work for cash, just as they differ from the intervention philosophy of development planners. Different value systems must be considered during planning.

Development projects that fail usually are either (or both) economically and culturally incompatible. For example, one South Asian project promoted the cultivation of onions and peppers, expecting this practice to fit into a preexisting labor-intensive system of rice-growing. Cultivation of these cash crops wasn't traditional in the area. It conflicted with existing crop priorities and other interests of farmers. Also, the labor peaks for pepper and onion production coincided with those for rice, to which the farmers gave priority.

Another naive and incompatible project was an overinnovative scheme in Ethiopia. Its major fallacy was to try to convert free-ranging nomadic herders into farm workers. Outsiders—commercial farmers—were to get much of the herders' territory, to convert to commercial farmland—plantations. The pastoralists were expected to settle down and start working on those plantations. The planners naively expected the herders to give up a generations-old way of life to work three times harder growing rice and picking cotton for bosses.

Underdifferentiation

The fallacy of **underdifferentiation** is planners' tendency to view "the less-developed countries" as more alike than they are. Often development agencies have ignored huge cultural contrasts (e.g., between Brazil and Burundi) and adopted a uniform approach to deal with very different sets of people. Planners also have tried to impose incompatible property concepts and social units. Most often, the faulty social design assumes either (1) individualistic productive units that are privately owned by an individual or couple and worked by a nuclear family or (2) cooperatives that are at least partially based on models from the former Eastern bloc and Socialist countries.

One example of using an inappropriate First World model (the individual and the nuclear family) was a West African project designed for an area where the extended family was the basic social unit. The project succeeded despite its faulty social design because the participants used their traditional extended family networks to attract additional settlers. Eventually, twice as many people as planned benefited as extended family members flocked to the project area. Here, settlers used the principles of their traditional society to modify the project design that had been imposed on them.

The second dubious foreign social model that is common in development planning is the cooperative. In the comparative study of rural development projects, new cooperatives fared badly. Cooperatives succeeded only when they harnessed preexisting local-level communal institutions. This is a corollary of a more general rule: *Participants' groups are most effective when they are based on traditional social organization or on a socioeconomic similarity among members.*

An alternative to such foreign models is needed: greater use of indigenous social models in economic development. These are traditional social units, such as the clans, lineages, and other extended kin groups of Africa, Oceania, and many other nations, with their communally held estates and resources. *The most humane and productive strategy for change is to base the social design for innovation on traditional social forms in each target area.*

Indigenous Models

Many governments are not genuinely, or realistically, committed to improving the lives of their citizens. Interference by major powers also has kept governments from enacting needed reforms. Occasionally, however, a government does act as an agent of and for its people. One historic example is Madagascar, whose people, the Malagasy, were organized into descent groups prior to indigenous state formation in the 18th century. The Merina, creators of the major precolonial state of Madagascar, wove descent groups into its structure, making members of important groups advisers to the king and thus giving them authority in government. The Merina state made provisions for the people it ruled. It collected taxes and organized labor for public works projects. In return, it redistributed resources to peasants in need. It also granted them some protection against war and slave raids and allowed them to cultivate their rice fields in peace. The government maintained the water works for rice cultivation. It opened to ambitious peasant boys the chance of becoming, through hard work and study, state bureaucrats.

Throughout the history of the Merina state—and continuing to some extent in postcolonial Madagascar—there have been strong relationships between the individual, the descent group, and the state. Local Malagasy communities, where residence is based on descent, are more cohesive and homogeneous than are communities in Latin America or North America. Madagascar gained political independence from France in 1960. Its new government had an economic development policy aimed at increasing the ability of the Malagasy to feed themselves. Government policy emphasized increased production of rice, a subsistence crop, rather than cash crops. Furthermore, local communities, with their traditional cooperative patterns and solidarity based on kinship and descent, were treated as partners in, not obstacles to, the development process.

In a sense, the descent group is preadapted to equitable national development. In Madagascar, descent groups pooled their resources to educate their most ambitious members. Once educated, these men and women gained economically secure positions in the nation. They then shared the advantages of their new positions with their kin. For example, they gave room and board to rural cousins attending school and helped them find jobs.

This Madagascar example suggests that when government officials are of "the people" (rather than the elites) and have strong personal ties to common folk, they are more likely to promote democratic economic development. In Latin America, by contrast, leaders and followers too often have been from different socioeconomic strata, with no connections based on kinship, descent, marriage, or common background. When elites rule, elites usually prosper. Recently, however, Latin America has elected some nonelite leaders. Brazil's lower class (indeed the entire nation) benefited socioeconomically when one of its own was elected president. Luis Inácio da Silva, aka Lula, a former factory worker with only a fourth-grade education, served two terms (ending in 2011) as one of the Western Hemisphere's most popular leaders.

Realistic development policies promote change but not overinnovation. Many changes are possible if the aim is to preserve things while making them work better. Successful economic development projects respect, or at least don't attack, local cultural patterns. Effective development draws on indigenous cultural practices and social structures. As nations become more tied to the world capitalist economy, it is not inevitable that indigenous forms of social organization will break down into nuclear family organization, impersonality, and alienation. Descent groups, with their traditional communalism and solidarity, have important roles to play in economic development.

Anthropology and Education

Attention to culture also is fundamental to **anthropology and education,** a field whose research extends from classrooms into homes, neighborhoods, and communities (see Levinson and Pollock, eds. 2011; Spindler 2000; Spindler and Hammond, eds. 2006). In classrooms, anthropologists have observed interactions among teachers, students,

Afghan girls attend a lesson at the secondary school in Sarkani village, Kunar Province, eastern Afghanistan. What do you see here that differs from classrooms in your country?

parents, and visitors. Jules Henry's classic account of the American elementary school classroom (1955) shows how students learn to conform to and compete with their peers. Anthropologists view children as total cultural creatures whose enculturation and attitudes toward education belong to a context that includes family and peers.

Sociolinguists and cultural anthropologists have worked side by side in education research. In one classic study of Puerto Rican seventh-graders in the urban Midwest (Hill-Burnett 1978), anthropologists uncovered some key misconceptions held by teachers. The teachers mistakenly had assumed that Puerto Rican parents valued education less than did non-Hispanics, but in-depth interviews revealed that the Puerto Rican parents valued it more. The anthropologists also identified certain practices that were preventing Hispanics from being adequately educated. For example, the teachers' union and the board of education had agreed to teach "English as a foreign language." However, they had provided no bilingual teachers to work with Spanish-speaking students. The school was assigning all students (including non-Hispanics) with low reading scores and behavior problems to the English-as-a-foreign-language classroom. This educational disaster brought together in the classroom a teacher who spoke no Spanish, children who barely spoke English, and a group of English-speaking students with reading and behavior problems. The Spanish speakers were falling behind not just in reading but in all subjects. They could at least have kept up in the other subjects if a Spanish speaker had been teaching them science, social studies, and math until they were ready for English-language instruction in those areas.

Urban Anthropology

For centuries, cities have been influenced by global forces, including world capitalism and colonialism (Smart and Smart 2003). However, the roles of cities in the world system have changed recently because of the time–space compression made possible by modern transportation and communication systems. That is, everything appears closer today because contact and movement are so much easier.

In the context of globalization, the mass media have joined local factors in guiding people's routines, dreams, and aspirations. Although people live in particular places, their imaginations are not locally confined (Appadurai 1996). Media-transmitted images and information help draw people to cities. People migrate partly for economic reasons, but also to be where the action is. Rural Brazilians routinely cite *movimento*, urban activity and excitement, as something to be valued. International migrants tend to settle in large cities, where a lot is going on, and where they can feel at home in ethnic enclaves. Consider Canada, which, after Australia, is the country with the highest percentage of foreign-born population: 71 percent of immigrants to Canada settle in Toronto, Vancouver, or Montreal. Nearly half of Toronto's citizens were born outside Canada (Smart and Smart 2003).

Urban living has increased steadily since the Industrial Revolution. The percentage of the world's population living in cities surpassed 50 percent for the first time in 2008 and is projected to rise to 70 percent by 2050 (Handwerk 2008). Only about 3 percent of people were city dwellers in 1800, compared with 13 percent in 1900, over 40 percent

One-sixth of the Earth's population lives in urban slums. Roçinha (shown here) is a populous shantytown city within the city of Rio de Janeiro, Brazil. How might anthropologists study slums?

in 1980, and over 50 percent today (see Handwerk 2008; Smart and Smart 2003). The More Developed Countries (MDCs) were 76 percent urbanized in 1999, compared with 39 percent for the Less Developed Countries (LDCs). However, the urbanization growth rate is much faster in the LDCs (Smart and Smart 2003). In Africa and Asia alone, a million people a week migrate to cities (Handwerk 2008). The world had only 16 cities with more than a million people in 1900, versus 314 such cities in 2005 (Butler 2005; Stevens 1992).

One billion people now live in urban slums, mostly without reliable water, sanitation, and public services (Handwerk 2008; Vidal 2003). If current trends continue, urban population increase and the concentration of people in slums will be accompanied by rising rates of crime, along with water, air, and noise pollution. These problems will be most severe in the LDCs.

As industrialization and urbanization spread globally, anthropologists increasingly study these processes and the social problems they create. **Urban anthropology,** which has theoretical (basic research) and applied dimensions, is the cross-cultural and ethnographic study of urbanization and life in cities (see Gmelch and Zenner, eds. 2002; Smart and Smart 2003; Stevenson 2003). The United States and Canada have become popular arenas for urban anthropological research on topics such as immigration, ethnicity, poverty, class, and urban violence (Vigil 2003, 2010).

Urban versus Rural

An early student of urbanization, the anthropologist Robert Redfield contrasted rural communities, whose social relations are on a face-to-face basis, with cities, where impersonality reigns. Redfield (1941) proposed that urbanization be studied along a rural–urban continuum. He described differences in values and social relations in four sites that spanned such a continuum. In Mexico's Yucatán peninsula, Redfield compared an isolated Maya-speaking Indian community, a rural peasant village, a small provincial city, and a large capital. Several studies in Africa (Little 1971) and Asia were influenced by Redfield's view that cities are centers through which cultural innovations spread to rural and tribal areas.

In any nation, urban and rural represent different social systems. However, cultural diffusion or borrowing occurs as people, products, images, and messages move from one to the other. Migrants bring rural practices and beliefs to cities and take urban patterns back home. The experiences and social forms of the rural area affect adaptation to city life. City folk also develop new institutions to meet specific urban needs (Mitchell 1966).

An applied anthropology approach to urban planning starts by identifying key social groups in specific urban contexts—avoiding the fallacy of underdifferentiation. After identifying those groups, the anthropologist might elicit their wishes for change, convey those needs to funding agencies, and work with agencies and local people to realize those goals. In Africa relevant groups might include ethnic associations, occupational groups, social clubs, religious groups, and burial societies. Through membership in such groups, urban Africans maintain wide networks of personal contacts and support. The groups provide cash support and urban lodging for their rural relatives. Sometimes such groups think of themselves as a gigantic kin group, a clan that includes urban and rural members. Members may call one another "brother" and "sister." As in an extended family, richer members help their poorer relatives. A member's improper behavior, however, can lead to expulsion—an unhappy fate for a migrant in a large, ethnically heterogeneous city.

One role for the urban applied anthropologist is to help people deal with urban institutions, such as legal and social services, with which recent migrants may be unfamiliar. In certain North American cities, as in Africa, ethnic associations are relevant urban groups. One example comes from Los Angeles, which has the largest Samoan immigrant community in the United States (over 50,000 people). Samoans in Los Angeles draw on their traditional system of *matai* (*matai* means "chief"; the matai system now refers to respect for elders) to deal with modern urban problems. One example: A white police officer once shot and killed two unarmed Samoan brothers. When a judge dismissed charges against the officer, local leaders used the matai system to calm angry youths (who have formed gangs, like other ethnic groups in the Los Angeles area). Clan leaders and elders organized a well-attended community meeting, in which they urged young members to be patient. The Samoans then used the American judicial system. They brought a civil case against the officer in question and pressed the U.S. Justice Department to initiate a civil rights case in the matter (Mydans 1992*b*). Not all conflicts involving gangs and law enforcement end so peacefully.

James Vigil (2003, 2010) examines gang violence in the context of large-scale immigrant adaptation to American cities. He notes that before the 1970s most gangs were located in white ethnic enclaves in eastern and midwestern cities. Back then, gang incidents typically were brawls involving fists, sticks, and knives. Today, gangs more often are composed of nonwhite ethnic groups, and handguns have replaced less lethal weapons. Gangs still consist mostly of male adolescents who have grown up together, usually in a low-income neighborhood, where it's estimated that about 10 percent of young men join gangs. Female gang members are much rarer. With gangs organized hierarchically by age, older members push younger ones (usually 14- to 18-year-olds) to carry out violent acts against rivals (Vigil 2003, 2010).

The populations that include most of today's gang members settled originally in poor urban areas. On the East Coast these usually were run-down neighborhoods where a criminal lifestyle already was present. Around Los Angeles, urban migrants created squatterlike settlements in previously empty spaces. Immigrants tend to reside in neighborhoods apart from middle-class people, thus limiting their opportunities for integration (Vigil 2003). In addition, many industries and jobs have moved from American cities to distant suburbs and foreign nations. Given their limited access to entry-level jobs, many urban minority youth pursue informal and illegal economic arrangements, of which drug trafficking in particular has heightened gang violence (Singer 2008; Vigil 2003, 2010). How might an applied anthropologist approach the problem of urban violence? Which groups would have to be involved in the study (see Vigil 2010)?

Medical Anthropology

Medical anthropology is both academic and applied and includes anthropologists from all four subfields (see Anderson 1996; Briggs 2005; Brown and Barrett 2010: Dressler, Oths, and Gravlee 2005; Joralemon 2010; Singer and Baer 2007; Trevathan, Smith, and McKenna, eds. 2008). Medical anthropologists examine such questions as which diseases and health conditions affect particular populations (and why) and how illness is socially constructed, diagnosed, managed, and treated in various societies.

Disease refers to a scientifically identified health threat caused genetically or by a bacterium, virus, fungus, parasite, or other pathogen. **Illness** is a condition of poor health perceived or felt by an individual (Inhorn and Brown 1990). Perceptions of good and bad health are culturally constructed. Various cultures and ethnic groups recognize different illnesses, symptoms, and causes and have developed different health care systems and treatment strategies.

The incidence and severity of *disease* vary as well (see Barnes 2005; Baer, Singer, and Susser 2003). Group differences are evident in the United States. Keppel, Pearch, and Wagener (2002) examined data between 1990 and 1998 using 10 health status indicators in relation to categories used in the U.S. census: non-Hispanic white, non-Hispanic black, Hispanic, American Indian or Alaska Native, and Asian or Pacific Islander. Black Americans' rates for six measures (total mortality, heart disease, lung cancer, breast cancer, stroke, and homicide) exceeded those of other groups by a factor ranging from 2.5 to almost 10. Other ethnic groups had higher rates for suicide (white Americans) and motor vehicle accidents (American Indians and Alaskan Natives). Overall, Asians had the longest life spans (see Dressler et al. 2005).

Hurtado and colleagues (2005) note the unusually high rates of early mortality among South America's indigenous populations, whose life expectancy at birth is at least 20 years shorter than that of other South Americans. The life expectancy of indigenous peoples in Brazil and Venezuela was lower than that in Sierra Leone, which had the world's lowest reported national life expectancy (Hurtado et al. 2005). What can applied anthropologists do to help improve health conditions among indigenous peoples? Hurtado and colleagues (2005) suggest three steps: (1) Identify the most pressing health problems that indigenous communities face; (2) gather information on solutions to those problems; and (3) implement solutions in partnership with the agencies that are in charge of public health programs for indigenous populations.

In many areas, the world system and colonialism worsened the health of indigenous peoples by spreading diseases, warfare, servitude, and other stressors. Traditionally and in ancient times, hunter-gatherers, because of their small numbers, mobility, and relative isolation from other groups, lacked most of the epidemic infectious diseases that affect agrarian and urban societies (Cohen and Armelagos, eds. 1984; Inhorn and Brown 1990). Epidemic diseases such as cholera, typhoid, and bubonic plague thrive in dense populations, and thus among farmers and city dwellers. The spread of malaria has been linked to population growth and deforestation associated with food production.

Certain diseases, and physical conditions such as obesity, have spread with economic development and globalization (Ulijaszek and Lofink 2006). Schistosomiasis or bilharzia (liver flukes) is probably the fastest-spreading and most dangerous parasitic infection now known. It is propagated by snails that live in ponds, lakes, and waterways, usually ones created by irrigation projects. The applied anthropology approach to reducing such diseases is to see if local people perceive a connection between the vector (e.g., snails in the water) and the disease. If not, such information may be provided by enlisting active local groups, schools, and the media.

The highest global rates of HIV infection and AIDS-related deaths are in Africa, especially southern Africa. As it kills productive adults, AIDS leaves behind dependent children and seniors (Baro and Deubel 2006). In southern and eastern Africa, AIDS and other sexually transmitted diseases (STDs) have spread along highways, via encounters between truckers and prostitutes. STDs also are spread through prostitution as young men from rural areas seek wage work in cities, labor camps, and mines. When the men return home, they infect their wives (Larson 1989; Miller and Rockwell, eds. 1988). Cities also are prime sites of STD transmission in Europe, Asia, and North and South America (see Baer et al. 2003; French 2002). Cultural factors also affect the spread of HIV, which is less likely to be transmitted when men are circumcised.

The kinds of and incidence of disease vary among societies, and cultures perceive and treat illness differently. Health standards are cultural constructions that vary in time and space (Martin 1992). Still, all societies have what George Foster and Barbara Anderson call "disease-theory systems" to identify, classify, and explain illness. Foster and Anderson (1978) identified three basic theories about the causes of illness: personalistic, naturalistic, and emotionalistic. *Personalistic* disease theories blame illness on agents, such as sorcerers, witches, ghosts, or ancestral spirits.

Naturalistic disease theories explain illness in impersonal terms. One example is Western medicine or biomedicine, which aims to link illness to scientifically demonstrated agents that bear no personal malice toward their victims. Thus Western medicine attributes illness to organisms (e.g., bacteria, viruses, fungi, or parasites), accidents, toxic materials, or genes. Other naturalistic systems blame poor health on unbalanced body fluids. Many Latin cultures classify food, drink, and environmental conditions as "hot" or "cold." People believe their health suffers when they eat or drink hot or cold substances together or under inappropriate conditions. For example, one shouldn't drink something cold after a hot bath or eat a pineapple (a "cold" fruit) when one is menstruating (a "hot" condition).

Emotionalistic disease theories assume that emotional experiences cause illness. For example, Latin Americans may develop *susto,* an illness caused by anxiety or fright (Bolton 1981; Finkler 1985). Its symptoms (lethargy, vagueness, distraction) are similar to those of "soul loss," a diagnosis of similar symptoms made by people in Madagascar. Modern psychoanalysis also focuses on the role of the emotions in physical and psychological well-being.

All societies have **health care systems** consisting of beliefs, customs, specialists, and techniques aimed at ensuring health and diagnosing and curing illness. A society's illness-causation theory is important for treatment. When illness has a personalistic cause, magicoreligious specialists may be good curers. They draw on varied techniques (occult and practical) that are part of their special expertise. A shaman may cure soul loss by enticing the spirit back into the body. Shamans may ease difficult childbirths by asking spirits to travel up the birth canal to guide the baby out (Lévi-Strauss 1967). A shaman may cure a cough by counteracting a curse or removing a substance introduced by a sorcerer.

If there is a "world's oldest profession" besides hunter and gatherer, it is curer, often a shaman. The curer's role has some universal features (Foster and Anderson 1978). Thus a **curer** emerges through a culturally defined process of selection (parental prodding, inheritance of the role, visions, dream instructions) and training (apprentice shamanship, medical school). Eventually, the curer is certified by older practitioners and acquires a professional image. Patients believe in the skills of the curer, whom they consult and compensate.

We should not lose sight, ethnocentrically, of the difference between **scientific medicine** and Western medicine per se. To be sure, there have been scientific advances in technology, genomics, molecular biology, pathology, surgery, diagnostics, and applications. However, many Western medical procedures have little justification in science, logic, or fact. Overprescription of drugs, unnecessary surgery, and the impersonality and inequality of the physician–patient relationship are questionable features of Western medical systems (see Briggs 2005 for linguistic aspects of this inequality). Also, overuse of antibiotics, not just for people but also in animal feed, seems to be triggering an explosion of resistant microrganisms, which may pose a long-term global public health hazard.

Still, biomedicine surpasses tribal treatment in many ways. Although medicines such as quinine, coca, opium, ephedrine, and rauwolfia were discovered in nonindustrial societies, thousands of effective drugs are available today to treat myriad diseases. Today's surgical procedures are much safer and more effective than those of traditional societies.

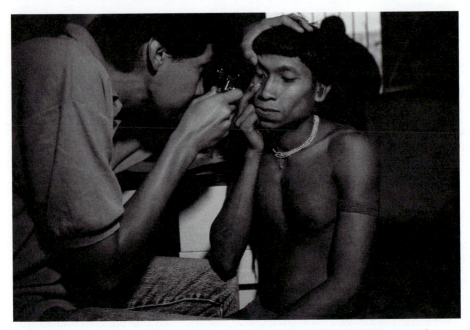

In Serra Parima, Brazil, a Yanomami Indian is examined at a field hospital. Treatment is available here for malaria, which has killed thousands of Yanomami. Such hospitals and clinics provide antibiotics, antimalarials, surgery, and preventive medicine.

But industrialization and globalization have spawned their own health problems. Modern stressors include poor nutrition, dangerous machinery, impersonal work, isolation, poverty, homelessness, substance abuse, and noise, air, and water pollution (see McElroy and Townsend 2009). Health problems in industrial nations are caused as much by economic, social, political, and cultural factors as by pathogens. In modern North America, for example, poverty contributes to many illnesses, including arthritis, heart conditions, back problems, and hearing and vision impairment (see Bailey 2000). Poverty also is a factor in the differential spread of infectious diseases.

In the United States and other developed countries, good health has become something of an ethical imperative (Foucault 1990). Individuals are expected to regulate their behavior and shape themselves in keeping with new medical knowledge. Those who do so acquire the status of sanitary citizens—people with modern understanding of the body, health, and illness. Such citizens practice hygiene and look to health care professionals when they are sick. People who act differently (e.g., smokers, overeaters, those who avoid doctors) are stigmatized as unsanitary and blamed for their own health problems (Briggs 2005; Foucault 1990).

Even getting an epidemic disease such as cholera may be interpreted today as a moral failure. It's assumed that people who act rationally can avoid "preventable" diseases. Individuals are expected to follow scientifically based imperatives (e.g., "boil water," "don't smoke"). People (e.g., gay men, smokers, veterans) can become objects of avoidance and discrimination simply by belonging to a group seen as having a greater risk of disease or poor health (Briggs 2005).

Health interventions always have to fit into local cultures and be accepted by local people. When Western medicine is introduced, people usually retain many of their old methods while also accepting new ones (see Green 1987/1992). Native curers may continue to treat certain conditions (spirit possession), while physicians deal with others. When patients are cured, the native curer and the physician share the credit.

A more personal treatment of illness that emulates the non-Western curer-patient-community relationship might benefit Western systems. Western medicine tends to draw a rigid line between biomedical and psychological causation. Non-Western theories usually lack this sharp distinction, recognizing that poor health has intertwined physical, emotional, and social causes. The mind–body opposition is part of Western folk taxonomy, not of science (see also Brown and Barrett 2010; Helman 2007; Joralemon 2010; Strathern and Stewart 2010).

Medical anthropology also considers the impact of new scientific and medical techniques on ideas about life, death, and *personhood* (what it means to be a person). For decades, disagreements about personhood—such as when life begins and ends—have been part of political and religious discussions of contraception, abortion, assisted suicide, and euthanasia (mercy killing). More recent additions to such discussions include stem cells, "harvested" embryos, assisted reproduction, genetic screening, cloning, and life-prolonging medical treatments. How long should a human body be kept alive if there is no hope of recovery?

Kaufman and Morgan (2005) emphasize the contrast between what they call low-tech and high-tech births and deaths. A desperately poor young mother dies of AIDS in Africa while half a world away an American child of privilege is born as the result of a $50,000 in-vitro fertilization procedure. Medical anthropologists increasingly are concerned with how the boundaries of life and death are being questioned and negotiated in the 21st century.

Anthropology and Business

For decades anthropologists have used ethnography to understand business settings (Arensberg 1987; Jordan 2003). Ethnographic research in an auto factory, for example, may view workers, managers, and executives as different social categories participating in a common system. Each group has characteristic attitudes and behavior patterns. These are transmitted through *microenculturation,* the process by which people learn particular roles within a limited social system. The free-ranging nature of ethnography takes the anthropologist back and forth from worker to executive. Each employee is both an individual with a personal viewpoint and a cultural creature whose perspective is, to some extent, shared with other members of his or her group. Applied anthropologists have acted as "cultural brokers," translating managers' goals or workers' concerns to the other group (see Ferraro 2010).

Carol Taylor (1987) stresses the value of an "anthropologist-in-residence" in a large, complex organization, such as a hospital or corporation. A free-ranging ethnographer can be a perceptive oddball when information and decisions typically move through a rigid hierarchy. If allowed to observe and converse freely with all types and levels of

At a major information technology company, Marietta Baba examines one of the world's fastest super-computers. She is studying that firm's adaptation to the rise of the service economy. Professor Baba, a prominent applied anthropologist and dean of the College of Social Science at Michigan State University, also has studied Michigan's automobile industry.

personnel, the anthropologist may acquire a unique perspective on organizational conditions and problems. Such high-tech companies as Xerox, IBM, and Apple have employed anthropologists in various roles. Closely observing how people actually use computer products, anthropologists have worked with engineers to design products that are more user-friendly.

Key features of anthropology that are of value to business include (1) ethnography and observation as ways of gathering data, (2) a focus on diversity, and (3) cross-cultural expertise. Businesses have heard that anthropologists are specialists on cultural diversity and observing behavior in natural settings, including home and office. Hallmark Cards has hired anthropologists to observe parties, holidays, and celebrations of ethnic groups to improve its ability to design cards for targeted audiences. Applied anthropologists routinely go into people's homes to see how they actually use products (see Sunderland and Denny 2007 and the "Anthropology Today" at the end of this chapter).

Careers and Anthropology

Many college students find anthropology interesting and consider majoring in it. However, their parents or friends may discourage them by asking, "What kind of job are you going to get with an anthropology degree?" The first step in answering that question is to consider the more general question, "What do you do with any college major?" The answer is "Not much, without a good bit of effort, thought, and planning." A survey of graduates of the University of Michigan's literary college showed that few had jobs that

Anthropology Today   *Culturally Appropriate Marketing*

Innovation succeeds best when it is culturally appropriate. This axiom of applied anthropology could guide the international spread not only of development projects but also of businesses, such as fast food. Each time McDonald's or Burger King expands to a new nation, it must devise a culturally appropriate strategy for fitting into the new setting.

McDonald's has been very successful internationally. Over 60 percent of its current annual revenue comes from sales outside the United States. One place where McDonald's has expanded successfully is Brazil, where 90 million middle-class people, most living in densely packed cities, provide a concentrated market for a fast-food chain. Still, it took McDonald's some time to find the right marketing strategy for Brazil.

In 1980 when I visited Brazil after a seven-year absence, I first noticed, as a manifestation of Brazil's growing participation in the world economy, the appearance of two McDonald's restaurants in Rio de Janeiro. There wasn't much difference between Brazilian and American McDonald's. The restaurants looked alike. The menus were more or less the same, as was the taste of the quarter-pounders. I picked up an artifact, a white paper bag with yellow lettering, exactly like the take-out bags then used in American McDonald's. An advertising device, it carried several messages about how Brazilians could bring McDonald's into their lives. However, it seemed to me that McDonald's Brazilian ad campaign was missing some important points about how fast food should be marketed in a culture that valued large, leisurely lunches.

A McDonald´s restaurant in Kazan, capital of the Republic of Tatarstan, within Russia. Can you see any evidence that McDonald's is adapting to this cultural setting?

continued

Anthropology Today *continued*

The bag proclaimed, "You're going to enjoy the [McDonald's] difference," and listed several "favorite places where you can enjoy McDonald's products." This list confirmed that the marketing people were trying to adapt to Brazilian middle-class culture, but they were making some mistakes. "When you go out in the car with the kids" transferred the uniquely developed North American cultural combination of highways, affordable cars, and suburban living to the very different context of urban Brazil. A similar suggestion was "traveling to the country place." Even Brazilians who owned country places could not find McDonald's, still confined to the cities, on the road. The ad creator had apparently never attempted to drive up to a fast-food restaurant in a neighborhood with no parking spaces.

Several other suggestions pointed customers toward the beach, where *cariocas* (Rio natives) do spend much of their leisure time. One could eat McDonald's products "after a dip in the ocean," "at a picnic at the beach," or "watching the surfers." These suggestions ignored the Brazilian custom of consuming cold things, such as beer, soft drinks, ice cream, and ham and cheese sandwiches, on the beach. Brazilians don't consider a hot, greasy hamburger proper beach food. They view the sea as "cold" and hamburgers as "hot"; they avoid "hot" foods at the beach.

Also culturally dubious was the suggestion to eat McDonald's hamburgers "lunching at the office." Brazilians prefer their main meal at midday, often eating at a leisurely pace with business associates. Many firms serve ample lunches to their employees. Other workers take advantage of a two-hour lunch break to go home to eat with the spouse and children. Nor did it make sense to suggest

that children should eat hamburgers for lunch, since most kids attend school for half-day sessions and have lunch at home. Two other suggestions—"waiting for the bus" and "in the beauty parlor"—did describe common aspects of daily life in a Brazilian city. However, these settings have not proved especially inviting to hamburgers or fish filets.

The homes of most Brazilians who can afford McDonald's products have cooks and maids to do many of the things that fast-food restaurants do in the United States. The suggestion that McDonald's products be eaten "while watching your favorite television program" is culturally appropriate, because Brazilians watch TV a lot. However, Brazil's consuming classes can ask the cook to make a snack when hunger strikes. Indeed, much televiewing occurs during the light dinner served when the husband gets home from the office.

Most appropriate to the Brazilian lifestyle was the suggestion to enjoy McDonald's "on the cook's day off." Throughout Brazil, Sunday is that day. The Sunday pattern for middle-class families who live on the coast is a trip to the beach, liters of beer, a full midday meal around 3:00 P.M., and a light evening snack. McDonald's found its niche in the Sunday evening meal, when families flock to the fast-food restaurant.

McDonald's has expanded rapidly in Brazil, where, as in North America, teenage appetites have fueled the fast-food explosion. As McDonald's outlets appeared in urban neighborhoods, Brazilian teenagers used them for after-school snacks, while families had evening meals there. As an anthropologist could have predicted, the fast-food industry has not revolutionized Brazilian food and meal customs. Rather, McDonald's is succeeding because it has adapted to preexisting Brazilian cultural patterns.

The main contrast with North America is that the Brazilian evening meal is lighter. McDonald's now caters to the evening meal rather than to lunch. Once McDonald's realized that more money could be made by fitting in with, rather than trying to Americanize, Brazilian meal habits, it started aiming its advertising at that goal.

were clearly linked to their majors. Most professions, including medicine and law, require advanced degrees. Although many colleges offer bachelor's degrees in engineering, business, accounting, and social work, master's degrees often are needed to get the best jobs in those fields. Anthropologists, too, need an advanced degree, almost always a PhD, to find gainful employment in academic, museum, or applied anthropology.

A broad college education, and even a major in anthropology, can be an excellent foundation for success in many fields. One survey of women executives showed that most had not majored in business but in the social sciences or humanities. Only after graduating from college did they study business, leading to a master's degree in business administration (MBA). These executives felt that the breadth of their college educations had contributed to their business careers. Anthropology majors go on to medical, law, and business schools and find success in many professions that often have little explicit connection to anthropology.

Anthropology's breadth provides knowledge and an outlook on the world that are useful in many kinds of work. For example, an anthropology major combined with a master's degree in business is excellent preparation for work in international business. Breadth is anthropology's hallmark. Anthropologists study people biologically, culturally, socially, and linguistically, across time and space, in various countries, in simple and complex settings. Most colleges offer anthropology courses that compare cultures, along with others that focus on particular world areas, such as Latin America, Asia, and Native North America. The knowledge of foreign areas acquired in such courses can be useful in many jobs. Anthropology's comparative outlook and its focus on diverse lifestyles combine to provide an excellent foundation for overseas employment (see Omohundro 2001).

For work in modern North America, anthropology's focus on culture is increasingly relevant. Every day we hear about cultural differences and about problems whose solutions require a multicultural viewpoint—an ability to recognize and reconcile ethnic differences. Government, schools, hospitals, and businesses constantly deal with people from different social classes, ethnic groups, and cultural backgrounds. Physicians, attorneys, social workers, police officers, judges, teachers, and students can all do a better job if they understand cultural differences in a nation that is one of the most ethnically diverse in history.

Knowledge of the traditions and beliefs of the groups that make up a modern nation is important in planning and carrying out programs that affect those groups. Experience in planned social change—whether community organization in North America or economic development overseas—shows that a proper social study should be done before a project or policy is implemented. When local people want the change and it fits their lifestyle and traditions, it has a better chance of being successful, beneficial, and cost effective.

People with anthropology backgrounds do well in many fields. Even if one's job has little or nothing to do with anthropology in a formal or obvious sense, a background in anthropology provides a useful orientation when we work with our fellow human beings. For most of us, this means every day of our lives.

Summary

1. Applied anthropology uses anthropological perspectives, theory, methods, and data to identify, assess, and solve problems. Applied anthropologists have a range of employers. Examples: government agencies; development organizations; NGOs; tribal, ethnic, and interest groups; businesses; hospitals; social services and educational agencies. Applied anthropologists come from all four subfields. Ethnography is one of applied anthropology's most valuable research tools.

2. Development anthropology focuses on social issues in, and the cultural dimension of, economic development. Not all governments seek to increase equality and end poverty. Resistance by elites to reform is typical. At the same time, local people rarely cooperate with projects requiring major and risky changes in their daily lives. Many projects seek to impose inappropriate property notions and incompatible social units on their intended beneficiaries. The best strategy for change is to base the social design for innovation on traditional social forms in each target area.

3. Anthropology and education researchers work in classrooms, homes, and other settings relevant to education and make policy recommendations based on their findings. Both academic and applied anthropologists study migration from rural areas to cities and across national boundaries. North America has become a popular arena for urban anthropological research on migration, ethnicity, poverty, and related topics. Although rural and urban are different social systems, there is cultural diffusion from one to the other.

4. Medical anthropology is a biocultural field that studies variation in health care systems, including disease, illness, health standards, and disease theories. In a given setting, the characteristic diseases reflect diet, population density, economy, and social complexity. Native theories of illness may be personalistic, naturalistic, or emotionalistic. In applying anthropology to business, the key features are (1) ethnography and observation as ways of gathering data, (2) a focus on diversity, and (3) cross-cultural expertise.

5. A broad college education, including anthropology and foreign-area courses, offers excellent background for many fields. Anthropology's comparative, cross-cultural outlook provides an excellent basis for overseas employment. Even for work in North America, a focus on culture and cultural diversity is valuable. Anthropology majors attend medical, law, and business schools and succeed in many fields, some of which have little explicit connection with anthropology.

Key Terms

anthropology and education, *423*

curer, *429*

development anthropology, *418*

disease, *427*

equity, increased, *419*

health care systems, *429*

illness, *427*

medical anthropology, *427*

overinnovation, *420*

scientific medicine, *429*

under-differentiation, *421*

urban anthropology, *425*

 Go to our Online Learning Center website at **www.mhhe.com/kottak** for Internet resources directly related to the content of this chapter.

Chapter 19

Anthropology's Role in a Globalizing World

Globalization: Its Meaning and Its Nature

Global Climate Change

Environmental Anthropology

Global Assaults on Local Autonomy

Deforestation

Interethnic Contact

Cultural Imperialism

Making and Remaking Culture

Indigenizing Popular Culture

A Global System of Images

A Global Culture of Consumption

People in Motion

Applying Anthropology to Popular Culture: ET Phone Home

Indigenous Peoples

Identity in Indigenous Politics

The Continuance of Diversity

Anthropology Today: Engulfed by Climate Change, Town Seeks Lifeline

This chapter applies an anthropological perspective to contemporary global issues. We begin by considering different meanings of the term *globalization*. The fact that certain risks now have global implications leads to a discussion of climate change, aka global warming. Next, we return to issues of development, this time alongside an intervention philosophy that seeks to impose global ecological morality without due attention to cultural variation and autonomy. Also considered is the threat that deforestation poses to global biodiversity. The second half of this chapter turns from ecology to the contemporary flows of people, technology, finance, information, images, and ideology that contribute to a global culture of consumption. Globalization promotes intercultural communication, through the media, travel, and migration, which bring people from different societies into direct contact. Finally, we'll consider how such contacts and external linkages influence indigenous peoples, and how those groups have organized to confront and deal with national and global issues, including their mobilization to promote human, cultural, and political rights.

Note that it would be impossible in a single chapter to discuss all or even most of the global issues that are salient today and that anthropologists have studied. Some such issues (e.g., war, displacement, terrorism, NGOs) have been considered in previous chapters. For timely anthropological analysis of a range of global issues, see recent books by John H. Bodley (2008*a*, 2008*b*) and Richard H. Robbins (2008). The current global issues these anthropologists consider include, but are not limited to, hunger, international interventions, peacekeeping, global health, and sanitation.

Globalization: Its Meanings and Its Nature

Chapter 2 characterized globalization as a series of processes that promote change in a world in which nations and people are increasingly interlinked and mutually dependent. Its forces include international manufacture, commerce, and finance; travel and tourism; transnational migration; the media, the Internet, and other high-tech information flows. Globalization deserves a closer look in this final chapter.

Mark Smith and Michele Doyle (2002) distinguish between two meanings of globalization:

1. *Globalization as fact:* the spread and connectedness of production, communication, and technologies across the world. This meaning is like the one described above and in Chapter 2.

2. *Globalization as ideology and policy:* efforts by the International Monetary Fund (IMF), the World Bank, and other international financial powers to create a global free market for goods and services.

In this second sense, for neoliberal economists, globalization is the way the world should go. For their opponents—anti-neoliberals—it is the way the world should *not* go (Lewellen 2010). It is this neoliberal view of globalization that has generated the protests described in Chapter 2.

The first meaning is more neutral. Globalization as *systemic connectedness* reflects the relentless and ongoing growth of the world system. In its current form, that system, which has existed for centuries, has some radical new aspects. Three are especially noteworthy: the *speed* of global communication, the *scale* (complexity and size) of global networks, and the sheer *volume* of international transactions.

The "Second World" opened to world capitalism with the fall of the Soviet Union in 1989–90. Once that happened a truly global economy could emerge (Lewellen 2010). According to Manuel Castells (2001), three key features of this new economy are as follows: (1) it is based on knowledge and information; (2) its networks of financing, production, management, and exchange are transnational; and (3) its core activities, even if dispersed, can proceed as a unit in real time.

The Internet has made possible the rapid, often instantaneous, transmission of information and resources distributed across the globe. Activities that are spatially dispersed can now be coordinated in real time. Activities that once involved face-to-face contact are now conducted impersonally and often across vast distances. For example, when you order something from the Internet, the only human being you might speak to is the delivery driver (Smith and Doyle 2002). The computers that take and process your order

Successful multinationals strive to make their brands part of how people see themselves. Shown here, an Apple store opens in Shanghai, China. If you own an Apple product, what does it mean to you?

from Amazon can be on different continents, and the products you order can come from a warehouse anywhere in the world.

Commenting on studies of commodities and globalization (e.g., Haugerud, Stone, and Little, eds. 2000), Ted Lewellen (2010) notes that the average food product now travels 1,300 miles and changes hands a dozen times before it reaches the American consumer. He suggests that for contemporary anthropologists who wish to develop a good "system-awareness," local fieldwork isn't enough. They also need to follow networks of production, processing, advertising, distribution, and consumption.

Michael Burawoy suggests that researchers shift "from studying 'sites' to studying 'fields,' that is, the relations *between* sites" (Burawoy 2000, p. xii). He observes that people increasingly live their lives across borders, maintaining social, financial, cultural, and political connections with either a "home" country or multiple countries. Such "multiplaced" folk would include business and intellectual leaders, development workers, and members of multinational corporations, as well as migratory domestic, agricultural, and construction workers (see Lewellen 2010).

By the beginning of the 21st century, multinational corporations accounted for a third of global output, and two-thirds of world trade (Gray 1999, p. 62). Profit-seeking multinationals move production, sales, and services to areas where labor and materials are cheap. This globalization of labor creates unemployment "back home" as industries relocate and outsource abroad.

Multinationals also seek out new markets, striving to create new needs among different target groups, especially the youth market. Young people increasingly construct their identities and relationships around consumption, especially of brand-name products. Successful multinationals, including Nike, Apple, Coca-Cola, and McDonald's, invest huge sums in promoting their brands. The goal is to make a particular brand an integral part of the way people see themselves. Savvy branders try to "get them young" (Klein 2000; Smith and Doyle 2002).

Multinational companies (e.g., General Motors) increasingly influence national policy and attempt to forge beneficial alliances with politicians and government officials, especially those who are most concerned with world trade. The influence of multinationals extends to key transnational players, such as the European Union and the World Bank. With the globalization of financial markets, nations have less control over their own economies. Such institutions as the World Bank, the International Monetary Fund, the European Union, and the European Central Bank routinely constrain and dictate national economic policy.

As capitalism has spread globally, the gap between rich and poor has widened both within and between nations. The widening gap in the United States was discussed in the chapter "The World System and Colonialism." David Landes (1999) calculated the difference in per capita income between the world's richest nation (he cited Switzerland) and the poorest nation (Mozambique) as 400 to 1, versus around 5 to 1 when the Industrial Revolution began. The key role of knowledge in today's global economy has accelerated this gap, because knowledge tends to be concentrated in core countries and certain areas within them. *Knowledge capitalism* describes the commercial value of generating new ideas and converting them into products and services that consumers want (Leadbeater 1999).

Another key component of globalization is the *globalization of risk* (Smith and Doyle 2002). Ecological risks have multiplied, as we saw in the "Anthropology Today" in the chapter "The World System and Colonialism." Hazards linked to industrial production or a cyber attack can spread quickly beyond their point of origin. Climate risks also have become globalized. Each consumer of fossil fuels makes his or her own individual contribution to global climate change, to which we now turn.

Global Climate Change

The year 2010 tied with 2005 as the hottest ever recorded by NASA's Goddard Institute for Space Studies (GISS), whose analysis covers 131 years. Earth's surface temperatures have risen about 1.48°F (0.78°C) since the early 20th century. (This chapter's "Anthropology Today" discusses how this rise has affected an indigenous group in Alaska.) About two-thirds of this increase has been since 1978 (Figure 19.1). Scientific measurements confirm that global warming is not due to increased solar radiation. The causes are mainly *anthropogenic*—caused by humans and their activities. It stands to reason that 7 billion people, along with their animals, crops, and machines, have more of an impact on the environment than the 5 million or so hunter-gatherers who lived on our planet 12,000 years ago—before the advent of food production.

Because Earth's climate changes constantly, the key question becomes: How much climate change is due to human activities versus natural climate variability. Most scientists agree that human activities play a major role in global climate change. How can the human factor not be significant given population growth and rapidly increasing use of fossil fuels, which produce greenhouse gases in the atmosphere?

The **greenhouse effect** is a natural phenomenon that keeps the Earth's surface warm. Without greenhouse gases—water vapor (H_2O), carbon dioxide (CO_2), methane (CH_4), nitrous oxide (N_2O), halocarbons, and ozone (O_3)—life as we know it wouldn't exist. Like a greenhouse window, such gases allow sunlight to enter and then prevent heat from escaping the atmosphere. All those gases have increased since the Industrial Revolution. Today, the atmospheric concentration of greenhouse gases has reached its highest level in 400,000 years. It will continue to rise—as will global temperatures—without actions to slow it down (National Academies 2007).

FIGURE 19.1   Global Temperature Change

Global annual-mean surface air temperature derived from measurements at meteorological stations has increased by 1.4°F (0.7°C) since the early 20th century, with about 0.9°F (0.5°C) of the increase occurring since 1978.

Source: Goddard Institute for Space Studies, from "Understanding and Responding to Climate Change: Highlights of National Academies Reports," http://dels.nas.edu/basc/Climate-HIGH.pdf.

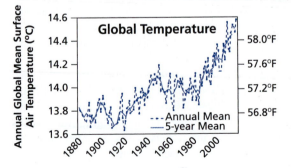

Scientists prefer the term **climate change** over "global warming." The former term points out that, beyond rising temperatures, there have been changes in sea levels, precipitation, storms, and ecosystem effects. The precise effects of climate change on regional weather patterns have yet to be determined. Land areas are predicted to warm more than oceans, with the greatest warming in higher latitudes, such as Canada, the northern United States, and northern Europe. Climate change may benefit these areas, offering milder winters and extended growing seasons. However, many more people worldwide probably will be harmed. Already we know that in the Arctic, temperatures have risen almost twice as much as the global average. Arctic landscapes and ecosystems are changing rapidly and perceptibly, as this chapter's "Anthropology Today" illustrates.

Coastal communities worldwide can anticipate increased flooding and more severe storms and surges. At risk are people, animals, plants, freshwater supplies, and such industries as tourism and farming. Along with many island nations, Bangladesh, one of the world's poorest countries, is projected to lose a significant portion (17.5 percent) of its land, displacing millions of people (National Academies 2008).

The U.S. National Academy of Sciences has issued several reports on climate change. Those reports are summarized in a downloadable brochure titled "Understanding and Responding to Climate Change, 2008 edition" (http://dels-old.nas.edu/dels/rpt_briefs /climate_change_2008_final.pdf), on which some of this discussion has been based (see also Crate and Nuttall 2008).

In the global economy India and China (shown here) in particular have increased their use of fossil fuels, and consequently their emissions of CO_2. This scene, near Beijing, shows the Shougang steel plant, a major source of air pollution in 1997. What's the most polluted place you've ever been?

FIGURE 19.2

Projected Emission of Greenhouse Gases, 2025

This figure compares CO$_2$ emissions per nation in 2000 and projections for 2025. In 2000, the largest emitter of CO$_2$ was the United States, which was responsible for 25 percent of global emissions. In 2025, China and the developing world may significantly increase their CO$_2$ emissions relative to the United States.

Source: Baumert, Harzog, and Pershing 2005.

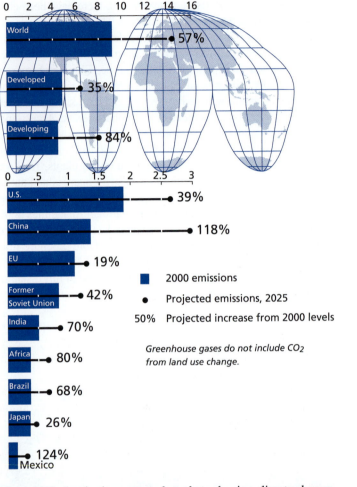

Trillions of tons of carbon equivalent

■ 2000 emissions

● Projected emissions, 2025

50% Projected increase from 2000 levels

Greenhouse gases do not include CO$_2$ from land use change.

Meeting global energy needs is the single greatest obstacle to slowing climate change. In the United States, about 80 percent of all energy used comes from fossil fuels. Worldwide, energy use continues to grow with economic and population expansion. China and India in particular are rapidly increasing their use of energy, mainly from fossil fuels, and consequently their emissions (Figure 19.2). Among the alternatives to fossil fuels are nuclear power and such renewable energy technologies as solar, wind, and biomass generators.

Environmental Anthropology

Anthropology always has been concerned with how environmental forces influence humans and how human activities affect the biosphere and the Earth itself. The 1950s–1970s witnessed the emergence of an area of study known as cultural ecology or **ecological**

anthropology. That field focused on how cultural beliefs and practices helped human populations adapt to their environments, and how people used elements of their culture to maintain their ecosystems.

Early ecological anthropologists showed that many indigenous groups did a reasonable job of managing their resources and preserving their ecosystems. Such groups had traditional ways of categorizing resources, regulating their use, and preserving the environment. An **ethnoecology** is any society's set of environmental practices and perceptions—that is, its cultural model of the environment and its relation to people and society. Indigenous ethnoecologies increasingly are being challenged as migration, media, and commerce spread people, institutions, information, and technology. In the face of national and international incentives to exploit and degrade, ethnoecological systems that once preserved local and regional environments increasingly are ineffective or irrelevant.

Anthropologists routinely witness threats to the people they study and their environments. Among such threats are commercial logging, industrial pollution, and the imposition of external management systems on local ecosystems (see Johnston 2009). Today's ecological anthropology, aka *environmental anthropology,* attempts not only to understand but also to find solutions to environmental problems. As aspects of the globalization of risk, such problems must be tackled at the national and international levels (e.g., global warming). Even in remote places, ecosystem management now involves multiple levels. For example, among the Antankarana of northern Madagascar (Gezon 2006), several levels of authority claim the right to use and regulate natural resources and local ecosystems. Actual or would-be regulators there include local communities, traditional leaders (the regional king or chief), provincial and national governments, and the WWF, the Worldwide Fund for Nature (formerly the World Wildlife Fund), an international NGO whose name attests to its global reach.

Local people, their landscapes, their ideas, their values, and their traditional management systems face attacks from all sides. Outsiders attempt to remake native landscapes and cultures in their own image. The aim of many agricultural development projects, for example, seems to be to make the world as much like a midwestern American agricultural state as possible. Often there is an attempt to impose mechanized farming and nuclear family ownership, even though these institutions may be inappropriate in areas far removed from the midwestern United States. As we saw in the previous chapter, development projects usually fail when they try to replace indigenous institutions with culturally alien concepts (Kottak 1990*b*).

Global Assaults on Local Autonomy

A clash of cultures related to environmental change may occur when development threatens indigenous peoples and their environments. A second clash of cultures related to environmental change may occur when external regulation aimed at conservation confronts indigenous peoples and their ethnoecologies. Like development projects, conservation schemes may ask people to change their ways in order to satisfy planners' goals rather than local goals. In places as different as Madagascar, Brazil, and the Pacific Northwest of the United States, people have been asked, told, or forced to abandon basic economic activities because to do so is good for "nature" or "the globe." "Good for the globe" doesn't play very well in Brazil, whose Amazon region has been a focus of international environmentalist attention. Brazilians complain that outsiders (e.g., Europeans and North Americans) promote "global needs" and "saving the Amazon" after having destroyed their own forests for economic growth. Well-intentioned conservation plans can be as insensitive as development schemes that promote radical changes without involving local people in planning and carrying out the policies that affect them. When people are asked to give up the basis of their livelihood, they usually resist.

The spread of environmentalism may reveal radically different notions about the "rights" and value of plants and animals versus humans. In Madagascar, many intellectuals and officials complain that foreigners seem more concerned about lemurs and other endangered species than about the people of Madagascar (the Malagasy). As a geographer there remarked to me, "The next time you come to Madagascar, there'll be no more Malagasy. All the people will have starved to death, and a lemur will have to meet you at the airport." Most Malagasy perceive human poverty as a more pressing problem than animal and plant survival.

On the other hand, who can doubt that conservation, including the preservation of biodiversity, is a worthy goal? The challenge for applied ecological anthropology is to devise culturally appropriate strategies for achieving biodiversity conservation in the face of unrelenting population growth and commercial expansion. How does one get people to support conservation measures that may, in the short run at least, diminish their access to resources? Like development plans in general, the most effective conservation strategies pay attention to the needs and wishes of the local people.

Deforestation

Deforestation is another expression of the globalization of risk. Forest loss can lead to increased greenhouse gas (CO_2) production, which contributes to global warming. Tropical forests contain at least half of Earth's species while covering just 6 percent of the planet's land surface. The ongoing destruction of tropical forests also is a major factor in the loss of global biodiversity.

Generations of anthropologists have studied how human economic activities (ancient and modern) affect the environment. Anthropologists know that food producers (farmers and herders) typically do more to degrade the environment than foragers do. Population increase and the need to expand farming caused deforestation in many parts of the ancient Middle East and Mesoamerica (see Hornborg and Crumley, eds. 2007). Even today, many farmers think of trees as giant weeds to be removed and replaced with productive fields.

Often, deforestation is demographically driven—caused by population pressure. For example, Madagascar's population is growing at a rate of 3 percent annually, doubling every generation. Population pressure leads to migration, including rural–urban migration. Madagascar's capital, Antananarivo, had just 100,000 people in 1967. The population stands at about 2 million today. Urban growth promotes deforestation if city dwellers rely on fuel wood from the countryside, as is true in Madagascar. As forested watersheds disappear, crop productivity declines. Madagascar is known as the "great red island," after the color of its soil. On that island, the effects of soil erosion and water runoff are visible to the naked eye. From the look of its rivers, Madagascar appears to be bleeding to death. Increasing runoff of water no longer trapped by trees

Applied anthropology uses anthropological perspectives to identify and solve contemporary problems that affect humans. Deforestation is one such problem. Here women take part in a reforestation project in coastal Tanzania near Dar es Salaam.

causes erosion of low-lying rice fields near swollen rivers as well as siltation in irrigation canals (Kottak 2007).

Causes of deforestation include demographic pressure (from births or immigration) on subsistence economies, commercial logging, road building, cash cropping, fuel wood needs associated with urban expansion, and clearing and burning associated with livestock and grazing. The fact that forest loss has several causes has a policy implication: Different deforestation scenarios require different conservation strategies.

What can be done? On this question applied anthropology weighs in, spurring policy makers to think about new conservation strategies. The traditional approach has been to restrict access to forested areas designated as parks, then employ park guards and punish violators. Modern strategies are more likely to consider the needs, wishes, and abilities of the people (often impoverished) living in and near the forest. Since effective conservation depends on the cooperation of the local people, their concerns must be addressed in devising conservation strategies.

Reasons to change behavior must make sense to local people (see Sillitoe 2007). In Madagascar, the economic value of the forest for agriculture (as an antierosion mechanism and reservoir of potential irrigation water) provides a much more powerful incentive against forest degradation than do such global goals as "preserving biodiversity." Most Malagasy have no idea that lemurs and other endemic species exist only in Madagascar. Nor would such knowledge provide much of an incentive for them to conserve the forests if doing so jeopardized their livelihoods.

To curb the global deforestation threat, we need conservation strategies that work. Laws and enforcement may help reduce commercially driven deforestation caused by burning and clear-cutting. But local people also use and abuse forested lands. A challenge for the environmentally oriented applied anthropologist is to find ways to make forest preservation attractive to local people and ensure their cooperation. Applied anthropologists must work to make "good for the globe" good for the people.

Interethnic Contact

Since at least the 1920s anthropologists have investigated the changes—on both sides—that arise from contact between industrial and nonindustrial societies. Studies of "social change" and "acculturation" are abundant. British and American ethnographers, respectively, have used those terms to describe the same process. *Acculturation* refers to changes that result when groups come into continuous firsthand contact—changes in the cultural patterns of either or both groups (Redfield, Linton, and Herskovits 1936, p. 149). Acculturation differs from *diffusion,* or cultural borrowing, which can occur without firsthand contact. For example, most North Americans who eat hot dogs ("frankfurters") have never been to Frankfurt, Germany, nor have most North American Toyota owners or sushi eaters ever visited Japan. Although *acculturation* can be applied to any case of sustained cultural contact and change, the term most often has described **Westernization**—the influence of Western expansion on indigenous peoples and their cultures. Thus, local people who wear store-bought clothes, learn Indo-European languages, and otherwise adopt Western customs are called acculturated. Acculturation may be voluntary or forced, and there may be considerable resistance to the process.

Different degrees of destruction, domination, resistance, survival, adaptation, and modification of native cultures may follow interethnic contact. In the most destructive encounters, subordinate cultures face obliteration. Often, when powerful outsiders (e.g., colonialists) threaten or conquer indigenous peoples, a "shock phase" follows the initial encounter (Bodley 2008*b*). Outsiders may attack or exploit the local people. Such exploitation may increase mortality, disrupt subsistence, fragment kin groups, damage social support systems, and inspire new religious movements, such as the cargo cults examined in the chapter "Religion" (Bodley 2008*b*). During the shock phase, there may be civil repression backed by military force. Such factors may lead to the group's cultural collapse (ethnocide) or physical extinction (genocide).

Cultural Imperialism

Cultural imperialism refers to the spread or advance of one culture at the expense of others, or its imposition on other cultures, which it modifies, replaces, or destroys—usually because of differential economic or political influence. Thus, children in the French colonial empire learned French history, language, and culture from standard textbooks also used in France. Tahitians, Malagasy, Vietnamese, and Senegalese learned the French language by reciting from books about "our ancestors the Gauls."

To what extent do contemporary global forces propel cultural imperialism? Some commentators see the spread of modern technology, the media, and global brands as erasing cultural differences, as homogeneous products reach more people worldwide. Others note that certain innovations have allowed social groups (local cultures) to express themselves and to survive (Marcus and Fischer 1999). For example, modern radio, TV, digital media, and increasingly the Internet (e.g., YouTube) constantly bring local happenings to the attention of a larger public. Susan Boyle's rendition of "I Dreamed a Dream" on a British TV show soon became an Internet sensation and made her a global star. Without YouTube, appreciation of Boyle's voice might have been confined to the United Kingdom. What have you watched lately on YouTube? Contemporary media play a role in stimulating and organizing local and community activities of many sorts. Think of ways in which this is done by YouTube, Facebook, and Twitter—global networks all.

In Brazil, local practices, celebrations, and performances have changed in the context of outside forces, including the mass media and tourism. In the town of Arembepe (Kottak 2006), TV coverage stimulated increased participation in a traditional annual performance, the Chegança. This is a fishermen's danceplay that reenacts the Portuguese discovery of Brazil. Arembepeiros have traveled to the state capital to perform the Chegança before television cameras, for a TV program featuring traditional performances from many rural communities, and cameras have come to Arembepe to record it.

In several towns along the Amazon River, annual folk ceremonies now are staged more lavishly for TV and video cameras. In the Amazon town of Parantíns, for example, boatloads of tourists arriving any time of year are shown a video recording of the town's annual Bumba Meu Boi festival. This is a costumed performance mimicking bullfighting, parts of which have been shown on national TV. This pattern, in which local communities preserve, revive, and intensify the scale of traditional ceremonies to perform for the media and tourists, is expanding. To see whether I could, I just managed to watch snippets of these annual events in Arembepe and Parantíns on YouTube!

The Brazilian mass media also have helped spread the popularity of holidays like Carnaval and Christmas (Kottak 1990a). TV has aided the national spread of Carnaval beyond its traditional urban centers. Still, local reactions to the nationwide broadcasting of Carnaval and its trappings (elaborate parades, costumes, and frenzied dancing) are not simple or uniform responses to external stimuli.

Rather than direct adoption of Carnaval, local Brazilians respond in various ways. Often they don't take up Carnaval itself but modify their local festivities to fit Carnaval images. Others actively spurn Carnaval. One example is Arembepe, where Carnaval has never been important, probably because of its calendrical closeness to the main local festival, which is held in February to honor Saint Francis of Assisi. In the past, villagers couldn't afford to celebrate both occasions. Now, not only do the people of Arembepe reject Carnaval; they also are increasingly hostile to their own main festival. Arembepeiros resent the fact that the Saint Francis festival has become "an outsiders' event," because it draws thousands of tourists to Arembepe each year. The villagers think that commercial interests and outsiders have appropriated Saint Francis.

In opposition to these trends, many Arembepeiros now say they like and participate more in the traditional June festivals honoring Saint John, Saint Peter, and Saint Anthony.

In the past, these were observed on a much smaller scale than was the festival honoring Saint Francis. Arembepeiros celebrate them now with a new vigor and enthusiasm, as they react to outsiders and their celebrations, real and televised. The national or the global only can become that if the local cooperates.

Making and Remaking Culture

In the process of globalization, people constantly make and remake culture as they evaluate, and assign their own meanings to, the information, images, and products they receive from outside. Those meanings reflect their cultural backgrounds and experiences.

Indigenizing Popular Culture

As global forces reach new communities, they are **indigenized**—modified to fit the local culture. This is true of cultural domains as different as fast food, music, movies, housing styles, science, terrorism, celebrations, and political ideas and institutions (Appadurai 1990; Fiske 1989). One classic example is how the movie *Rambo* (the first one in the series) was indigenized by Native Australians. Eric Michaels (1986, 1991) found Rambo to be popular among aborigines in the deserts of central Australia, who had manufactured their own meanings from the film. Their interpretation was very different from the one imagined by the movie's creators. The Native Australians saw Rambo as someone

Illustrating a process of indigenizing offerings of the modern world system, children dress as Colonel Sanders to promote egg tarts (a local dish now offered by an international restaurant chain) at a KFC store in Shanghai, China.

from the Third World battling white oppressors. This view expressed their resentment about white paternalism and inequitable race relations. The Native Australians also imagined that there were tribal ties and kin links between Rambo and the prisoners he was rescuing. Based on their experience, all this made sense. Native Australians are disproportionately represented in Australia's jails, and their most likely savior would be someone with a personal link to them.

A Global System of Images

All cultures express imagination—in dreams, fantasies, songs, myths, and stories. With globalization, however, more people in many more places imagine "a wider set of 'possible' lives than they ever did before. One important source of this change is the mass media . . ." (Appadurai 1991, p. 197). The United States as a global media center has been joined by Canada, Japan, Western Europe, Brazil, Mexico, Nigeria, Egypt, India, and Hong Kong.

Like print (see Anderson 1991), the electronic mass media can diffuse the cultures of different countries within (and sometimes beyond) their own boundaries, thus enhancing national cultural identity. For example, millions of Brazilians who used to be cut off (by geographic isolation or illiteracy) from urban, national, and international events and information now participate in a larger "mediascape" (Appadurai 1991) through the Internet and especially television (Kottak 1990a, 2009). Many Americans mistakenly think that American programs, when available abroad, inevitably triumph over local products. In fact, this usually doesn't happen when there is appealing local competition.

In Brazil the most popular network (TV Globo) relies heavily on its own productions, especially *telenovelas* (nightly serial melodramas often compared to American soap operas). Globo plays each night to the world's largest and most devoted audience (perhaps 80 million viewers throughout the nation and beyond—via satellite TV). The programs that attract this horde are made by Brazilians, for Brazilians. Thus, it is not the spread of North American culture through globalization, but a new form of pan-Brazilian national culture, that Globo is propagating. Illustrating once again the importance of cultural fit, as discussed in the previous chapter, we may generalize that programming that is culturally alien won't do very well anywhere if a quality local choice is available. Confirmation comes from many countries, including Japan, Mexico, India, and Nigeria, in all of which national productions are very popular.

The mass media also play a role in maintaining ethnic and national identities among people who lead transnational lives. Arabic-speaking Muslims, including migrants in several countries, follow the TV network Al Jazeera, based in Qatar, which helps reinforce ethnic and religious identities. As groups move, they can stay linked to each other and to their homeland through global media. **Diasporas** (people who have spread out from an original, ancestral homeland) have enlarged the markets for media, communication, brands, and travel services targeted at specific ethnic, national, or religious groups who now live in various parts of the world.

A Global Culture of Consumption

Besides the electronic media, other key global forces are production, commerce, and finance. Multinational corporations and other business interests look beyond national boundaries for profitable places to invest, manufacture, and sell. As Arjun Appadurai (1991, p. 194) puts it, "money, commodities, and persons unendingly chase each other around the world." Residents of many Latin American communities now depend on outside cash, remitted from international labor migration. The American economy is increasingly influenced by foreign investment and dependent on foreign labor—whether through the immigration of laborers or the export of jobs.

Globalization is driven by flows of people, technology, products, finance, information, images, and ideology (Appadurai 1990, 2001). Business, technology, and the media have increased the craving for commodities and images throughout the world (Gottdiener, ed. 2000). This has forced nation-states to accept a global culture of consumption. Almost everyone today participates in this culture. Few people have never seen a T-shirt advertising a Western product. American and English rock stars' recordings blast through the streets of Rio de Janeiro, while taxi drivers from Toronto to Madagascar play Brazilian music. Peasants and tribal people participate in the global economy not only because they have been hooked on cash, but also because their products and images are appropriated by world capitalism (Root 1996). They are commercialized by others (like the Quileute nation in the *Twilight* series). Furthermore, indigenous peoples also market their own images and products, through outlets like Cultural Survival (see Mathews 2000).

People in Motion

Globalization has both enlarged and erased old boundaries and distinctions. Arjun Appadurai (1990, p. 1) characterizes today's world as a "translocal" "interactive system" that is "strikingly new." Whether as refugees, migrants, tourists, pilgrims, proselytizers, laborers, businesspeople, development workers, employees of nongovernmental organizations, politicians, terrorists, soldiers, sports figures, or media-borne images, people appear to travel more than ever.

In previous chapters, we saw that foragers and herders are typically seminomadic or nomadic. Today, the scale of human movement has expanded dramatically. So important has transnational migration become that many Mexican villagers find "their most important kin and friends are as likely to be living hundreds or thousands of miles away as immediately around them" (Rouse 1991). Most migrants maintain their ties with their native land (phoning, Skyping, texting, e-mailing, visiting, sending money, watching home videos or "ethnic TV"). In a sense, they live multilocally—in different places at once. Dominicans in New York City, for example, have been characterized as living "between two islands": Manhattan and Hispaniola, where the Dominican Republic is located (Grasmuck and Pessar 1991). Many Dominicans—like migrants from other countries—migrate to the United States temporarily, seeking cash to transform their lifestyles when they eventually return to the Caribbean.

With so many people "in motion," the unit of anthropological study expands from the local community to the diaspora—the offspring of an area who have spread to many lands. Anthropologists increasingly follow descendants of the villages we have studied as they move from rural to urban areas and across national boundaries.

Postmodernity describes our time and situation: today's world in flux, these people on the move who have learned to manage multiple identities depending on place and context. In its most general sense, **postmodern** refers to the blurring and breakdown of established canons (rules or standards), categories, distinctions, and boundaries. The word is taken from **postmodernism**—a style and movement in architecture that succeeded modernism, beginning in the 1970s. Postmodern architecture rejected the rules, geometric order, and austerity of modernism. Modernist buildings were expected to have a clear and functional design. Postmodern design is "messier" and more playful. It draws on a diversity of styles from different times and places—including popular, ethnic, and non-Western cultures. Postmodernism extends "value" globally—well beyond classic, elite, and Western cultural forms. *Postmodern* now is used to describe comparable developments beyond architecture—in music, literature, and visual art. From this origin, postmodernity describes a world in which traditional standards, contrasts, groups, boundaries, and identities are opening up, reaching out, and breaking down.

New kinds of political and ethnic units have emerged along with globalization. In some cases, cultures and ethnic groups have banded together in larger associations. There is a growing pan-Native-American identity (Nagel 1996) and an international

With so many people on the move, the unit of anthropological study has expanded from the local community to the diaspora. This refers to the offspring of an area who have spread to many lands, such as the owners of this falafel shop in Paris, France.

What's your favorite science fiction movie or TV show? What images of other planets stand out in your memory? Can you easily visualize *Star Wars'* Death Star, poor old Alderan, Yoda's misty world in the Dagoba system, the two suns of Tatooine? How about *Avatar's* Pandora? Such movie images may be as familiar to you as those of real planets. Think, too, about how extraterrestrials have been portrayed in movies. On the one hand are *ET's* harmless plant collectors and *Avatar's* endangered Na'vi. More typical are Earth's would-be conquerors, as shown in *Independence Day, Starship Troopers, V,* and a hundred others. Still other films, most notably *The Day the Earth Stood Still* (either the 1951 or the 2008 version), feature omnipotent, omniscient guardians of interplanetary affairs. How, if at all, do the issues portrayed in such science fiction movies relate to the global issues examined in this chapter?

pantribal movement as well. Thus, in June 1992, the World Conference of Indigenous Peoples met in Rio de Janeiro concurrently with UNCED (the United Nations Conference on the Environment and Development). Along with diplomats, journalists, and environmentalists came 300 representatives of the tribal diversity that survives under globalization—from Lapland to Mali (Brooke 1992; see also Maybury-Lewis 2002). The meeting itself was a global forum, sponsored by the United Nations, perhaps the closest thing Earth has to a planetary council.

Indigenous Peoples

The term *indigenous people* entered international law with the creation in 1982 of the United Nations Working Group on Indigenous Populations (WGIP). This group, which meets annually, has members from six continents. The draft of the Declaration of Indigenous Rights, produced by the WGIP in 1989, was accepted by the UN for discussion in 1993. Convention 169, an ILO (International Labor Organization) document that supports cultural diversity and indigenous empowerment, was approved in 1989. Such documents, along with the global work of the WGIP, have influenced governments, NGOs, and international agencies to adopt policies aimed at benefiting indigenous peoples. Social movements worldwide now use "indigenous people" as a self-identifying label in their quests for social, cultural, and political rights (Brower and Johnston 2007; de la Peña 2005).

In Spanish-speaking Latin America, social scientists and politicians now favor the term *indígena* (indigenous person) over *indio* (Indian). The latter is a colonial term that European conquerors used for Native Americans, whose situation did not necessarily improve after Latin American nations gained independence from Spain and Portugal, mostly by the 1820s. For the white and *mestizo* (mixed) elites of the new nations, *indios* and their lifestyle seemed alien to (European) civilization (de la Peña 2005).

Until the mid- to late 1980s, Latin American public policy emphasized assimilation. Indigenous groups were associated with a romanticized past, but marginalized in the present, except for museums, tourism, and folkloric events. Indigenous Bolivians and Peruvians were encouraged to self-identify as *campesinos* (peasants). The past 30 years have witnessed a dramatic shift. The emphasis has shifted from assimilation—*mestizaje*—to cultural difference. In Ecuador, groups seen previously as Quichua-speaking peasants are classified now as indigenous communities with their own territories. Brazil has recognized 30 new indigenous communities in the northeast, a region previously seen as having lost its native population. Guatemala, Nicaragua, Brazil, Colombia, Mexico, Paraguay, Ecuador, Argentina, Bolivia, Peru, and Venezuela now are officially multicultural (Jackson and Warren 2005). Several national constitutions recognize the rights of indigenous peoples to cultural distinctiveness and political representation. In Colombia, indigenous territories have the same benefits as any local government (de la Peña 2005).

The indigenous rights movement exists in the context of globalization, including transnational movements focusing on human rights, women's rights, and environmentalism. Transnational organizations have helped indigenous peoples to influence legislation. Since the 1980s there has been a general shift in Latin America from authoritarian

La Paz, Bolivia: Bolivians claiming an indigenous identity rally for indigenous rights and the nationalization of that country's natural gas resources. In 2005 and again in 2009, Bolivians elected as their president Evo Morales, the candidate of the Indigenous Movement toward Socialism party. Morales, whose first language is Aymara, considers himself his country's first indigenous head of state.

to democratic rule. Still, inequality and discrimination persist, and there has been resistance to indigenous mobilization, including assassinations of leaders and their supporters. Guatemala, Peru, and Colombia have witnessed severe repression. There have been thousands of indigenous deaths, refugees, and internally displaced persons (Jackson and Warren 2005).

Ceuppens and Geschiere (2005) explore a recent upsurge, in multiple world areas, of the notion of *autochthony* (being native to, or formed in, the place where found), with an implicit call for excluding strangers. The terms *autochthony* and *indigenous* both go back to classical Greek history, with similar implications. Autochthony refers to self and soil. Indigenous literally means born inside, with the connotation in classical Greek of being born "inside the house." Both notions stress the need to safeguard ancestral lands (patrimony) from strangers, along with the rights of first-comers to special rights and protection versus later immigrants—legal or illegal (Ceuppens and Geschiere 2005).

During the 1990s, autochthony became an issue in many parts of Africa, inspiring violent efforts to exclude (European and Asian) "strangers." Simultaneously, autochthony became a key notion in debates about immigration and multiculturalism in Europe. European majority groups have claimed the label *autochthon*. This term highlights the prominence that the exclusion of strangers has assumed in day-to-day politics worldwide (Ceuppens and Geschiere 2005). One familiar example is the United States, as represented in debates over illegal immigration.

Identity in Indigenous Politics

Essentialism describes the process of viewing an identity as established, real, and frozen, so as to hide the historical processes and politics within which that identity was forged. Identities, emphatically, are not fixed. We saw in the chapter "Ethnicity and Race" that identities can be fluid and multiple. People seize on particular, sometimes competing, self-labels and identities. Some Peruvian groups, for instance, self-identify as *mestizos* but still see themselves as indigenous. Identity is a fluid, dynamic process, and there are multiple ways of being indigenous. Neither speaking an indigenous language nor wearing "native" clothing is required. Identities are asserted at particular times and places by particular individuals and groups and after various kinds of negotiations. Indigenous identity coexists with, and must be managed in the context of, other identity components, including religion, race, and gender. Identities always must be seen as (1) potentially plural, (2) emerging through a specific process, (3) ways of being someone or something in particular times and places (Jackson and Warren 2005).

The Continuance of Diversity

In our globalizing world, anthropology has a crucial role to play, by promoting a more people-centered vision of social change, one that respects the value of human biological and cultural diversity. The existence of anthropology is itself a tribute to the continuing need to understand similarities and differences among human beings throughout the world. Anthropology teaches us that the adaptive responses of humans can be more flexible than those of other species because our main adaptive means are sociocultural.

Anthropology Today *Engulfed by Climate Change, Town Seeks Lifeline*

The United Nations' Intergovernmental Panel on Climate Change estimates that 150 million people worldwide could become environmental refugees by 2050 (York 2009). The Alaskan villagers described in this news story are among the first climate change refugees in the United States. During the past 50 years, the state of Alaska has warmed at more than twice the rate of the rest of the United States (York 2009). Residents of Newtok, Alaska, belong to a federally recognized American Indian tribe. Decades ago, the U.S. government mandated that they (and other Alaskan natives) abandon a nomadic life based on hunting and fishing and settle down in what used to be a winter camp. What obligations does government have to local people whose lives have been disrupted not only by government decree but also by global warming?

NEWTOK, Alaska—The earth beneath much of Alaska is not what it used to be. The permanently frozen subsoil, known as permafrost, upon which Newtok and so many other Native Alaskan villages rest is melting, yielding to warming air temperatures and a warming ocean. Sea ice that would normally protect coastal villages is forming later in the year, allowing fall storms to pound away at the shoreline.

Erosion has made Newtok an island, caught between the ever widening Ninglick River and a slough to the north. The village is below sea level, and sinking. Boardwalks squish into the spring muck. Human waste, collected in "honey buckets" that many residents use for toilets, is often dumped within eyeshot in a village where no point is more than a five-minute walk from any other. The ragged wooden houses have to be adjusted regularly to level them on the shifting soil.

Studies say Newtok could be washed away within a decade. Along with the villages of Shishmaref and Kivalina farther to the north, it has been the hardest hit of about 180 Alaska villages that suffer some degree of erosion. Some villages plan to hunker down behind sea walls built or planned by the Army Corps of Engineers, at least for now. Others, like Newtok, have no choice but to abandon their patch of tundra. The corps has estimated that to move Newtok could cost $130 million because of its remoteness, climate and topography. That comes to almost $413,000 for each of the 315 residents. . . .

Newtok's leaders say the corps' relocation estimates are inflated, that they intend to move piecemeal rather than in one collective migration, which they say will save money. But they say government should pay, no matter the cost—if only there were a government agency charged with doing so. There is not a formal process by which a village can apply to the government to relocate.

"They grossly overestimate it, and that's why federal and state agencies are afraid to step in," said Stanley Tom, the current tribal administrator. . . . "They don't want to spend that much money." Still, Newtok has made far more progress toward moving than other villages, piecing together its move grant by grant.

Through a land swap with the U.S. Fish and Wildlife Service, it has secured a new site, on Nelson Island, nine miles south. It is safe from the waves on a windy rise above the Ninglick River. They call it Mertarvik, which means "getting water from the spring." They tell their children they will grow up in a place where E. coli does not thrive in every puddle, the way it does here.

With the help of state agencies, it won a grant of about $1 million to build a barge landing at the new site. Bids go out

continued

Anthropology Today *continued*

Thousands of indigenous people living on the Alaskan tundra derive 90 percent or more of what they eat annually from the land, the rivers, and the Bering Sea. Among them are Stanley and Elizabeth Tom and their children, shown here standing beside the Niutaq River in Newtok, Alaska. The local and regional effects of global warming have made the Toms and their fellow villagers climate change refugees.

this summer, and construction could be complete next year, providing a platform to unload equipment for building roads, water and sewer systems, houses and a new landing strip. . . .

The administrative leaders of Newtok are mostly men in their 40s, nearly all of them related. They are widely praised by outsiders for their initiative and determination to relocate.

Yet nearly any place would seem an improvement over Newtok as it exists today, and not all of its problems are rooted in climate change. Some are almost universal to Alaskan villages, which have struggled for decades to reconcile their culture of subsistence hunting and fishing with the expectations and temptations of the world outside.

Excrement dumped from honey buckets is piled on the banks of the slow-flowing Newtok River, not far from wooden shacks where residents take nightly steam baths. An elderly man drains kerosene into a puddle of snowmelt. Children pedal past a walrus skull left to rot, tusks intact, in the mud beside a boardwalk that serves as a main thoroughfare. There are no cars here, just snow machines, boats and all-terrain vehicles that tear up the tundra. Village elders speak their native Yupik more often than they speak English. They remember when the village was a collection of families who moved with the seasons, making houses from sod, fishing from Nelson Island in the summer, hunting caribou far away in the winter.

Many men still travel with the seasons to hunt and fish. Some will take boats into Bristol Bay this summer to catch salmon alongside commercial fishermen from out of state. But the waterproof jacket sewn from seal gut that Stanley Tom once wore is now stuffed inside a display case at Newtok School next to other relics.

Now Mr. Tom puts on a puffy parka to walk the few hundred feet he travels to work. He checks his e-mail messages to see if there is news from the corps . . . while his brother, Nick, sketches out a budget proposal for a nonprofit corporation to help manage the relocation, presuming the money arrives.

Source: William Yardley, "Engulfed by Climate Change, Town Seeks Lifeline," *New York Times,* May 27, 2007. Copyright © 2007 The New York Times. Reprinted by permission.

However, in the face of globalization, the cultural institutions of the past always influence subsequent adaptation, producing continued diversity in the actions and reactions of different groups. With our knowledge and our awareness of our professional responsibilities, let us work to keep anthropology, the study of humankind, the most humanistic of all the sciences.

Summary

1. Fueling global climate change are human population growth and use of fossil fuels, which produce greenhouse gases. The atmospheric concentration of those gases has increased since the Industrial Revolution, and especially since 1978. Climate change encompasses global warming along with changing sea levels, precipitation, storms, and ecosystem effects. Coastal communities can anticipate increased flooding and more severe storms and surges.

2. Anthropology always has been concerned with how environmental forces influence humans and how human activities affect the biosphere. Many indigenous groups did a reasonable job of preserving their ecosystems. An ethnoecology is any society's set of environmental practices and perceptions—that is, its cultural model of the environment in relation to people and society. Indigenous ethnoecologies increasingly are being challenged by global forces that work to exploit and degrade—and that sometimes aim to protect—the environment. The challenge for applied ecological anthropology is to devise culturally appropriate strategies for conservation in the face of unrelenting population growth and commercial expansion.

3. Deforestation is a major factor in the loss of global biodiversity. Causes of deforestation include demographic pressure (from births or immigration) on subsistence economies; commercial logging; road building; cash cropping; fuel wood needs associated with urban expansion; and clearing and burning associated with livestock and grazing. The fact that forest loss has several causes has a policy implication: Different deforestation scenarios require different conservation strategies. Applied anthropologists must work to make "good for the globe" good for the people.

4. Different degrees of destruction, domination, resistance, survival, and modification of native cultures may follow interethnic contact. This may lead to a tribe's cultural collapse (ethnocide) or its physical extinction (genocide). Cultural imperialism refers to the spread of one culture and its imposition on other cultures, which it modifies, replaces, or destroys—usually because of differential economic and political power. Some worry that modern technology, including the mass media, is destroying traditional cultures. But others see an important role for new technology in allowing local cultures to express themselves.

5. As the forces of globalization spread, they are indigenized to fit local cultures. The mass media can help diffuse a national culture within and beyond its own boundaries. The media, including the Internet, also play a role in preserving ethnic and national identities among people who lead transnational lives. Business, technology, and the media have increased the craving for commodities and images throughout the world, creating a global culture of consumption.

6. People travel more than ever. But migrants also maintain ties with home, so they live multilocally. With so many people "in motion," the unit of anthropological study expands from the local community to the diaspora. Postmodernity describes this world in flux, such people on the move who manage multiple social identities depending on place and context. With globalization, new kinds of political and ethnic units are emerging as others break down or disappear.

7. The term and concept *indigenous people* has gained legitimacy within international law. Governments, NGOs, and international agencies have adopted policies designed to recognize and benefit indigenous peoples. Social movements worldwide have adopted this term as a self-identifying and political label based on past oppression but now signaling a search for social, cultural, and political rights.

8. In Latin America, emphasis has shifted from assimilation to identities that value difference. Transnational organizations have helped indigenous peoples influence national legislative agendas. Recent use of the notion of autochthony (being native to, or formed in, the place where found) includes a call to exclude strangers, such as recent and illegal immigrants. Identity is a fluid, dynamic process, and there are multiple ways of being indigenous. No social movement exists apart from the nation and world that include it.

Key Terms

climate change, *443*	essentialism, *456*	postmodern, *453*
cultural imperialism, *443*	ethnoecology, *445*	postmodernism, *453*
diaspora, *451*	greenhouse effect, *442*	postmodernity, *453*
ecological anthropology, *444*	indigenized, *450*	Westernization, *448*

Go to our Online Learning Center website at **www.mhhe.com/kottak** for Internet resources directly related to the content of this chapter.

Glossary

A

A. (Australopithecus) afarensis Early form of *Australopithecus,* found in Ethiopia at Hadar ("Lucy") and in Tanzania at Laetoli; dating to the period between 3.8 and 3.0 m.y.a. (129)

A. africanus First *Australopithecus* discovered, in South Africa; dating to 3.0–2.5 m.y.a. (134)

A. anamensis Earliest form of *Australopithecus* yet discovered; found in Kenya and dating to 4.2 m.y.a. (129)

A. boisei Late, hyperrobust form of *Australopithecus,* found in East Africa and dating to the period between 2.6 and 1.2 m.y.a. (137)

A. garhi Found in Ethiopia in association with tools and dating to 2.5 m.y.a. (140)

A. robustus Robust form of *Australopithecus,* found in South Africa and dating to the period between 2.6 and 2.0 m.y.a., aka Paranthropus. (134)

absolute dating Dating techniques that establish dates in numbers or ranges of numbers; examples include the radiometric methods of ^{14}C, K/A, ^{238}U, TL, and ESR dating. (46)

acculturation The exchange of cultural features that results when groups come into continuous firsthand contact; the original cultural patterns of either or both groups may be altered, but the groups remain distinct. (34)

Acheulian Derived from the French village of St. Acheul, where these tools were first identified; Lower Paleolithic tool tradition associated with *H. erectus.* (148)

achieved status Social status that comes through talents, actions, efforts, activities, and accomplishments, rather than ascription. (279)

adaptation The process by which organisms cope with environmental stresses. (3)

adaptive Favored by natural selection in a particular environment. (76)

age set Group uniting all men or women (usually men) born during a certain time span; this group controls property and often has political and military functions. (281)

agriculture Nonindustrial system of plant cultivation characterized by continuous and intensive use of land and labor. (253)

allele A biochemical difference involving a particular gene. (73)

analogies Similarities arising as a result of similar selective forces; traits produced by convergent evolution. (99)

anatomically modern humans (AMHs) Including the Cro-Magnons of Europe (31,000 B.P.) and the older fossils from Skhūl (100,000) and Qafzeh (92,000); continue through the present. (158)

animism Belief in souls or doubles. (350)

anthropoids Members of Anthropoidea, one of the two suborders of primates; monkeys, apes, and humans are anthropoids. (100)

anthropology The study of the human species and its immediate ancestors. (2)

anthropology and education Anthropological research in classrooms, homes, and neighborhoods, viewing students as total cultural creatures whose enculturation and attitudes toward education belong to a larger context that includes family, peers, and society. (423)

anthropometry The measurement of human body parts and dimensions, including skeletal parts (*osteometry*). (49)

applied anthropology The application of anthropological data, perspectives, theory, and methods to identify, assess, and solve contemporary social problems. (12)

arboreal Tree-dwelling. (100)

archaeological anthropology The branch of anthropology that reconstructs, describes, and interprets human behavior and cultural patterns through material remains; best known for the study of prehistory. Also known as "archaeology." (7)

archaic *Homo sapiens* Early *H. sapiens,* consisting of the Neandertals of Europe and the Middle East, the Neandertal-like hominins of Africa and Asia, and the immediate ancestors of all these hominins; lived from about 300,000 to 30,000 B.P. (153)

Ardipithecus The earliest widely accepted hominin genus (5.8–4.4 m.y.a.); includes species *kadabba* (earlier) and *ramidus* (later). (120)

ascribed status Social status (e.g., race or gender) that people have little or no choice about occupying. (278)

assimilation The process of change that a minority group may experience when it moves to a country where another culture dominates; the minority is incorporated into the dominant culture to the point that it no longer exists as a separate cultural unit. (406)

australopithecines Varied group of Pliocene–Pleistocene hominins. The term is derived from their former classification as members of a distinct subfamily, the Australopithecinae; now they are distinguished from *Homo* only at the genus level. (128)

authority The formal, socially approved use of power, e.g., by government officials. (271)

Aztec Last independent state in the Valley of Mexico; capital was Tenochtitlan. Thrived between 1325 C.E. and the Spanish conquest in 1520. (215)

B

balanced polymorphism Two or more forms, such as alleles of the same gene, that maintain a constant frequency in a population from generation to generation. (77)

balanced reciprocity See *generalized reciprocity*. (264)

band Basic unit of social organization among foragers. A band includes fewer than one hundred people; it often splits up seasonally. (250)

behavioral modernity The advent of modern human behavioral capabilities based on

symbolic thought and language, in addition to modern anatomy. (162)

big man Figure often found among tribal horticulturalists and pastoralists. The big man occupies no office but creates his reputation through entrepreneurship and generosity to others. Neither his wealth nor his position passes to his heirs. (278)

biocultural Referring to the inclusion and combination (to solve a common problem) of both biological and cultural approaches—one of anthropology's hallmarks. (5)

biological anthropology The branch of anthropology that studies human biological diversity in time and space—for instance, hominid evolution, human genetics, human biological adaptation; also includes primatology (behavior and evolution of monkeys and apes). Also called *physical anthropology*. (10)

bipedalism Upright two-legged locomotion, the key feature differentiating early hominins from the apes. (101)

Black English Vernacular (BEV) A rule-governed dialect of American English with roots in southern English. BEV is spoken by African American youth and by many adults in their casual, intimate speech—sometimes called *ebonics*. (239)

blade tool The basic Upper Paleolithic tool type, hammered off a prepared core. (165)

bone biology The study of bone as a biological tissue, including its genetics; cell structure; growth, development, and decay; and patterns of movement (biomechanics). (48)

bourgeoisie One of Karl Marx's opposed classes; owners of the means of production (factories, mines, large farms, and other sources of subsistence). (375)

brachiation Swinging hand over hand movement through trees, characteristic of arboreal apes and some New World monkeys. (105)

bridewealth A customary gift before, at, or after marriage from the husband and his kin to the wife and her kin; see also *progeny price*. (315)

broad-spectrum revolution Period beginning around 20,000 B.P. in the Middle East and 12,000 B.P. in Europe, during which a wider range, or broader spectrum, of plant and animal life was hunted, gathered, collected, caught, and fished; revolutionary because it led to food production. (174)

bronze   An alloy of arsenic and copper or of tin and copper. (206)

C

call systems   Systems of communication among nonhuman primates, composed of a limited number of sounds that vary in intensity and duration. Tied to environmental stimuli. (222)

capital   Wealth or resources invested in business, with the intent of producing a profit. (371)

capitalist world economy   The single world system, which emerged in the 16th century, committed to production for sale, with the object of maximizing profits rather than supplying domestic needs. (370)

cargo cults   Postcolonial, acculturative, religious movements common in Melanesia that attempt to explain European domination and wealth and to achieve similar success magically by mimicking European behavior. (363)

caste system   Closed, hereditary system of stratification, often dictated by religion; hierarchical social status is ascribed at birth, so that people are locked into their parents' social position. (312)

catastrophism   View that extinct species were destroyed by fires, floods, and other catastrophes. After each destructive event, God created again, leading to contemporary species. (69)

chiefdom   Form of sociopolitical organization intermediate between the tribe and the state; kin-based with differential access to resources and a permanent political structure. A ranked society in which relations among villages as well as among individuals are unequal, with smaller villages under the authority of leaders in larger villages; has a two-level settlement hierarchy. (204, 273)

chromosomes   Basic genetic units, occurring in matching (homologous) pairs; lengths of DNA made up of multiple genes. (72)

clan   Unilineal descent group based on stipulated descent. (306)

climate change   Global warming, plus changing sea levels, precipitation, storms, and ecosystem effects. (443)

cline   Gradual shift in gene (allele) frequencies between neighboring populations. (80)

Clovis tradition   Stone technology based on a projectile point that was fastened to the end of a hunting spear; it flourished between 12,000 and 11,000 B.P. in North America. (167)

colonialism   The political, social, economic, and cultural domination of a territory and its people by a foreign power for an extended time. (378)

communism   Spelled with a lowercase *c*, describes a social system in which property is owned by the community and in which people work for the common good. (384)

Communism   Spelled with a capital *C*, a political movement and doctrine seeking to overthrow capitalism and to establish a form of communism such as that which prevailed in the Soviet Union (USSR) from 1917 to 1991. (384)

communitas   Intense community spirit, a feeling of great social solidarity, equality, and togetherness; characteristic of people experiencing liminality together. (349)

conflict resolution   The means by which disputes are socially regulated and settled; found in all societies, but the resolution methods tend to be more formal and effective in states than in nonstates. (275)

convergent evolution   Independent operation of similar selective forces; process by which analogies are produced. (99)

core   Dominant structural position in the world system; consists of the strongest and most powerful states with advanced systems of production. (371)

core values   Key, basic, or central values that integrate a culture and help distinguish it from others. (21)

correlation   An association between two or more variables such that when one changes (varies), the other(s) also change(s) (covaries); for example, temperature and sweating. (250)

creationism   Explanation for the origin of species given in Genesis: God created the species during the original six days of Creation. (68)

Cro-Magnon   The first fossil find (1868) of an AMH, from France's Dordogne Valley. (167)

cultural anthropology   The study of human society and culture; describes, analyzes, interprets, and explains social and cultural similarities and differences. (7)

cultural colonialism   Within a nation or empire, domination by one ethnic group or nationality and its culture/ideology over others—e.g., the dominance of Russian people, language, and culture in the former Soviet Union. (411)

cultural consultant   Someone the ethnographer gets to know in the field, who teaches him or her about their society and culture, aka *informant*. (55)

cultural imperialism   The rapid spread or advance of one culture at the expense of others, or its imposition on other cultures, which it modifies, replaces, or destroys—usually because of differential economic or political influence. (448)

cultural relativism   The position that the values and standards of cultures differ and deserve respect. Anthropology is characterized by methodological rather than moral relativism: In order to understand another culture fully, anthropologists try to understand its members' beliefs and motivations. Methodological relativism does not preclude making moral judgments or taking action. (32)

cultural resource management (CRM) The branch of applied archaeology aimed at preserving sites threatened by dams, highways, and other projects. (15)

cultural rights   Doctrine that certain rights are vested not in individuals but in identifiable groups, such as religious and ethnic minorities and indigenous societies. (32)

cultural transmission   A basic feature of language; transmission through learning. (224)

culture   Traditions and customs that govern behavior and beliefs; distinctly human; transmitted through learning. (2)

cuneiform   Early Mesopotamian writing that used a stylus (writing implement) to write wedge-shaped impressions on raw clay; from the Latin word for "wedge." (206)

curer   Specialized role acquired through a culturally appropriate process of selection, training, certification, and acquisition of a professional image; the curer is consulted by patients, who believe in his or her special powers, and receives some form of special consideration; a cultural universal. (429)

D

daughter languages   Languages developing out of the same parent language; for example, French and Spanish are daughter languages of Latin. (240)

descent   Rule assigning social identity on the basis of some aspect of one's ancestry. (398)

descent group   A permanent social unit whose members claim common ancestry; fundamental to tribal society. (305)

descriptive linguistics   The scientific study of a spoken language, including its phonology, morphology, lexicon, and syntax. (228)

development anthropology   The branch of applied anthropology that focuses on social issues in, and the cultural dimension of, economic development. (418)

diaspora   The offspring of an area who have spread to many lands. (451)

differential access   Unequal access to resources; basic attribute of chiefdoms and states. Superordinates have favored access to such resources, while the access of subordinates is limited by superordinates. (273)

diffusion   Borrowing between cultures either directly or through intermediaries. (34)

diglossia   The existence of "high" (formal) and "low" (familial) dialects of a single language, such as German. (235)

discrimination   Policies and practices that harm a group and its members. (410)

disease   A scientifically identified health threat caused by a bacterium, virus, fungus, parasite, or other pathogen. (427)

displacement   A linguistic capacity that allows humans to speak of things and events that are not present. (225)

domestic   Within or pertaining to the home. (331)

domestic–public dichotomy   Contrast between women's role in the home and men's role in public life, with a corresponding social devaluation of women's work and worth. (331)

dominant   Allele that masks another allele in a heterozygote. (72)

dowry   A marital exchange in which the wife's group provides substantial gifts to the husband's family. (315)

E

ecological anthropology   Study of cultural adaptations to environments. (444)

economy   A population's system of production, distribution, and consumption of resources. (256)

egalitarian society   A type of society, most typically found among foragers, that lacks status distinctions except for those based on age, gender, and individual qualities, talents, and achievements. (203)

emic   The research strategy that focuses on native explanations and criteria of significance. (55)

enculturation   The social process by which culture is learned and transmitted across the generations. (18)

endogamy   Marriage between people of the same social group. (312)

equity, increased   A reduction in absolute poverty and a fairer (more even) distribution of wealth. (419)

essentialism   The process of viewing an identity as established, real, and frozen, so as to hide the historical processes and politics within which that identity developed. (456)

estrus   Period of maximum sexual receptivity in female baboons, chimpanzees, and other primates, signaled by vaginal area swelling and coloration. (26)

ethnic group   Group distinguished by cultural similarities (shared among members of that group) and differences (between that group and others); ethnic group members share beliefs, values, habits, customs, and norms, and a common language, religion, history, geography, kinship, and/or race. (393)

ethnicity   Identification with, and feeling part of, an ethnic group, and exclusion from certain other groups because of this affiliation. (394)

ethnocentrism   The tendency to view one's own culture as best and to judge the behavior and beliefs of culturally different people by one's own standards. (31)

ethnocide   Destruction by a dominant group of the culture of an ethnic group. (411)

ethnoecology   A culture's set of environmental practices and perceptions. (445)

ethnography   Field work in a particular culture. (7)

ethnology   The theoretical, comparative study of society and culture; compares cultures in time and space. (7)

etic   The research strategy that emphasizes the observer's rather than the natives' explanations, categories, and criteria of significance. (56)

evolution   Descent with modification; change in form over generations. (69)

excavation   Digging through the layers of deposits that make up an archaeological site. (44)

exogamy   Mating or marriage outside one's kin group; a cultural universal. (309)

extended family household   Expanded household including three or more generations. (302)

F

family   A group of people (e.g., parents, children, siblings, grandparents, grandchildren, uncles, aunts, nephews, nieces, cousins, spouses, siblings-in-law, parents-in-law, children-in-law) who are considered to be related in some way, for example by "blood" (common ancestry or descent) or marriage. (298)

family of orientation   Nuclear family in which one is born and grows up. (299)

family of procreation   Nuclear family established when one marries and has children. (299)

fiscal   Pertaining to finances and taxation. (288)

focal vocabulary   A set of words and distinctions that are particularly important to certain groups (those with particular foci of experience or activity), such as types of snow to Eskimos or skiers. (232)

food production   Cultivation of plants and domestication (stockbreeding) of animals; first developed in the Middle East 10,000 to 12,000 years ago. (4)

fossils   Remains (e.g., bones), traces or impressions (e.g., footprints) of ancient life. (43)

G

gender roles   The tasks and activities that a culture assigns to each sex. (326)

gender stereotypes   Oversimplified but strongly held ideas about the characteristics of males and females. (326)

gender stratification   Unequal distribution of rewards (socially valued resources, power, prestige, and personal freedom) between men and women, reflecting their different positions in a social hierarchy. (326)

gene   Area in a chromosome pair that determines, wholly or partially, a particular biological trait, such as whether one's blood type is A, B, AB, or O. (73)

gene flow   Exchange of genetic material between populations of the same species through direct or indirect interbreeding. (78)

gene pool   All the alleles and genotypes within a breeding population—the "pool" of genetic material available. (74)

genealogical method   Procedures by which ethnographers discover and record connections of kinship, descent, and marriage, using diagrams and symbols. (54)

general anthropology   The field of anthropology as a whole, consisting of cultural, archaeological, biological, and linguistic anthropology. (4)

generality   Culture pattern or trait that exists in some but not all societies. (27)

generalized reciprocity   Principle that characterizes exchanges between closely related individuals: As social distance increases, reciprocity becomes balanced and finally negative. (264)

genetic evolution   Change in gene frequency within a breeding population. (75)

genocide   Policies aimed at, and/or resulting in, the physical extinction (through mass murder) of a people perceived as a racial group, that is, as sharing defining physical, genetic, or other biological characteristics. (411)

genotype   An organism's hereditary makeup. (73)

glacials   The four or five major advances of continental ice sheets in northern Europe and North America. (153)

globalization   The accelerating interdependence of nations in a world system linked economically and through mass media and modern transportation systems. (34)

gracile   Small, slight; opposite of *robust*. (134)

greenhouse effect   Warming from trapped atmospheric gases. (442)

H

H. (Homo) erectus   Hominin type that lived from approximately 1.9 to 300,000 m.y.a.; widely distributed throughout the Old World; immediate predecessor of *Homo sapiens*. (145)

Halafian   An early (7500–6500 B.P.) and widespread pottery style, first found in northern Syria; refers to a delicate ceramic style and to the period when the first chiefdoms emerged. (203)

haplogroup   Lineage or branch of a genetic tree marked by one or more specific genetic mutations. (83)

head, village   See *village head*.

health care systems   Beliefs, customs, and specialists concerned with ensuring health and preventing and curing illness; a cultural universal. (429)

hegemony   The internalization of a dominant ideology. (289)

Herto   Very early (151,000 m.y.a.) AMH fossils, found in Ethiopia. (159)

heterozygous   Having dissimilar alleles of a given gene. (73)

Hilly Flanks   Woodland zone that flanks the Tigris and Euphrates rivers to the north; zone of wild wheat and barley and of sedentism (settled, nonmigratory life) preceding food production. (178)

historical linguistics   Subdivision of linguistics that studies languages over time. (240)

holistic   Interested in the whole of the human condition: past, present, and future; biology, society, language, and culture. (2)

hominid   A member of the taxonomic family that includes humans and the African apes and their immediate ancestors. (23)

hominin   A member of the human lineage after its split from ancestral chimps; used to describe all the human species that ever have existed, including the extinct ones, but excluding chimps and gorillas. (23)

hominoid   Zoological superfamily that includes all fossil and living apes and hominins. (105)

Homo erectus   See *H. (Homo) erectus.* (145)

Homo habilis   Term coined by L. S. B. and Mary Leakey; ancestor or contemporary of *H. erectus;* lived from about 1.9 to 1.44 m.y.a. (137)

homologies   Traits that organisms have jointly inherited from their common ancestor. (97)

homozygous   Possessing identical alleles of a particular gene. (73)

horticulture   Nonindustrial system of plant cultivation in which plots lie fallow for varying lengths of time. (251)

human rights   Doctrine that invokes a realm of justice and morality beyond and superior to particular countries, cultures, and religions. Human rights, usually seen as vested in individuals, would include the right to speak freely, to hold religious beliefs without persecution, and not to be enslaved. (32)

hypodescent   A rule that automatically places the children of a union or mating between members of different socioeconomic groups in the less privileged group. (398)

I

illness   A condition of poor health perceived or felt by an individual. (427)

imperialism   A policy of extending the rule of a nation or empire over foreign nations and of taking and holding foreign colonies. (377)

incest   Sexual relations with a close relative. (309)

increased equity   See *equity, increased.*

independent assortment (Mendel's law of)   Chromosomes are inherited independently of one another. (74)

independent invention   Development of the same culture trait or pattern in separate cultures as a result of comparable needs and circumstances. (34)

indigenized   Modified to fit the local culture. (450)

indigenous peoples   The original inhabitants of particular territories; often descendants of tribespeople who live on as culturally distinct colonized peoples, many of whom aspire to autonomy. (387)

Industrial Revolution   The historical transformation (in Europe, after 1750) of "traditional" into "modern" societies through industrialization of the economy. (373)

informed consent   Agreement to take part in research, after the people being studied have been told about that research's purpose, nature, procedures, and potential impact on them. (60)

intellectual property rights (IPR)   Each society's cultural base—its core beliefs and principles. IPR is claimed as a group right—a cultural right, allowing indigenous groups to control who may know and use their collective knowledge and its applications. (33)

interglacials   Extended warm periods between such major glacials as Riss and Würm. (153)

international culture   Cultural traditions that extend beyond national boundaries. (30)

intersex   Pertaining to a group of conditions reflecting a discrepancy between the external genitals (penis, vagina, etc.) and the internal genitals (testes, ovaries, etc.). (339)

intervention philosophy Guiding principle of colonialism, conquest, missionization, or development; an ideological justification for outsiders to guide native peoples in specific directions. (382)

interview schedule Ethnographic tool for structuring a formal interview. A prepared form (usually printed) that guides interviews with households or individuals being compared systematically. Contrasts with a questionnaire because the researcher has personal contact and records people's answers. (54)

K

key cultural consultant An expert on a particular aspect of local life who helps the ethnographer understand that aspect. Also called *key informant*. (55)

kinesics The study of communication through body movements, stances, gestures, and facial expressions. (226)

L

law A legal code, including trial and enforcement; characteristic of state-organized societies. (275)

leveling mechanisms Customs and social actions that operate to reduce differences in wealth and thus to bring standouts in line with community norms. (358)

levirate Custom by which a widow marries the brother of her deceased husband. (317)

lexicon Vocabulary; a dictionary containing all the morphemes in a language and their meaning. (228)

life history Of a cultural consultant; provides a personal cultural portrait of existence or change in a culture. (55)

liminality The critically important marginal or in-between phase of a rite of passage. (354)

lineage Unilineal descent group based on demonstrated descent. (306)

linguistic anthropology The branch of anthropology that studies linguistic variation in time and space, including interrelations between language and culture; includes *historical linguistics* and *sociolinguistics*. (11)

longitudinal research Long-term study of a community, society, culture, or other unit, usually based on repeated visits. (57)

M

magic Use of supernatural techniques to accomplish specific aims. (352)

maize Corn; domesticated in highland Mexico. (186)

majority groups Superordinate, dominant, or controlling groups in a social–political hierarchy. (396)

mana Sacred impersonal force in Melanesian and Polynesian religions. (351)

manioc Cassava; a tuber domesticated in the South American lowlands. (186)

market principle Profit-oriented principle of exchange that dominates in states, particularly industrial states. Goods and services are bought and sold, and values are determined by supply and demand. (262)

matrilineal descent Unilineal descent rule in which people join the mother's group automatically at birth and stay members throughout life. (306)

matrilocality Customary residence with the wife's relatives after marriage, so that children grow up in their mother's community. (308)

means (or factors) of production Land, labor, technology, and capital—major productive resources. (258)

medical anthropology Unites biological and cultural anthropologists in the study of disease, health problems, health care systems, and theories about illness in different cultures and ethnic groups. (427)

meiosis Special process by which sex cells are produced; four cells are produced from one, each with half the genetic material of the original cell. (74)

melanin Substance manufactured in specialized cells in the lower layers of the epidermis (outer skin layer); melanin cells in dark skin produce more melanin than do those in light skin. (84)

Mendelian genetics   Studies ways in which chromosomes transmit genes across the generations. (72)

Mesoamerica   "Middle America," including Mexico, Guatemala, and Belize. (179)

Mesolithic   Tool-making tradition between Upper Paleolithic and Neolithic, based on very small stone tools—*microliths*. (174)

Mesopotamia   The area between the Tigris and Euphrates rivers in what is now southern Iraq and southwestern Iran; location of the first cities and states. (200)

metallurgy   Knowledge of the properties of metals, including their extraction and processing and the manufacture of metal tools. (206)

minority groups   Subordinate groups in a social–political hierarchy, with inferior power and less secure access to resources than majority groups have. (395)

mitosis   Ordinary cell division; DNA molecules copy themselves, creating two identical cells out of one. (74)

mode of production   Way of organizing production—a set of social relations through which labor is deployed to wrest energy from nature by means of tools, skills, and knowledge. (257)

molecular anthropology   Genetic analysis, involving comparison of DNA sequences, to determine evolutionary links and distances among species and among ancient and modern populations. (47)

monotheism   Worship of an eternal, omniscient, omnipotent, and omnipresent supreme being. (350)

morphology   The study of form; used in linguistics (the study of morphemes and word construction) and for form in general—for example, biomorphology relates to physical form. (228)

Mousterian   Middle Paleolithic tool-making tradition associated with Neandertals. (156)

multiculturalism   The view of cultural diversity in a country as something good and desirable; a multicultural society socializes individuals not only into the dominant

(national) culture, but also into an ethnic culture. (407)

multivariate   Involving multiple factors, causes, or variables. (196)

mutation   Change in the DNA molecules of which genes and chromosomes are built. (78)

m.y.a.   Million years ago. (111)

N

nation   Once a synonym for "ethnic group," designating a single culture sharing a language, religion, history, territory, ancestry, and kinship; now usually a synonym for "state" or "nation-state." (404)

nation-state   An autonomous political entity, a country like the United States or Canada. (404)

national culture   Cultural experiences, beliefs, learned behavior patterns, and values shared by citizens of the same nation. (30)

nationalities   Ethnic groups that once had, or wish to have or regain, autonomous political status (their own country). (405)

Natufians   Widespread Middle Eastern culture, dated to between 12,500 and 10,500 B.P.; subsisted on intensive wild cereal collecting and gazelle hunting and had year-round villages. (178)

natural selection   Originally formulated by Charles Darwin and Alfred Russel Wallace; the process by which nature selects the forms most fit to survive and reproduce in a given environment, such as the tropics. (70)

Neandertals   *H. sapiens neanderthalensis,* representing an archaic *H. sapiens* subspecies, lived in Europe and the Middle East between 130,000 and 30,000 B.P. (153)

negative reciprocity   See *generalized reciprocity.* (264)

neoliberalism   Revival of Adam Smith's classic economic liberalism, the idea that governments should not regulate private enterprise and that free market forces should rule; a currently dominant intervention philosophy. (383)

Neolithic   "New Stone Age," coined to describe techniques of grinding and polishing stone tools; the first cultural period in a region in which the first signs of domestication are present. (175)

neolocality Postmarital residence pattern in which a couple establishes a new place of residence rather than living with or near either set of parents. (302)

nomadism, pastoral Movement throughout the year by the whole pastoral group (men, women, and children) with their animals. More generally, such constant movement in pursuit of strategic resources. (256)

norms Cultural standards or guidelines that enable individuals to distinguish between appropriate and inappropriate behavior in a given society. (275)

O

office Permanent political position. (283)

Oldowan pebble tools Earliest (1.8–2.6 m.y.a.) stone tools; first discovered in 1931 by L. S. B. and Mary Leakey at Olduvai Gorge. (137)

opposable thumb A thumb that can touch all the other fingers. (101)

overinnovation Characteristic of development projects that require major changes in people's daily lives, especially ones that interfere with customary subsistence pursuits. (420)

P

paleoanthropology The study of hominin evolution and human life as revealed by the fossil record. (43)

Paleolithic Old Stone Age (from Greek roots meaning "old" and "stone"); divided into Lower (early), Middle, and Upper (late). (147)

paleontology Study of ancient life through the fossil record. (42)

paleopathology Study of disease and injury in skeletons from archaeological sites. (48)

pantribal sodality A non-kin-based group that exists throughout a tribe, spanning several villages. (280)

participant observation A characteristic ethnographic technique; taking part in the events one is observing, describing, and analyzing. (51)

particularity Distinctive or unique culture trait, pattern, or integration. (27)

pastoralists People who use a food-producing strategy of adaptation based on care of herds of domesticated animals. (255)

patriarchy Political system ruled by men in which women have inferior social and political status, including basic human rights. (334)

patrilineal descent Unilineal descent rule in which people join the father's group automatically at birth and stay members throughout life. (306)

patrilineal–patrilocal complex An interrelated constellation of patrilineality, patrilocality, warfare, and male supremacy. (333)

patrilocality Customary residence with the husband's relatives after marriage, so that children grow up in their father's community. (308)

peasant Small-scale agriculturist living in a state, with rent fund obligations. (262)

periphery Weakest structural position in the world system. (371)

phenotype An organism's evident traits; its "manifest biology"—anatomy and physiology. (75)

phenotypical adaptation Adaptive biological changes that occur during the individual's lifetime, made possible by biological plasticity. (93)

phoneme Significant sound contrast in a language that serves to distinguish meaning, as in minimal pairs. (229)

phonemics The study of the sound contrasts (phonemes) of a particular language. (229)

phonetics The study of speech sounds in general; what people actually say in various languages. (229)

phonology The study of sounds used in speech. (228)

physical anthropology See *biological anthropology*. (10)

Pleistocene Epoch of *Homo*'s appearance and evolution; began 2 million years ago; divided into Lower, Middle, and Upper. (153)

plural marriage   Marriage of a man to two or more women (polygyny) or marriage of a woman to two or more men (polyandry)—at the same time; see also *polygamy*. (316)

plural society   A society that combines ethnic contrasts, ecological specialization (i.e., use of different environmental resources by each ethnic group), and the economic interdependence of those groups. (406)

polyandry   Variety of plural marriage in which a woman has more than one husband. (316)

polygamy   Marriage with three or more spouses, at the same time; see also *plural marriage*. (316)

polygyny   Variety of plural marriage in which a man has more than one wife. (316)

polytheism   Belief in several deities who control aspects of nature. (350)

population genetics   Field that studies causes of genetic variation, maintenance, and change in breeding populations. (72)

postcolonial   Referring to interactions between European nations and the societies they colonized (mainly after 1800); more generally, "postcolonial" may be used to signify a position against imperialism and Eurocentrism. (382)

postmodern   In its most general sense, describes the blurring and breakdown of established canons (rules, standards), categories, distinctions, and boundaries. (453)

postmodernism   A style and movement in architecture that succeeded modernism. Compared with modernism, postmodernism is less geometric, less functional, less austere, more playful, and more willing to include elements from diverse times and cultures; *postmodern* now describes comparable developments in music, literature, and visual art. (453)

postmodernity   Condition of a world in flux, with people on-the-move, in which established groups, boundaries, identities, contrasts, and standards are reaching out and breaking down. (453)

potlatch   Competitive feast among Indians on the North Pacific Coast of North America. (265)

power   The ability to exercise one's will over others—to do what one wants; the basis of political status. (271)

prejudice   Devaluing (looking down on) a group because of its assumed behavior, values, capabilities, or attributes. (410)

prestige   Esteem, respect, or approval for acts, deeds, or qualities considered exemplary. (286)

primary states   States that arise on their own (through competition among chiefdoms), and not through contact with other state societies. (204)

primates   Monkeys, apes, and prosimians; members of the zoological order that includes humans. (96)

primatology   The study of the biology, behavior, social life, and evolution of monkeys, apes, and other nonhuman primates. (96)

productivity   The ability to use the rules of one's language to create new expressions comprehensible to other speakers; a basic feature of language. (224)

progeny price   A gift from the husband and his kin to the wife and her kin before, at, or after marriage; legitimizes children born to the woman as members of the husband's descent group. (315)

prosimians   The primate suborder that includes lemurs, lorises, and tarsiers. (100)

protolanguage   Language ancestral to several daughter languages. (240)

R

race   An ethnic group assumed to have a biological basis. (396)

racial classification   The attempt to assign humans to discrete categories (purportedly) based on common ancestry. (80)

racism   Discrimination against an ethnic group assumed to have a biological basis. (396)

random genetic drift   Change in gene frequency that results not from natural selection but from chance; most common in small populations. (78)

ranked society   A type of society with hereditary inequality but not social stratification; individuals are ranked in terms of their genealogical closeness to the chief, but there is a continuum of status, with many individuals and kin groups ranked about equally. (203)

recessive   Genetic trait masked by a dominant trait. (72)

reciprocity   One of the three principles of exchange. Governs exchange between social equals; major exchange mode in band and tribal societies. (263)

reciprocity continuum   Regarding exchanges, a range running from generalized reciprocity (closely related/deferred return) through balanced reciprocity to negative reciprocity (strangers/immediate return). (264)

redistribution   Major exchange mode of chiefdoms, many archaic states, and some states with managed economies. (263)

refugees   People who have been forced (involuntary refugees) or who have chosen (voluntary refugees) to flee a country, to escape persecution or war. (411)

relative dating   Dating technique (e.g., stratigraphy) that establishes a time frame in relation to other strata or materials, rather than absolute dates in numbers. (46)

religion   Beliefs and rituals concerned with supernatural beings, powers, and forces. (348)

revitalization movements   Movements that occur in times of change, in which religious leaders emerge and undertake to alter or revitalize a society. (362)

rites of passage   Culturally defined activities associated with the transition from one place or stage of life to another. (354)

ritual   Behavior that is formal, stylized, repetitive, and stereotyped, performed earnestly as a social act; rituals are held at set times and places and have liturgical orders. (353)

robust   Large, strong, sturdy; said of skull, skeleton, muscle, and teeth; opposite of *gracile*. (134)

S

sample   A smaller study group chosen to represent a larger population. (54)

Sapir-Whorf hypothesis   Theory that different languages produce different ways of thinking. (231)

science   A systematic field of study or body of knowledge that aims, through experiment, observation, and deduction, to produce reliable explanations of phenomena, with reference to the material and physical world. (11)

scientific medicine   As distinguished from Western medicine, a health care system based on scientific knowledge and procedures, encompassing such fields as pathology, microbiology, biochemistry, surgery, diagnostic technology, and applications. (429)

sedentism   Settled (sedentary) life; preceded food production in the Old World and followed it in the New World. (178)

semantics   A language's meaning system. (234)

semiperiphery   Structural position in the world system intermediate between core and periphery. (371)

settlement hierarchy   A ranked series of communities differing in size, function, and type of building; a three-level settlement hierarchy indicates state organization. (214)

sexual dimorphism   Marked differences in male and female biology, besides the contrasts in breasts and genitals, and temperament. (324)

sexual orientation   A person's habitual sexual attraction to, and activities with: persons of the opposite sex (*heterosexuality*), the same sex (*homosexuality*), or both sexes (*bisexuality*). (342)

sexual selection   Based on differential success in mating, the process in which certain traits of one sex (e.g., color in male birds) are selected because of advantages they confer in winning mates. (77)

shaman   A part-time religious practitioner who mediates between ordinary people and supernatural beings and forces. (350)

smelting   The high-temperature process by which pure metal is produced from an ore. (206)

social control   Those fields of the social system (beliefs, practices, and institutions) that are most actively involved in the maintenance of any norms and the regulation of any conflict. (288)

society   Organized life in groups; typical of humans and other animals. (2)

sociolinguistics   Study of relationships between social and linguistic variation; study of language in its social context. (11, 235)

sociopolitical typology   Classification scheme based on the scale and complexity of social organization and the effectiveness of political regulation; includes band, tribe, chiefdom, and state. (273)

sodality   See *pantribal sodality*. (280)

sororate   Custom by which a widower marries the sister of the deceased wife. (316)

speciation   Formation of new species; occurs when subgroups of the same species are separated for a sufficient length of time. (80)

species   Population whose members can interbreed to produce offspring that can live and reproduce. (79)

state (nation-state)   Complex sociopolitical system that administers a territory and populace with substantial contrasts in occupation, wealth, prestige, and power. An independent, centrally organized political unit; a government. A form of social and political organization with a formal, central government and a division of society into classes. (195, 273)

status   Any position that determines where someone fits in society; may be ascribed or achieved. (278)

stereotypes   Fixed ideas—often unfavorable—about what members of a group are like. (410)

stratification   Characteristic of a system with socioeconomic strata. (203)

stratigraphy   Science that examines the ways in which earth sediments are deposited in demarcated layers known as strata (singular, stratum). (46)

style shifts   Variations in speech in different contexts. (235)

subcultures   Different cultural symbol-based traditions associated with subgroups in the same complex society. (31)

subgroups   Languages within a taxonomy of related languages that are most closely related. (240)

subordinate   The lower, or underprivileged, group in a stratified system. (286)

superordinate   The upper, or privileged, group in a stratified system. (286)

survey research   Characteristic research procedure among social scientists other than anthropologists. Studies society through sampling, statistical analysis, and impersonal data collection. (58)

symbol   Something, verbal or nonverbal, that arbitrarily and by convention stands for something else, with which it has no necessary or natural connection. (18)

syntax   The arrangement and order of words in phrases and sentences. (228)

systematic survey   Information gathered on patterns of settlement over a large area; provides a regional perspective on the archaeological record. (43)

T

taboo   Prohibition backed by supernatural sanctions. (351)

taphonomy   The study of the processes—biological and geological—by which dead animals become fossils; from the Greek taphos, which means "tomb." (45)

taxonomy   Classification scheme; assignment to categories (*taxa;* singular, *taxon*). (96)

teosinte   Wild grass; apparent ancestor of maize. Also called teocentli. (188)

Teotihuacan   First state in the Valley of Mexico and earliest major Mesoamerican empire, 100 to 700 C.E. (214)

terrestrial   Ground-dwelling. (96)

theory   An explanatory framework, containing a series of statements, that helps us understand why (something exists); theories suggest patterns, connections, and relationships that may be confirmed by new research. (69)

totem An animal, plant, or geographic feature associated with a specific social group, to which that totem is sacred or symbolically important. (357)

transgender A category of varied individuals whose gender identity contradicts their biological sex at birth and the gender identity that society assigned to them in infancy. (340)

transhumance One of two variants of pastoralism; part of the population moves seasonally with the herds while the other part remains in home villages. (256)

tribe Form of sociopolitical organization usually based on horticulture or pastoralism. Socioeconomic stratification and centralized rule are absent in tribes, and there is no means of enforcing political decisions. (273)

typology, sociopolitical See *sociopolitical typology*. (273)

U

underdifferentiation Planning fallacy of viewing less developed countries as an undifferentiated group; ignoring cultural diversity and adopting a uniform approach (often ethnocentric) for very different types of project beneficiaries. (421)

uniformitarianism Belief that explanations for past events should be sought in ordinary forces that continue to work today. (69)

unilineal descent Matrilineal or patrilineal descent. (306)

universal Something that exists in every culture. (27)

Upper Paleolithic Blade tool-making traditions associated with AMHs; named from their location in upper, or more recent, layers of sedimentary deposits. (165)

urban anthropology The anthropological study of life in and around world cities, including urban social problems, differences between urban and other environments, and adaptation to city life. (425)

V

variables Attributes (e.g., age, occupation, income) that differ from one person or case to the next. (59)

village head Leadership position in a village (as among the Yanomami, where the head is always a man); has limited authority; leads by example and persuasion. (277)

W

wealth All a person's material assets, including income, land, and other types of property; the basis of economic status. (286)

Westernization The acculturative influence of Western expansion on other cultures. (448)

working class (or proletariat) Those who must sell their labor to survive; the antithesis of the bourgeoisie in Marx's class analysis. (375)

world-system theory Argument for the historic and contemporary social, political, and economic significance of an identifiable global system, based on wealth and power differentials, that extends beyond individual countries. (371)

XYZ

Zapotec state Mesoamerica's earliest state, which developed in Mexico's Valley of Oaxaca from a chiefdom by about 100 B.C.E. and lasted until its overthrow by Spain in the 1500s. (212)

Photo Credits

p. 238: © Jim Goldberg/Magnum Photos; p. 240: © Mike Nelson/epa/Corbis

Chapter 11: p. 252: © D. Halleux/Bios/ Photolibrary; p. 254: © Earl & Nazima Kowall/Corbis; p. 260: © Li Jianping/Imag-inechina/AP Images; p. 265: © American Museum of Natural History, Neg# 336116; p. 268: © Carl D. Walsh/Aurora Photos

Chapter 12: p. 272: © Joel Gordon; p. 274: © Joy Tessman/National Geographic Image Collection; p. 279: © Burt Glinn/Magnum Photos; p. 284: © John A. Novak/Animals Animals; p. 285: © Syracuse Newspapers/ D Lassman/The Image Works; p. 291: © University of Illinois Press; p. 293: © Kirsty Wigglesworth/AP Images

Chapter 13: p. 300: © Brenninger/Sueddeutsche Zeitung Photo/The Image Works; p. 301: © Katja Heinemann/Aurora Photos; p. 313: © Bill O'Leary/The Washington Post/ Getty Images; p. 319: © Earl & Nazima Kowall/Corbis Images

Chapter 14: p. 325: © Ziva Santop; p. 332: © Lindsay Hebberd/Corbis Images; p. 333: © George Holton/Photo Researchers; p. 335: © National Archives; p. 338: © Karsten Schoene/laif/Redux; p. 341: © Sinopictures/Maciej Dakowicz/Photolibrary; p. 344: © Patrik Giardino/Corbis

Chapter 15: p. 351: © Jose Luis Palaez Inc./Blend Images/Getty Images; p. 353: © David Zalubowski/AP Images; p. 356(top): © Thierry Secretan/COSMOS/Woodfin Camp &

Associates; p. 356(bottom): © Joe McNally/ IPNstock.com; p. 358: © North Wind Picture Archives/AP Images; p. 361: © Enrique Marcarian/Reuters/Corbis; p. 364: © Kal Muller/Woodfin Camp & Associates

Chapter 16: p. 371: © Michael Coyne/Lonely Planet Images; p. 372: © Rupert Conant/ Photolibrary; p. 374: © ARPL/Topham/The Image Works; p. 379: © Hulton Archive/Getty Images; p. 389: © Friedrich Stark/Das Fotoarchiv GmbH/Photolibrary

Chapter 17: p. 395: © Terrence Jennings/ Retna Ltd./Corbis; p. 397: © Shannon Stapleton/Reuters/Corbis; p. 401: © PJ. Griffiths/ Magnum Photos; p. 403(all): Conrad P. Kottak; p. 412(top): © Bradley Mayhew/ Lonely Planet Images; p. 412B: © Sergei Grits/AP Images

Chapter 18: p. 420: © Betty Press/Woodfin Camp & Associates; p. 423: © Oleg Popov/ Reuters; p. 425: © Antonio Scorza/AFP/Getty Images; p. 430: © Mark Edwards/Photolibrary; p. 432: Courtesy Professor Marietta Baba, Michigan State University; p. 433: © Philippe Michel/Age Fotostock/Photolibrary

Chapter 19: p. 440: © Eugene Hoshiko/AP Images; p. 453: © Lionel Derimais/Visum/ The Image Works; p. 443: © Fritz Hoffman/ The Image Works; p. 447: © Ed Parker/Photographers Direct/Chris Fairclough Worldwide Ltd.; p. 450: © Hu Sheng/EPA/Corbis; p. 455: © Jose Luis Quintana/Reuters/Corbis; p. 458: © Monica Almeida/Redux Pictures

Bibliography

Abelmann, N., and J. Lie 1995. *Blue Dreams: Korean Americans and the Los Angeles Riots*. Cambridge, MA: Harvard University Press.

Adams, R. M. 1981. *Heartland of Cities*. Chicago: Aldine.

Adherents.com 2002. Major Religions of the World Ranked by Number of Adherents. http://www.adherents.com/Religions_By_Adherents.html.

Ahmed, A. S. 1992. *Postmodernism and Islam: Predicament and Promise*. New York: Routledge.

————. 2004. *Postmodernism and Islam: Predicament and Promise,* rev. ed. New York: Routledge.

Aiello, L., and M. Collard 2001. Our Newest Oldest Ancestor? *Nature* 410 (March 29):526–527.

Akazawa, T. 1980. *The Japanese Paleolithic: A Techno-Typological Study*. Tokyo: Rippo Shobo.

Akazawa, T., and C. M. Aikens, eds. 1986. *Prehistoric Hunter-Gatherers in Japan: New Research Methods*. Tokyo: University of Tokyo Press.

Amadiume, I. 1987. *Male Daughters, Female Husbands*. Atlantic Highlands, NJ: Zed.

American Anthropological Association *Anthropology Newsletter*. Published 9 times annually by the American Anthropological Association, Washington, DC.

Anderson, B. 1991. *Imagined Communities: Reflections on the Origin and Spread of Nationalism,* rev. ed. London: Verso.

Anderson, R. 1996. *Magic, Science, and Health: The Aims and Achievements of Medical Anthropology*. Fort Worth, TX: Harcourt Brace.

Angier, N. 1998. When Nature Discovers the Same Design Over and Over, Lookalike Creatures Spark Evolutionary Debate. *New York Times,* December 15, pp. D1, D6.

Annenberg/CPB Exhibits 2000. Collapse, Why Do Civilizations Fall? http://www.learner.org/exhibits/collapse/.

Antoun, R. T. 2008. *Understanding Fundamentalism: Christian, Islamic, and Jewish Movements,* 2nd ed. Lanham, MD: AltaMira.

Aoki, M. Y., and M. B. Dardess, eds. 1981. *As the Japanese See It: Past and Present*. Honolulu: University Press of Hawaii.

Aoyagi, K., P. J. M. Nas, and J. Traphagan, eds. 1998. *Toward Sustainable Cities: Readings in the Anthropology of Urban Environments*. Leiden: Leiden Development Studies, Institute of Cultural and Social Studies, University of Leiden.

Appadurai, A. 1990. Disjuncture and Difference in the Global Cultural Economy. *Public Culture* 2(2):1–24.

————. 1991. Global Ethnoscapes: Notes and Queries for a Transnational Anthropology. In *Recapturing Anthropology: Working in the Present,* R. G. Fox, ed., pp. 191–210. Santa Fe, NM: School of American Research Advanced Seminar Series.

————. 1996. *Modernity at Large. Cultural Dimensions of Globalization*. Minneapolis: University of Minnesota Press.

Appadurai, A., ed. 2001. *Globalization*. Durham, NC: Duke University Press.

Applebome, P. 1996. English Unique to Blacks Is Officially Recognized. *New York Times,* December 20, http://www.nytimes.com.

Arensberg, C. 1987. Theoretical Contributions of Industrial and Development Studies. In *Applied Anthropology in America,* 2nd ed., E. M. Eddy and W. L. Partridge, eds. New York: Columbia University Press.

Arieff, I. 2001. Developing Nations' Share of World Population Rising. Reuters, February 28. http://www.forests.org/archive/general/denashw1.htm.

Arrighi, G. 1994. *The Long Twentieth Century; Money, Power, and the Origins of Our Times*. New York: Verso.

Asad, T. 2008 (orig. 1983). The Construction of Religion as an Anthropological Category. In *A Reader in the Anthropology of Religion,* M. Lambek, ed., pp. 110–132. Malden, MA: Blackwood.

Asfaw, B., T. White, and O. Lovejoy 1999. *Australopithecus garhi:* A New Species of Early Hominid from Ethiopia. *Science* 284 (April 23):629.

Ashcroft, B., G. Griffiths, and H. Tiffin 1989. *The Empire Writes Back: Theory and Practice in Post-colonial Literatures.* New York: Routledge.

Baer, H. A., and M. Singer 2008. *Global Warming and the Political Ecology of Health.* Walnut Creek, CA: Left Coast Press.

Baer, H. A., M. Singer, and I. Susser 2003. *Medical Anthropology and the World System.* Westport, CT: Praeger.

Bailey, E. J. 2000. *Medical Anthropology and African American Health.* Westport, CT: Bergin and Garvey.

Bailey, R. C. 1990. *The Behavioral Ecology of Efe Pygmy Men in the Ituri Forest, Zaire.* Ann Arbor: Anthropological Papers, Museum of Anthropology, University of Michigan, no. 86.

Bailey, R. C., G. Head, M. Jenike, B. Owen, R. Rechtman, and E. Zechenter 1989. Hunting and Gathering in Tropical Rain Forests: Is It Possible? *American Anthropologist* 91:59–82.

Banton, M. 1957. *West African City. A Study in Tribal Life in Freetown.* London: Oxford University Press.

Barber, B. R. 1992. Jihad vs. McWorld. *Atlantic Monthly* 269(3):53–65, March 1992.

———. 1995. *Jihad vs. McWorld.* New York: Times Books.

Barker, C. 1997. *Global Television: An Introduction.* Malden, MA: Blackwell.

———. 2003. *Cultural Studies: Theory and Practice.* Thousand Oaks, CA: Sage.

Barnaby, F., ed. 1984. *Future War: Armed Conflict in the Next Decade.* London: M. Joseph.

Barnard, A., ed. 2004. *Hunter-Gatherers in History, Archaeology and Anthropology.* New York: Oxford University Press.

Barnes, E. 2005. *Diseases and Human Evolution.* Albuquerque: University of New Mexico Press.

Baro, M., and T. F. Deubel 2006. Persistent Hunger: Perspectives on Vulnerability, Famine, and Food Security in Sub-Saharan Africa. *Annual Review of Anthropology* 35:521–538.

Barringer, F. 1992. New Census Data Show More Children Living in Poverty. *New York Times,* May 29, pp. A1, A12–A13.

Barth, F. 1968. (orig. 1958). Ecologic Relations of Ethnic Groups in Swat, North Pakistan. In *Man in Adaptation: The Cultural Present,* Yehudi Cohen, ed., pp. 324–331. Chicago: Aldine.

———. 1969. *Ethnic Groups and Boundaries: The Social Organization of Cultural Difference.* London: Allen & Unwin.

Bar-Yosef, O. 1987. Pleistocene Connections between Africa and Southwest Asia: An Archaeological Perspective. *African Archaeological Review* 5:29–38.

Baumert, K., T. Herzog, and J. Pershing 2005. Navigating the Numbers: Greenhouse Gas Data and International Climate Policy. World Resources Institute. http://www.wri.org/publication/navigating-the-numbers.

BBC News 2006. Neanderthal Yields Nuclear DNA, May 16. http://news.bbc.co.uk/go/pr/fr/-/2/hi/science/nature/4986668.stm.

Beeman, W. 1986. *Language, Status, and Power in Iran.* Bloomington: Indiana University Press.

Bell, W. 1981. Neocolonialism. In *Encyclopedia of Sociology,* p. 193. Guilford, CT: DPG Publishing.

Bellah, R. N. 1978. Religious Evolution. In *Reader in Comparative Religion: An Anthropological Approach,* 4th ed., W. A. Lessa and E. Z. Vogt, eds., pp. 36–50. New York: Harper and Row.

Bellwood, P. S. 2004. *The First Farmers: Origins of Agricultural Societies.* Malden, MA: Blackwell.

Benedict, R. F. 1940. *Race, Science and Politics.* New York: Modern Age Books.

————. 1946. *The Chrysanthemum and the Sword.* Boston: Houghton Mifflin.

Bennett, J. W. 1969. *Northern Plainsmen: Adaptive Strategy and Agrarian Life.* Chicago: Aldine.

Berkeleyan 1999. Berkeley Researchers Head Team That Discovers New Species of Human Ancestor: Earliest Evidence of Meat-Eating, Early Beings Has Been Unearthed in Ethiopia. April 28–May 4, 1999 (27,32); http://www .berkeley.edu/news/berkeleyan/1999/0428/ species.html.

Berlin, B., and P. Kay 1992 (orig. 1969). *Basic Color Terms: Their Universality and Evolution,* 2nd ed. Berkeley: University of California Press.

Bernard, H. R. 2002. *Research Methods in Anthropology: Qualitative and Quantitative Methods,* 3rd ed. Walnut Creek, CA: AltaMira.

————. 2006. *Research Methods in Anthropology: Qualitative and Quantitative Approaches.* 4th ed. Lanham, MD: AltaMira.

Bernard, H. R., ed. 1998. *Handbook of Methods in Cultural Anthropology,* Walnut Creek, CA: AltaMira.

Bicker, A., P. Sillitoe, and J. Pottier, eds. 2004. *Investigating Local Knowledge: New Directions, New Approaches.* Burlington, VT: Ashgate.

Binford, L. R. 1968. Post-Pleistocene Adaptations. In *New Perspectives in Archeology,* S. R. Binford and L. R. Binford, eds., pp. 313–341. Chicago: Aldine.

Binford, L. R., and S. R. Binford 1979. Stone Tools and Human Behavior. In *Human Ancestors, Readings from Scientific American,* G. L. Isaac and R. E. F. Leakey, eds., pp. 92–101. San Francisco: W. H. Freeman.

Bird-David, N. 1992. Beyond "The Original Affluent Society": A Culturalist Reformulation. *Current Anthropology* 33(1):25–47.

Bjuremalm, H. 1997. Rattvisa kan skippas i Rwanda: Folkmordet 1994 gar attt forklara och analysera pa samma satt som forintelsen av judarna. *Dagens Nyheter* [06-03-19777, p. B3].

Blackwood, E., and S. Wieringa, eds. 1999. *Female Desires: Same-Sex Relations and Transgender Practices across Cultures.* New York: Columbia University Press.

Blanton, R. E. 1999. *Ancient Oaxaca: The Monte Alban State.* New York: Cambridge University Press.

Blau, S., and D. Ubelaker, eds. 2008. *Handbook of Forensic Anthropology and Archaeology.* Walnut Creek, CA: Left Coast Press.

Bloch, M., ed. 1975. *Political Language and Oratory in Traditional Societies.* London: Academic Press.

Blommaert, J. 2010. *Sociolinguistics of Globalization.* New York: Cambridge University Press.

Blum, H. F. 1961. Does the Melanin Pigment of Human Skin Have Adaptive Value? *Quarterly Review of Biology* 36:50–63.

Boas, F. 1966 (orig. 1940). *Race, Language, and Culture.* New York: Free Press.

Boaz, N. T. 1997. *Eco Homo: How the Human Being Emerged from the Cataclysmic History of the Earth.* New York: Basic Books.

Boaz, N. T., and R. L. Ciochon 2004. Headstrong Hominids. *Natural History* 113(1): 28–34.

Bodley, J. H. 2003. *The Power of Scale: A Global History Approach.* Armonk, NY: M. E. Sharpe.

————. 2008a. *Anthropology and Contemporary Human Problems,* 5th ed. Lanham, MD: AltaMira.

————. 2008b. *Victims of Progress,* 5th ed. Lanham, MD: AltaMira.

Bodley, J. H., ed. 1988. *Tribal Peoples and Development Issues: A Global Overview.* Mountain View, CA: Mayfield.

Boellstorff, T. 2007. Queer Studies in the House of Anthropology. *Annual Review of Anthropology* 36:375–389.

Bogaard, A. 2004. *Neolithic Farming in Central Europe: An Archaeobotanical Study of Crop Husbandry Practices.* New York: Routledge.

Bogin, B. 2001. *The Growth of Humanity.* New York: Wiley.

Bogoras, W. 1904. The Chukchee. In *The Jesup North Pacific Expedition,* F. Boas, ed. New York: Memoir of the American Museum of Natural History.

Bolinger, D., and D. Sears 1981. *Aspects of Language,* 3rd ed. New York: Harcourt Brace Jovanovich.

Bolton, R. 1981. Susto, Hostility, and Hypoglycemia. *Ethnology* 20(4): 227–258.

Bonnichsen, R., and A. L. Schneider 2000. *Battle of the Bones.* New York Academy of Sciences, *The Sciences,* July–August, http://www.friendsofpast.org/forum/battle.html.

Bonvillain, N. 2001. *Women and Men: Cultural Constructions of Gender,* 4th ed. Upper Saddle River, NJ: Prentice Hall.

———. 2008. *Language, Culture, and Communication: The Meaning of Messages,* 5th ed. Upper Saddle River, NJ: Prentice Hall.

———. 2010. *Language, Culture, and Communication: The Meaning of Messages,* 6th ed. Boston: Prentice Hall.

Boserup, E. 1970. *Women's Role in Economic Development.* London: Allen & Unwin.

Bourdieu, P. 1977. *Outline of a Theory of Practice.* R. Nice (trans.). Cambridge: Cambridge University Press.

———. 1982. *Ce Que Parler Veut Dire.* Paris: Fayard.

———. 1984. *Distinction: A Social Critique of the Judgment of Taste.* R. Nice (trans.). Cambridge, MA: Harvard University Press.

Bourque, S. C., and K. B. Warren 1987. Technology, Gender and Development. *Daedalus* 116(4): 173–197.

Bowen, J. R. 2008. *Religion in Practice: An Approach to Anthropology of Religion,* 4th ed. Boston: Pearson/Allyn and Bacon.

Bowie, F. 2006. *The Anthropology of Religion: An Introduction.* Malden, MA: Blackwell.

Brace, C. L. 1995. *The Stages of Human Evolution,* 5th ed. Upper Saddle River, NJ: Prentice Hall.

Bradley, B., D. M. Doran-Sheehy, D. Lukas, C. Boesch, and L. Vigilant 2004. Dispersed Male Networks in Western Gorillas. *Current Biology* 14 (March):510–513.

Braidwood, R. J. 1975. *Prehistoric Men,* 8th ed. Glenview, IL: Scott, Foresman.

Braudel, F. 1981. *Civilization and Capitalism, 15th–18th Century,* Volume I, *The Structure of Everyday Life: The Limits.* S. Reynolds (trans.). New York: Harper and Row.

———. 1982. *Civilization and Capitalism, 15th–18th Century,* Volume II, *The Wheels of Commerce.* New York: Harper and Row.

———. 1992. *Civilization and Capitalism, 15th–18th Century,* Volume III, *The Perspective of the World.* Berkeley: University of California Press.

Bremen, J., and A. Shimizu, eds. 1999. *Anthropology and Colonialism in Asia and Oceania.* London: Curzon.

Brenneis, D. 1988. Language and Disputing. *Annual Review of Anthropology* 17:221–237.

Brettell, C. B., and C. F. Sargent, eds. 2009. *Gender in Cross-Cultural Perspective*, 5th ed. Upper Saddle River, NJ: Pearson/Prentice Hall.

Briggs, C. L. 2005. Communicability, Racial Discourse, and Disease. *Annual Review of Anthropology* 34:269–291.

Brooke, J. 1992. Rio's New Day in Sun Leaves Laplander Limp. *The New York Times,* June 1, p. A7.

Brower, B., and B. R. Johnston 2007. *Disappearing Peoples?: Indigenous Groups and Ethnic Minorities in South and Central Asia.* Walnut Creek, CA: Left Coast Press.

Brown, A. 2001. Communism. *International Encyclopedia of the Social & Behavioral Sciences,* pp. 2323–2326. New York: Elsevier.

Brown, D. 1991. *Human Universals.* New York: McGraw-Hill.

Brown, M. F. 2003. *Who Owns Native Culture?* Cambridge, MA: Harvard University Press.

Brown, P. J. 1998. *Understanding and Applying Medical Anthropology.* Mountain View, CA: Mayfield.

Brown, P. J., and R. L. Barrett 2010. *Understanding and Applying Medical Anthropology,* 2nd ed. New York: McGraw-Hill.

Brown, R. W. 1958. *Words and Things*. Glencoe, IL: Free Press.

Bryant, V. M. 1999. Review of Piperno, D. R., and D. M. Pearsall, *The Origins of Agriculture in the Lowland Neotropics* (1998), *North American Archaeologist* (26):245–246.

———. 2003. Invisible Clues to New World Domestication. *Science* 299 (February 14) 1029–1030.

———. 2007a. Artifact: Maize Pollen. *Archaeology* 60(4). www.archaeology.org/ 0707/etc/artifact.html.

———. 2007b. Little Things Mean a Lot: The Search for Starch Grains at Archaeological Sites. *Mammoth Trumpet* 22(4):3–4, 16.

Burawoy, M. 2000. Introduction. *Global Ethnography: Forces, Connections, and Imaginations in a Postmodern World*. Berkeley: University of California Press.

Burawoy, M. et al. 2000. *Global Ethnography: Forces, Connections, and Imaginations in a Postmodern World*. Berkeley: University of California Press.

Burns, J. F. 1997. A Year of Harsh Islamic Rule Weighs Heavily for Afghans. September 24. www.nytimes.com.

Butler, R. 2005. World's Largest Cities: [Ranked by City Population]. http://www .mongabay.com/cities_ pop_01.htm.

Buvinic, M. 1995. The Feminization of Poverty? Research and Policy Needs. In *Reducing Poverty through Labour Market Policies*. Geneva: International Institute for Labour Studies.

Cachel, S. 2006. *Primate and Human Evolution*. New York: Cambridge University Press.

Callaway, E. 2010. Fossil Genome Reveals Ancestral Link: A Distant Cousin Raises Questions about Human Origins. *Nature* 468, 1012 (2010) | doi:10.1038/4681012a, published online December 22, 2010.

Campbell, C. J., ed. 2011. *Primates in Perspective*, 2nd ed. New York: Oxford University Press.

Cann, R. L., M. Stoneking, and A. C. Wilson 1987. Mitochondrial DNA and Human Evolution. *Nature* 325:31–36.

Carey, B. 2007. Washoe, a Chimp of Many Words Dies at 42. *New York Times,* November 1. http://www.nytimes.com.

Carneiro, R. L. 1956. Slash-and-Burn Agriculture: A Closer Look at Its Implications for Settlement Patterns. In *Men and Cultures.* Selected Papers of the Fifth International Congress of Anthropological and Ethnological Sciences, pp. 229–234. Philadelphia: University of Pennsylvania Press.

———. 1968. (orig. 1961). Slash-and-Burn Cultivation among the Kuikuru and Its Implications for Cultural Development in the Amazon Basin. In *Man in Adaptation: The Cultural Present,* Y. A. Cohen, ed., pp. 131–145. Chicago: Aldine.

———. 1970. A Theory of the Origin of the State. *Science* 69:733–738.

———. 1990. Chiefdom-Level Warfare as Exemplified in Fiji and the Cauca Valley. In *The Anthropology of War,* J. Haas, ed., pp. 190–211. Cambridge: Cambridge University Press.

———. 1991. The Nature of the Chiefdom as Revealed by Evidence from the Cauca Valley of Colombia. In *Profiles in Cultural Evolution,* A. T. Rambo and K. Gillogly, eds. Anthropological Papers 85, pp. 167–190. Ann Arbor: University of Michigan Museum of Anthropology.

Carroll, R. 2008. Chimps 90 Percent Gone in a "Final Stronghold." *National Geographic News,* October 13, 2008. http://news.nationalgeographic .com/news/pf/69848470.html.

Carsten, J. 2004. *After Kinship*. New York: Cambridge University Press.

Carter, J. 1988. Freed from Keepers and Cages, Chimps Come of Age on Baboon Island. *Smithsonian,* June, pp. 36–48.

Cartmill, M. 1974. Rethinking Primate Origins. *Science* (April 26):436–437.

———. 1992. New Views on Primate Origins. *Evolutionary Anthropology* 1: 105–111.

Castells, M. 2001. Information Technology and Global Capitalism. In *On the Edge: Living with Global Capitalism*, W. Hutton and A. Giddens, eds. London: Vintage.

Cernea, M., ed. 1991. *Putting People First: Sociological Variables in Rural Development,* 2nd ed. New York: Oxford University Press (published for the World Bank).

Ceuppens, B., and P. Geschiere 2005. Autochthony: Local or Global? New Modes in the Struggle over Citizenship and Belonging in Africa and Europe. *Annual Review of Anthropology* 34:385–407.

Chagnon, N. A. 1967. *Yanomamo Warfare: Social Organization and Marriage Alliances.* Ann Arbor, MI: University Microfilms.

———. 1992 (orig. 1983). *Yanomamo: The Fierce People,* 4th ed. New York: Harcourt Brace.

———. 1997. *Yanomamo,* 5th ed. Fort Worth, TX: Harcourt Brace.

Chakrabarty, D. 2007. *Provincializing Europe: Postcolonial Thought and Historical Difference.* Princeton, NJ: Princeton University Press.

Chambers, E. 1987. Applied Anthropology in the Post-Vietnam Era: Anticipations and Ironies. *Annual Review of Anthropology* 16:309–337.

Champion, T., and C. Gamble, eds. 1984. *Prehistoric Europe.* New York: Academic Press.

Chang, K. C. 1977. *The Archaeology of Ancient China.* New Haven, CT: Yale University Press.

Chatterjee, P. 2004. *The Politics of the Governed: Reflections on Popular Politics in Most of the World.* New York: Columbia University Press.

Cheney, D. L., and R. M. Seyfarth 1990. In the Minds of Monkeys: What Do They Know and How Do They Know It? *Natural History,* September, pp. 38–46.

Childe, V. G. 1950. The Urban Revolution, *Town Planning Review,* 21:3–17.

———. 1951. *Man Makes Himself.* New York: New American Library.

Chiseri-Strater, E., and B. S. Sunstein. 2001. *Fieldworking: Reading and Writing Research,* 2nd ed. Upper Saddle River, NJ: Prentice Hall.

Chomsky, N. 1957. *Syntactic Structures.* The Hague: Mouton.

Christensen, L. 2003. The Politics of Correction. *Rethinking Schools Online.* Fall. http://www.rethinkingschools.org/archive/18_01/corr181.shtml.

Ciochon, R. L. 1983. Hominoid Cladistics and the Ancestry of Modern Apes and Humans. In *New Interpretations of Ape and Human Ancestry,* R. L. Ciochon and R. S. Corruccini, eds., pp. 783–843. New York: Plenum.

Ciochon, R. L., J. Olsen, and J. James 1990. *Other Origins: The Search for the Giant Ape in Human Prehistory.* New York: Bantam Books.

Coates, J. 1986. *Women, Men, and Language.* London: Longman.

Cody, D. 1998. British Empire. http://www.stg.brown.edu/projects/hypertext/landow/victorian/history/Empire.html, May 18.

Cohen, M. 1998. *Culture of Intolerance: Chauvinism, Class, and Racism.* New Haven, CT: Yale University Press.

Cohen, M. N., and G. J. Armelagos, eds. 1984. *Paleopathology at the Origins of Agriculture.* New York: Academic Press.

Cohen, P. 2008. The Pentagon Enlists Social Scientists to Study Security Issues. *New York Times,* June 18.

Cohen, R. 1967. *The Kanuri of Bornu.* New York: Holt, Rinehart & Winston.

Cohen, Y. 1974. Culture as Adaptation. In *Man in Adaptation: The Cultural Present,* 2nd ed., Y. A. Cohen, ed., pp. 45–68. Chicago: Aldine.

Colson, E., and T. Scudder 1975. New Economic Relationships between the Gwembe Valley and the Line of Rail. In *Town and Country in Central and Eastern Africa,* David Parkin, ed., pp. 190–210. London: Oxford University Press.

———. 1988. *For Prayer and Profit: The Ritual, Economic, and Social Importance of Beer in Gwembe District, Zambia, 1950–1982.* Stanford, CA: Stanford University Press.

Connor, W. 1972. Nation-Building or Nation-Destroying. *World Politics* 24(3).

Cooper, F., and A. L. Stoler, eds. 1997. *Tensions of Empire: Colonial Cultures in a Bourgeois World.* Berkeley: University of California Press.

Coppens, Y. 1994. East Side Story: The Origin of Humankind. *Scientific American* 270(5):88–95.

Council on International and Public Affairs 2006. How Many Dollars at the Top? *Too Much: A Commentary on Excess and Inequality.* New York, April 24, 2006. http://www.toomuchonline.org/articlenew2006/April24a.html.

Crapo, R. H. 2006. *Anthropology of Religion: The Unity and Diversity of Religions.* Boston: McGraw-Hill.

Crate, S. A., and M. Nuttall 2008. *Anthropology and Climate Change: From Encounters to Actions.* Walnut Creek, CA: Left Coast Press.

Cresswell, T. 2006. *On the Move: Mobility in the Modern West.* New York: Routledge.

Crosby, A. W., Jr. 2003. *The Columbian Exchange: Biological and Cultural Consequences of 1492.* Westport, CT: Praeger.

Cultural Survival Quarterly. Quarterly journal. Cambridge, MA: Cultural Survival, Inc.

Cunningham, G. 1999. *Religion and Magic: Approaches and Theories.* New York: New York University Press.

Dalton, R. 2006. Ethiopia: Awash with Fossils. http://www.nature.com/news/2006/060102/full/439014a.html.

DaMatta, R. 1991. *Carnivals, Rogues, and Heroes: An Interpretation of the Brazilian Dilemma.* Translated from the Portuguese by John Drury. Notre Dame, IN: University of Notre Dame Press.

D'Andrade, R. 1984. Cultural Meaning Systems. In *Culture Theory: Essays on Mind, Self, and Emotion,* R. A. Shweder and R. A. Levine, eds., pp. 88–119. Cambridge: Cambridge University Press.

Darwin, C. 1958 (orig. 1859). *On the Origin of Species.* New York: Dutton.

Das, V., and D. Poole, eds. 2004. *Anthropology in the Margins of the State.* Santa Fe, NM: School of American Research Press.

Degler, C. 1970. *Neither Black nor White: Slavery and Race Relations in Brazil and the United States.* New York: Macmillan.

de la Peña, G. 2005. Social and Cultural Policies toward Indigenous Peoples: Perspectives from Latin America. *Annual Review of Anthropology* 34:717–739.

DeMarco, E. 1997. New Dig at 9,000-Year-Old City Is Changing Views on Ancient Life. *New York Times,* November 11. http://www.nytimes.com.

DeNavas-Walt, C., B. D. Proctor, and J. C. Smith 2010. *Income, Poverty, and Health Insurance Coverage in the United States: 2009.* U.S. Census Bureau, Current Population Reports, P60-238. U.S. Government Printing Office, Washington, DC, 2010. http://www.census.gov/prod/2010pubs/p60-238.pdf.

Dentan, R. K. 1979. *The Semai: A Nonviolent People of Malaya,* Fieldwork edn. New York: Harcourt Brace.

Descartes, L., and C. P. Kottak 2009. *Media and Middle-Class Moms: Images and Realities of Work and Family.* New York: Routledge.

De Vos, G. A., W. O. Wetherall, and K. Stearman 1983. *Japan's Minorities: Burakumin, Koreans, Ainu and Okinawans.* Report no. 3. London: Minority Rights Group.

De Waal, F. B. M. 1995. Bonobo Sex and Society: The Behavior of a Close Relative Challenges Assumptions about Male Supremacy in Human Evolution. *Scientific American,* March, pp. 82–88.

———. 1997. *Bonobo: The Forgotten Ape.* Berkeley: University of California Press.

———. 1998. *Chimpanzee Politics: Power and Sex among Apes,* rev. ed. Baltimore: Johns Hopkins University Press.

Di Leonardo, M., ed. 1991. *Toward a New Anthropology of Gender.* Berkeley: University of California Press.

Diamond, J. M. 1990. A Pox upon Our Genes. *Natural History,* February, pp. 26–30.

———. 1997. *Guns, Germs, and Steel: The Fates of Human Societies.* New York: Norton.

Dickau, R., A. J. Ranere, and R. G. Cooke 2007. Starch Grain Evidence for the Preceramic Dispersals of Maize and Root Crops into Tropical Dry and Humid Forests of Panama. *Proceedings of the National*

Academy of Sciences of the United States of America 104(9):3651–3656. http://www.pnas.org/cgi/content/full/104/9/3651.

Dillon, S. 2006. In School Across U.S., the Melting Pot Overflows. *New York Times,* August 27. http://www.nytimes.com.

Divale, W. T., and M. Harris 1976. Population, Warfare, and the Male Supremacist Complex. *American Anthropologist* 78:521–538.

Dorward, D. C., ed. 1983. *The Igbo "Women's War" of 1929: Documents Relating to the Aba Riots in Eastern Nigeria.* Wakefield, England: East Ardsley.

Douglass, W. A. 1969. *Death in Murelaga: Funerary Ritual in a Spanish Basque Village.* Seattle: University of Washington Press.

———. 1975. *Echalar and Murelaga: Opportunity and Rural Exodus in Two Spanish Basque Villages.* London: C. Hurst.

———. 1992. Basques. *Encyclopedia of World Cultures,* V.4. Boston: G. K. Hall.

Dove, M. R., and C. Carpenter, eds. 2008. *Environmental Anthropology: A Historical Reader.* Malden, MA: Blackwell.

Draper, P. 1975. !Kung Women: Contrasts in Sexual Egalitarianism in Foraging and Sedentary Contexts. In *Toward an Anthropology of Women,* R. Reiter, ed., pp. 77–109. New York: Monthly Review Press.

Dreifus, C. 2000. Saving the Orangutan: Preserving Paradise. *New York Times,* March 21. http://www.nytimes.com/library/national/science/032100sci-animal-orangutan.html.

Dressler, W. W., K. S. Oths, and C. C. Gravlee 2005. Race and Ethnicity in Public Health Research. *Annual Review of Anthropology* 34:231–252.

Duffield, M., and V. Hewitt, eds. 2009. *Empire, Development, and Colonialism: The Past in the Present.* Rochester, NY: James Currey.

Durkheim, E. 1951 (orig. 1897). *Suicide: A Study in Sociology.* Glencoe, IL: Free Press.

———. 1961 (orig. 1912). *The Elementary Forms of the Religious Life.* New York: Collier Books.

———. 2001 (orig. 1912). *The Elementary Forms of the Religious Life.* Translated by Carol Cosman. Abridged with an introduction and notes by Mark S. Cladis. New York: Oxford University Press.

Durrenberger, E. P., and T. D. King, eds. 2000. *State and Community in Fisheries Management: Power, Policy, and Practice.* Westport, CT: Bergin and Garvey.

Earle, T. K. 1987. Chiefdoms in Archaeological and Ethnohistorical Perspective. *Annual Review of Anthropology* 16:279–308.

———. 1997. *How Chiefs Come to Power: The Political Economy in Prehistory.* Stanford, CA: Stanford University Press.

Eastman, C. M. 1975. *Aspects of Language and Culture.* San Francisco: Chandler and Sharp.

Echeverria, J. 1999. *Home Away from Home: A History of Basque Boardinghouses.* Reno: University of Nevada Press.

Eckert, P. 1989. *Jocks and Burnouts: Social Categories and Identity in the High School.* New York: Teachers College Press, Columbia University.

———. 2000. *Linguistic Variation as Social Practice: The Linguistic Construction of Identity in Belten High.* Malden, MA: Blackwell.

Eckert, P., and S. McConnell-Ginet 2003. *Language and Gender.* New York: Cambridge University Press.

Edelman, M., and A. Haugerud 2005. *The Anthropology of Development and Globalization: From Classical Political Economy to Contemporary Neoliberalism.* Malden, MA: Blackwell.

Edwards, D. N. 2004. *The Nubian Past: An Archaeology of Sudan.* New York: Routledge.

Elson, C. 2007. *Excavations at Cerro Tilcajete: A Monte Alban II Administrative Center in the Valley of Oaxaca.* Memoir 42 of the Museum of Anthropology, University of Michigan, Ann Arbor.

Ervin, A. M. 2005. *Applied Anthropology: Tools and Perspectives for Contemporary Practice,* 2nd ed. Boston: Pearson/Allyn & Bacon.

Escobar, A. 1991. Anthropology and the Development Encounter: The Making and

Marketing of Development Anthropology. *American Ethnologist* 18:658–682.

———. 1994. Welcome to Cyberia: Notes on the Anthropology of Cyberculture. *Current Anthropology* 35(3):211–231.

———. 1995. *Encountering Development: The Making and Unmaking of the Third World.* Princeton, NJ: Princeton University Press.

Eskridge, W. N., Jr. 1996. *The Case for Same-Sex Marriage: From Sexual Liberty to Civilized Commitment.* New York: Free Press.

Evans-Pritchard, E. E. 1970. Sexual Inversion among the Azande. *American Anthropologist* 72:1428–1433.

Fagan, B. M. 1996. *World Prehistory: A Brief Introduction,* 3rd ed. New York: HarperCollins.

———. 1998. *World Prehistory: A Brief Introduction,* 4th ed. New York: Longman.

———. 2002. *World Prehistory: A Brief Introduction,* 5th ed. Upper Saddle River, NJ: Prentice Hall.

———. 2003. *Archeology: A Brief Introduction,* 8th ed. Upper Saddle River, NJ: Prentice Hall.

———. 2004. *People of the Earth: A Brief Introduction to World Prehistory,* 12th ed. Upper Saddle River, NJ: Prentice Hall.

Farner, R. F., ed. 2004. *Nationalism, Ethnicity, and Identity: Cross-National and Comparative Perspectives.* New Brunswick, NJ: Transaction Publishers.

Farooq, M. 1966. Importance of Determining Transmission Sites in Planning Bilharziasis Control: Field Observations from the Egypt-49 Project Area. *American Journal of Epidemiology* 83:603–612.

Farr, D. M. L. 1980. British Empire. *Academic American Encyclopedia.* Princeton, NJ: Arete, volume 3, pp. 495–496.

Fasold, R. W. 1990. *The Sociolinguistics of Language.* Oxford: Blackwell.

Fearon, James D. 2003. Ethnic and Cultural Diversity by Country. *Journal of Economic Growth* 8:2 (June 2003):195–222.

Feder, K. 2011. *Frauds, Myths, and Mysteries: Science and Pseudoscience in Archaeology.* New York: McGraw-Hill.

Fedigan, L. M. 1992. *Primate Paradigms: Sex Roles and Social Bonds.* Chicago: University of Chicago Press.

Ferguson, R. B. 1995. *Yanomami Warfare: A Political History.* Santa Fe, NM: School of American Research Press.

———. 2002. *The State, Identity, and Violence: Political Disintegration in the Post-Cold War Era.* New York: Routledge.

Ferraro, G. P. 2010. *The Cultural Dimension of International Business,* 6th ed. Upper Saddle River, NJ: Prentice Hall.

Fields, J. M. 2004. America's Families and Living Arrangements: 2003. U.S. Census Bureau. *Current Population Reports,* P20–553, November. http://www.census.gov.

Fields, J. M., and L. M. Casper 2001. America's Families and Living Arrangements: Population Characteristics, 2000. U.S. Census Bureau. *Current Population Reports,* P20–537, June. http://www.census.gov/prod/2001pubs/p20–537.pdf.

Files, J. 2005. Report Describes Immigrants as Younger and More Diverse. *New York Times,* national ed., June 10, p. A11.

Finkler, K. 1985. *Spiritualist Healers in Mexico: Successes and Failures of Alternative Therapeutics.* South Hadley, MA: Bergin and Garvey.

Finnstrom, S. 1997. Postcoloniality and the Postcolony: Theories of the Global and the Local. http://www.stg.brown.edu/projects/hypertext/landow/post/poldiscourse/finnstrom/finnstrom1.html.

Fiske, J. 1989. *Understanding Popular Culture.* Boston: Unwin Hyman.

Fiske, J., and J. Hartley 2003. *Reading Television.* New York: Routledge.

Flannery, K. V. 1969. Origins and Ecological Effects of Early Domestication in Iran and the Near East. In *The Domestication and Exploitation of Plants and Animals,* P. J. Ucko and G. W. Dimbleby, eds., pp. 73–100. Chicago: Aldine.

———. 1973. The Origins of Agriculture. *Annual Review of Anthropology* 2: 271–310.

———. 1995. Prehistoric Social Evolution. In *Research Frontiers in Anthropology,*

C. R. Ember and M. Ember, eds., pp. 1–26. Upper Saddle River, NJ: Prentice Hall.

———. 1999. Chiefdoms in the Early Near East: Why It's So Hard to Identify Them. In *The Iranian World: Essays on Iranian Art and Archaeology,* A. Alizadeh, Y. Majidzadeh, and S. M. Shahmirzadi, eds. Tehran: Iran University Press.

Flannery, K. V., ed. 1986. *Guila Naquitz: Archaic Foraging and Early Agriculture in Oaxaca, Mexico.* Orlando, FL: Academic Press.

Flannery, K. V., and J. Marcus 2000. Formative Mexican Chiefdoms and the Myth of the "Mother Culture." *Journal of Anthropological Archaeology* 19:1–37.

———. 2003a. *The Cloud People: Divergent Evolution of the Zapotec and Mixtec Civilizations.* Clinton Corners, NY: Percheron Press.

———. 2003b. The Origin of War: New ^{14}C Dates from Ancient Mexico. *Proceedings of the National Academy of Sciences of the United States of America,* 100(20):11801–11805.

Flannery, K. V., J. Marcus, and R. G. Reynolds 1989. *The Flocks of the Wamani: A Study of Llama Herders on the Punas of Ayacucho, Peru.* San Diego: Academic Press.

Fleisher, M. L. 2000. *Kuria Cattle Raiders: Violence and Vigilantism on the Tanzania/Kenya Frontier.* Ann Arbor: University of Michigan Press.

Ford, C. S., and F. A. Beach 1951. *Patterns of Sexual Behavior.* New York: Harper Torchbooks.

Fortes, M. 1950. Kinship and Marriage among the Ashanti. In *African Systems of Kinship and Marriage,* A. R. Radcliffe-Brown and D. Forde, eds., pp. 252–284. London: Oxford University Press.

Fossey, D. 1983. *Gorillas in the Mist.* Boston: Houghton Mifflin.

Foster, G. M., and B. G. Anderson 1978. *Medical Anthropology.* New York: McGraw-Hill.

Foucault, M. 1979. *Discipline and Punish: The Birth of the Prison.* A. Sheridan (trans.). New York: Vintage Books.

———. 1990. *The History of Sexuality,* Volume 2, *The Use of Pleasure.* R. Hurley (trans.). New York: Vintage.

Fountain, H. 2002. Iceman's Last Meal. *New York Times,* September 17. http://www.nytimes.com/2002/09/17/science/17OBSE.html.

Fouts, R. S. 1997. *Next of Kin: What Chimpanzees Have Taught Me about Who We Are.* New York: William Morrow.

Fouts, R. S., D. H. Fouts, and T. E. Van Cantfort 1989. The Infant Loulis Learns Signs from Cross-Fostered Chimpanzees. In *Teaching Sign Language to Chimpanzees,* R. A. Gardner, B. T. Gardner, and T. E. Van Cantfort, eds., pp. 280–292. Albany: State University of New York Press.

Franke, R. 1977. Miracle Seeds and Shattered Dreams in Java. In *Readings in Anthropology,* pp. 197–201. Guilford, CT: Dushkin.

Freilich, M., D. Raybeck, and J. Savishinsky 1991. *Deviance: Anthropological Perspectives.* Westport, CT: Bergin and Garvey.

French, H. W. 2002. Whistling Past the Global Graveyard. *New York Times,* July 14, http://www.nytimes.com/2002/01/14.weekinreview/14FREN.html.

Fricke, T. 1994. *Himalayan Households: Tamang Demography and Domestic Processes,* 2nd ed. New York: Columbia University Press.

Fried, M. H. 1960. On the Evolution of Social Stratification and the State. In *Culture in History,* S. Diamond, ed., pp. 713–731. New York: Columbia University Press.

———. 1967. *The Evolution of Political Society: An Essay in Political Anthropology.* New York: McGraw-Hill.

Friedl, E. 1975. *Women and Men: An Anthropologist's View.* New York: Holt, Rinehart & Winston.

Friedman, J., ed. 2003. *Globalization, the State, and Violence.* Walnut Creek, CA: AltaMira.

Friedman, K. E., and J. Friedman 2008. *The Anthropology of Global Systems.* Lanham, MD: AltaMira.

Frisancho, A. R. 1993. *Human Adaptation and Accommodation.* Ann Arbor: University of Michigan Press.

Futuyma, D. J. 1995. *Science on Trial,* updated ed. New York: Pantheon.

Gal, S. 1989. Language and Political Economy. *Annual Review of Anthropology* 18:345–367.

Galdikas, B. M. 2005. *Great Ape Odyssey.* New York: Harry N. Abrams.

———. 2007. The Vanishing Man of the Forest. *International Herald Tribune,* January 7. http://www.nytimes.com/2007/01/07/opinion/ 07iht-edgald.4127210.html?_r=1&scp=1&sq=orangutan%20 endangered&st=cse.

Gardner, R. A., B. T. Gardner, and T. E. Van Cantfort, eds. 1989. *Teaching Sign Language to Chimpanzees.* Albany: State University of New York Press.

Gates, C. 2003. *Ancient Cities: The Archaeology of Urban Life in the Ancient Near East, Egypt, Greece, and Rome.* New York: Routledge.

Geertz, C. 1973. *The Interpretation of Cultures.* New York: Basic Books.

Geis, M. L. 1987. *The Language of Politics.* New York: Springer-Verlag.

Gellner, E. 1997. *Nationalism.* New York: New York University Press.

Gezon, L. L. 2006. *Global Visions, Local Landscapes: A Political Ecology of Conservation, Conflict, and Control in Northern Madagascar.* Lanham, MD: AltaMira.

Giddens, A. 1973. *The Class Structure of the Advanced Societies.* New York: Cambridge University Press.

———. 2000. *Runaway World: How Globalization Is Reshaping Our Lives.* New York: Routledge.

Gillespie, J. H. 2004. *Population Genetics: A Concise Guide,* 2nd ed. Baltimore: Johns Hopkins University Press.

Gilmore, D. D. 1987. *Aggression and Community: Paradoxes of Andalusian Culture.* New Haven, CT: Yale University Press.

———. 2001. *Misogyny: The Male Malady.* Philadelphia: University of Pennsylvania Press.

Gilmore-Lehne, W. J. 2000. Pre-Sumerian Cultures: Natufian through Ubaid Eras: 10,500–3500 B.C.E. http://www.stockton.edu/~gilbmorew/consorti/1bnear.htm.

Gimpel, J. 1988. *The Medieval Machine: The Industrial Revolution of the Middle Ages,* 2nd ed. Aldershot, Hants, England: Wildwood House.

Gledhill, J. 2000. *Power and Its Disguises: Anthropological Perspectives on Politics.* Sterling, VA: Pluto Press.

Gmelch, G. 1978. Baseball Magic. *Human Nature* 1(8):32–40.

———. 2001. *Inside Pitch: Life in Professional Baseball.* Washington, DC: Smithsonian Institution Press.

Gmelch, G., and W. Zenner, eds. 2002. *Urban Life: Readings in the Anthropology of the City.* Prospect Heights, IL: Waveland.

Goldberg, D. T. 2002. *The Racial State.* Malden, MA: Blackwell.

Golden, T. 1997. Oakland Revamps Plan to Teach Black English. *New York Times,* January 14, http://www.nytimes.com.

Goleman, D. 1992. Anthropology Goes Looking for Love in All the Old Places. *New York Times,* November 24, 1992, p. B1.

Goodall, J. 1986. *The Chimpanzees of Gombe: Patterns of Behavior.* Cambridge, MA: Belknap Press of Harvard University Press.

———. 1996. *My Life with the Chimpanzees.* New York: Pocket Books.

Gottdiener, M., ed. 2000. *New Forms of Consumption: Consumers, Culture, and Commodification.* Lanham, MD: Rowman & Littlefield.

Gough, E. K. 1959. The Nayars and the Definition of Marriage. *Journal of the Royal Anthropological Institute* 89:23–34.

Gould, S. J. 1999. *Rock of Ages: Science and Religion in the Fullness of Life.* New York: Ballantine Books.

Gowlett, J. A. J. 1993. *Ascent to Civilization: The Archaeology of Early Humans.* New York: McGraw-Hill.

Gramsci, A. 1971. *Selections from the Prison Notebooks.* Q. Hoare and G. N. Smith, ed. and trans. London: Wishart.

Grasmuck, S., and P. Pessar 1991. *Between Two Islands: Dominican International Migration.* Berkeley: University of California Press.

Gray, J. 1986. With a Few Exceptions, Television in Africa Fails to Educate and Enlighten. *Ann Arbor News,* December 8.

———. 1999. *False Dawn. The Delusions of Global Capitalism.* London: Granta.

Greaves, T. C. 1995. Problems Facing Anthropologists: Cultural Rights and Ethnography. *General Anthropology* 1(2):1, 3–6.

Green, E. C. 1992 (orig. 1987). The Integration of Modern and Traditional Health Sectors in Swaziland. In *Applying Anthropology,* A. Podolefsky and P. J. Brown, eds., pp. 246–251. Mountain View, CA: Mayfield.

Green, G. M., and R. W. Sussman 1990. Deforestation History of the Eastern Rain Forests of Madagascar from Satellite Images. *Science* 248 (April 13): 212–215.

Green, T. 2006. Archaeologist Makes the Case for Burying Dominant Theory of First Americans. Austin: University of Texas Research, http://www.utexas.edu/research/features/story. php?item/2006/01/collins16.xml.

Greenhouse, S. 2011. Union Membership in U.S. Fell to a 70-Year Low Last Year. *New York Times,* January 21.

Greenwood, D. J. 1976. *Unrewarding Wealth: The Commercialization and Collapse of Agriculture in a Spanish Basque Town.* Cambridge: Cambridge University Press.

Greiner, T. M. 2003. What Is the Difference between Hominin and Hominid When Classifying Humans? MadSci Network: Evolution. http://www.madsci.org/posts/ archives/Apr2003/1050350684.Ev.r.html.

Grekova, M. 2001. Postsocialist Societies. *International Encyclopedia of the Social & Behavioral Sciences,* pp. 11877–11881. New York: Elsevier.

Gremaux, Rene 1993. Woman Becomes Man in the Balkans. In *Third Sex, Third Gender: Beyond Sexual Dimorphism in Culture and History,* G. Herdt, ed. Cambridge, MA: MIT Press.

Griffin, P. B., and A. Estioko-Griffin, eds. 1985. *The Agta of Northern Luzon: Recent Studies.* Cebu City, Philippines: University of San Carlos.

Gudeman, S., ed. 1999. *Economic Anthropology.* Northhampton, MA: E. Elgar.

Gugliotta, G. 2002. Earliest Human Ancestor? Skull Dates to When Apes, Humans Split. *Washington Post,* July 11, p. A01.

———. 2004. New Evidence of Controlled Fire Is Unearthed: Israeli Team's Finds at Ancient Campsite Near Jordan River Suggest Humans Harnessed Blazes 790,000 Years Ago. *Washington Post,* May 10, p. A10.

———. 2005. Tools Found in Britain Show Much Earlier Human Existence. *Washington Post,* December 15, p. A24.

Gumperz, J. J., and S. C. Levinson, eds. 1996. *Rethinking Linguistic Relativity.* New York: Cambridge University Press.

Gupta, A., and J. Ferguson 1997a. Culture, Power, Place: Ethnography at the End of an Era. In *Culture, Power, Place: Explorations in Critical Anthropology,* A. Gupta and J. Ferguson, eds., pp. 1–29. Durham, NC: Duke University Press.

———. 1997b. Beyond "Culture": Space, Identity, and the Politics of Difference. In *Culture, Power, Place,* pp. 33–51.

Gupta, A., and J. Ferguson, eds. 1997c *Anthropological Locations: Boundaries and Grounds of a Field Science.* Berkeley: University of California Press.

———. 1997d. *Culture, Power, Place: Explorations in Critical Anthropology.* Durham, NC: Duke University Press.

Guyot, J., and C. Hughes 2007. Researchers Find Earliest Evidence for Modern Human Behavior. *Arizona State University Research Magazine.* http://researchmag.asu.edu/2008/ 02researchers_find_earliest_evid.html.

Hallowell, A. I. 1955. *Culture and Experience.* Philadelphia: University of Pennsylvania Press.

Hancock, G. 2011. *Fingerprints of the Gods.* New York: MJF Books.

Hancock, G., and R. Bauval 1996. *Message of the Sphinx: A Quest for the Hidden Legacy of Mankind.* New York: Three Rivers Press.

Handwerk, B. 2008. Half of Humanity Will Live in Cities by Year's End. *National*

Geographic News, March 13. www.national geographic.com/news/pf30472163.html.

Handwerker, W. P. 2009. *The Origins of Cultures: How Individual Choices Make Cultures Change*. Walnut Creek, CA: Left Coast Press.

Hansen, K. V. 2004. *Not-So-Nuclear Families: Class, Gender, and Networks of Care*. New Brunswick, NJ: Rutgers University Press.

Hansen, K. V., and A. I. Garey, eds. 1998. *Families in the U.S.: Kinship and Domestic Politics*. Philadelphia: Temple University Press.

Harcourt, A. H., D. Fossey, and J. Sabater-Pi 1981. Demography of Gorilla gorilla. *Journal of Zoology* 195:215–233.

Harlan, J. R., and D. Zohary 1966. Distribution of Wild Wheats and Barley. *Science* 153:1074–1080.

Harlow, H. F. 1971. *Learning to Love*. San Francisco: Albion.

Harper, J. 2002. *Endangered Species: Health, Illness, and Death among Madagascar's People of the Forest*. Durham, NC: Carolina Academic Press.

Harris, M. 1964. *Patterns of Race in the Americas*. New York: Walker.

———. 1970. Referential Ambiguity in the Calculus of Brazilian Racial Identity. *Southwestern Journal of Anthropology* 26(1):1–14.

———. 1974. *Cows, Pigs, Wars, and Witches: The Riddles of Culture*. New York: Random House.

———. 1978. *Cannibals and Kings*. New York: Vintage Books.

———. 2001 (orig. 1968). *The Rise of Anthropological Theory:* Walnut Creek, CA: AltaMira.

Harris, M., and C. P. Kottak 1963. The Structural Significance of Brazilian Racial Categories. *Sociologia* 25:203–209.

Harrison, G. G., W. L. Rathje, and W. W. Hughes 1994. Food Waste Behavior in an Urban Population. In *Applying Anthropology: An Introductory Reader,* 3rd ed., A. Podolefsky and P. J. Brown, eds., pp. 107–112. Mountain View, CA: Mayfield.

Harrison, K. D. 2007. *When Languages Die: The Extinction of the World's Languages and the Erosion of Human Knowledge*. New York: Oxford University Press.

Hart, C. W. M., A. R. Pilling, and J. C. Goodale 1988. *The Tiwi of North Australia* 3rd ed. Fort Worth, TX: Harcourt Brace.

Hart, D., and R. W. Sussman 2005. *Man the Hunted: Primates, Predators, and Human Evolution*. New York: Westview.

Hartl, D. L. 2000. *A Primer of Population Genetics,* 3rd ed. Sunderland, MA: Sinauer Associates.

Hartl, D. L., and E. W. Jones 2006. *Essential Genetics,* 4th ed. Boston: Jones and Bartlett.

Harvey, D. J. 1980. French Empire. *Academic American Encyclopedia*. Princeton, NJ: Arete, volume 8, pp. 309–310.

Hassig, R. 1985. *Trade, Tribute, and Transportation: The Sixteenth-Century Political Economy of the Valley of Mexico*. Norman: University of Oklahoma Press.

Hastings, A. 1997. *The Construction of Nationhood: Ethnicity, Religion, and Nationalism*. New York: Cambridge University Press.

Haugerud, A., M. P. Stone, and P. D. Little, eds. 2011. *Commodities and Globalization: Anthropological Perspectives*. Lanham, MD: Rowman & Littlefield.

Hawkes, K., J. O'Connell, and K. Hill 1982. Why Hunters Gather: Optimal Foraging and the Aché of Eastern Paraguay. *American Ethnologist* 9:379–398.

Hayden, B. 1981. Subsistence and Ecological Adaptations of Modern Hunter/Gatherers. In *Omnivorous Primates: Gathering and Hunting in Human Evolution,* R. S. Harding and G. Teleki, eds., pp. 344–421. New York: Columbia University Press.

Hedges, C. 1992. Sudan Presses Its Campaign to Impose Islamic Law on Non-Muslims. *New York Times,* June 1, p. A7.

Helman, C. 2007. *Culture, Health, and Illness* 5th ed. New York: Oxford University Press.

Henry, D. O. 1989. *From Foraging to Agriculture: The Levant at the End of the Ice Age*. Philadelphia: University of Pennsylvania Press.

———. 1995. *Prehistoric Cultural Ecology and Evolution: Insights from Southern Jordan*. New York: Plenum Press.

Henry, J. 1955. Docility, or Giving Teacher What She Wants. *Journal of Social Issues* 2:33–41.

Herdt, G. H. 1981. *Guardians of the Flutes*. New York: McGraw-Hill.

———. 1994. *Third Sex, Third Gender: Beyond Sexual Dimorphism in Culture and History*. Cambridge: MIT Press.

Herdt, G. H., ed. 1984. *Ritualized Homosexuality in Melanesia*. Berkeley: University of California Press.

Herskovits, M. 1937. *Life in a Haitian Valley*. New York: Knopf.

Heyerdahl, T. 1971. *The Ra Expeditions*. P. Crampton (trans.). Garden City, NY: Doubleday.

Hill, J. H. 1978. Apes and Language. *Annual Review of Anthropology* 7:89–112.

Hill, K., H. Kaplan, K. Hawkes, and A. Hurtado 1987. Foraging Decisions among Ache Hunter-gatherers: New Data and Implications for Optimal Foraging Models. *Ethology and Sociobiology* 8:1–36.

Hill-Burnett, J. 1978. Developing Anthropological Knowledge through Application. In *Applied Anthropology in America,* E. M. Eddy and W. L. Partridge, eds., pp. 112–128. New York: Columbia University Press.

Hinde, R. A. 1983. *Primate Social Relationships: An Integrated Approach*. Sunderland, MA: Sinauer.

Hobhouse, L. T. 1915. *Morals in Evolution,* rev. ed. New York: Holt.

Hoebel, E. A. 1954. *The Law of Primitive Man*. Cambridge, MA: Harvard University Press.

———. 1968 (orig. 1954). The Eskimo: Rudimentary Law in a Primitive Anarchy. In *Studies in Social and Cultural Anthropology,* J. Middleton, ed., pp. 93–127. New York: Crowell.

Hoge, W. 2001. Kautokeino Journal; Reindeer Herders, at Home on a (Very Cold) Range. *New York Times,* March 26, late ed.—final, sec. A, p. 4.

Holden, A. 2005. *Tourism Studies and the Social Sciences*. New York: Routledge.

Hole, F., K. V. Flannery, and J. A. Neely 1969. *The Prehistory and Human Ecology of the Deh Luran Plain*. Memoir no. 1. Ann Arbor: University of Michigan Museum of Anthropology.

Holst, I., J. E. Moreno, and D. R. Piperno 2007. The Identification of Teosinte, Maize, and *Tripsacum* in Mesoamerica by Using Pollen, Starch Grains, and Phytoliths. *Proceedings of the National Academy of Sciences USA* 104:17608–17613.

Hopkins, T., and I. Wallerstein 1982. Patterns of Development of the Modern World System. In *World System Analysis: Theory and Methodology,* by T. Hopkins, I. Wallerstein, R. Bach, C. Chase-Dunn, and R. Mukherjee, eds., pp. 121–141. Thousand Oaks, CA: Sage.

Hornborg, A., and C. L. Crumley, eds. 2007. *The World System and the Earth System: Global Socioenvironmental Change and Sustainability since the Neolithic*. Walnut Creek, CA: Left Coast Press.

Hornborg, A., J. R. McNeill, and J. Martinez-Alier, eds. 2007. *Rethinking Environmental History: World-System History and Global Environmental Change*. Lanham, MD: AltaMira.

Horton, R. 1993. *Patterns of Thought in Africa and the West: Essays on Magic, Religion, and Science*. Cambridge: Cambridge University Press.

Huffington Post 2009. Geneva WTO Protests 2009: Police Clash with Black Bloc Demonstrators. http://www.huffmgtonpost.conT/ 2009/ll/ 28/geneva-wto-protests-2009-_n_372855.html.

Hunt, R. C. 2007. *Beyond Relativism: Comparability in Cultural Anthropology*. Lanham, MD: AltaMira.

Hunter, M. L. 2005. *Race, Gender, and the Politics of Skin Tone*. New York: Routledge.

Hurtado, A. M., C. A. Lambourne, P. James, K. Hill, K. Cheman, and K. Baca 2005. Human Rights, Biomedical Science, and Infectious Diseases among South American Indigenous Groups. *Annual Review of Anthropology* 34:639–665.

Inda, J. X., and R. Rosaldo, eds. 2008. *The Anthropology of Globalization: A Reader*. Malden, MA: Blackwell.

Ingraham, C. 2008. *White Weddings: Romancing Heterosexuality in Popular Culture,* 2nd ed. New York: Routledge.

Inhorn, M. C., and P. J. Brown 1990. The Anthropology of Infectious Disease. *Annual Review of Anthropology* 19:89–117.

Iqbal, S. 2002. A New Light on Skin Color. *National Geographic Online Extra.* http://magma.nationalgeographic.com/ngm/0211/feature2/online_extra.html.

Jablonski, N. G., and G. Chaplin, 2000. The Evolution of Human Skin Coloration. *Journal of Human Evolution* (39):57–106.

Jackson, J., and K. B. Warren 2005. Indigenous Movements in Latin America, 1992–2004: Controversies, Ironies, New Directions. *Annual Review of Anthropology* 34:549–573.

Jenks, C. 2005. *Culture,* 2nd ed. New York: Routledge.

Johansen, B. E. 2003. *Indigenous Peoples and Environmental Issues: An Encyclopedia.* Westport, CT: Greenwood.

Johanson, D. C., and T. D. White 1979. A Systematic Assessment of Early African Hominids. *Science* 203:321–330.

Johnson, A. W. 1978. *Quantification in Cultural Anthropology: An Introduction to Research Design.* Stanford, CA: Stanford University Press.

Johnson, A. W., and T. K. Earle 2000. *The Evolution of Human Societies: From Foraging Group to Agrarian State,* 2nd ed. Stanford, CA: Stanford University Press.

Johnston, B. R. 2009. *Life and Death Matters: Human Rights, Environment, and Social Justice,* 2nd ed. Walnut Creek, CA: Left Coast Press.

Jolly, C. J., and R. White 1995. *Physical Anthropology and Archaeology,* 5th ed. New York: McGraw-Hill.

Jones, D. 1999. Hot Asset in Corporate: Anthropology Degrees. *USA Today,* February 18, p. B1.

Joralemon, D. 2006. *Exploring Medical Anthropology,* 2nd ed. Boston: Pearson.

Jordan, A. 2003. *Business Anthropology.* Prospect Heights, IL: Waveland.

Jungers, William L. et al. 2008. Descriptions of the Lower Limb Skeleton of Homo floresiensis. *Journal of Human Evolution* 57(5):538.

Kan, S. 1986. The 19th-Century Tlingit Potlatch: A New Perspective. *American Ethnologist* 13:191–212.

———. 1989. *Symbolic Immortality: The Tlingit Potlatch of the Nineteenth Century.* Washington, DC: Smithsonian Institution Press.

Kaneshiro, N. K. 2009. Intersex. Medline Plus. National Institutes of Health, U.S. National Library of Medicine. http://www.nlm.nih.gov/medlineplus/ency/article/001669.htm.

Katzenberg, M. A., and S. R. Saunders, eds. 2000. *Biological Anthropology of the Human Skeleton.* New York: Wiley.

Kaufman, S. R., and L. M. Morgan 2005. The Anthropology of the Beginnings and Ends of Life. *Annual Review of Anthropology* 34:317–341.

Kearney, M. 1996. *Reconceptualizing the Peasantry: Anthropology in Global Perspective.* Boulder, CO: Westview Press.

———. 2004. *Changing Fields of Anthropology: From Local to Global.* Lanham, MD: Rowman & Littlefield.

Kellenberger, J. 2008. *Moral Relativism: A Dialogue.* Lanham, MA: Rowman & Littlefield.

Kelly, R. C. 1976. Witchcraft and Sexual Relations: An Exploration in the Social and Semantic Implications of the Structure of Belief. In *Man and Woman in the New Guinea Highlands,* P. Brown and G. Buchbinder, eds., pp. 36–53. Special Publication no. 8. Washington, DC: American Anthropological Association.

Kelly, R. L. 1995. *The Foraging Spectrum: Diversity in Hunter-Gatherer Lifeways.* Washington, DC: Smithsonian Institution Press.

Kennickell, A. B. 2006. Currents and Undercurrents: Changes in the Distribution of Wealth, 1989–2004. FEDS Working Paper No. 2006-13. Accessed June 20, 2008. http://ssm.com/abstract=909206.

Kent, S. 1992. The Current Forager Controversy: Real versus Ideal Views of Hunter-gatherers. *Man* 27:45–70.

———. 1996. *Cultural Diversity among Twentieth-Century Foragers: An African Perspective.* New York: Cambridge University Press.

Kent, S., and H. Vierich 1989. The Myth of Ecological Determinism: Anticipated Mobility and Site Organization of Space. In *Farmers as Hunters: The Implications of Sedentism,* S. Kent, ed., pp. 96–130. New York: Cambridge University Press.

Kent, S., ed. 2002. *Ethnicity, Hunter-gatherers, and the "Other": Association or Assimilation in Africa.* Washington: Smithsonian Institution Press.

Keppel, K. G., J. N. Pearch, and D. K. Wagener 2002. Trends in Racial and Ethnic-Specific Rates for the Health Status Indicators: United States, 1990–98. *Healthy People Statistical Notes No. 23.* Hyattsville, MD: National Center for Health Statistics.

Kerbo, H. R. 2006. *World Poverty: Global Inequality and the Modern World System.* Boston: McGraw-Hill.

Kershaw, S. 2009. For Teenagers, Hello Means 'How About a Hug?' *New York Times,* May 28.

Keynes, J. M. 1927. *The End of Laissez-Faire.* London: L and Virginia Woolf.

———. 1936. *General Theory of Employment, Interest, and Money.* New York: Harcourt Brace.

Kimmel, M. S. 2007. *The Gendered Society,* 3rd ed. New York: Oxford University Press.

Kimmel, M. S., J. Hearn, and R. W. Connell 2004. *Handbook of Studies on Men and Masculinities.* Thousand Oaks, CA: Sage.

Kimmel, M. S., and M. A. Messner, eds. 2007. *Men's Lives,* 7th ed. Boston: Pearson/Allyn & Bacon.

Kimmel, M. S., and R. Plante 2004. *Sexualities: Identities, Behaviors, and Society.* New York: Oxford University Press.

Kinsey, A. C., W. B. Pomeroy, and C. E. Martin 1948. *Sexual Behavior in the Human Male.* Philadelphia: W. B. Saunders.

Kjaerulff, J. 2010. *Internet and Change: An Ethnography of Knowledge and Flexible Work.* Walnut Creek, CA: Left Coast Press.

Klass, M. 2003. *Mind over Mind: The Anthropology and Psychology of Spirit Possession.* Lanham, MA: Rowman & Littlefield.

Klein, N. 2000. *No Logo.* London: Flamingo.

Klein, R. G., with B. Edgar 2002. *The Dawn of Human Culture.* New York: Wiley.

Kleinfeld, J. 1975. Positive Stereotyping: The Cultural Relativist in the Classroom. *Human Organization* 34:269–274.

Kluckhohn, C. 1944. *Mirror for Man: A Survey of Human Behavior and Social Attitudes.* Greenwich, CT: Fawcett.

Komar, D. A., and J. E. Buikstra 2008. *Forensic Anthropology: Contemporary Theory and Practice.* New York: Oxford University Press.

Kopytoff, V. G. 1995. Meat Viewed as Staple of Chimp Diet and Mores. *New York Times,* June 27, pp. B5–B6.

Kottak, C. P. 1980. *The Past in the Present: History, Ecology, and Social Organization in Highland Madagascar.* Ann Arbor: University of Michigan Press.

———. 1990a. Culture and "Economic Development." *American Anthropologist* 93(3):723–731.

———. 1990b. *Prime-Time Society: An Anthropological Analysis of Television and Culture.* Belmont, CA: Wadsworth.

———. 1991. When People Don't Come First: Some Lessons from Completed Projects. In *Putting People First: Sociological Variables in Rural Development,* 2nd ed., M. Cernea, ed., pp. 429–464. New York: Oxford University Press.

———. 1999. The New Ecological Anthropology. *American Anthropologist* 101(1):23–35.

———. 2004. An Anthropological Take on Sustainable Development: A Comparative Study of Change. *Human Organization* (63, 4):501–510.

———. 2006. *Assault on Paradise: The Globalization of a Little Community in Brazil,* 4th ed. New York: McGraw-Hill.

———. 2007. Return to Madagascar: A Forty Year Retrospective. *General Anthropology: Bulletin of the General Anthropology Division of the American Anthropological Association* 14(2):1–10.

———. 2009. *Prime-Time Society: An Anthropological Analysis of Television and Culture,* updated ed. Walnut Creek, CA: Left Coast Press.

Kottak, C. P., and K. A. Kozaitis 2011. *On Being Different: Diversity and Multiculturalism in the North American Mainstream,* 4th ed. Boston: McGraw-Hill.

Kottak, C. P., L. L. Gezon, and G. Green 1994. Deforestation and Biodiversity Preservation in Madagascar: The View from Above and Below. *CIESIN Human Dimensions Kiosk*—an electronic publication. http://www.ciesin.com.

Kottak, N. C. 2002. *Stealing the Neighbor's Chicken: Social Control in Northern Mozambique.* PhD dissertation. Department of Anthropology, Emory University, Atlanta, GA.

Kreider, R. M., and J. M. Fields 2002. Number, Timing and Duration of Marriages and Divorces: 1996. U.S. Census Bureau. *Current Population Reports,* P70–80, February. http://www.census.gov/prod/2002pubs/p70–80.pdf.

Kretchmer, N. 1975 (orig. 1972). Lactose and Lactase. In *Biological Anthropology, Readings from Scientific American,* S. H. Katz, ed., pp. 310–318. San Francisco: W. H. Freeman.

Kuhn, S. L., M. C. Stiner, and D. S. Reese 2001. Ornaments of the Earliest Upper Paleolithic: New Insights from the Levant. *Proceedings of the National Academy of Sciences of the United States of America* 98(13): 7641–7646.

Kulick, D. 1998. *Travesti: Sex, Gender, and Culture among Brazilian Transgendered Prostitutes.* Chicago: University of Chicago Press.

Kuper, L. 2006. *Race, Class, and Power: Ideology and Revolutionary Change in Plural Societies.* New Brunswick, NJ: Transaction Publishers.

Kurtz, D. V. 2001. *Political Anthropology: Power and Paradigms.* Boulder, CO: Westview Press.

Kutsche, P. 1998. *Field Ethnography: A Manual for Doing Cultural Anthropology.* Upper Saddle River, NJ: Prentice Hall.

Labov, W. 1972a. *Language in the Inner City: Studies in the Black English Vernacular.* Philadelphia: University of Pennsylvania Press.

———. 1972b. *Sociolinguistic Patterns.* Philadelphia: University of Pennsylvania Press.

La Fraugh, R. J. n.d. Euskara: The History, a True Mystery. The La Fraugh Name History. http://planetrjl.tripod.com/LaFraughName/id5.html.

Laguerre, M. 1999. *The Global Ethnopolis: Chinatown, Japantown, and Manilatown in American Society.* New York: St. Martin's Press.

———. 2001. *Urban Multiculturalism and Globalization in New York City.* New York: Palgrave Macmillan.

Laird, S. A. 2002. *Biodiversity and Traditional Knowledge: Equitable Partnerships in Practice.* Sterling, VA: Earthscan.

Lakoff, G. 2008. *The Political Mind: Why You Can't Understand 21st-century Politics with an 18th-century Brain.* New York: Viking.

Lakoff, R. T. 2000. *The Language War.* Berkeley: University of California Press.

———. 2004. *Language and Women's Place: Text and Commentaries,* rev. ed., M. Bucholtz, ed. New York: Oxford University Press.

Lambek, M., ed. 2008. *A Reader in the Anthropology of Religion.* Malden, MA: Blackwell.

Lancaster, R. N., and M. Di Leonardo, eds. 1997. *The Gender/Sexuality Reader: Culture, History, Political Economy.* New York: Routledge.

Landes, D. 1999. *The Wealth and Poverty of Nations. Why Some Are So Rich and Some Are So Poor.* London: Abacus.

Lange, M. 2009. *Lineages of Despotism and Development: British Colonialism and State Power.* Chicago: University of Chicago Press.

Largent, F. 2007a. Clovis Dethroned: A New Perspective on the First Americans, Part 1. *Mammoth Trumpet* 22(3):1–3, 20.

———. 2007b. Clovis Dethroned: A New Perspective on the First Americans, Part 2. *Mammoth Trumpet* 22(4):1–2, 13.

Larsen, C. S. 2000. *Skeletons in Our Closet: Revealing Our Past through Bioarchaeology.* Princeton, NJ: Princeton University Press.

Larson, A. 1989. Social Context of Human Immunodeficiency Virus Transmission in Africa: Historical and Cultural Bases of East and Central African Sexual Relations. *Review of Infectious Diseases* 11:716–731.

Lassiter, L. E. 1998. *The Power of Kiowa Song: A Collaborative Ethnography.* Tucson: University of Arizona Press.

Laughlin, J. C. H. 2006. *Fifty Major Cities of the Bible.* New York: Routledge.

Leach, E. R. 1955. Polyandry, Inheritance and the Definition of Marriage. *Man* 55:182–186.

———. 1961. *Rethinking Anthropology.* London: Athlone Press.

Leadbeater, C. 1999. *Europe's New Economy.* London: Centre for European Reform.

Leakey, M. G., C. S. Feibel, I. McDougall, and A. Walker 1995. New Four-Million-Year-Old Hominid Species from Kanapoi and Allia Bay, Kenya. *Nature* 376: 565–571.

Lee, R. B. 1979. *The !Kung San: Men, Women, and Work in a Foraging Society.* New York: Cambridge University Press.

———. 1984. *The Dobe !Kung.* New York: Harcourt Brace.

———. 1993. *The Dobe Ju/'hoansi,* 2nd ed. Fort Worth, TX: Harcourt Brace.

———. 2003. *The Dobe Ju/'hoansi,* 3rd ed. Belmont, CA: Wadsworth.

Lee, R. B., and R. H. Daly 1999. *The Cambridge Encyclopedia of Hunters and Gatherers.* New York: Cambridge University Press.

Lehmann, A. C., J. E. Meyers, and P. A. Moro eds. 2005. *Magic, Witchcraft, and Religion: An Anthropological Study of the Supernatural,* 6th ed. Boston: McGraw-Hill.

Leman, J. 2001. *The Dynamics of Emerging Ethnicities: Immigrant and Indigenous Ethnogenesis in Confrontation.* New York: Peter Lang.

Lemonick, M. D., and A. Dorfman 1999. Up from the Apes: Remarkable New Evidence Is Filling in the Story of How We Became Human. *Time* 154(8):5–58.

Lenski, G. 1966. *Power and Privilege: A Theory of Social Stratification.* New York: McGraw-Hill.

Levine, N. E. 2008. Alternative Kinship, Marriage, and Reproduction. *Annual Review of Anthropology* 37:17–35.

Levinson, B. A. U., and M. Pollock, eds. 2011. *A Companion to the Anthropology of Education.* Malden, MA: Blackwell.

Lévi-Strauss, C. 1963. *Totemism.* R. Needham (trans.). Boston: Beacon Press.

———. 1967. *Structural Anthropology.* New York: Doubleday.

Levy, F. 2010. The World's Happiest Countries. *Forbes,* July 14. http://www.forbes.com/2010/07/14/world-happiest-countries-lifestyle-realestate-gallup.html.

Levy, J. E., with B. Pepper 1992. *Orayvi Revisited: Social Stratification in an "Egalitarian" Society.* Santa Fe, NM: School of American Research Press, and Seattle: University of Washington Press.

Lewellen, T. C. 2002. *The Anthropology of Globalization: Cultural Anthropology Enters the 21st Century.* Westport, CT: Bergin and Garvey.

———. 2003. *Political Anthropology: An Introduction,* 3rd ed. Westport, CT: Praeger.

———. 2010. Groping toward Globalization: In Search of Anthropology without Boundaries. *Reviews in Anthropology* 31(1):73–89.

Lie, J. 2001. *Multiethnic Japan.* Cambridge, MA: Harvard University Press.

Lieban, R. W. 1977. The Field of Medical Anthropology. In *Culture, Disease, and Healing: Studies in Medical Anthropology,* D. Landy, ed., pp. 13–31. New York: Macmillan.

Lindenbaum, S. 1972. Sorcerers, Ghosts, and Polluting Women: An Analysis of Religious Belief and Population Control. *Ethnology* 11:241–253.

Linton, R. 1943. Nativistic Movements. *American Anthropologist* 45:230–240.

Little, K. 1965. *West African Urbanization: A Study of Voluntary Associations in Social Change*. Cambridge: Cambridge University Press.

———. 1971. Some Aspects of African Urbanization South of the Sahara. Reading, MA: Addison-Wesley, McCaleb Modules in Anthropology.

Livingstone, F. B. 1969. Gene Frequency Clines of the b Hemoglobin Locus in Various Human Populations and Their Similarities by Models Involving Differential Selection. *Human Biology* 41:223–236.

Lockwood, W. G. 1975. *European Moslems: Economy and Ethnicity in Western Bosnia*. New York: Academic Press.

Lohr, S. 2005. Cutting Here, but Hiring Over There. *New York Times,* June 24. http://www .nytimes.com/2005/06/24/technology/24blue .html?pagewanted=print.

Loomis, W. F. 1967. Skin-Pigmented Regulation of Vitamin-D Biosynthesis in Man. *Science* 157:501–506.

Lowie, R. H. 1961 (orig. 1920). *Primitive Society*. New York: Harper & Brothers.

Lucentini, J. 2002. Bones Reveal Some Truth in "Noble Savage Myth." *Washington Post,* April 15, p. A09.

Lugaila, T. 1999. Married Adults Still in the Majority, Census Bureau Reports. http://www .census.gov/Press-Release/www/1999/cb9903 .html.

Lyell, C. 1969 (orig. 1830–1837). *Principles of Geology*. New York: Johnson.

MacKinnon, J. 1974. *In Search of the Red Ape*. New York: Ballantine Books.

Madra, Y. M. 2004. Karl Polanyi: Freedom in a Complex Society. *Econ-Atrocity Bulletin: In the History of Thought*. http://www.fguide .org/Bulletin/polanyi.htm.

Malinowski, B. 1927. *Sex and Repression in Savage Society*. London and New York: International Library of Psychology, Philosophy and Scientific Method.

———. 1929. Practical Anthropology. *Africa* 2:23–38.

———. 1961 (orig. 1922). *Argonauts of the Western Pacific*. New York: Dutton.

———. 1978 (orig. 1931). The Role of Magic and Religion. In *Reader in Comparative Religion: An Anthropological Approach,* 4th ed., W. A. Lessa and E. Z. Vogt, eds., pp. 37–46. New York: Harper and Row.

Malkin, C. 2004. Earliest Primate Discovered in China. *Science Now,* January 5, American Association for the Advancement of Science. http://cmbi.bjmu.edu.cn/news/0401/13.htm.

Malkki, Liisa H. 1995. *Purity and Exile: Violence, Memory, and National Cosmology among Hutu Refugees in Tanzania*. Chicago: University of Chicago Press.

Maquet, J. 1964. Objectivity in Anthropology. *Current Anthropology* 5:47–55.

Mar, M. E. 1997. Secondary Colors: The Multiracial Option. *Harvard Magazine,* May–June, pp. 19–20.

Marcus, G. E., and M. M. J. Fischer. 1986. *Anthropology as Cultural Critique: An Experimental Moment in the Human Sciences*. Chicago: University of Chicago Press.

———. 1999. *Anthropology as Cultural Critique: An Experimental Moment in the Human Sciences,* 2nd ed. Chicago: University of Chicago Press.

Marcus, G. E., and F. R. Myers, eds. 1995. *The Traffic in Culture: Refiguring Art and Anthropology*. Berkeley: University of California Press.

Marcus, J. 1989. From Centralized Systems to City-States: Possible Models for the Epiclassic. In *Mesoamerica After the Decline of Teotihuacan: A.D. 700–900,* ed. R. A. Diehl and J. C. Berlo, pp. 201–208. Dumbarton Oaks: Washington, D.C.

Marcus, J., and K. V. Flannery 1996. *Zapotec Civilization: How Urban Society Evolved in Mexico's Oaxaca Valley*. New York: Thames and Hudson.

Margolis, M. L. 1984. *Mothers and Such: American Views of Women and How They Changed.* Berkeley: University of California Press.

———. 2000. *True to Her Nature: Changing Advice to American Women.* Prospect Heights, IL: Waveland.

———. 2003. The Relative Status of Men and Women. In *Encyclopedia of Sex and Gender: Men and Women in the World's Cultures,* C. Ember and M. Ember, eds., pp. 137–145. New York: Kluwer Academic/Plenum.

Marshall, R. C., ed. 2011. *Cooperation in Economy and Society.* Lanham, MD: Rowman & Littlefield.

Martin, E. 1992. The End of the Body? *American Ethnologist* 19:121–140.

Martin, K., and B. Voorhies 1975. *Female of the Species.* New York: Columbia University Press.

Martin, S. M. 1988. *Palm Oil and Protest: An Economic History of the Ngwa Region, South-Eastern Nigeria, 1800–1980.* New York: Cambridge University Press.

Martinez, E., and A. Garcia 2000. What Is "Neo-Liberalism"? A Brief Definition. http://www.globalexchange.org/campaigns/econ101/neoliberalDefined.html.pdf.

Marx, K., and F. Engels 1976 (orig. 1848). *Communist Manifesto.* New York: Pantheon.

Mascia-Lees, F., and N. J. Black 2000. *Gender and Anthropology.* Prospect Heights, IL: Waveland.

Mathews, G. 2000. *Global Culture/Individual Identity: Searching for Home in the Cultural Supermarket.* New York: Routledge.

Maugh, T. H., III 2007. One Language Disappears Every 14 Days; About Half of the World's Distinct Tongues Could Vanish This Century, Researchers Say. *Los Angeles Times,* September 19.

Maybury-Lewis, D. 2002. *Indigenous Peoples, Ethnic Groups, and the State,* 2nd ed. Boston: Allyn & Bacon.

Mayell, H. 2003. Orangutans Show Signs of Culture, Study Says. *National Geographic News,* January 3. http://news.national

geographic.com/news/2002/12/1220_021226 _orangutan.html.

———. 2004a. Wild Orangs, Extinct by 2023? *National Geographic News,* March 9. http://news.national-geographic.com/news/2003/09/0930_030930_orangutanthreat.html.

———. 2004b. Is Bead Find Proof Modern Thought Began in Africa? *National Geographic News,* March 31. http://news.national -geographic.com/news/2004/03/0331 _040331_ostrichman.html.

Mayr, E. 2001. *What Evolution Is.* New York: Basic Books.

Mba, N. E. 1982. *Nigerian Women Mobilized: Women's Political Activity in Southern Nigeria, 1900–1965.* Berkeley: University of California Press.

McBrearty, S., and A. S. Brooks 2000. The Revolution That Wasn't: A New Interpretation of the Origin of Modern Human Behavior. *Journal of Human Evolution* 39:453–563.

McElroy, A., and P. K. Townsend 2003. *Medical Anthropology in Ecological Perspective,* 4th ed. Boulder, CO: Westview Press.

McKinnon, S. 2005. On Kinship and Marriage: A Critique of the Genetic and Gender Calculus of Evolutionary Psychology. In *Complexities: Beyond Nature and Nurture,* S. McKinnon and S. Silverman, eds., pp. 106–131. Chicago: The University of Chicago Press.

Mead, M. 1937. *Cooperation and Competition among Primitive Peoples.* New York: McGraw-Hill.

Meadow, R. H., ed. 1991. *Harappa Excavations 1986–1990: A Multidisciplinary Approach to Third Millennium Urbanism.* Monographs in World Archeology, no. 3. Madison, WI: Prehistory Press.

Meadow, R. H., and J. M. Kenoyer 2000. The Indus Valley Mystery: One of the World's First Great Civilizations Is Still a Puzzle. *Discovering Archaeology,* March/April 2000. http://www/discoveringarchaeology. com/0800toc/8feature1-indus.shtml.

Meigs, A., and K. Barlow 2002. Beyond the Taboo: Imagining Incest. *American Anthropologist* 104(1): 38–49.

Mercader, J., M. Panger, and C. Boesch 2002. Excavation of a Chimpanzee Stone Tool Site in the African Rainforest. *Science* 296 (May 24): 1452–1455.

Merry, S. E. 2006. Anthropology and International Law. *Annual Review of Anthropology* 35:99–116.

Michaels, E. 1986. Aboriginal Content. Paper presented at the meeting of the Australian Screen Studies Association, December, Sydney.

———. 1991. Aboriginal Content: Who's Got It—Who Needs It? *Visual Anthropology* 4:277–300.

Miles, H. L. 1983. Apes and Language: The Search for Communicative Competence. In *Language in Primates,* J. de Luce and H. T. Wilder, eds., pp. 43–62. New York: Springer Verlag.

Miller, B. D. 1997. *The Endangered Sex: Neglect of Female Children in Rural North India.* New York: Oxford University Press.

Miller, N., and R. C. Rockwell, eds. 1988. *AIDS in Africa: The Social and Policy Impact.* Lewiston, NY: Edwin Mellen.

Mintz, S. 1985. *Sweetness and Power: The Place of Sugar in Modern History.* New York: Viking Penguin.

Mitani, J. C., and D. P. Watts 1999. Demographic Influences on the Hunting Behavior of Chimpanzees. *American Journal of Physical Anthropology* 109: 439–454.

Mitchell, J. C. 1966. Theoretical Orientations in African Urban Studies. In *The Social Anthropology of Complex Societies*, M. Banton, ed., pp. 37–68. London: Tavistock.

Moerman, M. 1965. Ethnic Identification in a Complex Civilization: Who Are the Lue? *American Anthropologist* 67(5 Part I): 1215–1230.

Moncure, S. 1998. Anthropologist Assists in Police Investigations. *University of Delaware Update.* 17(39, August 20). http://www.udel .edu/PR/UpDate/98/39/anthrop.html.

Montagu, A., ed. 1997. *Man's Most Dangerous Myth: The Fallacy of Race.* Walnut Creek, CA: AltaMira.

Morgen, S., ed. 1989. *Gender and Anthropology: Critical Reviews for Research and Teaching.* Washington, DC: American Anthropological Association.

Morrill, C., D. A. Snow, and C. H. White, eds. 2005. *Together Alone: Personal Relationships in Public Places.* Berkeley: University of California Press.

Motseta, S. 2006. Botswana Gives Bushmen Tough Conditions. *Tulsa World,* December 14.

Moyà-Solà, S., M. Köhler, D. M. Alba, I. Casanovas-Vilar, and J. Galindo 2004. *Pierolapithecus catalaunicus,* a New Middle Miocene Great Ape from Spain. *Science* 306 (November 19):1339–1344.

Mukhopadhyay, C., and P. Higgins 1988. Anthropological Studies of Women's Status Revisited: 1977–1987. *Annual Review of Anthropology* 17:461–495.

Mukhopadhyay, C. C., R. Henze, and Y. T. Moses 2007. *How Real Is Race? A Sourcebook on Race, Culture, and Biology.* Lanham, MD: AltaMira.

Mullings, L., ed. 1987. *Cities of the United States: Studies in Urban Anthropology.* New York: Columbia University Press.

Murdock, G. P. 1934. *Our Primitive Contemporaries.* New York: Macmillan.

———. 1957. World Ethnographic Sample. *American Anthropologist* 59: 664–687.

Murdock, G. P., and C. Provost 1973. Factors in the Division of Labor by Sex: A Cross-Cultural Analysis. *Ethnology* XII(2):203–225.

Murray, S. O., and W. Roscoe, eds. 1998. *Boy-wives and Female Husbands: Studies in African Homosexualities.* New York: St. Martin's Press.

Mydans, S. 1992a. Criticism Grows over Aliens Seized during Riots. *New York Times,* May 29, p. A8.

———. 1992b. Judge Dismisses Case in Shooting by Officer. *New York Times,* June 4, p. A8.

Nadeem, S. 2011. *Dead Ringers: How Outsourcing Is Changing the Way Indians Understand Themselves.* Princeton, NJ: Princeton University Press.

Nafte, M. 2000. *Flesh and Bone: An Introduction to Forensic Anthropology*. Durham, NC: Carolina Academic Press.

Nagel, J. 1996. *American Indian Ethnic Renewal: Red Power and the Resurgence of Identity and Culture*. New York: Oxford University Press.

Nanda, S. 1999. *Neither Man nor Woman: The Hijras of India,* 2nd ed. Belmont, CA: Wadsworth: Cengage.

———. 2000. *Gender Diversity Crosscultural Variations*. Prospect Heights, IL: Waveland.

National Academies 2007. Understanding and Responding to Climate Change: Highlights of National Academies Reports. http://dels.nas.edu/basc/Climate-HIGH.pdf.

Naylor, L. L. 1996. *Culture and Change: An Introduction*. Westport, CT: Bergin and Garvey.

Nazarea, V. D. 2006. Local Knowledge and Memory in Biodiversity Conservation. *Annual Review of Anthropology* 35:317–335.

New York Times 1992. Alexandria Journal: TV Program for Somalis Is a Rare Unifying Force. December 18.

Ni, X., W. Wang, Y. Hu, and C. Li 2004. A Euprimate Skull from the Early Eocene of China. *Nature* 427 (January 1):65–68.

Nielsson, G. P. 1985. States and Nation-Groups: A Global Taxonomy. In *New Nationalisms of the Developed World,* E. A. Tiryakian and R. Rogowski, eds., pp. 27–56. Boston: Allen & Unwin.

Nolan, R. W. 2002. *Development Anthropology: Encounters in the Real World*. Boulder, CO: Westview Press.

———. 2003. *Anthropology in Practice*. Boulder, CO: Lynne Rienner.

Nordstrom, C. 2004. *Shadows of War: Violence, Power, and International Profiteering in the Twenty-First Century*. Berkeley: University of California Press.

Nugent, D., and J. Vincent, eds. 2004. *A Companion to the Anthropology of Politics*. Malden, MA: Blackwell.

Ohlemacher, S. 2006. 2006: The Year of the 300M Mark: Face of America Changes as Country Grows. *Charleston Post and Courier,* June 26, pp. 1A, 11A.

O'Leary, C. 2002. *Class Formation, Diet and Economic Transformation in Two Brazilian Fishing Communities*. Unpublished PhD dissertation, University of Michigan, Ann Arbor.

Omohundro, J. T. 2001. *Careers in Anthropology,* 2nd ed. Boston: McGraw-Hill.

Ong, A. 1987. *Spirits of Resistance and Capitalist Discipline: Factory Women in Malaysia*. Albany: State University of New York Press.

———. 1989. Center, Periphery, and Hierarchy: Gender in Southeast Asia. In *Gender and Anthropology: Critical Reviews for Research and Teaching,* S. Morgen, ed., pp. 294–312. Washington, DC: American Anthropological Association.

Ong, A., and S. J. Collier, eds. 2005. *Global Assemblages: Technology, Politics, and Ethics as Anthropological Problems*. Malden, MA: Blackwell.

Ontario Consultants on Religious Tolerance 1996. Religious Access Dispute Resolved. Internet Mailing List, April 12, http://www.religioustolerance.org/news_694.htm.

———. 2001. Religions of the World: Number of Adherents; Rates of Growth. http://www.religioustolerance.org/worldrel.htm.

Oriji, J. N. 2000. Igbo Women from 1929–1960. *West Africa Review* 2:1.

Ortner, S. B. 1984. Theory in Anthropology Since the Sixties. *Comparative Studies in Society and History* 126(1):126–166.

Ott, S. 1981. *The Circle of Mountains: A Basque Shepherding Community*. Oxford: Clarendon Press.

Owen, J. 2006. "Lucy's Baby"—World's Oldest Child—Found by Fossil Hunters. *National Geographic News,* September 20, 2006. http://news.nationalgeographic.com/news/2006/ 09/060920-lucys-baby.html.

Paine, R. 2009. *Camps of the Tundra: Politics Through Reindeer among Saami Pastoralists*. Oslo: Instituttet for sammenlignende kulturforskning.

Palmer, S. 2001. The Rael Deal. *Religion in the News* 4:2. Hartford, CT: Trinity College. The Leonard E. Greenberg Center for the Study of Religion in Public Life. http://www .trincoll.edu/depts/csrpl/PJNVol4No2/Rael.htm.

Parkin, R., and L. Stone, eds. 2004. *Kinship and Family: An Anthropological Reader.* Malden, MA: Blackwell.

Parsons, J. R. 1974. The Development of a Prehistoric Complex Society: A Regional Perspective from the Valley of Mexico. *Journal of Field Archaeology* 1:81–108.

———. 1976. The Role of Chinampa Agriculture in the Food Supply of Aztec Tenochtitlan. In *Cultural Change and Continuity: Essays in Honor of James Bennett Griffin,* C. E. Cleland, ed., pp. 233–262. New York: Academic Press.

Parzinger, H., et al. 2006. Declaration (on the Bosnia pyramid hoax). *The European Archaeologist,* December 11. http://www.e-a-a.org/ statement.pdf.

Patterson, F. 1978. Conversations with a Gorilla. *National Geographic,* October, pp. 438–465.

Paulson, T. E. 2005. Chimp, Human DNA Comparison Finds Vast Similarities, Key Differences. *Seattle Post-Intelligencer Reporter,* September 1, 2005. http://seattlepi. nwsource.com/local/238852_chimp01.html.

Peletz, M. 1988. *A Share of the Harvest: Kinship, Property, and Social History among the Malays of Rembau.* Berkeley: University of California Press.

Pelto, P. 1973. *The Snowmobile Revolution: Technology and Social Change in the Arctic.* Menlo Park, CA: Cummings.

Peplau, L. A., ed. 1999. *Gender, Culture, and Ethnicity: Current Research about Women and Men.* Mountain View, CA: Mayfield.

Peregrine, P. N., C. R. Ember, and M. Ember 2007. Modeling State Origins Using Cross-Cultural Data. *Cross-Cultural Research* 41:75–86.

Perlman, D. 2004. Fossil Find May Be the Father of Us All: It's Hailed as Last Common Kin of the Great Apes and Humans. *San Francisco Chronicle,* November 22, p. A-4.

http://www.sfgate.com/cgibin/article.cgi?file=/ chronicle/archive/2004/11/22/MNGIV-9VF3G1.DTL.

Peters-Golden, H. 2002. *Culture Sketches: Case Studies in Anthropology,* 3rd ed. New York: McGraw-Hill.

Petraglia-Bahri, D. 1996. Introduction to Postcolonial Studies. http://www.emory.edu/ ENGLISH/Bahri/.

Piddocke, S. 1969. The Potlatch System of the Southern Kwakiutl: A New Perspective. In *Environment and Cultural Behavior,* A. P. Vayda, ed., pp. 130–156. Garden City, NY: Natural History Press.

Piperno, D. R. 2001. On Maize and the Sunflower. *Science* 292(5525):2260–2261.

Piperno, D. R., and D. M. Pearsall 1998. *The Origins of Agriculture in the Lowland Neotropics.* San Diego: Academic Press.

Piperno, D. R., and K. E. Stothert 2003. Phytolith Evidence for Early Holocene *Cucurbita* Domestication in Southwest Ecuador. *Science,* February 14, 299(5609):1054–1105.

Plattner, S., ed. 1989. *Economic Anthropology.* Stanford, CA: Stanford University Press.

Podolefsky, A., and P. J. Brown, eds. 1992. *Applying Anthropology: An Introductory Reader,* 2nd ed. Mountain View, CA: Mayfield.

Pohl, M. E. D., D. R. Piperno, K. O. Pope, and J. G. Jones 2007. Microfossil Evidence for Pre-Columbian Maize Dispersals in the Neotropics from San Andrés, Tabasco, Mexico. *Proceedings of the National Academy of Sciences of the United States of America* 104(29):11874–11881.

Polanyi, K. 1968. *Primitive, Archaic and Modern Economies: Essays of Karl Polanyi,* G. Dalton, ed., Garden City, NY: Anchor Books.

Pollock, S. 1999. *Ancient Mesopotamia: The Eden That Never Was.* Cambridge: Cambridge University Press.

Pospisil, L. 1963. *The Kapauku Papuans of West New Guinea.* New York: Holt, Rinehart & Winston.

Potash, B., ed. 1986. *Widows in African Societies: Choices and Constraints.* Stanford, CA: Stanford University Press.

Potocki, E., and J. Krasinski, eds. 2009. *Primatology: Theories, Methods, and Research.* New York: Nova Science.

Prag, J., and R. Neave 1997. *Making Faces: Using Forensic and Archaeological Evidence.* College Station: Texas A&M University Press.

Price, R., ed. 1973. *Maroon Societies.* New York: Anchor Press/Doubleday.

Price, T. D., ed. 2000. *Europe's First Farmers.* New York: Cambridge University Press.

Radcliffe-Brown, A. R. 1965 (orig. 1962). *Structure and Function in Primitive Society.* New York: Free Press.

Raffaele, P. 2010. *Among the Great Apes: Adventures on the Trail of Our Closest Relatives.* New York: Smithsonian, Harper.

Rak, Y. 1986. The Neandertal: A New Look at an Old Face. *Journal of Human Evolution* 15(3):151–164.

Ramirez, R. R., and G. P. de la Cruz 2003. The Hispanic Population in the United States, U.S. Census Bureau. *Current Population Reports,* P20–545, March. http://www.census .gov/prod/2003pubs/p20-545.pdf.

Ramos, A. R. 1995. *Sanumá Memories : Yanomami Ethnography in Times of Crisis.* Madison, WI: University of Wisconsin Press.

Ranger, T. O. 1996. Postscript. In *Postcolonial Identities,* R. Werbner and T. O. Ranger, eds. London: Zed.

Rappaport, R. A. 1974. Obvious Aspects of Ritual. *Cambridge Anthropology* 2:2–60.

———. 1999. *Holiness and Humanity: Ritual in the Making of Religious Life.* New York: Cambridge University Press.

Rathje, W. L., and C. Murphy 2001. *Rubbish!: The Archaeology of Garbage.* Tucson: University of Arizona Press.

Rathus, S. A., J. S. Nevid, and J. Fichner-Rathus 2008. *Human Sexuality in a World of Diversity,* 7th ed. Boston: Pearson/Allyn & Bacon.

Redfield, R. 1941. *The Folk Culture of Yucatan.* Chicago: University of Chicago Press.

Redfield, R., R. Linton, and M. Herskovits 1936. Memorandum on the Study of Acculturation. *American Anthropologist* 38:149–152.

Reese, W. L. 1999. *Dictionary of Philosophy and Religion: Eastern and Western Thought.* Amherst, NY: Humanities Books.

Revkin, A. C. 2007. Dozens of Species of Primates Are Under Threat, Study Finds. *New York Times,* October 27. http://www.nytimes. com/2007/10/27/science/27primate.html?sq= endangeresd%20primates&st=cse&scp= 7&pagewanted=print.

Rice, P. 2002. Paleoanthropology 2001— Part II. *General Anthropology* 8(2): 11–14.

Rickford, J. R. 1997. Suite for Ebony and Phonics, *Discover,* December. http://www. stanford.edu/~rickford/papers/SuiteForEbony AndPhonics.html.

———. 1999. *African American Vernacular English: Features, Evolution, Educational Implications.* Malden, MA: Blackwell.

Rickford, J. R., and R. J. Rickford 2000. *Spoken Soul: The Story of Black English.* New York: Wiley.

Roach, J. 2007. "Hobbit" Human Was Unique Species, Wrist Bones Suggest. *National Geographic News,* September 20. http://news. nationalgeographic.com/news/pf/65255655.html.

Robbins, R. H. 2008. *Global Problems and the Culture of Capitalism,* 4th ed. Boston: Pearson/Allyn & Bacon.

Roberts, S., A. Sabar, B. Goodman, and M. Balleza 2007. 51% of Women Are Now Living without Spouse. *New York Times,* January 16. http:www.nytimes.com.

Robertson, A. F. 1995. *The Big Catch: A Practical Introduction to Development.* Boulder, CO: Westview Press.

Rodseth, L., R. W. Wrangham, A. M. Harrigan, and B. Smuts 1991. The Human Community as a Primate Society. *Current Anthropology* 32:221–254.

Romaine, S. 1999. *Communicating Gender.* Mahwah, NJ: Erlbaum.

———. 2000. *Language in Society: An Introduction to Sociolinguistics,* 2nd ed. New York: Oxford University Press.

Root, D. 1996. *Cannibal Culture: Art, Appropriation, and the Commodification of Difference.* Boulder, CO: Westview Press.

Rosaldo, M. Z. 1980a. *Knowledge and Passion: Notions of Self and Social Life.* Stanford, CA: Stanford University Press.

———. 1980b. The Use and Abuse of Anthropology: Reflections on Feminism and Cross-Cultural Understanding. *Signs* 5(3):389–417.

Roscoe, W. 1991. *Zuni Man-Woman.* Albuquerque: University of New Mexico Press.

———. 1998. *Changing Ones: Third and Fourth Genders in Native North America.* New York: St. Martin's Press.

Rose, M. 1997. Neandertal DNA. Newsbriefs. *Archaeology* 50 (September/October): 5. http://www.archaeology.org/9709/newsbriefs/dna.html.

Roth, N. L., and L. K. Fuller 1998. *Women and AIDS: Negotiating Safer Practices, Care, and Representation.* Binghampton, NY: Harrington Park Press.

Rothstein, E. 2006. Protection for Indian Patrimony That Leads to a Paradox. *New York Times,* March 29.

Rouse, R. 1991. Mexican Migration and the Social Space of Postmodernism. *Diaspora* 1(1):8–23.

Royal Anthropological Institute 1951. *Notes and Queries on Anthropology,* 6th ed. London: Routledge and Kegan Paul.

Ryan, S. 1990. *Ethnic Conflict and International Relations.* Brookfield, MA: Dartmouth.

Rylko-Bauer, B., M. Singer, and J. Van Willigen 2006. Reclaiming Applied Anthropology: Its Past, Present, and Future. *American Anthropologist* 108(1):178–190.

Sabloff, J. A. 2008. *Archaeology Matters: Action Archaeology in the Modern World.* Walnut Creek, CA: Left Coast Press.

Sahlins, M. D. 1968. *Tribesmen.* Englewood Cliffs, NJ: Prentice Hall.

———. 2004. *Stone Age Economics.* New York: Routledge.

Salzman, P. C. 1974. Political Organization among Nomadic Peoples. In *Man in Adaptation: The Cultural Present,* 2nd ed., Y. A. Cohen, ed., pp. 267–284. Chicago: Aldine.

———. 2004. *Pastoralists: Equality, Hierarchy, and the State.* Boulder, CO: Westview.

———. 2008. *Culture and Conflict in the Middle East.* Amherst, NY: Humanity Books.

Salzmann, Z. 2007. *Language, Culture, and Society: An Introduction to Linguistic Anthropology,* 4th ed. Boulder, CO: Westview.

Sanday, P. R. 1974. Female Status in the Public Domain. In *Woman, Culture, and Society,* M. Z. Rosaldo and L. Lamphere, eds., pp. 189–206. Stanford, CA: Stanford University Press.

———. 2002. *Women at the Center: Life in a Modern Matriarchy.* Ithaca, NY: Cornell University Press.

Santley, R. S. 1985. The Political Economy of the Aztec Empire. *Journal of Anthropological Research* 41(3): 327–337.

Sapir, E. 1931. Conceptual Categories in Primitive Languages. *Science* 74:578–584.

———. 1956 (orig 1928). The Meaning of Religion. In *Culture, Language and Personality: Selected Essays,* E. Sapir. Berkeley: University of California Press.

Schaik, C. V. 2004. *Among Orangutans: Red Apes and the Rise of Human Culture.* Tucson: University of Arizona Press.

Schaller, G. 1963. *The Mountain Gorilla: Ecology and Behavior.* Chicago: University of Chicago Press.

Scheidel, W. 1997. Brother-Sister Marriage in Roman Egypt. *Journal of Biosocial Science* 29(3):361–371.

Scheinman, M. 1980. Imperialism. *Academic American Encyclopedia.* Princeton, NJ: Arete, volume 11, pp. 61–62.

Schneider, D. M. 1967. Kinship and Culture: Descent and Filiation as Cultural Constructs. *Southwestern Journal of Anthropology* 23:65–73.

Scholte, J. A. 2000. *Globalization: A Critical Introduction.* New York: St. Martin's Press.

Scott, J. C. 1985. *Weapons of the Weak.* New Haven, CT: Yale University Press.

———. 1990. *Domination and the Arts of Resistance*. New Haven, CT: Yale University Press.

Scudder, T., and E. Colson 1980. *Secondary Education and the Formation of an Elite: The Impact of Education on Gwembe District, Zambia*. London: Academic Press.

Scupin, R. 2003. *Race and Ethnicity: An Anthropological Focus on the United States and the World*. Upper Saddle River, NJ: Prentice Hall.

Sebeok, T. A., and J. Umiker-Sebeok, eds. 1980. *Speaking of Apes: A Critical Anthropology of Two-Way Communication with Man*. New York: Plenum.

Senut, B., M. Pickford, D. Gommery, P. Mein, K. Cheboi, and Y. Coppens 2001. First Hominid from the Miocene (Lukeino Formation, Kenya). Comptes Rendus de l' Academie des Sciences, Series IIA - Earth and Planetary Science 332. 2 (January 30):137–144.

Service, E. R. 1962. *Primitive Social Organization: An Evolutionary Perspective*. New York: McGraw-Hill.

———. 1966. *The Hunters*. Englewood Cliffs, NJ: Prentice Hall.

Shaffer, M. S., ed. 2008. *Public Culture: Diversity, Democracy, and Community in the United States*. Philadelphia: University of Pennsylvania Press.

Shanklin, E. 1995. *Anthropology and Race*. Belmont, CA: Wadsworth.

Shannon, T. R. 1996. *An Introduction to the World-System Perspective,* 2nd ed. Boulder, CO: Westview Press.

Sharma, A., and A. Gupta, eds. 2006. *The Anthropology of the State: A Reader*. Malden, MA: Blackwell.

Shermer, M. 2002. *In Darwin's Shadow: The Life and Science of Alfred Russel Wallace*. New York: Oxford University Press.

Sherwood, R. J., Ward, S. C, and A. Hill 2002. The Taxonomic Status of the Chemeron Temporal (KNM-BC1). *Science Direct,* February 27. http://www.sciencedirect.com.

Shivaram, C. 1996. Where Women Wore the Crown: Kerala's Dissolving Matriarchies Leave a Rich Legacy of Compassionate Family Culture. *Hinduism Today.* http://www.spirit-web.org/HinduismToday/96_02_Women_Wore_Crown.html.

Shreeve, J. 1992. The Dating Game: How Old Is the Human Race? *Discover* 13(9):76–83.

Shryock, Andrew 1988. Autonomy, Entanglement, and the Feud: Prestige Structures and Gender Values in Highland Albania. *Anthropological Quarterly* 61(3):113–118.

Silberbauer, G. 1981. *Hunter and Habitat in the Central Kalahari Desert*. New York: Cambridge University Press.

Sillitoe, P., ed. 2007. *Local Science versus Global Science: Approaches to Indigenous Knowledge in International Development*. New York: Berghahn Books.

Simons, E. L., and P. C. Ettel 1970. Gigantopithecus. *Scientific American,* January, pp. 77–85.

Singer, M. 2008. *Drugging the Poor: Legal and Illegal Drugs and Social Inequality.* Long Grove, IL: Waveland.

Singer, M., and H. Baer 2007. *Introducing Medical Anthropology: A Discipline in Action.* Lanham, MD: AltaMira.

Sinnott, M. J. 2004. *Toms and Dees: Transgender Identity and Female Same-Sex Relationships in Thailand*. Honolulu: University of Hawaii Press.

Slade, M. 1984. Displaying Affection in Public. *New York Times,* December 17.

Smart, A., and J. Smart 2003. Urbanization and the Global Perspective. *Annual Review of Anthropology* 32:263–285.

Smith, A. T. 2003. *The Political Landscape: Constellations of Authority in Early Complex Polities*. Westport, CT: Praeger.

Smith, B. D. 1995. *The Emergence of Agriculture*. New York: Scientific American Library, W. H. Freeman.

Smith, C. S. 2006. Some See a "Pyramid" to Hone Bosnia's Image. Others See a Big Hill. *New York Times,* May 15.

Smith, M. E. 2009. V. Gordon Childe and the Urban Revolution: a Historical Perspective on a Revolution in Urban Studies. *Town Planning Review* 80(1). http://www.public.asu.edu/

~mesmith9/1-CompleteSet/MES-09-Childe-TPR.pdf.

Smith, M. K., and M. E. Doyle 2002. Globalization. The Encyclopedia of Informal Education. http://www.infed.org/biblio/globalization.htm.

Smitherman, G. 1986 (orig. 1977). *Talkin and Testifyin: The Language of Black America.* Detroit: Wayne State University Press.

Solway, J., and R. Lee 1990. Foragers, Genuine and Spurious: Situating the Kalahari San in History (with CA treatment). *Current Anthropology* 31(2):109–146.

Sotomayor, S. 2009 (orig. 2001). A Latina Judge's Voice. Judge Mario G. Olmos Memorial Lecture, University of California, Berkeley School of Law. Reprinted by the *New York Times,* http://www.nytimes.com/2009/05/15/us/politics/15judge.text.html.

Spencer, C. S. 2003. War and Early State Formation in Oaxaca, Mexico. *Proceedings of the National Academy of Sciences of the United States of America.* 100(20):11185–11187. http://www.pnas.org/cgi/doi/10.1073/pnas.2034992100.

Spencer, C. S., and E. M. Redmond 2004. Primary State Formation in Mesoamerica. *Annual Review of Anthropology* 33:173–199.

Spencer, E. T. 2010. *Sociolinguistics.* Hauppauge, NY: Nova Science Publishers.

Spickard, P., ed. 2004. *Race and Nation: Ethnic Systems in the Modern World.* New York: Routledge.

Spindler, G. D., ed. 2000. *Fifty Years of Anthropology and Education, 1950–2000: A Spindler Anthology.* Mahwah, NJ: Erlbaum.

Spindler, G. D. 2005. *New Horizons in the Anthropology of Education.* Mahwah, NJ: Erlbaum.

Spindler, G. D., and L. Hammond, eds. 2006. *Innovations in Educational Ethnography: Theory, Methods, and Results.* Mahwah, NJ: L. Erlbaum Associates.

Spoor, F., M. G. Leakey, P. N. Gathongo, F. H. Brown, S. C. Anton, I. McDougall, C. Kiarie, F. K. Manthi, and L. N. Leakey 2007. Implications of New Early Homo Fossils from Ileret, East of Lake Turkana, Kenya. *Nature* 448 (7154): 688–691. http://news.nature.com//news/2007/070806/070806-5.html.

Srivastava, J., N. J. H. Smith, and D. A. Forno 1998. *Integrating Biodiversity in Agricultural Intensification. Toward Sound Practices.* Washington, DC: World Bank.

Stack, C. B. 1975. *All Our Kin: Strategies for Survival in a Black Community.* New York: Harper Torchbooks.

Stanford, C. B. 1999. *The Hunting Apes: Meat Eating and the Origins of Human Behavior.* Princeton, NJ: Princeton University Press.

Stanford, C. B., and H. T. Bunn, eds. 2001. *Meat-eating and Human Evolution.* New York: Oxford University Press.

Statistical Abstract of the United States 1991. 111th ed. Washington, DC: U.S. Bureau of the Census, U.S. Government Printing Office.

———. 1996. 116th ed. Washington, DC: U.S. Bureau of the Census, U.S. Government Printing Office.

———. 1999. 119th ed. Washington, DC: U.S. Bureau of the Census, U.S. Government Printing Office.

———. 2001. http://www.census.gov/prod/www/statistical-abstract-us.html.

———. 2002. http://www.census.gov/prod/www/statistical-abstract-us.html.

———. 2003. http://www.census.gov/prod/www/statistical-abstract-04.html.

———. 2004–2005. http://www.census.gov/prod/www/statistical-abstract-04.html.

———. 2007. http://www.census.gov/prod/www/statistical-abstract.html.

———. 2008. http://www.census.gov/prod/www/statistical-abstract.html.

———. 2010. http://www.census.gov/prod/www/statistical-abstract.html.

———. 2011. http://www.census.gov/prod/www/statistical-abstract.html.

Statistics Canada 2001a 1996. Census. Nation Tables. http://www.statcan.ca/english/census96/nation.htm.

———. 2003. Religions in Canada. 2001 Census—Release 8, May 13, 2003.

http://www12.statcan.ca/english/census01/release/index.cfm.

Stein, R. L., and P. L. Stein, eds. 2008. *The Anthropology of Religion, Magic, and Witchcraft.* Boston: Pearson.

Stern, A. 2000. Experts Say 138 World Primate Species Endangered. *Reuters.* http://www.forests.org/archive/general/exsay138.htm.

Stevens, W. K. 1992. Humanity Confronts Its Handiwork: An Altered Planet. *New York Times,* May 5, pp. B5–B7.

Stevenson, D. 2003. *Cities and Urban Cultures.* Philadelphia, PA: Open University Press.

Stevenson, R. F. 1968. *Population and Political Systems in Tropical Africa.* New York: Columbia University Press.

Stoler, A. 1977. Class Structure and Female Autonomy in Rural Java. *Signs* 3:74–89.

Stone, L. S. 2004. Gay Marriage and Anthropology. *Anthropology News* 45(5). http://www.aaanet.org/press/an/0405if-comm4.htm.

———. 2010. *Kinship and Gender: An Introduction,* 4th ed. Boulder, CO: Westview.

Strathern, A., and P. J. Stewart 1999. *Curing and Healing: Medical Anthropology in Global Perspective.* Durham, NC: Carolina Academic Press.

———. 2010. *Kinship in Action: Self and Group.* Boston: Prentice Hall.

Strier, K. B. 2011. *Primate Behavioral Ecology,* 4th ed. Upper Saddle River, NJ: Prentice Hall.

Sunderland, P. L., and R. M. Denny 2007. *Doing Anthropology in Consumer Research.* Walnut Creek, CA: Left Coast Press.

Susman, R. L. 1987. Pygmy Chimpanzees and Common Chimpanzees: Models for the Behavioral Ecology of the Earliest Hominids. In *The Evolution of Human Behavior: Primate Models,* W. G. Kinzey, ed., pp. 72–86. Albany: State University of New York Press.

Suttles, W. 1960. Affinal Ties, Subsistence, and Prestige among the Coast Salish. *American Anthropologist* 62:296–305.

Swift, M. 1963. Men and Women in Malay Society. In *Women in the New Asia,* B. Ward, ed., pp. 268–286. Paris: UNESCO.

Tague, R. G., and C. O. Lovejoy 1986. The Obstetric Pelvis of A. L. 288-1 (Lucy). *Journal of Human Evolution* 15:237–255.

Tanaka, J. 1980. *The San Hunter-Gatherers of the Kalahari.* Tokyo: University of Tokyo Press.

Tannen, D. 1990. *You Just Don't Understand: Women and Men in Conversation.* New York: Ballantine Books.

———. 2005. *Conversational Style: Analyzing Talk among Friends,* new ed. New York: Oxford University Press.

Tannen, D., ed. 1993. *Gender and Conversational Interaction.* New York: Oxford University Press.

Tannen, D., S. Kendall, and C. Gordon., eds. 2007. *Family Talk: Discourse and Identity in Four American Families.* New York: Oxford University Press.

Taylor, C. 1987. Anthropologist-in-Residence. In *Applied Anthropology in America,* 2nd ed., E. M. Eddy and W. L. Partridge, eds. New York: Columbia University Press.

Terrace, H. S. 1979. *Nim.* New York: Knopf.

Thomas, L. 1999. *Language, Society and Power.* New York: Routledge.

Thomas, L., and S. Wareing, eds. 2004. *Language, Society, and Power: An Introduction.* New York: Routledge.

Thompson, W. 1983. Introduction: World System with and without the Hyphen. In *Contending Approaches to World System Analysis,* W. Thompson, ed., pp. 7–26. Thousand Oaks, CA: Sage.

Tice, K. 1997. Reflections on Teaching Anthropology for Use in the Public and Private Sector. In *The Teaching of Anthropology: Problems, Issues, and Decisions,* C. P. Kottak, J. J. White, R. H. Furlow, and P. C. Rice, eds., pp. 273–284. Mountain View, CA: Mayfield.

Tishkov, V. A. 2004. *Chechnya: Life in a War-Torn Society.* Berkeley: University of California Press.

Titiev, M. 1992. *Old Oraibi: A Study of the Hopi Indians of Third Mesa.* Albuquerque: University of New Mexico Press.

Tomlinson, J. 1991. *Cultural Imperialism: A Critical Introduction.* Baltimore: Johns Hopkins University Press.

———. 1999. *Globalization and Culture.* Chicago: University of Chicago Press.

Toner, R. 1992. Los Angeles Riots Are a Warning, Americans Fear. *New York Times,* May 11, pp. A1, A11.

Tougher, S. 2008. *The Eunuch in Byzantine History and Society.* New York: Routledge.

Trask, L. 1996. FAQs about Basque and the Basques. http://www.cogs.susx.ac.uk/users/larryt/basque.faqs.html.

Trevathan, W. R., E. O. Smith, and J. McKenna, eds. 2007. *Evolutionary Medicine and Health.* New York: Oxford University Press.

Trigger, B. G. 2003. *Understanding Early Civilizations: A Comparative Study.* Cambridge: Cambridge University Press.

Trivedi, B. P. 2001. Scientists Identify a Language Gene. *National Geographic News,* October 4. http://news.nationalgeographic.com/news/2001/10/1004_Tvlanguagegene.html.

Trudgill, P. 2000. *Sociolinguistics: An Introduction to Language and Society,* 4th ed. New York: Penguin Books.

Turnbull, C. 1965. *Wayward Servants: The Two Worlds of the African Pygmies.* Garden City, NY: Natural History Press.

Turner, V. W. 1974 (orig. 1967). *The Ritual Process.* Harmondsworth, England: Penguin Press.

———. 1995 (orig. 1969). *The Ritual Process.* Hawthorne, NY: Aldine de Gruyter.

Tylor, E. B. 1958 (orig. 1871). *Primitive Culture.* New York: Harper Torchbooks.

U.S. Census Bureau 2010. http://quickfacts.census.gov/qfd/index.html.

Ulijaszek, S. J., and H. Lofink 2006. Obesity in Biocultural Perspective. *Annual Review of Anthropology* 35:337–360.

Van Allen, J. 1971. *"Aba Riots" or "Women's War"?: British Ideology and Eastern Nigerian Women's Political Activism.* Waltham, MA: African Studies Association.

Van Cantfort, T. E., and J. B. Rimpau 1982. Sign Language Studies with Children and Chimpanzees. *Sign Language Studies* 34: 15–72.

Van der Elst, D., and P. Bohannan 2003. *Culture as Given, Culture as Choice,* 2nd ed. Prospect Heights, IL: Waveland.

Vayda, A. P. 1968 (orig. 1961). Economic Systems in Ecological Perspective: The Case of the Northwest Coast. In *Readings in Anthropology,* 2nd ed., volume 2, M. H. Fried, ed., pp. 172–178. New York: Crowell.

Veblen, T. 1934. *The Theory of the Leisure Class: An Economic Study of Institutions.* New York: The Modern Library.

Verdery, K. 2001. Socialist Societies: Anthropological Aspects. *International Encyclopedia of the Social & Behavioral Sciences,* pp. 14496–14500. New York: Elsevier.

Vekua, A., D. Lordkipanidze, and G. P. Rightmire. 2002. A Skull of Early Homo from Dmanisi, Georgia, *Science,* July 5, pp. 85–89.

Vidal, J. 2003. Every Third Person Will Be a Slum Dweller within 30 Years, UN Agency Warns: Biggest Study of World's Cities Finds 940 Million Already Living in Squalor. *The Guardian,* October 4, 2003. http://www.guardian.co.uk/international/story/0,3604,1055785,00.html.

Viegas, J. 2000. Planet of the Dying Apes: Conference Reveals Steep Decline in Primate Populations. http://abcnews.go.com/sections/science/DailyNews/apeconference000512.html.

Vigil, J. D. 2003. Urban Violence and Street Gangs. *Annual Review of Anthropology* 32:225–242.

———. 2010. *Gang Redux: A Balanced Anti-Gang Strategy.* Long Grove, IL: Waveland.

Viola, H. J., and C. Margolis 1991. *Seeds of Change: Five Hundred Years since Columbus, a Quincentennial Commemoration.* Washington, DC: Smithsonian Institution Press.

Von Daniken, E. 1971. *Chariots of the Gods: Unsolved Mysteries of the Past.* New York: Bantam.

Wade, N. 2004. New Species Revealed: Tiny Cousins of Humans. *New York Times,* October 28, national edition, pp. A1, A6.

———. 2005. For Gay Men, Different Scent of Attraction. *New York Times,* May 10, late ed.—final, p. A1.

———. 2007. Fossil DNA Expands Neanderthal Range. *New York Times,* October 2. www.nytimes.com.

Wade, P. 2002. *Race, Nature, and Culture: An Anthropological Perspective.* Sterling, VA: Pluto Press.

Wagley, C. W. 1968 (orig. 1959). The Concept of Social Race in the Americas. In *The Latin American Tradition,* by C. Wagley, pp. 155–174. New York: Columbia University Press.

Wallace, A. F. C. 1956. Revitalization Movements. *American Anthropologist* 58:264–281.

———. 1966. *Religion: An Anthropological View.* New York: McGraw-Hill.

———. 1969. *The Death and Rebirth of the Seneca.* New York: Knopf.

Wallerstein, I. M. 1982. The Rise and Future Demise of the World Capitalist System: Concepts for Comparative Analysis. In *Introduction to the Sociology of "Developing Societies,"* H. Alavi and T. Shanin, eds., pp. 29–53. New York: Monthly Review Press.

———. 2004a. *The Decline of American Power: The U.S. in a Chaotic World.* New York: New Press.

———. 2004b. *World-Systems Analysis: An Introduction.* Durham, NC: Duke University Press.

Ward, M. C. 2003. *A World Full of Women,* 3rd ed. Needham Heights, MA: Allyn & Bacon.

Ward, M. C., and M. Edelstein 2009. *A World Full of Women,* 5th ed. Needham Heights, MA: Allyn & Bacon.

Warms, R., Garber, J., and R. J. McGee, eds. 2009. *Sacred Realms: Readings in the Anthropology of Religion,* 2nd ed. New York: Oxford University Press.

Waters, M. R., and T. W. Stafford, Jr. 2007. Redefining the Age of Clovis: Implications for the Peopling of the Americas. *Science,* (February 23) 315:1122–1126.

Watson, P. J. 1983. The Halafian Culture: A Review and Synthesis. In *The Hilly Flanks and Beyond: Essays on the Prehistory of Southwestern Asia,* T. C. Young, Jr., P. E. L. Smith, and P. Mortensen, eds. Studies in

Ancient Oriental Civilization 36:231–250. Oriental Institute, University of Chicago.

Watzman, H. 2006. The Echoes of Ancient Humans. *Chronicle of Higher Education,* January 27. http://chronicle.com/weekly/v52/i21/21a01601.htm.

Weber, M. 1958 (orig. 1904). *The Protestant Ethic and the Spirit of Capitalism.* New York: Scribner.

———. 1968 (orig. 1922). *Economy and Society.* E. Fischoff et al. (trans.). New York: Bedminster Press.

Webster's New World Encyclopedia 1993. College Edition. Englewood Cliffs, NJ: Prentice Hall.

Wedel, J. 2002. Blurring the Boundaries of the State-Private Divide: Implications for Corruption. Paper presented at the European Association of Social Anthropologists (EASA) Conference in Copenhagen, August 14–17, 2002. http://www.anthrobase.com/Txt/W/Wedel_J_01.htm.

Weiner, J. 1994. *The Beak of the Finch: A Story of Evolution in Our Time.* New York: Alfred A. Knopf.

Weise, E. 1999. Anthropologists Adapt Technology to World's Cultures. *USA Today,* May 26. http://www.usatoday.com/life/cyber/tech/ctf256.htm.

Weiss, H. 2005. *Collapse.* New York: Routledge.

Weiss, R. 2005. More Evidence of Skull's Link to Humans: Remains Believed to Be from Earliest Known Ancestor. *Washington Post,* April 7, p. A03.

Wendorf, F., and R. Schild 2000. Late Neolithic Megalithic Structures at Nabta Playa (Sahara), Southwestern Egypt. http://www.comp-archaeology.org/WendorfSAA98.html.

Wenke, R. J., and D. I. Olszewski 2007. *Patterns in Prehistory: Mankind's First Three Million Years,* 5th ed. New York: Oxford University Press.

Weston, K. 1991. *Families We Choose: Lesbians, Gays, Kinship.* New York: Columbia University Press.

White, L. A. 1959. *The Evolution of Culture: The Development of Civilization to the Fall of Rome*. New York: McGraw-Hill.

Whorf, B. L. 1956. A Linguistic Consideration of Thinking in Primitive Communities. In *Language, Thought, and Reality: Selected Writings of Benjamin Lee Whorf,* J. B. Carroll, ed., pp. 65–86. Cambridge, MA: MIT Press.

Whyte, M. F. 1978. Cross-Cultural Codes Dealing with the Relative Status of Women. *Ethnology* XII(2): 203–225.

Wilford, J. N. 1995. The Transforming Leap, from 4 Legs to 2. *New York Times,* September 5, pp. B5(N), C1(L).

———. 2000. Ruins Alter Ideas of How Civilization Spread. May 23, http://www.nytimes.com.

———. 2002. When Humans Became Human. *New York Times,* February 26, late edition—final, sec. F, p. 1, col. 1. http://www.nytimes.com.

———. 2003. Big Teeth in Ancient Jaw Offer Clues About Our Ancestors. *New York Times,* September 30, 2003, late edition—final, sec. F, p. 4, col. 2.

———. 2005. For Neandertals and *Homo Sapiens,* Was It De- Lovely? *New York Times,* February 15. http://www.nytimes.com/2005/02/15/science/15nean.html?ex=1147492800&en=7d5fadb91364f1d5&ei=5070.

———. 2006. Improved Science Puts Modern Humans in Europe Earlier. *New York Times,* February 23.

———. 2007a. Fossils in Kenya Challenge Linear Evolution, *New York Times,* August 9, p. A6.

———. 2007b. Fossils Reveal Clues on Human Ancestors. *New York Times,* September 20. www.nytimes.com.

———. 2009a. Feet Offer Clue about Tiny Hominid. *New York Times,* May 9. http://www.nytimes.com/2009/05/07/science/ 07hobbit.html?_r=1&scp=1&sq=feet%20offer%20clues%20about%20tiny%20hominid&st=cse.

———. 2009b. Fossil Skeleton from Africa Predates Lucy. *New York Times,* October 2, pp. Al, A6.

Wilk, R. R. 1996. *Economies and Cultures: An Introduction to Economic Anthropology.* Boulder, CO: Westview Press.

Wilk, R. R., and L. Cliggett 2007. *Economies and Cultures: Foundations of Economic Anthropology,* 2nd ed. Boulder, CO: Westview.

Williams, L. M., and D. Finkelhor 1995. Paternal Caregiving and Incest: Test of a Biosocial Model. *American Journal of Orthopsychiatry* 65(1):101–113.

Willie, C. V. 2003. *A New Look at Black Families.* Walnut Creek, CA: AltaMira.

Wilmsen, E. N. 1989. *Land Filled with Flies: A Political Economy of the Kalahari.* Chicago: University of Chicago Press.

Wilson, D. S. 2002. *Darwin's Cathedral: Evolution, Religion, and the Nature of Society.* Chicago: University of Chicago Press.

Wilson, M. L., and R. W. Wrangham 2003. Intergroup Relations in Chimpanzees. *Annual Review of Anthropology* 32:363–392.

Wilson, R., ed. 1996. *Human Rights: Culture and Context: Anthropological Perspectives.* Chicago: Pluto Press.

Winter, R. 2001. Religions of the World: Number of Adherents; Names of Houses of Worship; Names of Leaders; Rates of Growth. http://www.religioustolerance.org/worldrel.htm.

Winzeler, R. L. 2007. *Anthropology and Religion.* Lanham, MD: AltaMira.

Witt, J. 2011 *Soc,* 2nd ed. Boston: McGraw-Hill.

Wittfogel, K. A. 1957. *Oriental Despotism: A Comparative Study of Total Power.* New Haven, CT: Yale University Press.

Wolcott, H. F. 2008. *Ethnography: A Way of Seeing,* 2nd ed. Lanham, MD: AltaMira.

Wolf, E. R. 1966. *Peasants.* Englewood Cliffs, NJ: Prentice Hall.

———. 1982. *Europe and the People without History.* Berkeley: University of California Press.

Wolf, E. R., with S. Silverman 2001. *Pathways of Power: Building an Anthropology of the Modern World.* Berkeley: University of California Press.

Wolpoff, M. H. 1980a. *Paleoanthropology.* New York: McGraw-Hill.

———. 1980b. Cranial Remains of Middle Pleistocene Hominids. *Journal of Human Evolution* 9:339–358.

———. 1999. *Paleoanthropology,* 2nd ed. New York: McGraw-Hill.

Wolpoff, M., B. Senut, M. Pickford, and J. Hawks 2002. Sahelanthropus or "Sahelpithecus"? *Nature* 419: 581–582.

World Malaria Report 2005. Roll Back Malaria. World Health Organization, UNICEF. http://rbm.who.int/wmr2005/pdf/WMReport_lr.pdf.

Worsley, P. 1985 (orig. 1959). Cargo Cults. In *Readings in Anthropology* 85/86. Guilford, CT: Dushkin.

Wrangham, R., W. McGrew, F. de Waal, and P. Heltne, eds. 1994. *Chimpanzee Cultures.* Cambridge, MA: Harvard University Press.

Wright, H. T. 1977. Recent Research on the Origin of the State. *Annual Review of Anthropology* 6:379–397.

———. 1994. Prestate Political Formations. In *Chiefdoms and Early States in the Near East: The Organizational Dynamics of Complexity,* G. Stein and M. S. Rothman, eds., *Monographs in World Archaeology* 18:67–84. Madison, WI: Prehistory Press.

Wright, H. T., and G. A. Johnson 1975. Population, Exchange, and Early State Formation in Southwestern Iran. *American Anthropologist* 77:267–289.

Yellen, J. E., A. S. Brooks, and E. Cornelissen 1995. A Middle Stone Age Worked Bone Industry from Katanda, Upper Semliki Valley, Zaire. *Science* 268:553–556.

York, A. 2009. Alaskan Village Stands on Leading Edge of Climate Change. Mother Nature Network, August 19. http://news21.jomc.unc.edu/index.php/stories/alaska.html.

Young, A. 2000. *Women Who Become Men: Albanian Sworn Virgins.* New York: Berg.

Yurchak, A. 2002. Entrepreneurial Governmentality in Postsocialist Russia. In *The New Entrepreneurs of Europe and Asia,* V. Bonnell and T. Gold, eds., p. 301. Armonk, NY: M. E. Sharpe.

———. 2005. *Everything Was Forever until It Was No More: The Last Soviet Generation.* Princeton, NJ: Princeton University Press.

Zimmer, C. 2010. Siberian Fossils Were Neandertals' Eastern Cousins, DNA Reveals. *New York Times,* December 22.

Zimmer-Tamakoshi, L. 1997. The Last Big Man: Development and Men's Discontents in the Papua New Guinea Highlands. *Oceania* 68(2):107–122.

Zou, Y., and E. T. Trueba 2002. *Ethnography and Schools: Qualitative Approaches to the Study of Education.* Lanham, MD: Rowman & Littlefield.

Zulaika, J. 1988. *Basque Violence: Metaphor and Sacrament.* Reno: University of Nevada Press.

Index

A

A. afarensis, 121–123
A. africanus, 134–136
A. anamensis, 129
A. boisei, 137, 141
A. garhi, 140, 141
A. robustus, 128, 133–136
A. sediba, 137, 139–140
AAA, 12
AAA code of ethics, 60–61
Aba Women's Riots of 1929, 291
Absolute dating, 46–47, 48
Abu Hureyra, 179
Academic anthropology, 417–418
Accelerator mass spectrometry, 193
Acculturation, 34, 448
Aché, 248
Acheulian, 148–149
Achieved status, 279
Adaptation, 3
Affinal, 314
African cattle complex, 183
Age grades, 281
Age set, 281
Agency, 29
Agricultural intensification, 254–255
Agriculture, 253–255. *See also* First farmers
AIDS, 428
Alexander the Great, 378
Ali Kosh, 178
Allele, 73
Alternative ends, 261–262
Alternative religious movements, 365
Amazon.com, 386
American Anthropological Association (AAA), 12
American Hispanics/Latinos, 394, 395
American Revolution, 378
American Sign Language (ASL), 223, 224
AMHs, 154, 158–162
Analogies, 99
Anatomically modern humans (AMHs), 154, 158–162

Anderson, Barbara, 428
Anderson, Benedict, 405
Anencephaly, 87
Animalia, 97
Animism, 350
Antankarana, 445
Anthropoid, 100
Anthropological archaeology, 41
Anthropology
    applied, 12, 15
    applying. *See* Applying anthropology
    archaeological, 7–10
    biological, 10–11
    cultural, 7
    current events. *See* Anthropology today boxes
    defined, 2
    development, 418–419
    dimensions, 12
    ecological, 266
    economic, 256–257, 261, 270
    environmental, 444–448
    ethics, 59–65
    forensic, 49
    general, 4–6
    kinds of, 45
    linguistic, 11
    medical, 427–431
    molecular, 47–48
    other academic fields, and, 11–12
    physical, 48–50
    popular culture. *See* Popular culture boxes
    public, 15
    science, as, 11–12
    sociology, contrasted, 50
    subdisciplines, 7–11
    urban, 424–427
    what they do. *See* Doing anthropology
Anthropology and business, 431–432
Anthropology and education, 423–424
Anthropology today boxes
    Betsileo, 267–269
    climate change refugees, 457–459

culturally appropriate marketing, 457–459
discovery of *A. sediba,* 139–140
displays of affection, 37
Italian Americans (guido), 413–414
linguistic diversity/Internet, 243–244
masculinity, 344–345
mining company/ sustainability institute, 388–390
Neandertal cannibalism, 170–171
New Orleans (post-Hurricane Katrina), 62–64
new world domestication, 192–193
Obama, Barack, 13–15
orangutans, 116–117
personal space, 36
polygamy (Turkey), 320–321
pseudo-archeology, 217–219
syphilis, 91–92
Yanomami, 292–294
yoga, 366–367
Anthropometry, 49
Apes, 105
    bonobos, 109
    chimps. *See* Chimpanzees
    gibbons, 106
    gorillas, 107–108
    human-like traits, 98
    language, 222–226
    Miocene era, 114
    orangutans, 106–107, 116–117
Apical ancestor, 306
Appadurai, Arjun, 452
Apple, 432
Applied anthropology, 12, 15, 416
Applied cultural anthropologists, 15
Applying anthropology, 416–437
    academia, 417–418
    anthropology and business, 431–432
    anthropology and education, 423–424

Applying anthropology, *(Cont.)*
  careers and anthropology,
    432–436
  development anthropology,
    418–419
  equity, 419
  ethnographic method, 416
  indigenous models, 422–423
  medical anthropology, 427–431
  overinnovation, 420–421
  role of applied anthropologist,
    417–418
  strategies for innovation,
    419–423
  underdifferentiation, 421–422
  urban anthropology, 424–427
  war zones/military
    intelligence, 417
Arago, 156
Arboreal monkeys, 104
Arboreal theory, 112
Archaeological anthropology,
  7–10
Archaeology, 416
Archaic *H. sapiens,* 152–153,
  154, 155–156, 158
Archaic (nonindustrial) states, 283
Ardi, 126, 127
Ardipithecus, 120, 121, 126–128
Ardipithecus kadabba, 126, 127
Ardipithecus ramidus, 126, 127
Arembepe, Brazil, 53, 54, 57,
  308, 449–450
Armelagos, George J., 91, 92
Arslan, Aga Mehmet, 320, 321
Arsuaga, Juan Luis, 155
Ascribed status, 278
Asexuality, 342
Asfaw, Berhane, 126, 127, 159
Ashanti, 311
ASL, 223, 224
Assimilation, 406
Association, 71, 280
Australopithecus afarensis,
  121–123
Australopithecus africanus,
  134–136
Australopithecus anamensis, 129
Australopithecus garhi, 140, 141
Australopithecus robustus, 128,
  133–136
Australopithecus sediba, 137,
  139–140
Autochthony, 456

Avatar, 387
Awls, 165
Azande, 343
Aztec period, 210, 215
Aztecs, 360

B

Baba, Marietta, 432
Balanced polymorphism, 77
Balanced reciprocity, 264
Band, 250, 273, 274–282. *See
  also* Political systems
Bar-Yosef, Ofer, 161
Barley, 180
Barlow, Kathleen, 311
Barry, Nancy, 14
Barth, Fredrik, 393, 406–407
Basarwa San Bushmen, 250, 274
Baseball, 352
Basseri, 282
Behavioral modernity, 162–164
Belize Valley Archaeological
  Reconnaissance Project, 44
Bellah, Robert, 360
Benedict, Ruth, 290
Berdache, 314, 341
Berger, Lee R., 139
Berger, Matthew, 139
Beringia, 167
Betsileo, 257, 267–269, 297–298,
  307, 319, 321, 358, 367
BEV, 239–240
BHP Billiton, 388–390
Biarchaeologists, 42
Big man, 278–280
Bilharzia, 428
Binford, Lewis, 178
Bingham, Hiram, 60
Biochemical genetics, 72
Biological anthropology, 5, 10–11
Biomedicine, 428–429
Bipedalism, 120–121
Bisexuality, 342
Black Death, 90
Black English Vernacular (BEV),
  239–240
Blades, 165
Boas, Franz, 7, 83
Bodley, John, 377, 382, 387,
  439, 448
Body mass, 49
Body mass index, 49

Body movements, 226–227
Body ornamentation, 163
Bolivia, 455
Bolshevik Revolution, 384
Bone biology, 48–49
Bones (TV program), 49, 50
Bonobos, 109
Border Cave, 160
Born-again Christians, 361–362
Botto, Carlos, 293
Bourdieu, Pierre, 239, 289
Bourgeoisie, 375
Bourque, Susan, 325
Boyle, Susan, 449
Brachiation, 105
Braidwood, Robert J., 178
Brain complexity, 102
Brain size, 23
Braudel, Fernand, 371
Brazil, 402–404, 449–450, 451
Brideprice, 315
Bridewealth, 315, 316
British colonialism, 378–380
British Empire, 378, 379
British law, 30
Broad happen-spectrum
  revolution, 174
Broad-spectrum revolution, 167
Bronze Age, 206
Brooks, Alison, 163
Broom, Robert, 134
Brown, Michael F., 60
Brunet, Michel, 125
Bryant, Vaughn, 42, 189
Bubonic plague, 90
Buganda, 321
Bumba Meu Boi festival, 449
Burakumin, 400–402
Burawoy, Michael, 441
Burins, 165
Bush, George H. W., 239

C

^{14}C dating, 46–47
Caesar, Julius, 378
Cahal Pech Maya (Belize), 44
Call systems, 222–223, 225
Campesinos, 455
Canada, 398–400
Candomblé, 365
Cann, Rebecca, 83, 161
Capital, 371

Capitalist world economy, 370
Capitalist world system, 376
Carbon-14 (^{14}C) dating, 46–47
Careers and anthropology, 432–436
Cargo cults, 363–365
Carnaval, 290, 449
Carneiro, Robert, 196, 197, 204, 283
Carnivora, 98
Carpine domestication, 176
Carter, Jimmy, 239
Caste, 312
Castells, Manuel, 439
Catal Hüyük, 201, 202
Catarrhines, 102, 113
Catastrophism, 68, 69
Cenozoic era, 111
Census, 398, 399
Ceremonial fund, 261
Chagnon, Napoleon, 277
Chakravartti, M. R., 90
Chambers, Erve, 12
Chaplin, George, 87, 88
Chavez, Hugo, 292
Cheganca, 449
Chemeron temporal, 136
Cherokee, 263
Chiefdom, 204, 205, 273, 283–286
Chiefly redistribution, 284
Childe, V. Gordon, 175, 198
Childhood dependency, 122
Chimpanzees, 108–109
    endangered species, as, 109
    human characteristics, 24
    humans, contrasted, 26
    hunting parties, 25
    overview, 26
Chlorofluorocarbons, 23
Cholera, 90
Chomsky, Noam, 231
Chopper, 137, 138
Chopra, Deepak, 366, 367
Christianity, 360–362
Chromosome, 72, 73
Chronology, 111
Ciochon, Russell, 115
CIS, 411
Cities. *See* First cities and states
Civic culture, 30
Civilization and Capitalism, 15th–18th Century (Braudel), 371

Clan, 307
Clark, Wesley, 280
Class consciousness, 375
Cleavers, 148
Climate change, 442–444
Climate change refugees, 457–459
Cline, 80
Clinton, Bill, 239, 280, 309
Clitoridectomy, 32
Cloning, 20
Cloth mills, 373
Clovis spear point, 168
Clovis tradition, 167, 168
Coca-Cola, 421, 441
Code of ethics, 60–61
Codes of morality and ethics, 359
Codominant, 74
Cohen, Yehudi, 246, 251
Collateral household, 302
Colonial archaeologists, 45
Colonialism, 377–382
Colson, Elizabeth, 57
Columbia-Cornell-Harvard-Illinois summer field studies program, 57
Columbus, Christopher, 372, 373
Columbus hypothesis, 91
Commonwealth of Independent States (CIS), 411
Communication. *See* Language and communication
Communism, 384
Communitas, 349, 356
Complex chiefdom, 283
Conservation schemes, 445
Contagious magic, 352
Continental glaciation, 153–155, 166–167
Continental shelf, 166
Continental slope, 166
Convergent evolution, 99
Copán, 215–216
Copper, 206
Core, 137, 138, 371
Core values, 21
Correlations, 250
Cosby Show, 304
Cowell, Simon, 30
Creationism, 68
Creole languages, 231
Crimes, 287
CRM, 15, 44, 418

Cro-Magnon, 158
Cuban Americans, 395
Cultural and archaeological anthropologists, 5
Cultural and biological adaptation, 3
Cultural anthropology, 4, 7, 41
Cultural colonialism, 411
Cultural consultant, 55
Cultural ecology, 266, 444
Cultural forces, 5
Cultural generality, 27
Cultural imperialism, 448–450
Cultural learning, 18
Cultural particularity, 27
Cultural relativism, 31
Cultural resource management (CRM), 15, 44, 418
Cultural rights, 31–32
Cultural rules, 29
Cultural transmission, 224
Culturally appropriate marketing, 457–459
Culture, 17–39
    adaptive, 21
    agency, 29
    all-encompassing, 20
    civic, 30
    cultural relativism, 31
    cultural rights, 31–32
    ethnocentrism, 31
    evolution, and, 23–26
    generality, 27
    globalization, 34–38
    human rights, 31
    ideal *vs.* real, 29
    instrumental, 21
    integrated, 20–21
    international, 30
    learned, 18
    levels of, 30–31
    maladaptive, 23
    mechanisms of cultural change, 34
    national, 30
    nature, and, 20
    particularity, 27–28
    popular, 30
    practice theory, 29
    public, 30
    shared, 19–20
    symbolic, 18–19
    universality, 27
Cuneiform, 206, 207

Curer, 429
Current events. *See* Anthropology today boxes

D

Dart, Raymond, 134
Darwin, Charles, 10
Darwin, Erasmus, 69
Dating the past, 45–48
Daughter languages, 240
Dawdy, Shannon Lee, 62–64
De facto discrimination, 410
De jure discrimination, 410
DeCarlo, John, 413, 414
Deforestation, 110, 215, 446–448
Demonstrated descent, 307
Denisovans, 162
DePalma, Donald A., 244
Depth perception, 23
Descartes, Lara, 304
Descent, 398
Descent groups, 299, 305, 306–307
Descriptive linguistics, 228
Desmond, Debbie, 366
Development anthropology, 416, 418–419
Dewey, Alice G., 14
Dexterity, 23
Diamond, Jared, 191
Diana, Princess, 200
Diaspora, 451, 453
Diffusion, 34
Diglossia, 235
Dillehay, Tom D., 192, 193
Direct rule, 380
Directional selection, 76
Disaster mortuary operational response team (Dmort), 63
Discrimination, 410
Disease, 88–92, 427–431
Disease-theory systems, 428
Disotell, Todd, 170
Displacement, 225
Displays of affection, 37
Disraeli, Benjamin, 380
Diversity on TV, 409
Divorce, 303, 304, 317–318
Djimdoumalbaye, Ahounta, 125
Dmanisi finds, 150–151
Dmort, 63
DNA testing, 313

dnaancestryproject.com, 84
Dobe Ju/'honsi San, 275
Doing anthropology, 40–66
    dating the past, 45–48
    ethics, 59–65
    ethnography. *See* Ethnography
    excavation, 44–45
    physical anthropology, 48–50
    research methods, 41–43, 51–52, 58–59
    survey research, 58–59
    systematic survey, 43
Domestic-public dichotomy, 331
Domesticated animals, 253
Domestication, 180–181, 190
Dominance, 73
Dowry, 315
Doyle, Michele, 439
Dry farming, 176
Dubois, Eugene, 151–152
Dunham, Ann, 13–15
Dunn, Janet, 58
Durable alliances, 316–317
Durkheim, Emile, 50, 348, 349, 357, 368

E

Early Cenozoic primates, 113
Early Hominins, 120–142
    Ardipithecus, 120, 121, 126–128
    australopithecines. *See*
        Australopithecines
    bipedalism, 120–121
    brain, skull, 122
    chronology of evolution, 123
    Oldowan tools, 137–141
    Orrorin tugenensis, 126
    overview, 124, 130
    Sahelanthropus tchadensis, 124–126
    teeth, 122–123
    tools, 122, 137–141
Early primates, 112–114
Ecological anthropology, 266, 444–445
Ecological niche, 407
Ecology, 9
Economic anthropology, 256–257, 261, 270
Economic development plans, 382

Economic liberalism, 383
Economic systems, 256–260
Economizing, 261–262
Economy, 256
Ecosystem, 9
Egalitarian society, 203
El Sidrón, 170
Elam, 200
Electron spin resonance (ESR), 47
Emic approach, 55
Emotionalistic disease theories, 429
Emshwiller, Eve, 192
Enculturation, 2
Endangered primates, 110
Endogamy, 312
Enduring Voices Project, 242
Energy consumption and industrial degradation, 386–390
Energy use, 444
Engels, Friedrich, 384
English industrialization, 374–375
English language, 27
Environmental anthropology, 444–448
Environmental circumscription, 196
Environmental refugees, 457–459
Environmental watchdogs, 388
Eocene, 111
Epoch, 111
Equity, 419
Era, 111
ESR, 47
Essentialism, 456
Ethics, 59–65
Ethnic expulsion, 411
Ethnic group, 393
Ethnic tolerance and accommodation, 406–409
Ethnicity and race, 393–415
    aftermaths of oppression, 411
    assimilation, 406
    Brazil, 402–404
    Canada, 398–400
    census, 398, 399
    chips in the mosaic, 410
    cultural colonialism, 411
    definitions, 393, 394, 396
    discrimination, 410
    ethnic expulsion, 411

ethnic majority, 405
ethnic tolerance and
    accommodation, 406–409
forced assimilation, 411
genocide, 411
hypodescent, 397–398
imagined communities, 406
Japan, 400–402
labels, 396
multiculturalism, 407–409
nation, 404
nationalities, 405
plural society, 406
prejudice, 410
roots of ethnic conflict,
    409–411
shifting status, 394–396
social construction of race,
    397–404
stratification, 396
U.S., 394–396, 397–399,
    407, 408
Ethnocentrism, 31
Ethnocide, 411, 448
Ethnoecology, 445
Ethnographers, 298
Ethnographic fieldwork, 1–2
Ethnographic techniques, 51
Ethnography, 7, 50, 51–58
    conversation, interviewing,
        53–54
    genealogical method, 54–55
    key cultural consultants, 55
    life history, 55
    local beliefs and perceptions,
        55–56
    longitudinal research, 56–57
    multisited, 57–58
    observation and participant
        observation, 52–53
    problem-oriented, 56
    team research, 57
    techniques, listed, 51
Ethnology, 7
Ethnomusicology, 12
Etic approach, 56
Etoro, 31, 343, 345
Eunuch, 340
European "Age of
    Discovery," 378
European colonialism, 378
European imperial expansion, 378
European industrialization, 373
Eve, 161

Evolution, genetics, and human
    variation, 67–95
    directional selection, 76
    disease, 88–92
    evolution, 69–71
    gene flow, 78–80
    genetic markers/phenotype,
        83–84
    genetics, 71–73
    human biological adaptation,
        88–93
    independent assortment, 74
    lactose tolerance, 93
    mutation, 78
    natural selection, 70,
        75–78, 84
    origin of species, 68–71
    population genetics, 74–75
    race, 80–83
    random genetic drift, 78
    sexual selection, 77
    skin color, 84–88
    stabilizing selection, 77–78
    uniformitarianism, 69
Excavation, 44–45
Exchange systems, 262–269
Exogamy, 309
Expanded family household, 302
"Experiencing Culture"
    (Kottak), 36
Experimental archaeologists, 45
Explanations, 71
Extended family, 299
Extended family household, 302
Extramarital sex, 330

F

Fa'afafine, 341
Facebook, 227
Factors of production, 258
Fakaleitis, 341
Families, kinship, and marriage,
    297–323
    adaptation to poverty,
        302, 304
    bridewealth, 315, 316
    caste, 312
    descent groups, 305, 306–307
    divorce, 303, 304, 317–318
    dowry, 315
    durable alliances, 316–317
    endogamy, 312

exogamy, 309
    family, defined, 298
    foraging societies, 305
    incest, 309–311
    industrialism and family
        organization, 301–302
    Leach's list of rights
        transmitted by marriage,
        312–313
    levirate, 317
    marriage, 308
    North American kinship,
        302–305
    nuclear and extended families,
        299–301
    plural marriages, 318–321
    polyandry, 321
    polygyny, 318–321
    postmarital residence
        rules, 308
    same-sex marriage, 308–309,
        313–315
    sororate, 316–317
Family of orientation, 299
Family of procreation, 299
Family Ties, 304
Farming. See First farmers
Father-daughter incest, 311
Fayum, 113
Fearon, James, 405
Federal Emergency Management
    Agency (FEMA), 62
Female genital modification
    (FGM), 32
Female labor force
    participation, 339
Feminine Mystique, The
    (Friedan), 336
Feminization of poverty, 337–338
FGM, 32
Fingerprints of the Gods
    (Hancock), 217
Finkelhor, David, 311
First cities and states, 195–220
    attributes of cities and states,
        198, 199
    chiefdoms, 204, 205
    Chinese state, 209
    collapse of states, 215–219
    hydraulic systems, 196
    Indus River Valley, 208–209
    long-distance trade
        routes, 196
    Mayan decline, 215–219

First cities and states, *(Cont.)*
  Mesoamerica, 210–215
  Middle East, 200–208
  population, war, and
    circumscription, 196–197
  pottery, 203
  river-valley states, 208
  social ranking, 203–204
  state as political system,
    286–288
  urban revolution, 198
  Valley of Mexico, 214–215
  Zapotec polity, 212–214
First farmers, 174–194
  African cattle complex, 183
  areas where food production
    was invented, 184, 185
  domestication, 180–181, 190
  geography and spread of food
    production, 191–193
  Hilly Flanks, 178–182
  irrigation systems, 182
  Mesolithic, 174–175
  Mexican Highlands, 189
  Middle East, 177,
    178–182, 190
  Nabta Playa, 183
  Natufians, 178, 179
  Neolothic, 175–177, 190–193
  new world farming, 185–189,
    192–193
  other Old World farmers,
    182–185
  sedentism, 178, 190
  vertical economy, 177,
    179–180
First World, 383
Fiscal support, 288
Fiske, John, 30
Fitness, 366
Flakes, 137, 138, 148–149
Flannery, Kent, 167, 174, 176,
  179, 181, 203, 204,
  212, 214
Flores, 168–169
Focal vocabulary, 232–234
Folate, 87, 88
Folklore, 12
Food production. *See* First farmers
Foraging, 247–251
Foraging bands, 274–276
Forced assimilation, 411
Ford, Gerald, 239
Forensic anthropology, 49, 416

Fortes, Meyer, 311
Fossey, Dian, 107, 108, 116
Fossil, 43
Fossil record, 45, 46
Foster, George, 428
Foucault, Michel, 289
Four-field anthropology, 4
Fouts, Roger, 224
FOXP2, 226
Franco, Francisco, 290, 411
Fraternal polyandry, 308
Frauds, Myths, and Mysteries:
  Science and Pseudoscience
  in Archaeology (Feder),
  217–218
"Frauds and Fantastic Claims in
  Archaeology," 217
Free trade, 383
French colonialism, 380, 381
French empire, 380, 381
Fried, Morton, 203, 271
Friedl, Ernestine, 315

G

Galdikas, Birute Mary, 116–117
Gangs, 426–427
Garbology, 9, 48, 416
Gardner, Beatrice, 224
Gardner, R. Allen, 224
Gaza province (Mozambique), 53
Geertz, Clifford, 18
Geico commercials ("So easy a
  caveman can do it"), 166
Gender, 324–347
  child care, 329
  division of labor, 327, 328
  domestic work, 329
  extramarital sex, 330
  female labor force
    participation, 339
  feminization of poverty,
    337–338
  masculinity, 344–345
  matriarchy, 331–333
  matrilineal-matrilocal
    societies, 331
  patrilineal-patrilocal societies,
    333–334
  premarital sex, 330
  primates, 346
  reproductive strategies, 329
  sexual orientation, 342–346

  single-parent households, 338
  speech, 236–237
  subsistence activities, 328
  transgendered persons,
    339–342
  violence, 334
  women's movement, 336
  work and happiness, 338–339
Gender roles, 326, 330–333
Gender stereotype, 326
Gender stratification, 326,
  330–334
Gene, 73
Gene flow, 78–80
Gene pool, 74
Genealogical method, 54–55
General anthropology, 4
Generalities, 27
Generalized reciprocity, 264
Genetic clocks, 48
Genetic evolution, 75
Genetics, 10, 71–73
Geneva WTO protests, 38
Genocide, 387, 411, 448
Genotype, 73, 75
Genus (genera), 97
Genus *Homo,* 124, 136–137,
  143–173
  AMHs, 154, 158–162
  archaic *H. sapiens,* 152–153,
    154, 155–156, 158
  behavioral modernity, 162–164
  Denisovans, 162
  H. antecessor, 155
  H. erectus, 145–147, 149–152,
    154, 158
  H. floresiensis, 168–172
  H. habilis, 144, 145
  H. heidelbergensis, 155
  H. rudolfensis, 144
  ice ages, 153–155, 166–167
  Neandertals, 153, 154,
    156–159
  Paleolithic tools, 147–148, 165
  settling the Americas,
    167–168
  tools, 164–166
Georgia (country), 412
Gibbons, 106
Gibson, McGuire, 205
Gigantophithecus, 114, 115
Gingrich, Newt, 397
Glacial, 153, 155
Glacial retreat, 166–167

Global climate change, 442–444
Global culture of consumption, 451–452
Global system of images, 451
Global temperature change, 442
Global warming, 443
Globalization, 34–38, 439–441
Globo, 451
Gmelch, George, 352
Golden rule, 359
González, Ramón, 292
Goodall, Jane, 24, 108, 109, 116
Gorilla, 107–108, 136
Gossip, 290–291
Gracile and robust australopithecines, 134–136
Gramsci, Antonio, 289
Grasping, 101
Great Depression, 383
Great Rift Valley, 47
Greco-Roman religions, 360
Greek empire, 377–378
Greenhouse effect, 442
Greenhouse gases, 444
Greenwashing, 388
Guido, 413, 414
Gullah, 231
Gwembe district, Zambia, 57

H

H. antecessor, 155
H. erectus, 137, 141, 145–147, 149–152, 154, 158
H. floresiensis, 168–172
H. habilis, 137, 138, 144, 145
H. heidelbergensis, 155
H. rudolfensis, 144
H. sapiens, 152–153, 154, 155–156, 158
Ha-sa-no-an-da, 5
Habitat destruction and fragmentation, 110
Haile-Selassie, Johannes, 127
Halafian ceramics, 203
Halafian period, 203, 205
Hallmark Cards, 432
Hancock, Graham, 217, 218
Handsome Lake, 363
Handsome Lake religion, 363
Hanumanthappa, Ram Prakash, 243

Haplogroup, 48, 83
Harappa, 8, 208, 209
Hard Times (Dickens), 375
Harper, Kristin, N., 91, 92
Harri, Illtud, 389
Harris, Marvin, 55
Harrison, K. David, 242
Hazel site (Arkansas), 49
Hb^A, 77
Hb^S, 77, 78
Health care systems, 429
Health problems, 427–431
Hegemony, 289
Heidelberg man, 155
Hemoglobin, 77
Hemudu, 184
Henry, Donald, 178
Henry, Jules, 424
Henshilwood, Christopher, 163
Herdt, Gilbert, 345
Hermaphroditism, 340
Herto, 159
Heterosexuality, 342
Heterozygous, 73
Heyerdahl, Thor, 217
Hicks, Edward, 68
Hidatsa, 328
Hidden transcript, 290
Hijra, 341
Hilly Flanks, 178–182
Hinderstein, Corey, 22
Hinduism, 360
Hip-hop lyrics, 263
Hispanics, 394, 395
Historical archaeologists, 45
Historical linguistics, 240–242
HIV/AIDS, 428
Hoebel, E. A., 275
Holism, 2
Holocene, 111
Holt cemetery, 62
Holy water, 19
Home-handicraft (domestic) system of production, 374
Hominid, 23, 100, 124, 130
Hominidae, 23, 99
Hominin, 23, 43, 100. *See also* Early Hominins
Hominin bipedalism, 120–121
Hominini, 100
Hominoid, 124
Hominoidea, 114
Homo. See Genus *Homo*
Homo antecessor, 155

Homo erectus, 137, 141, 145–147, 149–152, 154, 158
Homo floresiensis, 168–172
Homo habilis, 137, 138
Homo heidelbergensis, 155
Homo rudolfensis, 144
Homo sapiens, 152–153, 154, 155–156, 158
Homologies, 97
Homosexuality, 342
Homozygous, 73
Honorary men, 341
Hoodia, 33
Hopi, 318
Hopi language, 232
Horticultural villages, 276–277
Horticulture, 251–253
Hotel Rwanda, 381
HTS, 61, 64–65
Hugging, 37
Human adaptability, 2–4
Human biological adaptation, 88–93
Human rights, 31
Human terrain system (HTS), 61, 64–65
Hunter-gatherers, 247–251
Hussein, Saddam, 410
Hutus, 381
Hydraulic systems, 196
Hypodescent, 397–398

I

IBM, 432
Ice ages, 153–155, 166–167
Ideal culture, 29
Identical twins, 76
Ifugao, 253
Igbo, 315, 321
Igbo women's war, 291, 294
Il-khan, 282
Ileret finds, 145
Illness, 427
Imagined communities, 406
IMF, 383
Imitative magic, 352
Imperialism, 377
Inca, 210
Incest, 309–311
Income inequality, 376
Increased equity, 419
Independent assortment, 74

Independent invention, 34
Indiana Jones movies, 10
Indigenizing popular culture, 450–451
Indigenous intellectual property rights, 33
Indigenous models, 422–423
Indigenous peoples, 387, 405, 428, 454–456
Indirect rule, 380
Indus River Valley, 184, 208–209
Industrial alienation, 258–260
Industrial melanism, 70
Industrial Revolution, 373, 374
Industrial stratification, 375–377
Industrialization, 373–375
Infibulation, 32
Informed consent, 60
Intellectual property rights (IPR), 33
Intensive agriculture, 254–255
Inter-American Development Bank, 383
Interethnic conflict, 448–450
Interglacials, 153, 155
International culture, 30
International issues, 438–460
    climate change, 442–444
    continuance of diversity, 456, 459
    cultural imperialism, 448–450
    deforestation, 446–448
    environmental anthropology, 444–448
    global culture of consumption, 451–452
    global system of images, 451
    globalization, 439–441
    indigenizing popular culture, 450–451
    indigenous peoples, 454–456
    interethnic conflict, 448–450
    multinational companies, 441
    people in motion, 452–454
    transnational migration, 452–454
International Monetary Fund (IMF), 383
International Potato Centre (CIP), 187
Intersex, 339–342
Interstadials, 155
Intervention philosophy, 382

Interview schedule, 54
Inuit, 275–276
IPR, 33
Iranian pastoral nomadic tribes, 282
Iron Age, 207
Irrigation, 253
Irrigation systems, 182
Isiklar, Turkey, 320–321
Islam, 360, 361
Italian Americans, 413–414
Ivato, 267–269

J

Jablonski, Nina, 87, 88
Jackson, Michael, 200
Japan, 400–402
Jarmo, 178
Jati, 312
Java man, 150, 151
Jenkins, Leigh, 232
Jericho, 200–201, 202
Jersey Shore, 414
Jobless recovery, 386
Johanson, D. C., 129
Jomon people, 175
Ju/'hoansi San, 258, 275
Judiciary, 287
Jungers, William, 172

K

K/A dating, 47
Kabwe skull, 156
Kanuri, 319
Kaobawa, 277
Kapauku, 278
Kapauku big man, 278, 279
KE family, 226
Kelly, Raymond C., 343
Kent, Susan, 274, 275
Kershaw, Sarah, 37
Key cultural consultants, 55
Key informants, 55
Keynes, John Maynard, 383
Keynesian economics, 383
Khan, 282
Kids Are All Right, The, 313
Kimeu, Kimoya, 145
Kin-based societies, 55
Kinesics, 226

King, Rodney, 410
Kingdom, 97
Kinsey report, 342–343
Kinship, 26, 298. *See also* Families, kinship, and marriage
Kipling, Rudyard, 380
Kirsch, Stuart, 388–390
Klasies River, 160
Klinefelter's syndrome, 340
Kluckhohn, Clyde, 12
Knitting machine, 373
KNM-ER 1470, 143
KNM-ER 1813, 144
KNM-ER 42700, 145, 146
KNM-ER 42703, 145
Knuckle-walking, 105, 107
Koko, 224–226
Komodo, dragons, 169
Koobi Fora, 144
Kottak, Conrad, 36, 267, 285, 304, 385, 402, 407, 419, 445, 449
Kottak, Isabel Wagley, 57
Kottak, Nicholas, 288, 291
Krishna, Gopal, 244
Kuhn, Steven, 164
Kuikuru, 252
Kujundzic-Vejzagic, Zilka, 218
Kuria, 264
Kutse San, 275

L

L. S. B., 137, 144
La Chapelle-aux-Saints, 150
Labov, William, 237–239
Lactase, 93
Lactose, 93
Lactose tolerance, 93
Laissez-faire (hands-off) economics, 383
Lakher, 310
Lakoff, Robin, 237
Lalueza-Fox, Carles, 170, 171
Lambek, Michael, 349, 352
Landes, David, 441
Language and communication, 221–245
    BEV, 239–240
    call systems, 222–223, 225
    creole languages, 231
    focal vocabulary, 232–234

gender speech contrasts,
236–237
historical linguistics, 240–242
Internet, 243–244
language loss, 242
linguistic diversity within
nations, 235–236
nonverbal communication,
226–227
origin of language, 226
pidgins, 231
Sapir-Whorf hypothesis,
231–232
sign language, 223–226
social and linguistic variation,
234–235
speech sounds, 228–230
stratification/symbolic
domination, 237–239
Language loss, 242
Laplanders, 256
Lapps, 256
Late Miocene apes, 114
"Latina Judge's Voice, A," 397
Latinos, 394, 395
Law enforcement, 288
Leach, Edmund, 312
Leach's list of rights transmitted
by marriage, 312–313
Leakey, Louis B., 116
Leakey, Maeve, 129, 145
Leakey, Mary, 129, 131, 134,
137, 144
Leakey, Richard, 143, 145,
150, 159
Leave It to Beaver, 304
Lee, Richard, 248, 275
Lemurs, 102
Lenski, Gerhard, 376
Lesbian, gay, bisexual, and
transgender community
(LGBT), 342
Leveling mechanism, 358
Levirate, 317
Levy, Jerome, 318
Levy, Joe, 344
Lewellen, Ted, 440, 441
Lexicon, 228, 232
LGBT community, 342
Liberalism, 383
Life history, 55
Lightfoot, John, 68
Limbaugh, Rush, 397
Liminality, 354, 355

Lineage, 307
Linguistic anthropology, 5, 11,
222, 416
Linguistic displacement, 225
Linnaeus, Carolus, 68
Livelihood. See Making a living
Living Tongues Institute for
Endangered Languages,
242
Local beliefs and perceptions,
55–56
Long-distance communication, 35
Long-distance trade routes, 196
Longitudinal research, 56–57
Loomis, W. F., 87
Los Angeles riots, 410
Lovedu, 315
Lower Paleolithic, 147
Lower Pleistocene, 153
Lucy
chimp, 224
hominin skeleton, 129, 133
Lucy's baby, 130–131
Lyell, Charles, 69

M

Machu Picchu, 60
Macumba, 365
Madagascar, 55, 368, 422,
445–447
Magic, 352
Mahu, 341
Maize, 186, 188
Majority groups, 396
Making a living, 246–270
agriculture, 253–255
alternative ends, 261–262
economic systems, 256–260
economizing, 261–262
exchange systems, 262–269
foraging, 247–251
horticulture, 251–253
industrial alienation,
258–260
market principle, 262
maximizing, 261
means of production, 258
pastoralism, 255–256
potlaching, 265–269
reciprocity, 263–264
redistribution, 263
Malaria, 77, 428, 430

Malay peasants, 290
Malinowski, Bronislaw, 52, 291,
352, 417
Mammalia, 97
Mana, 351
Mandrill, 104
Manioc, 186
Manual dexterity, 23
Marcus, Joyce, 212, 214, 216
Mardi Gras, 290
Marean, Curtis, 164
Margolis, Maxine, 335, 336
Market principle, 262
Marriage, 26, 308. See also
Families, kinship, and
marriage
Marx, Karl, 259, 375, 384
Masai, 281
Masculinity, 344–345
Mass media, 451
Mass production, 385
Masturbation, 342
Matai, 426
Mating, 26
Matriarchy, 331–333
Matrilineal descent, 306, 307
Matrilineal-matrilocal
societies, 331
Matriliny, 331
Matrilocality, 308, 331
Maximizing, 261
Mayan decline, 215–219
McBrearty, Sally, 163
McCain, John, 280
McDonald's, 186, 434–435, 441
Mead, Margaret, 41, 290
Means of production, 258
Media and Middle-Class Moms:
Images and Realities of
Work and Family
(Descartes/Kottak), 304
Medical anthropology, 416,
427–431
Meigs, Anna, 311
Meiosis, 74
Mejía, Eduardo, 293
Melanesia, 351, 364, 365
Melanesians, 162
Melanin, 84, 87–88
Men and women. See Gender
Mende, 281
Mendel, Gregor, 72–74
Mendelian genetics, 72
Merina, 321

Mesoamerica
  archaeological evidence, 204
  domestication, 190
  intensive cultivation, 189
  maize, 191
  state formation, 210–215
  vertical economy, 179
  world's first states, 195
Mesolithic, 174–175
Mesopotamia
  cuneiform, 207
  increased food production, 205
  irrigation/intensive river
    valley agriculture, 200
  irrigation techniques, 181
  Uruk, 207
  world's first civilization,
    178, 195
Mesozoic era, 111, 112
Mestizaje, 455
Mestizo, 454, 456
Metallurgy, 206, 210
Mexican Americans, 395
Mexican Highlands, 189
Michaels, Eric, 450
Microenculturation, 431
Middle East
  chiefdoms, 204
  farming, 177, 178–182, 190
  state formation, 200–208
Middle Paleolithic, 147
Middle Paleolithic Mousterian
    tools, 165
Middle Pleistocene, 153
Middle Stone Age tools, 164
Middleton, Kate, 200
Migration, 409
Miller, Barbara, 334
Millet, 184, 185
Minangkabau, 332–333
Minerva, 61
Mining, 388–390
Minority groups, 395
Miocene, 111, 114
Miocene hominoids, 114–118
Mission civilisatrice, 380, 382
Mitochondrial DNA
    (mtDNA), 161
Mitosis, 74
Mode of production, 257
Modern world system.
    See World system
Mohenjo-daro, 208, 209
Molecular anthropology, 47–48

Monkey bars, 122
Monkeys, 102–105
Monocrop, 373
Monotheism, 350
Monte Alban, 212–214
Moral codes, 359
Morales, Evo, 455
Morphology, 228
Morwood, Michael, 169
Mountainous terrain, 3
Mousterian, 156
Multiculturalism, 407–409
Multinational companies, 441
Multisited ethnography, 56–58
Multivillage alliances, 204
Munns, Bill, 115
Muriqui, 103
Muslims and the media, 362
Mutation, 78
Mysorekar, Uma V., 367

N

Nabta Playa, 183
Nanchoc Valley, 192, 193
Nariokotome boy, 145, 147
Nation, 404
Nation-state, 404–405
National culture, 30
National Organization of Women
    (NOW), 336
Nationalities, 405
Nativistic movements, 362
Natufians, 178, 179
Natural selection, 70, 75–78, 84
Naturalistic disease theories, 428
Nayar, 27, 300–301
Ndembu, 354
Neandertal cannibalism, 170–171
Neandertals, 153, 154, 156–159
Negative reciprocity, 264
Négritude, 406
Nelson, Jim, 345
Neoliberalism, 383
Neolithic, 203
Neolithic Revolution, 198
Neolocality, 302
Neolothic, 175–177, 190–193
Neural tube defect (NTD), 87
New Age movement, 365
New and alternative religious
    movements, 365
New Deal, 383

New Orleans (post-Hurricane
    Katrina), 62–64
New world farming, 185–189,
    192–193
New World monkeys, 103–104
Newtok, Alaska, 457–459
Ngandong XI, 150
Ngeneo, Bernard, 143
Night monkey, 104
Nike, 441
Nilotes, 82
Nittano, 175
Nok Nok Tha, 210
Nomadic politics, 282
Nomadism, 256
Nonverbal communication,
    226–227
Norm, 275, 288
North American kinship,
    302–305
Nosso Senhor do Bomfim, 358
NOW, 336
NTD, 87
Nuclear family, 27, 299
Nuer, 308–309
Nut cracking, 24

O

Oaxaca, 189, 212
Obama, Barack, 13–15, 240, 280
Observation and participant
    observation, 52–53
Office, 283
OH9, 152
OH24, 145
OH62, 145
Ok Tedi copper mine, 389
Old World farming, 178–185
Old World monkeys, 103,
    104–105
Oldowan tools, 137–141
Oligocene, 111, 113–114
Oligocene anthropoids, 113–114
Olmec, 210
Omo 1, 159
Omo 2, 159
Omo Kibish, 159
On the Origin of Species
    (Wallace), 70
Ong, Aihwa, 259, 260
Opposable thumbs, 23, 101
Orangutans, 106–107, 116–117

Origin of species, 68–71
Orrorin tugenensis, 126
Ortner, Donald J., 92
Osmanagic, Semir, 218, 219
Osteology, 10
Osteomyelitis, 49
Osteoporosis, 87
Otto, Remzi, 320
Overfarming, 215
Overinnovation, 420–421
Owl monkey, 104
Ox-powered irrigation
    system, 182

P

Paabo, Svante, 162
Paint-pot theory, 72
Paleoanthropology, 10, 43
Paleocene, 111, 113
Paleoecology, 9
Paleoindians, 167
Paleolithic, 147
Paleolithic tools, 147–148, 165
Paleontology, 42
Paleopathology, 48
Paleozoic era, 111
Palynology, 42
Pan troglodytes, 108, 154
Pantheon, 359
Pantribal sodalities, 280–282
Papio sphinx, 104
Papua New Guinea, 31, 333–334,
    343–345
Paranthropus, 134
Parappil, Pradeep, 244
Parental investment, 102
Parker, Ely S., 5
Participant observation, 52–53
Particularity, 27–28
Passage rites, 354–357
Pastoralism, 255–256
Patriarchy, 334
Patrilineal descent, 306
Patrilineal-patrilocal societies,
    333–334
Patriliny, 331
Patrilocal extended family, 300
Patrilocality, 308, 331
Patterson, Penny, 224–226
Pawnee, 328
Pearsall, Deborah, 188
Peasants, 262

Pebble tools, 142. *See also*
    Stone tools
People in motion, 452–454
Peppered moth, 70
Peres, Dan, 345
Period, 111
Periphery, 371–372
Personal space, 36
Personalistic disease theories, 428
Personhood, 431
Peru, 187, 197, 210
Phenotype, 73, 75, 76, 402
Phenotypical adaptation, 93
Phoneme, 229, 230
Phonemics, 229
Phonetics, 229
Phonology, 228
Phylogeny, 97
Phylum (phyla), 97
Physical anthropology, 10–11,
    48–50
Physically circumscribed
    environment, 196
Phytolith, 42
Pickford, Martin, 126
Pidgin, 34
Pidgin English, 34
Pidgins, 231
PIE, 240
PIE family tree, 241
Pierolapithecus catalaunicus,
    115–118
Piperno, Dolores, 188
Pizzaro, Francisco, 218
Plains Indian societies, 281, 354
Planet of the Apes, 98
Plantation economy, 373
Platyrrhines, 102
Pleistocene, 111, 153
Pliocene, 111
Plural marriage, 308
Plural marriages, 318–321
Plural society, 406
Polanyi, Karl, 262
Political organization, 271
Political regulation, 272
Political systems, 271–296
    bands and tribes, 273–282
    big man, 278–280
    chiefdoms, 283–286
    definitions, 271–272
    foraging bands, 274–276
    hegemony and resistance, 289
    Igbo women's war, 291, 294

    nomadic politics, 282
    overview, 286
    pantribal sodalities, 280–282
    Service's typology, 272
    shame and gossip, 290–291
    social control, 288–294
    state systems, 286–288
    tribal cultivators, 276–277
    types and trends, 272–273
    village head, 277–278
    weapons of the weak, 290
Polyandry, 321
Polygyny, 318–321
Polynesia, 351
Polynesian chiefs, 283, 285
Polynesians, 82
Polytheism, 350
Popular culture, 30
Popular culture boxes
    Avatar, 387
    Bones, 50
    Coca-Cola, 421
    diversity on TV, 409
    Facebook, 227
    Geico commercials ("So easy
        a caveman can do it"), 166
    hip-hop lyrics, 263
    Indiana Jones, 10
    McDonald's, 186
    monkey bars, 122
    Muslims and the media, 362
    Planet of the Apes, 98
    popular songs, 21
    royalty, 200
    science fiction movies, 454
    The Simpsons, 337
    superheroes, 280
    TV families, 304
    Twitter, 227
    Winfrey, Oprah, 84
Popular resistance, 289
Popular songs, 21
Population control, 287
Population genetics, 72, 74–75
Poro, 281
Portuguese colonialism, 378
Pospisil, Leopold, 278
Postcolonial studies, 381–382
Postmarital residence rules, 308
Postmodernism, 453
Postmodernity, 453
Postsocialist societies, 384
Postsocialist transitions, 384
Pot irrigation, 189

Potassium-argon (K/A) dating, 47
Potato, 187
Potlaching, 265–269
Potsherds, 9
Pottery, 203
Potts, Rick, 140
Poverty, 430
Practice theory, 29
Prejudice, 410
Premarital sex, 330
Prepottery Neolithic, 203
Prestige, 286
Priesthood, 359
Primary states, 204
Primate evolution, 110–111
Primate family tree, 100
Primate taxonomy, 99
Primate tendencies, 100–102
Primates, 23, 96–119
  apes. *See* Apes
  call systems, 225
  early, 112–114
  endangered, 110
  evolution, 110–111
  family tree, 100
  homologies and analogies,
    99–100
  humans, and, 24–26, 100–102
  language, 222–226
  late Miocene apes, 114
  mates, 26
  Miocene hominoids,
    114–118
  monkeys, 102–105
  Oligocene anthropoids,
    113–114
  Pierolapithecus catalaunicus,
    115–118
  Proconsul, 114
  prosimians, 102
  sexual expression, 346
  taxonomy, 99
  tendencies, 100–102
Primatology, 11, 49–50, 96
Primitive Culture (Tylor), 17
Principles of Geology (Lyell), 69
Private-public contrast, 331
Problem-oriented
  ethnography, 56
Proconsul, 114
Progeny price, 315
Project Bhasha, 244
Project Minerva, 61
Proletarianization, 375

Proletariat, 375
Prosimian, 100
Prosimians, 102
Protestant nonconformists, 375
Proto-Indo-European (PIE), 240
Protolanguage, 240
Pseudo-archeology, 217–219
Public archaeology, 15
Public culture, 30
Public transcript, 290
Publicly traded companies, 376
Pygmies (Congo), 274

Q

Qafzeh, 160
Qashqai, 282
Quantifiable information, 59
Quaternary period, 111
Quillpad, 243

R

Ra Expeditions, The
  (Heyerdahl), 217
Rabe, Joseph, 297–298
Race, 80–83, 396. *See also*
  Ethnicity and race
Racism, 396
Radiometric dating, 46–47
Raelian movement, 365
Rakoto, 55
Ram, Prasad Bhaarat, 244
Rambo, 450
Random genetic drift, 78
Ranked societies, 203, 204
Rathje, William, 9
Reagan, Ronald, 239, 280
Real culture, 29
Real-life examples. *See*
  Anthropology today boxes
Recessive traits, 72
Reciprocity, 263–264
Reciprocity continuum, 264
Red Sox nation, 368
Redfield, Robert, 426
Redistribution, 263
Reese, David, 164
Refugees, 411
Regional surveys, 43
Reichs, Kathy, 49
Relative dating, 46

Religion, 348–369
  cargo cults, 363–365
  change, and, 362–365
  kinds, 359–360
  magic, 352
  major world religions,
    360–362
  new and alternative
    movements, 365
  powers and forces, 351
  revitalization movements,
    362–363
  rites of passage, 354–357
  rituals, 353–354
  secular rituals, 365–368
  social control, 357–359
  spiritual beings, 350
  totemism, 357, 368
  uncertainty, anxiety,
    solace, 352
  unofficial, 365
*Religion: An Anthropological
  View* (Wallace), 348
Religious fundamentalists, 362
Remote sensing, 43
Rent fund, 262
Replacement fund, 261
Reproductive technology, 313
Research methods, 41–43, 51–52,
  58–59
Resistance, 289
Resource depletion, 386–390
Respondents, 59
Revitalization movements,
  362–363
Rice, 183, 184, 185
Rickets, 87
Ridicule, 291
Rites of intensification, 355–357
Rites of passage, 354–357
Ritualized homosexuality, 346
Rituals, 353–354
River-valley states, 208
Robbins, Richard H., 439
Robinson, J. T., 134
Robust australopithecines,
  134–136
Roçinha, 425
Rodentia, 98
Roman empire, 378
Romance languages, 240
Rosaldo, Michelle, 326
Rosie the Riveter, 335
Royalty, 200

Rural *vs.* urban, 426
Rwanda, 381

S

Sahelanthropus tchadensis,
    124–126
Same-sex marriage, 308–309,
    313–315
Same-sex sexual activity, 343
Samis, 256
Samoans (Los Angeles), 426
Sample, 54
San, 82, 274–275
Sanday, Peggy, 332
Santeria, 365
Sapir, Edward, 231, 349
Sapir-Whorf hypothesis, 231–232
Satellite imagery, 43
Saturday Night Fever, 413
Savino, Diane J., 413
Scandinavian shell mounds, 175
Schistosomiasis, 428
Sciame, Joseph, 414
Science fiction movies, 454
Scientific medicine, 429
Scott, James, 290
Scrapers, 165
Scudder, Thayer, 57
SE, 229, 230, 236, 239–240
Seattle WTO protests, 38
Second World countries, 383–384
Secular rituals, 365–368
Sedentism, 178, 190, 275
Semantics, 234
Semaw, Sileshi, 140
Semiperiphery, 371
Senut, Brigitte, 126
Sequoia, 224
Serial monogamy, 318
Service, Elman, 272
Service's typology, 272
Settlement hierarchy, 214
Settling the Americas, 167–168
Seven Years' War, 378
Sex and gender, 324–326
Sexual dimorphism, 104, 135,
    146, 324
Sexual orientation, 342–346
Sexual selection, 77
Sexually transmitted diseases
    (STDs), 428
Shaheen, Jack, 362

Shahid, Sam, 344
Shaman, 359, 429
Shame, 290–291
Shang dynasty, 209
Shanidar Neandertals, 156
Sharecroppers, 262
Shifting cultivation, 252
Shiites, 410
Shock therapy, 384
Shoshone, 305
Shukla, Aseem, 366, 367
Sibling marriage, 311
Sickle-cell anemia, 77
Sign language, 223–226
Silent trade, 264
Silverman, Michael S., 91, 92
Simancas, Meydell, 294
Single-parent family, 304
Single-parent households, 338
Situational negotiation of social
    identity, 394
Skeletal biology, 48
Skhūl, 160
Skhūl V, 160
Skin color, 84–88
Slash-and-burn horticulture, 252
Slimane, Hedi, 344
Smallpox, 90
Smallpox vaccine, 89
Smelting, 206
Smith, Adam, 383
Smith, Mark, 439
Social circumscription, 196
Social construction of race,
    397–404
Social control, 288–294
Social fund, 261
Social indicators, 59
Social ranking, 203–204
Social strata, 285–286
Socialist internationalism, 411
Sociocultural anthropology, 4
Socioeconomic stratification, 375
Sociolinguistics, 11, 234–236
Sociology, 50
Sociopolitical organization, 272
Sociopolitical typology, 273
Sodalities, 280
Soetoro, Stanley Ann Dunham,
    13–15
Soetoro-Ng, Maya, 13–15
Sororate, 316–317
Sotomayor, Sonia, 396, 397
South Ossetia, 412

Spanish colonialism, 378
Speciation, 80
Species, 79
Speech sounds, 228–230
Spencer, Charles, 212, 213
Spina bifida, 87
Spirit possession, 260
Spiritual beings, 350
Stafford, Thomas, 168
Standard (American) English
    (SE), 229, 230, 236,
    239–240
Starch grain analysis, 42
State, 195, 273, 283
State formation. *See* First cities
    and states
State systems, 286–288
Statistical analysis, 59
Status, 278–279
STDs, 428
Stereotype, 410
Stiner, Mary, 164
Stipulated descent, 307
Stoler, Ann, 326
Stone picks, 148
Stone tools, 137–141
Stonehenge, 284
Stoneking, Mark, 83, 161
Stothert, Karen, 188
Stratification
    chiefdoms, 285–286
    ethnicity and race, 396
    gender, 326, 330–334
    industrial, 375–377
    inequality, and, 419
    socioeconomic, 375
    Weber's three dimensions, 286
Stratified societies, 203, 219
Stratigraphy, 46
Stratum (strata), 46
Stratum endogamy, 285
Stringer, Christopher, 46
Style shifts, 235
Stylus, 206
Subculture, 31
Subdisciplines of anthropology,
    7–11
Subordinate stratum, 286
Subsistence fund, 261
Subspecies, 97
Sudanese Azande, 343
Sugar, 373
Sugarcane, 373
Sukuma, 381

Sumer, 200
Sunnis, 410
Superheroes, 280
Superordinate stratum, 286
Superposition, 44
Survey research, 58–59
Susa, 200
Susto, 429
Suttles, Wayne, 266
Suwa, Gen, 126
Sweat lodge ceremonies, 365
Swimmers, 5–6
Sworn virgin, 341
Symbolic thought, 18
Symbols, 18, 19
Syntax, 228
Syphilis, 91–92
Systematic survey, 43

T

Taieb, M., 129
"Take Back Yoga," 366
Tannen, Deborah, 226, 235–237
Taphonomy, 45
Tarawad, 300
Tarsier, 102
Taylor, Carol, 431
Team research, 57
Teeth, 122–123
Tell el-Ubaid, 203
Tell es-Sawwan, 204
Tell Hamoukar, 205
Ten Commandments, 359
Tenant farmers, 262
Tenochtitlan, 215
Teosinte, 188
Teotihuacan, 214
Terminiting, 24
Terrace, Herbert, 225
Terracing, 253
Terrestrial monkeys and
    apes, 96, 105
Terrorism, 61, 64–65
Tertiary period, 111
The Simpsons, 337
Theory, 69, 71
Theory of the Leisure Class
    (Veblen), 266
Thermoluminescence (TL), 47
Third gender, 339–342
Third World, 384
Tice, Karen, 418

Tikal, 216
Titanic (movie), 45
Titiev, Mischa, 318
Tiwari, Sanjay, 244
TL, 47
Today's current events. See
    Anthropology today boxes
Toltec period, 214
Tom, Elizabeth, 458
Tom, Stanley, 457–459
Tomb-centered ceremonies, 368
Tonowi, 278, 279
Tools, 122, 164–166
    Acheulian, 148–149
    blade-core method, 165
    middle stone age, 164
    Neolithic, 176
    Oldowan, 137–141
    overview, 148
    Paleolithic, 147–148, 165
Totem, 357
Totemism, 357, 368
Toumai, 125
Tourism, 37
Transatlantic slave trade, 373
Transformism, 69
Transgendered persons, 339–342
Transhumance, 256
Transnational migration,
    452–454
Transsexual, 339–342
Transvestism, 343
Tribal cultivators, 276–277
Tribe, 100, 273, 274–282. See
    also Political systems
Tricarico, Donald, 413
Trickle down, 383
Triple X syndrome, 340
Trobriand Islands, 52
True Gonadal Intersex
    person, 340
Tuesdaysfather, 55
Tula, 214
Tunnel of Bones, 170
Turkana, 256
Turner, Victor, 349
Turner syndrome, 340
Tutankhamun, 199
Tutsis, 381
TV, diversity on, 409
TV families, 304
TV Globo, 451
Twentieth-century
    industrialization, 385

Twitter, 227
Tylor, Edward, 17, 350

U

Ubaid period, 203
Ubaid pottery, 203
Underdifferentiation, 421–422
"Understanding and Responding
    to Climate Change, 2008
    edition," 443
Understanding Popular Culture
    (Fiske), 30
Underwater archaeology, 45
Uniformitarianism, 69
Unilineal descent, 306
Unilocal rules of postmarital
    residence, 308
United Nations Working Group
    on Indigenous Populations
    (WGIP), 454
Universal grammar, 231
Universal life-cycle events, 28
Universals, 27
Unofficial religions, 365
Upper Paleolithic, 147
Upper Paleolithic blade tools, 165
Upper Paleolithic bone tools, 165
Upper Paleolithic tools, 164, 165
Upper Pleistocene, 153
Uranium series dating, 47
Urban anthropology, 424–427
Urban revolution, 198
Urban slums, 425
Uruk, 200, 207
Uruk period, 205
Ussher, James, 68

V

Valley of Mexico, 214–215
van Vugt, Janine, 53
Variables, 59
Varna, 312
Vayda, Andrew, 266
Veblen, Thorstein, 266
Verano, John W., 92
Vertical economy, 177, 179–180
Viagara, 20
Victorian Era, 380
Vietnam War, 417, 418
Vigil, James, 426–427

Viki, 223
Village fissioning, 277
Village head, 277–278
Virginal transvestite, 341
Vitamin D-deficiency diseases, 87
Vocabulary, 232–234
Vodoun, 365
Vogel, F., 90
von Daniken, Erich, 217
Voodoo, 365

W

Walker, Alan, 129
Wallace, Alfred Russell, 70
Wallace, Anthony F. C., 348, 359
Warrant chiefs, 294
Warren, Kay, 325
Washoe, 224, 225
Waters, Michael, 168
Wealth inequality, 376, 377
Wealth of Nations, The
    (Smith), 383
Weapons of the weak, 290
Weber, Max, 286, 375, 377
Weber's three dimensions of
    stratification, 286
Weretigers, 260
Western European
    nationalism, 405
Westernization, 448
WGIP, 454
Wheat, 180
When Languages Die
    (Harrison), 242
White, Leslie, 18, 19
White, Tim, 125, 126, 145, 159

Whorf, Benjamin, Lee, 231
William, Prince, 200
Williams, Linda M., 311
Williamson, Bonnie, 42
Wilmsen, Edwin, 274
Wilson, Allan C., 83, 161
Winfrey, Oprah, 84
Witchcraft accusations, 358
Wodaabe, 325
Women and men. See Gender
Women's movement, 336
Wood, Bernard, 125
Woolly spider monkey, 103
Work and happiness, 338–339
Working class, 375
World Bank, 383
World Conference of Indigenous
    Peoples, 454
World religions, 360–362
World stratification system, 377
World system, 370–392
    British colonialism, 378–380
    colonialism, 377–382
    communism, 384
    core, semiperiphery,
        periphery, 371–372
    current situation, 385–390
    development, 382–383
    emergence of, 372–373
    French colonialism, 380, 381
    income inequality, 376
    industrial stratification,
        375–377
    industrialization, 373–375
    neoliberalism, 383
    postcolonial studies, 381–382
    postsocialist transitions, 384
    resource depletion, 386–390

Second World countries,
    383–384
wealth inequality,
    376, 377
World-system theory, 371
Wright, Henry, 212
WT15,000, 145, 147
WTO protests, 37–38
Würm, 155

X

Xerox, 432
XX Intersex person, 340
XY Intersex person, 340

Y

Yanomami, 258, 277–278,
    292–294, 311, 430
Yanomami Health Plan, 293
Yanomami village headman, 277
Yeltsin, Boris, 384
Yoga, 366–367
Yoruba religion, 365

Z

Zadruga, 299–300
Zapotec, 212
Zapotec polity, 212–214
Zhoukoudian, 150, 152
Zoological taxonomy, 97, 98
Zoonomia (Darwin), 69
Zuni man-woman, 341